USS RANGER

ALSO BY ROBERT J. CRESSMAN

The Official Chronology of the U.S. Navy in World War II
A Magnificent Fight: The Battle for Wake Island
That Gallant Ship: U.S.S. YORKTOWN (CV-5)

By the Author with J. Michael Wenger,
Steady Nerves and Stout Hearts: The ENTERPRISE
(CV-6) Air Group and Pearl Harbor, 7 December 1941

By the Author with Donald M. Goldstein,
Katherine V. Dillon, and J. Michael Wenger
The Spanish-American War: The Story and Photographs

By the Author with Steve Ewing, Barrett Tillman,
Mark Horan, Clark G. Reynolds, and Stan Cohen
"A Glorious Page in Our History": The Battle of Midway
4–6 June 1942

USS RANGER

THE NAVY'S FIRST FLATTOP FROM KEEL TO MAST, 1934–46

ROBERT J. CRESSMAN

BRASSEY'S, INC.
Washington, D.C.

Copyright © 2003 by Robert J. Cressman.

Published in the United States by Brassey's, Inc. All rights reserved. No part of this book may be reproduced in any manner whatsoever without written permission from the publisher, except in the case of brief quotations embodied in critical articles and reviews.

Library of Congress Cataloging-in-Publication Data
Cressman, Robert.
　USS Ranger : the Navy's first flattop from keel to mast, 1934–46 / Robert J. Cressman.— 1st ed.
　　p. cm.
Includes bibliographical references and index.
　ISBN 1-57488-720-3 (cloth : alk.paper)
　1. Ranger (Aircraft carrier : CV-4)　I. Title.

VA65.R35C74 2003
359.9′435′0973—dc21

2003005159

Hardcover ISBN 1-57488-720-3

Printed in the United States of America on acid-free paper that meets the American National Standards Institute Z39-48 Standard.

Brassey's, Inc.
22841 Quicksilver Drive
Dulles, Virginia 20166

First Edition

10 9 8 7 6 5 4 3 2 1

To the officers and men of the United States Ship *Ranger*
(CV-4), 1934–46

"*RANGER* has stood this, her first test in Fleet maneuvers, very well, and I am satisfied that she will prove herself a very valuable ship."

Vice Adm. Henry V. Butler, USN
Commander Aircraft, Battle Force,
remarks at the critique of Fleet
Problem XVI, 15 June 1935

CONTENTS

	Acknowledgments	IX
	Abbreviations and Watches	XI
	Introduction	XIII

PART I—PRE-WORLD WAR II

1	"I Christen Thee *Ranger*"	1
2	"Set the Watch!"	8
3	"The Job Is a Diplomatic One"	19
4	"She Will Prove Herself a Very Valuable Ship"	30
5	"A Very Good Time Was Had by All"	44
6	"Have Reached a Marvelous Efficiency"	57
7	"When a Ship Breaks into the Movies"	68
8	"Bring Back Amelia and Fred!"	78
9	"An Everlasting Remembrance of Admiration and Friendship"	94
10	"The Officers and Men Know Their Business"	106
11	"The Probability of Air Attack on Carriers"	117
12	"*Ranger* Has Taken the Necessary Changes in Stride"	130
13	"Spreading the Butter a Little Thin"	139
14	"With Contagious Enthusiasm"	156

PART II—WORLD WAR II AND AFTER

15	"Our Only Striking Force against Raiders"	177
16	"There Is a Need for a Carrier in the Atlantic"	188
17	"We Could Take No Chances"	208
18	"A 'Red Ripper Special'"	222
19	"Looking for Targets of Opportunity"	232
20	"Morale Drops Quickly before an Enemy Who Is Clearly Superior"	249
21	"Eucalyptus, by the Smell"	260
22	"Well Done *RANGER*"	268
23	"You Have All Done a Grand Job"	286
24	"We Are Too Valuable as a Striking Force"	293
25	"I Am Fed Up with This Place"	309
26	"The Old Ship Came Across in Good Style"	323
27	"*Ranger* Could Be Made Into an Excellent Training Ship."	347
28	"She Didn't Need Headlines to Be a Great Ship"	379
	Notes	398
	Bibliography	425
	Index	429
	About the Author	453

ACKNOWLEDGMENTS

This voyage of research and writing has not been a solitary endeavor, for, if a historian is to recount a story with any degree of confidence, he needs the vital raw material from which the account must be fashioned. This raw material, primary documents, resides in facilities for their preservation, under the care of dedicated professional archivists and curators. I would like to thank the magnificent staff of the branches of the Naval Historical Center: in the Operational Archives, Kathy Lloyd, Mike Walker, Kenneth Johnson, Wade Wyckoff, John Hodges, Regina Akers, and Ariana Jacob, and, particularly, a former member of that staff, Kathy Rohr; in addition, I would also like to thank Roy Grossnick, Mark Evans, and Todd Baker of the Aviation History Branch and Archives; Charles R. Haberlein, Jack Green (now public affairs specialist at the Center), Ed Finney, and Mark Wertheimer of the Curator Branch; in the Navy Department Library, Jean Hort, Glenn Helm, Tonya Simpson, Davis Elliott, and Barbara Auman.

Hill Goodspeed of the Emil Buehler Aviation History Library at the Naval Air Station, Pensacola, Florida, proved of signal assistance. Likewise, the staff at the Still Pictures Branch of the National Archives and Records Administration (NARA) at College Park, Maryland, not only proved knowledgeable, but made doing research in the facility enjoyable. NARA archivists Barry Zerby and Sandy Smith (College Park) and Rebecca Livingston and Richard Peyser (Washington) saw to it that key documentation was pulled and waiting in the research rooms.

Special thanks, too, to Gerald Thomas, formerly of VT-4; Lloyd Edens, of VS-41/VB-4; Comdr. Clifford M. White, Jr., USN (Ret.), formerly of VF-4; the family of the late Aviation Radioman 3d Class George E. "Bugs" Biggs, Jr., USN, of VS-41: his sister, Mrs. Amy McQuade; and his nephew, Eugene Rowley, who contributed recollections and copies of relevant correspondence that shed some light on the short life of one of the two radio-gunners lost in Operation Torch; and Rudy Bakran, brother of the late Aviation Radioman 2d class Stephen D. Bakran, of VB-4.

Christopher Goscha proved invaluable in obtaining important material concerning the French Navy and French Air Force side of Torch; Jack Lambert shared records on the French Air Force that he had gathered in the course of his research for *Wildcats over Casablanca*; Peter Mersky shared photographs gathered in the course of his own research on Torch; Thomas E. Doll provided photographs of Commander, *Ranger* Air Group, aircraft; Larry Suid shared the fruits of his archival work in the records of the Navy's Motion Picture Board; James T. Rindt likewise shared material doggedly gleaned from RG-313; James C. Sawruk, his work in compiling strike rosters; and Steve Ewing, material he had obtained during his biographical research on James Flatley.

A special thanks to my wife, Linda, who lovingly and generously allowed me the time to write and rewrite and reflect on this manuscript, as it grew from source documents to finished product, as did our two children, Christine and Robert, Jr., who often graciously endured my moods as deadlines came and went. Nancy A. Hart, Margaret and Jim Cudney, Tom and Barbara Dolch, Joe and Susan Fisher, Lila Batdorff, and Scranton Nesbitt furnished needed prayer support. Others whose encouragement and kind words helped me in my intellectual voyage to complete this work include John B. Lundstrom, Pete Clayton, Jeffrey G. Barlow, John D. Sherwood, Sarandis Papadopoulos, and Laurie S. Ravin.

Special thanks to Richard A. Russell, erstwhile Contemporary History Branch colleague and good friend, for his patience as editor.

Robert J. Cressman

ABBREVIATIONS AND ACRONYMS

AAR	Aircraft Accident Report	CASU	Carrier Aircraft Service Unit
AARM	Aircraft Accident Report Microfilm	CinCLant	Commander in Chief, Atlantic Fleet
AC	Collier	CinCUS	Commander in Chief, United States Fleet (see ComINCH)
AD	Destroyer tender		
AF	Refrigerated storeship	CL	Light cruiser
AG	Miscellaneous auxiliary	CNO	Chief of Naval Operations
AH	Hospital ship	CO	Commanding Officer
AO	Oiler	ComAirBatFor	Commander Aircraft, Battle Force
AP	Transport	ComAirForLant	Commander Air Force, Atlantic
AR	Repair ship (or Action Report, in endnotes)	ComAirLant	Commander Aircraft, Atlantic Fleet
		ComBatFor	Commander Battle Force
AS	Submarine tender	ComCarDiv	Commander, Carrier Division
AV	Seaplane tender	ComINCH	Commander in Chief, United States Fleet (post-December 1941)
AvH	Aviation History Branch and Archives, Naval Historical Center		
		Conf	Confidential
		CRAG	Commander, *Ranger* Air Group
A-V(N)	USNR flight officer, detailed to active duty in the aeronautic organization of the USN following the completion of their training and designation as naval aviators	CV	Aircraft Carrier
		CVE	Aircraft Carrier, Escort
		CVEG	Escort Carrier Air Group
		CVG	Carrier Air Group
		DC	Dental Corps
		DD	Destroyer
AVP	Small seaplane tender	D-V(G) LCMD	USNR officer, qualified for general duty, afloat or ashore
BB	Battleship		
BuAer	Bureau of Aeronautics		
BuC&R	Bureau of Construction and Repair	GB	*Groupe de Bombardement* (French Air Force, Bombardment Group)
BuNav	Bureau of Navigation		
BuNo	Bureau Number	GC	*Groupe de Chasse* (French Air Force, Fighter Group)
BuShips	Bureau of Ships		
CA	Heavy cruiser	GPO	Government Printing Office

XI

GR	*Groupe de Reconnaissance* (French Air Force, Reconnaissance Group)	USCG	United States Coast Guard
		USMA	United States Military Academy
		USMC	United States Marine Corps
GT	*Groupe de Transport* (French Air Force, Transport Group)	USNA	United States Naval Academy
		USNR	United States Naval Reserve
HIA	Hoover Institution Archives	VB	Bombing Squadron ("Bombing [Number of Squadron]")
LCMD	Library of Congress Manuscript Division		
		VBF	Bombing Fighting Squadron
LSO	Landing Signal Officer	VC	Composite Squadron
Ltr	Letter	VF	Fighting Squadron ("Fighting [Number of Squadron]")
MC	Medical Corps		
MCHC	Marine Corps Historical Center	VF(N)	Fighting Squadron (Night)
Msg	Message	VGF	Escort Fighting Squadron
NA	National Archives	VGS	Escort Scouting Squadron
NAP	Naval Aviation Pilot	VJ	Utility Squadron
NARA	National Archives and Records Administration	VMF	Marine Fighting Squadron
		VMJ	Marine Utility Squadron
NAS	Naval Air Station	VMO	Marine Observation Squadron
NDL	Navy Department Library	VMS	Marine Scouting Squadron
NHC	Naval Historical Center	VMSB	Marine Scouting/Bombing Squadron
NOB	Naval Operating Base	VO	Observation Squadron
OA	Operational Archives Branch, Naval Historical Center	VOC	Observation Spotter Squadron
		VP	Patrol Squadron
SC	Supply Corps	VS	Scouting Squadron ("Scouting [Number of Squadron]")
SH	Ships' Histories Branch, Naval Historical Center		
		VT	Torpedo Squadron ("Torpedo [Number of Squadron]")
SS	Submarine		
TF	Task Force	WD	War Diary
TG	Task Group	WrNr	Werke Number (German term)
TU	Task Unit	XO	Executive Officer
USAAF	United States Army Air Force	ZRS	Rigid airship

WATCHES

All times in this book are based on the "watches" of a 24-hour clock. These are: first watch (2000–2400), mid watch (0000–0400), morning watch (0400–0800), forenoon watch (0800–1200), afternoon watch (1200–1600), first dog watch (1600–1800), second dog watch (1800–2000). Individual times are rendered in keeping with the 24-hour clock, that is, one o'clock in the afternoon is 1300, two o'clock is 1400, and so on, and, unless otherwise noted, reflecting the times observed by the ship during the course of her life.

INTRODUCTION

Norwegians in Bodø and Fagervika, near the Arctic Circle, may have often heard airplane engines since their country had fallen under the Nazi heel. On that memorable Monday morning, however—4 October 1943—the planes that swept in from over the cold Norwegian Sea at low level, like birds of prey bent on destruction, bore not black and white crosses or the swastika, but red-outlined blue and white stars and bars. They were not Heinkels or Junkers, but Grummans and Douglasses, roaring in at low level or pushing over into shallow glide-bombing runs to unleash bullets and bombs on unsuspecting German convoys in the leads of the fjords between Bodø and Sandnessjøen.

From Carrier Air Group (CVG) 4, they flew from the second-oldest aircraft carrier in the United States Navy's inventory, the United States Ship *Ranger* (CV-4), and carried out the only U.S. Navy carrier strike on Axis shipping above the Arctic Circle during World War II. More important, however, the strike carried out by CVG-4 heartened those living under the yoke of the Nazis and their Quisling allies. Norwegians who nurtured the flickering flame of freedom in their hearts never forgot the sight of the *Ranger*'s planes that day. The fleeting presence of American planes provided them with the hope to sustain them until they regained their freedom from tyranny. "Those of us in Fagervika who witnessed the battle that raged more or less on our doorstep," wrote one Norwegian observer later, "came to look upon the presence of the American aircraft as a reaching out of hands from the other side of the vast ocean—a reaching out of hands from brothers—a gesture which in itself bore promise of a new dawn, a new future for our beloved Norway."[1]

Aircraft carriers—virtually small floating, moving cities—provide a mobile base for a powerful striking group of aircraft, such as the Wildcats, Avengers, and Dauntlesses of CVG-4 that autumn day in 1943. More than with any other type of ship, a carrier's chronicle consists of two parallel stories, each reflecting facets of the personality of a "flattop": one deals with the ship and the other the air group for which she serves as home. Although the size of that seagoing city has increased over the years, and the capability for both fighting a war and keeping the peace has become more sophisticated, the basic mission has remained unaltered. The aircraft carrier and the power she projects remains viable as America combats global terrorism at the beginning of a new millenium.

United States Ship *Ranger* served the U.S. Navy continually from her commissioning in 1934 to her inactivation in 1946, and performed whatever task was assigned her. Strangely, there has never been a "biography" of the *Ranger*, the Navy's first aircraft carrier built as such from the keel up. She played a part in maintaining President Franklin D. Roosevelt's "Good Neighbor" policy toward Argentina, Brazil, and Uruguay, on her 1934 shakedown cruise. Beginning in 1935 and continuing through her participation in the 1939 war games, she participated in the yearly large-scale Fleet Problems, which testified to the growing importance of carriers and carrier aircraft. She continued the

Navy's work in cold weather operations in 1936, and, being the first carrier equipped with a director-controlled antiaircraft system, pioneered that work in carriers. Those familiar with the story know that planes from the aircraft carrier *Lexington* (CV-2) looked for the lost aviatrix Amelia Earhart in 1937, but few probably know that three of the six squadrons that operated from the *Lexington* during that search were actually from the *Ranger* Air Group.

All of the *Ranger*'s pre–World War II commanding officers went on to attain flag rank and directed larger forces during that global conflict. Although her design characteristics and limitations circumscribed the role she would play in the war, she occupied center stage in the carrier operations during Operation Torch in November 1942 and conducted the only U.S. Navy carrier air strikes above the Arctic Circle in Operation Leader in October 1943. Both operations reflected, in part, a problem that would confront the United States in later conflicts (in Vietnam and in more recent conflicts "other than war"): hitting legitimate military targets (Vichy French or German and Quisling shipping), while minimizing civilian casualties in proximity.

Many pilots and radio-gunners from CVG-4, who had participated in either Operation Torch or Leader, or both, went on to fly from the famous *Essex* (CV-9) and fight in the Pacific, but the *Ranger*, as she had done throughout her career, continued to train hundreds more pilots—her sole role from 1944 to 1946. In 1945, she served as a platform for the trials of new aircraft (the Ryan Fireball) and new technology (airborne early warning). The fact that her employment limited

The *Ranger*'s Utility Unit insignia, 17 January 1939: the 13 stars represent the original 13 colonies, surrounding a silhouette head of Captain John Paul Jones, who commanded the first *Ranger* in 1777, the year at the upper left; the year 1934 represents when the then-present *Ranger* was commissioned. (NA, 80-G-464912)

her combat use does not diminish the professionalism and courage of her officers and men. This, then, is the unique, never-before-told story of the USS *Ranger*, related as the biography of a great lady, in the context of momentous times.

PART I
PRE-WORLD WAR II

1

"I CHRISTEN THEE RANGER"

A festive atmosphere prevailed at Newport News that Saturday as Mrs. Herbert Hoover, wife of the outgoing President of the United States and the first First Lady to christen an aircraft carrier, declared, "I christen thee *Ranger*." She smashed a bottle of Prohibition-era grape juice on the bow of the ship that towered before her, while Secretary of the Navy Charles Francis Adams, Assistant Secretary of the Navy and Mrs. Ernest L. Jahncke, Mrs. William V. Pratt, the wife of the Chief of Naval Operations, and Homer L. Ferguson, president of the shipbuilding company, and his wife, all looked on. Rear Adm. William A. Moffett, Chief of the Bureau of Aeronautics (BuAer), who had battled for the ship in the bureau and congressional hearings, attended as well, his work vindicated.[1] Then the *Ranger*, her name bestowed in accordance with time-honored naval tradition, gathered momentum and slid down the building ways on 25 February 1933. A crescendo of appreciative applause joined the screeching whistles of nearby ships and boats, and the drone of airplanes overhead.[2]

Later, the First Lady, remembering gratefully how an Allied relief expedition of American sailors and marines had rescued the Hoovers, along with others besieged in Tientsin, China, during the Boxer Rebellion more than three decades before, explained why christening the *Ranger* had been a "most thrilling" experience: "I shall always have a soft spot in my heart for the Navy," she declared, "because the blue-jackets of the Navy once saved the life of my husband and myself from Oriental bullets and knives."[3]

Unofficial estimates numbered the crowd at around 15,000 people, no doubt because of the holiday that had been declared throughout the city. Doubtless, too, the news that future contracts would be headed to Newport News, thus furnishing work for many people, also helped the happy atmosphere. Among those witnessing the launching were Comdr. Charles A. "Baldy" Pownall and his wife Mary; Pownall, Navy people had it on good authority, was to be the *Ranger*'s executive officer.[4]

The road to the launch that Saturday morning had been fraught with difficulties.[5] Following the 1922 Washington Treaty, the U.S. Navy found itself with the problem of how to apportion its allotted aircraft carrier tonnage of 69,000 tons. The first U.S. carrier—an experimental ship—was the *Langley* (CV-1), converted from the collier *Jupiter* (AC-13). With the cancellation of battle cruiser construction as the result of the 1922 arms limitation treaty, two aircraft carrier conversions, the *Lexington* (CV-2) and the *Saratoga* (CV-3), followed. The Bureau of Construction and Repair began studying the matter of a built-for-the-purpose carrier in 1922, the year the *Langley* was commissioned and the *Lexington* and *Saratoga* were authorized. Two years later, the General Board, the Secretary of the Navy's highest policy advisory body, accelerated work on potential carrier designs, only to see its efforts rendered irrelevant when the bill for which the designs were produced failed to pass. Undeterred, the board resumed work during 1925–26 to prepare for the Fiscal Year 1929 building program. On 1 November 1927, the General Board recommended to the Secretary of the

Mrs. Hoover smashes a flask of grape juice on the *Ranger*'s bow during launching ceremonies, 25 February 1933, as Secretary of the Navy Charles Francis Adams (L) and Homer Ferguson, president of the shipyard, watch (R). (NA, 80-G-391490)

Navy military characteristics to be incorporated into the design of aircraft carriers included in the five-year building program submitted the previous September. A little over a fortnight later, the first battle cruiser conversion, the *Saratoga*, went into commission, followed a month later by the second, the *Lexington*.

The General Board believed that a 13,800-ton carrier satisfactorily embodied all of the necessary characteristics of larger ships, and would thus enable more of them to be built. The board also specified that the ship have a clear flying deck, be fitted for use as a flagship, and carry an air group in the ratio of three light planes (fighting, spotting, light bombing, and tactical scouting) for every one heavy (bombing and torpedo planes), for a total of 108. The board also specified twelve 5-inch antiaircraft guns and a "maximum number of machine guns that can be installed clear of [the] flying deck with effective arcs of fire."[6] Two catapults were to be fitted, athwartships, on the hangar deck.

After soliciting the comments of officers from the *Lexington* and the *Saratoga* on the initial operations of those ships, the General Board forwarded the original design for what would become CV-4, on 11 February 1928. The board had discussed with those carrier officers the relative disadvantages of open or closed hangars, the arrangement and size of arresting gear, the size and location of elevators, and the number, capacity, and character of the cranes and weight-handling appliances. Other elements of carrier design taken into account included the height of hangars, the location of catapults, gun arrangements, bomb and

As Old Glory streams from her flagstaff, the *Ranger*, scaffolding festooning her fantail and temporary wooden railings lining her elevator pits, gathers momentum as she is launched into the James River, 25 February 1933. A tug (R) stands toward the ship to assist in taking her to a fitting-out berth. (NA, 80-G-1007392)

torpedo stowage, and the location and arrangements of palisades (windbreaks), nettings and galleries, all of which went into the general arrangement drawings. The conferees made the size and arrangement of the flight deck and hangar space the primary feature: Those elements dictated sacrifices in other areas. To obtain a flight deck of maximum width (86 feet), the designers found it necessary to create a hull form of marked flare.

Congress finally authorized the aircraft carrier, known at the outset only by the alphanumeric hull number CV-4, on 13 February 1929, stipulating a total cost, "including armor and armament, not to exceed $19,000,000."[7] About 1 June 1929, however, the first summary of weights in the original design showed a margin of greater than 200 tons over the projected displacement. Utilizing men from the standard plans, war plans, and weight calculation sections, the Bureau of Construction and Repair redrew the plans to an accelerated timetable and accommodated a 400-ton margin. Before the year 1929 was out, however, a numbing depression began to grip the United States, and domestic economic concerns dominated the attention of the nation.

The Navy Department opened bids for CV-4's construction on 3 September 1930. Newport News Shipbuilding and Dry Dock Company of Newport News, Virginia, outbid the Bethlehem Shipbuilding Corporation of Quincy, Massachusetts, and New York Shipbuilding Company of Camden, New Jersey, and, in November 1930, received the contract to build her.

Secretary of the Navy Adams assigned the name *Ranger*—a name originally assigned to one of the projected battle cruisers eliminated by the 1922 Washington Treaty—to CV-4 on 10 December 1930. Four previous U.S. Navy commissioned ships had carried that name, beginning with the 18-gun sloop authorized and built by order of the Continental Congress and first commanded by Captain John Paul Jones.[8]

Workmen at Newport News laid the keel for the fifth *Ranger* on 26 September 1931. Further design changes followed, including the addition of an island structure for ship control, gunnery direction, and the control of flight deck operations, and including the elimination of catapults. Construction proceeded over the next 17 months, culminating in the launching on 25 February 1933.

Four months after the *Ranger* had slid down the ways, her nucleus crew began forming at the Receiving Station at Norfolk, with the establishment of the "*Ranger* Detail" on 23 June 1933. Chief Commissaryman Lloyd W. McDonald, transferred from the battleship *Idaho* (BB-42) on that day, became the carrier's first crewman. Six days later, the first staff officer, Lt. Comdr. Edwin D. Foster, Supply Corps, reported for duty. The 37-year-old Foster, who had been appointed assistant paymaster in June 1917, held a bachelor's degree from Princeton and a recently earned master's in business administration from Harvard, where he had become acquainted with Clarence Birdseye, a pioneer in the fields of processed and frozen foods. Foster was no stranger to aircraft carriers, having been supply officer in the *Langley*. Commander William G. Greenman, USNA 1912, reported to the *Ranger* Detail on 8 July 1933, establishing the office of "Prospective Commanding Officer, *Ranger*," on 22 July at the Newport News yard. Commander Pownall reported on 1 August and formally took over the duties of that office.[9]

As the *Ranger* took shape in her builders' skilled hands, she looked small when compared to the ex-battle cruisers

Fitting out at Newport News, 21 March 1934; fences surround the three elevator openings in the flight deck. (NA, 80-CF file)

Lexington and the *Saratoga*. The "Lex" and the "Sara" each measured 888 feet overall; the former displaced 39,056 tons and the latter 38,957. The *Ranger* would have a trial displacement of 15,575 and measure 728 feet in length at the waterline, but her clipper bow extended that length to 769; her extreme beam at the waterline measured 80 feet 1 inch; above, the main deck was 109 feet 6 inches. Her flight deck measured 709 by 86 feet; three elevators allowed easy movement of planes between flight and hangar decks. High-pressure Curtis-geared turbines and low-pressure Parsons-geared turbines, plus six oil-fired Babcock and Wilcox boilers, enabled the *Ranger* to attain a designed speed of 29.25 knots.

Unlike the massive islands of her twin predecessors, the *Ranger* had only a small structure on her starboard side, fitted with a light tripod mast and a pole mast. And, instead of the massive stacks that characterized the *Lexington* and *Saratoga*, the *Ranger*'s six "special swinging smoke pipes," installed three per side well aft, folded from the vertical to the horizontal to allow for a virtually uninterrupted space for plane operations, which was a feature that had been utilized in the *Langley*. Electric motors controlled the movement of each stack, and the smoke could be shifted to the lee side to permit a landing area free of stack gases. The principal weapons for her own defense—in addition to her air group—were eight 5 inch/25-caliber guns: a pair at the bow, a pair on the fantail, and one each in four galleries at the quarters, controlled by two Mk. 33 directors, the first such system installed in an aircraft carrier. Her designers, specifically wary of dive-bombing attacks, had made provision for forty .50-caliber Browning water-cooled machine guns as a close-in battery, sited in galleries just below the level of the flight deck. Her complement, including an embarked air group, consisted of 216 officers and 2,245 enlisted men. To feed the large company of men that made up the *Ranger*'s crew, cafeteria-style messing arrangements had been incorporated into her design. She was the first such combatant ship to be so equipped.[10]

2
"SET THE WATCH"

Less than a year after the *Ranger* slid down the ways, the Navy selected Capt. Arthur LeRoy "Roy" Bristol to command her. Classmates in the Naval Academy class of 1906 regarded the 47-year-old South Carolinian as a "calm and easy going cavalier from the 'Sunny South,'" who possessed "a manner of serious reserve that convinces without a hearing." Among his tours of duty ashore and afloat, Bristol had served as flag secretary and acting chief of staff to the commander of the Cruiser and Transport Force during World War I, for which service he had received the Navy Cross and the Distinguished Service Medal. He had also participated in the evacuation of refugees from the Crimea in the wake of the Russian Civil War in 1920; had attended and then instructed at the Naval War College, and had served as a member of the Naval Mission to Brazil. Completing flight training at Pensacola in February 1929 and awarded the wings of a naval aviator, Bristol assumed command of the seaplane tender *Jason* (AV-2), with additional duties as Commander, Aircraft Squadrons, Asiatic Fleet, soon thereafter. His most recent post had been the prestigious one of naval attaché in London. Regarded by his contemporaries as "an able planner and organizer" who "combined a capacity for hard work with a kindly geniality," capable and personable, "productive and easy to get along with," as well as an "excellent leader with high administrative abilities," Bristol reported for "duty involving flying" in connection with fitting out the *Ranger* on 9 April 1934.[1]

A week later, on 16 April, the carrier's Marine Detachment was formed at the Norfolk Navy Yard under the command of Capt. Clifford O. Henry, USMC. Like the ship's company, the Marines tapped for service in the *Ranger* reflected experience: First Sgt. Josiah D. Johnson, "the type of leader men need aboard [*sic*] ship," had formerly been the acting sergeant major at the Norfolk Navy Yard; Gunnery Sgt. Ora C. Harter had been an instructor on the rifle range at Parris Island; Cpls. Gulledge E. "Squads Right" Curry and Thomas H. "Pop" Simpson had earned ratings of first class gun pointer and gun pointer, respectively, on board the battleship *Texas* (BB-35). Other Marines who gave the detachment its character at the outset were Cpl. Lewis J. Fields, "drill-master extraordinary" of Parris Island and the "Gable of the USMC," and Cpl. Robert D. Cullum, a "professional chiseler," about whom it was said, "If you want it—tell Cullum. He will get it." In the event that the ship conducted a cruise to South American waters, Captain Henry, formerly the detail officer at Headquarters, Marine Corps, began conducting Spanish language classes "for those who are ambitious."[2]

Less than a month after the *Ranger*'s prospective commanding officer had arrived at the shipyard, Newport News put the ship through her paces off the Virginia capes on 1–2 May; the Navy then ran her through preliminary trials off Rockland, Maine, between 8 and 15 May. On 2 June, the ship's Marine Detachment reported on board. Manned and directed by shipyard people, with a nucleus crew of U.S. Navy officers and men alongside them as observers, the *Ranger* departed her builder's yard at 0740 on 4 June 1934, and arrived alongside Pier 7, Naval Operating Base (NOB)

Captain Arthur L. Bristol, having reported for duty as prospective commanding officer of the *Ranger* a little over a fortnight before, looks over his crew at NAS Norfolk, 25 April 1934. (NA, 80-G-391493)

Norfolk, at 0900, at which time the remainder of the ship's company, with bags and hammocks, reported on board.[3]

"Admiral Smith," said Homer Ferguson, the shipyard's president, as he presented his firm's latest warship to the Navy, "it gives me great pleasure to turn over to you the USS *Ranger*." Rear Adm. Arthur St. Clair Smith, Commandant of the Fifth Naval District, then presented Ferguson with a receipt, provisionally accepting her. A short time later, at 1043, in the presence of his white-uniformed ship's company, and the assembled guests, on the maroon and chrome-yellow flight deck, Captain Bristol read his orders to command the Navy's newest aircraft carrier. Turning to Comdr. Pownall, Bristol gave the crisp order: "Set the watch." The executive officer complied, and soon the shrill boatswain's pipe sounded over the loud speakers with the repeated words, "Set the watch!" The stars and stripes snapped up the halyards and unfurled in the breeze, as the *Ranger*'s Marines, who had stood "with burning necks and aching feet," smartly presented arms at Captain Henry's command, the band played the National Anthem, and the USS *Ranger* went into commission.[4]

Following engineering trials off the Chesapeake lightship shortly on the 18th, the *Ranger* shifted to Lynnhaven Roads on the 20th. She got underway a little over an hour into the morning watch on 21 June to carry out her initial flight operations off the Virginia capes. With the destroyer *Barry* (DD-248) steaming astern as plane guard, the *Ranger* went to flight quarters and, in the laconic prose of the ship's deck log, "commenced sending observation land planes into the air and receiving them on deck."[5]

Forty-one-year-old Lt. Comdr. Arthur C. Davis, the *Ranger*'s air officer, piloting U.S.S. RANGER-1, a Vought O3U-3 (BuNo 9318), plane number one of the ship's utility unit, with Aviation Chief Machinist's Mate H. E. Wallace, of the ship's V-2 division, in the rear seat, made the first takeoff and the first landing. After recovering planes over the bow later that afternoon—a practice that the *Ranger* would establish as "routine," because she was the first carrier equipped with both bow and stern arresting gear—she anchored for the evening off Virginia Beach. "Today was Air Department day," Captain Bristol told his crew upon the conclusion of the evolutions of 21 June, and heartily congratulated "the officers and men of the Air Department for their successful accomplishment of the day's operations." The Air Department had shone that day, but the captain recognized the work of all departments that had contributed to "this happy result."[6]

The following morning, with the *Barry* again in company, the *Ranger* got underway at 0732 and went to flight quarters at 0805, launching two of her utility unit planes to fly to the Naval Air Station (NAS) at Hampton Roads. They returned in an hour, U.S.S. RANGER-1 bearing Rear

Drydocked following builder's trials, Newport News, 2 May 1934. (NA, 80-CF-file)

Adm. Ernest J. King, the Chief of BuAer, who had flown down from Washington, and who remained on board for a little under an hour. After the *Ranger* had rendered him appropriate honors, King climbed into the O3U-3 and departed for NAS Norfolk, evidently pleased, congratulating Captain Bristol for his ship's good early showing. "What I have seen," King wrote, "gives every promise of a fine ship manned by a fine crew, which is a combination that cannot be beat. I have been happy to have been aboard and hope to come again."[7] That evening, the *Ranger* again anchored in Lynnhaven Roads.

Assisted by the harbor tugs *Mohawk* (YT-17), *Reindeer* (YT-115), and *Stallion* (YT-120), and the Wead Towing Corporation tugs *Helen* and *Nonpariel*, the *Ranger* moored at the Norfolk Navy Yard on 23 June to begin outfitting work that lasted through the following month. Private 1st Class Wallace V. "Tex" Fowler and Pvts. Davies E. Wakefield and Frank S. Brown, USMC, undoubtedly welcomed the ship's being moored, having been "practically prostated by the nausea of the sea" in the early going.[8]

While the ship to which it would be assigned lay in yard hands, a new squadron joined the Fleet—Bombing Squadron (VB) 5B—when 44-year-old Lt. Comdr. James D. Barner read his orders to take command on 2 July 1934. Barner, promoted from the warrant ranks, had received his commission in 1918. He won his wings at Pensacola in 1922 and, in the ensuing years, as the American public began to hear more about aviation, accumulated laurels as a test pilot.

The new squadron's early operations did not proceed wholly without incident. On 9 July, Ens. Victor H. Soucek, making his first flight in one of the squadron's Boeing F4B-4s, attempted a slow roll, but soon found "that the part of his anatomy through which an aviator is supposed to do his

During final acceptance trials off Rockland, Maine, 12 May 1934, all hands brace themselves as the *Ranger* heels to starboard as her rudder is put hard over. (NA, 80-CF-21148-1A)

best flying [the seat of his pants] suddenly parted company with its accompanying cushion." Soucek's safety belt had broken, but, possessing "the same tenacity of purpose and lightning intellect of his two famous cousins [Zeus and Apollo], he held on with his toes and eye teeth until he could right his plane" and make a normal landing.[9]

Nine days later, Lt. (jg) DeVere L. Day, after having made several hard landings during carrier landing practice, made an "eggshell" landing that aviators often dream of "and always claim, but seldom actually make," only to find at the end of his landing run that the landing gear V-strut had collapsed. "Off like a bloodhound on the scent of a new strut," Day, belonging to the materiel section of VB-5B, managed to locate one "from a secret cache and returned to the hangar with it." The squadron's engineering department had it installed by "secure" that afternoon, and the Boeing sat ready for the following day's evolutions.[10]

One mishap, however, had nearly disastrous consequences, as Lt. (jg) John G. "Jack" Burgess discovered on the morning of 23 July, while returning from a division formation tactics flight to land at Northwest Field, NAS Hampton Roads, in a Boeing F4B-4 (BuNo A-9030). Heading in an easterly direction as the sixth plane in the landing circle, and just before turning south, Burgess glanced at his air speed indicator. He saw that he was flying at about 80 knots. His altimeter showed about 150 feet. Seeing that all aircraft were landing well to the northeast side of the field, Burgess knew that he would have to make a sharp turn to keep clear of the other planes. As he started the turn, the controls and engine seemed to be functioning normally, and the Boeing felt secure.

At an altitude of about 75 feet, however, Burgess felt 5-B-9 wafted by the slipstream of the plane ahead. The nose of 5-B-9 "whipped up and then down in almost the same

Captain Bristol reads the orders designating him as commanding officer of United States Ship *Ranger*, NOB Norfolk, 4 June 1934. Looking on at left is Comdr. Charles A. Pownall, the *Ranger*'s executive officer. The ship's Marine Detachment stands at attention in the background. (NA, 80-G-391496)

instant.... The controls did not feel mushy, but... completely inefficient." Burgess instantly realized that a crash loomed: "My nose was so far down," he later wrote, "that I realized I was going to hit the ground, despite anything I could do." He pulled the control column back and to the left, hoping to coax some altitude out of his mount, and cut the engine. When he realized he was going to crash, it seemed like the attitude of his plane was "almost vertical to the ground." Striking on its right wing and on its nose, Five-Baker-Nine began to cartwheel. The engine struck a ditch and tore itself loose; the rest of the plane came to rest right-side up in the rough of the Norfolk Naval Station golf course. Burgess, who suffered only a cut above his left eye, either from his goggles or the windshield when he was thrown forward against it upon impact, groggily climbed out of the wrecked fighter unassisted. His foresight in cutting off his engine had forestalled a fire.[11]

Burgess's fellow pilots congratulated him not only upon his good fortune (his almost miraculously sustaining only a very minor injury) but also for his "civic enterprise in enlarging the golf course to a 'ten-holer.'" Burgess, known by his USNA classmates as "alive and full of fun" and the possessor of an "unfailing sense of humor," displayed those agreeable traits when he granted nonchalantly "that the landing was part of the day's work." He added, with tongue in cheek, that he was contemplating "entering the Civil Engineering field as a golf course expert." A trouble board, by contrast, evidenced no sense of humor, faulting the pilot's poor technique as the cause of the crash. Burgess had, however, only flown Boeings for about eight hours, and, as the trouble board remarked "the sensitivity of control of this model airplane is so much greater than that of the types which Lieutenant (jg) Burgess had been flying." The plane was concluded to be beyond salvage and was stricken.[12]

That same day, as the pilots earmarked to fly off the *Ranger* were practicing their trade and proving their mettle, so were the sailors who would man the ship. Seaman 1st Class John W. Sloan fell into the water off Pier 4 at the Norfolk Navy Yard. Fireman 1st Class Ernest G. Hewitt, from the *Ranger*'s M Division, immediately dove into the water and saved him. Hewitt, who had enlisted in the Navy in 1930 and re-enlisted in '34, would later receive a commendatory letter from the Secretary of the Navy, as well as a Silver Life Saving Medal from the Treasury Department. The medals proved another type of honor for "Spider" Hewitt, who had held the title of welterweight champion of the Navy since 10 March 1933. Having begun boxing about the time he joined the Navy, Hewitt had fought in 56 bouts, winning 51 of them.

The *Ranger* departed the Norfolk Navy Yard on 3 August, the planned yard work unaffected by a canteen storeroom fire that consumed 96¢ worth of candy bars on 27 July, and continued preparations to begin operating in the role for which she had been intended. At the beginning of the forenoon watch on 4 August, she embarked the men of Bombing Squadron (VB) 5B, VB-3B, and Fighting Squadron (VF) 3B, from NAS Hampton Roads.

VB-5B's men found the living and working quarters comfortable and easily accessible. Reaching the squadron office, store room, ready room, or living quarters, for example, did not require use of "the tedious 'follow the green line'" system. Not only could one find his way around the ship

Alongside Pier 7, NOB Norfolk, with (L–R) the minesweeper *Owl* (AM-2), the fleet tug *Allegheny* (AT-19), and the minesweeper *Robin* (AM-3), 11 June 1934. (NA, 80-CF-2114-2)

with relative ease, but "every effort has been made," VB-5B's scribe recounted, "to make as comfortable and easy as possible the obtaining of the vital information as to where the carrier is when one takes off and what is more important where she will be when one gets back."[13] Each squadron enjoyed its own ready room, to enable those plotting their navigation to be "immeasurably more successful . . . than trying to stand on one foot and look through the backs of several other people all seeking to get the same information from one board." Another innovation that excited comment was the "attention" howler that prompted one wit to observe, "It made quite a few of the boys homesick by its remarkable resemblance to hog-calling down on the farm." Despite its down-home sound, though, the *Ranger*'s people found it very effective.[14] Meanwhile, the first of VB-5B's new planes, the Curtiss XBF2C-1, reached the experimental division at NAS Hampton Roads, thus affording the squadron's pilots the chance to help put the required 150 accelerated service hours on the aircraft.

Underway early in the morning watch on 6 August to conduct her first operations with her assigned air group, minus the fourth squadron, Scouting Squadron (VS) 1B, the *Ranger* sounded flight quarters 32 miles off Cape Henry, a half hour before the start of the forenoon watch. She first landed her utility planes, then those from the three squadrons whose men she had embarked on the 4th. She carried out engineering runs on the 7th and into the 8th, commencing launch of the three squadrons' planes at 0735 that day.

At 0825, five minutes into the *Ranger*'s recovering VS-1B, Lt. Halstead L. Hopping, flying a Vought SU-4 (BuNo 9419), began his approach. Lieutenant Samuel H. Arthur, the landing signal officer (LSO), deemed it a bit

Lieutenant Comdr. Arthur C. Davis makes the first landing on the *Ranger*'s flight deck, in a Vought O3U-3 (BuNo 9318), off the Virginia capes, 21 June 1934, with Aviation Chief Machinist's Mate H. E. Wallace, of the ship's V-2 division, as his passenger. The O3U carries the legend "U.S.S. RANGER-1" on the after fuselage; red, white, and blue stripes adorn the rudder, markings specified for ship utility unit aircraft. (NA, 80-G-391498)

Lieutenant Comdr. Arthur C. Davis and Aviation Chief Machinist's Mate H. E. Wallace stand in front of U.S.S. RANGER-1, a Vought O3U-3 (BuNo 9318) used in the first take off and landing from the *Ranger*'s flight deck, 21 June 1934. (NA, 80-G-391499)

Fitting out, Norfolk Navy Yard, 13 July 1934; the battleship *Idaho* (BB-42) lies across the pier in this view taken from a *Lexington* (CV-2) plane. (NA, 80-CF file)

high and signaled "high." Hopping compensated and received an "R" ("roger"), but then dipped, receiving a "low" signal. Arthur saw Hopping's approach as "normal," although he noted that it was slightly off-center, which was, in his estimation, not unusual. Guiding 1-S-7 in the groove, Arthur signaled "cut," so indicating by drawing a paddle across his throat in a cutting motion.[15]

At that point, however, Hopping's SU-4 drifted to port, restricting the pilot's view of the LSO. Although Hopping had seen Arthur drawing a paddle across his throat and had closed the throttle, he realized almost simultaneously that he was "well to the left of the centerline." He tried to center 1-S-7, but inadvertently opened the throttle. Hopping's trailing tailhook caught the number nine wire, but parted it because of the load imposed by the SU-4's excess speed. Consequently, the unbridled SU-4 crashed into the barrier.

The impact buckled the fuselage, badly bent the landing gear strut fittings, broke the diagonal engine mount braces and the front spar of the lower right wing, cracked and buckled the left gasoline tank, and demolished the landing gear, as the *Ranger* logged her first flight deck mishap.[16]

In the meantime, while the *Ranger* had been conducting her first flight operations, preparations for her shakedown cruise, to "train the crew and . . . to test fully the machinery plants within six months of delivery to the Government while the contractors' guarantee is still in effect," continued. Originally, she had not been scheduled to proceed beyond the Gulf of Mexico. Captain Bristol, however, confident that her "special features" could be safeguarded, pressed for extending her cruise to Rio de Janeiro, Brazil (where he had served as a member of the U.S. Naval Mission between 19 January 1925 and 26 October 1926). Rear Adm. King,

Lieutenant (jg) Jack Burgess's Boeing F4B-4 (BuNo 9030) (5-B-9), after its crash on 23 July 1934, in the "rough" of the Norfolk Naval Station golf course. Note lack of squadron insignia on the fuselage. (NA, VF4B-4/ L11-1 file, Box 4918, RG-72)

Chief of BuAer, concurred, and the Department agreed to send the ship to Rio, reasoning that that would allow for a longer "free-route" cruise, as well as afford her crew a chance to visit a "large foreign port south of the Equator." Accordingly, on 14 July, as the *Ranger* lay in the Norfolk Navy Yard, continuing her fitting out, the Navy, in accordance with standard procedure, requested the Department of State to make the "usual diplomatic notifications" for the proposed visit.[17]

"Showing the flag" constituted part of the Navy's peacetime mission. With the inauguration of Franklin Delano Roosevelt as President in March 1933, soon after the *Ranger* had been launched, the United States had begun to institute a "Good Neighbor" policy with the nations that lay to the south. That approach differed significantly from that of "non recognition" (withholding diplomatic recognition from governments that had come to power in other than democratic means), practiced since the administration of Woodrow Wilson but relaxed under Roosevelt's predecessor, Herbert Hoover. Relations with each Latin American nation posed unique difficulties and unique challenges.

The Department of State informed the Navy on 6 August that the Brazilian authorities did not object to the *Ranger*'s visiting Rio. Following public announcement of the *Ranger*'s shakedown itinerary two days later, however, Alexander S. Weddell, U.S. Ambassador to the Argentine Republic, wired his superiors at State, expressing concern lest the Argentines feel slighted that the *Ranger* would visit Rio and not Buenos Aires, too. At about the same time, Comdr. Edmund W. Strother, the naval attaché accredited to Montevideo, Uruguay, and Buenos Aires, Argentina, pondered the effects of the perceived diplomatic slight. Regarded by his USNA classmates as "conscientious and hard-working, so earnest in everything he does," Commander Strother also urged that the *Ranger*'s cruise include Buenos Aires.[18]

Diplomatic concerns could not be easily dismissed given the importance of the relationship between the United States and Argentina especially in the realm of hemispheric leadership. The Navy had slated the new heavy cruiser *Tuscaloosa* (CA-37) to visit Buenos Aires in November on *her* shakedown as regional tensions in the wake of the assassination of Austrian chancellor Engelbert Dollfuss in July 1934 had prompted the Department to cancel the *Tuscaloosa*'s originally scheduled European voyage. Because lengthening the *Ranger*'s cruise would limit the operations that the carrier could conduct prior to her final acceptance trials, the service did not look favorably upon the extension. However, because the Navy wished to assist the Department of State in furthering the Good Neighbor policy, it

Boeing F4B-4s (VF-5B) and Martin BM-1s (VB-1B) sit spotted on the forward part of the flight deck, facing astern, as the *Ranger* prepares for a stern launch, 7 August 1934; the crew stands in the shade provided by the aircraft in the warm summer sun. (NA, 80-CF-54862-6)

Boeing F4B-4 (BuNo 9256) of VF-3B, Three-Fox-Seven, stowed on an outrigger on the port side of the flight deck, 7 August 1934. (NA, 80-G-13364)

Vought SU-4 (BuNo 9419) of VS-1B at NAS Hampton Roads, 9 August 1934, the day after its barrier crash—the *Ranger*'s first. (NA, VSU4/L11-1 files, RG-72, Box 5485)

granted the inclusion of Buenos Aires—and Montevideo, too, for good measure—on 14 August.

Two days later, Adm. William H. Standley, the Chief of Naval Operations (CNO), visited the ship in mufti. Six years before, when he had been director of fleet training in the office of the CNO, Standley had taken part in the hearings on the design of the ship that he was visiting. He spent a little over three hours on board, inspecting her thoroughly. He disembarked pleased with what he had seen.

A little less than an hour and a quarter into the afternoon watch on 17 August, the *Ranger*, with only a utility unit embarked (and VB-5B's 5-B-19, its Grumman SF-1 liaison plane), stood out of Hampton Roads. As she passed the *Lexington* and the *Saratoga*, the latter's band serenaded her with "There'll Be a Hot Time in the Old Town Tonight." After responding with the National Anthem, the *Ranger*'s musicians played "Auld Lang Syne." Outside the Roads, the *Ranger* met the battleships *Mississippi* (BB-41), *West Virginia* (BB-48), *Texas* (BB-35), and *New York* (BB-34), steaming in column. More salutes and men standing at attention ensued. Finally, "with them passed," a *Ranger* sailor later wrote, "we headed to sea, south and east! RIO AHEAD!"[19]

3

"THE JOB IS A DIPLOMATIC ONE"

The *Ranger*'s voyage proceeded uneventfully until the 20th, when the U.S. Shipping Board freighter *Collingsworth*, also Rio-bound, radioed the carrier, inquiring how to treat a case of epistaxis, or nosebleed. Nicholas de la Fuente, 44-year-old Argentine-born ship's cook, had a severe case, prompting the merchantman's request for assistance. The *Ranger*'s medical department responded with directions by radio and all—for a time—went well.

Two days later, however, the *Collingsworth* radioed again, this time more urgently. Accordingly, the merchantman turned northward, while the carrier bent on more speed, and the two ships met at dusk on 22 August. The *Ranger* sent over a boat with Lt. Jesse G. Wright (MC) and brought de la Fuente on board in a stretcher. A transfusion, with the blood provided by Pharmacist's Mate 1st Class A. E. Ruth, saved the cook's life. De La Fuente, who had recently taken out naturalization papers to become an American citizen, would remain a guest in the *Ranger*'s sick bay for the duration of the trip south. He provided the hospital apprentices ("Hossapps") with "a lot of information on Rio. Any of the crew desiring any particular[s]," a sailor in H Division suggested later, "might see the Hossapps."[1]

That night, as a balmy tropical breeze whipped through the hangar deck, the *Ranger*'s sailors enjoyed a "happy hour." One of the ship's two canine mascots, "Popeye," barked excitedly during the proceedings, which included exhibitions of boxing, weight lifting, magic acts with "The Mystic Wonder," tumbling, and a performance by the "Old Home Town Boys," in which one of the ship's mail clerks provided "a comedy dance garbed in female (?) attire." The ship's band played "The Star-Spangled Banner" to bring the night's entertainment, enjoyed by all hands who attended, to a patriotic conclusion.[2]

The *Ranger* continued on her voyage with expectation mounting. With Sergeant Fields of the Marine Detachment drilling the ship's landing force in preparation for its participation in the planned parade at Buenos Aires, marking Brazilian independence, another singular event occurred: the publication of the ship's newspaper, *The Ranger*. The inaugural issue, eight pages in length, featured articles about Brazil (the first country that the ship would visit), the visitors who had embarked for the ship's shakedown cruise, and a brief recounting of events between launching and commissioning.

Captain Bristol welcomed *The Ranger*, acknowledging that "it is no small task to get out a ship's paper; one which will have the support of the crew; which will be interesting and amusing and which will, lastly, reflect the spirit of our ship." He also wrote of the "tedious and anxious work" for editors and assistants, how a contributor, already "under press of other work, will find himself prodded to get in his material," and how, sometimes, printers "won't be able to see his way through." "Such is the story of all newspaper work and in a small community such as ours, only hearty cooperation by all hands will bring success."[3]

"It may be well asked if a ship's paper is necessary," Bristol wrote, "By no means a necessity, but it is one of those luxuries which our times and our facilities permit us to have, and which we can ill afford to do without. There are many intangible forces acting to affect the efficiency of our ship as well as the happiness and contentment of ourselves. The ship's paper is one that we can use to our own ends and if it produces only an occasional grin or even what has become to be known as a special cheer, we are well repaid." If asked "what is the good of a ship's paper," the captain concluded, "I would say: It serves and plays its due part in breathing life into the greatest word that the language of the sea has given us, and that word is 'shipmate.'" He asked all to join him in greeting *The Ranger* and "to work with me towards its success."[4] The pages of the maiden edition of *The Ranger* also served as the vehicle for more serious matters: both the captain and the exec each expressed their philosophies on what constituted a "smart" ship.

The *Ranger* having been in commission more than two months, Bristol acknowledged that all hands had

> "worked hard and faithfully. That which we have attempted to do, and that which it has been necessary to do have been accomplished in a smooth and timely manner. Our efforts have been crowned with no small success and we may be modestly proud. We may claim that we have passed through the 'teething stage' with the minimum of pain.... We are now entering into our adolescence. This long cruise to foreign ports must bring us to early manhood: to that stage where we can justly claim that we are a ship. So far we have had to content ourselves with the bare essentials of a day-to-day life. There has been little time for far-reaching planning; less time for considered contemplation and, least of all, time for leisure. It would seem that the opportunity is at hand and the occasion suitable to being planting the seeds of those activities which will develop the character of our ship.[5]

That each ship has its own individual character, you all know. That this character is definitely derived from the consciousness and acts of its crew, can be readily understood. A ship that has an outstanding character is called a smart ship. It is a word which has a special meaning to Naval men and which has been passed down to us as a heritage by generations of American Sailormen. To be a smart ship, we must be ready to perform any duty, at any time, anywhere. There are many things which form the visible attributes of smartness. In the days of sail its greatest outward sign was the manner in which sails were handled. Today, it is most evidenced by the manner in which all evolutions both in port and at sea are carried out. But there are also many other unfailing signs of smartness, which have pertained to all times. To mention some of these: appearance and conduct of officers and men; cleanliness and neatness of the ship; quietness and orderliness with which the daily life of the ship is conducted; and tidiness of ship's boats. But back of all such signs there must be the one which really tells the story, cheerfulness, self reliance and self respect in all of the ship's personnel.... This last you have already shown me. With that basis we can go forward in confidence that at an early date we will be greeted as a smart ship."[6]

Commander Pownall affirmed the captain's sentiments. "The USS *Ranger* has started to go places and to do things," he wrote, "She has made her speed. She has operated aircraft successfully. To be a grand ship of the Navy she must be more than simply a successful seagoing robot. She must possess a great spirit within. The Government gave her a proud and glorious name which typifies the finest of naval tradition." He had observed "sufficient evidence... to assure [us] that the grand old Navy spirit is asserting itself in the *Ranger*." He lauded those who had served in the precommissioning and commissioning days. "We now have before us another job, a harder and more exacting one than those which have gone before.... The job is a diplomatic one in which we meet people of other lands and tongues. We are on parade before their eyes and are required to inculcate confidence and respect not only to us but as representatives of American citizenship at its best." Reminding readers that visits "of this nature are not in the category of a joyride or yachting trip simply for our amusement," he emphasized that, in a foreign port, where "impressions go a long way," each officer and enlisted man was, in fact, on duty, "not really on 'liberty.'" Pownall declared that "two general classes of men" existed in the navy: "*Those who know how to take care of themselves on shore; and those who do not or cannot.*" The executive officer concluded: "Ask yourself the simple question—can I take this fellow called me ashore, have a good time and bring him back with credit to me, my shipmates, my ship and my country? I hope you can."[7]

Prior to the *Ranger*'s reaching Rio, her officers and men observed a time-honored tradition. On the morning of 24 August, "Davy Jones," portrayed in tonsorial splendor by Chief Electrician's Mate Terry W. Mize of the ship's E Division, came on board, presaging the ship's imminent arrival in the realm of "Neptunus Rex," as the *Ranger* "crossed the line", the equator, for the first time. The following day the *Ranger* observed the traditional rites as Captain Bristol welcomed the appropriately attired Neptunus Rex, portrayed by Chief Commissary Steward F. C. "Stew" Keller, on board his ship an hour before the end of the morning watch on 25 August. In the matter-of-fact prose of the ship's deck log: "Shellbacks began receiving pollywogs with appropriate ceremonies." First in line stood Chief Yeoman John Lusby, the "genial and efficient" chief yeoman from Commander Pownall's office. Next waited Comdr. George C. Rhoades, MC, the ship's senior medical officer, the ship's officers, chief petty officers, and the rest of the crew. The shellbacks duly initiated the pollywogs—which also included the entire Marine Detachment, except Capt. Charles C. Gill, USMC, its commander—and the ship continued her voyage. All pollywogs had been duly initiated by 1037. "If the *Ranger* fights as well as she plays," Commander Rhoades wryly observed after his initiation, "she will make a name for herself."[8]

Fog shrouded the "the far-famed beauty of Rio's harbor," as the *Ranger* stood in, a little less than an hour before the end of the morning watch on 30 August. As her officers and men soon discovered over the ensuing days, however, "if nature did not greet us kindly with clear weather and glorious views, surely the people did. The welcome was worthy of the fame of the city."[9] Over the course of the carrier's visit, one often saw small groups of Brazilians gathered around an American bluejacket "trying to talk with his hands," as Rio's inhabitants sympathized with the "mistakes in the language and our unfamiliarity with their customs."[10]

The *Ranger* anchored a half hour into the forenoon watch, rendering appropriate salutes to the host nation. She then delivered her patient, de la Fuente, to representatives of the American Steamship Agencies Company. Then, in keeping with diplomatic amenities, Captain Bristol called upon U.S. Ambassador to Brazil Hugh S. Gibson at 1025. A 24-year veteran foreign service officer then working toward mediating an end to the Gran Chaco War between Paraguay and Bolivia, Ambassador Gibson returned Captain Bristol's call the following afternoon.

The Brazilian government having granted her permission to do so, the *Ranger* hoisted out her small complement of utility planes and conducted flight operations on 1, 3, 4, and 5 September. Various aviators assigned to the ship took turns getting in flight time in the unit's Grumman JF-1s amphibians and float-equipped Vought O3U-3s. Storekeeper 3d Class J. E. Juracka, of the ship's S (Supply) Division, Lt. Marcel E. A. Gouin's passenger on one flight, had been to Rio in the *Utah* (BB-31), when President-elect Herbert Hoover had visited the port in 1928. Later, Juracka reflected that he had never appreciated the beauty of the city until viewing it from the air.

In keeping with diplomatic amenities, Captain Bristol and a party of his officers called upon President Getulio Vargas, a known aviation enthusiast, on 5 September—a

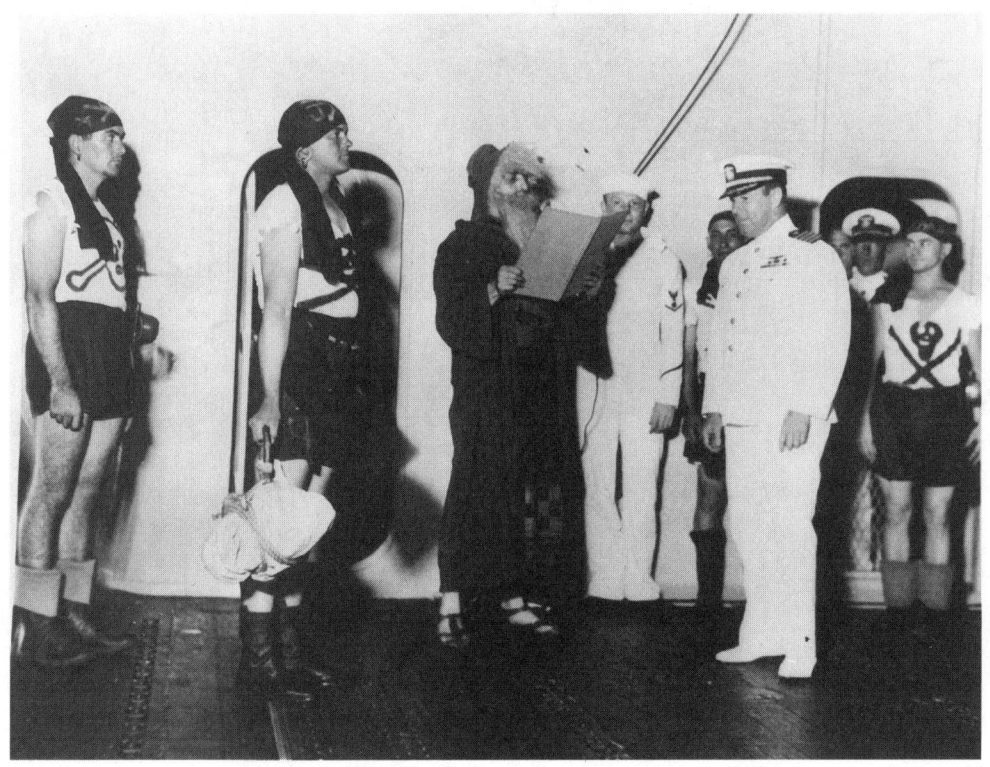

"Davy Jones" (portrayed by Chief Electrician's Mate Terry W. Mize) informs Captain Bristol of the imminent arrival of "Neptunus Rex" to cleanse the ship of "pollywogs" on the eve of crossing the equator, 24 August 1934. Photograph by Photographer's Mate 1st Class T. W. Busic. (NA, 80-G-391502)

call returned by that chief of state, with suitable pomp, on the 8th. Vargas's call came on the heels of an inspection of the ship by the Spanish Ambassador Vicente Salas, the Chilean Marcial Martinez, and the French Louis Hermite, and the Chinese minister to Brazil, Samuel Sung Young. The *Ranger*'s 160-man landing force, during that force, made up of the ship's Marine Detachment and bluejackets, participated in the parade honoring Brazilian independence, on the 7th.

Underway for Buenos Aires almost exactly midway through the first watch on 9 September, the *Ranger* reached her destination and moored starboard side to Pier 3, late in the afternoon of the 12th, to find the U.S. freighter *Western World* moored nearby, the presence of which soon prompted one *Ranger* sailor to exclaim: "There's mail from home!" Cpl. Leslie J. Hall, USMC, the ship's mail orderly, soon retrieved nine bags of mail from the U.S. legation. "After it came aboard [it] began to trickle out here and there," one observer later wrote. "Then came the word: 'One petty officer from each division report to the Post Office for division mail.'" After the precious letters had been distributed, men settled down at a table, stood by a port, and eagerly opened them, prompting one sailor to observe that "a man's face as he reads a letter from home is an interesting study."[11]

During the *Ranger*'s visit to Buenos Aires, Spider Hewitt, the U.S. Navy's all-welterweight champion, fought a bout against an Argentine boxer who had never been knocked out, before a capacity crowd of seamen from visiting merchantmen and dock workers, at the Mission for Seamen on Calle San Juan. In the "hazy, smoke-filled arena" Hewitt's fast left "which always seemed to pop up from nowhere"

President Getulio Dornelles Vargas of Brazil, the first head of state to visit the *Ranger*, comes on board, 8 September 1934 at Rio de Janeiro. (USN, NH 42319)

bewildered Albores, and the American floored the Argentine in the second round. "After [the] termination of the bout" by technical knockout, Chief Yeoman F. Bruhns of the *Ranger* recounted later, "Albores rushed over to Hewitt and grasped his hand, proving himself a game and sportsmanlike loser." As both boxers exited the ring, the 500 onlookers gave them "a great big hand."[12]

After hosting brief calls by the British and French naval attachés and the U.S. military attaché on the 13th, the *Ranger* hosted the U.S. consul general early on the 14th. Later that same day, Captain Bristol and a party of his officers called formally upon President Agustín P. Justo, who had come to power from the ranks of Argentina's Conservative Party in February 1932. Ambassador Weddell, whose wire to the State Department had helped extend the *Ranger*'s shakedown cruise, visited the ship briefly later on the 14th, but returned for a second call on the 17th. Like Hugh Gibson, Weddell was also deeply involved in the ongoing efforts to bring an end to the conflict between Bolivia and Paraguay. Later the same day, President Justo became the second foreign head of state to visit the *Ranger*, when he made a 25-minute call upon the ship during the forenoon watch. Concluding her visit to the Argentine capital midway through the morning watch on 18 September, the *Ranger* made the 10-hour passage to Montevideo, Uruguay—the last foreign port on her shakedown itinerary—arriving there later that afternoon.

Captain Bristol laid a wreath at the tomb of the Uruguayan patriot Jose Gervasio Artigas, on the 21st. That same day, less ceremonial pursuits occupied 600 of the crew, who visited the Swift meat company's ranch outside the capital city for an *asado*, a uniquely Latin American institution described by one observer as something "beside which the words 'picnic' and 'barbecue' are but colorless third cousins."[13] Three *Ranger* sailors sustained injuries while engaged in the distinctly unnautical avocation of horseback riding. Two horses collided, throwing one rider, Aerographer 3d Class J. F. Albert, who suffered a fractured right femur. Pharmacist's Mate 1st Class K. N. Flowers provided first aid treatment on the scene, before Albert was returned to the ship. Seaman 1st Class M. P. McGown, of the ship's V-2 Division, and Seaman 2d Class C. F. Cole, of the V-1 Division, suffered lesser injuries while seemingly trying to emulate *gaucho*s. All of those hurt reflected Ens. Lester R. Schulz's observation that "some returned to the ship worse for the wear—'sore horsemen.'"[14]

Meanwhile, as the heads of state of Brazil and Argentina had done, the President of Uruguay, Gabriel Terra, who had wielded dictatorial power since a coup d'etat the previous year, called briefly on the U.S. Navy's newest aircraft carrier on the afternoon of 23 September. The next morning, the *Ranger* sailed for home, as Secretary of the Navy Claude A. Swanson later reported, her visit having apparently created "most favorable impressions" in the three foreign capitals visited.[15] By the same token, for Sergeant Fields of the Marine Detachment, visiting Montevideo and Buenos Aires had been "quite an experience for a young guy who had grown up on the [Maryland] Eastern Shore not knowing too much beyond his county."[16]

In advance of her arrival at Norfolk, the *Ranger* launched five utility planes and 5-B-19 to land at NAS Hampton Roads on the afternoon of 4 October. "It was rather expected," one VB-3B observer later related, "that the plane crews would come flinging out of the planes doing a tango." All those who welcomed the returning *Ranger* men could get, however, "were a few garbled Spanish phrases."[17] The squadrons earmarked for assignment to the *Ranger* had not been idle in the ship's absence, doing their flying in other locales. VS-1B's Lt. (jg) John T. "Chick" Hayward even achieved a milestone on board another ship, when he made the *Saratoga*'s 23,000th landing, on 17 September.

The *Ranger* returned to NOB Norfolk on 8 October and began a period of postshakedown upkeep. Two days later, VB-5B flew to Anacostia in a "caravan" of nine F4Bs, one Grumman SF, and a Martin T4M, to witness a Curtiss-Wright pilot's demonstration of the new Curtiss BF2C-1, with which the squadron would be equipped. VB-5B's aviators, impressed by the BF2C's "smooth maneuverability and the high speed available," displayed by the test pilot's performing "slow and snap rolls at less than a thousand feet over the field," returned the same day with a "hopeful attitude that [they would] soon have a plane that [they would] all be proud to fly."[18]

As the fleet returned to the West Coast, the *Langley*, with three squadrons embarked, sailed on 12 October, serenaded as she did so by the *Ranger*'s band, on the opposite side of the pier. Two *Ranger* squadrons, VB-3B and VB-5B, remained at Norfolk, to join the ship upon completion of her postshakedown availability. On 17 October, VB-3B took delivery of the Great Lakes XBG-1 (BuNo 9220) from NAS Anacostia, "to prepare both pilots and mechanics for the surprise which awaits them when the BG's [were] delivered" to the squadron.[19]

The *Ranger* shifted to the Norfolk Navy Yard, Portsmouth, Virginia, on 23 October, and entered drydock number four that morning. The next day, planks slipped off the stages that had been erected along the hull, rudely dumping Pvt. R. M. Buchanan, USMC, Seaman 2d Class G. W. Winkle, Fireman 3d Class K. D. Klies, and Seaman

2d Class G. F. Moore about 15 feet to the floor of the dock. The ship's medical people treated Buchanan and Winkle and returned them to duty, but judged Klies and Moore injured badly enough to be retained in sick bay for further observation. On the 25th, Frank Harris, a yard workman, fell 15 feet to the drydock floor; he was taken to the Navy Yard dispensary for diagnosis and treatment. Ultimately, the necessary work, which had included the installation of new propellers, having been concluded by the forenoon watch on the 26th, the *Ranger* moved out into Hampton Roads.

The next day, VB-5B and VB-3B thrilled observers with an aerial demonstration at Richmond, Virginia, simulating an attack on the track thronged with fans who had turned out for a Navy Day automobile race. Returning from Richmond, VB-5B's Lts. Charles F. "Dutch" Greber, Edwin R. Peck, and Alfred C. Olney, Jr., conducted a display of flying that amused the crowd at halftime of the football game between the Norfolk Training Station "boots" and the team from the heavy cruiser *Northampton* (CA-26). An unintentional outside spin on the part of one of the trio, however, occasioned applause from the crowd who thought it was all part of the exhibition.

After conducting flight operations on 30 and 31 October and on 1 November, the *Ranger* embarked Rear Adm. George C. Day, the president of the Navy's Board of Inspection and Survey, on the 6th, along with a party of other officers, to witness the ship's final trials. Day and his party disembarked at 1430 on the 7th, and the *Ranger* returned to Norfolk Navy Yard for posttrial repairs and alterations, arriving there during the forenoon watch on the 8th. The necessity of replacing her gasoline tanks, which had proved to be not as resistant to corrosion as had been advertised,

In drydock, 26 October 1934. This unusual view shows to advantage not only the extreme flare of the *Ranger*'s sides (necessary to provide the widest possible flight deck), but the original location of the two 5-inch/25 guns at the bow, a position that would have made them virtually unserviceable in all but a calm sea. (NA, 80-CF file)

lengthened her yard completion date. One wag likened the evolution of taking out the old tanks to replace them with new as almost "Caesarean" in nature.[20]

As the *Ranger* lay in drydock and work progressed, the need apparently arose to find a new name for the ship's paper. Consequently, Seaman 2d Class N. C. Williams came up with the winning entrant, and Seaman 2d Class H. M. Pawlic prepared a stylistic rendition of the ship for the new masthead. And thus, on 24 November 1934, *The CV-4* came into being.

Moving into drydock number four again on 2 January 1935, the *Ranger* remained there until about an hour into the afternoon watch on 18 March, when she got underway to return to the NOB. During the ship's time in drydock, fumes overcame Willie Perkins and James Almond, two yard workmen, as they worked on the modification of the gasoline tanks on 26 February. They had to be transported by ambulance to a hospital.

While the *Ranger* had been yard-bound, however, her squadrons had not been idle, conducting a series of flights in January from Norfolk to Hartford, Connecticut, and Buffalo, New York, to see how well planes, equipment, and clothing stood up to adverse climate conditions. Upon completion of those tests on 2 February, BuAer began assessing the results, to plan for cold weather tests slated for the *Ranger* the following year.

VB-3B, in the interim, had ferried its new BG-1s from the Great Lakes' factory to Norfolk. "Most pilots have been through one or more aircraft factories," one observer later wrote, "but not such a high percentage have been able to see

Three Curtiss BF2C-1s from VB-5B, 18 March 1935. Five-Baker-One was normally assigned to the squadron's commanding officer, Lt. Comdr. James D. Barner; 5-B-2 to Lt. Rufus C. Young, Jr.; 5-B-3 to Lt. (jg) Victor H. Soucek. (NA, 80-G-424289)

the plane that they will fly during the next cruise in the actual process of fabrication from the hammering out by hand of intricate little parts to the machine stamping of others." Most pilots did not appreciate the "vast size of a factory necessary to produce a plane or the care necessary in its production when we nonchalantly explain that the thing just won't make a three-point landing."[21]

The *Ranger* received another visit from Admiral Standley on 23 March, the CNO accompanied by Rear Admiral King and a congressional party. On the 25th, the carrier ran her final official trials. She resumed flight operations the following morning, evolutions enlivened by Lt. (jg) William M. Freshour, who, upon receiving the "cut" signal for his first carrier landing, pulled back on the stick. Freshour's BF2C-1 (BuNo 9595) floated over all of the cross-deck pendants and, still airborne, slammed into the barrier. A major overhaul lay in store for 5-B-9; a trouble board later faulted "Mac" Freshour's inexperience for the accident. Lieutenant. (jg) Lorenz Q. "Lorry" Forbes, one of Freshour's USNA classmates, experienced difficulty with his landing gear while in the air, but flew to NAS Norfolk, where he landed without incident.

VB-3B and VB-5B assumed shipboard status on 27 March, a movement that had left the Naval Air Station at Norfolk "enshrouded in peace and quiet.... the first time in many moons that no unit of the Fleet has been on this station."[22] The

Lieutenant (jg) Theodore R. Frederick stands in front of the Vought O3U-3 in which he executed the *Ranger*'s 1,000th landing on 4 April 1935, after flying a photographic flight during the ship's gunnery drills out of Guantanamo Bay, Cuba. Note prominent markings, U.S.S. RANGER–3, and the winged turtle insignia that reflects the plane having been flown across the equator. Photograph by Chief Photographer W. L. Williams. (NA, 80-G-391523)

Anchored at Colon, Canal Zone, 6 April 1935, shortly before her maiden transit of the Panama Canal. Note the temporary "bridge" structure erected on the flight deck to provide the pilot with a centerline vantage point. (NA, 80-G-462861)

Ranger recovered 35 planes from the two squadrons that morning, and the destroyers *Leary* (DD-158) and *Herbert* (DD-160) served as plane guards. Late that afternoon, the *Ranger* anchored for the night off Virginia Beach.

Routine operations the next morning, with the *Leary* plane-guarding, showed that even experienced pilots could have trouble landing the BF2C. At 1059, Lt. Rufus C. Young, Jr., VB-5B's materiel officer, received the cut, but pushed 5-B-2's nose down to ensure that he caught a wire. The BF2C (BuNo 9588) landed wheels-first, in such an attitude that, normally, the tail hook would have engaged one of the pendants, but the hook bounced against the bumper and then bounced again, causing 5-B-2 to miss at least two wires. The bounding BF2C-1's hook missed other pendants, too, and Young's mount ended up in the barrier. Five-Baker-Two required a major overhaul.[23]

Commander Barner, coming in 15 minutes after "Ruf" Young, proved similarly unfortunate. Just before passing over the ramp, Barner saw the LSO give an advisory "high" shortly before he signaled "cut." Barner nosed the Curtiss down to ensure catching a wire, reprising Young's action. The commanding officer's BF2C-1 (BuNo 9512) settled into what would be a normal landing, but the tailhook struck just aft of number three wire, and bounced up, clearing it. Five-Baker-One cleared the number four wire, too, and bounced again, clearing the rest of the wires. Barner's BF2C-1 eventually came to rest in the barrier, shearing off both landing gear oleo struts, breaking oil lines, straining the engine mount, flattening the auxiliary fuel tank, and causing minor damage to the cowl. Contact with the deck curled up one propeller blade and bent the other.[24]

Subsequently, after the *Ranger* had exercised with the *Leary* during long range battle practice (LRBP)—gunnery exercises designed to enable the ship to use her 5-inch/25 battery to defend herself against surface adversaries—released the latter to proceed on other duties. The carrier dropped anchor in Hampton Roads, where she remained for the rest of the month of March, preparing for her movement to the West Coast.

During the afternoon watch on 1 April, the *Ranger* sailed, accompanied by the new destroyer *Dewey* (DD-349). Three days later, the carrier obtained tactical data and exercised off Guantanamo Bay, Cuba. The *Ranger* and her consort reached the Canal Zone on the morning of the 6th. Completing her initial transit of the Panama Canal in six and a half hours on the 7th, the *Ranger* tarried only briefly at Balboa before she sailing the next morning. She formally reported for duty (by radio) with Aircraft, Battle Force, her new type command, two hours into the forenoon watch. The next day, she experienced the only nonroutine landing evolution of that leg of her voyage, when Lt. Ward T. ("W.T") Shields made an emergency landing in 5-B-9.

The *Ranger* reached Coronado Roads during the first dog watch on the 14th and stood in to San Diego harbor the following morning, firing a salute to Vice Adm. Henry V. Butler, Commander Aircraft, Battle Force (ComAirBatFor), before she moored to the NAS pier at North Island. Butler, the first flag officer to hold that post with the rank of vice admiral, had graduated in the USNA Class of 1895; the first ship in which he served was the then-new battleship *Maine*. As aide to Capt. George V. Gridley, he had participated in the Battle of Manila Bay in 1898 on board the protected cruiser *Olympia*, and had heard Commodore George Dewey utter, "You may fire when ready, Gridley." His first

Vice Adm. Henry V. Butler, Commander Aircraft, Battle Force, 25 April 1935 (seen during an inspection of the *Lexington*), the first flag officer to use the *Ranger* as his flagship. (NA, 80-CF File)

command had been the gunboat *Mindoro*, during the Philippine Insurrection. During a career that included duty at sea in a succession of ships or ashore in various posts, he earned his observer's wings at NAS Pensacola in 1926, one of the first of the Navy's senior officers to do so, and attained flag rank the following year.[25]

The *Ranger*'s task, simply stated, was "to operate at once as a unit of the Fleet that can accomplish the mission for which she is built. Time will be short between her arrival and the severe test of the approaching Fleet Problem. The ship will do her best, and all hands devoutly hope, her stuff!"[26] A period of in-port upkeep followed, after which time she resumed flight operations on 23 April.

During her initial operations with the Battle Force off San Diego, the *Ranger* experienced her first mishap involving the Great Lakes BG-1. Some pilots acquainted with the type's tendency to bounce excessively when landed wheels-first, or with even a moderate amount of excess speed, had nicknamed the BG the "Bouncing Girl." Midway through the afternoon watch, Lt. Lucien A. Moebus of VB-3B, with Radioman 3d Class J. R. Charleton in the rear seat, made a normal landing in BuNo 9506. Getting the signal to taxi clear of the gear, he opened his throttle to move forward quickly. Unfortunately, his arrestor hook failed to lock in the up position, and "Fish" Moebus, thinking that he had hooked a wire, applied the brakes, causing the BG to "nose up," curling both propeller blades.[27]

The next day, Lt. (jg) James O. Vosseller of VB-5B was returning to the ship from a routine flight. He found the *Ranger*'s pitching deck more than he could handle in his limited carrier experience. As the stern began to drop, the LSO signalled "high." Unfortunately, "Jimmie" Vosseller throttled back "excessively," so that the BF2C settled rapidly before reaching the ramp. When the stern began to lift, the Curtiss hit the ramp tail wheel first, bending the oleo strut beyond repair.[28]

That same day, the *Ranger* conducted fueling exercises with the destroyers *Buchanan* (DD-131) and *Crowninshield* (DD-134), proving that her flared sides posed no obstacles to fueling a ship alongside at sea underway. She then conducted local flight operations during the last week of April, as her participation in her first major war games—Fleet Problem XVI—drew near. How she would perform in the role for which she was designed would be determined in the weeks to come.

4

"SHE WILL PROVE HERSELF A VERY VALUABLE SHIP"

Assigned to the Main Body of the White Fleet, the *Ranger* stood out of San Diego harbor a half hour before the end of the mid watch on 29 April, bound for San Francisco, as Phase I of Fleet Problem XVI began. Planes from Utility Squadron (VJ) 1F and from the Naval Reserve Air Base at Long Beach, but from neither the *Ranger* nor the *Saratoga,* nor from the battleships and cruisers, covered the sortie. Later that day, during the afternoon watch, the *Saratoga* put aloft an inner air patrol, but not over the Main Body itself. That tardy acknowledgment of the "enemy" submarine threat soon proved a case of closing the barn door after the horse had bolted: Black submarines were already inside the White formation.

Undeterred by the antisubmarine screen, the *Dolphin* (SS-169) fired six torpedoes at a *New Mexico*-class battleship at 1,300 yards; the *Narwhal* (SS-167) four at the *Pennsylvania* (BB-38) at 800 yards and two from her stern tubes at the lead battleship in the right flank column, 1,500 yards distant. The slowness of getting the patrols underway on 30 April allowed Black submarines to again approach undetected; the *Bonita* (SS-165) closed to within 500 yards and fired six torpedoes at the *Ranger* while she was recovering aircraft. The *Barracuda* (SS-163) fired four at the *Ranger* from 1,900 yards. Planes from the *Saratoga* and the *Ranger,* however, operated effectively against Black submarines during the daylight hours on 30 and 31 April. Dive-bombers caught the *Bonita* on the surface on the 30th, and carried out their attacks so efficiently that one plane had completed its run before the submarine, running on the surface, was even aware of the planes' presence.

Ultimately, the harried White Main Body entered San Francisco Bay under cover of darkness, during the mid watch on 1 May, under darkened ship conditions. In view of the submarine menace reflected in the attacks on the White Fleet during its passage up the California coast, Adm. Joseph M. Reeves, the Commander in Chief, U.S. Fleet (CinCUS), acting in his capacity as Commander, White Main Body, changed his force's operation order covering Phase II of the problem—the advance of the fleet toward the Hawaiian Islands–Aleutian Islands line. His ships would steam at higher speed than before, steer courses off a direct track to their next destination (Pearl Harbor), and mount intensive antisubmarine patrols by destroyers and aircraft. In addition, the White Fleet would employ a false screen of destroyers ahead and on the Main Body's flanks, and monitor Black communications traffic to determine the activities of his submarines. With those measures ready to be implemented, the White force sailed for Oahu on 3 May.[1]

Operating in company with the *Saratoga,* the *Ranger* alternated as duty carrier: the former maintained patrols as ordered on the odd days, the latter on the even. This represented the first time that duty and relief groups had been employed during a fleet's advance. The duty group maintained all daylight patrols and kept two divisions of nine planes, each armed with a 500-pound bomb, ready for launching on deck. The relief group maintained all planes in condition 13 readiness, with the carrier ready to proceed at 24 knots within 90 minutes of being notified. The system allowed better fuel economy, because only one carrier needed to have boiler power ready for flight operations, would permit checking of aircraft, and would permit pilots, although they would fly between 8 to 10 hours on the "duty" day, to rest on the "off" day, allowing them to "remain unfatigued over long periods."[2]

On the day of departure, a Black submarine was spotted 10 miles from the disposition about midday; planes from the *Saratoga*'s inner air patrol sped to the scene, but could not make contact. Although no contacts materialized the following day, radio bearings indicated Black submarines lurking to the north, as the fleet steamed toward Hawaiian waters. On 5 May, radio bearings indicated the probable presence of a Black sub close to the track of the carriers. The *Ranger* and the *Saratoga* immediately closed the White Main Body; soon thereafter, the carriers received orders to take station at high speed on the battle line's starboard quarter.

The *Ranger* remained with the fleet, her planes flying antisubmarine patrols ("tedious work . . . effective and well worth the effort," Vice Admiral Butler later contended), a mission in which she was engaged into 6 May.[3] On that day, the *Ranger* went to flight quarters at the end of the mid watch and turned into the wind. A little less than a half-hour into the launch, however, Aviation Chief Machinist's Mate Elmer B. Lloyd tripped over a line on deck and fell into a whirling propeller, suffering multiple fractures of his right forearm, arm, and shoulder. Flight operations continued as Lloyd's shipmates bore him below for treatment, and the *Ranger* brought those evolutions to a close at 0507.

Meanwhile, Lt. (jg) Harlan T. "Swede" Johnson of VB-3B had taken off in a BG-1 (BuNo 9508), with Aviation Chief Machinist's Mate Jerry F. Bartlett in back. After reaching an altitude of between 300 and 500 feet, Johnson nosed the plane over slightly to shift his propeller into high pitch. He immediately noticed the smell of gasoline. When he opened the throttle and began to climb, he felt a fine spray mixed with drops of gasoline, a mist appearing on his goggles. Not having joined formation, Johnson immediately dropped his tailhook and made a shallow dive, passing down the *Ranger*'s port side—the designated signal for a deferred forced landing—and then climbed to 1,000 feet. As he circled at that altitude at an airspeed of 90 knots, investigating the problem, he could smell only gasoline fumes while he sat upright, but, when he ducked his head down, he could again feel the spray. At that point, he later recounted, it seemed as if the gasoline was circulating "up along the front of the pilot's seat and down again under the instrument board," but he could not determine for sure where the fuel was coming from.[4]

The *Ranger* had in the meantime acted upon Johnson's dropping his hook and flying close aboard. She changed course at 0520 and rang down full astern to prepare for an emergency landing over the bow. Seeing the ship stern-to the wind, Johnson glided down to begin his first approach. After again feeling the fine gasoline spray in the upper part of the cockpit, he saw a loose cowling flap and erroneously assumed that the main gasoline tank had not been properly secured. As Johnson approached the ship twice more, as she gained speed, the mist intensified to the point that he found it necessary to wipe his goggles twice.[5]

During his fourth approach, Johnson received a "high" signal at medium distance from the LSO, a "roger," another "high," another "roger," another "high," followed by "cut," in rapid succession. Cutting his engine and nosing over, he pulled back on the stick just before reaching the deck. That maneuver proved successful in retarding the drop, and the BG-1 caught the second wire, in what Johnson later considered an "about average" landing. During the run-out, however, Johnson saw fire appearing along the left side of the plane and in the front cockpit. The plane burst into flames as raw aviation gasoline splashed onto the hot lower exhaust pipes. In his excitement, Johnson forgot the switch and reached for the handle to the fire extinguisher, but hit the propeller pitch control handle instead. As he later recounted, at that point the flames in the cockpit may have been "sufficiently high to be in front of my face, rendering it impossible to see the instrument board."[6]

"Believing myself on fire," Johnson later recounted, "I prepared to leave. As I expedited my departure I saw my mechanic opening his safety belt."[7] Posthaste, pilot and passenger exited the burning BG-1; Swede Johnson suffered a cut across the bridge of his nose in so doing, Jerry Bartlett had a burned left hand. The flight deck crew quickly converged on the scene and put out the blaze, but not before it had burned off the fabric of the lower left wing, left side of the fuselage, and left elevator and the rudder, and had destroyed electrical leads and connections: Fused metal indicated the fire's intense heat.

An investigation later revealed that, when the plane had been fueled under darkened ship conditions the night before, the cap on the auxiliary gasoline tank had not been properly screwed on. Only one lip had been caught, and the other rode on top of the locking groove, allowing an opening in the spout large enough for the fuel to splash out while the plane was in flight. The slipstream then carried it into the cockpit, through the openings around the bomb-release gear. Aviation Machinist's Mate 2d Class James N. Taylor, the plane captain, later testified to the fact that, when he had checked the fit of the cap by feel, during the predawn launch preparations that morning, he believed that it had felt tight. When the trouble board attributed the

Lieutenant (jg) Swede Johnson's BG-1 (BuNo 9508), after its fiery landing on 6 May 1935. (NA, VBG-1/L11-1 file, 5-1-35 to 9-30-35, RG-72, Box 4833).

fire to "personnel error," Commander Pownall disagreed, laying the blame on the "unsatisfactory design" of the gasoline cap. Vice Admiral Butler, however, ultimately concurred with the board. After citing examples of how the present equipment worked well under actual operating conditions, he observed simply that "personnel must exercise care in replacing filler caps, just as they do in most other activities in connection with airplanes."[8]

Two days after Swede Johnson's fiery landing, as the White Main Body pressed on toward Oahu, Lt. (jg) William A. Moffett, Jr., of VF-5B, son of the late chief of BuAer, made a normal approach for a routine landing during a tactics hop, on the morning of 8 May. As his BF2C neared the ramp, however, he allowed the Curtiss to "get a little low." Consequently, the LSO signalled a last-minute "low." Moffett tried to raise the plane's nose, but to no avail, as the tail wheel struck the ramp, it was crushed beyond repair, as was the rudder immediately above it.[9]

The *Ranger* reached Lahaina Roads off Maui, Territory of Hawaii, on the morning of 12 May, the White Main Body having made the passage from 'Frisco without being attacked once by Black submarines: Good weather had made possible daily antisubmarine patrols from the carriers. Black subs had located the White force, but planes from the Main Body's air patrol knocked *Bonita* and *Barracuda* out of action before they could attack.

After fueling from the oiler *Kanawha* (AO-1) the next morning, the *Ranger* shifted to Honolulu, anchoring off Diamond Head, along with the *Lexington* and the *Saratoga*, because the operations to dredge the channel into Pearl Harbor, particularly the waters between Hospital and Waipio Points, had not yet reached completion. On the 15th, the *Ranger* returned to the "wars"—Phase III of Fleet Problem XVI—when she departed Oahu as part of White's Advance Force and headed to the northwestward, bound for Midway Island, at the northwestern end of the Hawaiian chain. The other carrier assigned to the White force for Phase III, the *Saratoga*, proceeded to the southwestward.

Phase III of the problem represented a step in an overseas campaign, in which the White Fleet advanced west from the Hawaiian Islands, opposed by the Black Fleet from its bases in the Aleutians and Midway. Before the Black fleet could hope to engage the White Fleet, however, it had to carry out a campaign of attrition by use of submarines off Oahu and planes and destroyers operating from Midway. At the outset, White could attack Midway to reduce Black's strength, while a White landing force could secure the island. The problem as set up provided both White and Black commanders with a choice between two principal objectives: (1) the defense (or capture) of Midway and (2) the defeat of the opposing fleet. The White force commander chose to "defeat the Black Fleet without delay in order to gain a strategic advantage over Black"; the Black force commander decided "to hold Midway."

During operations north-northeast of Midway on 19 May, Lt. Comdr. Malcolm F. "Rojo" Schoeffel, VS-1B's

Although the flare of the *Ranger*'s sides concerned those who feared that she would be unable to fuel ships alongside while underway, she did so unhindered, as is demonstrated in this fine shot of the *Simpson* (DD-221) fueling on 7 May 1935, during Fleet Problem XVI. (NA, 80-CF File)

commanding officer, with Chief Radioman V. V. Thompson on board, returned from a scouting flight. Lieutenant William D. Johnson, Jr., the LSO, seeing Schoeffel coming in high and fast, signalled accordingly. Just short of the stern, Johnson gave Schoeffel the "low" signal. Schoeffel, anticipating the pitch of the ship in the long Pacific swells, gave his SU-4 the gun. As Johnson drew the flag across his throat, Schoeffel cut the engine as usual, and, nearing the deck, pulled back on the stick to ease the landing. The SU-4 bounced, however, the impact breaking the left landing gear oleo strut and brake rod, and dishing-in both wheels. In the postmortem of the crash, Lieutenant Johnson considered that the pilot had erred in "failing to answer my 'fast' signals," but candidly admitted that he had permitted Lieutenant Commander Schoeffel to land, "when he [Schoeffel] should have been waved off." Crash investigators agreed, apportioning the blame equally between the LSO and the pilot.[10]

As the White Attack Group steamed on a southeasterly course, scout planes from the *Ranger* contacted a Black submarine operating to the eastward of the heavy cruiser *Chicago* (CA-29), during the morning watch on 20 May. At about 0615, four *Ranger* planes bombed the *S-30* (SS-135); at 0748, 10 more aircraft from the carrier attacked the same quarry. Consequently, umpires judged the *S-30* "sunk." The *S-30*'s sistership, the *S-31* (SS-136), however, fared better, "sinking" the *Chester* (CA-27) and "damaging" the *Portland* (CA-33). Following the engagement with the two Black S-boats, the White Attack Force radically changed courses and speeds, proceeding south to contact the White Main Body.

The following day, Lt. (jg) Milton A. Nation of VS-1B, with Radioman 1st Class J. M. Snider in back, returned from a scouting flight for a bow landing—the first he had ever attempted—on the *Ranger*'s pitching deck. Lieutenant

The oiler *Kanawha* (AO-1) fuels the *Ranger* in Lahaina Roads, 13 May 1935. Open lighters (*YC-477* in the foreground), towed from Pearl Harbor and placed between the ships, provide the necessary buffer to prevent the carrier's tophamper from fouling the oiler's. The minesweeper *Bobolink* (AM-20) is moored to the *Kanawha*'s port side. (NA, 80-CF-318 file, Box 29)

Johnson deemed Nation's approach "normal, except for excessive speed," and had thrice wagged "fast." The landing appeared normal, until the landing gear gave way at the point of impact, Nation's SU-4 (BuNo 9424) sustaining damage that resulted in a major overhaul. Moving pictures of the landing, however, showed it to have been far from normal, with 1-S-2 alighting on its wheels, with the tail slightly higher than it should have been in the two-point position. Afterwards, Johnson expressed "surprise that this landing, which appeared to me almost normal, could have resulted so disastrously."[11]

A short time later, Lt. (jg) Walter C. Wingard of VS-1B brought in his SU-4 (BuNo 9428) for a landing over the bow. Lieutenant Johnson repeatedly wagged "fast," but observed that "Wing" Wingard appeared to be, in effect, ignoring the LSO's cautionary signals. As he came up the groove fast, Wingard saw Johnson's "cut" signal, too late for a wave off, but still coming on high and fast, nosed 1-S-18 down sharply, hitting the *Ranger*'s slightly pitching deck tail-high. With the right wing slightly down, Wingard's plane caught the number four wire, slammed down on the deck, collapsing the left oleo strut, then slid to a stop just short of the barrier. Like Nation's plane, Wingard's required a complete overhaul. In the postmortem of Wingard's crash, investigators faulted not only the pilot for his technique, but the LSO for not giving Wingard a wave-off.

Wingard's and Nation's crashes prompted Captain Bristol to complain of "two important difficulties about bow landings" in the *Ranger*. "The first is that the landing gear area is inherently and unavoidably too short, unless and until [the] *Ranger*'s flight deck can be extended to the length now made feasible by relocation of [the 5-inch/25] bow guns. The second is that the relative positions of bow arresting gear and #1 elevator further shorten the effective bow arresting gear area because of the resultant necessary barrier arrangement." Fundamentally, no plane should land with only one barrier up, unless the deck beyond was clear. The use of two barriers forward rendered the landing area unavoidably short. The *Ranger*'s limited backing speed, combined with the inability to count on sufficient real wind, would always be problematical in producing "an adequate apparent wind over the deck for bow landings." Emphasizing training in bow landings, Bristol wrote, would be only a stopgap. "Increase in flight deck length and barrier rearrangement," the *Ranger*'s captain concluded, "offer the only hope of justifying the use of the *Ranger*'s bow arresting gear for other than emergency situations."[12]

Meanwhile, as the climactic "battle" between White and Black forces loomed near Midway, a tragedy intervened to halt the war. In a bid to attack the White Main Body, the two Black patrol plane squadrons based on Midway took off before dark. Decreasing visibility conditions and the fact that the White ships were, in the main, running darkened, made it difficult to assess the actual "damage" inflicted. During the return flight in extremely poor flying conditions, one of VP-6F's planes, 6-P-10, made a forced landing. Six-Peter-Seven, a Martin PM-1 (BuNo 8295), piloted by Lt. Harry A. Brandenburger, signalled two of the accompanying flying boats that he was going to stand by the downed plane. About five hours later, Admiral Reeves cancelled all White air attacks on Midway to avoid interfering with the patrol planes searching the area, which eventually turned up evidence of the crash of 6-P-7 that resulted in the destruction of the plane and the loss of Lieutenant Brandenburger and his crew of five men.[13]

A surface action on the morning of 22 May effectively ended Phase III of the problem, with the White air operations against Midway and against the Black fleet having never been carried out, because of the disruption caused by the loss of 6-P-7 and the necessary search and rescue operations in the wake of it. As Vice Adm. Harris Laning of the White force commented later: "It was a disappointment to White that the action ended when it did and as it did. We had worked hard to attain the position we were in and were all set to strike with all of our forces. We had reached the point we hoped to reach and were in contact with the enemy fleet we were to destroy. Our air forces were intact and ready to strike with all they had, while our submarines were just where our plan called for them to be with the enemy ships all around them."[14] At 0638, Admiral Reeves made the signal: "Cease present exercises." Phase III of Fleet Problem XVI was over.

Phase IV involved the assembly of the fleet at Pearl Harbor, with the previous exception of the carriers returning to the waters off Diamond Head. The *Ranger*'s planes participated in an aerial parade over Honolulu on 25 May; she herself took part in a searchlight display off Diamond Head during the first 30 minutes of the first watch on the 29th. Underway the next morning, the *Ranger* then participated in Phase V of the Fleet Problem, a submarine-opposed departure from Hawaiian waters, and tactical exercises en route to the West Coast. During the passage, Lt. Comdr. George R. Fairlamb suffered a bad landing, when his BG-1, 3-B-1, crashed into the barrier, and a broken arresting wire inflicted minor bruises on Lt. (jg) Edward C. Renfro of VB-5B.

The Fleet arrived off San Diego on 10 June, "exactly in accordance with schedule," although the planned fleet review and arrival at its anchorage had had to be postponed until later in the day, because of dense fog. The *Ranger* moored at the NAS dock at North Island during the first dog watch.

The four carriers that had participated in Fleet Problem XVI—the *Langley*, the *Lexington*, the *Saratoga*, and the *Ranger*—had allowed a better distribution of planes throughout the various forces involved in the exercises, as well as their massed use in Phase V. "The employment of such large masses of aircraft under one command on the same mission," Vice Admiral Butler observed in the critique of the fleet problem, "is a difficult tactical problem for which future experience will give us an opportunity to solve."[15]

Butler believed that all units of the Fleet had acquitted themselves well during the maneuvers, but he recommended that greater effort be expended to develop cooperation between type commands. He noted that the aircraft under him rarely had the opportunity to operate either for or against heavy cruisers, or to work directly with destroyers or submarines. Although he acknowledged that problems and tactical exercises covered such features to a limited extent, he posited that more specialized operations between types should supplement the general fleet exercises.

Butler also believed that all officers and men should familiarize themselves with the "appearance and operating methods of our own aircraft." "Those of us in the carriers," the admiral declared, "whether aviators, other line officers, or enlisted men" could differentiate between squadrons at "very great distances," so that it was "seldom necessary to challenge our airplanes." The number of false reports during the fleet problems reflected the lack of ability on the

Anchored off Honolulu in berth 5, with 135 fathoms of chain to the port anchor, 28 May 1935. Diamond Head looms in the distance. (NA, 80-CF File)

part of the nonaviation people to recognize "friendly" planes. Rerouting friendly aircraft around concentrations of friendly ships posed problems of navigation and safety; going around the friendly fleet delayed the planes from carrying out their missions and introduced the potential for navigational errors. Warning planes away from friendly vessels did not constitute the solution to the problem: Butler believed that the matter had to be approached boldly. He urged that officers and men on lookout duty be required to familiarize themselves with the appearance and formations employed by friendly planes, in the same manner in which pilots and plane crews were required to differentiate between ships of U.S. and foreign navies. "With a little practice and judgment," Butler concluded, "it is easy enough to tell whether or not airplanes are friendly or hostile."[16]

Butler also called upon the nonaviators to not dismiss the contributions that aviators could make to the fleet's efficiency. He declared that officers of the aircraft squadrons stood "eager to participate and to assist" in developing tactics. Butler, who had been involved in aviation matters for almost a decade, had seen aviation's usefulness to the fleet expand "far beyond our original conception." He invited the other communities in the fleet to "let us [aviators] work more closely with you in the development of tactical effectiveness of the U.S. Fleet."[17]

As far as the *Ranger* went, ComAirBatFor declared that she had stood "her first test in Fleet maneuvers, very well, and I am satisfied that she will prove herself a very valuable ship to the Fleet." He noted, however, that the *Ranger*'s characteristics of roll and pitch resulted in her having difficulty, under "certain conditions of wind and sea," in both launching and recovering planes. Butler noted, however, that only time would tell "what the real state of affairs" was in those respects.[18]

The rookie *Ranger* had indeed performed with the poise of a practiced veteran—something that did not escape the

VB-1B's Martin BM-1s and -2s fly over the *Ranger* and her two plane guard destroyers, 5 June 1935, showing the "toy-like appearance of ... ships maneuvering or steaming majestically in formation on the glassy surface of the sea." It also shows how small a carrier looks from aloft. (NA, 80-CF-393-26)

notice of Admiral Reeves, CinCUS, and a man who, during the 1920s, had helped to lay the groundwork for carrier operations. The *Ranger* had joined the fleet only a few days before the war games commenced, Reeves noted, "but she embarked her squadrons and participated very satisfactorily in the Fleet Problem."[19] By the end of the fiscal year, the admiral could report that carrier operations in general had attained a "high degree of proficiency." He particularly lauded the increased number of night landings and nocturnal operations, which exceeded the previous year's.[20]

After the increased tempo of operations incident to the war games at sea, life returned to a more prosaic in-port pace at San Diego, with the *Ranger* "dressing ship" in honor of Independence Day at 0800 and firing a national salute at noon. Two days later, the *Ranger*'s fire and rescue party turned in an alert performance, after the gig from the *Wright* (AV-1) caught fire following an explosion in its engine compartment. As flames began to envelop the seaplane tender's boat, the *Ranger*'s number four motor launch arrived on the scene and rescued Fireman 2d Class M. M. Barlau, the *Wright* boat's engineer, and men in the carrier's number two motor boat extinguished the blaze. The *Ranger*'s practiced efficiency contrasted markedly with that of the San Diego water taxi *Blue Bell*. The *Ranger*'s officer of the deck noted disgustedly that the civilian craft passed within 20 feet of the *Wright*'s burning gig and "made no attempt to render aid in spite of the fact that four persons, one of whom was a woman, were struggling in the water."

The *Ranger*'s subsequent port visit to Los Angeles was not without incident. On 9 July, Lt. Jack Brand made a normal landing in a slightly choppy sea as he was ferrying one of the utility unit JF-1s (BuNo 9440) out to the ship, with

Captain Bristol, front and center, with members of his crew and their guests at the ship's dance, held on the hanger deck, 26 June 1935. (NA, 80-CF file, Box 170)

Aviation Chief Ordnanceman Pargen and Radioman 2d Class Grace embarked. The plane struck the water at the top of a small swell, and, as the Grumman rode down the swell, the tail surfaces absorbed the upward force of the wave, buckling and fracturing the leading and trailing edges of the right stabilizer strut and denting and buckling the skin of the right horizontal stabilizer, damage not apparent until the *Ranger* had hoisted the plane on board.[21]

With VB-5B, VF-3B, and VS-1B (VB-3B being temporarily assigned to the *Lexington*) embarked, the *Ranger* returned to San Diego. During flight operations on 14 August, Lt. William H. Hamilton of Observation Squadron (VO) 3B, the unit normally assigned to the battleship *Idaho*, made a carrier refresher landing in an amphibian-configured O3U-1 (BuNo 8574). He landed off-center and caught a wire, but the Vought then bounced about two feet into the air, the hook whipping the tail sharply to starboard. The abrupt impact caused the main strut to collapse, the propeller blade chewing into the top of the float, and buckled the after end of the float. A trouble board faulted Lieutenant Hamilton's technique, but it also assigned a part of the blame for the accident upon the design of the landing gear.[22]

Lieutenant (jg) Charles M. Jett, bringing in a Grumman FF-1 (BuNo 9376) assigned to VF-5B, had troubles that day, too, as he landed with Seaman 2d Class A. C. Murray on board. Trying to get into the arresting gear without a radical dive for the deck, well aware of the tendency of the FF-1's gear to collapse if landed too hard, Jett managed to catch the ninth wire, but the Grumman went into the after barrier, taking damage that required a major overhaul. The trouble board found that some fault lay in the plane's equipment, but leveled blame upon both pilot and LSO.

The *Ranger* later participated in the aerial review that accompanied the entry of the Fleet into San Diego Bay on

23 August. Subsequently, beginning on 9 September, as the carrier lay alongside the pier at San Diego, in preparation for training and firing antiaircraft practices, the officers and men who manned the ship's gun directors used one of the *Ranger*'s utility planes as a target and recorded the pertinent data, such as altitude and speed and course.

Although shipboard landing accidents accounted for a percentage of damage to naval aircraft as a matter of course, mishaps ashore accounted for their share also. On 19 September, 15 of VS-1B's SU-4s were being warmed up on the ramp at North Island, preparatory to flying out to the *Ranger* for exercises. With the regular line crew and mechanics being on board ship, Aviation Chief Ordnanceman A. L. Christensen was supervising the radiomen, who were normally assigned to the aircraft, as they started the planes. All pilots, meanwhile, gathered in the ready room receive last-minute instructions for the flight.

Radioman 1st Class Hobart B. Sullivan, in the cockpit of 1-S-13 (BuNo 9433), started the aircraft, but, with his head down and his eyes on the fuel valves, did not notice that the SU-4 had vibrated its right wheel out of its chocks. Because of the propeller wash from 1-S-14 (BuNo 9432) parked two feet to the rear, Sullivan's SU-4 edged forward, the whirling prop slashing into the tail of 1-S-12 (BuNo 9414) parked two feet ahead, damaging the rudder and elevator beyond repair, partially severing the starboard elevator and rudder wires, and sheering off the horizontal stabilizer and elevator hinge fittings. Flying fragments perforated the vertical stabilizer and stabilizer adjusting post in 1-5-12 as well as damaging two other SU-4s (BuNos 9418 and 9420) in the next line. "It all happened so fast," Sullivan recounted later. "As soon as I saw what was happening I cut off the motor and secured the plane."[23]

Mitigating circumstances resulted in no disciplinary action for either Christensen (under whose supervision the planes were being prepared for flight) or Sullivan (who had been preoccupied with shifting 1-5-13's gas tanks and testing the magnetoes). Henceforth, however, orders came down for pilots to start their own planes in the absence of the regular ground crew, until radiomen had received thorough instructions. In addition, a bungee to hold the wheel chock in its proper position was added to that to prevent a recurrence of the incident.

The *Ranger* participated in the Fleet Review off San Diego on 3 October for President Roosevelt and Admiral Reeves, embarked in the heavy cruiser *Houston* (CA-30), obliging the Chief Executive by launching VB-5B's BF2C-1s as she passed close aboard the presidential flagship. Preparation for the review had proved "extremely valuable in the tactical exercises incident thereto," wrote one informed observer, and "probably made an interesting spectacle for the President who is thoroughly informed in regard to the work of the Navy."[24]

Meanwhile, the *Ranger*'s gunnery officer, Lt. Comdr. Heman J. Redfield, had drilled his crews well. The *Ranger*'s 5-inch battery scored 61 hits of 68 shots during day short-range battle practice (SRBP), racking up a percentage of 89.7% and achieving a merit of 64. She thus out-shot the larger *Lexington* and *Saratoga*, with the latter earning a final merit of 52.6 and the former 48.267. Night battle practice, however, proved another matter, as the gunnery drills tested the effectiveness of 5-inch/25 batteries in repelling night destroyer attacks; the *Ranger* finished second to the *Lexington* in Run A (star shell illumination) and to the *Saratoga* in Run B (searchlights). Concerning the Second Battle Antiaircraft Practice, Redfield concluded that daily drills with an aircraft target led to excellent results, and graded rapid fire as inferior to timed fire, principally because the blasts from adjacent guns interfered with nearby gun crews. "Timed fire" allowed the crews to develop a rhythm "which makes a smoother battery performance." Furthermore, during all gunnery drills, simulated casualties allowed gun and director crews to train to meet eventualities in the event of battle, and the men developed confidence in the ship's installed guns and directors.

At the same time that the *Ranger*'s gun crews drilled to develop their proficiency, Marine aviators, in keeping with the advance base mission of the Corps, continued their routine training in carrier landings. On 4 November, the *Ranger* carried out refresher training for Aircraft Two, based at NAS San Diego. Major Lewie G. "Griff" Merritt, USMC, brought in a BG-1 (BuNo 9548) from VJ-7M; instead of the more customary sandbag, however, Brig. Gen. Douglas C. McDougal, USMC, Assistant to the Major General Commandant, occupied the back seat. Merritt had already made one landing that morning; and Lt. Warren K. Berner, the LSO, believed that the major's second approach looked "satisfactory," so gave him an "OK" signal. Just before he reached the ship, however, Merritt pushed the throttle forward, "which made the plane faster than normal," Berner later noted, "but not too fast for a successful landing." The pilot nosed the plane down at the cut and his wheels touched the deck near the number one wire. The Bouncing Girl struck hard and tail-high before catching the second cross-deck pendant, bounced about 10 feet into the air, and finally came to a stop at number six wire, the impact causing the BG-1 to nose up, bending both propeller blades. The 59-year-old General McDougal, unaccustomed to carrier landings, had braced himself rigidly. Although he had noticed nothing unusual about the landing,

Machine gun practice with .50-caliber M-2 Brownings, 8 October 1935; the guns are in group VII, with what appears to be predominantly Marine crews. (NA, 80-CF file, Box 30)

he called out to his pilot, when the plane sat on the elevator and was being taken below, that "his [McDougal's] back was hurt." Helped out of the plane by the *Ranger*'s surgeon and put to bed, the general had sustained a contusion of the spine in the sacrolumbar region. That painful back injury would keep the general on the sick list for a week.[25]

Merritt's, however, proved to be not the only mishap that day, as the flying leathernecks practiced their trade on the *Ranger*'s deck. First Lt. Wilfred J. Huffman, USMC, had made his first landing without incident. His second approach in a BG-1 (BuNo 9536), from VB-4M, looked normal as he came up the groove with his tailhook extended. Upon landing, however, Huffman's hook bounced off the deck and into the retrieved position, where it stayed. The BG-1 rolled into the barrier and came to an abrupt halt, receiving damage to a cylinder rocker box housing, the forward landing gear fairings, upper engine mounts, both propeller blades, and the lower left wing. Huffman sustained a small cut on his lower lip.[26]

Huffman's misfortune prompted a quick warning to the pilots who had more landings to carry out. One who had heard the word to lock his tailhook in the "down" position, Capt. Vernon M. Guymon, USMC, had recently completed a tour of duty at the U.S. Army Air Corps Tactical School at Maxwell Field, Montgomery, Alabama. Guymon's previous two landings that day had occurred without incident. After giving the "cut" signal, the LSO lost sight of the BG-1 for a moment, and, when he next saw it, it was in a landing attitude about a foot from the deck at about wire number four. With his hook in the retrieved position, Guymon's BG-1 (BuNo 9534) rolled into the barrier, suffering damage to the propeller blades, the lower left wing, the fairing of the forward landing gear struts, and guide bracket assembly brake rods.[27]

Captain Vernon Guymon, USMC, exits his BG-1 (BuNo 9534), after it came to grief on 4 November 1935. (Author)

A little over a week and a half later, following a tactics hop, Lt. George C. Montgomery, of VF-3B, landed his F2F-1 (BuNo 9652) and taxied out of the gear, up the flight deck, to a spot aft of number one elevator. Montgomery cut his engine and remained in the cockpit to man the brakes as plane handlers began pushing BuNo 9652 toward the elevator. Meanwhile, squadronmate Lt. (jg) Myron T. "Empty" Evans was bringing his F2F (BuNo 9654) on board. The LSO had signaled "roger" for most of Evans's coming up the groove, but flashed a "fast" signal twice to show the pilot that he was slightly too fast in his approach. Evans responded correctly in both instances. As Evans was about to catch the wire, however, he brought the F2F's nose up abruptly and missed the third pendant. Evans's tailhook caught the top wire of the second barrier and broke off. The hookless Grumman dropped to the deck, knocking down the third barrier, then charged unchecked toward George Montgomery's plane. Evans's F2F swung to the right, his propeller coming to rest in the port side of Montgomery's cockpit. Fortunately, Montgomery suffered only a cut and bruised right forearm when he was hit by the prop blade; Evans received a slight cut on the forehead when his head hit the windshield.[28]

Another highlight of the *Ranger*'s training that autumn was her participation in a landing exercise at San Clemente Island on 15 November. As part of the attack force comprising the battleships *West Virginia*, *Colorado* (BB-45), *Maryland* (BB-46), and *California* (BB-44), her planes laid smoke to conceal the ship-to-shore movement of Marines from "transports" portrayed by the auxiliary vessel *Utah* (AG-16), storeship *Bridge* (AF-1) and submarine tender *Holland* (AS-3). The exercise showed the ability of the Fleet to concentrate rapidly and put a considerable force ashore in a timely fashion, as well as to carry out well-timed supporting aircraft operations, naval gunfire, and boat movements.

With the coming of the new year 1936, the *Ranger* resumed operations with four squadrons: her own VS-1B and VF-5B and two temporarily assigned *Lexington* squadrons, VB-1B and VF-3B (the *Ranger*'s other two squadrons being transferred temporarily to the *Lexington*) embarked their men on 2 January. Underway later that same day, the *Ranger* conducted carrier qualifications for the *Saratoga*'s Torpedo Squadron (VT) 2B and Bombing Squadron (VB) 2, evolutions that did not proceed entirely without incident.

One of VT-2B's enlisted pilots, Aviation Chief Machinist's Mate (NAP) E. A. O'Donnell, with Aviation Machinist's Mate 1st Class (NAP) R. L. Nichols and Aviation Machinist's Mate 1st Class E. Hasty on board, brought his Great Lakes TG-2 (BuNo A-8702) up the groove. Just as the veteran enlisted pilot received the cut, however, the TG-2 suddenly "crabbed" to the left. O'Donnell applied full left rudder, but the plane did not answer the controls in time.

It bounced, then slammed into the deck, the right landing gear carrying away at a faulty weld.²⁹

Soon thereafter, the *Ranger* exercised with the *Lexington*, then, on 6 January, participated in Fleet Tactical Exercise No. 1-36, which, among other training, involved carrier plane searches for a battleship division, followed by an attack on those ships. It also involved the Fleet units being divided into Black and Blue forces, each proceeding to an assigned initial point, then attempting to locate and attack the other.

During flight operations that day, Lt. (jg) Charles R. Carroll of VB-1B, flying a BM-2 (BuNo 9174), with Aviation Machinist's Mate 2d Class E. C. Hamby on board, made a normal landing. His tailhook bounced, however, and remained nearly in the up position. Applying the brakes retarded the BM-2's forward motion, but did not stop the plane from crashing into the barrier; it nosed up, then fell back to the normal three-point position. Later, those who investigated the accident found no fault with Carroll, who had checked the hook locking device during his approach and found it to be locked in the correct position. When ordered to taxi the plane out of the barrier, however, Carroll noted that the device was unlatched, leading to the conclusion that the accident had been caused by material failure.³⁰

The next morning, Ens. John T. Nolan, USNR, of VF-3B, returning to the *Ranger* in an F2F-1 (BuNo 9651), found the ship rolling and pitching considerably. Nolan received a "fast" signal from Lt. Cecil B. Gill, the LSO, when about 100 yards astern, made the necessary adjustments, and came up the groove with a "roger." When he landed, however, Nolan saw the "cut" signal accompanied by a "high," which prompted him to nose over and pull back on the stick. Unfortunately, 3-F-6's nose failed to rise enough to check the rapid descent, and the Grumman landed hard, wheels-first, collapsing the left landing gear strut and allowing the lower left wing to scrape the deck, bending both spars. Nolan's hook caught the first wire and brought the stubby biplane to a halt. Crash investigators leveled part of the blame on Lieutenant Gill's signals, part to the pilot, and part to the weather and the *Ranger*'s short landing area, because F2Fs had made the same type on landings on board the larger *Lexington* with no problems.³¹

Those same factors figured in two mishaps that occurred during VF-3B's operations on 8 January. In the first, Lt. (jg) James J. McRoberts turned just forward of the planeguard destroyer steaming astern of the carrier, and responded to Lieutenant Gill's "low" signal with a slight increase in altitude. At Gill's "low-fast" signal, McRoberts reduced his rpms and made a slight increase in altitude. After compen-sating for a second "low-fast" signal, he crossed the ramp, looking directly at Gill, who gave him a "high" signal, followed by the flag being drawn across the LSO's throat. Cutting the throttle and dipping the nose, McRoberts felt the Grumman respond sluggishly. His hauling back hard on the stick caused the F2F-1 (BuNo 9650) to land in about a three-point position. The right landing gear gave way upon impact, and the right wing hit the deck.³²

The *Ranger*'s plane-handlers had no sooner cleared away McRoberts's Grumman when Lt. (jg) George S. "Buck" James, Jr. made his approach. Although appropriately adjusting to the LSO's "high-fast" signals, he felt the plane flying "uncomfortably slow," so throttled back only slightly in response to the "fast" signals. As James crossed the ramp, the LSO signaled "high," then "cut." Buck James nosed down slightly, closed the throttle, and brought the stick back. The last maneuver had little effect, and James's F2F-1 (BuNo 9664) landed wheels-first, slightly on the right wheel. The right landing gear strut link failed and BuNo 9664 crashed.³³

The three accidents for VF-3B, occurring so close together, occasioned the usual investigation. A trouble board concluded that the cause lay in "(1) the airplane's having been brought in too high above the deck, and at too low an airspeed, and (2) the pilots' failure to ease their planes into the gear." The F2F-1 could be "'hung on the prop" and controlled at a speed considerably below that which it can be controlled when the slipstream is removed from the tail surfaces by cutting the throttle. The practice on board the *Ranger*, those who investigated the crashes wrote, was to bring F2Fs in high, and just above a full stall, with "gun" on. Under those conditions, when the pilot closed the throttle, the plane tended to drop rapidly, and employing the elevators had little effect. Unless the pilot brought back the stick "smartly," the plane would strike the deck "with considerable force." Finding himself high above the deck when the LSO gave him the cut, a pilot of "average experience and ability" would "duck for the deck"—pushing the stick forward for a moment before pulling it back to land, to eliminate any possibility that the F2F would float over the gear. If the LSO gave the "high–cut" signal, the reaction would be more positive. Those who looked into the crashes of the three F2Fs posited that a safe landing could be made from the "high stalled position," in which the plane was habitually placed by the LSO, only by a burst of throttle just before the wheels touched the deck (which was a forbidden practice) or by the pilot's carefully manipulating the controls to hold the nose up while preventing a spin. The investigators believed that the LSO had placed the pilot in the unenviable predicament of requiring "unusual airmanship" to land without damage to the airplane.[34]

Lieutenant Comdr. Miles R. Browning, commanding officer of VF-3B, however, believed that the F2F-1s were being brought in "too high and too slow" on board the *Ranger*. After observing landings for the previous six months, Browning believed that F2F-1 landings on board the *Ranger* were "generally more uncomfortable and . . . harder on the airplanes . . . than has been the experience of the squadron," when it operated from either the *Lexington* or the *Langley*. Browning noted that the question of "approach procedure and landings [on board the *Ranger*] has been the subject of repeated discussion and study by the ship and her squadrons, and all criticism and suggestion[s] by pilots has received full consideration . . . ." In light of the three recent mishaps that had crystallized the discussion of the matter, VF-3B's skipper recommended modifying "the general practice in approaches and landings by F2Fs and similar types . . . to result in a reduction of the altitude when crossing the ramp, and a slightly increased speed to permit better control." Further, Browning recommended that no alterations be made in the design of the F2F-1's landing gear, believing it to be "of sound design and satisfactory strength."[35]

Reflecting on the crashes of the three F2F-1s, Captain Bristol suggested that the pitching of the ship contributed to the accidents, noting the appreciable movement of the stern upward when the planes were about to touch down. "It is quite possible," he wrote, "that the upward motion of the deck caused the plane to touch before the pilot had sufficient time to level off." He concurred with the observation that the landings did not appear to be abnormally hard, but believed that the failure of certain parts of the landing gear be investigated. Bristol promised to give Browning's suggestions "careful study for the purpose of preventing similar crashes of this nature." ComAirBatFor, in his endorsement, noted that any attempt to modify the F2F-1's landing gear "would probably result in fuselage failures under similar circumstances." He believed that the failures were the cumulative effect of hard landings, not necessarily abnormally hard in any case, and the result of the "landing signal technique peculiar to the *Ranger*."[36] ComAirBatFor concurred in Captain Bristol's belief that the "excessive motion of the ship" played a role in the mishaps.[37]

5

"A VERY GOOD TIME WAS HAD BY ALL"

Following that stint of local operations, the *Ranger* embarked the Cold Weather Test Detachment, formally established on 25 November 1935 and placed under the command of Lt. George Van Deurs of VS-1B, an officer who had received commendations for his innovations in organization and methods that had resulted in time- and money-saving aircraft overhauls (methods widely adopted by other stations as a consequence), while serving at NAS San Diego prior to his joining VS-1B.[1] The detachment, constituted from various units from Aircraft Squadrons, Battle Force, boasted an aircraft complement that consisted of three O3U-3s, two JF-1s, three SBU-1s, six F2F-1s, six BG-1s, and three BF2C-1s.[2] Between the date upon which the detachment was established and its departure for Alaskan waters, it installed and tested its special equipment, while its people familiarized themselves with that equipment and proper operating procedures.[3]

As part of the evaluation work, the *Ranger* also embarked 16 observers (5 military and 11 civilian), each of the latter required to sign a statement certifying that the information obtained during the *Ranger*'s Cold Weather Cruise be kept confidential within the interests of the government and the firm the individual represented. U.S. Army Majs. W. T. Larson and K. W. Walker, and 1st Lt. R. E. Giavannoli; 1st Lt. William D. Saunders, Jr., USMC; and Lt. Clarence F. Edge, USCG formed the visiting military contingent. The civilians included C. F. Becker (Associated Oil Company), Rudolph Gagg (Wright Aeronautical Corporation), George Hausaman (Eclipse Aviation Corporation), R. A. Coffman (Federal Laboratories), R. E. Ellis (Standard Oil Company of New Jersey), A. H. Kobelmann (Walter Kidde Company), J. W. Townsend (Solas Engineering Company), A. W. DeChard (Scintilla Magneto Company), W. Thomas and Lorenzo Snow (Pratt and Whitney Aircraft), and M. A. Lott, a mechanical engineer from the Naval Aircraft Factory.

The *Ranger*, in company with the destroyers *Lea* (DD-118) and *Roper* (DD-147), departed San Diego an hour before the end of the first watch on 13 January. With the two destroyers in company, the *Ranger* turned into the Strait of San Juan de Fuca during the morning watch on 17 January, and conducted flight operations to thoroughly impregnate "all engine bearing surfaces with the special test oils" being used during the Cold Weather Test Detachment's work.

As the *Ranger* approached Port Angeles, Washington, Lt. (jg) Lorry Forbes, flying a BG-1 (BuNo 9505), with Aviation Chief Machinist's Mate F. Kast on board, tried to lower his tailhook, but found that the control handle jammed halfway up the slide. Unable to lock the hook either up or down, he contacted the ship. Instructed to fly to NAS Sand Point, Seattle, accompanied by Lt. (jg) William H. Ashford in another BG-1, Forbes landed and inspected the hook cable. After replacing the kinked and frayed cable and finding the change satisfactory, Forbes and Ashford would return to the *Ranger* during the forenoon watch the following day.[4]

Lieutenant (jg) Norman M. "Bus" Miller, meanwhile, with Aviation Machinist's Mate 2d Class H.W. Dye in back, brought in his BG-1 (BuNo 9504) slightly fast, hitting the deck wheels-first between number two and three wires, then bouncing. The tailhook failed to engage the wires, and the BG-1 charged forward, penetrating the barrier. When it then reached a point abreast the forward end of the island, Bus Miller's mount spun to the left, through 270 degrees, and came to rest on the port side of the flight deck, facing inboard. Although damaged beyond immediate repair and unflyable until it had been overhauled, the BG-1, minus its wings and placed on the hangar deck, would still serve a useful purpose in engine-starting tests.[5]

Soon thereafter, the *Ranger* reached her destination, during the forenoon watch, to top off fuel and pick up stores for the work that lay ahead. Knowing that their destination afforded little opportunity for rest and recreation ashore, Captain Bristol granted liberty for the Port Watch. The next day, the *Ranger* sailed for Cook Inlet, having recovered Forbes and Ashford from Sand Point.

After an uneventful passage, the carrier detached the *Lea* and the *Roper* on the morning of 22 January, to allow the destroyers to proceed to Seward, Alaska, to fuel. Proceeding independently, the *Ranger* ultimately made landfall on Barren Island, located at the entrance to Cook Inlet and, after encountering currents as high as three knots in the waters that lay between Barren and Chugach Islands, anchored in the inner arm of Kachemak Bay, a little over an hour and a quarter into the afternoon watch. Lowering two motor whaleboats, two motor launches, and a dinghy soon occupied the deck force; Ens. Clarence A. Keller, Jr., in the number two motor whaleboat, took a party of men in two motor launches to drag the area that lay to the northward of the ship's anchorage; Lt. Comdr. Van H. Ragsdale took a party of men in the number one motor whaleboat and the dinghy to investigate potential emergency landing field locations. "Careful reconnaissance of the region," however, "disclosed no suitable terrain of sufficient extent," finding mountainous topography "with glaciers and deep ravines."

Lieutenant Theodore R. Frederick took up U.S.S. RANGER-4, a Grumman JF-1, and overflew possible field sites, photographing Kasilof, Ninilchuk, Kenai, and a lake on the north shore of Kachemak Bay, before he returned to the ship shortly before the end of the afternoon watch. The latter place proved to be the only one deemed suitable for emergency landings, with an area 1,120 by 860 feet on a surface of ice 18 inches thick. Those who evaluated the sites believed Kasilof "unfit even for [an] emergency landing," Ninilchuk covered with ice and snow and fit only for landings ("planes probably would be unable to take off again"), and Kenai "practicable for planes equipped either with wheels or skis."

Continuing the dragging operations begun the previous afternoon, Captain Bristol dispatched two parties of men ashore to reconnoiter and look for potential landing sites, during the forenoon watch on 23 January, and one of the ship's utility planes was sent out on a reconnaissance flight, before threatening weather compelled the ship to haul it on board less than an hour into the afternoon watch. Rain was soon lashing the area, with strong, gusty winds that occasionally reached gale force. It was the *Ranger*'s first encounter with what those familiar with local weather conditions referred to as a "williwaw" (strong, gusty winds blowing down from the mountains and glaciers through passes leading to the water). Such conditions rendered the inner reach of Kachemak Bay a poor anchorage.

At 1340, the *Ranger* dispatched Lt. (jg) Cecil B. Gill to Homer Spit to retrieve one reconnoitering party from the beach, as well as to bring back one of the motor whaleboats and a punt. A little less than an hour and a half later, she sent Ens. Earl E. Schneider with a motor launch and a dinghy to recover a second reconnoitering party four miles northeast of the inboard end of Homer Spit. Lieutenant Comdr. Ralph W. Christie, the ship's navigator, returned 40 minutes later in a motor boat, with a party that had been reconnoitering Seldovia. Lieutenant (jg) Gill, however, had had to return without the motor whaleboat and the punt, which had been blown onto the beach.

At 1750, with one party of men still stranded ashore, Comdr. Bill Greenman, the carrier's first lieutenant, took the ship's number three motor launch to attempt to bring them off; the ship maintained a searchlight beam to aid the rescue party, as well as to provide a reference point for the *Lea* and the *Roper* to anchor off Homer Spit. As the *Ranger* stood by, her engineering force ready to answer all signals from the bridge and to get underway because of the unsettled conditions, Greenman continued in his efforts to recover the officers and men trapped ashore, rewarded at last by success toward the end of the mid watch on 24 January. "No injury to personnel," reads the laconic prose of the *Ranger*'s log, "except exposure which was not considered dangerous." Within an hour and half of the afternoon watch, the ship had recovered all of her boats and hoisted them in. That day ended as it had begun, with the *Ranger* ready to get underway, prepared for heavy weather.[6]

Over the next several days, the *Ranger* operated out of Kachemak Bay and Cook Inlet, sending up her utility planes as the weather permitted. On the same day that the intrepid Commander Greenman established a shore base for cold weather operations (27 January), the *Ranger* encountered a "local squall of considerable violence," with winds gusting between 50 and 55 knots, and blowing

The *Ranger*, with the planes from the Cold Weather Test Detachment spotted on deck, anchored in the inner reach of Kachemak Bay, Alaska, 26 January 1936, with the snow-covered mountains of the southeastern shore visible in the distance. (AUTHOR)

steadily between 35 to 40, which compelled Captain Bristol to get the *Ranger* underway. Standing out of Kachemak Bay soon after the squall forced her to drag her 22,500-pound anchor and 105 fathoms of chain to leeward about 700 yards, the *Ranger* reached a safe haven between Anchor Point and Seldovia.

The *Ranger* conducted various tests of planes (all except the BF2C-1s, which were not maintained in flying status during the cruise) and equipment into the second week of February, conducting flying operations on 3, 4, 5, and 9 February. She conducted airplane engine-starting tests, machine gun firings for not only her own weapons, but those of her embarked BF2C-1s, and firings of her 5-inch batteries. The F2F-1 pilots logged 53.8 hours of flight time and 29 deck landings, the BG-1 pilots 49.2 hours aloft and 25 landings, JF-1 pilots 46.4 hours and 13 landings, O3U-3 pilots 23.3 hours and 12 landings and the SBU-1s 23.2 hours and 13 landings.

Although little opportunity existed for regular leave and liberty, Lieutenant Commander Redfield, the *Ranger*'s gunnery officer, engineered a "scenic trip" to the Grewingk Glacier, on Sunday morning, 2 February, to punctuate the period of work. Organized as a landing force, the 32 officers and 388 men, all garbed in special winter clothing, landed in tiny Halibut Cove, near a deserted fish cannery, and trekked over a rocky ridge to the foot of the glacier. "I'm sure no one who saw it," wrote Musician 2d Class C. H. Channing later, "could help but feel a sense of amazement and awe at its immensity and beauty. Hundreds of feet thick and stretching back to the horizon and beyond, lay this

Sailors from the *Ranger*'s starboard watch—25 officers and 388 enlisted men strong—visit Grewingk Glacier, 2 February 1936. (AUTHOR)

huge mass of blue and green," surrounded by the peaks of the Kenai Range that rose to the clouds.[7] "The party seemed to thoroughly enjoy this diversion," Captain Bristol wrote later, although several "glacier climbers" were heard to mutter as they sank, bone weary, into their bunks that night, "they wouldn't have missed it for five dollars and wouldn't go again for another five."[8]

Once a week, the *Ranger* sent a large motor launch over to the *Lea* and the *Roper* with fresh provisions and stores. Additionally, when boating conditions permitted, she provided the destroyers with "a supply of all articles of food" on her general mess menu. "The consideration and assistance rendered by the *Ranger* to the plane guard destroyers," Lt. Comdr. William M. Reifel, the *Lea*'s commanding officer, later wrote, surpassed "anything which might be expected from a vessel not equipped as a tender." Consequently, Reifel asked that Commander Destroyers, Battle Force, "make special note of this greatly appreciated service rendered by the *Ranger*."[9]

Thus far in the life of the ship, there had been no mishaps involving her unique "hinged smoke pipes." The morning before the *Ranger* was to sail for San Diego, 10 February, however, the Cold Weather Detachment's planes had been spotted on deck for starting tests, among them an SBU-1 (BuNo 9771) secured with its right wingtip over the lowered starboard after stack platform. Everyone topside with duties to perform that day wore heavy winter clothing. Somehow, someone unknown to the flight control officer brushed past him on the fly control station on the bridge and accidentally hit the exposed button. Eight seconds later, the upward movement of the stack attracted attention. Apprised of the situation, the fly control officer soon

Ranger sailors easily remove the fine and dry snow from the flight deck after the 32-hour blizzard, 7 February 1936. The fine precipitation, however, sifted into cockpits, posing "a menace for which the only known remedy [was] to send the planes to a heated hangar deck." (AUTHOR)

pushed the "stop" button that arrested the stack's motion within another 11½ seconds. Unfortunately, a quick investigation soon revealed that the after spar of the SBU-1's right lower wing was fractured and the forward spar bent and fractured. The left lower wing was twisted out of line, and the upper wing was deemed "questionable." The true nature of the damage to the upper wing, investigators believed, could not be determined on board ship. Covers over the local stack controls had prevented any accidental depression of the buttons there, leading investigators to conclude that "some person, whose identity is unknown" had inadvertently hit the exposed switch on the bridge. Soon thereafter, a sheet metal cover, fabricated on board, appeared over the stack operating buttons on the bridge. Captain Bristol considered that solution "satisfactory" for preventing that kind of accident from happening again.[10]

Underway for San Diego on 11 February, the *Ranger* sighted the familiar shape of San Clemente Island on the morning of the 18th. A little over an hour into the afternoon watch, she launched planes allocated to the Cold Weather Test Detachment (which would be formally disbanded on 25 February, one week after its return to North Island), as well as the ship's utility aircraft, and anchored in Coronado Roads during the first watch. She shifted thence to the NAS pier at North Island the next morning and broke Vice Admiral Butler's flag an hour before the end of the morning watch.

"An extended winter cruise in northern regions," Captain Bristol wrote soon afterward of the cruise just concluded, "with an outlook for considerable exposure, discomfort and hard work and no opportunity in sight for liberty and shore recreation, constituted a new experience for a large percentage of the officers and men of the USS *Ranger*." Naturally, he added, at the outset, some harbored apprehension about the enterprise. "On the other hand," Bristol noted, "a feeling and spirit of adventure, quite common to the average American youth, prevailed."[11]

As the cruise progressed and conditions became more severe, Bristol had observed "no apparent slack-up of effort, efficiency or interest in the job." In fact, he perceived not only a "general feeling of contentment, but a cheerful and keen outlook...decidedly in evidence," reflected in the excellent general conduct of the crew and the absence of courts-martial or brig sentences. "Briefly," the *Ranger*'s captain concluded, "it may be fairly accurately stated, from the standpoint of the personnel as a whole, a very good time was had by all, despite the absence of habitual liberty and shore recreation facilities."[12]

"A modern vessel, with modern improvements," the *Ranger* possessed adequate heating and ventilating systems, which made it possible for temperature and ventilation conditions to be controlled for the comfort of the officers and men. Additionally, "by virtue of the cafeteria messing system and adequate food supply," the *Ranger*'s crew enjoyed hot meals "to suit any special situation at variance

Planes of the Cold Weather Test Detachment, 7 February 1936. (NA, 80-CF-5487-4)

with the ship's routine," which meant that those subjected to exposure to the elements had a hot breakfast, for example, before going to work. "Early breakfast for the Air Department," Bristol noted, "became almost a matter of routine." The mess cooks kept a constant supply of that Navy staple, coffee, "available at practically all hours of the day," and the ship's soda fountain sold hot chocolate. Furthermore, the "supply and ready issue of special winter clothing" meant that officers and men did not suffer undue "hardship and discomfort through lack of adequate protection."[13]

To provide the crew with recreational opportunities, "the hangar deck became invaluable," with the enlisted men enjoying basketball, volleyball, and handball; the officers could play volleyball and badminton. Interdivisional contests in volleyball, basketball, tugs-of-war, and acey-ducey (a variant of backgammon) took place, the crew manifesting considerable interest in the competition. Movies began nightly an hour and a quarter into the second dog watch, preceded by a "Bureau of Navigation Educational Slide Film." Both the motion pictures and the slide shows proved a big draw, with "invariably large" attendance. The ship also held a happy hour, with "mass singing, boxing, and comedy" programs, attended by a large group of guests from the *Lea* and the *Roper*.[14]

The Bureau of Aeronautics had initiated the cold weather operations to "test power plant starting and [the] operation of arresting gear; to determine [the] most suitable clothing for flight deck crews; and to determine the general efficiency of cold weather operation." Although the *Ranger* encountered no subzero temperatures, Captain Bristol felt that his men had accumulated valuable data. "The present cruise of the *Ranger* in so far as aviation is concerned," Bristol concluded, "has been of the nature of shop test work,"

Pilots of the Cold Weather Test Detachment, 8 February 1936. Seated in front (L–R): Lt. (jg) Milton A. Nation (VS-1B), Lt. (jg) Lorenz Q. "Lorry" Forbes (VB-3B), Lt. (jg) William H. Ashford (VB-3B), Lt. (jg) Eugene "Gene" Tatom (VF-3B), Lt. (jg) Ward T. "W. T." Shields (VB-5B), and Lt. (jg) William F. "Red" Raborn, Jr. (VF-5B). Seated in the middle row (L–R): Lt. (jg) Theodore R. "Ted" Frederick (*Ranger*), Lt. John W. C. "Jack" Brand (*Ranger*), Lt. (jg) Joseph T. "Joe" Thornton (VB-3B), Lt. Apollo "Soakem" Soucek (*Ranger*), Lt. George Van Deurs (VS-1B) (commanding officer), Lt. Frederick M. "Freddie" Hughes (VB-3B), Lt. George C. Montgomery (VF-3B), and Lt. (jg) Herbert D. Riley (VF-3B). Standing (L–R): Lt. (jg) Charles L. Westhofen (VF-3B), Lt. (jg) William M. "Mac" Freshour (VB-5B), Lt. (jg) Baylies V. Clark (VB-1B), Lt. (jg) Harlan T. "Swede" Johnson (VB-3B), Lt. (jg) Karl E. "Jug" Jung (VF-3B), Lt. (jg) Alden H. "Rusty" Irons (VF-3B), Lt. (jg) Albert H. "Jock" Wilson, Jr. (VS-1B), and Lt. (jg) John H. Morse, Jr. (VF-5B). (NA, 80-CF-8005-3)

trying out and analyzing equipment and methods of operation. Although he acknowledged that operating only 23 airplanes was a far cry from the full four operating squadron complement, he believed that the work that his ship had just completed had been significant, and that the conclusions applied to a full-strength air group. Much depended on the availability of flight and hangar deck space. "Cold weather in itself need cause no great worry," he concluded, "but cold, bad weather—snow, ice, and sleet—is a most serious problem and much study and experience is in order."[15]

The *Ranger* resumed local operations in the balmy climes of San Diego soon thereafter. On 28 February, Lt. (jg) William Miller, Jr., of VS-1B, with Radioman 2d Class H. L. Casey on board, returned from a bombing hop in an SU-4. As Miller approached the ramp, he could not discern the LSO's signals until nearly at the ramp itself, when he saw the LSO wag a frantic "low." Miller pulled up sharply, but the Vought, with insufficient speed, struck the ramp, the impact carrying away all of the bracing for the tail wheel inside the after fuselage bay. The trouble board assessed the damage as 100% human error—but the LSO's, not the pilot's.[16]

Landing an airplane on a carrier deck poses enough of a challenge in the daytime; nocturnal operations more so. On 31 March, Lt. (jg) Henry H. "Bill" Hale of VF-3B, making his second night qualification landing in an F2F-1, watched the illuminated movements of the LSO and followed them explicitly, as the ship pitched in the Pacific swells. Crossing the ramp in a decidedly high attitude, Hale saw the LSO give him the "high cut" signal. Realizing he was coming in

Checking flotation bag operation on a BG-1 (BuNo 9505), 11 February 1936. Note "LT. (jg) L. Q. Forbes" beneath the cockpit, showing that the practice of painting pilots' names on aircraft is not a recent phenomenon. (AUTHOR)

high, Hale dove for the deck, but being unable to see it, could not cushion his descent. His F2F-1 (BuNo 9651) hit the deck "with considerable force and speed," catching the number three wire near the broad chrome yellow deck stripe running down the starboard side of the flight deck. Both landing gear link struts collapsed; the barrel-fuselaged Grumman slid down the deck on its belly, the impact of the crash throwing Hale forward in the cockpit and opening the throttle. The propeller chewed into the deck, demolishing both blades. Disassembling and inspecting the engine, the trouble board posited, would reveal what damage had been done there; a quick inspection of the fuselage showed it to be wrinkled, with a buckled firewall, a collapsed landing gear and a broken prop. Bill Hale, who had always wanted to be a naval officer since growing up on the shores of Lake Michigan, spent three days on the sick list with a strained back.[17]

Anticipation reigned in VB-5B, which had operated only nine Boeing F4B-4s since the previous September, when it found itself with a full complement of 19 airplanes. On 10 April, the squadron received nine Grumman F2F-1s from VF-5B; over the next week, VB-5B's men completed all checks and repainted the aircraft, and experienced the "grand and glorious feeling to again have a full squadron in the air." On 23 April, the squadron, possessing its full complement of planes, embarked for the upcoming fleet problem. Although the squadron had its planes, however, it almost did not have the number of pilots necessary to fly them, for urgent dental work, a case of the mumps, and two last-minute transfers took four VB-5B pilots, including the exec and the personnel officer. Fortunately, other squadrons provided the necessary replacements: Lt. (jg) Maxwell F. Leslie from VF-5B, Lt. (jg) Eugene Tatom from VF-3B, and Lt. (jg) John D. "Mike" Shea and Ens. Brian O. Sparks, USNR, from VF-6B.

A Washington, D.C., native, Mike Shea particularly impressed his new squadronmates. Fresh from Pensacola, he came to VB-5B after it had embarked in the *Ranger*. "Thanks to the excellent training he had received in Fighting Six and the carrier training received from the *Saratoga* signal officer," a shipmate later observed, Shea "was able to take his place in this squadron on its first flight off the carrier and although he was in a strange airplane, in a strange squadron; landing for the first time on a strange and smaller carrier; and being signaled to by a strange signal officer he had never seen before, Lieutenant Shea acted like a veteran," who would make "as pretty landings as have been seen aboard the *Ranger* for a long time."[18] Such success would not have surprised his classmates, one of whom wrote that Shea had surmounted all obstacles at the Naval Academy (including academics—he graduated ninth from the bottom of the Class of 1932) "with the tenacity of an Irish terrier."[19]

On the eve of the *Ranger*'s departure for the upcoming fleet problem, Lt. (jg) Sylvius Gazze of VF-3B, flying the

Martin BM-1 of VB-1B in flight, 14 April 1936. (NA, 80-G-462944)

squadron's SBU-1 liaison plane (BuNo 9776), came in after a routine familiarization hop on 26 April. With good visibility, a moderate sea, and only slight pitch on the ship, all boded well for a good landing. Gazze made a normal approach, pulled up slightly just prior to receiving the LSO's "cut" signal, and received the LSO's "high–cut" signal. Slightly high, with his landing speed just above stall, however, Gazze inadvertently let the nose drop, so that 5-F-19 hit the deck wheels-first, just short of number one wire. Bouncing into the air, the Vought continued up the deck until the arresting wire brought it to an abrupt stop, collapsing the landing gear. Those who investigated the accident believed that Gazze had nosed his plane over slightly, believing that he was coming in high and, not sensing the slow airspeed, had simply waited too long before trying to cushion the landing by using his elevators.[20]

On the morning of 27 April, the *Ranger* sailed to take part in Fleet Problem XVII, standing out in company with the *Lexington*, the *Saratoga*, and the *Langley*. Embarked on board the *Lexington*, the pilots of VF-3B, after serving in the *Ranger*, clearly had to adjust to the sheer size of the larger ship. "It seemed like an endurance run," one pilot recounted with tongue in cheek, "to taxi from the gear up to the island." In the same vein, one observer later reported overhearing "several of the pilots...debating the advisability of tracing out their courses with chalk whenever they go below in order that they might find their way back to daylight." As VF-3B's men acquainted themselves with a much larger ship than they had been used to, they also continued to gain experience with their new Grumman F3F-1s—a transition made easier by the presence of Harry Larsen, the Grumman factory representative, who was making the cruise to give the squadron the benefit of the manufacturer's familiarity with his product.[21]

"A VERY GOOD TIME WAS HAD BY ALL" ■ 53

Between 28 April and 3 June, the Battle Force "fought" the augmented Scouting Force (each side employing two carriers), in waters that ranged from those off the U.S. West Coast to Panama to the western coast of central America. Fleet Problem XVII included evolutions designed to exercise submarines in offensive operations, continue the development of antisubmarine operations, develop techniques for aircraft and surface ship scouting, test communication systems, and provide training for patrol plane squadrons in extended fleet operations.

For the *Ranger*'s flight deck crews, however, matters of grand naval strategy assumed second place to practical considerations in day-to-day operations, as the glare off the ship's painted flight deck began to lead to "head aches, blurred vision, and 'sun grins,' which materially reduced their efficiency." Flying helmets without visors proved no help, nor did white hats with the brims turned down because the brims reflected the glare into the eyes (not to mention the fact that the hats themselves proved liable to being blown off and into a plane's oil cooler). Some sailors even tried dark glasses, but "discarded them for various reasons."[22]

During the first day of the problem, Aviation Chief Machinist's Mate J. T.O. Marquis (NAP) of VB-1B, returning from a tactical hop in a BM-1 (BuNo 8883) during the forenoon watch, throttled back and eased the stick forward a little as he neared the ramp. After receiving the cut, he expected to catch the fifth or six wire. When he did not, Marquis thought that his hook had failed, and pushed the stick forward until he had gained the deck. Catching the last wire, Marquis's BM-1 encountered the barrier abruptly, damaging the propeller and the tailwheel assembly, the barrier wire slightly denting the right lower wing. Marquis walked away from the crash with a bump on the forehead; Seaman 1st Class R. F. Baker, his passenger, nursed a fractured right elbow.[23]

Later, during the first watch, Lieutenant Hopping of VS-1B (who had been involved in the very first deck crash in the *Ranger*'s history) returned from a night flight in an SBU-1 (BuNo 9803), with Radioman 2d Class C. L. Evans on board. Seeing Hopping approach too far to starboard in the groove, the LSO "walked" the pilot to the left. After receiving a "fast" signal, Hopping dropped 1-S-7's left wing, blanking the LSO from his view, and overcontrolled, a maneuver that threw the right wing down at a 30 degree angle and caused those on deck to think that Hopping was taking a waveoff to the right. Hopping opened his throttle, threw the left wing down, then cut the throttle as the SBU-1 leveled off, passing over the arresting wires and through the first two barriers, skidding along the deck for a short distance before coming to a stop. Among the extensive damage to the aircraft, the bomb displacement gear fork and right drag strut pierced the fuselage and wrecked the pilot's foot boards, rudder pedals, front stick bearing supports, and adjacent fuselage members. A subsequent trouble board faulted Hopping for "error of judgment" and "poor technique."[24]

Returning from a scouting mission during the forenoon watch on 4 May, Lt. (jg) Warren R. Thompson of VS-1B, with Seaman 1st Class M. L. Hoover in back, drifted to the left of the centerline as he approached in his SBU-1 (BuNo 9811). Applying right rudder to regain the center, Thompson took the cut and landed, but his applying the rudder caused the SBU-1 to catch a wire while in a skid. The impact threw the right wingtip to the deck, crumpling the lower right wing and bending the right lower aileron.[25]

Two days further into the maneuvers, Lt. John P. Whitney of VF-3B, flying an F2F-1 (BuNo 9649), took the cut from the LSO, and settled down to the deck just short of the number one wire, just to port of the broad center stripe. Observers saw 3-F-4's hook strike the deck, but at that instant one of the elevator signal bell cover plates flew up and hurtled over the side of the ship abreast the stacks. Whitney's hook caught number two wire, but failed; the unbridled Grumman, thus allowed "free gangway" up the deck, rolled into the barrier and turned over. The fact that the signal bell cover plate had been in a position to foul Whitney's hook mystified the trouble board, who surmised that the only possibility was that a previous landing had caused the plate to jump out of its usually flush housing. An overhaul lay in store for the F2F-1, but Whitney sustained only minor bruises and a small cut on his scalp just above the forehead, requiring one stitch.[26]

VS-1B's woes continued during the afternoon watch on 6 May, when Lt. (jg) Lucian F. Dodson, returning from a tactics hop, with Radioman 1st Class W. L. McAlister in back, in an SBU-1 (BuNo 9771), made a normal, but slightly left-of-centerline approach. After receiving the cut from the LSO, Dodson attempted to better center the airplane by applying right rudder, a move that only arrested the plane with a skidding motion that threw the right wing down to scrape the deck, buckling the right lower wingtip.[27]

Pilot error accounted for mishaps, as did materiel failure, but so too could weather phenomena over which a flier could exercise no control. A little over an hour into the afternoon watch on 14 May, 34-year-old Aviation Chief Machinist's Mate Thomas M. Neal (NAP), one of the ship's enlisted pilots, took off from Coco Solo in U.S.S. RANGER-4, a Grumman JF-1 (BuNo 9454), with two passengers: Lt. (jg) Harold P. Richards (SC), from Vice

Admiral Butler's staff, in the second seat and Storekeeper 2d Class Henry Melville in the lower passenger compartment. "Pay" Richards carried a black box containing $20,000. Just prior to departure, Neal had read the weather report telling of satisfactory conditions on his flight path, with a 500-foot ceiling at Darien.[28]

With a 600-foot cloud ceiling over Darien, Neal maintained altitude at 500, following the canal, keeping the channel bouys in sight on his port side. Although rain continued to fall, the weather improved slightly as Neal flew on, getting even better as he arrived at Gamboa. Suddenly, as he neared a point about a quarter of a mile opposite the Gamboa Bridge, Neal saw a "brilliant flash" around the nose of the plane and slightly to the right. A quick look at his airspeed indicator showed 160 knots or better, but Neal immediately felt that he had lost nearly all of his air speed, as well as "a terrific pancaking sensation." Thinking that he had lost his prop, he cut the switch. Seeing that had not been the case, he cut it in again and pushed the throttle forward. The Grumman, however, refused to go faster than idling speed, and Neal felt his controls go limp. As the JF-1 pancaked, the nose suddenly whipped down at an angle of 45 degrees. The acceleration of the dive prompted Neal to try the elevator controls, decreasing the glide angle and leveling off his wings as the water rushed inexorably nearer. The Grumman, with a nose-down attitude of about 30 degrees, richocheted across the waves before overturning, violently, the abrupt impact of the plane on the unyielding water jamming the sliding hood over Lieutenant (jg) Richards's head and slamming the passengers around like dice in a box.

"As soon as all motion of the plane had stopped," Neal, holding his breath, unfastened his parachute and safety belt, then kicked himself out from under the plane. Bobbing to the surface, Neal could see U.S.S. RANGER-4's tail assembly and a small portion of the after fuselage. Seeing no other survivors, Neal dove to the lower passenger compartment, the entrance to which lay about a foot below the water. Sliding back the door, Neal reached in and grabbed the unconscious Melville by the hair and pulled him through the opening, holding his head above water. Melville's parachute straps, however, tethered him fast to the slowly sinking plane.

Providentially, a Panama Canal dredging division launch, southward bound at the time of the crash, arrived, with Supervisor P. A. White, Asst. Eng. E. P. Haw, and Charles Hill, Jr., master of the dredge *Paraiso*, on board. Seeing Neal desperately holding Melville's head above the water but helpless to free him, White dove in and freed the chute straps that kept the assistant paymaster with the plane. With Melville safely on board the launch, Neal pulled himself down along the overturned amphibian and tried to open the after cockpit hood. Unable to hold his breath long enough to do so, he came to the surface. White dove in again, but could not locate Pay Richards, trapped in the plane.

Neal suggested to the boat crew that they tie a line around the tail and try to tow the plane to shallow water to facilitate salvage. White did so, but as soon as the boat took a strain on the line, it parted. The supervisor refastened the rope to one of the struts, but the strut again gave way under the strain; as the JF-1 slid deeper into the water, a float came to the surface. Neal recognized it immediately, and told the boat crew that the line was attached to a black satchel "containing some $20,000." After recovery of the payroll, the launch headed for Paraiso, because there were no signs of life, "such as bubbles coming up from the plane" to indicate that Pay Richards was still alive.

The launch arrived at Paraiso about 1400, where Storekeeper 2d Class Melville was transferred to a waiting ambulance and rushed to Gorgas Hospital. Neal proceeded to the nearest telephone, called the Fleet Air Base at Coco Solo, reported the crash, and requested that they notify the *Ranger* what had happened. About 1445, Neal called the minesweeper *Teal* (AM-23), moored at the submarine base at Coco Solo, and recounted the events he had survived. Ultimately, Aviation Chief Machinist's Mate Neal and Storekeeper 2d Class Melville went to the hospital ship *Relief* (AH-1) for treatment; a Sergeant Lewis of the Canal Zone Police took the payroll satchel to Balboa. Neal's only injury was a lacerated right upper eyelid, and he returned to duty the next day. Melville's diagnosed intracranial injuries resulted in 22 days on the sick list; he did not return to duty until 5 June.

The *Teal*, steamed to Gamboa, arriving there a little over four hours later, to begin efforts to locate the sunken amphibian. The *Teal*'s sailors, assisted by a party from the U.S. Navy's radio station at Darien, worked throughout the night without success. Eventually, divers from the Canal Zone barge *Atlas* located the JF-1 at the end of the morning watch on the 15th. Soon thereafter, the seaplane wrecking derrick *YSD-8* arrived from the Fleet Air Base and hoisted the Grumman from the water and onto its deck at 1430, where, soon thereafter, a pharmacist's mate from the *Teal* supervised the removal of the corpse of Lieutenant (jg) Richards from the after cockpit.

Ironically, the previous afternoon, Bombing Squadron Two, then embarked in the *Saratoga*, had been in the process of typesetting a newsletter of appreciation for the work of the Fleet Air Disbursing Office, which had performed its vital fiscal function under Pay Richards's able direction. "Although working under the handicap of having their [pay]rolls scattered throughout the four Aircraft Carriers at sea and many more squadrons ashore," VB-2's correspondent wrote, "his force nevertheless contrived to give every assistance and thorough cooperation at all times." All hands accorded Pay Richards sincere admiration and respect. The Bombing Two eulogist wrote that Richards's personal and professional life exemplified "a good life devoted to worthy ideals."[29]

The resulting trouble board found it difficult to reconstruct what had happened. Neal had related "a rapid succession of unusual events difficult to realize and more difficult to describe." The board supposed that "the plane encountered an area of very unusual weather phenomena, caused by an electrical disturbance in close proximity." It believed that "this disturbance was in the nature of a severe pressure wave followed by a sharp and equally intense rarified wave" and that those conditions "might have affected the carburetor to the extent that the engine failed to pick up above idling speed." The board concluded that "the conditions were such that the skill of the pilot could not have affected the outcome."

The fleet sailed to resume the "wars" on 16 May. After completing tactical exercises for that particular phase of Fleet Problem XVII on 17 May, VF-3B was returning to the ship in good visibility and moderate sea conditions. Lieutenant (jg) Gazze, again flying the squadron's BuNo 9776, with Chief Radioman J. J. Ward in back, made a normal approach and had properly answered the LSO's "fast" signal. The LSO gave the "cut" signal when Gazze was about 40 feet from the ramp, to allow for the pilot's fast approach. Gazze, however, settled in rapidly and 5-F-19's wheels gently touched the deck between number two and number six pendants. Onlookers soon saw, however, that the tail did not settle toward the deck, and the propeller seemed to be turning at an excessive rate. Tail-high, BuNo 9776 charged down the deck, hook fully extended, but clearing the arresting wires by several inches. Gazze's hook engaged number nine wire, but 5-F-19 fouled the number two barrier soon thereafter, the impact tearing off the landing gear. The number nine wire, however, soon parted, allowing the SBU to charge into number three barrier. The still-revolving prop struck that barrier, then cut through the wooden deck and the steel one beneath it, to a distance of about 14 inches. Gazze walked away from the crash with a slight bruise on his forehead; McAlister had a bruise in the middle of his back.[30]

On 19 May, "in order that the ship's companies might conduct ceremonies incident to crossing the Equator," Admiral Reeves, who himself had first crossed the "line" as a naval cadet during the voyage of the *Oregon* (Battleship No. 3) in 1898, temporarily suspended the war games. Reaching 00° latitude late in the morning watch, all ships

Lt (jg) Sylvius Gazze's SBU-1 (BuNo 9776), 5-B-19, its propeller embedded in the deck after a hard landing on 17 May 1936, during Fleet Problem XVII. (AUTHOR)

stopped a half hour later, fired a three-gun salute, and broke out the skull and crossbones flag of Neptunus Rex. "This fleet," one observer later confided to his diary, "composed of 9 battleships, 11 heavy cruisers, 4 airplane carriers, 5 light cruisers and 72 destroyers, probably carries more candidates for Neptune's initiation than ever before crossed the Equator at one time."[31] The *Ranger* had initiated all of her pollywogs by 1040, and later exchanged movies with the *Langley*.

The Fleet Problem soon resumed in earnest. After taking part in squadron tactical maneuvers on 26 May, Lt. John W. King returned to the ship in a BM-2 (BuNo 9184), with Aviation Chief Machinist's Mate R. F. Sutton on board, during the first dog watch. Coming in high and fast, King overcorrected in response to the LSO's signals. Distracted by the plane that had landed just ahead, King responded too slowly to the "low and slow" signals, coming in too close to the ramp to prevent his plane from striking it as he came on board, the impact breaking the tail wheel post at the point at which the oleo strut was attached. He most likely sensed his position too late to correct it. An otherwise normal landing ensued, with King catching the number one wire.[32]

The Fleet observed Memorial Day at sea in the Gulf of Tehuantepec, 200 miles off shore, in clear tropical weather, with a heavy swell running from the northwest. At noon, all ships half-masted their colors, and gun salutes honored the "memory of those sailors and soldiers whose work is done." For the living, that work resumed soon thereafter, and, ultimately, the Fleet returned to Long Beach on 6 June, "after a most profitable six weeks at sea and at Balboa," one observer wrote, "during which time fleet war problems and continuous training in fleet tactics measurably improved the efficiency of the Battle Force."[33] The *Ranger* dropped anchor in the channel at San Diego that same day, and shifted alongside the NAS pier on 8 June.

Soon thereafter, the business of evaluating the lessons learned of the yearly fleet problem began in earnest. Those who did so saw the need to address the critical issue of communications people to handle the greatly increased message traffic incident to wartime situations: Captain Bristol complained that, on board the *Ranger* during Phase II of the problem, some of his radiomen had stood watch 15 hours out of 24, and 29 out of 48.[34]

In the wake of the Fleet Problem, high command changes occurred that involved the *Ranger*. Vice Adm. Frederick J. Horne, a knowledgeable and efficient officer who displayed such consideration for his subordinates that the latter worked for him to the peak of their efficiency, relieved Vice Admiral Butler as ComAirBatFor, on the morning of 9 June. In the letter circulated to his former command, Butler expressed his "sincere appreciation for their loyal attention to duty and hard work [which had] characterized the efforts of all hands in carrying out the orders and policies of this Force." He further declared that the "advancing progress of the Air [Battle] Force as a task group speaks most eloquently for its high state of efficiency. Every problem, every task, and every experiment has been met cheerfully, faithfully, and honestly—truly, it has been an inspiring force to command." Although Butler regretted hauling down his flag, he wished all hands "happy landings and continued success in the spirit of carrying on in the years to come." "You people who have done the work deserve the credit," Butler then declared, in his farewell remarks before the microphones, "and I thank you. I know that you will give to my successor the same cooperation and support which you have given me. Good luck."[35] Butler's three-starred flag fluttered down from the *Ranger*'s truck, as saluting guns boomed the appropriate number of times. After Vice Admiral Horne read his orders, his flag ascended, the saluting guns spoke once more, and the "change of command" ended. That same day, Baldy Pownall, the *Ranger*'s affable and likeable executive officer, turned over his duties to Comdr. Earl W. "Win" Spencer, Jr., USNA 1910 and Naval Aviator No. 20, a man described by an Academy classmate as "fiery and able...brimming with happy spirits."[36]

6

"HAVE REACHED A MARVELOUS EFFICIENCY"

In the laconic prose of the *Ranger*'s plan of the day for Wednesday, 10 June 1936: "1015—Quarters for muster, hangar deck parades." Reading those words, however, every officer and man on board knew what that meant. At the appointed time, Captain Bristol approached the microphone, and read his orders. After a brief pause, he thanked all hands for their "loyal support, cooperation, and efficiency." He paused again before concluding in an emotion-filled voice, "God bless you all." The *Ranger*'s crew "knew he meant every word of it, and wished it back to him."[1]

Captain Patrick N. L. Bellinger, Naval Aviator No. 8, then stepped before the microphone and read his orders relieving Captain Bristol. A contemporary of the *Ranger*'s new commanding officer remembered him as "a very nice guy...with a dimpling, boyish smile; and the guts, initiative, and persistence to become a submarine skipper and then start flying in the fall of 1912." One Academy class behind the man he relieved, Bellinger gained early fame in commanding the aviation detachment assigned to the *Mississippi* (Battleship No. 22) during the occupation of Vera Cruz, Mexico in 1914, where he had been the first U.S. Navy pilot to take hostile fire. He also set an altitude record for seaplanes in 1915 and stood among the pioneers of U.S. Navy night flying in 1917. He held the Navy Cross for commanding the flying boat *NC-1* in the attempted transatlantic flight in 1919.

Despite being "slow to learn, and never an idea man," a contemporary wrote, Bellinger "was always ready to try out an idea." An "adequate" flier, Bellinger "never worried long about anything, believed that time would solve most problems without his help, and seldom acted 'til he had to. Then he was prone to drop his deliberateness and react like a bull, rapidly, persistently, and instinctively along the course of his first reaction." Although his indecision sometimes frustrated his juniors, no one "actively disliked Pat Bellinger."[2] Classmates joked that Bellinger possessed "more names [four: Patrick Neison Lynch Bellinger] per inch immersion than any man in the class." He was also described as an "open-faced lad from Dixie, with a sunny smile" that won feminine hearts.[3]

Underway for the Puget Sound Navy Yard on 19 June, the *Ranger* reached her destination on the 23d. Remedying the serious defect in the ship's flight deck assumed a high priority: the paint applied to that surface had, over time, "formed a glazed surface on which footing was never secure." During early morning flight operations, for example, rain or dew rendered it difficult for men to "barely stand up and perform necessary work in a strong wind." Such insecure footing endangered life if the slipstream from a propeller could "blow a man into the propeller of another plane just astern." In addition, the sun reflecting off the painted deck resulted in the men contracting a form of "snow blindness," or at least the "sun grins" which had occurred during Fleet Problem XVII. The eyestrain thus created contributed to normal fatigue "and undoubtedly decreased personnel efficiency." Efforts would be made to remove the paint and replace it with stain or dye, since the replacement of paint with stain on the *Lexington*'s flight deck had reportedly improved footing under wet deck conditions.[4]

The *Ranger* arrived with plans in place to utilize a recreation camp on Kitsap Lake, a project that "aroused the enthusiasm of the entire crew." Men would be sent to the camp for a period of a week, and "all hands will have an opportunity to enjoy this recreation at some time during the ship's stay in the Navy Yard."[5] Rechristened "Camp Craven," in honor of Rear Adm. Thomas T. Craven, Commandant of the 13th Naval District and the Puget Sound Navy Yard, the facility presented "real recreation for tired men-of-wars-men" and proved extremely popular.[6] Word that the ship had won the Aircraft, Battle Force, communication competition, carrier division, for 1935–36, finishing ahead of the *Langley*, the *Lexington*, and the *Saratoga*, also buoyed her morale, as the yard work at Puget Sound proceeded apace.[7] Even happier were the 53 men (radiomen, signalmen, quartermasters, and yeomen) who received prize money that accompanied the ship's award. The communication force thanked the squadrons "for their whole-hearted cooperation," which materially aided their winning the award for the *Ranger*.[8]

In the meantime, the *Ranger*'s squadrons operated from North Island, as usual. When the *Ranger* had departed for Bremerton, she also left behind with the air group Lt. Jack Brand, the LSO, who began training two assistants, Lts. (jg) Walter F. Rodee and Edward A. Hannegan. "By the time [the *Ranger*'s] flight operations are resumed," one observer wrote, it was hoped that the ship would have "at least one signal officer that will suit the exacting demands of the most temperamental pilot."[9]

Natural impediments proved an exacting adversary and made one authorized extended flight more of an adventure than anticipated, when a bad gas leak forced Ens. Robert B. Hoyt, A-V(G), USNR, to land his BM-1 (BuNo 8880), 1-B-3, at the emergency landing field at Pierce's Ferry, Arizona, located about 43 miles east of Boulder Dam, while flying back from the Grand Canyon. The pilot accompanying Hoyt landed there, too, but both pilots discovered that the sandy field was actually only a few inches of sand over countless small boulders that "completely destroyed the immediate usefulness of [the] rudder and landing gear." Fortunately, the rugged Ford trimotored transports of Grand Canyon Airways maintained a regular service between Grand Canyon and Boulder City. One of the Fords landed and transported the four aviators from VB-1B to Boulder City, where, "after a hurried crash report" to North Island by telephone, they awaited reinforcements.[10]

The NAS San Diego Douglas transport plane soon brought parts and artisans to Boulder City, whence Lt. (jg) Anderson Offutt, flying a TG from the *Saratoga*'s VT-2B, would fly them to Pierce's Ferry. Offutt dragged the field once, picked out what looked like the best spot, then landed. "He offloaded his supplies," one observer later wrote with tongue in cheek, "and thinking what duds these VB-1 pilots must be, volunteered to go for the remainder of [the] needed parts." A second trip to Boulder City and Offutt returned to Pierce's Ferry. "A glance at the tail of his plane revealed that his tail wheel assembly had collapsed. The moral of this story," VT-2B's correspondent admonished his readers, "is for aircraft to stay out of Pierce's Ferry" because of the deceptive nature of the field.[11] Repairs to Lieutenant (jg) Offutt's plane had to be effected at night, because of the intense heat of the day.[12]

Although extended flights inland, such as VB-1B's to Pierce's Ferry, taxed the patience of naval aviators, VS-1B's carrying out bombing practice at Miramar Field revealed their versatility. One of the first section's pilots noticed that one of the miniature bombs dropped during the evolution had ignited dry stubble grass on the field. Lieutenant Comdr. Vernon F. Grant, VS-1B's diminutive but energetic commanding officer, a former bantamweight wrestling champion, sized up the situation and quickly realized what danger a fire, if unchecked, could pose to the nearby Scripps Estate and the Camp Kearney Mesa. Consequently, Grant, whom a USNA classmate at the Academy once described as "small, but highly charged," landed along with his section. VS-1B's commander, "assuming the role of Fire Chief, led his men to quick conquest of the flames."[13]

Carelessness figured in two VF-3B mishaps in August. Less than an hour and a half into the forenoon watch on the 4th, Lt. (jg) Empty Evans had taken off in an F2F-1 (BuNo 9650), with his section leader, and had proceeded to South Ream Field, where he practiced landings until 1000. Proceeding thence to Miramar, to conduct squadron tactics, Evans was flying over Spanish Bight, approaching North Island, when his engine suddenly failed. At an altitude of about 300 feet, he immediately looked for a landing place. Finding none, he opted to head for the deep water off East Beach. As the F2F descended toward the waves, he knocked off his goggles and braced himself with his left arm to avoid being thrown forward. The Grumman touched the water and immediately somersaulted onto its back. Evans managed to free himself from the cockpit with no difficulty and swam to the surface. The trouble board subsequently concluded that a low fuel supply had caused

VF-3B's pilots pose at North Island for a squadron portrait in front of one of the unit's Grumman F2F-1s, 18 August 1936. Seated (L–R): Lt. (jg) Charles R. Fenton, Lt. Seymour A. Johnson, Lt. (jg) Henry H. Hale, Lt. (jg) Karl E. "Jug" Jung, Lt. Comdr. Cato D. Glover (commanding officer), Lt. (jg) Herbert D. Riley, Lt. (jg) Charles E. Perkins, Lt. George C. Montgomery, Lt. (jg) Herschel A. House. Standing (L–R): Lt. (jg) Howard E. Shelton, Lt. (jg) George L. Kohr, Lt. Sylvius Gazze, Lt. (jg) James H. "Jimmy" Flatley, Jr., Lt. (jg) George S. James, Lt. Harold L. Meadow, Lt. (jg) James J. McRoberts, Lt. (jg) Paul D. Buie, Lt. Claude F. Sullivan, Lt. Myron T. "Empty" Evans, and Lt. Thomas B. Neblett. (NA, 80-CF-8002-1)

a lack of suction on the main fuel tank, resulting in the engine's sudden stoppage. Disciplinary action for Empty Evans ensued.[14]

Only four days after the Navy Department had announced that VF-3B would, along with the Marines' VO-8M, be giving "demonstration flights" at the National Air Races at Los Angeles early the following month, Lt. (jg) James H. "Jimmy" Flatley, Jr., on temporary duty with that squadron from VF-5B, in which he had served as assistant engineering and materiel officer, returning from a navigation hop on the afternoon of 31 August, approached NRAB Long Beach to land.

Unfortunately, Flatley neglected to crank his wheels down, and his stubby Grumman F2F-1 (BuNo 9665), which had, up to that point, been "functioning normally in all respects," came in in "a full stall attitude" on its belly. The Grumman skidded for about 65 feet before it turned over on its back, coming to rest on its wings and vertical tail surfaces, the abrupt crash throwing Flatley forward in the cockpit. His head smashed into the after end of the telescopic gunsight, breaking the right lens of his goggles on impact with the rubber buffer. With a lacerated upper right eyelid caused by the broken lens, Flatley required 13 days on the sick list before he returned to

Grumman F2F-1s of VF-3B, landing gear extended, prepare to land at North Island, 28 August 1936. (NA, 80-CF-54547-2)

duty. The F2F-1 required a major overhaul before it could be flown again.[15]

As the result of his experience, Flatley recommended rethinking the design of safety belts, noting that those installed in the F2F-1s and F3F-1s crossed the pilot's thighs and did not prevent the body "from being thrown forward from the hips up." Flatley considered it imperative "that the position of this safety belt be changed." Subsequently, in his endorsement, Capt. John H. Towers (whose survival of a crash, when nobody else had done so previously, had led to the employment of safety belts for pilots in the first place), writing for ComAirBatFor, noted that several existing safety belts had been returned to the Naval Aircraft Factory at Philadelphia "for incorporation of recommended modifications." Should those remodeled belts be modified and ready for trial, Towers recommended "that they be issued...at least one...to VF Squadron Three-B for test."[16]

VF-3B, commanded by Lt. Comdr. Cato B. Glover, who had relieved Miles Browning, and a U.S. Marine squadron, VO-8M, were to demonstrate "regular service maneuvers and tactical flying as practiced in the United States Fleet," before the throngs at the National Air Races at Los Angeles, California, between 4 and 7 September. The squadron rehearsed various tactical exercises and conducted forenoon and afternoon drills, in their efforts to perfect their aerial technique. The squadron soon logged experience in "high speed formation dives and maneuvers."[17] The squadron's training emphasized flying a formation "N," which, "although comparatively easy to fly...require[d] a good deal of practice. For the first attempt, however, the maneuver was very successful" and elicited favorable comment.[18]

Vought SBU-1 (BuNo 9802), 1-S-6, of VS-1B, in flight over the southern California countryside, 28 August 1936. The number of "gadgets" in the cockpit of the SBU intrigued new pilots, one of whom suggested with tongue in cheek that "an extensive ground course in pipe-organ playing" would qualify a pilot "temperamentally and physically" to operate the plane. (NA, 80-G-5637)

VF-3B Flight Demonstrations, Los Angeles, California

Lt. Comdr. Cato D. Glover	
Lt. Sylvius Gazze	Lt. Harold L. Meadow
Lt. Claude F. Sullivan	Lt. Myron T. Evans
Lt. Seymour A. Johnson	Lt. George C. Montgomery
Lt. (jg) George L. Kohr	Lt. (jg) James H. Flatley, Jr.*
Lt. (jg) George S. James, Jr.	Lt. (jg) James J. McRoberts
Lt. (jg) Charles R. Fenton	Lt. (jg) Paul D. Buie
Lt. (jg) Henry H. Hale	Lt. (jg) Karl E. Jung
Lt. (jg) Herbert D. Riley	Lt. (jg) Charles E. Perkins
Lt. (jg) Herschel A. House	

*Did not fly.

For the *Ranger*'s pilots who participated, not all went smoothly once they got back on terra firma. On the afternoon of 5 September, after the day's scheduled demonstration flight, the squadron taxied to its parking line. VF-3B taxied in single file up the oiled runway, up to the line, when the first section stopped to permit the planes of the second and third sections to taxi to their parking area in inverse division order. The second section, led by Lieutenant Montgomery, stopped behind the second, and the third proceeded to its parking area.

Montgomery noticed, however, that his number three wingman had failed to follow the third section as he was supposed to, and immediately radioed his errant squadronmate to pull ahead. Montgomery turned his head and looked to the rear to see if his instructions were being complied with, but unconsciously released the brakes as he did so. Montgomery's F2F-1 (BuNo 9658) rolled forward, its

Lycoming-Smith propeller slashing through the rudder and the left horizontal stabilizer, stabilizer strut, and elevator of Lt. (jg) Karl E. "Jug" Jung's F2F-1 (BuNo 9648). A trouble board faulted Montgomery for the mishap; BuNo 9658 required a new propeller, and BuNo 9648 a new rudder and repairs to the damaged stabilizer.[19]

Jimmy Flatley, although the injury suffered in the crash at the end of August had prevented his joining his shipmates in flying during the air races, nevertheless earned a commendation for his "ability, enthusiasm and loyal efforts" that "contributed in a large measure" to VF-3B's performance during that period. In fact, Vice Admiral Horne later expressed his appreciation to the officers and men of VF-3B for their "excellent performance of duty." He complimented the squadron on its exhibition of flying that reflected "a high state of discipline."[20] As one observer later wrote, "all [VF-3B] pilots derived a great deal of benefit from watching the maneuvers and acrobatic flying of others in attendance, and conversely learned what not to try and do in our F2F-1 airplanes."[21]

Mishaps, however, continued to bedevil VF-3B, once it resumed its normal training. On the evening of 8 September, during a night flight, Lt. Claude "Sully" Sullivan, flying an F2F-1 (BuNo 9645), was making his final landing to return to the flight line at NAS San Diego on a "one ball" (east to west) course, in a six-knot northwesterly breeze. The field's east floodlight illuminated the landing area, as it usually did when an incoming pilot followed the one ball course, thus obviating the need for Sullivan to employ his F2F-1's landing light. Although Sully Sullivan had logged over 2,475 hours of flight time, he had had only 3.9 hours of nocturnal flight operations in the previous three months. As he slowed after his landing, he apparently did not realize "in sufficient time" that his Grumman was not rolling on a straight course, as he was deccelerating. The F2F-1 ground-looped to the right, causing damage to the trailing edge of the lower left wing; a trouble board subsequently attributed the accident to Sullivan's "temporary poor reaction" and his "lack of recent special experience."[22]

The *Ranger* had completed her yard period at Puget Sound, the flight deck having been refinished, gasoline tanks having been modified, and experiments with flight deck headgear begun, and prepared to return to San Diego. Before she left the yard, however, her hangar deck served as the venue for a singular event, when, an hour before the end of the forenoon watch on 20 September, Mrs. Charles Head, the State Regent for the State of Washington of the National Society, Daughters of the American Revolution, presented Captain Bellinger with the D.A.R. Anti-Aircraft Trophy for the *Ranger*'s obtaining the highest merit in anti-aircraft gunnery for the 1935–36 gunnery year. In his acceptance speech, Bellinger praised the "intelligent leadership and hard work of the officers of the Gunnery Department and of the men who man the guns and the control stations." Bellinger designated Lt. John B. Dimmick as the custodian of the trophy. "The officers and men in the Gunnery Department," Dimmick declared, "are confident that with the whole-hearted support of other departments of the ship, the name USS *Ranger* will be engraved on this trophy again next year, and, we hope, for many years to come."[23]

The *Ranger* sailed for San Diego on 21 September. She moored to the NAS pier at North Island on the 25th and resumed the familiar cycle of operations three days later, off Point Loma. Contrasting with the maroon-stained flight deck and the chrome yellow and white deck striping were the new sweaters—actually, "surveyed small store woolen undershirts, dyed to the desired shade"—worn by the plane directors and spotters (yellow) and the arresting gear crew (green). Warm enough for wear off the coast of California, they would prove too warm to wear in the tropics, prompting the ship to ready a complete set of surveyed summer-type undershirts for use in the "lower latitudes."[24]

The first four days of that cycle of qualification and refresher training, carried out in conditions that included a moderate roll, light pitch, and light varying winds, proceeded mostly without incident. During the forenoon watch on 1 October, however, Lt. Thomas B. Neblett, flying VF-3B's lone SBU-1 (BuNo 9776), on his first carrier landing since his initial qualification on board the *Lexington* in 1933, apparently did not realize the amount of throttle needed to regain level flight once an SBU-1 started to settle. Neblett cleared the ramp, but did so in a left skid, forcing the LSO to scramble out of the way to avoid decapitation by the oncoming 5-B-19. Neblett's hook caught number one wire, but the tailwheel assembly collapsed after hitting the ramp. A trouble board faulted the pilot's poor technique.[25]

Later that day, during night qualifications, Bill Hale of VF-3B had completed one landing successfully and was coming in for his second. Taking the LSO's cut with proper speed and altitude, Hale landed, but his left wheel absorbed the impact of the descent as he caught the number one wire. The left upper compression link in the landing gear failed after the F2F-1 (BuNo 9655) had traveled an appreciable distance up the deck. A trouble board later assigned only 25% of the immediate causes to Hale (faulting "poor technique"), assigning the rest to the landing gear itself (25%) and hazards "incident to night carrier operations" (50%). Other than the mishaps that had occurred during Tom Neblett's and Bill Hale's landings, however, VF-3B had fared well in its 80 landings.[26]

Looking down and aft from a dockyard crane: The *Ranger* lies alongside Pier 6, Puget Sound Navy Yard, 18 September 1936. Note details of the after portion of the flight deck, the unique arrangement of her stacks, her identification marking, "R N G R," on the ramp, aft, as well as the position of number two elevator, flush against the island. (AUTHOR)

Lieutenant (jg) Sherman W. "Sherry" Betts, flying a BM-1 (BuNo 8879), floated over the arresting gear after twice attempting to descend far enough, after taking the cut, to engage the wires, ending up crashing in full flight into number two barrier.[27] It proved to be VB-1B's only mishap in 94 landings, the most carried out by any squadron on board during that particular week of operations. Bombing One had qualified on board the *Saratoga* in the *Ranger*'s absence, where the size of the former's flight deck impressed them. The new nonglare aspect of their own ship's flight deck, however, in the wake of the refurbishing at Puget Sound, prompted expressions of appreciation. "One pilot," one observer later wryly wrote, "even went so far as to cut himself a piece of it."[28]

The following day, Capt. Lawton H. M. Sanderson, USMC, of VO-8M, was returning to the ship from tactical exercises in an O3U-3 (BuNo 9734), with Technical Sgt. William E. Word, USMC, in back. Cutting the throttle and dropping to the deck, Sanderson hooked a wire, but his tailhook broke. Before the Marine could employ the brakes to stop the rampaging Vought, it hit the barrier, bending the propeller blades, and damaging the lower wings and landing gear struts beyond economical repair, in what proved to be VO-8M's only mishap in 35 landings that week.[29] Later, during the second dog watch, Lt. (jg) J. Clark Riggs, Jr., of the *Lexington*'s VF-1B, approached for his first night carrier landing in an F4B-4 (BuNo 9041), but realized too late that he had not lowered his tail hook. The LSO had given him the cut, after he had been informed by his assistant that the hook had been in fact lowered. The plane suffered minor damage when it struck

Fine detail photo of the *Ranger*'s unique island, Puget Sound Navy Yard, 18 September 1936; note Bogen flight deck loudspeakers on the light tripod mast, and the two Mk. 33 directors for the 5-inch/25 battery, each of which sports a gunnery "E". Also note the communications excellence "C" (the ship's first) on the flag bag. (AUTHOR)

the barrier, but not severe enough to prevent its being flown off to North Island without further incident. That had been the *Lexington* squadron's only mishap in 50 landings on board the *Ranger* that week.[30]

The next period of the *Ranger*'s operations (5–10 October) proceeded uneventfully, as she conducted tactical exercises off the southern California coast. She logged 136 more landings, bringing her total since commissioning to 7,486. VS-1B took top honors with 36 landings, followed by VF-5B (35), VB-1B (34), and VF-3B (31). VF-5B logged a take-off interval of one every 13 seconds, followed by VF-3B (13.8 seconds), VS-1B (15.4), and VB-1B (15.6). Captain Bellinger later reported that, on Tuesday afternoon, 6 October, the *Ranger* experienced the greatest conditions of pitch she had ever experienced, averaging about 8 degrees, which resulted in an up and down movement of the ramp for a span of some 20 feet. "This displacement and the careful technique required in the landing of planes," Bellinger wrote, "caused the landing intervals of all squadrons to be abnormally slow."[31]

Operating from North Island, Lt. Seymour S. Johnson of VF-3B conducted individual battle practice (fixed guns), run on the morning of 21 October, over the waters off San Diego. Completing his firing run on an overhead rear approach, Johnson inadvertently shot the towline in two. The line parted as Johnson's F2F-1 (BuNo 9667) passed so close astern of the target that there was no way the pilot, who had been peering into his telescopic sight, could avert a collision. When one became imminent, Johnson instinctively pushed the stick forward to try to pass below the target. Feeling no shock, he felt that he had been successful. It was not until he returned to North Island that a check revealed the fabric on the leading edge of the upper wing had been cut through to the front spar, most likely by the shot-away portion of the towline. The resulting trouble board assigned blame for the accident to factors "incident to fixed gunnery operations."[32]

Two days later, Lt. (jg) Robert L. "Strick" Strickler of VF-5B completed his gunnery practice and was approaching South Field, North Island, a little after midway through the afternoon watch. Returning to the field singly, having been accustomed to landing in a section, the pilot found his attention distracted by an airplane taxiing across the landing mat and stopping in the line of his approach. That combination of factors contributed to Strickler's not remembering to crank down his landing gear. The F3F-1 (BuNo 0220) hit tail-first, then slid on its belly for almost 60 feet before it turned over and skidded about 10 feet on its upper wing. The Grumman came to rest with its center section struts collapsed, the upper wing folded forward, the vertical stabilizer and rudder smashed, and Strickler pinned in the cockpit. A major overhaul lay in store for BuNo 0220; disciplinary action (for "carelessness") and treatment for a cut above his right eye awaited the pilot.[33]

The *Ranger* departed Coronado Roads on 9 November, bound for San Francisco in company with the *Lexington*. During the afternoon watch on 10 November, Lt. (jg) William E. "Slim" Townsend of VF-5B, returning to the ship from a tactics flight, cut his throttle after getting the cut from the LSO, but attempted to nose down slightly. His F3F-1 (BuNo 0228) struck the deck wheels-first, as the deck rose beneath him when the *Ranger* pitched, and blew both tires.[34]

Soon thereafter, tragedy reminded all of the dangers inherent in the calling of naval aviators. Aviation Cadet William H. Jones, USNR, of VF-5B, with only 24.4 hours in F3Fs in the past three months, flying an F3F-1 (BuNo 0221), inadvertently reduced his altitude to below 100 feet before he turned into the groove. In his descent, Jones apparently lost sight of the *Trever* (DD-339), the plane guard, as he entered the groove, because at 1531, 5-F-10 collided with, and shattered, the *Trever*'s foretopmast. Jones's F3F-1 made "a complete turn about the vertical axis," then splashed into the sea close aboard the *Trever*'s starboard side.[35] The *Ranger* stopped her engines immediately, then maneuvered to recover the small amount of floating wreckage from the stubby fighter, which had sunk to the bottom within 30 seconds of impact. Searchers found no sign of the pilot. A trouble board attributed the accident to an error in judgment on Jones's part, when he had evidently lost sight of the *Trever* during his approach.

The next day, VF-3B's landing woes continued, as Lt. (jg) George M. "Joe" Greene made a landing that mirrored Slim Townsend's the day before. As in Townsend's case, the trouble board lay 90% of the cause of the crash on equipment; 10% on "poor technique."[36] Landing operations continued to be difficult the next day, as, beneath a hazy overcast, the *Ranger* encountered long, rolling swells off San Francisco Bay on 12 November, causing the ship to roll a maximum of 10 degrees. She then brought that coastwise trip to an end, when she dropped anchor in San Francisco Bay during the afternoon watch.

During the forenoon watch on 16 November, the *Ranger* embarked Adm. William D. Leahy, Commander, Battle Force (ComBatFor), and Capt. Ralston S. Holmes, Leahy's chief of staff, and Lt. Joseph H. Wellings, his flag lieutenant, so that Leahy could observe "the tactics and operations of our sea borne air arm."[37] Underway with the *Lexington* and the destroyers *Hale* (DD-133), *Crowninshield*, *Zane* (DD-337) and *Trever*, and wearing ComBatFor's four-starred flag at the main, the *Ranger* sailed for San Diego, and, over the next few days, took part in Fleet Sortie and Fleet Tactical Exercises.

During the admiral's passage in the ship, two deck landing accidents occurred during the forenoon watch on 17 November. The first involved a Vought SBU-1 from VS-1B. Lt. (jg) Reginald R. McCracken, returning to the *Ranger* after a routine tactics hop, put down his hook before entering the groove, and diligently checked to see that the locking pin was engaged. After getting the cut from the LSO, McCracken, a former USNA lacrosse star, made what appeared to be a normal landing. The pilot, however, did not feel the hook pick up a wire, so he fully applied the brakes. The SBU-1 (BuNo 9810), however, had too much momentum to stop before hitting the barrier, and thus went up on its nose, with the propeller blade sticking into the deck. Taking stock in the cockpit, Mac McCracken noticed that the hook lever had moved forward, but had not locked itself in the up position. Neither McCracken, whose aggressive style of play on the lacrosse field while a midshipman had usually resulted in his sporting a bump on his head, nor Radioman 2d Class H. Wilson, his passenger, suffered any injuries. The trouble board deemed the cause of the accident to have been 100% materiel failure ("arresting appliance on aircraft"): the only mishap among the 27 landings carried out by the squadron during that stint of tactical exercises.[38]

Lieutenant (jg) Marshall T. Martin, coming on board less than an hour later, bringing in his BM-2 (BuNo 9185), with Aviation Chief Machinist's Mate W. A. Carls in back, after taking part in squadron tactics, engaged the number two wire. The BM-2 bounced slightly, then landed on its left wheel, the entire impact being absorbed by the left side of the landing gear and its appendages, breaking a fuselage longeron on the left side, breaking off a fitting from the fuselage members on the upper left side of the fuselage, and bending a lower athwartships member of the fuselage frame. The trouble board, divided in its opinion on what caused the accident, leaned toward incipient metal fatigue (90% materiel) and less on an error in judgment on landing (10% personnel), in VB-1B's sole mishap of 31 landings during the week.[39]

The *Ranger*'s performance in the three tactical exercises conducted en route, amidst the clear, fresh winds and moderate conditions of pitch and roll encountered off the California coast, impressed Admiral Leahy, who disembarked off San Pedro during the first dog watch on 18 November. Later, he confided to his diary that there was "no doubt whatever that American carrier-based naval airplanes have reached a marvelous efficiency considering the short time that has elapsed since their introduction into the Navy." He attributed that to the fact that U.S. naval aviation lay in the hands of "seagoing naval personnel," and was not treated as a separate air service as was the case "in England and other naval powers."[40]

Despite the "marvelous efficiency" that indeed existed, so, too, did the possibility of something going wrong as the result of inexplicable circumstances. Less than a month after Aviation Cadet Jones's death during carrier qualifications, tragedy again visited the *Ranger*'s air group, this time during VB-1B's operations with the target ship *Utah*. On the morning of 7 December, Aviation Cadet Maynard D. Smith, USNR, took off in a BM-1 (BuNo 9174), with Aviation Machinist's Mate 3d Class Lloyd M. Barnes as his passenger. At 1107, Smith pushed over into a dive at 10,000 feet to carry out a dive bombing attack on the maneuvering *Utah*. Observers saw Smith make a low release, at approximately 1,000 feet, then pull the nose up slightly. The Martin, however, slanted down and crashed into the Pacific some 12 miles off Point Loma. Neither the crew nor the plane was recovered, so what exactly had caused the crash would remain a mystery.[41]

Little mystery, however, attended the investigation of difficulties experienced by two young pilots during night field carrier landings later the same day. A trouble board faulted Aviation Cadet Arthur N. Kelly, USNR, of VF-5B, for poor technique and carelessness, in a mishap that resulted in Kelly's F2F-1 (BuNo 9659) ending up on the filled-in area comprising the western edge of North Island, hitting an empty oil drum and going over on its back. The plane suffered extensive damage; Kelly walked away unhurt, although he would face disciplinary action.[42] On the other hand, Aviation Cadet Robert C. Loomis, USNR, of VF-3B, seemed to be committing the "unpardonable sin" in failing "to close his throttle, take charge of his airplane and land in the gear." Flying an F2F-1 (BuNo 9663), Loomis tried to close his throttle after receiving the cut, but found that he could not

Commander Earl W. Spencer, Jr., the *Ranger*'s second executive officer (seen here in December 1932), and a very troubled man. (NA, 80-G-428104)

do so. Gaining 500 feet of altitude, Loomis tried several times to close the throttle, later stating that it felt like there was a spring tending to reopen it. Finally, he managed to make a landing by cutting his switch and returning to the flight line. An investigation later revealed that a small piece of sponge rubber, mounted on the bracket on a voltage control box, had fallen down and lodged between the firewall and the arm on the lower end of the throttle control jackstaff. VF-3B's mechanics soon installed larger pieces of sponge rubber, secured with bolts and washers, to prevent that from happening again in the squadron's airplanes.[43]

Meanwhile, for Win Spencer, the *Ranger*'s exec, the year's end brought scrutiny of a different sort. The intense media coverage surrounding the abdication of King Edward VIII of England to marry Wallis Warfield Simpson, the American divorcee, inextricably involved Spencer: Wallis had been Win Spencer's first wife. As Pat Bellinger, who had been present when Spencer and his bride-to-be had

Christmas party, 24 December 1936. Chief Storekeeper Webber, attired as "Santa Claus," distributes presents to children (over 150 of whom, under the age of 13, attended) of the *Ranger*'s officers and men; Commander Montgomery and Captain Bellinger (background, L) look on. (Bellinger Collection, AvH)

announced their engagement in 1916, later recalled: "Spencer was now [November–December 1936] bothered by reporters who tried by all methods and means to get him to make a statement. When I offered him my assistance he told me not to worry."[44] "She is a lovely person," Spencer said in describing his ex-wife to reporters, "intelligent, witty, and good company. 'Stimulating' is the word which best describes her charm. In whatever future she may choose— into whatever places it may take her—I wish her my very best. She will always hold my respect and admiration.... She is a most attractive woman and has one of the strongest characters I have ever known any person to possess."[45] Subsequently, while on weekend leave, Spencer suffered a fractured leg. Because Spencer faced a lengthy recuperation at the Naval Hospital at San Diego and would not be returning to the ship soon, Comdr. Alfred E. "Monty" Montgomery, Vice Admiral Horne's operations officer, soon received orders to the *Ranger* as her exec.[46]

7
"WHEN A SHIP BREAKS INTO THE MOVIES"

Lieutenant (jg) Dimmick, officer of the deck during the mid watch on 1 January 1937, inaugurated the new year in rhyme. Known by his naval academy classmates to possess "everlasting good humor...always ready for fun," Dimmick proved to have been well placed to compose the mid watch verse, as he was "pounding pitch" [standing watch] at that hour, along with the quartermaster and the anchor watch:

> Once more the start of a New Year by the clock
> Finds the *Ranger* moored to the Air Station Dock
> Starboard side to in a drizzling rain
> With twelve stout lines and a cable of chain
> To furnish the ship with heat and light
> Number four boiler is steaming this night
> With fresh water we are being supplied
> Through a hose connection from the dock to our side
> Various Fleet Units are anchored in the Bay
> And COMAIRBATFOR in *Ranger* is S.O.P.A.
> At the stroke of midnight all the ships started in
> Whistles and sirens seemed to screech as one
> To '37—welcome—To '36—well done.[1]

The *Ranger* began the new year's training slate by getting underway on Tuesday morning, 5 January, for local operations that included antiaircraft machine gun exercises; VB-1B and her own utility unit provided services for the training the following day. Gunnery exercises occupied the ship and her crew the following week, as well, carrying out the latter training in company with the *Saratoga*.

Her air group operated from North Island during that time. Lt. (jg) Harmon T. Utter, of VF-5B, noticed an abnormal rise in oil pressure as he climbed to take part in gunnery practice that afternoon in his F3F-1 (BuNo 0217). On the return to North Island, the pressure rose alarmingly, then dropped to zero, forcing Utter to run the engine with no pressure and glide to a landing without further incident. An investigation revealed that a rag, inadvertently left there after a previous period of repairs to the firewall, had stopped the oil outlet.[2]

For Lt. (jg) Herschel A. "Colonel" House of VF-3B, who had been commended for excellence in aerial gunnery in 1936, the new year brought matrimony. Regarded by his Academy classmates as having a "serious nature, an active mind and a good sense of humor," House had "done well in the classroom, [had] distinguished himself socially, and...worked hard at academics." He had also "delighted" his classmates with his "attractive drags [dates]." Thus, no one was probably surprised when he made the acquaintance of Hollywood's Anita Page, regarded as "one of the screen's all-time great beauties." In *The Flying Fleet* (1929) Page had played a young woman who fell "madly in love with a young naval officer." In a case of life imitating art, after a whirlwind courtship of 19 days, the pilot and the starlet eloped, tying the proverbial knot in Yuma, Arizona, on 9 January.[3]

During night landing practice on 14 January, Lt. (jg) Finley E. "Pete" Hall, flying an SBU-1 (BuNo 9801), with Aviation Machinist's Mate 2d Class F. J. Elkins on board, came in without difficulty, but, blinded by the glare of the field's west floodlights, did not see the truck, used by the LSO for radio purposes, parked to the right of the laid-out landing area. Just before the irrepressible Mississippian touched down, his SBU accidentally grazed the truck's cab, buckling the front and rear spars and splintering the ends of the ribs of the lower right wing. A trouble board faulted Hall's judgment.[4]

The *Ranger* put to sea on Monday morning, 18 January, for carrier qualifications. Aviation Cadet James O. Taylor of VS-1B, flying with a sandbag (to represent the weight of a passenger without hazarding a human being with a tyro pilot) in the back seat of his SBU-1 (BuNo 9804), landed tailwheel-first, after getting the cut from the LSO. The impact bent the wheel assembly, a mishap that the trouble board subsequently blamed more on the equipment (75%) than on the young pilot's technique (25%).[5]

During flight operations the following afternoon, Pete Hall, flying the same SBU-1 that had grazed the truck four days before at North Island, did not have to face the glare of a floodlight, but did have to contend with strong and gusty winds, a rough sea, and a pitching flight deck. Zooming slightly after getting the cut from the LSO, Hall's SBU caught a wire, but then slammed to the deck, the impact splitting the right oleo landing strut longtitudinally. The trouble board in this case faulted Hall's poor technique, but gave equal consideration to the weather and the pitching flight deck.[6]

During the second dog watch on 19 January, Vice Admiral Horne broke his flag in the *Ranger*, and she sailed the following morning for tactical exercises off the California coast, in company with the *Saratoga*. Completing a scouting mission during the forenoon watch on the 20th, Lt. (jg) David J. Welsh, with Radioman 2d Class H. L. Casey on board in the SBU-1 (BuNo 9807), made a good approach under the same conditions that had plagued his Academy classmate and squadronmate Pete Hall on the 18th: strong and gusty conditions, a rough sea, and a pitching deck. Taking the cut, Welsh descended, but, as he did so, the deck dropped from beneath him, causing the plane to drop from a "greater than normal" height in a three-point attitude, breaking the tailwheel assembly. In this case, however, the trouble board found no fault with the pilot, who had done all he could humanly do, but with the tail wheel assembly (75%) and a combination of the weather and the pitching deck.[7]

Soon thereafter, Lt. (jg) Richard R. Briner of VB-1B, piloting a BM-2 (BuNo 9185), with Lt. (jg) Joseph H. Kimpler in back, took the cut from the LSO, but suddenly felt a gust of wind lift the plane. Sensing that he was too high, Briner pushed the nose down slightly to compensate and gain the deck, but could not recover sufficiently to prevent the BM-2 from bouncing when it encountered the gear, resulting in damage to the fuselage and landing gear. The resulting trouble board allowed for the weather (60%), but still assessed the pilot for an error of judgment.[8]

Bad landing conditions the following day (21 January) accounted for a pair of mishaps. In the first, Lt. Comdr. Harold L. "Reverend" Meadow, VF-5B's skipper, took the cut and crossed the ramp, slightly high and to the right of the broad chrome yellow stripe on the flight deck. As the F2F-1 (BuNo 9643) settled toward the deck, turbulent air, probably caused by the ship's island, caused the right wing to drop, and pushed the stubby Grumman toward the starboard side. Meadow applied full left aileron, in an attempt to pick up the right wing, but the effort made little difference, as the fighter's right wheel hit first, almost simultaneously with the tailhook catching the number three wire. The right landing gear failed first, then the left, and the F2F slid up the deck a distance of 57 feet, before it stopped. The weather proved the culprit (50%), but the pilot's error of judgment (25%) and the landing gear (25%) played their part in the accident as well.[9]

Aviation Cadet Taylor, again flying the same SBU-1 in which he had had the accident on the 18th, took the cut and nosed the plane over. Hitting the deck wheels-first, the SBU bounced, its hook catching a wire almost simultaneously. Slammed to the deck, the plane suffered a buckled right landing gear strut. Fortunately, neither Taylor nor his passenger, Aviation Machinist's Mate 3d Class L. R. Smith, suffered any injuries.[10]

Following the conclusion of flight operations on the 22d, the *Ranger* anchored off San Diego a little over an hour into the afternoon watch; Vice Admiral Horne shifted his flag ashore, to the administration building, a little over an hour later. The ship shifted to a berth alongside the carrier pier at North Island on the 26th. Three days later, Commander Aircraft, Battle Force held a surprise military inspection of the *Ranger*, which revealed the ship and her people to be "in all respects ready."[11]

Part of a naval aviator's training involved extended flights over land for training purposes. Lt. (jg) William H. "Mac" McClure, designated as the senior member of a proposed cross-country flight on Saturday, 30 January, after receiving an unfavorable weather report of conditions around San Francisco by telephone from the aerologist at North Island, visited Lt. Philip R. Coffin, the officer of the day at NAS San Diego, and discussed the proposed flight. With weather conditions still unfavorable, McClure went to VF-3B's office and informed the other members of the flight, Lt. (jg)

Jug Jung and Aviation Cadet Bob Loomis, that the flight would most likely be cancelled. Learning from the aerological officer at North Island that the weather around the bay area was still bad, McClure went to Lieutenant Coffin and cancelled the proposed flight.[12]

After returning home, however, McClure tuned in all of the available weather broadcasts on his radio. Finding conditions much improved, he called Lt. Comdr. Charles J. McGuire, the aerological officer at NAS San Diego, and learned that later reports could permit a flight to Bakersfield, instead. Getting a release from Lt. Coffin to fly to Bakersfield, instead of to San Francisco, McClure returned to North Island and readied his flight. McClure climbed into 3-F-2, Jung into 3-F-3 and Loomis into 3-F-8. Armed with the available weather information and strip maps for their route, they took off at 1115.

McClure took his section to 14,000 feet and placed himself on the south leg of the Los Angeles radio beam; soon thereafter, they lost sight of the ground beneath a blanketing cloud layer 4,000 feet below them. Finding a fair-sized hole in the clouds over Long Beach enabled McClure to get a good position, and he radioed Jung and Loomis that he was shifting to the north L.A. beam; both flew formation on the leader. Coming out of a cloud layer about a quarter of an hour after leaving the skies over Long Beach, at 5,000 feet, however, McClure, although slightly familiar with Bakersfield and knowing he was to the east of it, radioed Jung: "Where do you think we are?"

"I believe we are over the Mojave Desert," Jug Jung responded, "in the vicinity of the town of Mojave."

Since their maps showed two large lake beds, Jung's assumption had been correct. Noticing a railroad track beneath them, Jung suggested that they use it: aviators commonly referred to railroad tracks as the "iron compass." They followed it 25 miles until they came to a town. Flying low, they could read the station sign: Kramer. McClure, then, knowing that he had flown too far to the east (Kramer, "the sunburned home of the main plant of a large Borax company," which also contained a small hotel and a few filling stations as "concessions to the tourist trade," was not even on their strip maps), looked in vain for a landing field.[13]

With a storm evident to the west, broken clouds lay above them, punctuated by large clear holes. Jung suggested to McClure that they climb above the clouds and set course 210 degrees toward San Diego, taking into account the strong westerly wind. After checking with Jung and Loomis and learning that the minimum gasoline left was 65 gallons in any plane, McClure, having learned that weather conditions at Bakersfield had suddenly changed for the worse, including icing conditions, steered southwesterly courses until he could find a clear spot on the coast side of the mountains; radio beam schedules reported weather over San Diego unlimited and broken high clouds over Oceanside. Climbing to 13,500 feet, above the clouds, McClure placed himself on the Los Angeles 200 degree beam, with the section intact. Clear skies extended above, with a cloud layer at 10,000 feet below. Seeing a very large cloud looming ahead, McClure decided to stay on the beam and fly through it.

As McClure and Loomis climbed, Jug Jung had a difficult time keeping up, and radioed McClure to slow down. Soon thereafter, however, the cloud enveloped the leader and his aviation cadet wingman; Loomis flew up close to 3-F-2. Jung lost sight of them. Losing sight of Jung as the flight encountered sleet and snow that soon coated their windshields, McClure asked Loomis if he could see him. Soon, snow static rendered radio reception almost impossible, and McClure lost the radio signals he had been following. His airspeed meter rendered useless by sleet, McClure made a radical turn, reversing course and heading back toward the desert. Loomis asked him where he was going.

Good instrument flying in an F2F-1 required utmost concentration; to answer Loomis's query would have meant that McClure would have had to take his eyes off his dials and guages. Instead, he ordered Loomis, the least experienced of the three pilots in the flight, to take the lead with the course he had given him, so that McClure could check his navigation. "I...had some difficulty," Loomis later admitted, "shifting from formation flying to instrument flying." McClure radioed Loomis to slow down, but soon lost sight of him in the snow that reduced visibility to only 700 feet.

McClure, now alone, headed west for three minutes, then south, assuming that 3-F-3 was to the east of 3-F-8 and wanting to reduce the chance of collision in the storm. After going into a spin at 14,000 feet and emerging at 11,000, he held his course and kept his turn and bank indicator steady. Losing altitude steadily, he soon found himself at 7,500 feet. Knowing that mountains towered nearby and with the Grumman heavily coated with ice, McClure decided to bail out. Rolling Three-Fox-Two on its back, he pushed forward on the stick, but stuck halfway out of the cockpit. After recovering from another spin, McClure tried again, this time kicking the stick forward and clearing the plane.

Landing in brush on a mountainside, McClure, who had been semiconscious after pulling his rip-cord, regained his full faculties 15 or 20 minutes after landing. Making his way to the Pine Canyon fire station, McClure telephoned

North Island and gave them what information he could about the crash.

Aviation Cadet Loomis, meanwhile, had dared not reduce speed to allow McClure to catch up, since he had already reached cruising speed. Five minutes later, Loomis could neither see nor hear McClure. Fearing that the section leader's engine had most likely iced up, Loomis firewalled the throttle and tried to climb, heading in an easterly direction. Topping the cloud bank at 18,000 feet, he flew east for another 45 minutes, believing the Los Angeles area completely covered over, and found himself over a desert. To determine his location, Loomis landed in a farmer's field, obtained directions to Lancaster, and flew there through a heavy rain, arriving at 1440. Remaining overnight there, Loomis left there at noon the following day, and arrived at North Island an hour later.

Jug Jung, after losing sight of McClure and Loomis, shifted immediately to fly on instruments. A heavy sleet storm coated his windshield with ice soon thereafter. His airspeed indicator performed erratically after being clogged with sleet, so Jung spun and recovered six times. Settling on a roughly south-southwesterly course, Jung topped a cloud layer at 19,500 feet. With his gas gauge showing only five gallons, he peered down through a hole in the overcast and cut the throttle. Diving down through, he soon found himself over Long Beach harbor. Pulling out at 1,500 feet, he headed for Seal Beach, the resort town with its fishing pier "hemmed in by power plants and gas storage tanks."[14] Keeping clear of the center of the city, Jung finally landed at NRAB Long Beach at 1455.

"I got my section into more trouble than I was able to get them out of," McClure later admitted, through his "over-confidence and lack of cross country experience." In his own defense, however, he wrote that "the storm in question moved about twenty-four hours faster than contemplated by any meteorologists on this coast." The increase in speed of its movement only became noticeable after he had been released to fly to Bakersfield. The resulting trouble board faulted McClure for "losing contact with the ground and flying 'on top,'" when inclement weather rendered it probable that he could be "out of contact with the ground for some eighty to ninety miles," in "following a 20 degree radio beam out of Los Angeles when it should have been apparent from his compass that he had taken the wrong beam," in attempting to follow an "unreliable beam away from the beacon station, over mountainous country, while flying out of contact with the ground," and in "attempting to lead a section through a cloud of 14,000 feet where icing conditions should have been expected, rather than going around the cloud."[15]

Captain Bellinger agreed fully with the trouble board in its laying the blame for the accident on Lieutenant (jg) McClure. "The pilot's decision to lead his section through a solid bank of clouds," he wrote, "was not only an error in judgment but extreme bad judgment inasmuch as he certainly should have realized that by doing so he was not only placing himself in a precarious position, but he was showing utter disregard for the other two pilots in his section, one of whom was an Aviation Cadet with very limited experience."[16]

Training continued. The *Ranger* put to sea on 8 February to continue flight operations. During qualification landings during the forenoon watch, Aviation Cadet James J. Richardson of VF-5B, flying 5-F-1, caught the number seven wire, but his tailhook broke, allowing his F3F-1 (BuNo 0252) to continue on into the barrier, scratching a propeller blade and wrinkling the skin of the leading edge of the lower right wing. A trouble board found no fault in Richardson, who suffered abrasions on his nose and left eyelid, but solely on the defective tailhook.[17] A little over two hours later, Aviation Cadet Calvin Y. Dyer of VS-1B, flying an SBU-1 (BuNo 9811), with a sandbag in the back seat, lined up perfectly in the groove in textbook fashion, in his first-ever carrier landing, but landed in a skid, after taking the cut, and caught number three wire near the port side of the ship. Rocked athwartships by the skidding landing, BuNo 9811's lower right wingtip hit the deck, buckling the aileron. A trouble board cited "poor technique" as the immediate cause of the accident.[18]

Flight operations continued over the next four days; on the 9th, the *Ranger* launched 60 planes, recovering them after a simulated attack on the ship. Her operations that day proved flawless. On the 10th, only one mishap occurred, when Aviation Cadet George B. Randolph, USNR, of VF-5B, brought in his F3F-1 (BuNo 0223) slightly fast and bounced upon landing. Pushing the stick forward to get back on deck caused Randolph to miss five wires before his hook caught the sixth. The Grumman nosed slightly down, bending both propeller blades.[19]

On Friday, 12 February, the last day of that particular period of flight operations that week, Aviation Cadet A. S. Gowen, USNR, of VS-1B, flying a BM-1 (BuNo 8881), with Aviation Cadet Emerson D. Gerhardt, USNR, as his passenger, inadvertently dipped his left wing upon landing. Catching number three wire, Gowen pulled back the stick, causing the Martin to land hard on its left wheel, collapsing the left landing gear, damaging the propeller beyond repair, and causing some fuselage damage. A trouble board faulted Gowen's pulling back the stick ("poor technique") as the root cause, because landing conditions had been good, with a smooth sea, and 25 knots of wind over the deck. That proved to be the only mishap of the 62 landings that day.[20]

The following week began routinely enough, with the *Ranger* steaming out on Monday, 15 February, for another cycle of underway operations with her air group, conducting 57 flawless qualification landings that day and launching and recovering planes with a three-degree list to starboard during the afternoon watch. She conducted 59 incident-free landings later that day. The following day, she operated in company with the *Saratoga*, then returned to North Island and moored to the NAS pier during the first dog watch.

The third week of February 1937 proved to be memorable for the *Ranger* for another reason. "Most people who break into the movies," one *Ranger* wit observed, "have to go to Hollywood to do it, but when a ship breaks into the movies, well, Hollywood has to come to the ship." In December 1936, Universal Pictures Corporation had submitted a screenplay, *Wings Over Honolulu*, to the Navy for its approval. Finding too many inaccuracies and elements of the story that presented a negative image of the service, especially those that might remind people of the "Massie Case," which had strained race relations between the Navy and the Honolulu community in 1932, the Navy's Motion Picture Board recommended that "cooperation *not* be extended to Universal Pictures."[21]

Subsequently, however, Universal effected enough changes and the Navy agreed to cooperate with the studio in the making of the film. For more than two weeks, Universal worked "on location" at North Island, with the Navy's permission, filming not only on the air station, but on board the *Ranger* during part of the third week of February. "In addition to the *Ranger* herself," the editor of the ship's paper later wrote, "several officers and enlisted men of the

Captain Bellinger (L), with veteran character actor Samuel S. Hinds (C) and actress Polly Rowles (R), during the filming of Universal Pictures's *Wings Over Honolulu* on board the *Ranger* at North Island, February 1937. Hinds, whose later roles would include that of James Stewart's father in the Christmas movie classic *It's a Wonderful Life*, played "Admiral Furness," Rowles played his daughter. (Bellinger Collection, AvH)

ship's company made movie debuts; and a number of the *Lexington* pilot's [*sic*] wives and others faced the celluloid strip in the making."[22]

At one point in the production, the scene required the presence of two more naval officers, but director Henry C. "Hank" Potter, a former Broadway producer, had neglected to bring a "captain" with him from Hollywood. Unwilling to delay the filming, Potter persuaded an interested observer to take the part. Thus, Captain Bellinger, cool and handsome, faced the camera, received an order from "Admiral Furness," played by Samuel S. Hinds, the veteran character actor, saluted, and responded with a snappy "Aye, Aye, Sir." The director also gave Lt. Comdr. Valentine H. Schaeffer, operations officer at NAS North Island and the liaison officer between the Navy and the film company, a role in the same scene. Potter later expressed gratitude "for the friendly and helpful spirit of the officers and men of the *Ranger*. We are working hard to make 'Wings Over Honolulu' a picture of which we and the Navy can be proud. And, if we achieve that end it will be because of the splendid cooperation of the Navy and the Navy people."[23] Critic Frank S. Nugent later accorded the movie "a bit above fair rating, being gayly played, attractively mounted, and directed with surprising confidence and skill."[24]

Transitioning from the "reel" world to real flight operations the next week, the *Ranger* logged only one landing mishap during that period, when Lt. Allen Smith, Jr., of VS-1B, with Radioman 1st Class T. U. Tighe on board, returned from a scouting mission on 24 February. Coming up the groove slightly to the left of the centerline, but not dangerously so, Smith landed without incident, until a gust of wind dropped the right wing; attempting to compensate, Smith landed hard on the left gear and wing.[25]

At Hunter's Point, the first time an aircraft carrier had been drydocked with her air group embarked, 2 March 1937. (NHC, NH 51826)

Proceeding to San Francisco on 27 February, the *Ranger* dropped anchor there during the forenoon watch. She shifted to Hunter's Point on 1 March, entering the drydock there with her entire air group embarked (the first time such an evolution had been conducted). The evolution captivated some of the new aviation cadets and some of the new enlisted men, who deemed it a "revelation and a novelty," never having seen a large ship in drydock. "Few had ever seen a carrier, with its planes aboard [*sic*]," wrote one observer, "sitting on blocks with no water below."[26]

Maneuvering free of the drydock at the end of the afternoon watch the following day, the *Ranger* took departure for San Diego. After launching her planes during the afternoon watch, she moored to the NAS dock a half hour into the first dog watch. There she remained into the fourth week of March, flying Vice Admiral Horne's flag. Operations of her air group continued from North Island, as well as on board the *Saratoga*. During that time, the ship's newspaper received a new name in response to "why not rename the baby?" After those who mulled over submissions had rejected *Rangerion*, *Quiberion*, or the *Ranger Maverick* (among others), *The CV-4* became simply *The Bull Horn* on 12 March 1937, with the new masthead artwork featuring two of the prominent Bogen flight deck loudspeakers.[27]

Occasionally, pilots from other air groups, unused to the *Ranger*'s characteristics, experienced difficulty on her flight deck, but the same held true in reverse. During qualifications on board the *Saratoga* on 24 March, Aviation Cadet

The *Ranger*'s scrappy "basketeers," 13 March 1937, made up of both bluejackets and Marines. Seated in the front row: 1st Lt. John A. "Jack" White, USMC (coach), Commander Montgomery (ship's executive officer), Captain Bellinger, Capt. Edwin J. Farrell, USMC (commanding officer of the ship's Marine Detachment and the ship's athletic officer), Ens. Chester A. Briggs (coach). "No other team," Ensign Briggs declared, "showed more fight, spirit, or sportsmanship than this aggregation." (NA, 80-G-391526)

Edmund O. Carmody, USNR, of VF-3B, making his first carrier landing, took the cut slightly to the left of the centerline. Inadvertently dropping his left wing, Carmody headed further to port, his arrestor hook catching the number two wire outboard of the yielding element. The arresting action of the wire caused the F2F-1 (BuNo 9645) to head toward the *Saratoga*'s port side. Had Carmody not opened the throttle inadvertently, the Grumman might have come to a stop in the port waterway, but his accidental action caused BuNo 9645 to continue over the side of the flight deck and end up in the gun gallery beneath, causing extensive damage to the plane.[28]

Gunnery training occupied the *Ranger* during the fourth week of March, in the operating areas off the coast of Southern California. Flight operations and tactical exercises continued into April, as the fleet prepared for the imminent large-scale war games. She sailed for the Hawaiian Islands on the morning of 16 April, to participate in Minor Joint Army and Navy Exercises and Fleet Problem XVIII.

As 23 April dawned, the forces en route to Hawaiian waters began a series of joint exercises leading up to a simulated attack on the defenses of Oahu.[29] Flight operations that day proceeded uneventfully, until Lt. (jg) Archibald W. "Bill" Greenlee, of VS-1B, flying a gunnery observation hop in an SBU-1 (BuNo 9805), with Radioman 3d Class W. Schlatz on board, made what appeared to be a normal approach, but took the cut high. The combination of the high cut and low speed resulted in 1-S-9 dropping to the deck; the impact bent both propeller blades and both landing flaps and broke both landing gear oleo and rear struts.[30]

Although Bill Greenlee's poor technique had been partly to blame for that accident, occasionally flight deck people

Pitching and rolling in the Pacific swells, 17 April 1937, as seen from the *Lexington*, en route to Hawaii and Fleet Problem XVIII. This view illustrates the *Ranger*'s "lively" tendencies. (NA, 80-CF file)

Beneath the *Ranger*'s number one plane, the O3U-3 (BuNo 9168), U.S.S. RANGER-1, sits one of the ship utility unit's J2F-1s (BuNo 0176) U.S.S. RANGER-5, 21 April 1937. Another J2F-1 (BuNo 0172), U.S.S. RANGER-4, sits in right foreground. Doors in background (L) lead to squadron offices. (NA, 80-CF-54867-3)

made mistakes, too. A half hour before the end of the afternoon watch on 24 April, Lt. (jg) DeWitt W. "Dave" Shumway, of VS-1B, was seated in the front cockpit of his SBU-1 (BuNo 9832), which sat parked opposite the island and on the port side of the flight deck, with its engine turning over. When the time came for Shumway to be spotted for launch, the flight deck handling crew cast off his wing lines. One of the plane directors, however, misjudged the distance between the SBU-1 and 5-F-3, an F3F-1 parked immediately astern and to the left, and signalled the VS-1B pilot to "turn right to come to the center line." Shumway did so, but, in so doing, the tail of his plane swung too far to port and the Grumman's whirling propeller sliced into the Vought's left elevator. Soon thereafter, Shumway recounted later, "I was then signalled out of the spot and to #1 elevator" to be sent below.[31]

Assigned to the "Hilo Force," along with her plane-guard destroyers, the *Ranger* launched planes during the mid watch on 25 April. The takeoff proceeded beneath the "light of a full Hawaiian moon," which shone so brightly "that it almost seemed to exert itself especially for the benefit of aviators." One VF-3B pilot wryly allowed later that the moon in Hoboken, New Jersey, "is sometimes just as large, but doesn't have the tremendous advantage of shining down on a high tropical island surrounded by a limitless expanse of glistening ocean."[32]

The general plan for the Minor Joint Army and Navy Exercises called for the *Saratoga*'s group (as part of the "Oahu Bombardment Force") to attack coast defenses between Pearl Harbor and Diamond Head, and the *Lexington*'s (as part of the "Northern Force") to neutralize Wheeler Field. The *Ranger*'s group received the task of knocking out the Pearl

Harbor Navy Yard. The *Ranger*'s planes encountered "enemy" bombers and patrol planes off Barber's Point, the running lights forming "gay triangular colored patterns shuttling back and forth over the dark sea," while "mobile batteries of searchlights…simulated antiaircraft fire." Mock dogfights with the "enemy" aircraft occurred, a VF-3B pilot wrote,"activity [that] added just the right amount of zest to the morning and made everyone feel very much alive," after which the sky began to lighten, affording "all hands…the privilege of witnessing a gorgeous sunrise…[wherein] the moon and the sun staged a contest of beauty to gain approval that morning, the former using only black and silver for its effects, while the latter made use of every shade of brilliant and pastel color…. After two hours of such sights it is no wonder that faces were glowing and the ready room buzzing with talk" upon the return to the *Ranger*. "It was the most perfect of preludes to the visit to Maui."[33]

Standing in to Lahaina Roads later that day, the *Ranger* dropped anchor in the 26-fathom depth of berth "A," early in the afternoon watch. The next day, Pat Bellinger sent a letter to his immediate superior, Vice Admiral Horne, requesting permission to embark his son, Frederick Wells Bellinger, who was 15 years, 4 months old at the time, for the trip from San Francisco to San Diego, when the fleet returned there after the fleet problem. "This request," Bellinger wrote, "is submitted in view of my detachment from the *Ranger* about 5 June, as this is the last opportunity my son will have to gain experience in the ship board [*sic*] life in the Navy."[34] On 28 April, the letter found its way up the chain of command via the guard mail, as the fleet lay off Lahaina, passed favorably from ComAirBatFor to ComBat For to CinCUS, thence on its way to Washington to the Bureau of Navigation, from whom the final word would have to come.

8
"BRING BACK AMELIA AND FRED"

On the eve of the impending fleet problem, on the morning of 2 May, the *Ranger* hoisted out three of her utility planes (two J2F-1s and an O3U-3) for familiarization flights. "Monty" Montgomery, the ship's exec, piloted a J2F-1 (BuNo 0176), U.S.S. RANGER–5, with Aviation Machinist's Mate 1st Class J. L. Andrews and Photographer 2d Class M. Hitchcock on board. Lieutenant Jack Brand took off that Sunday morning in the other Grumman amphibian, (BuNo 0172), U.S.S. RANGER–4, with Aviation Chief Machinist's Mate D. F. Powers and Aviation Ordnanceman 1st Class O. A. Kuper as passengers.[1]

During the course of his flight, Montgomery noted oil splashing down the side of his plane. To investigate the cause, he made for Maalea airport, near Lahaina. Knowing the shortness of the runways there, he tried to compensate by landing "short." Coming in from over the water, Montgomery, with only 4.8 hours in the cockpit of utility-type planes in the previous three months, found himself too low for comfort, and pushed the throttle forward, attempting to get enough airspeed to pull up. Unfortunately, the engine did not respond, and the J2F-1's hull and right wheel fouled a sandbank at the water's edge and broke off the wheel in so doing. The Grumman bounced twice, cleared a four-foot ditch, and slewed to a stop off in the soft mud that lay off the edge of the runway, coming to rest on its right wingtip pontoon. The impact had buckled the forward right cabane strut, and the wheel knocked off on the sandbank had dented the leading edge of the lower right wing. "Too much cannot be said for the Grumman hull," one observer later wrote, "Number 0176 bumped and slid along on its keel over rough terrain and mud for 60 to 70 yards and the hull hasn't a wrinkle or dent in it."[2]

Less than a half hour later, Jack Brand saw the exec's J2F-1 "in apparent trouble" and, after lowering his landing gear, "dragged the field downwind to view [Commander Montgomery]'s predicament." Brand turned and made another pass, the second time, however, floating the length of the runway. His wheels touched the very end of the strip. Finding himself in a bad situation, he, like the exec before him, tried to get out of trouble by pushing the throttle forward, but the engine would not "take," and the Grumman, after bouncing over the ditch and sand bank at the end of the field, "slowly squashed into Maalea Bay," about a mile offshore. Landing downwind, with a wind of about 25 knots, the amphibian flipped over on its back, the impact of the crash tearing the wings loose from the fuselage. Brand, having suffered contusions to his face and a blackened left eye, and his two passengers, Kuper with a scalp wound and a broken left clavicle and Powers with a lacerated finger on his right hand, clung to the wreckage until a local fishing sampan towed it, bottom-up, to a pier at Kehei. A working party from the *Ranger* later arrived, righted the hull, and towed it to Maalea airport, three miles away. Those who assessed the damage noted the demolished wings, badly damaged wingtip floats and hull sides, and bent propeller blades. Other than immersion in salt water, the engine appeared undamaged. Those who assessed blame for the crash faulted Brand for poor technique (75%), but allowed that the fuel system seemed to have played a role (25%) in the mishap. A working party also attended to U.S.S. RANGER–5 and, after putting a new right wheel on and installing a new front cabane strut, flew it back to the ship.

A little over an hour into the first dog watch on 3 May, Rear Adm. Ernest J. King, Commander Aircraft, Base Force (ComAirBaseFor), embarked on board the *Ranger*, accompanied by Comdr. Charles A. Pownall, his chief of staff (and the *Ranger*'s first exec), and other members of his staff, to use her as his flagship "and so to know at firsthand the characteristics of that ship." For the exercises, King was slated to serve as "Commander Aircraft, White Force." That evening, Bellinger invited the admiral to dine with him. During the course of the meal, King allowed that "he knew that having an Admiral on board was apt to be resented by the Captain," but told Bellinger that he should consider him [King] "as being on another ship." Bellinger appreciated King's gracious statement.[3]

Less than a half hour into the first watch on 4 May, the *Ranger* weighed anchor off Lahaina and stood out, to take part in Fleet Problem XVIII, as part of the White force. With the U.S. Fleet almost equally divided (the fleet's submarines were all assigned to one of the opposing forces), the *Ranger* took part in the nine-phase evolution, which depicted an offensive campaign in a chain of islands defended by a home fleet; she was to serve as one of the defenders. The destroyers *Fox* (DD-234) and *Brooks* (DD-232) joined her an hour before the end of the morning watch on 5 May, to serve as her plane guards.[4]

Rear Admiral King wanted planes launched at first light on 7 May. Squally weather, however, with rain and fog, gave Bellinger pause, the captain deeming it "suicide for a plane to go up" in those conditions. Bellinger and Lt. Comdr. Frederick A. Davisson, the *Ranger*'s aerological officer, watched the weather "like hawks" for signs of abating conditions that would permit planes to be launched. Bellinger climbed to flag plot, to determine if there were any changes of orders in light of the unrelenting poor weather conditions. Noticing what he later called a "peculiar hushed silence," the *Ranger*'s captain bid a cordial "Good morning" to the admiral and his staff.

"When," King asked, his voice breaking the uneasy quiet, "are you going to launch planes?"

"As soon as the weather gets satisfactory," Bellinger replied as he began to go below to his bridge, privately in a cold fury. "It wasn't what Admiral King said," Bellinger allowed in later years, "[as] much as the manner in which he said it that made one bite nails."

With the weather still poor, Bellinger, concern for his aircrews paramount, adhered to his intention of launching planes when conditions improved. Returning to the flag bridge later, Bellinger heard Admiral King repeat his

Join the Navy and See the World: *Ranger* sailors take in the "never ending abundance of scenic beauty" on Maui, May 1937. (NA, 80-CF file, Box 169)

question: "When are you going to launch planes?" Bellinger repeated that he would launch when the weather was satisfactory, but asked King whether or not he [the admiral] felt that the weather would permit launch. "If I was in command of this ship," King declared, "those planes would be gone by now."

"Well," Bellinger responded respectfully, "I don't think the weather is satisfactory."

By less than an hour into the afternoon watch, however, the weather conditions improved, so that, at 1241, the *Ranger* launched 10 F2F-1s from VF-3B, to provide combat air patrol (CAP) over the carrier. Soon thereafter, she received word from the heavy cruiser *New Orleans* (CA-32) of three carrier aircraft scouting in her vicinity. At 1244, the *Ranger* began launching 18 SBU-1s from VS-1B to scout a geographical rectangle between longitude 160° and 160°30′, and between latitudes 20° and 22°, and to develop any contacts made.

The pace of "battle" soon accelerated. About a half-hour later, the sixth section of VS-1B sighted and attacked three scout planes from the *Saratoga* group; a short time later, the *Ranger* recovered the nine SBU-1s from VS-1B's second division. Less than two hours into the afternoon watch, VS-1B's first section spotted five "enemy" scout planes at 1330, and two submerged submarines four minutes later. Soon thereafter, however, VS-1B's fourth section sighted the Black Main Body only 42 miles from the *Ranger*.

Word of the discovery of the enemy fleet prompted King to order a strike launched; at 1347, the *Ranger* turned into the wind and commenced putting 18 planes from VB-1B and 9 planes from VF-5B aloft. At 1350, VS-1B's fifth section reported the presence of the Black fleet 40 miles to the north-by-northwest. At about the same time, Black reconnaissance planes spotted the *Ranger* at 160°45′, 20°42′ "with all planes on deck."

At 1355, VS-1B's commanding officer sighted the *Saratoga* and a heavy cruiser roughly northwest, 90 miles from the *Ranger*. At 1356, the latter carrier launched nine planes from VF-3B to serve as a CAP. At 1359, the pilot of 1-S-13 spotted three battleships, the carriers *Lexington* and *Saratoga*, and "many DD's," roughly northwest-by-north of the *Ranger*'s position. At 1405, the *Ranger* directed the airborne VB-1B to attack Black transports steaming with the enemy main body.

A quarter of an hour later, because the *Ranger* had been spotted, the *Saratoga* turned into the wind to launch planes to attack her smaller adversary. To carry out the mission, she launched VS-4 and VS-2. In the carrier-versus-carrier duel, however, it was the *Ranger* that drew first blood, when VF-5B, armed with 100-pound bombs, pushed over to assault the *Saratoga* at 1427. The *Saratoga*'s assistant umpire, however, Comdr. Frederick C. Sherman, considered the attack "very poorly made," noting that the attacking F3F-1s passed over three heavy cruisers in the *Saratoga*'s screen and, during the approach and attack, had come under fire of the concerted antiaircraft fire of a trio of heavy cruisers and a trio of battleships. Nevertheless, the *Ranger*'s intrepid pilots managed to place the *Saratoga*'s number one rangefinder, number one antiaircraft director, and two 5-inch antiaircraft guns out of commission, killing six men and wounding 18. The damage, however, had been wreaked at high cost, for the umpire assessed 11 of VF-5B's planes destroyed.[5] The remainder of the squadron attacked the "transport" *Holland*, loosing 15 100-pounders in an unopposed assault.

Less than a half hour later, VB-1B, unable to reach the Black transports because of the heavy antiaircraft fire from the screen, attacked the heavy cruiser *San Francisco* (CA-38) instead, dropping eighteen 1,000-pounders, but "losing" three planes in the process. In about a quarter of an hour, VF-5B engaged a succession of Black divisions, from VF-6B, VB-5B, and VB-3B, assessed the loss of six planes in those aerial engagements.

Soon after the *Ranger* pilots had bombed the unsuspecting *San Francisco*, which neither maneuvered nor opened fire until after the attack had been completed, the *Saratoga*'s two scouting squadrons (VS-4B and VS-2B) arrived in the vicinity of the object of their search, and reported the presence of "rain squalls and poor visibility conditions."[6] Meantime, the *Lexington*'s planes having already been employed on attack missions against other White objectives precluded their use against the *Ranger*. The *Saratoga*'s pilots attacked a White "battle cruiser" with ten 500-pound bombs, around 1519, but had not been able to locate the *Ranger*, which had been effectively shielded by the weather. Lieutenant Commander John F. "Jack" Gillon, VS-2B's commanding officer, radioed that the area around the *Ranger* "has many rain squalls in which flying was dangerous."[7]

One hour before the end of the afternoon watch, the *Ranger* recovered VB-1B's first division. About three-quarters of an hour later, the ship turned into the wind and launched eight SBU-1s from VS-1B as an attack group, the Vought pilots shaping their courses toward the Black transports. Eight minutes later, the *Ranger* began landing her first attack group: VB-1B and VF-5B, the second division of VF-3B, followed by VS-1B's second division.

During the recovery of VF-5B, 15 minutes into the first dog watch, Lt. (jg) Roland H. Dale made a "fair" approach. The LSO adjudged the attitude of Dale's F3F-1 (BuNo 0225) as "satisfactory," although a little on the high side when he gave him the cut. Dale nosed the plane down slightly, dipping the left wing, however, when he was about to make contact with the deck. At that moment, with the *Ranger* pitching some two or three degrees in the Pacific swells, the F3F hit the deck nose-down and left wheel first, which "greatly magnified" the usual forces present at that important moment. The impact ruptured the weld in the left axle: "the compression link failed three inches above the lower hinge joint [and] the front and rear torque tubes were distorted and twisted." In addition, the lower left wing scraped the deck, receiving repairable damage, and contact with the deck damaged the tips of the propeller blades. Roland Dale walked away from his 66th carrier landing, unhurt.[8]

After a flight of less than an hour, VS-1B's first division of eight SBU-1s began pushing over to attack the *Holland*. Six of the eight *Ranger* pilots fought their way through an inner air patrol of VB-2B from the *Saratoga*; umpires later assessed all VS-1B planes destroyed, at the cost of one *Saratoga* plane rendered out of commission. The umpire on board the *Holland* assessed the attack as having been made on the "constructive" transport in the disposition, and assessed 11.5% damage against the imaginary auxiliary.[9]

Less than three-quarters of an hour into the first dog watch, the *Ranger* landed her second CAP, VF-3B's first division, then brought on board VS-1B's two sections, thus winding up her flight operations for the day. Soon thereafter, the *Saratoga* began recovering her planes. After having led VS-2B's unsuccessful efforts to find the *Ranger* earlier that afternoon, Lt. Comdr. Jack Gillon of VS-2B made a tight flipper turn, to fly around the *McCormick* (DD-223), the port plane guard destroyer. Two-Sail-One, however, inexplicably stalled and the nose dropped sharply. Gillon's SBU-1 (BuNo 9779) then flew directly into the water at full throttle in a geyser of spray just astern of the *McCormick*, the Vought disappearing from sight in about a half a minute. Neither Jack Gillon nor Radioman 1st Class Glen M. Beal, his passenger, survived the crash.[10] Their loss reminded those who carried on that naval aviation, whether carrier-based, in flying boats, or in the unsung utility squadrons, proved a dangerous profession in peacetime as well as in war.

A little over a half an hour into the morning watch on 8 May, the *Ranger* began launching her first attack group, putting aloft 6 F3F-1s from VF-5B and 15 Martins from VB-1B. Soon thereafter, 9 SBU-1s began taking off, each Vought carrying a 500-pound bomb to allow them to augment the attack group. She soon launched an additional 6 SBU-1s to serve as "smokers." Putting aloft 15 BM-1s and -2s from VB-1B at 0440, the *Ranger* wound up that particular portion of flight operations by launching a CAP of 19 planes from VF-3B.

Before the morning watch was out, VS-1B's pilots had found Black transports to attack, six planes carrying out their attacks at 0545 and encountering the *Saratoga*'s VF-6B. Two Vought pilots attacked a transport five minutes later and encountered six *Saratoga* fighters, with the resulting loss of both VS-1B planes. "Constructive" casualties continued to mount, as the *Ranger* recovered "out of action" planes from VF-5B, soon after the mid point in the morning watch.

At 0629, six VF-5B pilots pushed over in dive-bombing attacks against the *Argonne* (AG-31), portraying a Black "transport," dropping ten 100-pounders and one 500-pounder. Although they had attacked unopposed, retiring from the scene proved a difficult proposition, because the *Saratoga*'s VF-6B "bounced" them upon conclusion of the attack. Outnumbered nine to six, the *Ranger*men lost three planes to the determined attacks of the *Saratoga*'s fighter pilots. Their sacrifice had not, however, been in vain, for VF-5B's engaging VF-6B had allowed VB-1B to attack the *Argonne* without hindrance.

As the morning watch continued, the *Ranger* maintained a busy pace. She recovered the 6 smokers, beginning at 0635, followed within the hour by 9 SBU-1 scouts from VS-1B, and, a quarter of an hour later, her attack group of BM-1s and -2s from VB-1B. Striking the returning planes below, the *Ranger* spotted her flight deck for launch, and, beginning 10 minutes into the forenoon watch, began putting the first of another attack group into the air: 11 SBU-1s and 14 BM-1s and -2s. Once the deck had been cleared, the ship recovered the VF-5B attack group, starting at 0820. Within another half-hour's time, the *Ranger* recovered VF-3B's combat patrol and a pair of SBU-1s from VS-1B. Beginning at 0858, the *Ranger* launched 3 F3F-1s from VF-5B and 19 F2F-1s from VF-3B to serve as a CAP over the carrier.

Soon the *Ranger* would again tackle the *Saratoga*, damaging her bigger adversary. At 0900, the seven SBU-1s began deploying to dive-bomb the big carrier, catching her with planes on deck and scoring one 100-pounder hit that "jammed" Turret III in train and put it out of action for two hours. The 14 Martins of VB-1B began pushing over into the dives soon thereafter, scoring two hits, destroying two-thirds of the planes on deck and putting the *Saratoga*'s flight deck out of commission for two hours. "Antiaircraft fire" claimed three Voughts and three Martins.

Meanwhile, the Black patrol planes sought the *Ranger*. At 0938, the ship intercepted a transmission from a Black patrol plane: "*Ranger* bears 135 degrees distance 75 miles from LAHAINA—am tracking her."

Although the shadower's reported bearing for the ship proved to be off—it should have been 195 degrees—the plane, lurking in the distance on the starboard quarter, soon hove into sight, spotted at 0946 by the *Ranger*'s lookouts. Fighting Three's first division soon bore in on the attack, nine F2F-1s swarming upon the shadowing PBY, which turned out to be 11-P-11. Soon thereafter, while the PBY bore in on her, the *Ranger* recovered VB-1B's BM-1s, fresh from their triumph over the *Saratoga*.

Eleven-Peter-Eleven, meanwhile, approached from 10,000 feet and "bombed" the *Ranger*, which took the attacking PBY under fire for three minutes, expending 30 rounds of 5-inch ammunition. VF-3's first division knocked the PBY out of action soon thereafter, but the lumbering Catalina had performed her duty: umpires assessed 3.6% damage forward to the *Ranger*'s flight deck, rendering one-quarter of it out of commission. The *Ranger* "shot down" another PBY, crossing the carrier's bow to attack her, after three minutes' fire, at about the same time she was recovering the seven SBU-1s from her attack group. Fighting Three, in the interim, pounced on the three other flying boats lurking in the vicinity; the squadron's second division "splashed" two.

Backing engines, the *Ranger* spotted her air group forward and launched seven SBU-1s from VS-1B and eight BM-1s from VB-1B over the stern ramp, between 1024 and 1045, because the umpires had declared the forward part of the flight deck out of action from the PBY's earlier attack. After completing the evolution, she went ahead on both engines. Soon thereafter, however, the ubiquitous Black patrol planes put in their appearance, swiftly pounced-on by VF-3B's first division. Despite the best efforts of the fighters, however, six flying boats managed to press home their attacks, the ship receiving 21.5% damage, with three-quarters of her flight deck "out of commission."

Soon thereafter, however, less than an hour before the end of the forenoon watch, three patrol planes "bombed" the ship, although the *Ranger* had taken them "under fire" during their approach. The ship's misfortunes during that phase of the "battle" soon multiplied, as her lookouts spotted six patrol planes off her starboard bow. Only minutes later, a group of five flying boats attacked from astern; although the *Ranger* maneuvered and opened up with her antiaircraft batteries on her tormentors, the big boats had scored what umpires ruled, at 1126, was 43% damage in the encounter. The umpires later heightened the assessment to 48% and declared the flight deck out of commission.

The *Ranger*'s attack group, however, doggedly flew toward the enemy. VB-1B's pilots pushed over against the *Lexington* at 1105, catching her bigger adversary recovering planes. However, Comdr. Wadleigh Capehart, the umpire on board the *Lexington* (and her executive officer), assessed "no damage" as a result of the attack, contending that VB-1B had been destroyed the previous afternoon by VB-5B. If the destruction of the *Ranger* squadron was disallowed, however, Capehart assessed the destruction of 48% of the flight deck forward, five planes, all six forward 5-inch anti-aircraft guns, and the loss of the emergency radio room and its four transmitters, at the cost of the loss of two of VB-1B's Martins to fighters from the *Lexington*'s VF-1B. Less than 15 minutes later, the seven SBU-1s from VS-1B pushed over into their dives over the *Saratoga*, losing their 500-pounders, which scored an addition 5% damage to that ship, knocking out a quarter of the planes on deck, and rendering the flight deck out of action for an additional two hours, at the cost of two SBU-1s. Unhappily for the *Ranger*men, after the "destruction" of the *Ranger*'s flight deck by the flying boats, the umpires had no choice but to render the ship's air group out of action when they returned to find no place to land.

During the afternoon watch, Black torpedo planes launched from the "repaired" flight deck of the *Saratoga* caught up with the *Ranger*. Five BM-2s from VT-2 skillfully pressed home their attacks through a smoke screen, at moderate range and enjoying a favorable attack angle. Although the *Ranger*'s 5-inch batteries put out 90 rounds and the ship maneuvered to avoid the "fish," VT-2 had done its work well, scoring one hit, causing a further 12% damage to the ship. Commander Montgomery, an assistant umpire for the Fleet Problem, assessed the damage to the ship by that point as 64%.

At last, at 1450, the Fleet received the signal "cease present exercises," which ended Fleet Problem XVIII. Soon, Rear Admiral King (who would relieve Horne as ComAirBatFor) returned to his regular flagship, the *Wright*. He had found the *Ranger* to be a "tender" ship that would heel noticeably in a turn, and small enough that the air department had to develop careful procedures for getting her planes aloft. Her flight deck crew, however, had become so adept at their tasks that they had put her planes in the air faster than either the larger *Lexington* or *Saratoga*.[11]

Anchoring off Honolulu the following day, the *Ranger* again participated in a fleet searchlight extravaganza for the benefit of the local residents on 12 and 13 May (the latter, the day upon which Pat Bellinger received permission to embark his son for the San Francisco-to-San Diego trip), remaining off the capitol of the Hawaiian territory until she sailed for San Diego with the rest of the fleet on 20 May. The majority of the *Ranger*'s sailors, one wrote, considered that "the stay in Honolulu, although pleasant [was also] somewhat extensive, considering the fact that the ordinarily delightful city of Honolulu lost most of its charm through no fault of its own but by an overcrowded condition" brought about by the entire fleet "being on liberty there at one time."[12]

The voyage back to the West Coast proved mostly uneventful, until 25 May, when Aviation Cadet Robert M. Stanley, USNR, of VB-1B, with Seaman 2d Class W. J. McNally on board, experienced some difficulty landing his BM-1 (BuNo 8885), late in the afternoon watch on 25 May, after a tactics flight. Making a normal approach, Stanley took the cut for a normal landing and came on in, buffetted by the turbulent air and gusts at the ramp and allowing for the roll of the ship. Stanley made a three-point landing between number four and five wire, but the temporary removal of the latter meant that the BM-1 came down hard on its right wheel, demolishing the right side of the landing gear, crumpling the lower right wing, and bending both propeller blades, after the plane's hook engaged number six pendant. The trouble board, however, concluded that the major cause of the accident had been the absence of the wire; they assigned 50% of the mishap to factors of weather and the pitching deck.[13]

That same day, during rehearsal for the aerial parade that was scheduled to take place upon arrival at San Francisco, Lt. Joseph B. Dunn of VS-1B, with Radioman 2d Class D. W. Blazer on board, made a slightly high approach that resulted in his landing heavily on the right wheel, carrying away the right seat of the landing gear and causing the SBU-1 (BuNo 9800) to slide on its lower right wing and bending the propeller tips. The resulting trouble board faulted Joe Dunn's "poor technique" for the accident, but admitted that the pitching deck had been a problem, too.[14]

The next day, 26 May, the *Ranger* sighted a Japanese tanker broad on the port bow some 15 miles distant, which remained in company throughout the afternoon watch, maneuvering to keep pace with the Americans' movements.

"The morning of 28 May found all hands up and about early," a *Ranger* sailor wrote later, "peering furtively into the usual San Francisco haze." The *Ranger* launched three squadrons to conduct refresher training, as well as to take part in an aerial parade to coincide with the festivities surrounding the opening of the Golden Gate Bridge. All told, twelve squadrons "passed over a parade route covering the bay area, crossing the bridge again upon completion of the parade, and then breaking up in formation to land aboard [*sic*] their respective carriers."[15]

The rough weather, however, made recovery a difficult proposition, with strong, cold winds and a heavy sea. A little over a half hour into the afternoon watch, Lt. (jg) Dave Shumway, flying an SBU-1 (BuNo 9799), with Lt. Comdr. William H. Rafferty, ChC, the ship's chaplain, in the back seat, approached the pitching carrier. Getting a "high" signal from Lt. Jack Brand, the LSO, Shumway compensated by losing altitude. Brand signalled "roger" and Shumway maintained his course toward the ship. Given a "low," he raised the nose and received a "roger." Although both pilot and LSO later agreed that Shumway had been a little high at that point, he was nevertheless in excellent position to make a safe landing. Immediately after Brand had signaled cut and Shumway began to drop to catch a wire, the latter saw the deck begin to drop away. From Brand's vantage point, it looked as if Shumway was going to catch number five wire, but the tail seemed to raise up because of the wind gusting across the deck. The pilot managed to get his wheels on the deck, but the unbridled Vought crashed into the barrier. Fearing fire, Shumway cut the engine, pulled the fire extinguisher, and exited the plane. Although 1-S-3 suffered class B damage and the pilot emerged without a scratch, the 41-year-old chaplain suffered a contusion of his left eyebrow and two small lacerations on his nose.[16]

Sighting San Francisco light at 1444, the *Ranger* entered the dredged channel into San Francisco Bay a little less than an hour later and, after steering various courses and speeds to approach her berth, dropped anchor at 1729. The next day, the *Ranger* participated in another searchlight extravaganza for the local citizenry as the celebration of the completion of the Bay Bridge continued.

Underway at 0648 on 3 June, in company with the *Lexington*, the *Saratoga*, and plane-guard destroyers, the *Ranger* moored in San Diego harbor the following day. The following morning, Capt. John S. McCain, fresh from a tour of duty as commanding officer, of the Fleet Air Base at Coco Solo, Canal Zone, relieved Pat Bellinger as the carrier's commanding officer, in a simple ceremony before the ship's company drawn up on the flight deck.[17]

A Naval Academy classmate of Roy Bristol, the *Ranger*'s first commanding officer, "Mac" McCain was described by one wit in '06 as the "skeleton in the class [of '06] family closet." His classmates, perhaps with tongue in cheek, considered him "a living example of the beneficial course of physical training at the N.A. [Naval Academy] having gained 1⅜ ounces since he entered," and a "man of exemplary habits which make him very popular, his 'den' having been a favorite resort for 'all hands' since the days of plebe rough-houses." He was also described as laughing "with an open-face movement" that reminded those who saw it of the Luray Cave. Unlike Pat Bellinger, who had been in on naval aviation from the beginning, the Mississippi-born McCain had come into the profession late, not receiving his orders to proceed to the Naval Air Station, Pensacola, "for duty under instruction in heavier-than-air aircraft" until 30 April 1935. Reporting on 20 June 1935, he completed the course of instruction and was given the wings of a naval aviator (heavier-than-air) on 19 August 1936. Detached from Pensacola on 16 September, he reported to the Fleet Air Base, Coco Solo, on 19 October. On 15 April 1937, he received his orders to the *Ranger* "for duty involving flying in command."[18]

Over the next three months, the *Ranger* operated locally in the San Diego–Coronado area, with her air group, as usual, basing at NAS San Diego when the ship was in port, her pilots honing their skills. The occasional error in judgment continued to punctuate the training, as Lt. (jg) Clayton L. Miller demonstrated on 17 June, when he overshot the landing area at North Island in his F3F-1 (BuNo 0216), and 5-F-5 rolled into two F2F-1s (2-F-15 and 2-F-17) from VF-2B, which sat parked in the warm-up area, damaging both.[19] On the other hand, a trouble board exonerated Aviation Cadet C. E. Jones, USNR, from being blamed for poor technique during a landing in his SBU-1 (BuNo 9808), with Radioman 3d Class S. P. Von Achen on board, on 21 June, when his tail wheel assembly collapsed during a landing at Camp Kearney. The board viewed the cause of the trouble as the assembly itself.[20]

In the meantime, the business of digesting the lessons learned during Fleet Problem XVIII reached a conclusion. The pace of carrier operations had particularly concerned Vice Admiral Horne, ComAirBatFor, who noted that the conclusion of the war games had found both carrier pilots and flight deck crews "exhausted." He decried the tendency "to operate [that type of ship] too steadily without sufficient regard for the theoretical and practical risks involved." Lengthy, sustained operations "without sufficient rest for pilots and flight deck crews," he wrote, "produced fatigue and consequent increase in actual hazards." In attempting to "crowd too much into a few days we create false impressions of our capacity for sustained operations."[21]

Whether or not an aircraft carrier should operate with the fleet's Main Body also continued to be a bone of contention. Horne posited that, if that feature was "considered essential [then] a carrier with a special complement of aircraft types should be detailed," recommending that the number of planes "be less than at present and proportionately the number of personnel for planes and for the carrier flight deck should be greater." If a carrier operated with the Main Body, however, Horne warned that "Fleet Problem XVIII again proved that evasive movements at high speed are a carrier's best protection against air attack and the old, oft repeated lesson—a carrier tied down to a slow formation is quite certain to be put out of action." Perhaps particularly mindful of the damage wreaked by the *Ranger*'s pilots upon both the *Saratoga* and the *Lexington*, Horne invited "particular attention" to the last comment: "There is nothing new in either the comments or the objections—yet plans and orders continue to be issued which foredoom carriers to certain loss before they can strike one telling blow." Maintaining that the mission of Aircraft, United States Fleet, lay in *offense*—"to obtain and maintain control of the air in the theater of Naval operations"—not *defense*, Horne argued that "a multiplicity of lesser, *defensive* [Horne's italics] missions" dissipated "the energies and strengths of the air arm." Once an enemy carrier lay "*within striking distance of our fleet no security remains until it—its squadrons—or both, are destroyed*, and our carriers, if with the Main Body are at tremendous disadvantage in conducting the necessary operations."[22]

"Offensive carrier operations at a distance from our own Main Body," ComAirBatFor observed, "do[es] reduce the strength of that Main Body. Under this condition the Main Body may be, for the time being, without aircraft services—even the important services of anti-submarine patrols and air scouts—if battleship and cruiser based aircraft cannot operate. It is a gamble for the Fleet Commander who detaches his carriers in this manner but he is playing for high stakes. It is no gamble, on the other hand if they are kept with the Main Body for their certain loss is only a matter of time—and usually a short time at that."[23]

Horne's observations came under the careful scrutiny of Adm. Claude C. Bloch, Commander, Battle Force (Commander, Black Fleet, Fleet Problem XVIII). Bloch regarded the *Lexington* and the *Saratoga* as "a vital part of the Black Main Body, contributing powerfully to its strength by their presence and leaving a pronounced weakness when absent. Their planes enabled Black to project offensive operations well beyond the limits of the disposition, not only against surface ships but against submarines, [patrol planes] and other aircraft." He accepted the "damage" inflicted by the *Ranger* planes upon the *Lexington* and the *Saratoga* as part of the "normal expectation in warfare, and as all types shared in the damage sustained, the carriers may be said to have borne no more than their part of the brunt of the battle."[24]

Bloch noted the arduous nature of the duty performed by the carriers, and the excellent performance of the squadrons involved, but observed that the duties were "limited and would not be required for protracted periods." He allowed that the work had proved "of great advantage to the carrier personnel in their training for the quick and almost continuous handling of planes."[25]

Concerning the matter of a carrier operating with the Main Body, Bloch decried the "'evasive tactics' [used] by the carriers" that had come to mean "independent operations, largely against the enemy carrier group. This," the admiral wrote, "results in a private war between the opposing air forces, often with complete disregard of the part [that] the air forces were intended to play in the furtherance of the plans" proposed by the officer in tactical command. Should carriers operate independently, Bloch complained, commanders would seek to replace destroyers with cruisers as plane guards, which would lead to a demand for more cruisers, then for new fast battleships to support the cruisers. "Pursued to its logical conclusion," the admiral contended, "means the carriers belong with the Fleet," where they could give, as well as receive, "mutual support."[26]

"It is essential," Bloch believed, "that the carriers judge the success of their operations, not by the damage inflicted on or received from enemy carriers, but by their contribution to the success of the entire operation. In other words," he continued, "it is better for the carriers to be sunk incident to winning a fleet victory than to escape from a defeat or an indecisive engagement." Given the interest expressed again in the "battle line carrier" concept, Bloch suggested that the "time has now arrived to try this scheme again, using the *Ranger*," which, in the admiral's estimation, because of her "small size, lack of protection, small battery, and forward arresting gear" made her "most suitable for such [a] purpose." Additionally, he noted that the *Ranger* possessed none of the "speed disadvantages which militated against the *Langley*," when she had been employed in that role in earlier Fleet Problems. Adding the *Yorktown* (CV-5) and the *Enterprise* (CV-6) to the fleet (both ships then building at the same yard that had built the *Ranger*) would increase the number of carriers in the fleet "to warrant the assignment of at least one carrier to duty with the Battle Line."[27]

Matters of how carriers would be employed in the future continued to be contemplated at higher levels, but, as the month of June waned, the *Ranger* received "some new and some old additions" to her assigned complement of planes, when, on 21 June, she received a Grumman J2F-1 to replace U.S.S. RANGER–4, which had been wrecked at Lahaina back in early May. She was also given an N2Y-1 for use by the ship's LSO, and an O3U-3 "which, from all appearances, even to the insignia on the side of the fuselage," one wag observed, "has spent its best days on the *Langley*."[28]

On the last day of June, many pilots from the *Lexington* and the *Ranger*, as well as the Marine flyers of Aircraft Two, completed intensive carrier landing practice. The day's evolutions held a little more zest for Lt. (jg) Vernon R. "Rex" Hain of VB-3B (the soon-to-be-redesignated VB-4), who took off from North Island in a BG-1 (BuNo 9504), with Aviation Machinist's Mate 3d Class G. P. Hanley as his passenger, for an oxygen familiarization flight.[29]

As Rex Hain took off, he observed a small puff of white smoke from an exhaust stack. He thought the occurrence of little import, because the engine had just received its 30-hour check, and he believed that consequently a small amount of grease or oil may have found its way onto the exhaust collector rings. Climbing at about 65% power, Hain reached an altitude of 8,000 feet over Camp Kearney, when he and his passenger felt a sudden jolt. A large puff of white smoke came from the engine, followed by another jolt; soon all exhaust stacks were emitting gouts of white smoke. Giving the deferred forced landing signal, Hain returned to North Island at reduced power.

When he arrived over the field, however, his engine was putting out so much smoke and making so much noise that he decided to cut his switch and make a dead stick landing. Climbing out of the aircraft, once back safely on the ground, Hain and Hanley could see that oil covered the entire left side of the aircraft, and was dripping from the exhaust stacks on the right side. A check of the oil sumps soon thereafter revealed finely ground steel and brass parts; a further check of the engine yielded the fact that the number two cylinder head had been cracked, from the center of the head through the hole for the sparkplug. Investigators also found the combustion chamber badly battered and a valve stem missing, the holed piston indicating that the missing piece had most likely penetrated the piston and gone into the crankcase.

Amidst the routine of flight operations, the Navy redesignated its carrier-based squadrons effective 1 July. The new system, decided upon the previous March, matched each assigned squadron with its parent ship and did away with the "B" (for Battle Force) suffix after the individual squadron number. Thus, the *Ranger*'s VB-1B became VT-2 and went to the *Lexington*; the latter's VB-3B became VB-4 and went to the *Ranger*. The *Saratoga*'s VS-2B became VS-42 and went to the *Ranger*. Re-marking and repainting the aircraft accompanied the alteration. Similar changes occurred in battleship- and cruiser-based squadrons, as well as Marine Corps and U.S. Naval Reserve units. "Due to the big shift occurring on 1 July," one observer wrote later, "the *Lexington* group included *Ranger* pilots and the *Ranger* group included *Saratoga* pilots. To add to the chances of confusion the majority of the pilots had just reported and many of the officers who had kept their squadrons running smoothly for the last year had been detached."[30]

That same day, while the *Ranger* and her air group were pursuing their training and acclimating themselves to the administrative paperwork headaches incident to the redesignations, on 2 July 1937 (west longitude date), the famed aviatrix Amelia Earhart [Putnam] and her navigator, Fred J. Noonan, took off from Lae, New Guinea, in their Lockheed Model 10-E Electra, bound for Howland Island, the next stop on their transpacific flight. Concern for their safety arose once they failed to reach Howland, and around midday on 3 July the Navy Department directed Adm. Arthur J. Hepburn, CinCUS, to hold a carrier in readiness, have her take on fuel, and make all preparations for a thorough search of the region in which Earhart's Lockheed Electra was thought to have gone down. Hepburn in turn directed ComAirBatFor to have a carrier ready to proceed to sea within four hours time.[31]

Vice Admiral Horne chose the *Lexington* for the duty (the *Ranger* lay off Santa Monica for the 4th of July), as well as the necessary carrier scouting squadrons, and directed the *Lexington*, the destroyer tender *Rigel* (AD-13), and NAS San Diego "to make the necessary preparations."[32] ComAirBatFor ordered the squadrons—which would include three from the *Ranger*'s air group and one from the *Saratoga*'s—to prepare to embark in the *Lexington*, and orders went out recalling the units' officers and men from leave and liberty; when the *Lex* arrived in Coronado Roads during the forenoon watch on 4 July, tugs brought a lighter alongside with squadron people and baggage and three tons of spare parts and operating spares sufficient for a four-week cruise.

As an example of what had been required in the emergency mobilization over the holiday weekend, the *Ranger*'s VS-41 managed to muster 19 pilots and 71 men, by dint of

The *Lexington* (CV-2) underway in San Francisco Bay, 12 November 1936, as she essentially appeared at the time of the search for Amelia Earhart and Fred Noonan eight months later. (NA, 80-CF-21123-3)

"many telephone calls," to locate the members of the squadron from beaches to mountain lakes. The *Lexington*'s VS-2, "deeply involved in the process of moving to new office spaces and changing its name, with all the accompanying difficulties and new problems," found itself "blasted from the serenity of the usual squadron composure by the unexpected orders to report aboard [*sic*] the carrier with their planes."[33]

Soon thereafter, Capt. Jonathan S. "Dad" Dowell, Jr., Commander, Destroyer Squadron Two, a 55-year old Texan who had been known to his Academy classmates as "rugged and remarkably energetic" (as well as having once possessed and used a "varied vocabulary of cuss words"), embarked in the *Lexington*. He had spent the majority of his career in destroyers or battleships, or in ordnance duty, with a particular specialty in fire control.[34] He assumed command of the search group, which consisted of the carrier and the destroyers *Lamson* (DD-367) and *Drayton* (DD-366). Two additional destroyers, the *Cushing* (DD-376) and the *Perkins* (DD-377), sisterships to the *Lamson* and the *Drayton*, were to fuel and provision at San Pedro and join later. Soon after Dowell arrived to take command, accompanied by his radio officer, Lt. William L. Pryor, Jr., Chief Yeoman J. H. Cannon, and Mess Attendant 2d Class F. Roa, Paul Brook of the International News Service, his presence approved by the Bureau of Navigation, reported on board just as the *Lexington* got underway.

The *Lamson* and the *Drayton*, the latter sailing 40 men (chiefly seaman and fireman rates) short of her allowance because of the emergency nature of the departure, stood out of Coronado Roads one hour into the afternoon watch on 4 July, as did the *Lexington*. With the destroyers *Southard* (DD-207) and *Chandler* (DD-209) serving as plane guards, the *Lexington* recovered 9 BM-2s from VT-2 and 11 SBU-1s from VS-2 from her own air group, 9 SBU-1s from the *Saratoga*'s VS-3, and 14 SBU-1s from VS-41, 9 SU-4s from VS-42, and 10 BG-1s from VB-4 from the *Ranger*'s air group.[35] One O3U-3 from the *Lexington*'s utility unit rounded out the aircraft complement, which, for this search mission, included no fighters. "The mobilization of these units," wrote one observer later, "was considered well done, particularly in view of the fact that it occurred during a holiday period."[36]

Lieutenant (jg) Benjamin B. C. Lovett, flying 4-B-4, could not lower his tailhook and was directed to return to North Island for repairs, accompanied by Lt. (jg) Everett O. Rigsbee, Jr., in Four-Baker-Seven. After quick repairs, both returned in time to make the voyage. Lt. George L. Hutchinson, however, who had brought 4-B-5 out to the ship, became seriously ill with what proved to be a gastric ulcer; the *Lexington* recalled the *Chandler*, which had just been released from plane guard duty at 1530, 20 minutes later. Stopping her engines and maneuvering to create a lee, the carrier transferred the ailing officer to the destroyer's boat, so that he could be transported back to San Diego for treatment.

Another officer who had had medical attention at North Island a short time before was Lt. Donald A. Lovelace, VS-41's gunnery officer, who, to the delight of his daughter Sally and son Donald, Jr., had lit off some fireworks to celebrate the Fourth of July in their back yard on J Avenue in Coronado. One firecracker, however, had exploded prematurely in Lovelace's hand, splitting a finger and necessitating a trip to the dispensary. Apparently, the injury proved minor enough to not prohibit flying. "Daddy is searching for Amelia Earhart," his wife Helen told their children, while he was at sea in the *Lexington*.[37]

Earhart Search Group, *Lexington* (CV-2)

Squadron	Commanding Officer	No. of Planes	Type
VT-2	Lt. Comdr. William Sinton	9	BM-2
VS-2	Lt. Donald F. Smith	11	SBU-1
VS-3*	Lt. Comdr. Frederick W. McMahon	9	SBU-1
VS-41**	Lt. Comdr. Herbert W. Taylor, Jr.	14	SBU-1
VS-42**	Lt. John M. Hoskins	9	SU-4
VB-4**	Lt. Comdr. Paul E. Roswall	10	BG-1
Lexington Utility Unit	Lt. (jg) Lamar P. Carver	1	O3U-3

* *Saratoga* Squadron; ** *Ranger* Squadron

Lieutenant Donald A. Lovelace flew an SBU-1 in the VS-41 detachment deployed on board the *Lexington* during the Earhart search. He is pictured during what was most likely his 1939–40 tour at the Naval Aircraft Factory at Philadelphia. He would die in a tragic accident on board the *Yorktown* (CV-5) on 30 May 1942, on the eve of the Battle of Midway. (Comdr. Donald A. Lovelace, II, USN, Retired)

Severe vibrations in her port high pressure turbine, however, prevented the *Perkins* from being able to exceed 17 knots, so she received orders to proceed to San Diego for repairs. Although that resulted in the *Perkins* being deleted from the search group, the *Cushing* joined up about 10 miles south of China Point, three-quarters of an hour into the second dog watch, and the four ships set course for the Hawaiian Islands.

Arrangements having been made by dispatch, the *Lexington* proceeded directly to Lahaina Roads, where she anchored shortly before the end of the forenoon watch on 8 July, to await the arrival of the small seaplane tender *Avocet* (AVP-4) and the latter ship's cargo of 10,600 gallons of aviation gasoline and aircraft engine spares. The destroyers proceeded to Pearl Harbor, where they fueled and provisioned to capacity and took on, between them, seven tons of stores to be transferred to the *Lexington*. At Pearl, the short-handed *Drayton* received a draft of 20 seamen, 20 firemen, and one chief pharmacist's mate, courtesy of the Commandant of the 14th Naval District, to bring her complement up to strength.

The *Lexington* took on gasoline from the *Avocet* during the afternoon watch on 8 July, and, during the darkness of the mid watch on the 9th, her three escorts joined her at Lahaina. The oiler *Ramapo* (AO-12), recalled from a voyage to Guam, arrived at 0628 on the 9th and immediately began fueling the carrier; the destroyers began the task of transferring the stores they had brought from Pearl. Providing for a minor, but necessary (for morale purposes) item of business also took place at that time, when the *Lex* exchanged movie programs with the destroyers, the latter having sailed from the West Coast in such haste as to preclude that being done beforehand and none having been available at Pearl Harbor. At the same time, two more Bureau of Navigation-approved newsmen, Earl M. Welty of the Associated Press and Charles Mounce of the United Press, embarked on board the carrier.

Planning conferences ensued on board the *Lexington*, as she continued fueling from the *Ramapo;* the destroyers got underway shortly before the end of the forenoon watch and one by one calibrated their radio direction finders to signals transmitted by the carrier. The *Lexington* completed fueling at 1456, having taken on board 903,784 gallons from the *Ramapo*. A little over a quarter of an hour later, at 1515, the big carrier got underway and set course for Howland Island, the last reported destination of Amelia Earhart and Fred Noonan, the destroyers in company.

As the *Lexington* and her consorts headed for Howland, Herb Taylor, Paul Roswall, and Johnnie Hoskins, and the commanders of the two *Lexington* squadrons and the sole *Saratoga* squadron, together with ships' officers, evaluated the information at hand. Together, they evolved a search plan to scout the open ocean stretching westward from Earhart and Noonan's destination, "a backtrack of the final corridor [they] would have flown to reach Howland from Lae."[38]

Lieutenant (later Lt. Comdr.) Paul E. Roswall, December 1927; he commanded VB-4's detachment based in the *Lexington* during the Earhart search. The father of two, he perished in an automobile accident at Coronado on 4 May 1938, soon after the squadron returned to the West Coast following Fleet Problem XIX. (NA, 80-G-465673)

At 0636 on 13 July, the *Lexington* reached 02°30′N latitude, 177°W longitude, the point of origin for search operations, having begun launching aircraft 20 minutes earlier. She put 60 planes aloft to begin searching for any sign of the Electra or its crew. The *Lexington*'s planes fanned out to the east and west, conducting their searches, although hampered by heavy rain squalls. "Although," as then-Lt. (jg) Francis D. Foley of VS-42 later recalled, "this was 11 days after Earhart and Noonan had been lost, there are many instances of people surviving at sea much longer than that." The lost fliers having provided for that eventuality fueled optimism about their chances of survival.[39] The first search, however, proved unsuccessful, with the last plane coming on board at 1018.

One landing mishap marred the morning's operations, when Aviation Cadet Walter A. Hibbs, USNR, of the *Lexington*'s VT-2, flying a BM-2 (BuNo 9170), with Aviation Machinist's Mate 3d Class E. M. Yonts on board, erred not only in his judgment of his fore-and-aft alignment, when he received the cut from Lt. Thurston B. Clark, the *Lexington*'s LSO, but also in correcting his alignment afterwards. Two-Tare-Thirteen ended up with its left wing overlapping the after port gun gallery, and required repairs to the damaged lower left wing and landing gear.[40]

The next search began a little over an hour into the afternoon watch, the *Lexington* putting aloft 27 planes in seven minutes, the departing aircrew accompanied, as one newsman wrote, by shouts of "bring back Amelia and Fred."[41] Bad flying conditions, however, resulted in a recall, and *Lexington* began recovering her brood about an hour later, between 1356 and 1411. What searching had been carried out had found Howland obscured by heavy rains. Despite the lack of success, the effort had been noteworthy. "It was quite impressive," Francis Foley later wrote, "to see aircraft stretched out at low altitude as far as the eye could see over the horizon." While each pilot searched toward the guide plane, the passenger in back would search the opposite direction, using binoculars.[42]

A half hour before the end of the morning watch on 14 July, with the *Lamson* steaming on the left flank, *Drayton* on the right, and the *Cushing* bringing up the rear as plane guard, the *Lexington* turned into the wind, her clipper bow cleaving the smooth sea, and began launching 42 planes. "In fierce equatorial heat," one newsman wrote, "fliers of the *Lexington* continued their increasingly hopeless search" for the Electra and its crew "missing twelve days on a world-girdling flight." The *Lexington* recovered the 42 planes an hour before the end of the forenoon watch; the returning aircrew reported "that they would [have] seen any wreckage or boat if such had been afloat."[43] Operating along the equator, an observer wrote, compelled the aviators to take special precautions against sunburn, "and the slightest shade was priceless on the unsheltered decks of the *Lexington*." Lessening the number of aircraft involved in the search, a reporter observed, "came as a relief to the *Lexington*'s mechanics, who had been working long hours under the hot equatorial sun to keep the air fleet in shape."[44]

Almost midway into the afternoon watch, the *Lexington* commenced flight operations anew, Captain Dowell noting that it was the first time that a U.S. Navy ship had operated in latitude 00°00′ and longitude 180° in recent memory. Rain squalls in the western portion of the search area compelled some of the planes assigned that sector to skirt them. After almost four hours, the afternoon search, 42-planes strong, returned, again empty handed. During the night, the *Lamson* and the *Cushing* exchanged places, with the *Lamson* becoming the plane guard for the next day. During that time, Dowell directed all ships to use their searchlights "for at least five minutes during each night watch."[45]

The *Lexington* utilized 41 aircraft on 15 July, beginning launch at 0719 with the *Cushing* and the *Drayton* steaming on the flanks. Recovering the planes at 1023, the carrier launched the afternoon flight at 1356, recovering them at 1636. Having encountered light rain squalls, the aircrew reported having no difficulty in seeing through them, and that, in their estimation, the search had been "satisfactory." During the dog watches, and the first and mid watches, the *Lexington* and her consorts maneuvered to take their places to commence the next day's work.

Those operations proved as unsuccessful as the previous ones had been. The *Lexington* began flight operations an hour before the end of the morning watch on the 16th, launching 40 planes to search north and south from the point of origin at 04°N, 178°E; she recovered her brood at

Lieutenant Thurston B. Clark, the *Lexington*'s LSO, seen here on 9 May 1937, an indispensable man in the process of bringing the searching planes back on board safely. (NA, 80-CF-54858-1)

Rex Hain's BG-1, 4-B-8, somewhat the worse for wear after encountering the *Lexington*'s Turret IV during the Earhart search, 17 July 1937. (AUTHOR)

1042. Launching the second search of the day, about an hour into the afternoon watch, the *Lexington* brought on board all aircraft a half hour into the first dog watch.

Three hours into the morning watch on the 17th, the *Lexington* began launching 41 planes, as she stood toward eastward from her point of origin, 01°00′N, 175°40′E. Soon thereafter, recovering two with mechanical difficulties, she began recovery operations for the remainder at 1012. Shortly, Rex Hain of VB-4, with Aviation Machinist's Mate 2d Class C. E. Pierce in back, made a normal approach, but came over the *Lexington*'s stern ramp "slightly fast." After seeing Lieutenant Clark bring a paddle across his throat, Hain nosed his BG-1 (BuNo 9508) down to ensure catching a wire. Unfortunately, 4-B-8's hook struck the deck about six feet forward of number two wire. Almost simultaneously, Hain's wheels came down upon wire number three with "considerable force." The Bouncing Girl again showed that the type had been aptly nicknamed, for the big biplane bounded three to four feet into the air and, slightly nose-high, "floated" forward.

Its tail hook having missed the number eight wire by two to three feet, Hain's plane charged up the deck. The BG-1's upper right wing collided with the *Lexington*'s after 8-inch turret, shearing off the wingtip and causing Four-Baker-Eight to slew around into the barrier. The abruptness with which the mishap unfolded clearly took the *Lexington*'s motion picture camera operator, who had not thought anything amiss until the "bounce" occurred, by surprise. Consequently, those who investigated the crash possessed no pictorial evidence of 4-B-8's first contact with the deck. The sailor manning number three wire declared that he had seen the tail hook hit the yielding element of that particular pendant, but no one else could either prove or disprove that man's version of events.

Four-Baker-Eight suffered class B damage to its engine, as well as to its landing gear (right wheel broken off at the lower end of the struts), engine cowling (its lower side smashed), propeller (one blade bent), bomb displacement gear (bent), oil radiator (punctured), wings (upper right wingtip sheared off outboard of the interplane struts, both lower right wing main spars bent, and the leading edge crushed), and fuselage (structure sprung out of alignment). Fortunately, neither Hain nor Pierce suffered any injuries, and recovery operations proceeded without further incident. The subsequent trouble board attributed the accident to a "peculiar combination of pilot error, signal officer error, [and the] characteristics of this type of airplane."[46]

A little under an hour into the afternoon watch on the 17th, the *Lexington*, still steaming eastward, began putting aloft 41 planes for the second search of the day. Her aircraft searched to the north and to the south, but, again finding nothing but open sea, landed on board an hour into the first dog watch. Dave Shumway of the *Ranger*'s VS-41, with Radioman 2d Class K. M. Bledsoe on board, landed slightly fast and low, which resulted in his not being able to raise the nose soon enough to prevent a bounce after catching the arrestor gear. Consequently, Shumway's SBU-1 (BuNo 9798) cracked the left oleo landing strut and blew the left tire.[47]

The *Lexington* and her consorts wound up search operations on the 18th, with the carrier launching both morning and afternoon flights that had, like those conducted on the previous days, come up empty-handed. With the recovery of the last plane at 1653 on the 18th, the Earhart search officially came to an end; three minutes later, the *Lexington* steadied on the Great Circle course for San Diego. The following day, midway through the second dog watch, in accordance with naval tradition, Capt. Leigh Noyes, commanding officer of the *Lexington*, welcomed "Davy Jones," emissary of King Neptune, and a boisterous "Neptune Party"—postponed by the exigencies of the urgent mission upon which she had been embarked—began. In the course of the rough-and-tumble festivities, six *Lexington* sailors suffered serious enough injuries to prompt them to report to sick bay the following day.[48]

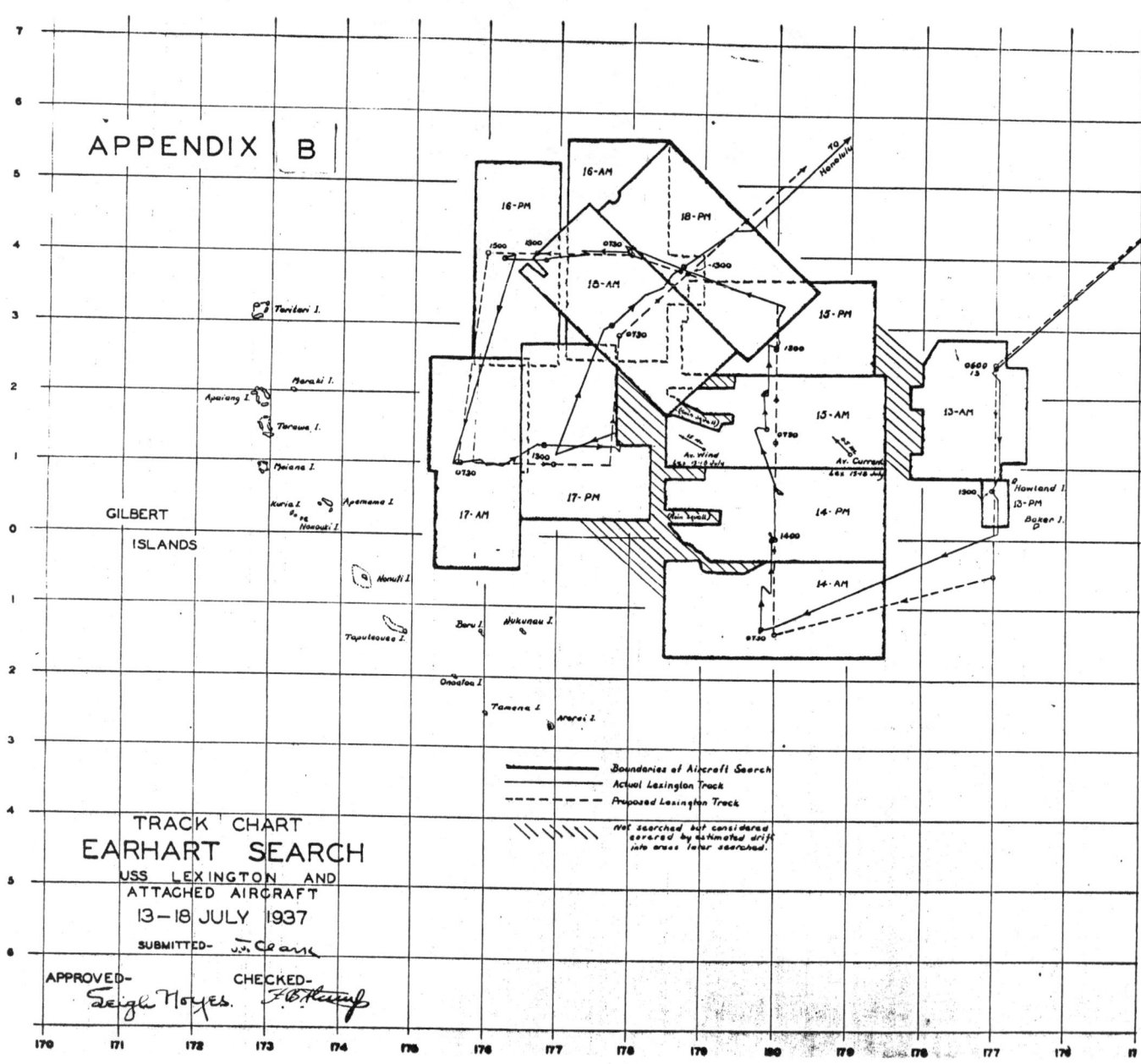

Track Chart of the Earhart search; heavy black lines indicate the boundaries of the aircraft searches from the *Lexington*, 13–18 July 1937. (Appendix B to Commander, *Lexington* Group to Commandant, Fourteenth Naval District, Subj: Report of Earhart Search, forwarding, 20 July 1937, AvH).

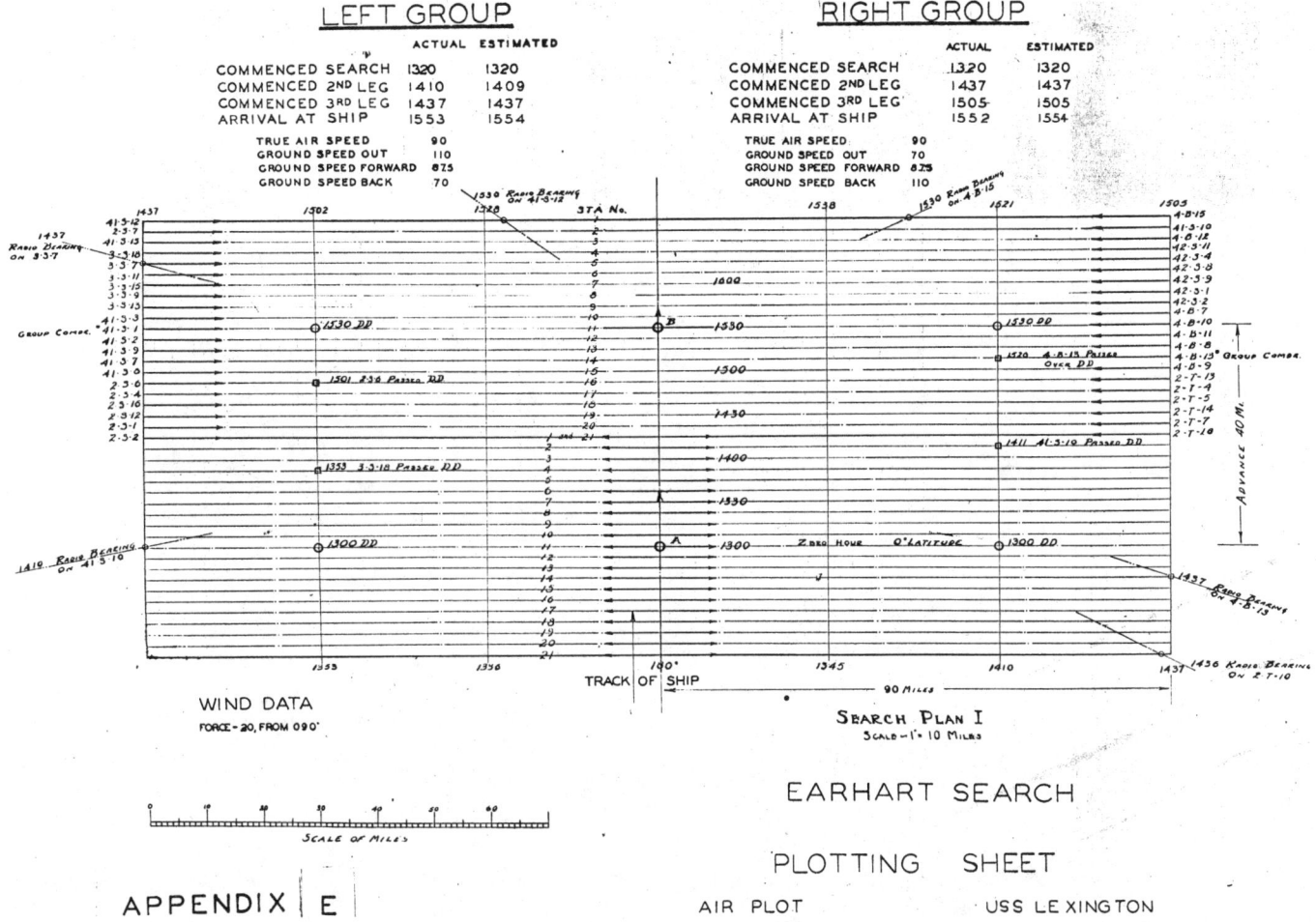

Plotting Sheet for the Earhart search; left group includes planes from the *Ranger*'s VS-41 and the *Lexington*'s VS-2 and the *Saratoga*'s VS-3; right group, the *Ranger*'s VB-4, VS-41, and VS-42, and the *Lexington*'s VT-2. (Appendix E to Commander, *Lexington* Group to Commandant, Fourteenth Naval District, Subj: Report of Earhart Search, forwarding, 20 July 1937, AvH).

Captain Dowell transferred his pennant to the *Lamson* at 1400 on 21 July, thus officially terminating the "*Lexington* Group." Consequently, the *Lexington* continued on to San Diego, and the three destroyers shaped a course for Pearl Harbor "for fuel, provisions, and voyage repairs." Despite the best efforts of all concerned, neither Amelia Earhart and Fred Noonan, nor their Lockheed Electra, were ever found.

"Although unfortunately the fate of the missing flyers remains a mystery," Captain Noyes later reported, "it is considered that the search made was efficient and that the areas covered were the most probable ones, based on the facts and information available."[49] As "Navy" Foley put it, the search had covered an area more than half the size of the state of Texas, to a density of a half-mile. The *Ranger*'s pilots and aircrew had helped search 151,556 miles, fly 143,242 miles, and amass 1,591 hours of flight time, in what the Associated Press representative in Honolulu called "the greatest mass rescue effort ever undertaken for a lost plane."

9

"AN EVERLASTING REMEMBRANCE OF ADMIRATION AND FRIENDSHIP"

At the same time that a large part of the *Ranger*'s air group had been at sea involved in the Earhart search, the remainder had continued its scheduled training. Four of VS-41's pilots had not yet qualified for carrier landings, so they had remained behind, with a like number of planes. "Very much irritated at not being able to come anywhere near the target" during dive-bombing practice, one pilot learned later that he had been diving upwind instead of downwind, and that "his allowances were therefore increasingly farther away."[1] One learned through experience.

Two VS-42 pilots and their passengers, however, experienced something not found in the syllabus. On the morning of 14 July, a Soviet RD 25-1 monoplane landed in a cow pasture near San Jacinto, California, after a 6,262-mile, 62 hour and 17 minute flight from Moscow. The transpolar flight had established a new record for distance and the media wrote approvingly of the modesty and friendliness of Mikhail Gromov (pilot), Andrei Yamashev (copilot) and Sergei Danilin (navigator), the RD 25-1's three-man crew.[2]

Hundreds of people of all ages thronged to the farm, from far and near, to see the big red monoplane: among them was Aviation Cadet Horace F. Amrine, USNR, of VS-42, flying a familiarization hop on the morning of 16 July, in a Vought SU-4 (BuNo 9419), with Aviation Cadet Frederick H. Spear, USNR as his passenger. After dragging over the area twice at an altitude of about 40 feet, Amrine landed, at 1050, in the pasture adjacent to the field where the RD 25-1 sat. He had done so, however, without permission, and his joyride onto an unauthorized field had its consequence: his Vought suffered a blown left tire and the left wheel rim tore loose from the axle.[3]

Later that day, VS-42's acting commanding officer (Lieutenant Hoskins being at sea in the *Lexington* on the Earhart search) detailed Lt. (jg) Clifford M. Campbell to fly to San Jacinto with a spare wheel and tire for the crashed SU-4. He was to "carefully examine the field in which the SU-4 crashed," to see "whether or not a safe landing and take off could be made." Consequently, with Aviation Machinist's Mate 1st Class F. E. Kelly on board in a Vought SBU-1 (BuNo 9770), Campbell took off for his destination, which lay about 66 miles from North Island. If the field looked unsuitable, he was to fly to the Army Air Corps' March Field and "endeavor to arrange for transportation by Army truck" for the material he was carrying for the damaged SU-4.[4]

Campbell prudently reconnoitered the field from an altitude of 10 feet and deemed it suitable for a landing. As the SBU-1 rolled about 300 feet after touching down, however, the terrain grew rougher and the ride more jarring. Finally, the wheels encountered a sharp bump. The right landing gear crumpled beneath the plane, the right wing tip scraped the ground and the Vought ground-looped, coming to rest on the left wheel, tail wheel, and right wingtip, after having turned completely around to face the direction from whence it had come. Campbell's plane suffered damage to the landing gear (ironically including a blown tire—the reason the flight had been undertaken in the first place), the

![Soviet RD 25-1 monoplane]

Soviet RD 25-1 monoplane at San Jacinto, California, 14 July 1937, the irresistible tourist attraction for a young *Ranger* aviation cadet two days later. (NA, 80-G-464645)

fuselage, and the wings. Disciplinary action in the wake of the damage to two of the squadron's planes swiftly followed for Aviation Cadet Amrine.

The main mission of an aircraft carrier revolved around her planes, but gunnery also assumed proper place in the training year, with healthy competition between the ships within the type command. The *Ranger*'s 5-inch/25-caliber batteries outshot the *Lexington* and *Saratoga* in SRBP earning a merit of 61.467 (the *Lexington* achieved 47.400 and the *Saratoga* 32.533). The *Ranger*'s gunners developed an excellent rate of hitting—12.16 hits per gun per minute—achieving 51 hits out of 68 shots. More important, however, during the 1936–37 gunnery year, although the performance of the gunnery drills fired by the Battle Force's carriers had been "generally satisfactory," the *Ranger* continued to "contribute effective performance and constructive develop-

ments to progress in antiaircraft control." The Experimental D Practice, which she had fired during the year, "contributed much to [the] development of [the] use of 5-inch/25-caliber batteries against dive bombers." The ensuing report of the exercise, deemed "unusually complete," expeditiously prepared, went out to all antiaircraft gunnery schools.[5]

Lieutenant Commander Timothy J. O'Brien, USNA 1921-A, who held a master's degree in aerology from Harvard and the Massachusetts Institute of Technology, headed the *Ranger*'s gunnery department. He concluded that the 5-inch/25-caliber battery, and its associated fire control equipment, possessed great potential for repelling a horizontal bombing attack, the *Ranger*'s experience proving that "our equipment if properly operated can be counted upon to obtain hits sometime before the plane can reach correct bomb-release position."[6]

Sharing the pier at North Island with the *Langley*, showing to advantage the sizes of the two ships, the *Langley* (by this point a seaplane tender) having been the U.S. Navy's first aircraft carrier and the *Ranger* the first carrier built as such from the keel-up. (NHC, NH 91368)

The first few bursts from the *Ranger*'s port battery inevitably shot down the target; on one occasion, the first shell burst at the mouth of the sleeve. O'Brien attributed the noteworthy results to (1) the excellent stereoscopic range-finders and the Mk. 10 range-keeper, (2) the *Ranger*'s method of ripple fire, (3) the practice of frequently holding tracking drills while in port, when the opportunity offered, using ship's planes to make regular runs, and (4) to the *Ranger*'s "care and attention...to accurate and frequent determinations of data" for computations of "ballistic wind and ballistic density."[7]

O'Brien, on the strength of his aerological experience (he had come to the *Ranger* from heading BuAer's Aerological Section), posited that "all ships recognize the importance of accurate determinations of ballistic wind" for antiaircraft firings. Neglecting that important factor, he wrote, could greatly reduce the chance of hitting the target in the initial bursts, reflecting the opinion of the *Ranger*'s antiaircraft control officer, Lt. Eugene F. May, who insisted that "we must concentrate on hitting with initial salvoes."[8] Thanks to the work of O'Brien and his department, the *Ranger* again received the D.A.R. Trophy for Antiaircraft Gunnery for the 1936–37 gunnery year, with O'Brien receiving a commendation for his work.[9]

The *Ranger* had performed well in night battle practice, too. Lieutenant Commander O'Brien, who had been chiefly assisted by Ens. Marion F. Ramirez de Arellano and Firecontrolman 3d Class R. Pevahouse, had good reason to be proud of his men. The 5-inch/25-caliber battery scored 22 hits on the battle raft target, 15 of which were on the lower half of the target; investigation revealed 6 green hits (the first third of the target projectiles had been painted green), 4 on the lower half of the target and 2 on the upper, indicating that the *Ranger*'s gunners had established hits early, without a casualty or without missing a firing buzzer. Even so, while he had been in command, Captain Bellinger had commented that the *Ranger*'s maneuvering ability constituted her best defense against attacks by enemy destroyers, positing that his ship should "avoid becoming involved in a night melee if possible since her lack of protective armor" rendered her "susceptible to destruction in a torpedo attack." That being the case, Bellinger had believed that "'Remain darkened, turn and run' appear[ed] to be the best doctrine for *Ranger* in a night torpedo attack." He had also considered the ship's 5-inch/25-caliber battery as an "effective weapon against enemy destroyers as demonstrated by rapidity with which hitting was established, volume of fire, and number of hits obtained" during night battle practice.[10]

As the month of July 1937 drew to a close, the *Ranger* conducted qualification landings for *Lexington* and *Saratoga* Air Group pilots. On Monday, the 26th, Lt. (jg) Charles F. Garrison, of VB-2, brought in his F4B-4 (BuNo 9253) for his second carrier landing. All proceeded well during the approach, and Garrison closed the throttle at the LSO's "cut" signal. Unaccustomed to carrier landings, however, Garrison felt that he was coming in high and slow, so he nosed the Boeing over to increase speed and reduce altitude. The F4B's right wing dropped and the plane hit the deck, right wheel first, at the same time that the tail hook engaged. The combination of factors caused the fighter to further nose up, with one propeller blade striking the deck. The trouble board called the "immediate cause... poor technique due to total lack of experience."[11]

Lieutenant (jg) James O. Cobb, from the *Saratoga*'s VB-3, made a proper approach in his Curtiss BFC-2 (BuNo 9332), but, after taking the LSO's cut, landed in a slightly nose-down attitude, the BFC-2 hitting the deck wheels-first, then bounced with the hook engaged. BuNo 9332 blew its right tire, bending the wheel when it hit the deck. Lieutenant (jg) Joseph B. H. Young made a normal approach, as his squadronmate had done, and, like Cobb, had landed in a slightly nose-down attitude. Joe Young's BFC-2 (BuNo 9333) blew a tire, bent a wheel, and suffered a damaged left landing gear.[12]

Three other *Saratoga* pilots likewise experienced difficulty on board the *Ranger* that day, perhaps unaccustomed to her smaller flight deck. Lieutenant Commander Marion E. Crist, commanding VT-3, made a normal approach, but, after receiving the cut from the LSO, believed that he had come in too high and attempted to compensate. His TG-2 (BuNo 8725) landed wheel-first and bounced, buckling both right upper K struts and the right jury strut. Later, Naval Aviation Pilot J. W. Haas, one of VT-3's enlisted pilots, like his commanding officer, mistakenly believed that he had come in too high, and nosed up. Haas's TG-2 (BuNo 8715) suffered identical damage to Lieutenant Commander Crist's, in addition to several rivets being sheared off in the vicinity of the forward K strut fuselage fitting and cracking the rear K strut fitting.[13]

Lieutenant Commander Irving D. Wiltsie, of VB-3, however, experienced the worst day of anyone. Upon receiving the LSO's cut, he nosed his BFC-2 (BuNo 9274) over slightly, to catch a wire. Unfortunately, he landed wheels-first, causing the Curtiss to nose up, damaging the propeller. Taking off later in another BFC-2 (BuNo 9338), Wiltsie again made a normal approach, but, when the *Ranger*'s LSO gave him the cut, the Curtiss was slightly high. Wiltsie obeyed the signal, but the BFC-2 nosed over abruptly; he waited too long to pull the stick back, resulting in BuNo 9338's hitting the deck wheels-first near number three wire. The BFC-2 then bounced without the hook engaging a wire, floating over the other pendants, following an almost undeviating course up the deck. Finally, the plane hit the barrier and somersaulted onto its back, damaging the upper wing, rudders, elevators, lower right wing, the landing gear, strut cowling, ring cowling, windshield, and propeller blades and hub, and sustaining indeterminate engine damage. Wiltsie, once extracted from the plane, limped away with a ruptured muscle in his left calf.[14]

The next day, 27 July, the *Ranger* again hosted the Marines, as she conducted carrier qualifications for the San Diego-based Marine Aircraft Group Two (VMF-2, VMS-2, and VMB-2). VMB-2's BG-1s, like the Navy's, continued to live up to the type's nickname. After having flown predominantly fighters over the previous year, 1st Lt. William K. Pottinger, USMC, brought in BuNo 9510, but nosed over too sharply, upon getting the LSO's "cut" signal. Landing wheels-first, the BG-1 bounced. Pottinger tried to hold the Bouncing Girl's nose up, but, in so doing, caused the big biplane to float over all of the cross-deck pendants and crash into the barrier, damaging the landing gear, brake rods, fairing assembly brackets, engine mount, lower right longeron, cylinder, and propeller shaft.[15]

Soon thereafter, 2d Lt. Michael Sampas, USMC, of VMB-2, made a normal approach to the ramp, as he wound up a qualification hop, answering all of the LSO's signals. When he received the cut, Sampas nosed his BG-1 (BuNo 9538) over slightly, but brought up the nose in time to make what observers thought looked like a perfect three-point landing, but BuNo 9538 bounced after catching the wire and came down with enough force to allow the propeller tips to hit the deck, damaging one tip and bending the other.[16]

A trouble board apportioned part (50%) of the blame for Pottinger's accident on his "poor technique," but it also believed that "the failure of the engine to throttle down completely" contributed to "keeping the plane in the air after the bounce." Had the engine idled properly, the board said, "the plane might have settled back into the restraining gear in time to avoid the barrier crash." Additionally, however, the board also believed that the design of the BG-1 landing gear contributed to the accident because that type was "conducive to excessive bouncing." With a "normal type of landing gear," BuNo 9510 "probably would not have bounced high enough to clear all the wires of the restraining gear." Although the board likewise faulted Sampas for poor technique (75%), the LSO testified to the pilot's making a normal approach and landing. In his estimation, the accident had been caused by "the inherent characteristics of the BG-1 airplane."[17]

The next day, after Lt. (jg) John N. Ogle of VS-42 had made a hard landing in an SBU-1 (BuNo 9764), which resulted in a collapsed tail wheel, the pilots of Bombing 4 found that their BG-1s were just as susceptible to landing accidents as the marines had found the day before. At 1330, Aviation Cadet Keith F. Schader, with Aviation Machinist's Mate 1st Class C. R. Palmer on board, was making his second landing in his carrier refresher operations. The LSO adjudged his approach as "normal" and purposely brought Schader on board "slightly high and slow" over the ramp.

Seeing the LSO signal "cut," Schader cut the throttle, but landed slightly wheels-first, between number two and three wires. The plane bounced, however, without catching a wire, prompting Schader to ease forward on the stick to try to get into the gear. His attempt to catch one of the cross-deck pendants, however, failed, and the BG-1 broke the barrier cables and nosed over as it did so, sliding up the deck some 30 to 40 feet, bending the propeller and smashing the lower part of the engine cowling. Soon thereafter, Aviation Cadet Robert I. Erickson, USNR, of VB-4, with Aviation Cadet Walter L. Meili, USNR, in back, made a normal approach and answered the LSO's signals. Like 2d Lt. Sampas the previous day, however, Erickson nosed the plane over slightly at the cut, but recovered in time to make a three-point landing. His BG-1 (BuNo 9507), however, bounced, as the others had done, the propeller striking the deck, one tip being nicked and bent when it most likely struck a metal deck fitting. The trouble board assessed Aviation Cadet Schader's accident as 75% "personnel" and 25% "material" ("excessive bounce"), but it lay the entire blame for Erickson's as 100% "excessive bounce."[18]

The following day proved a breeze by comparison to the three previous ones. During the afternoon watch, Lt. (jg) Burden R. Hastings brought in his BM-1 (BuNo 8879) for a refresher landing, with Aviation Machinists's Mate 3d Class C. E. McGeorge in the after cockpit. BuNo 8879 had been used for a total of eight landings that day and the day before, and had, each time, been assessed by inspection crews as possessing no structural defects; it had been used for 36 landings since its last overhaul. Hastings's mount suffered damage to two upper longerons, and the skin of the fuselage aft of the rear cockpit buckled. Because the trouble board found no fault with Hastings' technique, it fixed the cause of the accident as 100% materiel.[19]

The accidents that had occurred on board the *Ranger* during the last week of July 1937 had resulted in no human casualties, but, a few days later, during carrier landing practice on 3 August, *Ranger* men topside, in a position to do so, witnessed an event that "gave all hands the most unpleasant thrills."[20] Lieutenant (jg) Louis J. Kirn, of the *Saratoga*'s VT-3, flying a Great Lakes TG-2 (BuNo 8713), with Aviation Machinist's Mate J. Buehlman and Aviation Machinist's Mate 3d Class J. W. Bamber on board, saw the LSO's "low" signal, then "come on." Kirn correctly interpreted them, but, as he neared the ship, he tried to center his plane in the groove, by banking into a slight left turn. The LSO gave him the cut, but Kirn was still heading slightly to port, a condition that could, ordinarily, be corrected with little trouble. The turbulent air over the wake of the ship, caused by the *Ranger*'s ramp, prevented Kirn from straightening out. He continued banking the TG-2 to port and crossed over the side of the flight deck. After the plane's right wing hit the deck, the TG-2 slowed and veered back to the right, before the nose hit the side of the ship, and the aircraft dropped into the water on its back, tail first.

Kirn fought for his life against the torrent rushing into the open cockpit; experiencing "considerable difficulty" in extricating himself from his predicament, he did not pull the flotation toggle. The automatic gear failed to function properly (although a subsequent check of the records showed that a routine test of the flotation gear in March had been made and reported satisfactory), most likely because the impact of the crash had either jammed the bag doors or buckled lines. In any event, the TG-2 sank in less than a minute, nearly entombing Kirn, who, utilizing the determination that had enabled him to become a standout football player during his time at the Naval Academy, finally managed to exit the foundering plane. Neither Buehlman nor Bamber, Kirn's crewmen, experienced any trouble swimming free. The plane guard destroyer *Smith* (DD-378) promptly lowered her motor whaleboat and, in "expeditious" and "commendable" manner, picked up all three men. Kirn had suffered contusions of his chest and inhaled a good deal of water.

Dangers of other kinds lay in wait for carrier pilots aloft. The *Ranger*'s embarked fighting squadron, VF-4, was operating out of South Miramar Field, San Diego, during the third week of August 1937, conducting dive-bombing practice. On the morning of the 18th, Aviation Cadet Vincent F. Casey, USNR, flying an F3F-1 (BuNo 0220), 4-F-12, in the third position of a five-plane formation, pulled up abruptly in the path of Aviation Cadet George D. Gibson, USNR, who was flying another F3F-1 (BuNo 0236), 4-F-16, in the number four position. The two Grummans collided, Casey's plane suffering a damaged left stabilizer and strut, vertical stabilizer, rudder, and tail hook housing, and Gibson's, the upper right wingtip panel. Fortunately, both pilots managed to land safely and no injuries resulted. A trouble board faulted Casey, remarking that his action of "pulling up sharply while flying in a formation was... not only unnecessary under the existing circumstances in avoiding a collision with the plane ahead but also a violation of a fundamental principle of formation flying."[21]

Formation flying figured in a mishap the next day. Aviation Cadet William W. Moss of VB-4, flying a BG-1 (BuNo 9511), with Aviation Machinist's Mate 3d Class R. B. Collins in back, was flying the number three position in a section landing at Los Angeles Municipal Airport, on the afternoon of 19 August. He closed his throttle just before landing, but the engine's not idling properly forced him to overrun his leader. Maneuvering to stay clear, Moss diverted his attention from the actual landing long enough to stall out several feet above the ground. The left lower wingtip struck the ground upon landing, and, although neither Moss or Collins suffered any injuries, the rear spar of the left lower wing was buckled out of alignment (class C damage). A trouble board faulted the aviation cadet's "poor technique" as the cause of the accident.[22]

Providence had obviously smiled on the two VF-4 pilots involved in the aerial collision on the 18th, and it did likewise a week later, concerning a pilot and an enlisted man from VS-42 and a Marine pilot from VMF-2. Shortly before noon on 25 August, Lt. (jg) William C. Fortune of VS-42, flying an SBU-1 (BuNo 9765), prepared to put his training to good effect for the camera gun official firing. Radioman 3d Class John R. McDaniel, Fortune's radioman-gunner, had fired his string of shots for the record, at the target airplane, a Grumman F3F-1 (BuNo 0251) from VMF-2; Fortune wanted to score fixed gun hits during the allotted time limit. Captain Lawson H. M. Sanderson, USMC, pilot of the F3F, reached a position ahead and above Fortune's SBU, then did a wing-over and instituted a head-on diving approach directly at the navy scout bomber. Fortune brought his sights to bear on Sanderson's Grumman and took some pictures with his camera gun. When about 100 yards away from the Vought, Captain Sanderson, seeing a collision imminent, pulled up to clear it. Almost simultaneously, Fortune, worried as he saw the same situation unfolding, pulled up sharply to the right.[23]

Sanderson's F3F, however, squashed into the left wing of Fortune's SBU as it flew in a steep right bank. The left wing of Sanderson's plane struck the left wing of Fortune's, tearing it off at the fuselage. John McDaniel, facing to the rear, heard the crash, looked to the left and saw fabric floating by, before the SBU whipped into a left roll, throwing him out of the cockpit. Tethered by his safety belt, however, McDaniel, realizing that a crash had occurred, undid the belt, and dropped free.

Fortune, meanwhile, instinctively fought to free himself from his mortally wounded aircraft. He pulled open his safety belt, kicked out, struck a part of the plane, then, upside down, dropped free. Jerked abruptly right-side-up by his parachute popping open, Fortune saw two other parachutes and breathed a sigh of relief because that meant that his passenger and the pilot of the other plane had gotten free, too. Captain Sanderson had bailed out of his crippled Grumman, which crashed in a full dive near the southwest corner of Rancho Santa Fe; Fortune's SBU crashed about two miles away, four miles east of Cardiff. Sanderson suffered slight scratches on his face, hands, and ankles, in the landing; Fortune sprained his left knee in his landing and received small scratches on his legs and hands, but nothing that warranted hospitalization. Freeing himself of his parachute, he looked for his radioman.

Although McDaniel had drawn up his legs to cushion the impact of the landing, his oscillating parachute threw him toward the bank of a steep ravine. He straightened his legs, trying to keep his head from hitting the bank, but in so doing fractured his left hip as he hit the ground. Raising himself up, he rolled over and winced in pain. He signalled to the other planes in the air that he was all right; as Fortune scrambled down to the side of Escondido Creek and shouted to his radioman, McDaniel responded that his leg had been hurt in the landing. Fortune had indeed been aptly surnamed, for the result of the aerial collision in which he had been involved could have been a lot worse. All three men involved lived to fly another day.

Having been selected for another diplomatic mission to South American waters, the *Ranger* wound up carrier qualifications on the eve of her departure. On 3 September, Lt. (jg) Murray Hanson made a normal landing in 42-S-14, but came out of the gear too fast and had to apply his brakes to avoid fouling the plane ahead of him. His SBU-1 (BuNo 9763) nosed up, damaging both propeller blades. Soon thereafter, Lt. (jg) Howard T. E. Anderson brought in 42-S-2, in his third qualification landing of the day, but apparently neglected to lock his hook in the down position, as he had the previous two occasions. His SBU-1 (BuNo 9798) consequently landed between wires number three and four, but his hook hit the deck and bounced into the housed position. The Vought continued on down the deck and ended up in the barrier, with damage to the left lower wing, both flaps, propeller, cowling, exhaust stacks, and bomb displacement gear. Ensuing trouble boards wrote off Hanson's mishap as caused by "poor judgment," Anderson's, by "carelessness."[24]

Subsequently, air group embarked and, "fully provisioned, fuel tanks and gasoline tanks filled to capacity," the *Ranger*, accompanied by the destroyers *Worden* (DD-352) and *Hull* (DD-350), cleared San Diego on 4 September for Callao, Peru. The cruise had been authorized in response to the Peruvian government's request that the United States send aircraft to participate in the erection of a monument in Lima to the Peruvian aviator Jorge Chavez. Unofficially, "scuttlebutt" hinted that the *Ranger*'s presence would offset Italian propaganda activities in South America, for a crack Italian aerial demonstration team was to participate as well. Because the ship needed to make the trip to Peru and back without refueling, the *Ranger* needed to conserve fuel, conducting only such flight operations "in which conditions were such that it did not require the ship to run off its course for any great distance."²⁵

Even a paucity of flight operations, however, did not guarantee smooth ones. On 7 September, Aviation Cadet Amrine (of the unauthorized landing in the cow pasture near San Jacinto in July) attempted his first landing on a carrier deck in an SBU-1 (BuNo 9759). As Amrine entered the groove, Lt. Edward A. Hannegan, the LSO, gave him a "roger," followed soon thereafter by a "fast" signal. Easing back on the throttle, Amrine saw Hannegan signal "roger." A "low–dip" signal prompted the aviation cadet to pull the nose of 42-S-9 up slightly. Hannegan signalled "cut."²⁶

Amrine, however, who had last landed a plane (an SU-4) on a carrier deck on 21 May, felt that the Vought was slightly high and fast, so he compensated by easing back on the stick, trying to stall the SBU on deck, to reduce his excess speed. Unfortunately, 42-S-9 levelled off at about two feet over the deck, flew over the arresting wires without engaging any of them, and fouled number one barrier, for the first flight mishap of the cruise.

On Sunday morning, 12 September, the *Ranger* crossed the equator and launched her entire air group, as well as the ship's utility unit, to allow as many men as possible the opportunity to fly over the line. As a result, the ship's entire complement of willow-green-tailed aircraft would be decorated with a black "flying turtle" insignia, to denote their having been across the equator.

Because the flight operations of the previous day had prevented the colorful rites that usually accompanied a line-crossing, Captain McCain welcomed Neptunus Rex, portrayed by Chief Electrician's Mate Terry W. Mize of the ship's "E" Division (who had portrayed "Davy Jones" in the *Ranger*'s first Neptune Party) and his party for the traditional initiation ceremonies on the 13th, about an hour into the forenoon watch. With the Royal Court drawn up majestically before him on

Captain John S. McCain turns the ship over to "Neptunus Rex," who is portrayed by Chief Electrician's Mate Terry W. Mize, 12 September 1937. Commander Montgomery, the exec, looks on (R). (NA, 80-CF file)

Ship's company, embarked air group, and passengers all participated in crossing-the-line observances: 1st Lt. Nathan Bedford Forrest, Air Corps, U.S. Army, a passenger, and Comdr. John W. Vann, MC, the *Ranger*'s senior medical officer, stand on the flight deck awaiting the next step of the ceremonies, 12 September 1937; behind them stands the "Pollywog Honor Guard." Forrest (USMA 1928) would ultimately attain the rank of brigadier general. He would be the first U.S. general to die in combat, killed in action when the B-17 Flying Fortress in which he was riding as an observer was shot down over Kiel, Germany, on 13 June 1943. (NA, 80-CF file)

his flight deck, McCain declared: "Your gracious majesty, the ship is yours today." Looking up to the signal bridge, he ordered: "Break Neptune's flag," and the "Jolly Roger" soon streamed from the *Ranger*'s port yardarm.[27]

"Much to the surprise of those who had not crossed the equator in the immediate vicinity of this particular longitude," one *Ranger* sailor later wrote, "the weather was far from what might be expected of an equator crossing," overcast and cold, with a mean temperature of 70°F. The weather dictated Captain McCain's authorizing the shift in uniforms from whites to blues, which would be worn until well after the ship crossed the line on her northbound course.

The next morning, when shipboard routine returned to normal and the new shellbacks gingerly adjusted to their transformation from pollywogs, Aviation Cadet Lane A. Hurst, USNR, took off in an SBU-1 (BuNo 9777), 42-S-11, for a tactics hop, during the forenoon watch, with Radioman 3d Class Charles J. Herriot on board. At the completion of the flight, Hurst made a gradual turn into the groove, about 200 yards astern of the ship. After the usual succession of signals from Lieutenant Hannegan, all of which Hurst answered properly, Hannegan gave Hurst a vigorous "come on" as he neared the ramp, at which the pilot "gave the engine a sharp burst of gun." The LSO signalled "cut," and Hurst responded properly and started the landing.[28]

"I saw that I would get down all right," Hurst later wrote, "but that I was still to the left of the centerline of the deck and crabbing still more to the left." Too low to attempt to get back to the centerline, the pilot put 42-S-11 "about astraddle of the broad yellow fore and aft line on the port side." BuNo 4777 slowed down as its hook caught the number four wire. Under normal circumstances, the plane's catching the wire should have resulted in a safe landing, but, after a run of between 30 and 35 feet, its tailhook broke clear and the unbridled Vought kept going, over the side of

With lines attached to Aviation Cadet Lane Hurst's Vought SBU-1 (BuNo 9777), a 26-foot motor whaleboat prepares to bring the downed plane, its flotation gear deployed, alongside for salvage, 14 September 1937. (NA, 80-CF-5494-14)

the ship, almost in slow motion, and splashed alongside in a left slip attitude, nose slightly downward. The plane submerged briefly before the flotation gear deployed and brought it to the surface. The SBU received further damage to the upper part of its fuselage as the *Ranger* stopped and hoisted it on board.[29]

Aviation Cadet Hurst suffered a contusion on the left side of his forehead, an abrasion on his left forearm, a sprained right thumb, and a cut finger; Herriot had only a slight scratch on his left thigh. Crash investigators apportioned 100% blame to "arresting appliance on aircraft," with the tail hook having broken off in mid-weld. "Had the hook not failed," Hannegan later observed, "the plane would have arrested normally."[30]

The *Ranger* and her two consorts reached their destination on the afternoon of the 15th, and the usual rounds of calls and entertainments proceeded apace, with officers and officials abounding. The American colony tendered the ship a reception at the Lima Country Club that evening, and, as one observer in the *Ranger* wrote later, "From then on during the entire stay at Callao, the days and evenings were filled with cocktail parties, dinners, receptions and balls. Every form of uniform in the book, with the exception of whites, was in vogue at one time or another."[31]

U.S. Ambassador to Peru Laurence A. Steinhardt visited the ship on the morning of the 17th. Steinhardt, a lawyer by profession, had performed particularly valuable service in the successful efforts to secure the nomination of Franklin Roosevelt to be the Democratic Party's presidential candidate in 1932, and had been on the finance and executive committees during the campaign that eventually saw Roosevelt victorious in the 1932 election. Subsequently appointed U.S. Minister to Sweden, Steinhardt served two years in that post before being given the ambassadorship to Peru.

The *Ranger* Air Group over Lima, Peru, 17 September 1937; VF-4 flies at center (top), over VB-4's BG-1s; VS-41's and VS-42's SBU-1s fly on the flanks. (NA, 80-CF file, "Peru," Box 125)

Later that same day, The *Ranger* got underway to launch her air group to take part in an aerial parade over Lima, followed by a landing at Lima Tamba airport. One of the *Ranger*'s utility unit planes flew on ahead to the airport to keep the ship and incoming planes informed as to what weather conditions lay ahead.

"[The whole air group] launched under a 1,500 foot overcast," then-Aviation Cadet C. Addison Pound later recalled,

"joined up in a squadron 'diamond' parade formation and headed inland, some eight miles, to perform...over Lima Tamba airport. VB-4 had the 'point,' VS-41 and VS-42 on the 'wings' and VF-4 in the 'diamond.' By the time the group was nearing the airport, [Lt. Comdr. Wendell G.] 'Windy' Switzer [VF-4's commanding officer] was screaming that VF-4 was in the clouds and [Lt. Comdr. Paul E.] Roswall was scraping VB-4 in the trees. Unfortunately, the President's mounted guard was drawn up alongside the grass landing area and as the vertically 'compressed' air group passed over, the horses bolted...Nevertheless, somehow, the air group broke up under the...700 foot overcast and landed without a single casualty—what a show for the U.S. Navy!"[32]

During their brief period of operations at Lima, the *Ranger* Air Group came under the gaze of Ambassador Steinhardt, as well as of Peruvian ministers of navy, war, and air. The group received numerous compliments concerning not only the formation flight, but the manner in which the planes landed and parked on a "small and very dusty field" in less than 20 minutes, then took off again in less than 28.

U.S. Ambassador to Peru Laurence A. Steinhardt, Gen. Oscar R. Benavides, the President of Peru, Capt. McCain and Comdr. Montgomery, and an unidentified Peruvian military officer, Callao, 20 September 1937. (NA, 80-G-391537)

Hearing how the Peruvians had praised the air group's performance, one *Ranger* scribe wondered "what these same observers might think could they see the normal operations as conducted at North Island!"[33]

General Oscar R. Benavides, the President of Peru, who had ruled his country since 1933, visited the *Ranger* and called upon Captain McCain on the 20th. Three days later, the *Ranger* hosted delegates from the Aeronautical Conference, as she got underway and conducted flight operations off Callao, and her air group participated in the flyover to commemorate the dedication of the monument to the Peruvian aviator Jorge Chavez. The *Ranger's* aviators found the flying conditions even less favorable than before, with a lower ceiling than on the 17th, but performed their portion of the parade as planned.

After a reception given by Ambassador and Mrs. Steinhardt for all of the *Ranger*'s officers who were able to attend, the *Ranger* bid Peru adios on the morning of the 24th. "The presence of the USS *Ranger* in Peruvian waters and the brilliant aerial demonstration of its squadron [*sic*—air group] of planes," President Benavides later wrote to President Roosevelt, "have left in Peru an everlasting remembrance of admiration and friendship."[34]

The *Ranger*'s homeward voyage (the *Worden* and the *Hull*, which had been detached upon departing Peruvian waters to fuel, rejoined on 1 October) proceeded uneventfully until early in the afternoon watch on 2 October, when Lt. (jg) Robert L. Strickler's Grumman F3F-1 (BuNo 0222) skidded over the port side, upon landing, caught fire, and hung suspended between number four and six smokepipes. While Strick Strickler, "a man of strong character and generous impulses," scrambled free from 4-F-11, the *Ranger* went to fire quarters and stopped all engines, extinguishing the fire inside of eight minutes.

Coming back from a tactics hop, Lt. (jg) James M. Elliott, of VB-4, had reported that the engine of his BG-1

(BuNo 9502) had "sputtered and popped" shortly before he landed. Turning up the engine on deck revealed nothing other than a loss of rpms on each magneto at 1,200 rpm. Hearing no popping or sputtering, Elliott considered the engine performance satisfactory, and thus had no qualms about taking up that particular BG-1 for another tactics flight. Taking off again, with Radioman 2d Class M. T. Crowder on board, Elliott had gotten 20 minutes into the flight, when he heard the engine emitting "popping" noises and losing revolutions. Seeing Elliott signal for a deferred forced landing, the *Ranger* brought him back on board without incident. An examination of the engine revealed two small bits of nonmagnetic metal in the main sumps; they were forwarded to NAS San Diego for evaluation.[35]

Two days later, one day out of San Diego, one hour before the end of the afternoon watch, Aviation Cadet Calvin Dyer, USNR, flying an SBU-1 (BuNo 9804), attempted his first bow landing. His approach, carried him somewhat to the right of deck centerline, approximately in line with the wide yellow stripe, but, as an observer noted dryly, he "did not appear to be exactly lined up with the deck."[36] To those watching the evolution, the attitude and speed of Dyer's SBU-1 seemed normal, but a bit too far to the right. Radioman 2d Class C. L. Evans, looking out of the left side of 41-S-8's after cockpit, "could see both wide yellow stripes on the deck [but] saw that we were going to land outside the arresting gear."[37]

As Evans braced himself, Dyer answered the cut promptly, but apparently hesitated in centering his plane on the deck and, consequently, BuNo 9804 touched down at an acute angle just beyond number three cross-deck pendant, forward, the left wheel hitting the deck hard and the right barely skimming a grating in the waterway along the port side of the flight deck. The SBU-1 then bounced over the 5-inch gun gallery; the left wheel struck the outboard lip of the waterway immediately aft of the gallery, collapsing the left landing gear strut. The tailhook engaged the elbow of a fire main riser and, thus having caught a much less moveable object than an arrestor cable, sheared off two feet from its end. After bending several lifeline stanchions along the gun gallery, the plane fell into the water, striking on its nose and right wing. The *Ranger* immediately released two Franklin life buoys. The impact with the sea, in the meantime, properly activated 41-S-8's flotation gear, but the left bag, punctured by an undetermined sharp object (possibly the left struts attached to the wheel) or subjected to too great a pressure, deflated precipitously. As Dyer and Evans swam for the life buoys, the right bag then blew out, too, and the SBU-1 sank irretrievably in 1,200 fathoms. The *Hull* quickly recovered Dyer, who suffered slight facial lacerations in the crash, and Evans, who had suffered a cut on his right arm, as well as scalp abrasions.[38]

Lieutenant Jules F. Schumacher, who had been attached to VB-4 for about three and a half months, after recently earning his wings, enjoyed a unique perspective on the crash. Standing on the forward end of the port machine gun platform, watching the bow landings near Lieutenant Hannegan, Schumacher, "for his own instruction was calling the landing signals" softly to himself. Four times he had said "wave off" to himself, when Hannegan had brought the planes in.[39] Planes had made safe landings in each instance, except Aviation Cadet Dyer's. Subsequently, the trouble board, after hearing Schumacher's testimony and evaluating the motion pictures, assessed the LSO 25% of the responsibility for Dyer's crash.

10

"THE OFFICERS AND MEN KNOW THEIR BUSINESS"

Reaching San Diego on 5 October, the *Ranger* operated locally into the last week of October. Underway for Puget Sound on 27 October, she arrived there on the last day of the month, to undergo various items of work, including the recaulking of her flight deck and the cleaning of her gasoline storage tanks, which, when opened, proved to be "remarkably clean... [with] very little corrosion evident."[1] Good weather allowed for the work on the flight deck to proceed rapidly. To allow that particular work to continue in inclement weather, yard cranes placed three large sheds over the deck, giving the *Ranger* the appearance of a covered wagon, from a distance.

Not only did the *Ranger* undergo yard work while at Bremerton, but she served as the arena for a strange battle in the wardroom. A rat had taken up residence in that particular compartment, behind the electric water cooler, where several members of the wardroom mess trapped him with brooms, transom pillows, and deck swabs. When none of those weapons could reach the furry intruder in his hiding place, one of the air department officers rushed to his stateroom. He soon returned with his dress sword and, using the thrust-and-parry method, flushed out the rodent, minus an inch or so of its tail, where he could be subdued with a broom handle. "Which is better for hand to hand combat," the *Bureau of Aeronautics Newsletter* asked, "sword or broom handle?"[2]

The *Ranger* remained in yard hands at Bremerton until 28 January 1938, when she sailed for San Diego. She anchored in Coronado Roads on 31 January, then shifted to the NAS pier at North Island the next morning. Her respite, however, proved brief, for she was soon underway on 2 February, sounding flight quarters off San Clemente Island, where she recovered VB-4, VF-4, and the group commander, for fleet tactics.

Within a week, she logged her first aircraft mishap of the new year, when 1st Lt. Joseph P. Fuchs, USMC, flying 2-MB-4, a Great Lakes BG-1, crashed over the side on 8 February, during carrier qualifications of Marine pilots. The plane guard destroyer *Truxtun* (DD-229), however, picked up Fuchs, and the *Ranger* recovered the aircraft. Later that day, she brought VS-41 and VS-42 on board for refresher and qualifying operations off San Pedro and San Diego, until 11 February.

The *Ranger* continued to operate locally until 15 March 1938, when she sailed for the Hawaiian Islands and participation in Fleet Problem XIX, the large-scale fleet maneuvers that would again take place in the northern Pacific between Alaska and the Hawaiian Islands. With the U.S. Fleet divided into various task forces, the *Ranger* took part in the 12-phase evolution that saw an attack on the fictitious White coast by the Black fleet. There were also phases devoted to attacking and defending the Hawaiian Islands, and attacking and defending the West Coast of the United States against an invader. Bad weather, restricted visibility, and fairly heavy seas, however, hampered much of the exercises, the operating conditions proving so bad on 26–28 March as to cancel operations entirely.

The *Ranger*'s lively tendencies made flight operations on 17 March memorable. An hour and a half into the morning

Captain McCain (R) accompanies Sen. David I. Walsh (Democrat-Massachusetts), Chairman of the Naval Affairs Committee (C), and Vice Adm. Horne (L), as they inspect the *Ranger*, 15 October 1937. (NA, 80-CF file)

watch, Lieutenant (jg) Fortune sat in the cockpit of his SBU-1 (BuNo 9783), with Radioman 3d Class W. A. Gmyr in back; the Vought had been spotted aft on the port side of the flight deck, with its left wing projecting well over the side. Through his controls, Fortune could feel unusually strong the wind over the deck; he maintained his rudder and ailerons in neutral, his tail wheel locked, and his stick well back. His plane captain and the chief of the repair crew had been holding onto the wings, but the former ducked down to release the chocks preparatory to Fortune's taxiing forward. When the *Ranger* heeled to starboard as she turned into the wind, the wind lifted 42-S-5 over onto its right

On a foggy day in Bremerton, the *Ranger* prepares to sail for San Diego, 28 January 1938, her flight deck showing the recent replanking job accomplished during her stay in the Puget Sound Navy Yard. The extent of the work shows clearly the wear and tear that can occur on a wooden flight deck over time. (AUTHOR)

As the *Ranger* rolls in the whitecap-flecked Pacific swells, 41-S-13, normally assigned to Lt. (jg) Francis D. Foley, passes over the bow ramp, 17 March 1938, during Fleet Problem XIX. Spotted along the starboard side of the flight deck are BG-1s from VB-4. (NA, 80-G-44503)

wing, and threw its tail surfaces into the rotating propeller of 42-S-7, parked astern, causing extensive damage to the rudder and both elevators. Captain McCain later supposed that the wing lines and chocks had been removed too soon.[3]

Aviation Cadet Thomas A. Jaeger, USNR, brought in 42-S-6 (BuNo 9805), after three hours in the air, at the start of the forenoon watch on 17 March, favoring the right side of the groove. Lieutenant Hannegan gave him the cut, but a gust of wind caught the SBU-1 and caused it to drift to starboard. Jaeger managed to catch the number four wire about five feet from the edge of the deck, and 42-S-6 had almost rolled to a stop at the edge of the deck, before the

Flight deck plane-pushers respot VB-4's BG-1s, 17 March 1938. (NA, 80-CF-54862-11)

starboard as Wagner's SBU-1 (BuNo 9781) came out of the gear, 42-S-16 rolled, too, its wings crushing and lacerating the tail surfaces of the previously damaged 42-S-6.

Lieutenant (jg) Charles B. Lanman of VS-41, with Radioman 2d Class E. Wilson on board, landed his SBU-1 (BuNo 9790), after a scouting flight, soon after Wagner's mishap, finding the *Ranger* "rolling and pitching heavily with a strong wind over the deck." Retrieving his hook, Lanman's 41-S-11 moved out the gear "smartly and at a moderate speed," as Lt. Charles L. Lee, in Fly I, watched what happened next.

"Just as I crossed the first barrier," Lanman later recounted, "the ship rolled to starboard and a gust of wind lifted my left wing, at the same time lifting the left wheel clear of the deck and the plane swerved to the right and headed for the island." Lanman tried to apply left aileron, but 41-S-11 continued to lumber ahead on its right wheel, "finally hitting the island with the tip of the upper right wing which swung the plane further to the right forcing the propeller against the island." Just before the SBU hit, the pilot cut the switch, but the prop continued to turn, hitting several glancing blows before stopping. Those who assessed the damage to Lanman's mount noted the right wingtip crushed to the aileron bracket, the right upper aileron crumpled, the lower right wingtip bent upwards, the bent propeller blades, the crimped engine mount struts and the crimped gasoline tank.[5]

Conditions did not improve for the night recoveries, with the *Ranger* rolling and pitching. Aviation Cadet Roger C. Santee, USNR, of VS-42, made a satisfactory approach, but came over the ramp with excessive speed, floating across the deck until he engaged number nine wire. With a run-out of 29 feet, Santee's SBU-1 (BuNo 9799) struck the barrier, damaging the propeller.[6] VS-41's SBU pilots had difficulties that night, too: Lt. (jg) George R. Luker, in BuNo 9759; Lt. (jg) Lemuel M. Stevens, Jr., in BuNo 9795; and Aviation Cadet James M. Leslie, in BuNo 9766.[7]

The *Ranger*'s friskiness came to the fore again the following morning, as the ship turned into the gusty wind to launch planes. Spotted first for a scouting flight, Lt. Comdr. Johnnie Hoskins, Scouting Forty-Two's skipper, saw the plane dispatcher give him the signal to launch, and removed his feet from the brakes. As he started 42-S-1 forward, however, the *Ranger* rolled to starboard, then, abruptly, to port. The Vought began to turn to the left at the first roll; Hoskins's putting on full left rudder, then the right brake on full, failed to arrest the Vought's altered course toward the port bow. Hoping to stop BuNo 9764 before it ran out of flight deck, Hoskins applied both brakes. When that did not work, he released the brakes and pushed the throttle full

Aviation Cadet Thomas A. Jaeger, USNR's SBU-1 (BuNo 9805), 42-S-6, "wings in a vertical position, wheels caught between the deck and the rail…tail at the edge of the deck" during flight operations during Fleet Problem XIX, 17 March 1938. A plane landing later veered into this one and demolished its rudder and elevators. Destroyer *Conyngham* (DD-371) is visible at upper left. (NA, VSBU-1/L11-1 files, Vol.11, RG-72, Box 5407)

two-to-three-degree roll of the ship, coupled with considerably pitching, disposed events. Forty-Two-Sail-Six lurched over the edge of the flight deck and came to rest on its right side, the wings vertical and the wheels caught between the deck and the rail, the upper right wingtip touching the stack below, and the tail just at the edge of the deck. Tom Jaeger and Radioman 3d Class C. R. Congdon scrambled out of the plane unhurt.[4]

The flight deck crew secured 42-S-6 in place and the *Ranger* continued recovering planes. Soon thereafter, Lt. Edwin O. Wagner, with Radioman 1st Class Glen A. Herndon on board in 42-S-16, made a normal landing, slightly to the right of the broad chrome yellow stripe on the centerline of the flight deck, catching the number four wire—the same one that Tom Jaeger had caught a short time before. The undesirable air and sea conditions, however, again exerted control. When the *Ranger* rolled deeply to

Vought SBU-1 (BuNo 9759), Forty-One-Sail-Five, normally assigned to Lt. (jg) George R. "Luke" Luker, 22 March 1938. Note bombing "E" on forward fuselage and the squadron's "walking duck on roller skates" insignia just below the pilot's cockpit. (NA, 80-G-391546)

Four-Fox-Three, a Grumman F3F-1 (BuNo 0235), normally assigned to Aviation Cadet George B. Randolph, USNR, 22 March 1938. The plane bears the "Boar's Head" insignia of VF-4 ("The Red Rippers"), and a maintenance "E" on the fuselage just below the cockpit windshield. (NA, 80-CF-54854-2)

forward, giving the SBU-1 enough speed to clear the port gun gallery and attain an almost horizontal attitude before it splashed alongside. The automatic flotation gear functioned as advertised and a boat from the *Conyngham* (DD-371) rescued Hoskins and Chief Radioman L. Stancell without injury. The *Ranger* subsequently recovered the plane intact, although it suffered from salt-water immersion.[8]

Later, after examining his tire tracks on deck, thinking that his left brake had failed to release, Hoskins eventually surmised that his tail wheel, which had been unlocked in accordance with current operating instructions, had rolled to starboard when the ship did so. He postulated that, after 42-S-1 had begun to turn to port, the right wings "received considerably more lift (due to wind over the deck) than did the left wings, thereby taking enough weight off the right wheel to prevent the braking power of that wheel from being effective." The trouble board subsequently considered Hoskins's explanation "most logical" and recommended that, in the future, tail wheels be locked prior to takeoff, to prevent a recurrence of the accident.

On 31 March 1938—the day after umpires had declared the *Ranger* "out of action" for the remainder of that phase of the exercises—Aviation Cadet Lane A. Hurst and Radioman 1st Class C. J. Mahoney rode 42-S-13 (the SBU normally assigned to Lt. David B. Overfield) into the water on the carrier's port quarter. The *Lamson* picked up the two men, with Hurst (who found himself in the water for the second time in a little over six months) suffering a lacerated nose and a cut over one eye.

The *Ranger* rested briefly at Lahaina from 1 to 4 April, before resuming work in Fleet Problem XIX on 4–5 April, logging 218 landings during that time, with no barrier crashes. A second respite came soon thereafter, when she joined the *Lexington* and the *Saratoga* off Honolulu—Pearl Harbor's channel still not dredged deep enough to allow the carriers to proceed into the harbor itself.

The Fleet's visit to Hawaiian waters in the spring of 1938 took on a different aspect than previously. The Navy closed the entire Pearl Harbor area to all vessels, "fishing and otherwise," stationed an armed patrol around the

A BG-1, hook down and wearing the "Diving Panther" insignia of VB-4, descends for a landing, 22 March 1938. The small winged turtle insignia on the fin indicates that the plane had been flown across the equator. (NA, 80-CF-54854-4)

harbor, as well as maintained two destroyers underway continually off the entrance channel, keeping all ships and craft at a distance of a mile off the buoys marking the entrance to Pearl. "This is a new departure," Adm. Claude C. Bloch, CinCUS, informed Adm. Harry E. Yarnell, who had been Commandant, 14th Naval District from 1933 to October 1936, "and one that I considered necessary for the security of the fleet at all times while here." Bloch explained that "I would like to try it this time... hoping that there would not be too many complaints from interested persons owning land in the lochs."[9]

During her time off Diamond Head, the *Ranger* again took part in a searchlight display an hour into the first watch on 14 April. Underway on the 21st, she took part in the final phases of the problem—again being rendered out of action by 26 April—and eventually reached San Diego on the 28th. During that time (21–28 April), the *Ranger* operated VF-3 and its F3F-1s as a second fighting squadron, and logged 333 landings during that period, with no barrier crashes. The fleet, of which the *Ranger* had been a part returned to the West Coast, in CinCUS's estimation, "in splendid condition. The officers and men know their business," Admiral Bloch wrote proudly to Admiral Leahy, the Chief of Naval Operations, "are well trained and highly contented."[10]

The *Ranger* remained in the San Diego area over the next few months. During that time, she embarked the Marines from Aircraft Two: VMJ-2 (equipped with O3U-6s and BG-1s), VMF-2 (F3F-2s), VMS-2 (O3U-6s), and VMB-2 (BG-1s), in addition to her utility unit O3U-3, for training and carrier qualifications (25–26 May), and conducted rearming drills with the Marines (27 May). The leathernecks' performance (287 landings without a barrier crash) impressed Vice Admiral King, ComAirBatFor—no easy man to impress—for he lauded them as "well-trained and thoroughly indoctrinated," particularly noting their "especially good... radio discipline." King praised their high spirit and morale and concluded, "It was a pleasure to have them in *Ranger*."[11] Soon thereafter, the *Ranger* conducted damage control practices in the light, variable winds and moderate seas off San Diego, her air group making 72 landings with no mishaps.

The *Ranger* sailed for Monterey on 1 July, with King embarked. Because the admiral's family had gone east for part of that summer, he rode the ship down to Monterey to witness the carrier suitability trials of the Brewster XSBA-1 mid-wing monoplane scout bomber, a type that he had approved evaluating as a promising design when he had been chief of BuAer about two years earlier.[12] That day, the XSBA-1 made six takeoffs and six landings, taking the number one and two wires once each and numbers three and four twice each. The trials of the XSBA-1, King later wrote to Rear Adm. Arthur B. Cook, the Chief of BuAer, "seemed to me to go along very well," although he noted that the Brewster seemed "'blind' [so that] the pilot has to slew the plane in order to see the signal officer." Outside of "a little trouble" with one of the oleo gears sticking (something that, in King's estimation, "can readily be remedied"), "I think the ship [the XSBA-1] made a very favorable impression on all who saw the carrier landing trials."[13]

The *Ranger* then hosted general visiting on Independence Day, but got underway early the following morning to return to San Diego, reaching her home port on the morning of the 6th. She operated in the San Francisco–San Diego area between 8 and 16 July, punctuating that period with participation in the presidential review in San Francisco Bay on 14 July. During that time, she operated an air group that included detachments from her own VF-4 and VS-41, as well as F3F-1s (VF-3) and SBC-3s (VS-3) from the *Saratoga* group and VB-2 (SB2U-1s) and VT-2 (TBD-1) from the *Lexington*. A misunderstanding as to the location of planes spotted on the flight deck resulted in damage to one TBD-1 (BuNo 0309), 2-T-10, when one of the starboard stacks was raised, crushing and tearing the right horizontal stabilizer, crushing the right elevator and tearing the fabric.[14]

Following the presidential review, the *Ranger* returned to North Island with her squadrons to continue the cycle of training, conducting qualification and refresher training (1–5 August) (467 landings without a mishap). She then participated in fleet tactical exercises (9–12 August), logging 258 accident-free recoveries and bringing her total number of landings to date to 16,186.

By the end of the fiscal year, the performance of the *Ranger*'s gunnery department had elicited favorable comment from CinCUS. Carrier gunnery that year (1938–39) had been, with the exception of the *Ranger*'s, generally disappointing. Her continuing efficiency in antiaircraft firings, however, as well as in SRBP, proved considerably gratifying to those who observed it.

Among the practice that her gunners had received was that which had been occasioned by the demand in some quarters for realistic targets to lend more authenticity (and less artificiality) to gunnery drills. Admiral Bloch selected the *Ranger* to carry out the first test-firing against a radio-controlled target plane. The radio control group, under Lt. Comdr. Delmar S. Fahrney, made two practice runs over the *Ranger* on 15 and 16 August, in preparation for the scheduled tests. The *Ranger* continued the training, utilizing an

Balancing themselves against the roll of the ship, flight deck crews respot 41-S-14, the SBU-1 normally assigned to Lt. (jg) Lemuel M. Stevens, Jr., April 1938. (NA, 80-CF-3232-1)

aircraft that simulated the drone's runs. After passing overhead, the plane maneuvered as if to evade shell bursts. Two rehearsal runs on 22 August preceded two antiaircraft training runs. Examination of the towed sleeve afterward revealed that the starboard battery had scored three hits, the port, four. The results satisfied Captain McCain, on the eve of the scheduled test with the drone, that his fire control people had been well trained.[15]

Training came to the fore that day in another area. Lieutenant (jg) James M. "Jim" Wright, of VS-41, took off at 1440 in an SBU-1 (BuNo 9759), for prescribed fixed gunnery training, with Pvt. R. G. Killerece, USMC, in back. After

An SBU-1 about to touch down on the flight deck, while the LSO watches the landing by the ramp and hookmen prepare to disengage the tailhook from the cross-deck pendant; destroyers steam astern, April 1938. Note sailor (L) who appears to be leaning on a lifeline (a practice not encouraged!) over the stacks. (NA, 80-CF file)

The *Ranger* (below) with the *Saratoga* (vertical black stripe) and the *Lexington*, off Honolulu, 8 April 1938. (NA, 80-G-410056)

rendezvousing with the towing plane, Wright made one pass, but did not fire. Coming around to rejoin the echelon of firing planes, he suddenly heard "a grinding sound" and his engine began to vibrate violently. In less than half a minute, his SBU's engine "ceased to deliver power" and he soon saw that his oil pressure had dropped to zero. Aviation Cadet Alfred L. Gurney, USNR, close behind in the next plane, saw "a large amount of smoke coming from [Wright's] engine."[16]

Wright coolly nosed the Vought down, executed a spiral to the left, turning 180 degrees and, as Gurney watched admiringly, made a "perfect stalled landing directly into the wind" off Point Loma, about the length of a football field from the submarine *Porpoise* (SS-172).[17] Wright actuated the flotation gear by hand, keeping the waterborne SBU-1 on an even keel. He then took in a heaving line from the submarine and hauled over an 8-inch manila line that he slipped over both propeller blades.

Lieutenant John M. Will, the *Porpoise*'s captain, informed Wright "that he [Will] could not back with any degree of control and wished to work me astern." The bight of the line to the plane, however, tended to pull it against the side of the boat, despite the best efforts of the submariners to fend off the Vought, and the *Porpoise*'s stern crushed the SBU's top wing in two places. Jim Wright and Private Killerece then boarded the *Porpoise*, "filed a despatch report and a request for instructions," and watched as the plane, allowed to drift astern about 100 yards, "appeared to be towing easily," as the submarine, in the uncharacteristic role of towboat, crept toward North Island at 2½ knots. Seeing the Vought's port wing high out of the water, however, Wright took another 8-inch line out to the plane, by boat, and attached it to the port N-strut. Ultimately, the NAS San Diego crash boat arrived alongside the *Porpoise* and embarked Wright and his passenger at 1730, and continued salvaging the crashed plane.[18]

The next day, Lt. Jules F. Schumacher of VB-4 made a water landing of a different sort. After completing a *Ranger* Group flight, during which his engine ran perfectly, Schumacher was flying a BG-1 (BuNo 9534) at an altitude of 3,500 feet over mountainous country, five miles east of the Sweetwater Reservoir, just outside of San Diego, conducting a homing drill with the Aircraft, Battle Force radio truck, when his engine began running erratically. Losing power compelled Schumacher to set the BG-1 down in the reservoir, the only possible place within gliding distance, and he did so with minimal injury to himself (a slight cut on the bridge of his nose) and his passenger, Seaman 2d Class A. F. Puel (three small cuts on one hand), and damage to his plane (fresh water submersion for five hours until salvagers arrived).[19]

In the meantime, test preparations for the *Ranger*'s special gunnery exercises reached a conclusion, and, one hour into the forenoon watch on 24 August, the carrier, with 100 officer observers on board for the occasion, steamed to the firing area. At about 1140, she began her first run, and soon her starboard five-inch guns began to bark at a slant range

Vice Adm. Ernest J. King, Comdr. Aircraft, Battle Force, inspects the *Ranger* upon the conclusion of Fleet Problem XIX, 4 June 1938. "On the job," contemporaries remembered, he "seemed always to be angry or annoyed." In this view, he seems to be the latter. (NA, 80-G-391553)

of 4,400 yards, at an elevation of 50 at the radio-controlled Stearman-Hammond JH-1, simulating a screening vessel's firing at a bomber that had flown over the ship, toward the fleet center.

The *Ranger*'s starboard crews had expended their target ammunition by the time the range had opened to 4,850 yards. Observers noted that the bursts, although they had followed the changes of course, had been so far behind as to cause doubt that any had actually hit the target. Lieutenant Commander Fahrney could see that, at "'cease firing' the nearest bursts were a thousand feet or so away on either side in deflection."[20] Because the batteries had not scored any hits, thus obviating the need to return to base to photograph the results, the control party stationed the drone for the next run. The *Ranger*'s port battery opened fire at a slant range of 4,000 yards, and continued out to 6,200. The first

Flight deck hoisting-boom rigged and in operation, 8 June 1938. Note covered .50-caliber machine gun mounts along the gallery in foreground (R). (NA, 80-CF-21148-2)

bursts, Captain McCain later admitted, had "followed the target but were never able to catch up."[21]

McCain also noted that, "after the target reached a certain altitude on the approach it was necessary to train the director so rapidly that the solution obtained became virtually useless." The director crew had to compute a new solution between the time the drone was directly overhead and the time it had reached the 4,000 yard slant range. Had the drone kept a steady course, the *Ranger*'s captain continued, the first bursts "would have been sufficiently close as to have damaged the drone—on the first run in was apparent that the range-keeper alone was not capable of keeping the bursts on target or of providing an initial hitting solution." Summing up, McCain observed that "the antiaircraft training received from firing on a target similar to a drone is the most valuable and instructive firing that any ship equipped with an antiaircraft battery can have." McCain urged that, even if other practices had to be curtailed to permit it, funds should be made available to provide drones as targets in simulated dive-bombing attacks.[22]

The Chief of the Bureau of Ordnance dismissed the practice, but Rear Admiral Cook, Chief of BuAer, noted that the drone practices offered "very great possibilities." Although noting how the "target practice attitude" was perfectly natural, Cook pointed out "that the object in battle will be to shoot down airplanes rather than to be reduced...to claims of what would have happened if the enemy had followed a simple plan already known" to the antiaircraft crews. BuAer's chief condemned the "necessary artificialities of antiaircraft firing to date, dictated by both safety considerations and some regard to competitive records and scores" which had "inevitably narrowed and conventionalized the antiaircraft problem." The drone firings, Cook believed, provided the first opportunity to instill a "fresh viewpoint" in the process. "Our antiaircraft provision is not primarily for the purpose of developing maximum competitive skill and making fine-drawn comparisons of results in standardized unnatural problems," he concluded, "but for maximum war effectiveness under *all* conditions." He submitted that continued employment of radio controlled targets would help greatly in achieving "maximum effectiveness" in antiaircraft training, and expressed satisfaction that, if drones continued to be employed, the "initial antiaircraft readiness of the Fleet in [a] war emergency will be high."[23]

Although the drone had fallen into a steep spiral dive and crashed to destruction at the conclusion of the test, the exercises had proved the potential of the radio-controlled target drone in making gunnery training more realistic. As Lieutenant Commander Fahrney later noted, "all feel that the first drone firing has been useful in pointing out changes that are necessary in the technique of handling both the control of antiaircraft firing and the director." Observers conceded that "the realism, the maneuvering ability, the effectiveness of the simulated attacks...and the antiaircraft training values in a radio controlled target definitely off-set the costs that may be involved in supplying the large number to the fleet each year."[24]

While her gun crews had shown their proficiency at their craft, *Ranger* pilots continued to become proficient at water landings, as Jules Schumacher and Jim Wright had proved—whether they wanted to or not. During night carrier landing practice at NAS San Diego on 25 August, Lt. (jg) Robert B. Moore of VS-42 had just taken off in his SBU-1 (BuNo 9750), when the engine jerked to a stop; a shower of sparks, followed by flames, flashed from beneath the engine cowling on the port side. Moore made a full-stall landing with the flaps down, and the flotation gear functioned automatically, but, as the bags inflated, the plane rose to the surface, inverted. After only about 30 seconds, the bags abruptly pulled out of the plane and BuNo 9750 sank in 60 feet of water. Dragging operations eventually salvaged the Vought, 40 hours later, revealing that the head of number 12 cylinder had broken off, and only the exhaust pipe and intake held it in place. Moore suffered a contusion of his back, and his passenger, Seaman 1st Class Harold Stang, emerged from the crash unscathed.[25]

Providentially, individual battle practice and camera gunnery on 2 September ended differently than it could have. Aviation Cadet Richard C. Coar of VF-4, at the controls of an F3F-1 (BuNo 0216), as the "target" for Lt. Comdr. Charles F. Greber of VS-3, approached from 1,200 feet ahead and above, about 6,000 feet over La Mesa, California. As a head-on collision seemed imminent, both pilots took last-second evasive action, but Coar's F3F collided with Dutch Greber's SBC-3 (BuNo 0571), damaging the upper right wing and right aileron, and cutting and crushing the outboard four feet of the Curtiss's lower right wing, cutting through the forward spar to a point 15 inches outboard of a wing strut fitting, and slightly bending the landing flaps. Greber's passenger, Radioman 1st Class J. W. LeCompte, received a minor cut on his right knee in the impact.[26]

Both pilots maintained control of their damaged aircraft. Aviation Cadet Coar attempted an emergency forced landing at Camp Kearney. Coming in with his gear retracted, Coar's F3F hit the ground, skidded about 100 feet and turned over. Although his plane required a major overhaul before it could be flown again, the fortunate cadet Coar walked away uninjured. A subsequent trouble board faulted both pilots, assigning 80% of the blame to Coar (poor technique) and 20% to Greber (bad judgment), in that both pilots "approached within too close a range in a head on condition and were unable to avoid a collision."[27]

Punctuating her training with a drydocking at Hunter's Point (6–8 September), the *Ranger* conducted day and night refresher landings between 31 October and 2 November; during that time, the ship's air group commander made the transition from the previously assigned SBU-1 to a Vought SB2U-1 monoplane scout/dive-bomber. Between 7 and 10 November, as the *Ranger*'s air group made 330 accident-free landings, running the ship's total number of recoveries to 17,031, the ship participated in fleet tactical exercises out of San Diego. During that stint, the *Ranger*'s prize-winning communications department (which had won "C"s three years running) established contact with the Vought-Sikorsky XPBS-1 *Flying Dreadnought*, as it departed Anacostia, District of Columbia, at 0700 (Eastern Standard Time) on 9 November. The *Ranger*'s communicators maintained contact until the flying boat landed at San Diego at 1855 (Pacific Standard Time) that day, doing so while keeping up with the traffic load imposed during tactical exercises taking place at the same time.

Yet inherent in the pace of carrier operations, even in peacetime, was the possibility that tragedy could occur without warning. During the second day of refresher and squadron gunnery training (29 November), VS-42's second division had just taken off from the *Ranger*, and the lead section, led by Lt. Ralph W. D. Woods, the squadron's exec in 42-S-10, had just joined up. It flew back toward the ship at an altitude of about 700 feet—the usual practice—to allow the other sections to join. Lt. (jg) Bob Moore, in 42-S-16, had just fallen into the normal position to the right and behind the first section. Forty-Two-Sail-Seventeen joined next.[28]

Radioman 1st Class Glen Herndon, Moore's radioman, suddenly noticed 42-S-15 (BuNo 9780), flown by Aviation Cadet Tom Jaeger, cutting over toward 42-S-16 from about 50 degrees on the port bow, and about 20 feet above. Radioman 1st Class S. F. Hogge, Lieutenant Woods's radioman in 42-S-10, then saw 42-S-15 make a left flipper turn, with the nose slightly down, directly behind 42-S-10. Jaeger's left wing then apparently hit Woods's slipstream, which tossed 42-S-15 completely over. The nose dropped and the SBU-1 made a slow descent, out of control. Glen Herndon saw 42-S-15 hit the water "at an estimated speed in excess of 100 knots" and "completely disintegrate upon impact." Lieutenant (jg) Moore began to send a crash report, but only the word "CRASH..." came out before he heard Radioman 1st Class Hogge broadcasting over voice radio to the *Ranger*. As Lieutenant Woods flew over the slick, Hogge dropped a float light to mark the spot. Forty-Two-Sail-Fifteen, from which neither Tom Jaeger nor Seaman 2d Class L. R. Swanson had escaped, sank into 330 fathoms, 14 miles off Point Loma. The *Ranger* and the plane guard destroyer *Clark* (DD-361) both proceeded at full speed and lowered boats upon arrival on the scene, but searchers found only a wheel and a portion of a landing gear strut floating on the edge of a large oil slick, and nothing else. Both ships remained, searching the area thoroughly, but, finding nothing more, headed for home in the gathering darkness.

Nine days before Christmas of 1938, the *Ranger* carried out night landing practices off San Diego. Aviation Cadet Howard W. Crews, USNR, of VS-42, had completed his scheduled evolutions and returned to a wet South Field, and made a normal landing. After he had rolled only about 150 feet, however, Crews noticed his SBU-1 (BuNo 9756) angling to the right. Remedying the situation with "left rudder and a touch of left brake," Crews felt the plane again angling to the right. Using the left brake in increasing amounts, as required, did little to arrest the Vought's swing, until the left lower wing dragged on the field. He felt a bump soon thereafter, most likely from the landing gear as it broke during the ground loop. BuNo 9756 came to a stop, angled about 90 degrees from the landing course.[29]

Crews immediately cut the switch, but soon noticed flames spreading across the top of the engine. In the excitement of the moment, and in the darkness, the pilot could not locate the fire extinguisher handle. Grabbing a small hand extinguisher from the cockpit, Crews called out to Radioman 3d Class W. H. Jones, his passenger, "to try and find the fire extinguisher handle," which the latter soon did. Jones's activating the extinguisher, however, failed to put out the fire.

Taking his parachute clear of the plane, Crews handed Jones the Pyrene extinguisher to battle the flames, while he turned off the light switches and opened the cowling "in order to get at the fire better for by now the flames were back along the fire wall." Soon the station fire truck arrived on the scene and, after using CO_2 on the flames, managed to bring them under control after several minutes. A major overhaul lay in that SBU's immediate future, before it could be flown again. A trouble board blamed the crash on Crews's landing technique, but acknowledged that the wind, blowing in from the west, played its role in disposing events, too.

Keeping the planes in top condition lay in the hands of the plane captains and mechanics of the squadrons. Scouting Forty-Two's plane captains, on most occasions, received the criticisms and suggestions from the squadron's pilots with a ready ear. However, after one night flight, a pilot informed one of the mechanics that an odor of burning pancakes had filled the SBU-1's cockpit. A quick check revealed nothing out of the ordinary. A closer inspection the following morning, however, yielded the sight of two "guillotined, crushed, baked ducks...tightly wedged" against the lower engine cylinders with "various duck appurtenances...plentifully strewn elsewhere about the plane and engine." The pilot later "concluded that his passengers [had] embarked on their last flight when he first took off from the South Field mat."[30]

11

"THE PROBABILITY OF AIR ATTACK ON CARRIERS"

New challenges lay ahead for the new year 1939. With VF-4 (Grumman F3F-1s), VB-3 (Vought SB2U-1s) (which replaced the BG-1-equipped VB-4), VS-41 and VS-42 (Vought SBU-1s) embarked, the *Ranger* departed San Diego for Panama on 4 January, bid "Godspeed by the fluttering hankies of the about-to-become 'cruise widows' assembled on the dock, the cheers and cries of excited children and the complacent grins of the land sailors waiting for the next nickel ferry to San Diego."[1] Although the ship's pitching for the first two days slowed operations somewhat, the *Ranger* commenced her first flight operations of the new year on 5 January. Her flight deck crews showed no appreciable lack of finesse in handling VB-3's new monoplane Vought SB2U-1s with their "wide-span, hand-operated, folding wings," and each squadron made complete landings without a single wave-off from the LSO, Lt. David J. Welsh.[2]

The group's proficiency at bombing a towed spar with 100-pound water-filled practice bombs likewise impressed observers; VF-4, under Lt. Comdr. Windy Switzer, appreciably bettered its takeoff intervals, from 19.8 seconds to 15.1, during the periods of fleet tactics conducted en route to the Canal Zone.[3] Lieutenant (jg) Frederick R. "Fritz" Schrader, however, flying an F3F-1 (BuNo 0217), on 10 January, exhibited poor technique when trying to come on board that morning from a tactics hop, making a hard landing that resulted in the left wing scraping along the deck.[4]

Transiting the Panama Canal on 13 January, the *Ranger* stood in to Limon Bay the same day. Anchoring in her assigned berth in Colon harbor, the *Ranger* soon sent her men ashore to sample what Panama had to offer in the way of diversion. "Those who have, in the days of prohibition at home," wrote one *Ranger* scribe, "observed the expeditious manner in which the combination of Isthmian heat and rum transformed hundreds of clean, bright-faced young lads to dirty, sick, patrol-fighting beachcombers, could not but marvel at the change." Orderly, quiet young men, "carrying their liquid refreshments as steadily as their carefully selected purchases," had replaced the "yelling, fruit-heaving mob" that had to be loaded into ships' boats at the expiration of liberty. "And so passes the old conception of the roystering sailorman ashore in a foreign port," crowed a *Ranger* chronicler, when the carrier's crew proved well-behaved on liberty.[5]

The *Ranger* remained at Colon until the 19th, when she turned her clipper bow into the Caribbean chop which proved "somewhat disturbing to those of her crew accustomed only to the long rollers of the Pacific," and sailed for Guantanamo Bay.[6] She fell in astern of the *Lexington*, and the near-twin sisters *Yorktown* and *Enterprise* followed in the *Ranger's* wake.[7] Her flight operations continued to be flawless, logging 238 landings, without any mishaps, during the brief trip to Guantanamo. She dropped anchor at her destination on the 21st.

During the *Ranger's* time at Guantanamo, athletics provided an outlet for friendly intercarrier competition. Bombing Three and the *Lexington's* Bombing Two met for baseball and beer at Deer Point, where softball diamonds had

The *Ranger* in Pedro Miguel locks en route to Limon Bay, Canal Zone, 13 January 1939. SBU-1s of VS-42 are spotted forward on the starboard side, SBUs from VS-41 on the port, accompanied by a Vought SB2U-1, 3-B-18, in the foreground. Interested spectators line the flight deck and the galleries, regarding the ship's progress through the isthmian waterway. (NA, 80-G-391555)

been laid out among the trees and brush. Officers and enlisted men each fielded a team. Despite the good pitching of Aviation Cadet Walter L. "Moose" Kelsch, Jr., USNR, and Lt. Comdr. John G. Crommelin, VB-3's highly respected exec, Bombing Two edged out VB-3, 3–2, in the officers' contest. Bombing Three's enlisted men, however, bested Bombing Two's highly touted hurler ("a pitcher with a reputation") behind Seaman 1st Class J. W. Hennekes, pounding out an 8–0 win.[8]

The *Ranger*'s baseball team beat the diamond nine from the battleship *California* (BB-44) team, 5–2, earning a steak dinner in the process, and played a "thriller" of a game with the ballclub from the *Pennsylvania* (BB-38). In the latter contest, which took place on 29 January, the *Ranger*'s team pulled off a triple play—rare even for the major leagues.

Commander Osborne B. Hardison, the executive officer, Lt. Comdr. Edward R. Gardner, Jr., the gunnery officer, Comdr. Wilson S. Hullfish (SC), the supply officer, and Lts. Jesse G. Johnson (flight deck officer) and Albert E. Chapman (assistant gunnery officer), and 25 enlisted men sat among the spectators who saw the *Pennsylvania*'s team with men on first and second, and no outs. Sensing a bunt, Robinson, the *Ranger*'s catcher, called for a pitch out. The battleship sailor reached for the pitch, but popped it up instead. Robinson snagged the fly ball and fired to first baseman Tope, who threw to second baseman Borkowski. Robinson's heads-up play caught both runners off base and unable to get back in time. The *Ranger*'s team also pulled off three double plays as well, and neither team's pitching allowed a runner to reach second from the fourth through eleventh innings. In an effort

The *Lexington* leads the *Ranger*, the *Yorktown*, and the *Enterprise* out of Limon Bay, 19 January 1939. (NA, 80-G-1061652)

to spur the *Ranger*men on to victory, Lieutenant Johnson "was ready to put a case of beer on the line if the team could finally win." But the *Pennsylvania*'s team outlasted the *Ranger*'s, breaking a 6–6 deadlock in the 12th stanza, to win, 9–6. "Boy," wrote a *Ranger* chronicler, "what a ball game!"[9]

The *Ranger* sailed for Gonaives, Haiti, on 30 January. Over the next several days, her air group continued training, conducting aircraft bombing practice between Gonaives and Guantanamo. VS-41, VS-42, and VB-3 all bettered their takeoff intervals during that time, but VF-4, for some reason, slowed down. No mishaps marred the training conducted from 30 January to 4 February and on 6 and 7 February, but, on the morning of 14 February, a near-tragedy occurred on the flight deck.

Seaman 1st Class Clinton R. Downing had just completed energizing the inertia starter on an SB2U-1 (BuNo 0776). As he stepped back along the wing to give the plane captain the "all clear," he failed to realize how close BuNo 0776 was to another SB2U-1 (BuNo 0743) that sat spotted nearby and slightly astern. As the inertia starter engaged the engine of the latter, the propeller began to spin; Downing stepped directly into the propeller arc, the blade hitting him in the head and knocking him to his knees. Reacting quickly, other crewmen nearby pulled Downing clear just as the engine caught and the prop began to revolve under its own power. Fortunately, Downing's injuries did not prove fatal, as might have happened had the prop been at full power. As things stood, his slight scalp laceration required only three stitches to close.[10]

The *Ranger* took departure for Culebra, Puerto Rico, on 15 February, and there joined the fleet for Fleet Problem XX. As part of the Black fleet, she quit Culebra at the start

Leeward Field, Guantanamo Bay, Cuba, ca. 1939. Three SBU-1s from VS-42 are parked near the triangular encampment. The largest crowd seems to be gathered around the SB2U at right. (NA, 80-G-391557)

of the mid watch on 20 February, in company with the heavy cruiser *Astoria* (CA-34) and the destroyer *Somers* (DD-381), her antisubmarine screen. During the period including the morning through afternoon watches, patrol planes took station around the little force, serving as an antisubmarine screen, as it transited the waters off St. Croix and between the islands of Monserrat and Guadalupe.[11]

The "loss" of the light cruiser *Philadelphia* (CL-41) to the Black force during the day's "action" on 21 February put the *Ranger*'s Captain McCain in the position of "senior surviving officer" of Black's Task Force Three. Because the "surviving" ships had received orders to join the Black Main Body, however, he had very little to command. At sunset, the *Ranger* and her two consorts received word that a Black patrol plane had spotted a White destroyer force within striking distance. During the first watch on 21 February, the *Ranger* received orders to establish a radio watch on the frequencies of Black task groups and to assist in the destruction of a White destroyer reported off Leeward Island.

Shortly before sunrise on the 22d, the *Ranger* went to flight quarters, and, while the *Somers* steamed astern as plane guard and the *Astoria* took station on antisubmarine screen ahead of the carrier, she began launching planes, beginning with the first division of VS-41's SBU-1s for antisubmarine patrol, out to a distance of 15 miles. VS-42 (SBU-1s) and the second division of VS-41 took off to fly an outer air patrol circling the ship 75 miles out.

Slowed only briefly by the *Somer*'s suffering a casualty to her main feed pump, which reduced speed to 15 knots for a time, the *Ranger* landed VS-41 and VS-42 during the forenoon watch. That evolution having been completed, she put aloft VF-4's second division to fly antisubmarine patrol 15 miles out.

After maintaining her airborne antisubmarine patrols into the afternoon, the *Ranger* received a dispatch midway through the afternoon watch, from a Black patrol plane reporting the presence of White ships: a destroyer (DD) and a destroyer leader (DL), within range. Beginning those preparations an hour before the start of the first dog watch, the *Ranger* interrupted those preparations to recover an SBU-1 in the bow arresting gear, because of her full-spotted deck aft. Soon thereafter, resuming her course of 314 degrees at 25 knots, she abandoned plans to attack the two White ships, because there was simply not enough daylight remaining for the air group to make the attack and return by sunset. She thus recovered the first and second divisions of VS-42 during the first dog watch, then darkened ship at sundown. The *Astoria* took position on the *Ranger*'s port bow, the *Somers* on the starboard, to serve as antisubmarine screen for the night.

Flight operations began afresh with the dawn on 23 February, with one division of VS-42's SBU-1s launched for antisubmarine patrol; VS-42's second division took off soon thereafter, accompanying VS-41 to conduct a 100-mile-radius search completely around the ship. VF-4's first division relieved VS-42's first division during the forenoon watch on antisubmarine patrol out to 15 miles. At noon, the *Ranger* received orders to attack two White heavy cruisers located in Semana Bay, and set course accordingly. By the beginning of the first dog watch, however, it was obvious that an attack upon the two White warships was beyond the range of the strike group. The Commander of the Black force later cancelled the strike anyway, when further investigation revealed that the "cruisers" were in fact destroyers that had already been ruled out of action. Soon thereafter, in response to the request by Lt. Comdr. Morton T. Seligman, the Commander, *Ranger* Air Group (CRAG), the *Astoria* launched two Curtiss SOCs to conduct searches around the carrier, to a distance of 10 miles out. The heavy cruiser recovered the two floatplanes less than two hours later, and within a half hour, the ships of the little task group once more darkened ship and took their night steaming stations.

"War time" jitters prevailed the following morning, 24 February. Early during the morning watch, the *Ranger* went ahead full, and directed the *Astoria* back to investigate a strange destroyer that had come in on the starboard quarter and taken up a trailing position. The "DD" turned out to the *Somers*, which had left her screening position to take up plane guard position for the morning's flight operations. Resuming 18 knots, the *Ranger* soon spotted the Black fleet on the horizon. She launched her air group to search out to 100 miles on an 80-mile front. That having been accomplished, the *Ranger* changed course to take up a position 50 miles southwest of the Black fleet. Shortly before the start of the forenoon watch, the destroyer *Patterson* (DD-392) reported to the *Ranger* for duty as plane guard.

At 1015, Lt. Harper D. Scrymgeour, VS-42's flight officer, returned from a scouting mission with Radioman 1st Class H. F. Grace as his passenger in an SBU-1 (BuNo 9806). "Spark" Scrymgeour taxied up the deck, past the lowered number one and number two barriers. Number one elevator's being in use to strike planes below, however, necessitated Scrymgeour's taxiing forward along the port side. As the *Ranger* rolled heavily to port in the seaway, the wind across the deck lifted the right wing, throwing the weight of the airplane onto the left wheel; striking the number four barrier broach soon thereafter, 42-S-4 swerved sharply to the left. Scrymgeour tried to apply the brakes, but with the right wheel barely touching the deck, his efforts proved unavailing, and the Vought went over the side into the water.[12]

The *Patterson* promptly plucked Scrymgeour and Grace, (the latter suffering a slight contusion to the muscles of his right hip in the crash) out of the sea soon thereafter, and assisted while the *Ranger* recovered 42-S-4, between 1113 and 1157. The *Somers*, meanwhile, maintained an antisubmarine patrol in the vicinity; the *Astoria* was released to rejoin the Black fleet. In the afternoon, the *Ranger* launched VS-41 to conduct antisubmarine patrols astern of the Black Main Body.

Turning into the wind at 0632 on 25 February, the *Ranger* launched VS-42, its numbers diminished by one, after the damage to 42-S-4 the previous day, to search the 275 to 060 degree sector out to a distance of 100 miles, followed by three planes from VF-4 for antisubmarine patrol. After recovering two SBU-1s in the bow gear, one having made an emergency landing, the *Ranger* resumed her base course.

She soon received a report from 42-S-7, telling of "one enemy carrier and two plane guard destroyers." Less than a half hour later, 42-S-10 reported contact with a White submarine; a two-plane section "attacked" the enemy boat with two "500-pound bombs" and "strafed" it. Identifying the "enemy" as the *Enterprise*, the *Ranger* began launching her strike at 0752. Within 18 minutes, she put aloft VB-3 (18 SB2U-1s), VS-41 (18 SBU-1s), escorted by 15 F3F-1s from VF-4; during that time, she received a report from 42-S-10 telling of another White submarine in the vicinity.

Soon thereafter, however, Moose Kelsch, flying an SB2U-1 (BuNo 0744), with Aviation Machinist's Mate 3d

Class D. L. Stepp of VF-4 as his passenger, returned with a malfunctioning engine. Every time Kelsch attempted to throttle down, the engine would cut out, violently. After making a safe landing without further incident, Kelsch cut the engine, which torched excessively. A malfunctioning carburetor proved the culprit.[13]

In the meantime, the *Ranger*'s air group had reached its objective and had begun to deploy to attack, VS-42's first section joining VB-3 and VS-41. Pushing over from out of the sun, the *Ranger*'s pilots expended thirty 100-pound bombs, twenty-one 500-pounders and seventeen 1,000-pounders, and "sank" the *Enterprise*, "losing" two SB2U-1s, four F3F-1s, and five SBU-1s in the process. The *Ranger* group then fought its way out of the skies over the enemy ships, encountering 15 SBCs from VS-3 and 9 planes from VF-3. In the aerial engagement that followed, it "lost" one SB2U and three F3Fs. The Chief Umpire, however, upped the damage received by the *Ranger* group, assessing the "loss" of seven fighters, five SBU-1s (three from VS-41 and a pair from VS-42), and three SB2Us from VB-3.

A little over two hours into the forenoon watch, the *Ranger* launched two SBU-1s for antisubmarine patrol and recovered her victorious strike group. She then recovered the antisub patrol at the end of that period. Subsequently, she received orders to "investigate and attack" what was reported to be a carrier and four destroyers south of Point OPTION. The *Ranger* responded that the carrier sighted was, in fact, *hors de combat*, and the vicinity of Mona Island probably served as a rendezvous for ships declared by the umpires to be out of action. The Black officer in tactical command agreed with the *Ranger*'s assessment, but to be on the safe side ordered one squadron to investigate.

Consequently, the *Ranger* turned into the wind, and, between 1238 and 1243, launched 18 SBUs, 15 from VS-41, and 3 from VS-42. The search yielded four destroyers and two submarines in Mona Passage, all of which were indeed out of action, but the *Ranger*'s pilots also found the *Preston* (DD-379), an active White adversary. Their quarry proved a worthy foe, however, "damaging" eight planes with antiaircraft fire, before hoisting the "out of action" signal after being pounded by eighteen 500-pound bombs and 17,000 rounds of .30-caliber machine gun fire. The *Ranger* recovered her search in nine minutes, beginning at 1520, and joined the Black Main Body soon thereafter. At the end of the first dog watch, the *McCall* (DD-400) relieved the *Somers* as plane guard.

The "wars" continued on the 26th, with the *Ranger* launching VS-42's 17 SBU-1s, four sections for sector searches out to 100 miles from the Black fleet center and two sections to patrol ahead of the fleet out to 25 miles.

Once she had completed putting the searches aloft, the *Ranger* zig-zagged at 16 knots, steering a rough quadrangle in the vicinity of the launch position. A little less than a half an hour after they had taken off, VS-42's pilots began spotting White submarines; VS-42's fourth section attacked three between 0720 and 0816; the third section, three between 0740 and 0855; and the fifth, one at 0843. Given the obvious White submarine activity, the *Ranger* launched VF-4's fourth and fifth sections to patrol in the path of the Black Main Body, out to 25 miles.

During the recovery of VS-42's scouting sections over the bow, Lt. (jg) William E. Gaillard, VS-42's assistant gunnery officer, with Radioman 2d Class John McDaniel as his passenger, made a hard wheels-first landing, nosing over slightly on impact. Observers noted the SBU-1's fuselage fabric wrinkled as BuNo 9763 taxied out of the gear, the damage most likely the result of indeterminate stresses applied to the fuselage, perhaps from hard landings during a period of sustained operations. Others had landed hard as well, something attributed, by a subsequent trouble board, to a combination of factors: a slight crosswind approach, stack gases and island wash, and turbulent air close to the deck, the last-named factor most likely caused by the planes spotted aft. The same combination of factors came into play soon thereafter. During the recovery of VS-42's patrol sections, Lt. Ralph Woods, VS-42's exec, with Radioman 1st Class Hogge in back, landed his SBU (BuNo 9793) hard, too, his lower left wing striking the deck as his hook engaged number two wire, necessitating replacement of the wing. Neither Lieutenant (jg) Gaillard nor Lieutenant Woods emerged unscathed from subsequent evaluations: Investigators faulted Woods 85% and Gaillard 50% for poor landing technique.[14]

Operations against White submarines, however, continued unabated. VS-42's sixth section attacked an "enemy" boat 30 miles from the Black fleet center; the *Ranger*, backing at 12 knots and completing the recovery of VS-42's patrol sections, spotted a submarine just 4,500 yards distant. The *Patterson* sped to the attack, dropping 12 "depth charges" and ending up in a position to have "rammed" the enemy boat. Another sub advertised her presence with a smoke bomb soon thereafter, prompting the *McCall* to attack, dropping 10 charges. Umpires ruled that the boat that the *Patterson* attacked had managed to get off a shot at the *Ranger*, inflicting 8% damage to the carrier.

Following the action with the White submarines, the *Ranger* launched VS-41's first division, two sections for antisubmarine patrol ahead of the Black fleet and one section to patrol around the *Ranger*. Sighting a submarine on the surface 14,000 yards ahead, early in the afternoon watch, the carrier directed VS-41's first section and the *Patterson* to investigate. Finding the boat to be "enemy," Scouting 41's SBUs dropped three 500-pound bombs and expended 3,000 rounds of .30-caliber; the *Patterson* contributed 40 rounds of 5-inch fire to force the submarine to submerge. A smoke bomb indicated that the sub had fired at the *Ranger*, but umpires ruled that the carrier had not been hit. VS-41 carried out antisubmarine patrols during the afternoon, with the *Ranger* recovering the last SBUs early in the first dog watch, joining the Black Main Body soon thereafter.

The next morning, less than an hour before the end of the morning watch, before she had launched aircraft, the *Ranger*, which had left the Black fleet disposition only a short time before, came under attack by planes from the *Yorktown*. Three SBC-3s (VS-5), 12 TBD-1s (VT-5), and 16 BT-1s (VB-5) approached from 8,000 feet. Opposed by gunfire, however, from the time they were spotted until reaching attack position, the *Yorktown*ers, in the view of the umpires, scored no hits. Subsequently, Captain McCain posited that the *Yorktown*'s attack on the *Ranger* "well demonstrated...the probability of air attack on carriers remaining with or in the close vicinity of the Fleet Disposition after daylight." When attacked, McCain wrote, the *Ranger* was en route to taking a position 40 miles away from the fleet. Although "justified in not leaving the formation earlier under the conditions of the problem [the *Ranger*'s] vulnerability in this position is demonstrated by this incident."[15]

Later, during the forenoon watch, after dodging rain squalls, the *Ranger* turned into the wind to launch planes. She put up VF-4 to provide combat air patrol over the Black Main Body, and a strike group to seek out and attack White battleships. Aiding VF-4 in its watch over the Black fleet was VMF-1, the Marine fighting squadron based at San Juan. A little over two hours into the forenoon watch, the *Ranger*'s SB2Us and SBUs spotted the White Main Body, and began maneuvering to keep out of gun range and attain an attack position at 12,500 feet. An hour later, a formation of SBCs from VS-3 arrived over the Black Main Body; VF-4 engaged them at 10,000 feet, suffering four planes downed in the encounter. At 1125, the *Ranger* ordered her air group to attack, and the 34 SBUs and 18 SB2Us pushed over, the latter losing "1,000-pound bombs" and the former "500-pound bombs." During the course of the action, the *Ranger*men suffered the "loss" of two SB2Us and five SBUs in their attack on the three leading White battleships. Early in the afternoon watch, while the *Ranger*'s air group was setting a return course to the ship, VF-4 engaged fighters from VF-3 at 15,000 feet over the Black Main Body, losing two of their number in defense of the fleet.

"Weather conditions during this operation," Commander Seligman, the *Ranger*'s air group commander, reflected on the attack on the Black Main Body on 27 February, "were ideal for dive bombing attacks." The availability of ample cloud cover, together with the fact that the clouds themselves "were sufficiently scattered to enable pilots to see and identify enemy vessels" proved beneficial for the *Ranger*'s group as they arrived in the vicinity of the White fleet. Appreciating the Black fleet commander's desire to coordinate the *Ranger*'s air attack with the Black Main Body's engaging the White, however, Seligman posited that "an immediate attack after contacting [the White] main body would have been most effective." In all probability, he added, "the group could have returned to the carrier and rearmed in time to deliver another attack in an actual engagement." The weather conditions, although favorable for the attackers in one sense, could also have aided the defenders, allowing an enemy combat air patrol to appear suddenly from beneath the clouds to intercept the attack group. Maintaining his group in a wide approach formation, Seligman believed, made it probable that, in an actual engagement, the *Ranger*'s planes "would have been under fire on several occasions during the hour and ten minute interval."[16]

Commenting later on Seligman's observations, McCain attributed the practical limitations in air group attacks to the "limited radius of current carrier aircraft types when operated under full war load." He also added that one had to carefully weigh the "value of delaying an air attack to coordinate it with a main action...against the desireability of attacking earlier with the possibility of making a second attack later." He urged recognition of the danger "of losing our aircraft either on their carriers or in the the air by delaying their attacks."[17]

Returning from the attack mission, Lt. (jg) Fred D. Pfotenhauer, with Aviation Cadet James D. Arbes, USNR, riding in the back seat, in an SB2U-1 (BuNo 0737), slid into the groove astern of the *Ranger* and made his approach. It seemed normal in all respects, until he neared the ramp, when, in the gusty conditions prevailing and with the *Ranger* pitching in the seaway as she often did, the SB2U seemed to be displaced abruptly to starboard. By the time Pfotenhauer received the cut from the LSO, he was well to starboard of the centerline. Turning slightly to port, Pfotenhauer engaged number one wire, but the Vought came down hard, wrinkling the skin on the wings and damaging both tires.[18]

After calling briefly at Bridgetown, Barbados, from 4 to 9 March, the *Ranger* resumed training. Two days after leaving

The *Ranger* (L) and the *Lexington* in Carlisle Bay, off Bridgetown, Barbados, 7 March 1939. (NA, 80-G-463147)

Barbados, the ship was conducting flight operations in gusty winds and through a choppy sea, when VS-41's Lt. (jg) Charles Blenman, Jr., with Radioman 2d Class R. Schreffler on board, returned to the ship from a group tactics flight in an SBU-1 (BuNo 9309), approaching slightly to the right of the centerline. Blenman took the cut, but nosed over and tried to land in the center of the flight deck. Landing on its right wheel, the SB2U soon lost the right oleo, drag, and axle struts, then dropped its right wing, damaging the lower portion of the right aileron and right flap beyond repair, as well as bending both prop blades.[19]

The same gusty, choppy conditions also accounted for another mishap soon thereafter, when Lt. William S. Harris of VB-3, Radioman 2d Class Reginald A. Miner riding as passenger, approached the cut position in a flat attitude and with apparent excess speed. Once he got the cut from the LSO, Harris dipped the nose of his SB2U-1 (BuNo 0739) and eased back on the stick. As the motion pictures of the landing showed later, the Vought's arrestor hook struck the deck between number two and three wires and bounced up against the buffer. In an instant, the SB2U touched the deck in an approximate three-point attitude near number three wire, bounced some six feet in the air, tail high, and floated up the deck, finally engaging number nine wire. The Vought's landing gear and prop fouled the barrier and the plane nosed-up violently. Bill Harris suffered a fractured cheekbone as the SB2U slammed to the deck.[20]

Fleet Problem XX had provided ample opportunity for the practicability of forming plans and orders and of conducting varied operations geared toward strategic and tactical fleet training. Cruisers, supported by carrier planes and submarines, opposed by destroyers and patrol planes, carried out distant raiding operations that eventually led to a clash between the respective main bodies. Force, type, and intertype actions mirrored investigations into the increased use of aircraft, destroyers, and submarines in wartime scenarios. Additionally, the fleet acquainted itself with Atlantic and Caribbean Sea areas and ports of strategic importance to possible future operations. The exercises also confirmed a need for increased base facilities in Caribbean waters.

Upon the conclusion of Fleet Problem XX in mid-March, the *Ranger* carried out operations in the Gonaives–Guantanamo Bay areas into early April. Underway on 8 April for Norfolk, the *Ranger* conducted tactical evolutions with the *Lexington* and her erstwhile adversaries from the recently concluded war games, the *Yorktown* and the *Enterprise*, en route, and dropped anchor in Hampton Roads on the morning of 12 April.

As the fleet had steamed toward the Tidewater region, however, events in Europe reached a crisis, triggered by Italy's sending troops into its tiny neighbor, Albania, in an action that prompted Britain to gather her fleet in the Mediterranean and extend her defensive alliances. Germany and Italy scornfully rejected President Roosevelt's fervent appeal to their respective leaders, Adolf Hitler and Benito Mussolini, to pledge a decade of peace. The prospect of Japan taking advantage of an American preoccupation with European affairs to cause trouble in the Pacific, many speculated, had prompted Roosevelt to order the Fleet back to that ocean.

Shifting to NOB Norfolk on 20 April—the day the rest of the Fleet left to return to the Pacific, six weeks ahead of schedule—the *Ranger* moored to Pier 7, where she remained for a week. Assigned to the Atlantic Squadron, the *Ranger* continued north to New York City, which was then hosting the 1939 World's Fair. Underway for her destination on 27 April, she stood up the Hudson River on the morning of the 29th, and reached Pier 32 later that day, where she moored to await the onslaught of the curious, who descended upon the ship between 1 and 15 May. She logged a peak 9,975 visitors on 7 May. VF-4 and VB-3 both participated in observing the first annual "National Aviation Day" at the Fair. Inclement weather postponed the actual flight for two days, and, despite the presence of a front over the New York metropolitan area that compelled VF-4 to layover at Lakehurst to await clearing weather, the squadrons flew the parade on time. "Following a delightful lunch at Floyd Bennett [Field] as guests of the World's Fair," both squadrons made the quick return flight to Norfolk.[21]

Rear Adm. Alfred W. Johnson, Commander Atlantic Squadron, observed that the squadron's visit to New York City had been "interesting" and that "all hands had a good time though a rather strenuous one." The ships' officers and men had "acquitted themselves well," Johnson reported to Admiral Bloch, "and I am sure created a good impression and reflected credit on the navy." There had been no arrests, and "everyone showed great interest in our ships and genuine friendliness for the navy." Noting that over a half million people visited the ships, Johnson noted that the only disappointment had been "that thousands who wanted to see the ships had to be turned away because we could not safely handle more." New York City had proved "most hospitable," the men "particularly" enjoying the ball games, the dance at the Astor, and the trip to West Point, where they reviewed the Cadets.[22]

Finally departing New York on 17 May, the *Ranger* launched her air group to assume shore-based status at NOB Norfolk, later that afternoon. Arriving at its destination at

Rear Admiral Alfred W. Johnson, Commander Atlantic Squadron, 2 February 1939, San Juan, Puerto Rico. (AUTHOR)

1550 on the 17th, the group thus preceded the ship, which did not moor at Pier 7 until the following morning. She subsequently shifted to the Norfolk Navy Yard on the morning of 31 May, to begin her scheduled overhaul, which included the application of Mare Island Plastic Shipbottom Paint over two coats of corresponding anticorrosive paint. That work constituted the first time that the Norfolk Navy Yard had ever applied plastic paint to a large ship. Difficulties encountered in the operation of the specially designed spraying equipment resulted in a rough and irregular surface.[23]

While she teemed with the usual noisy busy-ness of a shipyard overhaul, the *Ranger* received a new captain on 3 June, as she lay alongside Pier 4, when Comdr. (Captain-selectee) Ralph F. Wood (USNA 1911), relieved Captain McCain. Wood had qualified in both lighter- and heavier-than-air, and had, like Pat Bellinger, commanded a submarine, the *Shark* (Submarine No. 8) early in his career. Among his tours of aviation duty afloat and ashore, Wood had commanded the Navy's first helium-inflated nonrigid airship *C-7*, NAS Coco Solo, and VF-1, prior to serving as the *Saratoga*'s air officer. After a tour as the *Lexington*'s exec under Capt. Arthur B. Cook, he had served as aviation aide to the Commandant of the 9th Naval District, then commanded the seaplane tender *Wright,* before being tapped, on 3 April 1939, to command the *Ranger.* In recommending Wood for the post of naval attaché for air to the embassy in Rome in 1926, then-Capt. Joseph M. Reeves had praised him as "an officer of outstanding ability...of broad views upon subjects other than those with which is immediately concerned...of character and force....He is a seaman as well as an [*sic*] naval aviator."[24] As commanding officer of a carrier, the last-mentioned traits were good to have. Yet, although Wood evidenced those traits to some, to others there was another side, one in which the written record did not reflect the reputation he held in the service. Arthur B. Cook, for example, later admitted to having a guilty conscience for not giving Wood an unsatisfactory fitness report when he had been exec of the *Lexington*. Wood eventually garnered a reputation as being overbearing toward his juniors.[25]

The assignment of the *Ranger* and the four *New Orleans*-class heavy cruisers of Cruiser Division 7 proved the first infusion of modern combatants into the U.S. Navy's forces in the Atlantic. A significant augmentation, it also presented major operational headaches in terms of training, because the *Ranger* and the cruisers had been separated from their type commands. With the *Ranger* the lone aircraft carrier in the Atlantic Squadron until the *Wasp* (CV-7) reached completion, Admiral Bloch feared that that would engender difficulties for type, intertype, and fleet training schedules. If an aircraft carrier and modern heavy cruisers were to be retained in the Atlantic, Bloch recommended, at the end of June 1939, that they should be relieved annually, so that "training of these units apart from their type organizations will not be continued too long."[26]

As the *Ranger* lay in the yard, her air group, as was customary, continued operating from ashore. On the afternoon

Standing up the Hudson, 29 April 1939, bound for Pier 32, during her visit to New York City for the 1939 World's Fair, flying her radio call sign from her starboard flag hoist (top to bottom): N A B F. (NHC, NH 81194)

of 29 June, Lt. Charles C. Howerton, the ship's assistant LSO flying a Grumman J2F-1 (BuNo 0169) from the ship's utility unit, with Aviation Machinist's Mate 3d Class R. J. Phelps and Seaman 1st Class J. A. Black on board, made a landing at Whitehurst Farms Field, near Norfolk, with his propeller in high pitch. "Chick" Howerton took off again, but neglected to change the propeller pitch to "low," as required by the instructions on the instrument board in the cockpit. Unable to gain sufficient altitude to clear the power lines that posed a hazard to operations from that field, Howerton opted to go under them, only to encounter a telephone wire strung halfway up the poles. The Grumman's propeller severed the wire and it damaged the left interplane strut. Had Howerton not decided to fly under the wires, however, he would have most likely struck the power lines and a serious accident would have resulted.[27]

For the ship, the yard routine proved just that—until the afternoon watch on 12 July. A fire broke out on the water alongside, between the ship, abreast frame 70, and the dock. The *Ranger* sounded fire quarters soon afterward, at 1445, following that with the general alarm and a call for the yard fire apparatus. Within a half hour, the blaze had been brought under control, but not before the starboard side, between frames 50 and 80, and an elevated gravity tank's insulation had been burned, the number one motor launch scorched, and the wiring beneath the flight deck at about frame 60 badly burned. Fortunately, only three men suffered smoke inhalation, and only one of those—Seaman 1st Class J. R. Smith—required extended treatment in sick bay. At 1602, all divisions opened their doors and ports for ventilation, and the electricians restored power to the ship by 1711.

The next day, as Bombing 4 (which had been redesignated from VB-3 on 1 July) carried out dive-bombing exercises, Ens. Robert R. Delareuelle, A-V(N), with Aviation Machinist's Mate 1st Class E. W. Deloache riding in back, began recovery from his first dive, of what was to be a second series of them that day, when he felt "excessive vibration throughout the plane." Quickly checking his SB2U-1 (BuNo 0743), Delareuelle saw that both of his flotation bags had deployed: the left one had split open and was flapping against the wing, the right had carried completely away. Pulling out of his dive at 2,000 feet, Delareuelle used full right rudder and considerable right aileron to maintain level flight back to NAS Norfolk, landing safely without further incident.[28]

Scouting Forty-Two carried out free gunnery runs on the 14th, off Virginia Beach. Ens. Lane Hurst was flying an SBU-1 (BuNo 9771), with Lt. William E. Pennewill in back, who shot holes in the horizontal stabilizer and the left elevator.[29]

On 27 July, Ens. Charles R. Elmore, A-V(N), checked his controls prior to takeoff as number three in section formation, in his SB2U-1 (BuNo 0731), for a gunnery flight. Finding stick and rudder operating normally, Elmore took off, with Aviation Machinist's Mate 1st Class C. L. Schooler in the rear cockpit. Attempting to apply left aileron as the Vought lifted off the ground, Elmore soon found the movement of his stick restricted, a short distance to the left of the neutral aileron position. After a second unsuccessful attempt to apply left aileron, Elmore, with the plane just five feet off the ground and rapidly nearing the east edge of the field, closed the throttle and landed. Applying a hard brake, he intentionally ground-looped the plane to avoid going into Willoughby Bay. Ground-looped 270 degrees to the left, the SB2U-1 dragged its right wing and right aileron, wrinkling both; the right tire wore through. Cutting the switch, Elmore climbed out of the Vought and inspected the controls. He found them unrestricted in movement. A trouble board declared 100% "material" cause of the accident.[30]

Scouting Forty-One logged an incident similar to that recounted by VS-42 on 14 July, off Virginia Beach on 7 August, when Radioman 2d Class B. A. Polen, radio-gunner in the SBU-1 (BuNo 9754) flown by Aviation Cadet Arthur J. Brassfield, USNR, put a bullet through the left horizontal stabilizer and the left elevator, while firing at a towed sleeve target. Scouting Forty-Two logged its second such incident four days later, when Radioman 2d Class Harold Stang, the passenger in the SBU-1 (BuNo 9807) flown by Ens. Edward J. Murphy, A-V(N), fired through the Vought's horizontal stabilizer and left elevator.[31]

The *Ranger* (Ralph Wood having received promotion to captain on 31 July), departed Norfolk Navy Yard on 23 August, and, over the ensuing days, ran her postrepair trials. She calibrated her radio direction finders on 28 August, and ship-handling exercises consumed the waning days of August, as she operated out of Lynnhaven Roads.

On the morning of 31 August, eight aviation machinist's mates from VF-4 embarked in a Sikorsky JRS-1, assigned to NAS Anacostia, for transportation. With Lt. Edward M. Blessman at the controls and with a crew of three, the seaplane took off with no trouble, but, when Blessman had reached the vicinity of the James River Bridge, he noted a "dull pounding" in the port engine, followed by considerable vibration. Heading back to NAS Norfolk, Blessman and his crew and passengers noted continuing pounding and vibration; as he approached the station to make a water landing, the pilot noted white smoke coming from the engine. As the Sikorsky alighted on the water, white smoke suddenly began pouring from the engine; the port engine cut out as Blessman approached the ramp, requiring him to make the ramp with the starboard engine only and also a tractor to tow him up on the ramp itself. VF-4's octet of petty officers, together with their hosts, walked away with no injuries.[32]

Sadly, another mishap, less than two hours later, did not end as happily. Ensign James H. Eoff, A-V(N), of VB-4, flying an SB2U-1 (BuNo 0776), took off for a navigation and radio training flight, with Radioman 3d Class Joseph T. George as his passenger. At about 1022, an eyewitness on the ground heard the sudden silence of an engine cutting out, something that attracted his attention.[33]

Eoff, apparently realizing that BuNo 0776 was in extremis and over terrain that would not permit a forced landing, ordered his passenger to bail out. Tragically, George's parachute became fouled on a part of the plane, for he appeared to be dangling some 15 feet behind and below it. Eyewitnesses then saw the plane sway from side to side, as if the pilot was trying to dislodge his trapped passenger. In staying at the controls in an effort to free George, however, Eoff sacrificed his own chance to jump clear of the Vought in its terminal dive. The SB2U-1, without power, plunged to earth in a near-vertical attitude near Stony Creek, Virginia, and crashed, killing both men instantly. The engine's being buried in five feet of mud and water testified not only to the force of impact, but defied any effort to determine what had happened. Investigators logged "undetermined" causes as the reason for the crash. In

Aviation Cadet James H. Eoff, 15 February 1936, with Class 83-C at NAS Pensacola, Florida. (NA, 80-G-450925, cropped)

courageously remaining on board to attempt to save his passenger's life, Ensign Eoff was awarded the Distinguished Flying Cross, posthumously.[34]

Far to the east, however, events on a grand scale would soon dwarf the *Ranger*'s routine and the sadness felt by shipmates who mourned the loss of Jim Eoff and Joe George. The *Ranger* lay anchored in Hampton Roads on 1 September 1939; that same day, Adolf Hitler's German mechanized legions, supported by a powerful tactical air arm, were smashing across the Polish frontier, demonstrating to the world in dramatic and chilling fashion, the Blitzkrieg—the speed and destructive power of modern warfare. How those events would effect the *Ranger*, and would determine the role she would play in the conflict that lay ahead, would soon be determined by the course of that conflagration that had begun to consume Europe.

12

"*RANGER* HAS TAKEN THE NECESSARY CHANGES IN ITS STRIDE"

The U.S. Navy's concentration on the West Coast in September 1939, where it had been since the spring, reflected America's traditional interest in the Far East and in its isolationist yearnings to keep out of European affairs. Although State and Navy Department people had discussed the matter as hostilities loomed on the horizon late in August, they made no plans to use U.S. Navy ships to repatriate American citizens, except in collecting small groups of them in the Mediterranean area, so they could be transported to safe ports for embarkation.

Rear Adm. Alfred W. Johnson, as Commander Atlantic Squadron, soon had his sailing orders on 4 September. On that day, the office of the Chief of Naval Operations (OpNav) ordered him to establish, as soon as possible, a combined air and ship patrol to observe and report, in cipher, the movements of warships of warring nations, east from Boston along a line to 42°30′N, 65°00′W, then south to 19°N, and around the seaward outline of the Windward and Leeward Islands to Trinidad, a British possession.

President Roosevelt proclaimed America's neutrality in the conflict, and, on 5 September, ordered the Navy to form a "Neutrality Patrol." To carry out that order, Adm. Harold R. Stark, the Chief of Naval Operations, directed Admiral Johnson to maintain an offshore patrol to report "in confidential system" the movements of all foreign men-of-war approaching or leaving the east coast of the United States and approaching and entering or leaving the Caribbean. U.S. Navy ships were to avoid making a report of foreign men-of-war or suspicious craft, however, on making contact or, when in their vicinity, to avoid the performance of unneutral service "or creating the impression that an unneutral service is being performed." The patrol was to extend about 300 miles off the east coast of the United States and along the eastern boundary of the Caribbean. Additionally, U.S. naval vessels were to report the presence of foreign warships sighted at sea to the district commandant concerned.

Along with Battleship Division 5, the *Ranger* formed a portion of the reserve for the Neutrality Patrol. Until needed, she continued her training, evolutions that continued to be characterized by occasional accidents that were part and parcel of the dangerous and demanding business of carrier aviation. On the same day that Admiral Stark ordered the establishment of the Neutrality Patrol, Lt. (jg) Richard S. Bull, Jr., of VS-41, flying an SBU-1 (BuNo 9811) on his third carrier qualification landing of the day, came in high. Given the cut, Bull attempted to hold the plane off and ease the landing, but, in so doing, the SBU floated over the arresting wires and crashed into the barrier, shearing off both landing gear, warping the wings, buckling the fuselage, pushing back the engine oil sump, damaging an engine cylinder, and bending both propeller blades.[1]

The following day, 6 September, Rear Admiral Johnson began to deploy the modest assets of the Atlantic Squadron, sending the small seaplane tenders *Gannet* (AVP-8) and *Thrush* (AVP-3) to establish a base at San Juan. The *Ranger* continued operations off the Virginia capes. Returning from a tactics hop during the afternoon watch, Lt. (jg) Clarence M. White, Jr., of VF-4, made his approach normally, and the LSO gave him the cut. White nosed down slightly, then kept easing back the stick, until his F3F-1 (BuNo 0217) flew into number three barrier in a full stall, the encounter with the barrier destroying the landing gear, springing and crushing both lower wing panels, and bending the propeller blades. White walked away from the barrier crash with a scratch on his left cheek when he hit the windshield.[2]

On the day after the heavy cruisers of Cruiser Division 7 sailed to begin patrols off the eastern seaboard between Newport, Rhode Island, and Norfolk, the *Quincy* (CA-39) and the *Vincennes* (CA-44) departing first, followed by the *San Francisco* (CA-38) and the *Tuscaloosa*, President Roosevelt, on 8 September, proclaimed a "limited national emergency" and ordered an increase in the enlisted strength of all of the armed forces. He also authorized the recall to active duty of officers, men, and nurses on the Navy and Marine Corps retired lists.

As the shadows of war lengthened over Europe and Asia, America clung tenaciously, but tenuously, to its neutrality. Against that backdrop of watchful waiting and the stirrings of preparedness, and with Captain Wood having been charged with overseeing the training of the *Ranger* and *Wasp* air groups (the latter having reported for duty with the Atlantic Squadron "for duty in connection with training, equipping, and organizing" on 12 July 1939), the *Ranger* conducted carrier qualifications off the Virginia capes with VB-4, VF-4, VS-41, and VS-42, and with VB-7, VF-7, VS-71, and VS-72, over the next three weeks. During the latter part of September, the *Ranger* also conducted SRBP and other training, before winding up those evolutions on the 29th.

After upkeep at NOB Norfolk, the *Ranger* sailed on 16 October for exercises. That same day, Rear Adm. Hayne Ellis (who had relieved Rear Admiral Johnson as Commander, Atlantic Squadron, on 30 September) issued contingency plans in case the German tanker *Emmy Friedrich*, then at Tampico, Mexico, tried to make a break for the Atlantic. One part of the plan specified that the *Ranger* and her planes were to search the Mexican gulf coast to locate and trail the German ship, which carried, among her cargo, carbonic acid, a necessary ingredient in shipboard refrigeration systems, such as that which cooled the magazines in the armored ship *Admiral Graf Spee*, which had begun commerce-raiding operations in the South Atlantic less than a fortnight before. President Roosevelt himself took an "intense interest" in the fate of the *Emmy Friedrich*.[3]

The *Ranger* returned to Hampton Roads on 20 October—the same day that the *Emmy Friedrich* sailed from Tampico to rendezvous with the *Admiral Graf Spee*. The British light cruiser HMS *Orion* and the Canadian destroyer HMCS *Saguenay*, however, turned back the German tanker in the Yucatan Channel soon thereafter, guiding another light cruiser, HMS *Caradoc*, to the scene. The *Emmy Friedrich*'s crew frustrated the British attempt to capture her when they scuttled her on 23 October, thus rendering unnecessary the *Ranger*'s having to proceed to the Gulf of Mexico.

On the same day that the waters closed over the *Emmy Friedrich*, the *Ranger* put to sea and conducted local operations off the Virginia capes which lasted until the 26th. Two days later, she departed Hampton Roads for Guantanamo, with destroyers *Fairfax* (DD-93) and *Badger* (DD-126) plane-guarding as she recovered her air group. A short time later, the *Gilmer* and the *Reuben James* relieved the *Fairfax* and the *Badger*. The three ships eventually reached their destination on 3 November.

For the next three weeks, the *Ranger* exercised in Cuban waters, and during a part of that time, her air group operated ashore from McCalla Field. On the last day of that stint of operations (28 November), a "fitful" wind from astern hampered recovery operations, lengthening landing intervals and causing "a few harder-than-average landings," as the ship brought her total number of recoveries to date to 21,658.[4]

With her sailors looking forward to their first real liberty in five weeks, the *Ranger* sailed for Havana the next day. While she was en route, however, "Miss Fortune" took a hand and dashed *Ranger*men's hopes of ever reaching the Cuban capital, when the *Ranger*'s former plane guard, the *Reuben James*, ran aground near the Old Bahama Channel. The *Ranger* bent on speed and arrived on the scene that same afternoon.

As the carrier was assisting her consort, her presence near the Old Bahama Channel was apparently prompting concern. In a telephone conversation concerning the *Reuben James*'s predicament on the afternoon of 30 November, Comdr. James L. Holloway, the chief of staff for the Commander Atlantic Squadron, asked Rear Adm. Robert L. Ghormley, in OpNav, if "anything [had been] settled about the *Ranger* coming north?"[5]

"I haven't gotten definite word yet," Ghormley responded.

"Well," Holloway continued, "I would sort of like to get that ship back up under mother's wing."

"Well, I think we probably will, but then we can't get that until..."

"Until we square this away, of course."

"We'll let you know about that as soon as we can," the admiral assured ComAtRon's chief of staff, "but this [the matter of the *Reuben James*] has got to be squared up first."

"Yes sir, I understand that," Holloway responded with a can-do attitude. "We'll sit on this until it is finished." Holloway promised to get the information that they discussed earlier, which involved the dispatch of more properly equipped salvage vessels, "right out to [Captain] Wood."

During the morning watch on 1 December, the *Ranger* hoisted out her number one motor launch, and pumped oil to form a slick around the grounded *Reuben James*. The *Ranger* remained in the destroyer's vicinity during the forenoon watch, as if standing a vigil. During the latter period, the carrier brought on board three torpedoes, ammunition, and depth charges to lighten the *Reuben James* and aid in refloating her. The salvage tug *Warbler* arrived on the scene about midway through the morning watch. Soon thereafter, Captain Wood left the *Ranger*, in the ship's number one motor launch, to board the destroyer.

At 1145, a signal from the *Reuben James* to the *Ranger* provided welcome news: the destroyer was afloat. The carrier took on board more ordnance material, however, 128 rounds of 4 inch/50 ammunition; nine more Mk. 8 torpedoes; and 14 more depth charges. Soon thereafter, Captain Wood returned to his ship. Later, during the first dog watch, the small seaplane tender *Lapwing* (AVP-1) reported for duty; three-quarters of an hour into the second dog watch, the *Ranger* went ahead two-thirds and set course for Charleston, South Carolina, in company with the damaged destroyer and her sistership *Fox* (DD-234). The small seaplane tender *Gannet* arrived an hour and a quarter into the first watch on the 1st, bringing with her Lt. Comdr. William J. Murphy, Construction Corps, and she soon transferred Murphy, a salvage specialist, to the *Ranger*, where he remained overnight. The carrier transferred him to the *Reuben James* midway through the morning watch the next day. The little convoy reached its destination on the 5th. Departing Charleston two days later, the *Ranger*, accompanied by the *Fox*, moored alongside Pier 7, NOB Norfolk, the next afternoon, after disembarking her 68-plane air group. "Anyway," one *Ranger* sailor sighed, philosophically, of the lack of liberty in Havana, "Home is more welcome than Cuba any day."[6]

In the Christmas issue of *The Bull Horn*, Captain Wood informed his crew that "recent world events have extended their influence into our world and lives and may be expected to continue this influence for an indefinite future. *Ranger* has taken the necessary changes in its stride, with increased efforts and in a hearty and cheerful spirit. We are able at this time to repay the nation for the years of preparation. We have the opportunity to prove that the nation's confidence and pride in its first line of defense is not misplaced. So, with a sense of accomplishment, based on past performances, we face the New Year with lively anticipation. For the year past, Well Done, for the next year may it be for All Hands—A Happy New Year."[7]

The *Ranger* rang in 1940 with operations off Cape Henry, qualifying the pilots of the *Wasp* Air Group. On 4 January, the ship conducted 81 landings, with VF-7 (Grumman F2F-1/F3F-1) and VS-72 (SB2U-2); the first mishap of the year occurred that day, when Lt. (jg) Joseph L. "Joe" Evans of VS-72, flying an SB2U-2 (BuNo 1358), with a sand bag in the rear seat for the carrier landing qualification, made a "slightly slow approach." The LSO wagged an emergency "come on," which went unanswered. Settling too rapidly, Evans's SB2U hit the ramp with both wheels and bounced on its tail, bending the tailwheel oleo piston tube. Fortunately, the aircraft's arrestor hook caught one of the cross-deck pendants, stopping the plane's forward motion. Careless handling in the wake of the accident, however, added further damage. A trouble board placed the blame on Joe Evans, onetime star football and lacrosse player at the Naval Academy, for not properly answering the LSO's signals.[8]

Between 9 and 11 January, the *Ranger* logged 368 landings, as she conducted individual and squadron qualifications for not only part of her own air group (VB-4 with its SB2U-1s, VS-41 with its SBU-1s, and the CRAG with his SB2U-1), but the *Wasp*'s as well. Off Hampton Roads on the first day of that stint, Ens. George S. Leonard, A-V(N), of VB-7, made a normal approach in his BG-1 (BuNo 9501), but was slightly to the left of the centerline of the flight deck. Upon touching down, Leonard, who had had 52.3 hours in the cockpits of BG-1s over the previous three months, inadvertently allowed the big biplane "to assume a skidding attitude to [the] right," causing the right landing gear strut to fail, because of the side thrust forces exerted upon it.[9]

Operating between Cape Henry and Charleston, South Carolina, the *Ranger* continued qualification and refresher landings, as well as experimental fighter and scout plane operations, between 15 and 18 January, logging 522 landings during that week. Things began badly the first day out, at the start of the afternoon watch on 15 January. Ensign Howard F. Dostal, A-V(N), of VF-4, was in takeoff position in his F3F-1 (BuNo 0253), when he received the "turn up" signal from the flight deck officer. In anticipation of the takeoff signal, however, Dostal started forward, tail high. Unfortunately, Dostal's propeller bit into the deck, bending the blades and causing internal damage to the engine.[10]

The next day, the *Wasp* Air Group experienced its own woes. During the forenoon watch, Lt. (jg) Richard A. Teel

In a scene reminiscent of Kachemak Bay four years earlier, snow whitens the *Ranger*'s flight deck, Hampton Roads, 9 January 1940. (NA, 80-CF-5487-5)

of VB-7, flying a BG-1 (BuNo 9506), with Aviation Machinist's Mate A. V. Cobb in back, moved his stick neither forward nor aft in response to the LSO's cut, but involuntarily eased back as he neared the deck, allowing the BG-1 to float up the deck and hit the barrier. Less than a half hour later, Ens. Spencer D. Wright A-V(N), flying another BG-1 (BuNo 9543), with Aviation Machinist's Mate 2d Class R. V. Stokes in back, held off after the cut, a display of "poor technique" that resulted in Wright's BG-1 catching the eighth wire. The resulting short run-out permitted the plane to go into the barrier, damaging both blades of the propeller.[11]

During the afternoon watch, however, tragedy marred bow carrier landing practice. Ensign Malcolm C. Kirby, A-V(N) of VF-7, flying a Grumman F2F-1 (BuNo 9673), had made five approaches, each time getting a wave-off from the LSO. Kirby failed to line up his sixth approach properly, also, and again the LSO gave him a wave-off. Kirby, however, turned left instead of right, toward, instead of away from, the island. Investigators later posited that Kirby apparently realized his mistake and tried to clear the island, but lost control of 7-F-17 and crashed. Sinking immediately, the stubby Grumman biplane took the 27-year-old pilot, who may have been knocked unconscious in the crash and thus unable to extricate himself from the aircraft, to the bottom. Neither man nor machine was recovered.[12]

Kirby's loss seemed to set the tone for the rest of the day for the *Wasp* Air Group. Lieutenant Charles H. Ostrom, flying an SBU-1 (BuNo 9817), with Radioman 1st Class

A.E. Pottage in back, dove for the gear in his sixth carrier landing; motion pictures of the landing showed that the SBU had floated for some distance over the arresting wires, with wheels and hook at about the same level, until going into the barrier, with resultant damage that required a major overhaul to fix. Later, Lt. Frank Turner of VS-72, flying an SB2U-2 (BuNo 1360), with Radioman 2d Class G. T. Blalock in back, shared part of the blame for a mishap that occurred about an hour later, when he responded to the LSO's "come on" signal with more throttle. The SB2U touched down at about the number three wire, but continued up the deck in a tail-high attitude, until it hit the barrier.[13]

Flying out to the *Ranger* from Norfolk the following day (17 January), Lt. (jg) Clarence M. White, Jr., of VF-4, came in slightly fast, but landed wheels-first about wire number three. His F3F-1 (BuNo 0263) bounced and floated the remaining distance into the second barrier, causing considerable damage to the plane. White emerged from the accident with a slight scratch above his left eyebrow. VF-4's woes continued the next day, when Ens. Carl W. Peterson, A-V(N), turned into the groove in his F3F-1 (BuNo 0229), at about a 75-foot altitude. Hitting the slipstream of the plane directly ahead of him, Peterson lost control as his Grumman made a half-roll to the left, hitting the water nose-first. In the crash, Peterson suffered a lacerated wound over his left eye and a hematoma on his left eyelid; he was picked up by a plane-guard destroyer.[14]

During February, the *Ranger* Air Group operated from shore bases; Lt. (jg) Fritz Schrader, flying an SB2U-1 (BuNo 0745) assigned to VF-4, experienced trouble with his landing gear, in a mishap later attributed entirely to material failure. Neither Schrader nor his passenger, Chief Radioman M. D. Corson, suffered any injuries in the incident which occurred at Chambers Field, Norfolk, on 8 February.[15] Five days later, Lt. (jg) Eugene W. Davis, with Radioman 2d Class R. Shreffler on board in an SBU-1 (BuNo 9775), took off from NAS Norfolk, but soon found himself wind-blown into the slipstream of the plane that had taken off just ahead. Making a sharp turn and ground-looping soon thereafter, the Vought nosed over, gasoline spilling from the carburetor and catching fire. The plane's own CO_2 system, and a quickly arriving station fire crew, managed to extinguish the blaze. Although a trouble board faulted Davis's poor takeoff technique, it also apportioned part of the blame upon the tower duty officer.[16]

Ferrying an SB2U-1 (BuNo 0746) to Stratford, Connecticut, Municipal Airport, on 16 February, Ens. Moose Kelsch taxied across a patch of snow after landing and found it difficult to turn the plane. Coming to a complete stop, Kelsch surveyed the ground from the cockpit and decided to taxi through the snow that appeared to be only about six inches deep. Meanwhile, Kelsch's passenger, Ens. Billy V. Gates, A-V(N), clambered down out of the after cockpit and began to push on the wing to help turn the aircraft. Kelsch applied the throttle and the SB2U moved ahead only about six feet, before it slowly nosed up into the wind. The pilot cut the switch, but not before his propeller was damaged. Changing the prop subsequently enabled it to be flown back to NAS Norfolk without further incident.[17]

Before the month was out, the *Ranger* Air Group logged its last mishap for February, when Lt. James A. Haley, Jr., released a target sleeve after towing for individual battle practice gunnery over the National Guard field at Virginia Beach on the morning of 27 February. After making a pass around the field, Haley forgot to crank down his gear. Descending in a three-point attitude, the F3F-1 (BuNo 0261) slid about 40 feet before the left wing dug into the ground, the Grumman slewing to the left, coming to a stop in an upright position. Although the soft condition of the field limited the damage to the plane, a trouble board faulted Haley for "carelessness."[18]

Carelessness figured in another mishap that occurred even before the *Ranger* sailed for the next stint of underway training. On 4 March, Ens. William R. Harlow, A-V(N), of VS-72, had the predawn task of taxiing an SB2U-2 (BuNo 1373) from West Field to the operating base where the ship lay moored alongside Pier 7. In the conditions of semidarkness prevailing at that hour, Harlow apparently lost track of his route and ended up in soft sand, the wheels sinking far enough that it permitted the propeller blades to strike the ground, bending and breaking the tips before the pilot pulled back on the throttle and cut the engine. A trouble board faulted Harlow for negligence, but it also took into account "miscellaneous" factors, including darkness and low visibility.[19]

The *Ranger* continued her operations off Charleston, again conducted qualifications for the *Wasp* Air Group; her own group continued operating from West Field. During the first stint, on 6 and 7 March, she logged 350 landings with VF-7's F2F-1 and F3F-1s, VS-71's SB2U-1s, VS-72's SB2U-2s, VB-7's BG-1s, the Comdr. Wasp Air Group's SB2U-1 and 7-F-19, the SB2U-2 assigned to VF-7. Ensign James F. Rigg, A-V(N), of VF-7, on his third qualification landing, brought in his F3F-1 (BuNo 0257), only to have his left landing gear fail upon landing, resulting in a scraped lower left wing and a nicked propeller.[20]

That same day, Ens. Alfred I. Boyd, A-V(N), of VF-4, flew in to West Field after a gunnery hop. Bringing in his

Vought SBU-1 (BuNo 9820), 41-S-8, displaying the "walking duck on roller skates" insignia below the cockpit, a maintenance "E" above the landing gear, and the "neutrality star," applied in accordance with the directive of 19 March 1940, adorning the engine cowling. (NA, 80-G-5636)

F3F-1 (BuNo 0219) fast, he floated half the distance of the strip before his wheels even touched the ground. Boyd tried his brakes, but, after running about 50 yards, the Grumman bounced. Coming down again near the sea wall, Boyd quickly realized that he would go over the wall if he did not take drastic action—and soon—so he deliberately ground-looped to the left. The Grumman nosed over, suffering damage to all wings, struts and fittings, and demolishing the vertical fin and rudder, buckling the fuselage, and bending the propeller blades. Boyd suffered no injuries in the accident, which the trouble board blamed entirely on his error in judgment.[21]

During the second stint off of Charleston, carried out between 11 and 15 March, the *Ranger* qualified only the *Wasp*'s scout and bomber pilots (VS-71, VS-72, and VB-7), before fog and rain, followed by wind that gusted from varying directions, curtailed flying on 15 March. Resuming again on 18 March, the *Ranger* logged 407 landings that week, before the evolutions ended on the 22d. Only one mishap spoiled an otherwise perfect record, however, when Ens. Benjamin M. Lakin, A-V(N), of VF-7, displayed poor technique in landing, causing his F3F-1 (BuNo 0242) to land wheels-first, collapsing the left landing gear.[22]

Operating in Lynnhaven Roads, the *Ranger* resumed work with her own air group on 1 April, and, over the next four days, logged 590 individual and squadron qualification landings. That first afternoon, Ens. Maynard M. "Bud" Furney, A-V(N), flying an F3F-1 (BuNo 0227), took the cut but dropped the nose and made a hard landing. The Grumman bounced, catching a wire, the latter

Four-Baker-Six, a Vought SB2U-1 (BuNo 0760) from VB-4 in flight, with "neutrality star," prominent "Top Hat" insignia on the fuselage, and practice bomb rack visible beneath the port wing. (Emil Buehler Aviation History Library)

Vought SB2U-1 (BuNo 0773) with the white-edged Willow Green diagonal stripe on the fuselage indicating its assignment to the Comdr., *Ranger* Air Group (CRAG), and the two-foot diameter "neutrality star" on the cowling. Lettering on the fuselage beneath the cockpit sill is LT. CDR. O. A. WELLER. Lieutenant Commander Oscar A. "Tex" Weller commanded the *Ranger* group from 30 June 1939 to 7 June 1940. Note Grumman F3F-2 from VMF-1 in the background (L). (Harry S. Gann Collection, via Thomas E. Doll)

NOB Norfolk, 28 March 1940; the *Ranger* shares Pier 7 (top) with the battleship *New York* (BB-34) (Comdr. Atlantic Squadron flagship) and the heavy cruiser *Tuscaloosa* (CA-37). At lower piers lie the transport *Chaumont* (AP-5), the ammunition ship *Nitro* (AE-2), the light cruiser *Omaha* (CL-4), gunnery training ship (ex-battleship) *Wyoming* (AG-17) and the destroyers *Gilmer* (DD-233), *Truxtun* (DD-229), *Borie* (DD-215), *Broome* (DD-210), *Simpson* (DD-221), *Greer* (DD-145), *Yarnall* (DD-143), and *Upshur* (DD-144). (NA, 80-G-454474)

slamming the plane to the deck and collapsing the left landing gear, in the only accident for VF-4 in its 128 landings that week.[23]

During the next stint of training, the *Ranger*'s air group practiced for, and conducted, live firing and bombing drills on 9, 10, and 11 April; pilots of the F3F-1s, SB2U-1s, and SBU-1s all conducted their takeoffs with bomb loads. During the forenoon watch on the 10th, Ens. Charles M. King, A-V(N), in an SB2U-1 (BuNo 9812), climbed to 13,000 feet for a practice dive-bombing run. Pushing over at 12,000 to begin his dive, he saw smoke issuing from his engine at 6,000 feet. He released one of his 100-pound practice bombs at 4,500, and pulled out at 2,500. Pulling alongside 42-S-17, King indicated his predicament to his squadronmate, keeping his motor idling and giving it a burst of "gun" to avoid fouling the plugs. As stifling smoke filled his cockpit, King overtook and flew alongside the *Ranger*'s starboard side at an altitude of 400 feet, rocking his wings. He banked across the path of the ship; observers saw flames not only coming from beneath the engine, but trailing along the fuselage underneath. Leveling off at 10 feet above the waves, King made a full stall water landing. The SB2U turned over soon after impact; although King suffered no injuries, his passenger, Hospitalman 3d Class C. T. Stuart, suffered a fractured clavicle. A major overhaul lay in store for King's plane.[24]

Later that same day, Lt. Joseph C. Clifton of VF-4 reprised Bud Furney's poor technique of nine days before, ironically in the same F3F-1. On this occasion, however, Joe Clifton's landing saw the right wheel hitting first, collapsing the right gear, allowing the prop and the right lower wing to hit the deck. This proved to be the only deck crash in 390 landings logged during the 9–11 April period.[25]

Early in May of 1940, the *Ranger*'s air group operated from NAS Norfolk, conducting gunnery and squadron tactics. During the former, on 8 May, Ens. Howard Dostal spun in from 20 feet when his F3F-1 (BuNo 0259) stalled after clearing a building during his approach to West Field, suffering a bruised left arm in the process. On 10 May, Lt. (jg) Everett M. Link, Jr., spun in from 30 feet, after he approached Chambers Field too close astern of the plane ahead of him; his F3F-1 (BuNo 0220) got caught in the slipstream. Link suffered scalp lacerations and several small contusions.[26]

The *Ranger* conducted night qualification and squadron refresher landings with her own air group (13–17 May), logging 346 landings; on the first day of that stint (13 May), Ens. Roger R. Hedrick, A-V(N), of VF-4, logged his 100th arrested landing on board the same ship. The *Ranger* then carried out individual and squadron qualifications with her own and the *Wasp* Air Group (20–24 May), logging 133 landings, with only one crash into the barrier during that time: Lt. (jg) Charles D. Hoover's engine began running roughly soon after takeoff on an individual qualification flight during the first dog watch on 21 May. He radioed the *Ranger* and informed the ship that he had to make a deferred forced landing. Hoover took the cut, but could not reduce his altitude to catch a wire. His F3F-1 (BuNo 0262) floated over the arresting gear, carrying away number two barrier and crashing into barrier four. A major overhaul lay in store for the Grumman, but Hoover walked away from the crash with a slight scratch under his right eye.[27]

Alone of the *Ranger*'s squadrons during the latter period of operations at sea, VS-41 operated from NAS Norfolk. It logged one mishap on 21 May, when Ens. Thomas D. Harris, A-V(N), experienced engine failure, during a night tactics hop in an SBU-1 (BuNo 9787), while at an altitude of 800 feet over Hampton Roads. Working the wobble pump vigorously gave Harris a momentary reprieve, but, when the engine quit again, the pilot dropped a flare before he resumed working the wobble pump. Descending to 200 feet, Harris began to prepare to land, turning 135 degrees out of the wind, to land in the light of his flare. The SBU landed hard, throwing Harris clear; the BuNo 9787's turned over and sank in about 20 feet of water. Harris survived his dunking, with no injuries, in an accident that the resulting trouble board blamed squarely on the plane's fuel system.[28]

13

"SPREADING THE BUTTER A LITTLE THIN"

Concluding exercises on the Southern Drill Grounds on 31 May, the *Ranger* arrived at the Norfolk Navy Yard later the same day, to begin an overhaul that would last through the end of July. During that time, she would receive six 3-inch/50-caliber antiaircraft guns, installed in lieu of a like number of 1.1-inch/75-caliber quadruple-mount machine guns, which would be shipped when available. Installation of the guns, together with the expected heavier aircraft that would soon be reaching carrier air groups, however, meant that eventually the arresting gear and the flight deck barriers would need to be rearranged.

Painting the ship's underwater hull was among the work to be performed. Although the ship had been able to make full power with little hindrance after inspections by the ship's divers had revealed the application of plastic paint on her underwater hull to have been substandard, correspondence ensued that revealed a difference of opinion as to whether or not the situation warranted drydocking the ship. Mirroring the opinion of Vice Adm. Charles A. Blakely, Commander Aircraft, Battle Force, that the corroded areas of the *Ranger*'s underwater hull be "*thoroughly cleaned* [emphasis original] and repainted with appropriate anticorrosive and Mare Island plastic" paints, the Bureaus of Construction and Repair and Engineering approved and authorized the necessary work.[1]

Ralph Wood's tour as commanding officer was drawing to a close. The high number of casualties in the *Ranger*'s training operations had prompted an investigation. Although the board convened to look into the matter did not specifically recommend it, Wood was relieved.[2] Soon after the *Ranger* entered the yard, Wood turned over command to Capt. Alfred E. Montgomery on 6 June, in ceremonies on the hangar deck.

The *Ranger*'s new captain was no stranger to the ship, having been Pat Bellinger's exec. Regarded by some as "impatient, sarcastic, irascible," Montgomery occasionally suffered from migraine headaches, which may have accounted for the apparent impatience, sarcasm, and irascibility. Considered "difficult to please," "not popular but highly respected," he had graduated from the Naval Academy a year after Ralph Wood (who apparently had been neither popular nor respected), and, like many early aviators, had seen service in submarines, serving as exec in the *E-1* (Submarine No. 24) and commander of the *F-1* (Submarine No. 20), until the latter was sunk in a collision with a sistership on 17 December 1917. Subsequently, he commanded the *R-20* (Submarine No. 97), during which time, while the ship was based in Hawaiian waters, he took elementary flight training in seaplanes at Pearl Harbor. Although he had been slated for command of a new "S" boat, the *S-32* (SS-137), he was transferred to superintend new ships under construction at the Mare Island Navy Yard.

After flight instruction at Pensacola, Montgomery received his naval aviator's wings on 8 June 1922. His aviation duty followed patterns similar to his contemporaries, as he served in aviation units and ships, in billets of increasing responsibility. These included air officer in the *Langley*,

Captain Ralph F. Wood reads his orders detaching him from command, 6 June 1940. (NA, 80-G-391566)

heading the aviation section of OpNav's Ship Movement Division, serving as operations officer on the staff of ComAirBatFor, serving as the *Ranger*'s exec, executive officer of NAS San Diego, and finally heading the Flight Division of BuAer, before getting orders to command the *Ranger*.

While the *Ranger* had been in the Navy Yard, her air group had continued its training from ashore. Ensign Albert B. Christman, A-V(N), of VB-4, had completed an instrument training flight in good weather, with Lt. (jg) Ralph A. Embree as his passenger. Christman, who in civilian life had assisted cartoonist Milt Caniff draw the popular comic strip "Terry and the Pirates," landed his SB2U-1 (BuNo 0745) at Whitehurst Auxiliary Field, Norfolk, when he noticed flames coming from the engine. Although he applied the throttle, the engine did not respond and stopped. Turning off the gas, Christman activated the CO_2 fire extinguisher and cut the ignition. As the pilot attempted to restart the engine, the fire broke out anew. Fortunately, neither Christman nor Embree suffered any injuries.[3]

As the second full week of June ended, VF-4 wound up operations out of West Field. Lieutenant Jack I. Bandy took off on a practice bombing hop in an F3F-1 (BuNo 0238), from an unsurfaced field, on 13 June. As he did so, however, the right landing gear buckled, causing the aircraft to ground-loop to the right, damaging the lower right wingtip.[4] The next afternoon, Lt. (jg) Clarence M. White, Jr., flying VF-4's sole Curtiss SBC-3 (BuNo 0508), with Aviation Ordnanceman 1st Class D. F. Asmus in back, returned from a familiarization flight; White reduced his speed to the point that the Curtiss biplane began to "squash" from an altitude of 30 feet, and landed on his left wheel, damaging the left wingtip and flap. The resulting trouble board faulted White's "poor technique."[5]

Brix Christman figured in another incident involving another SB2U-1, a little over a fortnight after his first. After completing an instrument flight on a cloudy, warm day, through very light winds and drizzling rain, Christman was approaching Whitehurst Auxiliary Field on 25 June, so that he could land and change places with his passenger, Ens. Frank Malinasky, A-V(N), so that Malinasky could get in his flight time. Coming in from the north, Christman made almost a three-point landing on the wet grass of the field, but could not get the plane to stop. The rampaging Vought rolled about 350 yards to the edge of the field, where two ditches fortuitously arrested its progress, bringing it to a stop just short of a house. Both Christman and Malinasky walked away from the accident unhurt, but the aircraft (BuNo 0736) required a major overhaul before it could be flown again.[6]

Training had been part of the mission of the *Ranger* and her squadrons, and of the Atlantic Squadron to which she had been assigned. During the spring of 1940, the situation in Europe had taken an alarming turn, and by the end of June, Germany stood as master of the European continent. As the reporting year ended, Rear Adm. Ellis wrote that, during the period from 1 July 1939 to 30 June 1940, the Atlantic Squadron's peacetime mission had developed into a dual one: (1) enforcement of American neutrality and (2) the training of people. As constituted, Ellis wrote, the Atlantic Squadron was "entirely adequate to the performance of... Peace Time Tasks." The "Primary War Mission" of the squadron, however, was to defend and further American interests in the Atlantic. "The present composition of this Squadron," Ellis concluded, "is quite inadequate to cope with the forces which the progress of events in Europe may soon release to operate against it."[7]

The demands of the Neutrality Patrol duty, plus the lack of necessary services, combined to prevent the *Ranger* from completing all of the target practices required for the 1939–40 gunnery year; changes in operating schedules, lack of services, and a shift of bases (the assignment of the *Enterprise* to the Hawaiian Detachment in the autumn of 1939) hampered the training of the other carriers, as well. Although Adm. James O. Richardson, Commander Battle Force, considered the *Ranger*'s antiaircraft battery's score "highly unsatisfactory" for SRBP the *Ranger* again won the DAR Antiaircraft Trophy for her creditable performance in antiaircraft practices for the 1939–40 gunnery year,[8] Mrs. Henry M. Robert, President General of the DAR, presented the trophy to Captain Montgomery, who received it on behalf of the ship.

Shifting to Pier 7, NOB Norfolk, on 1 August, the *Ranger* operated locally for the next several weeks, exercising on the Southern Drill Grounds into mid-September.

On 5 August, during aerial gunnery exercises off Virginia Beach, Lt. (jg) John M. "Count" DeVane of VB-4, with Radioman 2d Class L. A. Curtis in back, inadvertently flew his SB2U-1 (BuNo 0750) too close to a sleeve target and collided with it. The resulting bent wing rib and bent aileron caused "moderate wing heaviness at low air speed," but DeVane managed to land without further incident.[9] VB-4 logged its second mishap before the month was out, when Ens. James D. Arbes, A-V(N)'s left landing gear failed to lower on the 22d. His SB2U-1 (BuNo 0746) suffered damage to the left wing in the resulting ground loop, but neither Arbes nor his passenger, Aviation Chief Ordnanceman C. T. Bradley, suffered any injuries.[10]

Operating in Lynnhaven Roads from 3 to 6 September, the *Ranger* conducted individual squadron and group qualifications and group refresher landings, logging 557 landings of her own air group (including the group commander, who had been assigned an SBC-3 biplane in place of the monoplane SB2U-1) plus VMS-1, a Marine unit that operated the familiar Bouncing Girls. Two mishaps occurring the same day (5 September) punctuated that stint of operations.

The first occurred during the forenoon watch, when Lt. (jg) Lloyd A. Smith of VS-42, flying an SBU-1 (BuNo 9751), with Radioman 1st Class J. A. Anderson in back, made a normal landing and put his hook up. The officer in charge at the cross-deck pendants signalled for him "to get out of the gear quickly." Applying full gun to get the plane rolling, Smith throttled back slightly and moved the Vought forward at normal speed, then slowed as he rolled past the first lowered barrier. Still being vigorously waved up the deck, however, Smith glanced up the deck to see the next signalman, but none was in sight. He continued to slow down, and was about at normal taxiing speed as he passed the forward barrier. At that point, he noticed the tail of another aircraft dead ahead, about 20 feet away. Smith applied the brakes quickly, and BuNo 9751 skidded a short distance, then nosed up, with the propeller striking the deck several times, the force of that action stopping the plane from going over on its nose, and the tail then fell back to the deck with considerable force. A trouble board apportioned part of the blame upon Smith for an error of judgment (40%), but faulted the flight deck crew more for its share (60%).[11]

The second incident that day occurred in recovery operations during the afternoon watch, when Ens. Walter F. "Wally" Madden, A-V(N), made a normal approach, but, after receiving the cut, dove for the gear in his F3F-1 (BuNo 0219). He landed in a slight skid, and slightly right-wheel-first, buckling the landing gear compression link. The trouble board faulted Madden for his technique, but made an allowance for the landing gear design as well.[12]

Fighting four experienced another accident before the month was out, when Ens. Bud Furney, after taking off on a bombing hop on the morning of 20 September, in an F3F-1 (BuNo 0452), noticed that his oil tank filler cap had not been properly seated. Returning immediately to West Field at NAS Norfolk, Furney failed to lower his landing gear. The Grumman slid along on its belly for about 110 feet before it turned over, and the pilot received minor abrasions of the forehead and his right forearm in the crash. "In view of the fact that this approach to West Field is normally difficult," Lt. Comdr. Elton C. "Billy" Parker, VF-4's commanding officer, allowed later, "and recently rendered moreso by the new construction in the landing area, Ensign Furney's preoccupation with the landing is understandable." Nevertheless, the resulting trouble board faulted Furney for negligence in not cranking down his gear before landing.[13]

Following two weeks of in-port upkeep, the *Ranger* left Norfolk in her wake on 2 October for Guantanamo, which she reached on the 5th. Upon arrival, the *Ranger*'s air group assumed shore-based status at McCalla Field. The *Ranger* conducted night battle practice runs, flight operations, and other training evolutions into the second week of November 1940. During that time, Rear Adm. Arthur B. Cook, who had reported as Commander Aircraft, Atlantic Squadron, and Commander, Carrier Division 3, on 23 October, shifted his flag from the light cruiser *Memphis* (CL-13) to the *Ranger* on 30 October. With the subsequent change in designation from Atlantic Squadron to Patrol Force on 1 November, Cook's title changed to Commander Aircraft, Patrol Force.

Only two mishaps marred the *Ranger*'s flight operations during that time, and each illustrated the hazards inherent in carrier work. In the first, during the afternoon watch on 11 October, Capt. Robert O. Bisson, USMC, of VMS-1, made a normal approach for a qualification landing, flying a Grumman J2F-4 (BuNo 1652). After the LSO gave Bisson the "cut" signal, the Marine pilot kicked the Grumman into a skid, apparently to get a better view of the deck. The last-minute compensation caused Bisson to make a bad landing, bending the right compression strut, holing the right wingtip pontoon, blowing the right tire, and starting rivets in the vicinity of the right wheel recess, and slightly damaging the keel.[14]

The second mishap occurred a month later, on 12 November, when, during bombing practice, Lt. Abraham L. Baird, with Ens. William E. Rouse, A-V(N), as his passenger, landed his SB2U-1 (BuNo 0771) and taxied it forward. With the deck for some reason more crowded than usual, Baird had been signaled to stop his plane. Baird did so. Soon, he saw the flight deck officer motion him forward. Unfortunately, Baird had just started to answer the signal when Ens. Robert R. Marks, A-V(N), with Aviation Machinist's Mate 1st Class N. G. Weatherman in the rear seat, brought his SB2U-1 (BuNo 0767) out of the arresting gear "with more speed than the situation would warrant." Events unfolded swiftly, and Marks's SB2U was traveling too fast for the brakes to have any effect. In an instant, Marks's propeller tore into the tail section of Baird's plane, tearing the rudder fabric and damaging the starboard horizontal stabilizer and elevator beyond repair; flying metal punctured the vertical stabilizer in three places. Marks's plane nosed up, with the prop blades digging into the deck and causing engine damage from the sudden stoppage. A trouble board leveled blame for the accident in equal parts on Ensign Marks's "poor technique," but also faulted the flight deck crew for bringing him out of the gear too soon.

The *Ranger*'s work-up for the nocturnal gunnery shoot paid off, as she earned an accolade for her "outstanding" work in that particular exercise. Then, in company with the *Wasp* and plane guard destroyers *Moffett* (DD-362) and *Trippe* (DD-403), the *Ranger* departed Guantanamo on 18 November to operate off Culebra, Puerto Rico. She returned to Gitmo on 23 November.

During the time that the *Ranger* lay anchored at Guantanamo, her captain addressed an issue of concern on 28 November. With the ship's next overhaul scheduled for the following March, Captain Montgomery signed a request to the Bureau of Ships that all three of his ship's aircraft elevators be replaced or designed to permit them "to operate at a speed commensurate with that obtainable in recent aircraft carrier design." The operating cycle of *Yorktown*-class carriers was 45 seconds, identical to the proposed *Essex* (CV-9)-class ships. The growing size of carrier planes, Montgomery explained, dictated constant use of the *Ranger*'s hangar stowage "with the consequent use of elevators during launching and landing operations." Additionally, the small size of the elevator precluded moving more than one aircraft at a time. The 20 seconds it took to get the elevator up and 19 down, with a 10-second loading or unloading interval on the flight and hangar deck (making a total of 59 seconds—14 seconds longer than the *Yorktown* and *Essex* classes) hampered the handling of planes and reduced the flexibility of aircraft operations. Rear Admiral Cook concurred in Montgomery's request, considering the alteration "a military necessity."[15]

Departing Cuban waters for Culebra on 2 December, the *Ranger* reached her destination on the 4th. She sailed in the predawn darkness of 6 December, and participated in

The *Ranger*, Guantanamo Bay, Cuba, 12 January 1941, with two of her starboard smoke pipes lowered. (NA, 80-G-391583)

Fleet Landing Exercise No. 2, conducting flight operations that day and again on the 8th. Returning to Culebra on the 9th, the carrier departed the following morning for Norfolk, mooring at Pier 7 late on the afternoon of the 13th. Four days later, the *Ranger* steamed out of her berth, bound for Plantation Flats, where she conducted degaussing runs and tested her paravane gear en route. That work completed on the 19th, she stood in to Hampton Roads, shifting to NOB Norfolk the next morning, where she remained through year's end.

Three days into the year 1941, VB-4, VF-4, and VS-72 embarked on board the *Ranger*, shifting their status from shore-based at the Fleet Air Depot to ship-based; VS-41 and VS-42 remained at NAS Norfolk. Shifting from the NOB to a berth in the stream at Hampton Roads on 6 January, the *Ranger* sailed for Guantanamo the following afternoon, in company with other units of the Atlantic Fleet, arriving on the morning of the 11th. Six days later, the *Ranger* embarked VMO-1, VMS-1, and VMJ-1, as well as from the First Marine Aircraft Group headquarters and service element, and, the following day, transferred VF-4 to temporary duty ashore at McCalla Field.

The *Ranger* sailed for Jamaica on 18 January, in company with the heavy cruiser *Tuscaloosa* and the destroyers *O'Brien* (DD-415) and *Trippe*. On the same day, Capt. Robert O. Bisson, USMC, flying a J2F-1 (BuNo 0187) of the *Ranger*'s utility unit, exhibited what a trouble board considered "poor technique" in landing, when his hook failed to catch a wire and the Grumman amphibian passed over the first barrier, with the hook finally catching number four barrier. Seaman 1st Class M. J. Mayer and Aviation Machinist's Mate 1st Class F. V. Lovell, at their flight quarters stations, suffered injuries in the accident.[16]

Reaching Portland Bight, Jamaica, the following morning, the *Ranger* conducted maneuvers with Cruiser Division 7, as well as flight operations the following day. On 21 January,

Ens. James D. Arbes, A-V(N), of VB-4, logged his 100th landing on the same ship. Arriving back in Puerto Rican waters on the 22d, she spent the remainder of January engaged in carrying out flight and gunnery exercises off Culebra. During that time, on 23 January, Maj. Thomas C. Green, USMC, flying a BG-1 (BuNo 9514) from VMO-1, for a gunnery flight, with Technical Sgt. V. E. Murphy, USMC, in back, noticed his engine smoking badly, and with a loss in power, brought the plane back to the ship for a normal landing.[17]

During VF-4's operations from McCalla Field, Ens. Robert C. Jones, A-V(N), had been the last to land on the first approach during squadron tactical operations on 29 January. He had no sooner retracted his gear and formed up to rendezvous when the rest of VF-4 cranked down their gear to land. Jones did likewise, following the movements of the others, but, upon making the next landing approach and taking the cut from the LSO, the wheels retracted upon touchdown, breaking both landing gear chains. The F4F-3 (BuNo 1863) consequently settled onto its barrel-fuselage and cowling, damaging the propeller. The resulting trouble board faulted Jones for negligence.[18]

Meanwhile, the *Ranger*'s squadrons left behind at Norfolk carried out the work set forth in their syllabi of training. Normally, pilots could often consider ferrying a plane from one place to another a routine affair, devoid of drama. One such flight, however, proved memorable for Ens. Tom Harris of VS-41. En route to Atlanta, he suddenly executed a steep spiral and landed on what looked like the only flat field in the vicinity, behind a peaceful-looking farmhouse. The field had once been used by a local flying enthusiast, but not for some years. Two of Harris's squadronmates landed, but proved unable to assist him or ascertain what was wrong, and had taken off and continued on their way.

Tom Harris, now alone, stripped off the engine cowling to try to fathom the problem. He soon became aware of his growing audience, as local inhabitants showed up from far and near, including children, as school had been dismissed for the day. While Harris inspected his engine, the watching townsfolk had remained silently at a respectful distance, offering neither aid nor recognition. Still not having uncovered the problem, the perplexed pilot propped an elbow on a wingtip and began to return the silent stares of the locals.

Finally, an elderly woman stepped forward. "This is my field," she began, breaking the awkward silence. Harris quickly mentally reviewed BuAer's policy on respecting private property. "And I want you to know that I'm mighty proud to have you land your airyplane on it." Harris, greatly relieved, replied, "Madam, I'd like you to know that I'm mighty proud your field was here for me to land on."[19]

The ice having been broken, a young boy suddenly sidled up to Harris and quickly interrogated him with youthful boldness: "You a Yankee?" Harris, born in Los Angeles and a graduate of the University of California, but fully cognizant of the hopeful expressions on the faces of those who surrounded him, "forsook a California origin for one of more recent date." He announced with a prominent and appropriate drawl (reflecting his being based in Norfolk): "Ah'm from Vuh'gin'yuh, suh."

As the onlookers nodded and smiled approvingly, Harris told the lad: "You are now guarding 'U.S. Navy United States Federal Government Property [*sic*].'" With "eyes [as] big as saucers," the youngster ran to a nearby house. Returning with a loaded shotgun, he posted the watch.[20]

The town undertaker "although disappointed that his occupational services were not required," took Tom Harris in tow, basking in the glory "of such a prominent personage." Harris spent three days as the guest of the hospitable little town, and later insisted that, while repairs were being effected, "he met every inhabitant older than six months." When the time came for Harris to leave, all of the locals turned out "to give him a happy send-off."[21]

Meanwhile, on 1 February 1941, the Patrol Force became the U.S. Atlantic Fleet, and Adm. Ernest J. King broke his flag in the battleship *Texas*, a short distance away

Aviation Cadet (later Ensign) Thomas D. Harris, Pensacola, 12 March 1938. (NA, 80-G-450937, cropped)

from where the *Ranger* lay anchored. Underway from Culebra on the morning of 2 February, the *Ranger* rendezvoused with the *Wasp* soon thereafter (the two carriers comprising Carrier Division 3) and, after she had transferred VMO-1 and VS-72 to the *Wasp*, recovered her own VF-4 from the latter. Returning to Culebra on the 4th, the *Ranger* remained there only a short time, before she got underway to take part in Fleet Landing Exercise (FLEX) No. 7 as part of the "attacking" force.

FLEX No. 7 began in the Culebra–Vieques, Puerto Rico, area, on 4 February, with all available ships of the Atlantic Fleet and elements of the 1st Marine Division and the U.S. Army's First Division taking part. The objective was to train "Army and Navy Forces in the amphibious operations incident to a Joint Overseas Expedition." Unlike FLEX No. 6 the previous year, bona fide transports participated in the maneuvers. "The exercise," one observer later wrote, "provided excellent training and served a most useful purpose in exposing the lack of necessary services and equipment then available to conduct such an expedition."[22]

Two days before the conclusion of FLEX No. 7, during flight operations off St. Thomas on 12 February, VF-4 began experiencing problems with its F4Fs. At 1515, Lt. Comdr. Billy Parker, the squadron's commanding officer, was making a formation training dive in an F4F-3 (BuNo 1565), using the *Ranger* as target, during escort practice. Pushing over at 16,000 feet, Parker reached a dive angle of 50 degrees and was just about to pull out when his right windshield panel suddenly disintegrated at 5,000 feet. His right cheek cut by flying fragments of plexiglass, the 38-year-old Georgian, in momentary shock, experienced further surprise when his canopy immediately burst out on the right side. Small holes and dents in the tail surfaces ensued, as did "one impressive hole of fair size...drilled near the center of the pilot's head rest." Noting "no peculiarities in the flight performance of the airplane," however, the plucky Parker managed to land without further incident.[23]

Fifteen minutes later, Ens. Wally Madden, flying BuNo 1854, entered into a dive at 18,000 feet. He pushed over at about 13,000, picked up the objective on his telescopic sight and steadied on with a dive angle identical to the commanding officer's. As he leaned back to observe his airspeed and altitude, however, he heard a loud noise and "immediately felt a great deal of pain in my face." Removing his sunglasses, finding them covered with blood, Madden saw that the "left hand panel of the windshield and the sliding hatch" had shattered. Feeling a sharp pain at the back of his head, he reached back and discovered that the frame for the sliding canopy, which had been locked open one notch, had also broken on the left side and wrapped itself around his head, cutting his forehead and knocking his goggles off. Managing to extricate himself from the malevolent strip of metal, he "executed a very moderate pull-out and climbed up through the clouds." Calling the ship, he repeated "Mayday. Mayday..."[24]

Although he heard no acknowledgment, Madden could see the *Ranger* beginning to turn into the wind. Lowering his landing hook and wheels, he descended, passing the ship low on the starboard side, gunning his engine, the signal for a deferred forced landing. He then flew directly into the landing circle and lowered his flaps. As Madden began his approach, Lt. Jimmie Vosseller, the LSO, noted that the wind was 20 degrees on the starboard bow, at about 28 knots. Unaware of the "real nature of the emergency landing," Vosseller deliberately "signalled a somewhat high and fast approach," knowing that that permitted a pilot with a malfunctioning aircraft to have sufficient altitude and speed to take a wave-off if necessary.[25]

"I experienced some difficulty in watching the signal officer," Madden recounted subsequently, "due to the air blast and the blood" from the deep cut that blanked one eye. "I received a 'cut,'" he remembered, "but recall no exact details of the landing."[26]

Vosseller later wrote admiringly that the pilot "answered all signals in the groove perfectly." The LSO gave Madden an "informatory high signal, followed immediately by a cut, an early one...to compensate for his excess speed and altitude."[27] Dropping his nose, Madden caught the number two wire; the Wildcat came down hard on the left wheel. "Despite the major damage suffered by the airplane," Captain Montgomery commended the young ensign for his "landing on board under severe and adverse conditions of physical fitness."[28]

Before the month was out, VF-4 would temporarily lose the services of another of its F4F-3s, when Lt. Jack I. Bandy (in BuNo 1859) erred in judgment and displayed poor technique during group refresher training on 22 February. Overshooting the groove to the right, early in his approach, Jack Bandy overcorrected to the LSO's signals, crossing diagonally to the left. The LSO ran toward the center of the ramp, but, in an effort to keep him in view, the pilot applied additional right rudder. The fighter's right wing dropped and Bandy cut the engine; the wing remained down until it made contact with the deck just before the right wheel, damaging both the right wing panel and bending the upper drag link, damaging the wheel and cutting the tire.[29]

The *Ranger* operated in West Indian waters through mid-March 1941, punctuating her operations with visits to Ponce, Puerto Rico; Culebra, Guantanamo, as well as

View of some of the damage to Wally Madden's F4F-3, after the windshield and cockpit hood disintegrated during a dive. (NA, VF4F-3/L11-1 Vols. 1–2 to February 28, 1941, RG-72 Box 4930)

St. Thomas and Charlotte Amalie, Virgin Islands. During that time, the success achieved by the German battle cruisers *Scharnhorst* and *Gneisenau*, most notably on 22 February, when the two sank five merchantmen dispersed from a west-bound convoy approximately 500 miles east of Newfoundland, prompted U.S. Navy planners to confront the problem squarely. As long as the *Scharnhorst* and *Gneisenau* remained a threat, they felt, the Navy's concept for ocean escort required a battleship and an old cruiser, plus two to four destroyers. The escort force's obviously being weaker than the 15-inch-gunned German capital ships necessitated the employment of "heavy ships [battleships] and carriers." The then-present composition of the U.S. Atlantic Fleet allowed two carrier groups to be based at Bermuda, formed around the *Ranger* and the *Wasp*, two heavy cruisers and four destroyers.[30]

Consequently, on 1 March 1941, the Navy established the Support Force under Rear Adm. Arthur L. Bristol (the *Ranger*'s first captain). The destroyers and patrol plane squadrons and supporting auxiliaries under his command would protect convoys in the North Atlantic. Ten days later, Congress passed the "Lend-Lease Act," which changed the "cash and carry" provisions of the Neutrality Act of 1939 to permit the transfer of munitions to the Allies. Although criticized by isolationists, Lend-Lease would be the primary means by which the United States could provide Great Britain, the Soviet Union, and other belligerents with war material, food, and financial aid, without the United States having to enter combat. The Support Force would see that those cargoes reached their destinations.

Yet, while the United States was aligning itself ever closer to Britain, problems with the fighter aircraft U.S. naval aviators would have to fly from carriers in the event of hostilities began to prompt justifiable concern. VS-41 (soon to become VF-42) was working in its new F4F-3s out of Norfolk. On 13 March, Lt. (jg) Richard S. Bull, Jr., took up BuNo 2526, to test the reinforcements installed in the wake of the windscreen failures that had vexed Lieutenant Commander Parker and Ensign Madden of VF-4, off St. Thomas the month before. Bull made his first dive with his cockpit hood wide open, without incident. He began the second with his hood only partially open. All went well until the plane's flotation bottle discharged and the bags in the wing inflated, then tore open, as the F4F plummeted toward Smithfield.

Thinking that his Grumman was about to shed its violently fluttering wings, Bull unfastened his lap belt and attempted to bail out. Thrown back into his seat by what was either the slipstream or the intense vibration of his plane, however, Bull tried once more to rein in the plummeting F4F-3. "Six-feet, two hundred pounds of brawn," Bull grabbed the stick and with a tenacious display of strength like that that he had shown many times on the gridiron at the Naval Academy, managed to pull out of what had looked like a fatal dive. Expending so much energy in the attempt, however, he blacked out. When he regained consciousness, the altimeter read 4,100 feet and his airspeed indicator showed 250 knots. Finding that he could still control the plane, however, Bull managed to make a safe landing at Chambers Field.[31]

The *Ranger*'s pilots, however, were not alone in experiencing serious problems with the new F4F-3s, for pilots in the *Wasp* Air Group were beginning to encounter them, too. Rear Admiral Cook, Commander Aircraft, Atlantic Fleet (formerly Commander Aircraft, Patrol Force), took up the matter with Admiral King, Commander in Chief, Atlantic Fleet. Serious structural weaknesses in the F4F-3 model, Cook wrote on 17 March, required immediate correction. A hurried inspection of VF-72's Grummans on board the *Ranger*, which were due to return to their parent carrier, showed "no indication of similar failures but there is no reason to suppose they will not eventually occur." In addition, he continued, "all the F4F-3s are restricted from diving pending a redesign and strengthening of windshields; also serious wear and cracks in engine cowling[s], engine cowling attachment brackets and in carburator [sic] intake ducts have developed." An "unsatisfactory aerodynamic condition" also existed. "The whole situation," Cook wrote, "is pretty bad, and the fact that the pilots are beginning to get the wind up and are losing confidence in the plane doesn't help much, although I cannot blame them." Upon arrival at St. Thomas, Cook promised to make a careful inspection of the planes assigned to VF-41 (redesignated from VF-4 on 15 March), to determine whether or not "they should also be grounded."[32]

The SB2Us, with which the *Ranger* and *Wasp* air groups had been equipped, continued to give good service, however, proving "good old wheel horses." All had been concentrated in the Atlantic Fleet carriers by March 1941, because their folding wings alleviated stowage concerns on board the smaller *Ranger* and *Wasp*. During the 15 March redesignation of the *Ranger*'s squadrons, VB-4 became the new VS-41.[33]

Fighting Forty-Two, redesignated from the old Scouting Forty-One on 15 March, continued to break in its Grumman F4F-3s. Ens. Elbert S. "Doc" McCuskey, A-V(N), was conducting field carrier landings at Monogram Field in BuNo 2530 on 22 March, when his negligence or carelessness resulted in his landing gear collapsing, dropping the plane onto its belly.[34] Two days later, on the afternoon of 24 March, Ens. Harry E. "Pete" Howell, known affectionately to his classmates (USNA 1938) as a "fair-haired son of steel mills and railroads," was engaged in section tactics, flying BuNo 2521, when both flotation bags inflated. Howell climbed to try to shake them loose; the left bag carried away at 5,500 feet, the right at 3,000. The Grumman then went into a violent right spiral and plunged to earth, diving into the ground from about 2,000 feet, some six miles east-southeast of Chambers Field, killing Howell upon impact.[35]

Arriving back at Norfolk on the afternoon of 23 March, the *Ranger* shifted soon to NOB Norfolk, where she underwent upkeep alongside Pier 7 until the 25th, when she moved to the Norfolk Navy Yard for repairs and alterations. On the morning of 27 March, Comdr. Robert N. S. Baker, the planning officer for the Norfolk Navy Yard, met with Comdr. Duane L. Taylor, Lt. Stanley M. Alexander, and Lt. Junius W. Millard, USNR, the BuShips representative from Washington, to discuss the alterations to be carried out during the *Ranger*'s forthcoming overhaul, "having in mind a possible reduction in the 3-month overhaul period." The ensuing discussion revealed two major "limiting alterations in the militarily-urgent class: (1) the installation of improved arresting gear and (2) the auxiliary operation of elevators." The Norfolk yard people "felt that under no circumstances could they make the installation of arresting gear in less than three months, but felt that a delay of one month in overhaul date would enable them to procure the special motors needed for the auxiliary operation of the elevators and, these motors being on hand, the installation could be made in a 2-month period."[36]

The conferees also discussed the carrier's critical weight situation, with Lieutenant Millard pointing out that "the limitation of 20,300 tons on the displacement of the *Ranger* could not be exceeded" and that the installation of bombs, ammunition, etc., above that tonnage would have to be compensated for by removal of either fixed or variable weights." All present agreed "that a reasonably accurate determination of weights on and weights off would be necessary during the overhaul."[37]

After that "discussion of the *Ranger*'s problems" Commander Baker, Commander Taylor, and Lieutenants Alexander and Millard discussed the proposed overhauls of the British aircraft carriers, HMS *Illustrious* and HMS *Furious*, before the BuShips representative visited the *Ranger*. Once on board, Lieutenant Millard met with Comdr. Thomas L. Sprague, the *Ranger*'s executive officer, and Lt. Comdr. William H. Hamilton, Commander Aircraft, Atlantic Fleet, gunnery officer, and four of the *Ranger*'s heads of departments: Lt. Comdr. Jefferson D. Beard (damage control officer and first lieutenant), Lt. Comdr. John R. Van Nagel (gunnery officer), Lt. Comdr. Warren W. Johnson (chief engineer), and Lt. Comdr. Johnnie Hoskins (air officer). They discussed thoroughly the subjects of weights on and weights off and talked over possible methods of compensation, the latter having been anticipated by Captain Montgomery, who had already had a report prepared on the subject. Lieutenant Commander Beard and Lieutenant Millard then visited various parts of the ship, discussing the various proposed alterations as they did so.

Millard returned to the drydocked *Ranger* the next day and, again in company with the carrier's first lieutenant, inspected her underwater hull. With the exception of an area some 30 to 40 feet long on either side of the bow, where contact with the anchor chain had "more or less completly removed it" they found the plastic paint in excellent condition. Although they found several small barnacles and marine growth along the waterline, the bottom was clean, with very little corrosion evident. Only the leading edges and some surfaces of the rudder, repairs to which had been effected with "welding in the past with a rod that which [had] caused electrolytic action," showed some pitting. As Millard later reported to his superiors in BuShips, repairs were to remedy that defect in that docking period.[38]

In addition, because the *Ranger* had experienced difficulty in launching paravanes, Millard, for BuShips, authorized an alteration to the forefoot skeg, to accommodate a sliding shoe of the kind fitted to the new battleship *Washington* (BB-56). Later that afternoon, before the BuShips representative was to leave Norfolk, Captain Montgomery discussed the "matter of weights in general" with him, with Commander Sprague and Lieutenant Commander Beard joining them in the captain's cabin.[39]

Events elsewhere which would have an impact on the *Ranger*'s future operations, had occurred early in the ship's brief yard period. On the same day that the conference had taken place in the office of the Norfolk Navy Yard's planning officer—27 March—staff conversations between U.S, British, and Canadian military and naval representatives ended in Washington. The ABC-1 Staff Agreement that emerged from those talks concerned the basic strategic direction of the war in the event of U.S. entry, according the defeat of Germany a priority and establishing a Combined Chiefs of Staff. The U.S. Atlantic Fleet would help the Royal Navy convoy ships across the Atlantic. "We have begun intensive training of forces for all of this work," Secretary of the Navy Frank Knox had told the President on 20 March, "Our Navy is ready to undertake it as soon as directed, but could do it more effectively were we to have six to eight weeks for special training."[40]

Shortly after the start of the afternoon watch on 3 April, the *Ranger*, her major overhaul having been deferred to permit substantial design work in advance of the work to be performed, returned to Pier 7. During the continuing air group operations from shore stations, that same day VF-42 suffered damage to another of its Grummans, when Ens. Richard M. Plott's propeller malfunctioned, compelling him to make a forced landing, in BuNo 2533, one mile northeast of Monogram Field, landing in a nose-high stall with wheels and flaps down. Plott's F4F-3 turned over on its back. The plane required a major overhaul; Plott received treatment for shock and exposure and a puncture wound of his right forearm.[41]

Ensign Wally Madden of VF-41 suffered a mishap a little over a week later, when landing his F4F-3 (BuNo 1886) at Chambers Field on 11 April. He ground-looped the Grumman, in an accident the trouble board assessed as equally the fault of the pilot (poor technique) and the narrow-track landing gear.[42]

By April 1941, continued concern over the potential depradations by German capital ships or auxiliary cruisers (raiders) prompted more thought to be given to the ability of the Atlantic Fleet, as it was then constituted, to provide the minimum ocean escort. With the *Scharnhorst* and *Gneisenau* at large, U.S. Navy planners considered two carriers, two cruisers, and four destroyers "the minimum for an effective striking force." To provide "a proper degree of safety for convoys in the western Atlantic, and to provide an important striking unit for catching raiders," the situation required *New Mexico*-class battleships, one carrier (*Lexington* preferred), six destroyer leaders, twelve destroyers, and four modern light cruisers. If the movement was undertaken, "it should be done with the utmost possible secrecy." If the U.S. Navy were "to take an effective part in the Atlantic," the risks, vis-a-vis the Japanese, had to be accepted.[43]

Admiral Stark had included the foregoing thoughts in a memorandum drawn up primarily for President Roosevelt, to give him "a picture of what is now being done, what we would propose to do if we convoyed, and of our ability to do it." As the CNO informed Adm. Husband E. Kimmel, Commander in Chief of the U.S. Pacific Fleet, on 4 April, the matters dealt with in the memorandum concerned CinCPac directly "in the detachment from your command of what I believe to be necessary for King to have, to do the job. I feel it is only a matter of time before King is directed to convoy or patrol or whatever form the protective measures take."[44]

"You may not agree with me on this move," Stark continued, "I can only hope that I am right. The situation is obviously critical in the Atlantic. In my opinion, it is hopeless except as we take strong measures to save it. The effect on the British of sinkings with regard to both the food supply and essential material to carry on the war is getting progressively worse." Without America giving "effective aid," the CNO believed, "I do not believe the British can much more than see the year through, if that. The situation," he declared, "is much worse that the average person has any idea."[45]

The *Ranger*, meanwhile, had moved out into Hampton Roads on 5 April, and sailed, at the end of the mid watch the following day, for Bermuda. Accompanied only by the destroyer *Kearny* (DD-432), the *Ranger* reached Murray's Anchorage on the morning of the 8th, the day after the formal establishment of the naval operating base there. Her arrival also came a day after OpNav had informed CinCPac of the impending transfer of ships from the Pacific Fleet to the Atlantic, part of that transfer occasioned by the *Ranger's* recently deferred overhaul. "The *Ranger* is scheduled for Navy Yard overhaul from July 1st to September 1st for essential alteration of arresting gear and for routine work. The Chief of Naval Operations considers that this overhaul cannot be indefinitely postponed."[46] The *Ranger's* being out of action for that period necessitated the transfer of a carrier from the Pacific Fleet to fill the gap.

Underway again on the morning of the 10th, in company with the heavy cruisers *Wichita* (CA-45) and *Tuscaloosa* and the destroyers *Livermore* (DD-429), *Kearny*, and *Eberle* (DD-430), the *Ranger* conducted flight operations that afternoon. She then returned to Murray's Anchorage briefly on the 11th, before sailing for Hampton Roads the same day, accompanied only by the *Kearny* and the *Eberle*. Reaching her destination on the morning of the 13th, the *Ranger* then conducted flight operations off the Southern Drill Grounds, before she proceeded north, accompanied by the *Wasp* and the destroyers *Livermore* and *Sampson* (DD-394), to visit Newport, Rhode Island, on 18 and 19 April. The *Ranger* returned to Norfolk on the 20th.

While the *Ranger* had been at sea, on 15 April, President Roosevelt had signed an unpublicized executive order allowing individuals serving in the Navy, Marine Corps, or Army Air Corps to sign contracts with the "Central Aircraft Manufacturing Company" (CAMCO) in China for one year, with the proviso that they could rejoin their respective services with no loss in rank. Authorized to seek candidates for what would become known as the "American Volunteer Group," CAMCO recruiters found themselves with carte blanche to interview prospective pilots. Among those in VS-41 who found the fiscal inducements to fly for China appealing was Ens. Edward F. Rector, A-V(N), a 24-year-old North Carolinian who had been designated a naval aviator on 12 April 1940, and whose first preference for duty upon graduation from Pensacola had been fighters on a West Coast carrier. Other pilots from Scouting Forty-One who would join CAMCO were Ens. David L. "Tex" Hill, A-V(N), "a long-legged Texan who had been born in Korea, the son of a Presbyterian missionary," and Ens. Brix Christman, the cartoonist; Ens. John E. Petach, A-V(N), of VS-42, did likewise.[47]

Fighting Forty-Two's adventures with its F4F-3s continued, this time at sea on board the *Wasp*. Ensign Christopher A. Nolan, Jr., A-V(N), making his first refresher landing at 1027 on 15 April, soon found his tail hook and carriage pulling out after he had engaged number two wire. The unbridled Grumman (BuNo 2524) then crashed into and broke the first barrier, nosing over into the second barrier and striking the propeller against the deck; although the plane suffered class "C" damage, Nolan walked away from the mishap (deemed 100% "arresting appliance on aircraft") unhurt. Doc McCuskey's first landing proved a bit more unnerving, when his hook pulled out, too, permitting his F4F-3 (BuNo 2536) to bounce into the *Wasp's* island, knocking off the right wing and swinging the propeller into the island; the Grumman then dropped onto the deck on its back. McCuskey's F4F-3 suffered class B damage, and the pilot suffered minor contusions and abrasions.[48]

At the time that the *Ranger* lay off Newport, Admiral Stark sought to keep Admiral Kimmel informed on events that lay ahead. Referring again to the imminent transfer of part of the Pacific Fleet to the Atlantic, the CNO referred to the detachment, mentioned previously, as the "first echelon of the 'Battle of the Atlantic,'" and noted that the "entire world set-up" had been gone into "very carefully" by all concerned, before the movement had been ordered. "This detachment," the CNO wrote Kimmel on 19 April, "was one of the first means of implementing what we had every reason to anticipate here." President Roosevelt, Stark explained, had "agreed to, authorized, and directed in its detail," but had also cancelled it, limiting the detachment at that time to a single carrier and a division of destroyers. Although adhering to an Atlantic-first strategy, the CNO went on, the President had not wanted to give Japan any ideas that they could operate with impunity in the Far East. "I am telling you," Stark concluded of the transfer of the carrier and escorting destroyers, "not arguing with you" about it.[49]

Patrol operations with Atlantic Fleet carriers began from Hampton Roads and Bermuda, although the latter featured "limited facilities for liberty." With so many men involved, a sailor could unwind ashore only once in 10 days "which is pretty rough," Admiral Cook observed, "after two weeks at sea." Obviously, "even if the liberty limit is raised there will still be a number of men who for purposes of health and morale should be given a chance to get away from the ship." After a conversation he had had with Capt. Jules James,

Commandant of the Naval Operating Base at Bermuda, concerning the expense of renting a facility to convert to a canteen that would sell 'short orders,' beer, soft drinks, American cigarettes, candy, etc.," Cook exclaimed: "My God, what is $25,000 more or less a year to us now, especially when it has so much to do to make our men fit to properly fight the billions of dollars of ships we are building.[50]

Even given Bermuda's limitations, the work of the Neutrality Patrol needed to proceed from that place, and the inaugural operation began on 26 April, as the limits were extended southward to 20° south longitude. On that day, the *Wasp*, with VF-72, VS-71, and VS-72 embarked, stood out of Hampton Roads, accompanied by the heavy cruiser *Quincy* and the destroyers *Livermore* and *Kearny*. Two days later, the *Ranger*, wearing Rear Admiral Cook's flag, sailed for Bermuda with the heavy cruiser *Vincennes* and the destroyer *Sampson*, arriving there on the 30th. She shifted from Grassy Bay to Murray's Anchorage on 8 May. Soon thereafter, shortly before the *Ranger* was to put to sea again, Cook received word that the Governor of Bermuda had, under the Defense of the Realm Act, closed all pubs on the island from roughly 1400 to 1730 daily. "This is sort of bad news," the admiral observed, "because the men will do their best to fill up before the bars close with the result that many of them will probably get drunk who wouldn't have otherwise."[51]

The *Ranger* got underway at 0712 on the 9th, with VF-41 (F4F-3s), VS-41 (SB2U-1s and -2s), VS-42 (SB2U-1s, -2s and TBD-1s), and her utility unit (SOC-1s and J2F-1s, and the CRAG's SBC-3) embarked, sailing in company with the *Vincennes*, the *Sampson*, and the *Eberle*. She launched planes a half hour into the forenoon watch, the *Ranger* Air Group passing in review to seaward of Admiralty House, as the task group stood out to sea. Poor visibility conditions, however, compelled a cancellation of firing exercises scheduled by the group that morning.

"The first two days out," Rear Admiral Cook later recounted, "the *Vincennes* and the *Eberle* each held an anti-aircraft practice, [with] a *Ranger* J2F towing. We have also had considerable drill for other gunnery practices and each day the combat air patrol flies over the formation for an hour on specified courses and altitudes for aircraft tracking drill. While I am afraid to say anything and hereby tap wood and whistle, our air operations are going surprisingly well.... We launch three fighters and six scouts [all planes armed with machine gun ammunition but not bombs] each day at dawn and while the fighters cover the rear the scouts cover a front

Ensign Brainard T. Macomber, A-V(N), in the cockpit of his F4F-3, after making the *Ranger*'s 29,000th landing, 17 May 1941. Note part of the "Red Rippers" insignia on the side of the fuselage beneath the cockpit. Photograph taken by Photographer 3d Class Metley. (NA, 80-G-391578)

of about 100 miles to a distance of 75 miles. I will send them out further soon. They are pretty green but are coming along fast."[52] The task group operated under radio silence, with the planes reporting contacts by message drops (a weighted bean bag dropped on deck) or landing. Reflecting on part of the mission of the task group, Cook acknowledged the difficulty of detecting Axis armed merchant cruisers, or raiders. "Unless we see a man-of-war and identify it as German," he wrote, "or see a merchant ship actually fueling from a tanker or sinking a ship we can never be sure."[53]

As far as the composition of task groups operating in the Atlantic, Cook believed that "the ideal set-up for this kind of an expedition is one long-legged fast carrier, two heavy cruisers, and four destroyers. They should be able to take care of themselves and make trouble for any unit [that] they are apt to meet. One cruiser and two destroyers is spreading the butter a little thin." The task group had conducted several exercises "in which the *Ranger* took the part of a combatant raider superior in force to the *Vincennes* while the latter with her two destroyers attempted to protect a hypothetical carrier in her rear until the latter could get sufficient sea room to launch her planes. If the contact is a surprise one and the enemy ship has speed equal to our own (she probably will have more than the *Ranger*), there isn't much the *Vincennes* can do but stand and take it, under which circumstances she wouldn't last long. With two cruisers and four destroyers, it would be a different story."[54]

Unhappily, three days after Admiral Cook had reflected on how the air operations were going "surprisingly well," during the preparations to launch the dawn search on 19 May, Seaman 2d Class Douglas Gordon inadvertently walked into the nearly invisible propeller arc among the planes spotted aft on the flight deck, and died instantly. The pace of operations, however, even those short of war, continued, and the ship launched three fighters to carry out a search covering the 60–300 degree sector, out to 15 miles; two sections of scouts (six planes) searched sectors out to 65 miles and out to 85. The ship recovered the search three and a quarter hours later. Nothing had been sighted. In the meantime, a board of investigation, of which Lieutenant Commander Parker was senior member, convened to look into Gordon's death, meeting for almost five hours before adjourning. "Although the fatal accident [that involved Seaman Gordon] could not be definitely laid to the wet and slippery deck," Captain Montgomery later wrote, "there were numerous instances of men who lost their footing when caught in the slip stream of a propeller." Such incidents, he added, merely accentuated the need for "non-skid shoes" for the sailors who had to negotiate the occasionally treacherous flight deck.[55]

Shortly before the *Ranger* recovered the dawn patrol, she launched a second search that consisted of three fighters and five scouts. The three fighters searched the same relative area as those from the dawn launch; three of the scouts searched out to 75 miles to the left and right of the 248-degree bearing, and two conducted inner air patrol while the *Vincennes* fueled the *Eberle*. The only sighting of any consequence occurred during the latter, when the pilot of 41-F-13 saw a capsized life boat (but no signs of life) bearing 320 degrees, about two miles from the ship.

Upon arrival at Bermuda on the 23d, the *Ranger*'s task group having steamed 4,675 miles and her pilots logging a total of 1,490.7 hours flown (more than the *Wasp*'s air group accumulated during the patrol they brought to a close on 12 May), the *Ranger* flew off VF-41, VS-41, and VS-42 to the *Yorktown* (which had arrived at Bermuda on 12 May) and recovered the latter's VB-5 (equipped with Northrop BT-1s), VS-5 (Curtiss SBC-3s), and VF-5 (Grumman F3F-3s), after which time Rear Admiral Cook transferred his flag to the *Yorktown*.[56] The *Ranger*'s way of doing things had obviously impressed Cook. "He [Cook] continually criticized Capt. [Elliott] Buckmaster [the *Yorktown*'s commanding officer]," then-Comdr. Joseph J. "Jocko" Clark [then the *Yorktown*'s exec] wrote later, "always concluding with his favorite remark, 'We didn't do it this way in the *Ranger*.'"[57]

Reflecting upon the patrol just concluded, Captain Montgomery observed that the 14-day period of operations had tested the mettle of his crew "to maintain the condition of readiness required under the material condition specified." The ship had gone to general quarters daily, 45 minutes before sunrise, and, after the first day, "all stations reported manned and ready in less than 10 minutes." Air Department and squadron people were summoned to their stations 30 min before general quarters; the "necessary cooks, mess cooks, and mess attendants" an hour before, to begin serving breakfast at 0530, instead of the more customary 0630. The ship's mess people continued serving the morning meal until 0900, to accommodate those coming off the end of the morning watch. Radio gunners in VS-41 and VS-42 ate in the galley an hour before dawn; all pilots began breakfast in the wardroom an hour and 15 minutes before sun-up. "The necessity for serving meals at such early hours made a very long day for mess cooks and mess attendants," Montgomery admitted, but those who had been called early "to prepare and serve early breakfasts were given an opportunity to get some rest during the afternoon watch." The conditions encountered by the patrol limited the measures to maintain morale, but, when air operations permitted, all hands who wanted to do so watched motion pictures in the evening. Given the

Panoramic view of the funeral of the late Seaman 2d Class Douglas Gordon, the victim of an accident the previous day, on the morning of 20 May 1941. Lieutenant Commander Edward J. Robbins, ChC, conducts the service, while all hands, bareheaded, pay their respects to their dead shipmate. Note uncamouflaged SB2Us in the background on the hangar deck, with the prominent "neutrality star" on the nose. The dark shade of paint on the lowered stack in the left background indicates that the ship is wearing Measure 1 dark gray camouflage by this point. Among those gathered to pay their respects at right is Comdr. Thomas L. Sprague, the ship's executive officer, and Boatswain's Mate 1st Class R. M. Commick, a member of the ship's master-at-arms force. [NA, 80-G-391579 (left) and 80-G-391581 (right)]

wartime pace of operations, men off-watch preferred to sleep, rather than use the crew's lounge.[58]

The *Ranger* Air Group logged a total of 533 landings: VF-41 garnering the most, with 181, followed by VS-41 (174), and VS-42 (172) (the *Ranger* Air Group commander logged two and the target-towing Utility Unit four), with no barrier crashes during the two weeks at sea. Scouting Forty-One led the group in average landing intervals (one every 28.43 seconds), followed by VF-41 (30.42) and VS-42 (31.03), as well as in average launching intervals (one every 15.1 seconds) (Scouting Forty-Two put one plane aloft every 15.6 seconds and VF-41, one every 17.2). Two VF-41 landings accounted for the longest pull-outs (the pilots of 41-F-11 and 41-F-15 catching the number three wire with a 115-foot pull-out). The ship logged a daily launching interval of 16.1 seconds per plane, increased to 24.5 seconds during group operations in patrol periods, and recovered one plane every 30.25 seconds as the average landing interval.[59]

VF-42, back ashore, continued its training. Ensign Theodore A. Grell, flying in formation during division tactics on the afternoon of 22 May, noticed his engine suddenly losing power and vibrating excessively. As other pilots in the formation noticed puffs of black and white issuing from the engine exhausts, Grell eased the throttle and cut

the switch. Restarting the engine to assist in landing, Grell brought BuNo 2528 to earth safely five miles southwest of Portsmouth, Virginia. The subsequent trouble board deemed the power plant as the culprit in the accident; Mr. J. F. Walker of Portsmouth, however, later billed the Navy $42.50 for damage to a portion of his rye crop growing in the field where Grell landed.[60]

Six days later, however, during field carrier landing practice, Ens. J. A. Hirsch, A-V(N), was flying BuNo 1862, in good weather, one mile northwest of Cape Henry light. Eyewitnesses later testified to seeing Hirsch flying in a slight left bank, at moderate speed, at an altitude of about 10 feet for about a mile and a half, before the F4F-3's left wing dipped, caught the water, and cartwheeled, pivoting on the left wing. It sank immediately, entombing Ensign Hirsch. Seven days of grappling operations followed, until the plane, found to be a complete wreck, was recovered.[61]

The *Ranger*, with the *Yorktown* squadrons embarked, lingered in Bermuda until 29 May, when she and her consorts, the *Tuscaloosa* and the destroyers *McDougal* (DD-358) and *Eberle*, sailed to conduct another Neutrality Patrol. During flight operations, the first afternoon out, Ens. Charlie N. Conatser, A-V(N), of Bombing 5, took off, with Radioman 3d Class Walter D. Straub as his passenger. Conatser, in his first flight off the *Ranger* (and his first in over a month), eased 5-B-14 (BuNo 0614) to the right as he took off, as he could have done without any problems on the *Yorktown*, because of her wider flight deck. With the *Ranger*'s narrower deck, however, before he even reached the bow Conatser's right wheel went over the side of the deck into the waterway, hitting the forward LSO platform. The BT-1's right landing gear brace broke, and the right side of the wing center section buckled directly above the right gear, blowing the tire and crushing the wheel. Conatser regained control after the mishap and landed 10 minutes later.

Captain Montgomery (center, seated) with the *Ranger*'s heads of departments, 10 June 1941. Seated (L-R): Lt. Comdr. Herbert W. Taylor, Jr., Comdr. Francis G. Ulen (DC) (dental officer), Comdr. Francis W. Carll (Medical Corps) (medical officer), Captain Montgomery, Comdr. Thomas L. Sprague (executive officer), Comdr. Allen H. White (Supply Corps) (supply officer), Comdr. John M. Hoskins (air officer). Standing: Capt. Thomas B. Hughes, USMC (Marine Detachment commander), Lt. Comdr. Warren W. Johnson (engineer officer), Lt. Comdr. Edward J. Robbins (Chaplain Corps) (chaplain), Lt. Comdr. Jefferson D. Beard (damage control officer and first lieutenant), Lt. Comdr. John R. Van Nagell (gunnery officer), Lt. John H. Brockway. Spotted on the flight deck behind these officers are Grumman F3F-3s from VF-5, still painted in peacetime colors, the squadron having been transferred from the *Yorktown* (CV-5), which had recently arrived in the Atlantic. (NA, 80-CF-8005-1)

Although a trouble board, chaired by Lt. John S. "Jack" Tracy, Bombing 5's exec, met on 1 June and faulted Conatser for not carefully surveying the deck ahead of him before and during takeoff, it also praised the ensign (who held a bachelor's degree in business administration from the University of Texas at Austin) for his "exceptional skill" in bringing in the BT-1 so as to minimize further damage—the already crippled Northrop only suffered a bent right landing flap, in addition to the gear damage sustained on takeoff. Consequently, however, VB-5's pilots received the admonition to "take off down the center line of the deck while *Ranger* based, to prevent a recurrence of this type of accident."[62]

Bombing 5 suffered its second mishap of the cruise on the morning of 4 June. Ironically, it involved Jack Tracy, who had headed the trouble board that looked into Charlie Conatser's adventure on 29 May. Seeing Tracy's approach as "unsteady and to the right of the centerline," Lieutenant Norwood A. "Soupy" Campbell, the LSO who had accompanied the *Yorktown*'s squadrons on board the *Ranger*, signalled "wave-off." To avoid overheating his engine, Tracy closed his flaps, and also partially retracted his wheels as he brought his BT-1 (BuNo 0610) around for a second try. Tracy, however, knowing that the wave-off had put him last in the landing circle, later admitted candidly that he was "over-anxious to avoid delaying the carrier." Receiving the report "Hook, wheels, and flaps down," Campbell gave Tracy the cut, unaware that Bombing 5's exec had in fact entered the groove without completing his landing check-off list. Soon after giving that signal, however, Campbell noted that Tracy's wheels were not, in fact, fully extended, but "streaming aft of their proper position by about six (6) inches." Consequently, when his Northrop landed, Tracy caught a wire and rolled forward without any difficulty, but nearing the end of the run-out, the BT-1's gear collapsed to the retracted position, and the propeller imbedded itself in the deck, bringing the engine to an abrupt stop. Fortunately, as in Charlie Conatser's accident on 29 May, the *Ranger*'s medical people had no injuries to treat, and both Tracy and his passenger, Radioman 2d Class Clyde S. Mortensen, walked away from the accident unhurt.[63]

Over the next several days, the *Ranger* steamed 4,355 miles, and the pilots logged 1,068.4 hours of flight time. Returning to Bermuda on the morning of 9 June, the *Ranger* sailed later that same day for Norfolk. That same day, Rear Adm. Manley H. Simons, Commandant of the Norfolk Navy Yard, mindful of the *Ranger*'s pending arrival, was informing BuShips that the yard had "just resurveyed the probabilities of the situation on the basis of the progress made to date and of the conflicting demands of its heavy and urgent workload, insofar as those demands can be forecast; and has come again to the conclusion that two months will probably, though barely, suffice for the job (working three shifts and without any required diversions of attention or force from duly scheduled work comparable to those currently encountered)." Simons sought to point out the risk of undertaking a job "of such complexity and magnitude on a schedule figured so closely that there is no allowance for any one of the many unfavorable developments that can arise under current overload and rush-work conditions." If the ship "cannot share with the yard that risk of a possible...delay," the commandant believed it "of doubtful wisdom to undertake the subject alteration at this time." Simons, however, felt that the work should proceed, figuring in two weeks at the end of the overhaul before the *Ranger* resumed operations to test the installation of the new equipment. The commandant also pointed out that the period scheduled for the work (1 July–30 August) "does not quite allow the full two months...particularly with the Independence Day holiday intervening." To that end, Simons urged that the CNO consider 1 September as the completion date, instead of the "readiness date."[64]

14

"WITH CONTAGIOUS ENTHUSIASM"

After launching her air group to assume shore-based status, the *Ranger* stood into Hampton Roads on 11 June, and soon put out her mooring lines to the familiar Pier 7. That day, Capt. William K. Harrill reported on board to begin the required process of familiarizing himself with his new command, and on 13 June relieved Monty Montgomery, who fleeted up to become Rear Adm. Cook's chief of staff. "Keen" Harrill, a graduate of the USNA Class of 1914, came to the *Ranger* from command of Patrol Wing One. Designated as a naval aviator on 30 December 1921, Harrill had accumulated considerable administrative experience, gaining it in positions of responsibility that ranged from the navigation of a carrier to her housekeeping and upkeep. He had served as navigator, then exec, of the *Langley* from 23 May 1930 to 25 June 1932, and had had successive duty as navigator, first lieutenant, and damage control officer of the *Saratoga*, serving under the colorful Capt. William F. "Bill" Halsey, Jr., from 30 March 1935 to 22 March 1937. He had also served in London as assistant naval attaché and naval attaché (as Roy Bristol, the *Ranger*'s first captain, had done), from 11 May 1937 to 14 June 1939. After being detached from his prestigious posting abroad, Harrill reported to the *Wright*, which he then commanded from 11 July 1939 to 3 July 1940. Less than a fortnight later, he assumed command of Patrol Wing One.

While correspondence and long-distance telephone conversations between BuShips and the Norfolk Navy Yard addressed the impending overhaul (and the important matters of weight reduction, and the ship's highly stressed condition, among other things), the *Ranger*, under her new skipper, operated locally in the Norfolk area. As occasionally happened with Navy pilots, the Marines from the First Marine Aircraft Wing at Quantico encountered mishaps, too. On 18 June, VMSB-131's Capt. Nathaniel S. Clifford, USMC, with Sgt. M. L. Kreuter, USMC, on board, landed his Vought SB2U-3 (BuNo 2082), with 28 knots of wind over the deck, visibility clear and unlimited. But Clifford had landed too fast, and number eight landing wire carried away. The SB2U charged up the deck and nosed through barriers three and four, before coming to rest. Although neither Captain Clifford nor Sergeant Kreuter suffered any injuries, the *Ranger*'s medical people treated Apprentice Seaman C. E. Pierce, Seaman 2d Class Eugene Elliott, Seaman 1st Class F. C. Anderson, USNR, and Seaman 2d Class D. T. Shaw, all for lacerations or fractures received in scrambling out of the way of the wayward Vought.[1]

The *Ranger* embarked VMO-1 and VMF-111 on 22 June, for temporary duty to conduct flight operations on the Southern Drill Grounds. Three days later, leatherneck misfortunes continued, as 2d Lt. John P. Haines, USMC, with Pvt. F. E. Thompson, USMC, on board, had just landed his Curtiss SBC-4 (BuNo 1313) and taxied forward. As Haines was waiting for the signal to take off again, Capt. John C. Munn, USMC, with Cpl. B. A. Paglia, USMC, as passenger, landed in another SBC-4 (BuNo 1816), which touched down well aft. The tail of Munn's plane, however, never came down and the extended hook failed to catch a wire. Consequently, his

Captain William K. Harrill (pictured here as a commander in April 1935), became the *Ranger*'s sixth commanding officer on 13 June 1941. (NA, 80-G-466317)

SBC-4 crashed through the number two barrier and collided with Haines's, crumpling the vertical stabilizer, left horizontal stabilizer, and left elevator, as well as the lower left wing and flaps, and slightly damaged the upper wing. Munn's SBC suffered a twisted propeller, a broken engine mount, a crumpled left lower wing and an upper right wingtip, and a broken bomb rack.[2]

VF-41 logged two incidents during its shore-based time: Ens. John R. "Jawn" Sweeney, exhibited what a trouble board deemed as carelessness on 26 June, when he made a dive in his F4F-3 (BuNo 1853) and placed the propeller control in manual, thus putting it very close to the low-pitch setting. The engine, as a consequence, over-speeded in the dive "and probably pounded out the main bearing," because an examination at Monogram Field revealed large pieces of bearing metal in the strainer, upon landing.[3] That same day, returning from a familiarization flight in BuNo 1879, Ens. Edgar R. "Red" Bassett, A-V(N), a stout, cheerful Pennsylvanian, overshot the strip at East Field and ended up on a runway under construction, bending the propeller, badly buckling the left wing, and tearing up the left aileron, and shearing off the left wheel and side of the landing gear. A trouble board faulted his error in judgment.[4]

Scouting Forty-Two carried out its training syllabus shore-based, as well. Flying into Chambers Field after night section tactics on 27 June, Ens. Charles M. King, flying an SB2U-2 (BuNo 1346), with Seaman 2d Class W. W. Offenhauser in back, made a wheels-first landing and bounced three feet in the air, reaching a full stall. The left wing dropped, and the Vought swerved to the right; the left landing gear gave way and the plane skidded to a stop on its nose; the impact of the crash gave Seaman Offenhauser a cut on the bridge of his nose. Although a subsequent trouble board faulted King for his technique, it allowed that the field floodlights had illuminated a light haze, causing a tendency for the pilots to land high.[5]

Marine misfortunes on board the *Ranger* continued on the afternoon of 30 June: Capt. Ernest R. West, USMC, of VMF-111, exhibited what a trouble board later termed "poor technique," as he abruptly pulled back the control column as he landed. His F4F-3A (BuNo 3955) floated over all the wires and crashed on deck, shearing off the tip of one propeller blade and nicking the other two, bending the main landing gear strut, and bending and tearing the right side of the fuselage. Although his plane looked somewhat the worse for wear, Captain West emerged from the accident unhurt.[6]

Ensign Herman T. Krol, A-V(N), of VS-41, flying his first carrier qualification flight on 7 July, with the obligatory sandbag in the rear seat, came in in such a fashion as to prompt the LSO to wig-wag a frantic "come on" signal. In response, Krol applied full throttle, giving him much more speed than he needed to make the deck. As a result, his SB2U-1 (BuNo 0749) floated up the deck without catching any of the cross-deck pendants, and slammed into the first barrier. As the impact of the crash threw Krol forward, his left hand hit the throttle, giving the Vought even more speed, and the plane carried away two more barriers before finally coming to a stop. Fortunately, Krol suffered no injuries, but the SB2U suffered class B damage. The trouble board attributed the crash to poor technique and inexperience.[7]

The *Ranger* shifted to the Norfolk Navy Yard on the morning of 12 July, and her air group assumed shore-based status. Soon, the usual tumult of a yard overhaul would be familiar to the ears of the ship's company, as the ship began to undergo repairs and alterations which included the installation of 1.1-inch quadruple-mount antiaircraft machine guns to replace the 3-inch/.50-caliber guns, a CXAM-1 radar, and YE homing gear. In addition, the ship was to receive new camouflage (Measure 12, graded system).

Other work sought involved bomb stowage and improving the operation of the ship's elevators.

During the *Ranger* Air Group's time ashore, the occasional mishap occurred, as the ceaseless and unremitting training continued, both day and night. After a gunnery hop on 16 July, Ensign Sweeney of VF-41 made a normal landing in an F4F-3 (BuNo 1870) at Elizabeth City, North Carolina, but the plane started a ground loop. Although Sweeney applied the brakes properly, the Grumman, with its peculiar handling qualities, charged off the runway and turned over on its back, in soft ground 25 yards off the airstrip. Sweeney emerged from the accident unhurt, although the plane suffered class B damage, in a mishap a trouble board blamed on poor technique and the F4F-3's handling qualities.[8]

Three days later, as VS-42 underwent carrier qualifications on board the *Wasp*, Ens. Joseph P. Keigher, A-V(N), took the cut on his third landing of the day. Unlike his previous two, however, his SB2U-2 (BuNo 1348) passed over all the cross-deck pendants, about two feet above the deck, in a normal landing attitude, and slammed into barriers four and five. A trouble board assessed Keigher's poor technique as the sole cause for the mishap; he had not previously qualified in carrier landings.[9]

Scouting Forty-Two lost one of its aircraft on 28 July, at Ocean View, Virginia, when Lt. (jg) Charles E. Gibson, with Radioman 3d Class E. Gawlik on board his SB2U-1 (BuNo 0774), was making an approach for a night field carrier landing practice. With his wheels and flaps down, Gibson shifted his propeller to low pitch, and noticed a normal speed-up of the engine. Soon, however, he noticed an abrupt drop in power, and something that what was by no means normal: his exhausts emitting flames and sparks. As Gibson attempted to bring the Vought in for a landing, its wing clipped a telephone pole, the chimney of a house, and, as it descended further, the garage at the rear of the dwelling whose chimney had been struck. After the plane came to rest, the engine caught fire, and the plane burned. Fortunately, Gibson and Gawlik emerged from the mishap with only the former suffering lacerations and minor abrasions.[10]

During that time, squadrons from the *Ranger* Air Group deployed on Neutrality Patrols in the *Yorktown*: VF-42 and VS-42 operated alongside two Marine squadrons, VMO-1 and half of VMS-1, during the 29 June–12 July patrol which began and ended at Hampton Roads. When VF-42 made a second cruise from 30 July to 10 August, beginning at Hampton Roads and ending at Bermuda, VS-41 joined it and served alongside VT-5. Those same three squadrons operated from the *Yorktown* during the 15–27 August cruise out of Bermuda.

Operations on board the "The Mighty Y" proved, in the main, routine, except when Ens. Joe Keigher, who had only worn his wings for a little over two months (and who had experienced difficulty during carrier qualifications on board the *Wasp* a little less than a fortnight before), made a short approach that necessitated a short turn near the ramp, as he returned from a group refresher flight on 30 July. Barely crossing the ramp and headed about 30 degrees to the center line, nose high, left wing low, Keigher's SB2U-1 (BuNo 0759) dragged its left wing, as the tail hook engaged number one cross-deck pendant. The SB2U swung around another 30 degrees and plunged over the side, with the propeller and the left wing hitting the *Yorktown*'s side, tethered there by the wire, as the nose dragged in the water. Keigher jumped free; he was rescued soon thereafter. His passenger, Radioman 3d Class Arthur L. Kaster, was hoisted on board without further incident.[11]

Admiral Cook wore his flag in the *Yorktown* while the *Ranger* lay at the Norfolk Navy Yard. At sea, he addressed an issue of increasing importance. "Recent war experience," Cook wrote, "covering encounters between airplanes and combatant ships have demonstrated the effectiveness of the torpedo-carrying airplane." Noting that the present authorized operating strength of the two scouting squadrons each assigned to the *Ranger* and the *Wasp* included six torpedo planes in each ship (TBDs earmarked for the high-level bombing role), Cook considered that alteration of the *Ranger* and the *Wasp* "to permit stowage and maintenance of at least six fully ready [Mk. 13–Mod. 1] torpedoes with some adjustment facilities available and stowage for six more in standby status" would greatly enhance the "striking power and flexibility" of those two carriers.[12] Admiral King, in his endorsement on Commander Aircraft, Atlantic Fleet's recommendation, noted that the "provision of torpedo stowage—in carefully considered numbers for each aircraft carrier not so equipped—has become a prime military requirement," and seconded the proposed alterations to the *Ranger* and the *Wasp*, "subject to removal in each case of required compensating weights."[13]

During part of the time that the *Ranger* was yard-bound, VF-41, under Lt. James J. McRoberts, and VS-42, under Lt. Comdr. David B. Overfield, served in unfamiliar climes. They operated alongside the *Wasp*'s VF-72 and the *Yorktown*'s VS-5 and four Marine squadrons (VMF-111, VMSB-131 and -132, and VMO-151) in the U.S. Army's General Headquarters (GHQ) maneuvers held in Louisiana between 10 and 30 September, the U.S. Navy's participation having been occasioned by the Army Air Force's long-standing neglect of ground-support aviation.

Lieutenant Comdr. Thomas B. Williamson, Commander, *Ranger* Air Group, served as liaison officer at the Third Air Task Force headquarters and Officer in Charge of the Navy squadrons attached to that command. VF-41 based at Beaumont, Texas, and VS-42 at Shreveport, Louisiana, the former being singled out for surmounting not only bad weather, but primitive operating conditions, as well. The participating Navy and Marine Corps squadrons flew a total of 4,071.7 hours on tactical missions, with VS-42 putting in 465 of those hours and VF-41, 416.8. At the end of the maneuvers, Lt. Gen. Delos C. Emmons, USA, commended the Navy and Marine Corps squadrons for performing their many tasks "in a most creditable manner with contagious enthusiasm" and lauded their "uniformly excellent" performance in tactical maneuvers. That spoke well, Emmons wrote, for the "training and state of readiness of Naval Aviation."[14]

Naval aviators proved their versatility in the close air support role. "Dive bombing tactics as employed on land," Lieutenant Commander Overfield of VS-42 observed, "may have to be modified somewhat from the tactics used in naval aviation." Locating a target on land, as opposed to a ship that stood out easily at sea, required flying at lower altitudes. Smaller targets required more low-altitude flying, and pilots making that kind of attack would, he believed, encounter less heavier-caliber antiaircraft fire. A normal high-altitude approach could suffice, if the land target were larger and "well protected with antiaircraft batteries." Overfield proved a visionary in another important respect, recommending that the Navy adopt the Army's assigning nonflying officers to operating squadrons. Nonflying officers, Overfield suggested, could be used for personnel officers, office managers, communication officers, and administrative assistants to flight and engineering officers (tasks then performed by flying officers—pilots—who performed them in addition to their flight duties). Each carrier squadron, he concluded, could benefit from at least three nonflying officers, who could also assist in air intelligence work.[15]

During the same period, the situation in the Atlantic grew more dangerous. Although Adolf Hitler had specifically forbidden attacks on American ships, German submariners could not distinguish between active U.S. Navy

Major General Herbert A. Dargue (L) at his Lake Charles, Louisiana, headquarters during the Army's GHQ maneuvers, with Lt. Comdr. Thomas B. Williamson (R), the Navy liaison officer for the exercises (and the *Ranger*'s Air Group Commander), ca. 18 September 1941. (NHC, NH 42314)

destroyers identical to their sisters that had been transferred to the British in the autumn of 1940. The German submarine *U-652*, thinking her shadower to be a British warship, in light of the "flush deckers" known to have been transferred to the Royal Navy, fired a torpedo at the destroyer *Greer* (DD-145) on 4 September, 175 miles west of Iceland, as the latter shadowed the U-boat. The incident, coming almost two years after the inception of the Neutrality Patrol, prompted President Roosevelt to give the Navy "shoot on sight" orders on 11 September. A week later, U.S. Navy ships began escorting eastbound British convoys.

The *Ranger*'s overhaul lasted through mid-September. The "inexact stability information now available" dictated an urgent inclining experiment at the yard on 16 September (the only previous inclining work conducted on the ship dated back to 30 March 1935) to collect the necessary data. Although strenuous weight-reduction efforts had removed 56 tons prior to the start of the yard work, concern over the *Ranger*'s stability (especially with the inevitable assignment of heavier aircraft in the near future) prompted BuShips to decide to not install splinter protection in the *Ranger*, "the greatest weight which could possibly be spared for this purpose," Rear Adm. A. H. Van Keuren, the Assistant Chief of BuShips, declared, "would afford such scant protection to personnel as not to be worth its installation."[16]

Prior to the scheduled completion date for the *Ranger*'s overhaul, the yard completed the new arresting gear installation, and began testing several of the units, as instructed verbally by a BuAer representative. As the tests proceeded, however, it soon became evident that they would not be completed on time. On the morning of 15 September, the last day of the scheduled availability, a yard representative telephoned BuAer, prompting the hurried dispatch of an engineer from the Naval Aircraft Factory (NAF) in Philadelphia to assist the Norfolk people. Upon arrival that day, the engineer revealed that the tests ordered by BuAer's representative a few days before had not been necessary (the valves involved in the installation had been manufactured by the NAF and shipped completely assembled) and had probably damaged the valves. All 18 of the valves in question were removed that afternoon and 3 were found to have been damaged. The yard workmen reinstalled the 15 undamaged valves and began work on manufacturing new seats for the 3 damaged ones, as well as ordering 3 new seats from the NAF.[17]

More unpleasant surprises remained. The yard installed the CXAM-1 radar (an improved model of the CXAM, which employed amplidyne, instead of thyraton, control) and YE homing beacon equipment. The limited time available for the installation work, however, compelled yard engineers and workmen to engage in a lot of overtime on the CXAM-1 and YE equipments under unfavorable conditions work that, although appreciated by Captain Harrill, was still not completed by the time the ship left the yard on 17 September. That state of affairs necessitated a yard engineer and an RCA representative's remaining on board to instruct the *Ranger*'s radio people in its use, to check the performance of the equipment, and to determine the maximum attainable ranges.

As for the auxiliary operation of the ship's elevators, the Norfolk Navy Yard had adopted "the most unusual expedients . . . to get explosive-proof motors delivered in time." When those steps failed, the yard attempted a redesign "to utilize more readily obtainable motors; and all possible steps taken to obtain promise of sufficiently early deliveries." Although the yard managed to secure satisfactory bids for the motors and the material needed which would have perhaps allowed the work to have been undertaken and completed, the contractor failed to meet the required date. "All the required material," Rear Adm. Felix X. Gygax, Commandant of the Norfolk Navy Yard, later promised the CNO, "will be assembled at this yard for installation at a future availability."[18]

As that work went ahead, the *Ranger* put to sea to conduct test-firings of her newly installed "Chicago Pianos" (as sailors sometimes called the noisy and temperamental 1.1s). The ship's gunnery department soon found that the remote control equipment for the ship's searchlights had not, in fact, been installed. The ship proceeded to carry out the firing tests of the 1.1s, off the Chesapeake Lightship, on the 17th, then depermed at Plantation Flats on the 18th. She returned to Pier 7 on the afternoon of the 19th, and took delivery of the three arresting gear valves that had been repaired by the yard for installation by the ship's force, so that she could sail with her arresting gear in operable condition. The next day, the *Ranger* requested assistance from the yard to determine the problem with the directors. As things turned out, the control panels for the remote control of the searchlights, ordered under a BuShips contract, had arrived late, after the *Ranger* had left the yard on 17 September. Within 24 hr of the ship's trouble call on 20 September, the necessary work had been accomplished.

Ordered to proceed to Argentia, Newfoundland, at the earliest practicable time, the *Ranger* departed NOB Norfolk on 21 September, in company with the *Sterett* (DD-407). "Headed north," wrote Seaman 2d Class Ernest L. Crochet in his diary, "Rough sea and getting cold."[19] Despite the "strenuous and continuous efforts" of the Norfolk Navy Yard and RCA

"WITH CONTAGIOUS ENTHUSIASM" ■ 161

Norfolk Navy Yard, 10 September 1941: with the Wood Towing Company tugs *Alice* and *Reliance* alongside, the recently refitted transport *McCawley* (AP-10) runs her dock trials during the forenoon watch on 10 September 1941; in the background, work continues on the *Ranger*, including the foundation for the installation of the CXAM-1 radar at the top of the tripod foremast (upper right). The open lighter *YC-270* lies alongside the carrier, which appears to be painted in Measure 12 camouflage by this time (NA, 19-LCM, AP-1 to AP-10, Box 110)

engineers, however, the installation of the YE equipment remained incomplete, and the lack of time had prevented a test of the CXAM-1 at sea. Soon joined by the *Stack* (DD-406), the *Ranger* arrived at Placentia Bay on the 24th, where, the following day, Rear Admiral Cook shifted his flag back to the *Ranger* from the *Yorktown*.

The *Ranger* got underway later the same day, again accompanied by the *Stack* and the *Sterett*, and carried out flight operations that afternoon, as she shaped a course home to Hampton Roads, arriving there on the 28th. Her time in port, however, proved brief: Again in company with the *Stack* and the *Sterett*, she sailed for Bermuda, with her air group consisting of VF-41, VS-41, and VS-42, on the afternoon of 2 October, transporting a draft of men to join the light cruiser *Nashville* (CL-43).[20]

The *Ranger* also hosted other passengers: Rear Adm. Arthur L. St. George Lyster, CVO, DSO, ADC, the Fifth Sea Lord, Wing Comdr. Eric R. S. Jackson, Fleet Air Arm, Comdr. James I. Robertson, RN, and Lt. Comdr. Richard M. Smeeton, RN, to observe American carrier operations. Comdr. Steadman Teller, who had been a U.S. Naval Observer with the Royal Navy, and Lt. Comdr. John G. Crommelin, also reported on board for transportation. Robertson, formerly the Commander (Air) in the carrier

Alongside Pier 7, NOB Norfolk; the *Ranger* hoists on board a Grumman J2F-3 (marked USS RANGER–4) from her utility unit, during the afternoon watch on 20 September 1941; two F4F-3s and an SOC-1 (one of the two assigned to the utility unit, alongside the single J2F) wait in the distance. Gunnery training ship *Wyoming* (AG-17) (upper right) and the fleet oiler *Santee* (AO-29) (lower right) lie on the opposite side of the pier. Note the two SOC floats on the dock, family members at lower right, waiting for a loved one, and the wide variety of makes and models of vehicles (including a "woodie" station wagon). (NA, 80-G-391586)

HMS *Illustrious* (then undergoing repairs at Norfolk), was slated to command the Royal Navy's second "aircraft escort vessel," HMS *Archer*, then being completed at Norfolk.

During flight operations on 3 October, two mishaps punctuated the routine. Lieutenant Guy J. Anderson of VS-42, with Radioman 3d Class Joseph T. Rushing in back, ran low on fuel during a group tactics flight and signalled for a deferred forced landing, lowering his hook as required. Returning it to the up position, Anderson made his approach, but failed to lower it again in preparation for the landing. The pilot proved careless, but the crewman assigned the task of informing the LSO that Anderson's hook was still housed failed to do so, compounding the problem. Receiving the cut from the LSO, Anderson's unbridled SB2U-1 (BuNo 0747) rolled up the deck and crashed into the barrier, damaging landing gear fairings, twisting the stub wing and loosening rivets, springing the left wheel retracting gear, and badly bending the propeller.[21]

Ensign William E. Rouse, A-V(N), of VS-41, returning to the ship from patrol with Radioman 3d Class Arthur Kaster in back, signalled for a deferred forced landing, because of a rough running engine. Making a higher and faster approach than normal under the circumstances, Rouse did not react quickly enough to the cut from the LSO and could not catch a wire in time. Consequently, the SB2U-1 (BuNo 0763) crashed into the barrier, damaging

Lieutenant Commander William E. G. Taylor (R) lectured on board the *Ranger* on combat tactics and fighter direction, and passed on information on the use of search radar for fighter direction purposes, drawing upon his experience in the Royal Navy's Fleet Air Arm (1939–40), and the Royal Air Force (1940–41). He converses with Charles Codman, a *Saturday Evening Post* correspondent, and the *Ranger*'s air officer, Lt. Comdr. John Hoskins, September 1941. Note lack of splinter protection around the 1.1-inch/.75 quad ahead of the bridge, and Grumman F4F-3 from VF-5 in the background. (AUTHOR)

both landing gear fairings, crushing the lower portion of the nose cowling, straining the forward section of the fuselage, breaking the engine mount ring, and bending the propeller at both tips.[22]

The *Ranger* reached Bermuda early in the afternoon watch on 4 October and disembarked her passengers soon afterward. "The handling of aircraft on deck," Admiral Lyster later noted of his cruise in the *Ranger*, "is well organised and the day technique of flying off and landing on [recovering] a large number of aircraft has been developed to a high degree." The Fifth Sea Lord, however, although impressed with the thoroughness of the U.S. Navy's training, wrote of his concern over the Americans' "tendency to accept these two operations [handling of aircraft on deck and the launch/recovery process] as a major function of carrier borne aircraft, and that not enough consideration has been given as to the handling of this large number of aircraft over a long period of day to day flying in war time." The admiral thought that carrier operations involved continuous antisubmarine patrols, two or three searches each day, a small fighter patrol when in reach of possible enemy observation planes, and "other occasional small requirements, such as forced landings, refuelling and re-arming fighters, etc.," all of which required "great fluidity of the organisation." Lyster believed that "the continuous moving of aircraft on the deck may prove to be an embarassment."

Rear Admiral Arthur L. St. George Lyster, CVO, DSO, ADC, Fifth Sea Lord, shakes hands with Comdr. John J. Ballentine, to whose right stands Capt. Montgomery, the chief of staff for Comdr. Aircraft, Atlantic Fleet, and the *Ranger*'s Captain Harrill, 5 October 1941. Rear Adm. Arthur B. Cook, ComAirLant and Comdr. Carrier Division 3, looks on, right. (NHC, NH 42331)

On the basis of his observation of American carrier operations, Lyster believed that British carriers could operate more planes by adopting methods similar to the Americans, but believed that the Americans could not operate "the large numbers usually carried except for special operations." He did allow, however, that that remained to be proved, and expressed hesitancy "to make any drastic reductions until they are dictated by war experience."[23]

Soon thereafter, to inspect the landing field under construction in Castle Harbor, Bermuda, Rear Admiral Cook sent Lieutenant Commander Williamson, the *Ranger*'s air group commander, and Lt. Comdr. Jesse S. McClure, of the admiral's staff, ashore on 13 October, where they met Major White of the Army Engineer Corps. White had arrived in Bermuda in November 1940, had started the project, and hoped to be there to finish the job. The officers from the *Ranger* conferred with him in his office, looked over plans for the project, and later visited the field itself. The base, which at that point had no garrison, had been named Fort Bell; the airstrip, Kindley Field.

Built on Long Bird Island, Kindley consisted of three runways: "A," 3,200 feet long; "B," 2,400 feet, and "C," 4,800. A and B had been completed, except for the final surfacing of asphalt, and Major White informed them that planes could make an emergency landing at any time. His workmen toiled in two 10-hour shifts, meaning that people were there 20 hours out of every day. White promised Lieutenant Commanders Williamson and McClure that he would instruct his foremen to allow any U.S. Navy "landplanes" to use the field "any time they indicate a desire to do so." All the pilot had to do was fly low and parallel to the runway, signalling his need to land by opening and closing the throttle, gunning the engine. The foreman would then signal for all rolling stock to get off the runway that the pilot wanted to use.[24]

As McClure later noted, the Joint Board plans had called for Kindley Field to be able to handle one carrier air group consisting of 81 airplanes, 125 officers and 550 men. Major White had told them that those facilities, however, would most likely not be ready before January or February of 1942. "There is no place men could be berthed before these facilities are ready," McClure later reported to Admiral Cook, "as he [Major White] is already hard pressed to take care of the workmen" he had assigned, having to put them up in a former Hudson River excursion boat that had been brought down to serve as a floating barracks.[25]

With no Air Corps people, and no defenses, Major White told the two officers from the *Ranger* that he had contemplated obstructing the runways with such items as large sewer pipes, to prevent any enemy force from landing and taking possession of the field before a garrison arrived to defend it. "He was very anxious to know," Lieutenant Commander McClure later noted, "how our planes could be identified." McClure told Major White that "they would carry the standard U.S. Aviation Insigne." Reflecting on the army officer's worried expression, McClure suggested to Admiral Cook that, "when dragging the field pilots should be instructed to let men on the field get a good look at the markings of the plane." He also suggested advance word of a plane's arrival to the U.S. District Engineer's Office via the Naval Operating Base or the signal station.[26]

During the afternoon watch on 22 October, Ens. Benjamin M. Lakin, A-V(N), of VF-41, took off on a practice interception, upon the conclusion of which he returned to the ship. Receiving the cut from the LSO, Lakin held off putting his F4F-3 (BuNo 2538) on the deck until touching down at the number five wire. The Wildcat bounded, tail-high through the number three barrier and engaged number four forward barrier, running it out 30 feet, until the plane ended up on its nose and left wing tip. The barrier cables had mutilated the engine cowling and bent the prop blades; the sudden stoppage of the engine, when the propeller hit the deck, necessitated a major overhaul to the plane's powerplant. Repairs to the outboard ribs of the left wing, and to the landing gear, rounded out the overhaul items needed in the wake of Lakin's mishap, which a trouble board deemed 100% pilot error (poor technique).[27]

Even experienced aviators occasionally encountered difficulties landing on board. Lieutenant John R. Yoho (USNA 1929) of VS-42, with over a decade of flight time under his belt, returned to the ship on 28 October, with Radioman 1st Class W. T. Hugget in back, and made a normal approach, but was slightly higher than usual. Yoho, believing himself abnormally high, nosed the SB2U-1 (BuNo 0746) abruptly for the deck. Not pulling the stick back in time meant that the Vindicator struck the deck "very hard" and bounced about five feet into the air. Yoho's tail hook hit the deck between wires four and five, but failed to engage either pendant; finally it caught wire ten, but that failed to prevent the nose from going into the barrier, bringing the engine to an abrupt stop, slightly bending both landing gear retracting oleos, bending the engine mount and the propeller, damaging the right wingtip, and bending and tearing the engine cowling.

Soon after Major White had informed Tom Williamson that his pilots could use Kindley Field in an emergency, one of VF-41's aviators put the offer to the test. When the pilot fouled a towline during aerial gunnery exercises, and a carrier landing appeared unduly hazardous, the *Ranger* directed him to land at the Castle Harbor field. He thus became a celebrity when he made the first landing on the island's airstrip and was, as Admiral Cook later reported, "besieged by autograph seekers."[28]

The *Ranger's* troublesome YE gear had necessitated the dispatch of O. C. Dresser, a radio engineer from the Naval Research Laboratory (NRL). Dresser arrived on board on 27 October, the day after a Radio Corporation of America (RCA) representative, Jacobs, had arrived in the *Yarmouth*, to service the CXAM-1 radar. He inspected the equipment and soon found that it had been improperly installed, and that the main difficulty lay in the installation of the transmission line. Open circuits and short circuits existed within the system. Among the many defects was that the yard workmen had installed the antenna higher above the mast than had been recommended, resulting in additional strain, permanently bowing the topmast and thus creating additional bearing strain. The NRL engineer, assisted by the ship's radio gang, set to work to put the equipment in operation, as best they could. Urgent dispatches soon went from ComAirLant to BuShips, requesting the desired materials for the work be shipped to Portland, Maine, for delivery on 3 November.[29]

At the time that the *Ranger* was training out of Bermuda, the undeclared conflict in the Atlantic entered a new phase. U.S. Navy destroyers, convoying British merchantmen, engaged German U-boats for the first time. During the battle to protect convoy SC-48 southwest of Iceland, the *U-658* torpedoed the destroyer *Kearny*. On 30 October, the *U-106* torpedoed the oiler *Salinas* (AO-19), as the auxiliary was proceeding with convoy ON-28, 700 miles east of Newfoundland. Most serious of all was the *U-552's* torpedoing and sinking the destroyer *Reuben James* on Halloween

Night 1941, as the *Reuben James* had been escorting convoy HX-156 off western Iceland. As reflected in recruiting efforts soon thereafter, the soberingly heavy loss of life among the *Reuben James*'s officers and men gave many individuals second thoughts, who had been contemplating joining the Navy.

Among the shipping traversing the North Atlantic sealanes was a convoy bringing a large contingent of British troops to Halifax, Nova Scotia, escorted by a task force formed around the *Yorktown*. Upon reaching Halifax, the soldiers reembarked in six U.S. Navy transports: the *West Point* (AP-23) (formerly the U.S. liner *America*), the *Mount Vernon* (AP-22) (formerly the liner *Washington*), the *Wakefield* (AP-21)(formerly the liner *Manhattan*), the *Leonard Wood* (AP-25), the *Joseph T. Dickman* (AP-26), and the venerable *Orizaba* (AP-23), which had transported American Expeditionary Force doughboys to Europe in World War I.

As those events were transpiring, the *Ranger* sailed for Portland, in company with the destroyers *Rhind* (DD-404) and *Mayrant* (DD-402), on 31 October, and arrived on 2 November, during the afternoon watch, dropping anchor at 1424. While the ship lay at Portland, Captain Harrill responded to the Commandant of the Norfolk Navy Yard's request for comment on the low-visibility deck stain and marking paint (Norfolk Formula No.L-81-3m), which had been provided by that yard and applied to the

One sailor works intently on the tail of one of VS-42's Vought SB2U-2s (BuNo 1328), while a shipmate looks on, 3 November 1941. The plane bears the large single number marking from the Vindicator's previous unit, the Advanced Carrier Training Unit, Atlantic, from which it had been transferred on 31 October 1941. (NA, 80-CF File)

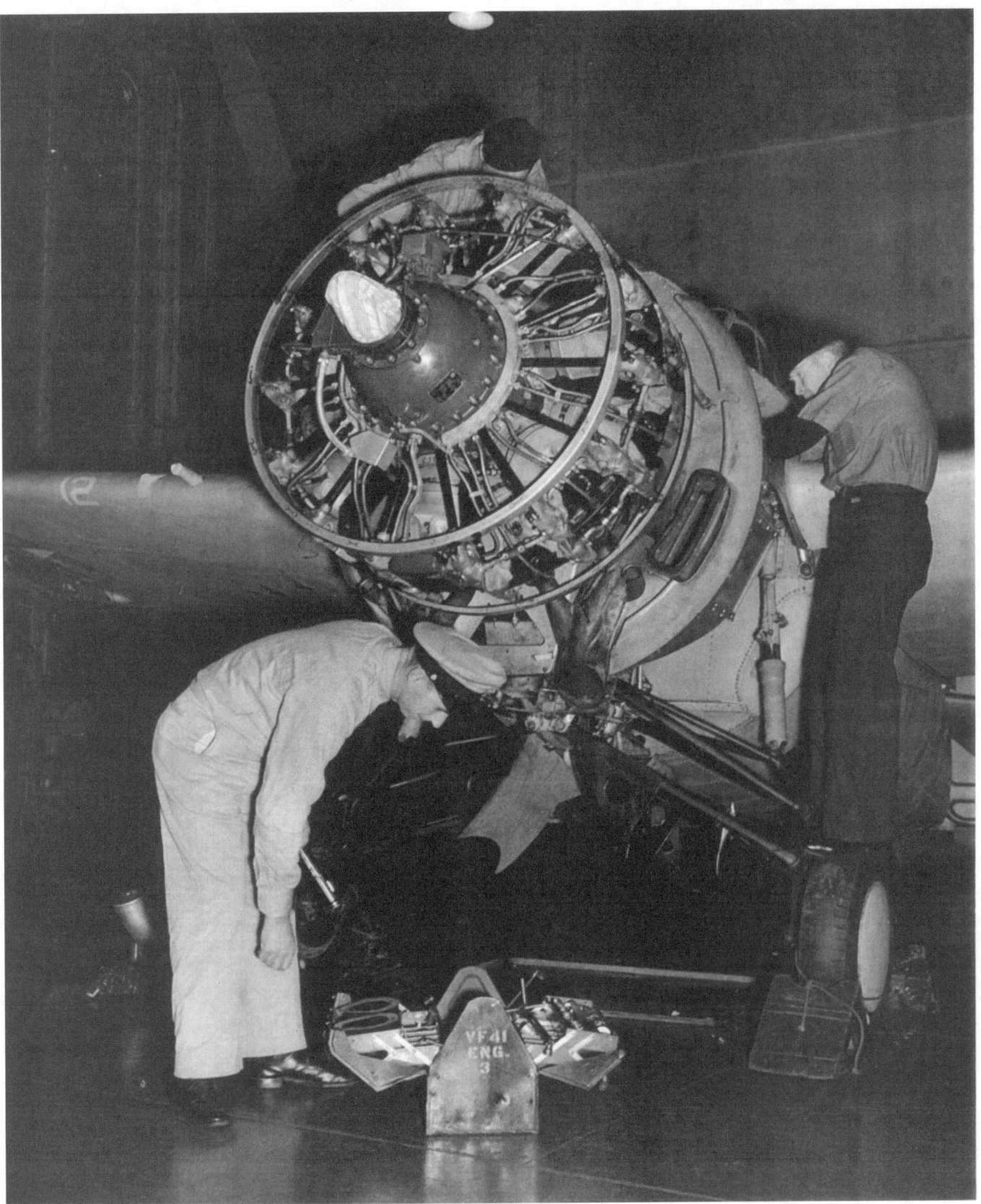

Servicing 41-F-12, an F4F-3, on the hangar deck, 3 November 1941. (NA, 80-CF File)

Forty-Two-Sail-Thirteen prepares to taxi forward to take off, while SB2Us from VS-41 and an F4F-3 (41-F-5) from VF-41 wait their turn, 10 November 1941. Note use of high contrast white markings against the dark blue gray "war color." (NA, 80-G-391590)

ship's flight deck. He noted that the ship had experienced no difficulties in applying and drying the experimental lot that had been supplied, and that pilots experienced no problems aligning planes during the landing approach, taxing, or taking off. Under low visibility conditions, Harrill noted, "the carrier deck is much more difficult to see, from the air, in comparison with the red stain and yellow markings as used heretofore. This," he continued, "constitutes an important advantage in that concealment of the carrier against detection and observation by enemy aircraft is greatly improved." In view of the ease of application and the concealment factors, Harrill "recommended that it be adopted for all aircraft carriers."[30]

The *Ranger*, earmarked to provide air cover for one phase of that movement of the British troops from Halifax, along with the heavy cruisers *Quincy* and *Vincennes* and seven destroyers, quit Portland for the open sea late in the afternoon watch on 9 November. She sailed with the troublesome YE gear at least having been flight tested, the operators attaining results comparable to what had been possible with the YE gear on board the *Yorktown*. Dresser, the NRL engineer who had spent two weeks on board engaged in the work, praised the *Ranger*'s radio people as having "done everything possible to correct the deficiencies, but, due to the original installation containing so many defects of a serious nature, it [had been] impossible to take proper corrective action while the vessel was at sea." He also recommended that the gear be "completely overhauled at the first opportunity. While every effort had been made to overcome the existing difficulties, many of the repairs were necessarily of a temporary nature, and the installation in its present condition will undoubtedly develop future troubles."[31]

VF-41's F4F-3s line the starboard side of the flight deck, aft, and predominantly SB2U-1s or –2s from either VS-41 or VS-42 the port. Note how the old deck markings are visible beneath the Norfolk Formula No. L-81-3m stain, the tire tracks illustrating the Norfolk product's durability problems. The transport *Orizaba* (AP-24) plows along off the carrier's port quarter; the *Joseph T. Dickman* (AP-26), in the shadow of a cloud, steams in the *Orizaba*'s wake, 25 November 1941. (NA, 80-G-464157)

When the *Ranger* sailed, one of her Marines, Pvt. Andrew J. Nemeth, a detachment clerk, for some reason, unfortunately missed her departure. He dutifully turned himself over to the senior shore patrol officer, however, a half hour before the end of the forenoon watch on the 9th. Furnished the first available government transportation—passage in the oiler *Sangamon* (AO-28)—Nemeth eventually arrived at the Marine Barracks, NOB Norfolk on the 25th, to await the return of his ship.

An hour and a half into the afternoon watch on 10 November, 50 miles south of the Halifax lightship, the *Ranger* and her consorts joined the six transports assigned to their protection. The *Ranger*, wearing Rear Admiral Cook's flag, served as flagship for convoy WS-12X (the "WS" denoting "Winston's Specials"), as it steamed southward into the Atlantic.

By and large, flight operations proceeded uneventfully. As the *Ranger* neared Trinidad, however, during the forenoon watch one week later, on 17 November, Ens. Edward J. Murphy, returning from a scouting flight in an SB2U-1 (BuNo 0756), with Radioman 2d Class Ammon E. Capshaw in back, made a normal landing, but slightly wheels-first. The tail wheel assembly, however, incident to progressive material failure, collapsed when the tail hit the deck.[32]

Anchoring at Port of Spain later during the forenoon watch on the 17th, the *Ranger* fueled from the British tanker *Servitor* and departed during the afternoon watch on the 19th. That same day, Keen Harrill elaborated further in response to the Norfolk Navy Yard's seeking comment on the stain that had been applied to the *Ranger*'s flight deck. He noted that the Norfolk stain covered the old red deck

The *Ranger*, painted in Measure 12 camouflage, recovering planes, 2 December 1941. The demarcation between the colors of the camouflage parallel the horizon along the main deck level. (NA, 80-G-212976 courtesy of David Shaddell)

Forty-Two-Sail-Seventeen banks to starboard as the *Ranger* prepares to launch F4Fs, 2 December 1941. (NA, 80-G-457881)

stain satisfactorily, but that only one coat had been applied to the greater portion of the flight deck. He observed, however, that the penetration into new wood was poor and the depth slight, whereas penetration into the older wood was satisfactory, prompting his recommendation that the Norfolk Navy yard undertake experiments to improve their product's penetration qualities. The new stain's slipperiness in wet weather, he noted, was the same as the old red stain, but he went on that the new deteriorated more in wet weather than the old. "Sliding of aircraft tires on the deck, covered by one coat of [the] subject stain," Harrill wrote, "shows definite tracks, i.e., the red stain shows through." Insufficient information could not permit any definite conclusion as to the relative resistance to corrosion of the Norfolk stain.[33] Inside a week's time, Admiral Cook concurred in Captain Harrill's earlier comments about the Norfolk stain's suitability for carrier decks, and, considering it "highly desirable that this stain be applied to all other aircraft carriers as soon as practicable," directed the commanding officers of the *Wasp*, the *Yorktown*, and the aircraft escort vessel *Long Island* (AVG-1) to have the stain applied "to the flight decks of their respective vessels."[34]

The *Ranger*'s routine continued as she escorted her valuable convoy. Two days out of Port of Spain, Lt. (jg) Cecil V. "Johnny" Johnson, of VS-41, was returning from a patrol in his SB2U-1 (BuNo 0757), with Radioman 3d Class L. R. Smith on board, only to encounter difficulty lowering his landing gear, because of a frozen control valve. Using the emergency release, Johnson managed to land without incident, but, when taxiing out of the gear, moved the flap control handle to the up position and thus inadvertently retracted the wheels. The trouble board assessed

SB2Us and F4Fs are spotted forward, an F4F taxies up the deck, and an SB2U is about to land, aft, as the *Ranger*, rolling easily to starboard, nears Port of Spain, Trinidad, 3 December 1941. (NA, 80-CF-5485-3)

most of the blame for the accident on Johnson, faulting his poor reaction.[35]

The *Ranger* continued to provide air cover until 26 November, at which time she and the destroyers *Trippe* and *Rhind* were detached, at 6°30′S, 33°W. The convoy proceeded on, command passing, with Rear Adm. Cook's departure, to Capt. Donald B. Beary, commanding officer of the *Mount Vernon*. Ensign Donald H. Dorris, on board the heavy cruiser *Vincennes*, noted the carrier's departure with her two consorts and the effect that that had on the routine observed by the heavy cruisers' aviation units. "The *Ranger* turned back yesterday," Dorris wrote in his diary on 27 November, "so now the pilots of the *Quincy* and the *Vinnie Maru* will have a lot of patrolling to do. Our aviators will start earning their money for a change."[36]

The *Ranger*'s continued to earn theirs, sometimes at great risk to life and limb. On 28 November, flight operations had proceeded uneventfully until the last. Ensign David M. Glass, A-V(N), in 42-S-8, with Radioman 3d Class Dale I. Jacobson on board, began his approach very close to the plane ahead. The LSO could see that Glass was coming in too slow, and that the SB2U-1 was beginning to settle. Consequently, with the Vindicator about 300 feet astern, the LSO signalled "wave-off." Glass started a climbing turn, banked about 60 degrees, and turned about 45 degrees from his landing course, but continued rolling to the left as he lost control. Forty-Two-Sail Eight inverted, dipped its left wingtip into the ocean, and crashed at 0952.[37]

The impact not only threw Glass into the left side of the cockpit, causing contusions and abrasions to his left arm and left leg, but slammed his face into the instrument panel, causing multiple lacerations. Radioman 3d Class Jacobson suffered multiple contusions of both arms, the laceration of his lower lip, and a sprained and lacerated right thumb. As both men freed themselves from 42-S-8, the *Rhind* immediately altered course and lowered her motor whaleboat, promptly rescuing both men. The SB2U-1 (BuNo 0754), beyond salvage, sank. The *Ranger* reembarked the two injured men from the *Rhind* soon thereafter and admitted them to sick bay immediately. Doctors who treated the 27-year-old Glass feared that he would lose his vision, because of the severity of his facial lacerations, which had occurred principally to the structure of the face surrounding the eyes. They believed further observation necessary to determine the extent of his injuries in the crash that had been due to 100% pilot error.[38]

Up to that point, the *Ranger*'s operations had been, excepting the accidents incident to flight deck operations, mostly devoid of incident. The readiness of the ship and her air group for war, however, found expression on 30 November, when Ens. Ed Murphy, flying 42-S-2, dropped a depth bomb on a "suspected submarine" during the forenoon watch.

Returning to Port of Spain to fuel on 3 December, the *Ranger* and her two consorts sailed the following morning for Hampton Roads. At about 0700 on 5 December, the *Ranger* intercepted a report broadcast by the British freighter *Wolfe* of a "suspicious vessel" at 16°00′N, 65°00′W, roughly 100 miles astern of the carrier. Shortly the *Ranger* intercepted a dispatch from the light cruiser *Cincinnati* (CL-6) that the latter was steaming toward the position given by the British merchantman. Assuming that the Commandant, Tenth Naval District, and the *Cincinnati* had been in receipt of "information relative to the suspicious vessel above that received in *Ranger*," Rear Admiral Cook ordered his flagship to proceed toward the contact at her best speed and to conduct an air search covering possible 1100–1600 positions. At the same time, he sent a dispatch to the Commandant, Tenth Naval District, and to the *Cincinnati*, requesting additional information.[39]

The *Ranger* went to general quarters at 1018 and altered course roughly southeast by east at 1042. Securing from general quarters at 1107, the air department remained at condition 1; changing speed at 1118, the carrier began launching planes at 1130, an evolution completed in three minutes. But, about a half hour later, the Commandant, Tenth Naval District, radioed the *Ranger* that the report of the suspicious vessel had been cancelled. The *Ranger* then recovered her aircraft and "proceeded on duty assigned."[40]

Two days later, while still en route to Norfolk, the *Ranger* received electrifying news. Lieutenant David L. McDonald, aide and flag secretary to Rear Admiral Cook, had just returned to his stateroom and shed his white coat when a Marine orderly brought him a message that told of Pearl Harbor being bombed by the Japanese. Donning the coat he had just taken off, McDonald hurried to the admiral's cabin to inform Cook of the news. Neither the admiral nor his aide doubted the authenticity of the tidings.[41]

PART II
WORLD WAR II AND AFTER

15

"OUR ONLY STRIKING FORCE AGAINST RAIDERS"

Despite the "scuttlebutt" that speculated whether or not the *Ranger* would immediately be sent to the Pacific, she reached Norfolk on 8 December and anchored in Hampton Roads, about midway through the first dog watch. Shifting to Pier 7 during the forenoon watch of the following day, and thence to the Norfolk Navy Yard during the forenoon watch on the 10th, the *Ranger* remained there, undergoing a restricted availability, until four days before Christmas. During that time in the yard, vigorous weight-reduction efforts proceeded on board to allow future installation of the splinter protection that BuShips had not approved during her previous overhaul in the summer of 1941. Material removed included the wooden decks in the captain's and admiral's galleys (2.9 tons in each), arresting gear repair stations and workshops, wooden mess tables and benches, bunk rails from officers' rooms, a winch platform and a wing stowage locker. That work lightened the ship by some 51.9 tons.[1] In addition, the ship landed some 4.5 tons of paint from storerooms on her second and third decks.

In war as well as in peace, aircraft accidents continued to take their toll, and did not exempt the *Ranger*'s air group from their cold grasp. On 11 December, Ens. William C. May, A-V(N), of VS-42, lost control of his SB2U-1 (BuNo 0743) while on a familiarization flight. The Vought crashed and burned, killing May and his passenger, Aviation Machinist's Mate 3d Class T. W. Lincoln, Jr. A trouble board concluded that the crash had been caused by May's going into an unrecoverable spin after having executed or recovered from a loop.[2]

Amidst the sobering events of national and global import that had been occurring since Pearl Harbor, tragedy of a different nature touched a family that had two brothers serving in the *Ranger*. During the first watch on 20 December, the ship received word from the Norfolk Shore Patrol station that Coxswain M. S. Youngblood, from the ship's Second Division, and a shipmate, Seaman 1st Class D. L. Hutsell, had suffered injuries in a car accident between Hertford and Edenton, North Carolina. Youngblood had died in the Albemarle Hospital, Elizabeth City, North Carolina; Hutsell clung to life. A Norfolk woman had perished in the accident as well. When the *Ranger*, accompanied by the *Lang* (DD-399) and the *Rhind*, stood out of Hampton Roads during the afternoon watch the following day, 21 December, bound for Bermuda, Boatswain's Mate 1st Class J. F. Youngblood remained behind to accompany his brother's body home for burial.

During the time that the *Ranger* had been in the yard, one of her old squadrons, the F4F-3-equipped VF-42, deployed on board the *Yorktown*, as she sailed for the Pacific on 16 December.[3] Fighting Forty-One had remained behind. Its commanding officer, Lt. Comdr. James J. McRoberts, and two other U.S. Navy pilots, flew F4F-3s out to the newly commissioned British aircraft escort vessel HMS *Archer*, during the forenoon watch on 23 December. The flight deck crew spotted McRoberts's F4F-3 (BuNo 1853) first to be catapulted. Tragically, the catapult bridle parted as VF-41's skipper took off, and the unassisted Grumman plunged into the cold waters off Cape Henry.

177

Able Seaman A. Giddings promptly dove into the sea to attempt to rescue McRoberts, but without success. The *Archer* subsequently flew off the other two Wildcats, and proceeded to the Philadelphia Navy Yard for repairs to the damaged catapult.[4]

The *Ranger*, with the *Wasp*'s VF-72 (VF-41 temporarily based at Norfolk), and her own VS-41 and VS-42, reached Bermuda almost midway through the forenoon watch on 23 December, and anchored in berth Fox-9, with seven fathoms of water beneath her keel. She remained there for almost 24 hours, getting underway at 0702 on 24 December, followed immediately by the *Rhind*, the *Lang*, and the light cruiser *Savannah* (CL-42). She conducted flight operations during the forenoon, afternoon, and first dog watches, logging only one mishap during the day's evolutions, when Ens. Andrew J. Lowndes, A-V(N), of VF-72, came in for a landing, but held his plane too high off the deck, with the result that his F4F-3 (BuNo 3862) missed the cross-deck pendants, penetrated the barriers, and crashed into the forward clipping house.

Returning to Bermuda in a heavy rain, the *Ranger* dropped anchor in Berth "A," Grassy Bay, at 1225 on Christmas Day, and brought the British tanker *War Brahmin* alongside to fuel, less than an hour before the end of the afternoon watch. Completing that necessary logistics evolution inside five hours' time, the carrier remained at anchor until the following morning, when she got underway, assisted by the harbor tug *Montezuma* (YT-145), and returned to sea to conduct further flight operations, accompanied by the *Rhind* and the *Lang*. She returned and anchored in Berth "A" during the first dog watch, and remained there until the morning of the 29th.

During the time a portion of the air group operated ashore, VF-72 experienced its second mishap of the cruise. Lieutenant (jg) Edward W. "Red" Hessel, a man whom his Academy classmates considered the possessor of "infectious good nature" and a "jovial disposition," as well as being a "fighting and capable tackle" for three of his four years at Annapolis, ground-looped his F4F-3 (BuNo 2518) on take off, in a crosswind, on 28 December, with both plane and engine suffering class B damage.[5]

The *Ranger* operated out of Grassy Bay on 29 December and Murray's Anchorage the following day, with the *Rhind* serving as plane guard each day. Only one mishap occurred during those operations, when 71-F-12 hit number four clipping room on landing, during the forenoon watch on 30 December, with no casualties and only slight damage to the F4F's right wing.

Subsequently, VT-4 (with its six Douglas TBD-1s) was formally activated on board on 10 January 1942, under Lt. Wallace A. Sherrill, who had been flight officer in Scouting Forty-One. For the first time in her career, the *Ranger* had an operational torpedo squadron, which expanded her capabilities and allowed more flexibility of employment.

While at Bermuda, the *Ranger*'s shore patrol (SP) detail found ample employment, either in assisting sailors who encountered unforeseen circumstances or, when the situation demanded it, serving notice that, even in wartime, breaches of regulations governing deportment or the wearing of the uniform would not be tolerated. During the afternoon watch on 2 January 1942, Constable L. Burge and George Petty, Arthur Trott, and Samuel Lighthouse, four British subjects, came on board the *Ranger* to "further establish the facts and to determine the actual status" of Radioman 2d Class G. P. Blakemore and Radioman 3d Class C. E. Vernadakis, "in the matter of a reported unauthorized use of a horse and buggy." In a verdict that seemed more reminiscent of the old west than the western Atlantic, both Blakemore and Vernadakis received 20 hours extra duty for horse theft.

A little over a week after the radiomen-rustlers had received their just desserts, the shore patrol apprehended Fireman 3d Class W. N. Well, speeding on a bicycle through the streets of Hamilton—without lights. A week later, they found Apprentice Seaman W. J. Sheets "under [the] influence of intoxicating liquor," as well as being out of uniform, with his cuffs rolled up and his hat perched jauntily (but not in accordance with regulations) on the back of his head. That same day, Gunner's Mate 3d Class W. S. Horton returned to the *Ranger* with a lacerated right hand—he had been playing with a dog and the animal had bitten him. After treatment, Horton performed light duty for two days. During the afternoon watch on 18 January, Fireman 1st Class J. F. Powers reported in to the SP headquarters with a torn and dirty uniform; he had been overleave since 1830 the previous day. Private Anthony Dawidowski, USMC, having overstayed his leave by seven minutes, turned himself in to the SPs ashore at 1852. Fireman 1st Class C. L. Bulwack reported on board at 2245, "in an intoxicated condition," as well as being absent over leave. Occasionally, a man would attempt to smuggle liquor on board ship: Mess Attendant C. L. Williams tried on 16 January, but the watch discovered three pints of Canadian Club whiskey in a shoe box he was carrying. A summary court martial sentenced Williams to one month of "extra police duty," to lose pay amounting to $108.00, and a bad conduct discharge. Convening authority approved the sentence, but lessened the loss of pay to $60 and remitted the bad-conduct discharge, providing that "Johnson's conduct remain[ed] satisfactory to his Commanding Officer for six months."

While the officer of the deck, megaphone in hand, watches for the next boat to come alongside and the gangway sentry looks toward the camera, three sailors turn to to the task of toting bulging mail sacks, Bermuda, January 1942. (NA, 80-G-464197)

Training, meanwhile, continued with the squadrons based ashore. Near the end of the morning watch on 28 January, VF-72 launched a dawn patrol. As pilots who flew the Bethpage, Long Island, product could readily attest, the Grumman Wildcat proved unforgiving with its narrow-track landing gear, if a pilot momentarily suffered a lapse in concentration. Lieutenant Stevan Mandarich took off from Kindley Field in an F4F-3 (BuNo 3863), but ground-looped to the left and plowed into one of VS-41's parked SB2U-3s (BuNo 0759), which sat parked in its assigned dispersal area near the edge of the field, some 50 yards to the left of the runway. Both planes burst into flames upon impact, forcing Mandarich, (who suffered a fractured nose and right clavicle, bilateral maxilla, as well as lacerations of his right cheek in the accident) to hastily exit his burning F4F. A trouble board blamed 25% of the accident on the F4F's handling qualities, but assessed 75% of the mishap as due to poor judgment (25%) and poor technique (50%) on the pilot's part.[6]

The *Ranger* weighed in her port anchor at 1246 on 4 February and stood out of Shelly Bay to conduct flight operations. Later, at 1533, she turned into the brisk wind to bring her air group on board. A little over a quarter of an hour later, Ens. Royal C. Carrington, A-V(N), VS-42's navigator, with Radioman 3d Class Henry H. Reed in back, approached the ramp in 42-S-12, "slightly high and fast." The LSO gave the 25-year-old Tennessean the "cut" signal, but, because of the pitching deck, the SB2U-1 (BuNo 0726) made a hard landing and bounced, missing a wire. The right wing dipped and the unbridled Vindicator drifted toward the starboard side of the deck, Carrington tried to regain the center of the deck, but 42-S-12 hit the clipping house aft of the island and belatedly engaged the number eight wire. The engine and engine mount broke off forward of the firewall and fell on deck.[7]

Fire, which carrier sailors rightly dread, flared up immediately, and the *Ranger* sounded fire quarters as she turned to provide a lee. In five minutes' time, the blaze had been brought under control, but not before 31 men, including Ensign Carrington, a former Decatur County, Tennessee, schoolteacher, had received foamite burns on eyes and eyelids; Carrington's passenger, Radioman 3d Class Reed, survived without a scratch. The flight deck crew, who had been unable to quell the blaze at the outset, pushed the crashed plane to the stern and rolled it over the ramp into the sea at 0948.

Misfortune again visited the ship the following day. Lieutenant (jg) Allen W. Smith, A-V(N), VS-42's engineering officer, made a good approach in 42-S-14 (BuNo 0751), with Radioman 2d Class Ammon Capshaw on board. Given the cut, Smith closed the throttle and nosed over before making the landing. Leveling off with his hook slightly above the cross-deck pendants, he unfortunately missed all the wires and continued up the deck, hitting number three barrier. All would have been well had it ended there, but 42-S-14 nosed up when it engaged the barrier, and the high winds disposed events from there, carrying the Vindicator aft and to starboard, heading toward the edge of the flight deck just forward of the stacks. Smith and Capshaw scrambled out of the plane onto the flight deck before the SB2U careened over the edge into the choppy sea below.[8]

While the *Ranger* was operating from Bermuda, Captain Harrill addressed the issue of the ship's next overhaul. The strenuous weight-reduction efforts that the *Ranger* had carried

Douglas TBD-1 Devastator from VT-4 takes off, while the *Ranger* lies at anchor, Bermuda, 15 January 1942. (80-G-2012)

out prompted him to inform BuShips that the net reductions carried out at the Norfolk Navy Yard in December 1941, together with the reduction in paint stocks, indicated that the ship had carried out "more than necessary" weight removal to meet the bureau's criteria "to improve damage resistance."[9]

Back in Washington, the *Ranger*'s future employment came under discussion in the wake of a desperate dispatch from Batavia requesting the services of a carrier to ferry Curtiss P-40 fighters to the Netherlands East Indies. Admiral Ernest J. King, who had been made Commander in Chief, United States Fleet, in the wake of the disaster at Pearl Harbor, in explaining the existing carrier situation to President Roosevelt on 12 February, pointed out that, as far as the Atlantic Fleet's flattops were concerned, the *Hornet* (CV-8) was "about to be assigned to Fleet duties, where she is urgently needed," and the *Wasp* and the *Ranger* "constituted our only striking force against raiders."[10]

The existing situation in the Atlantic, King believed, precluded "the detachment of either one [the *Wasp* or the *Ranger*] for . . . two or three months." As for the Pacific Fleet's carriers, other than the *Saratoga*, which was undergoing repairs after being torpedoed by a Japanese submarine on 11 January 1942, the *Lexington*, the *Yorktown*, and the *Enterprise* represented the "only offensive air striking power in the Pacific and our principal means of holding the Hawaiian Islands and maintaining our lines of communication to the Anzac and ABDA areas. They are urgently required for offensive action in fighting carriers," King declared, "and cannot logically be spared for use as ferry boats."[11]

Operations continued for the *Ranger*, with the occasional mishap punctuating the routine. On 18 February, at Grassy Bay, one of the ship's two Utility Unit Grumman J2F-5s, flown by an enlisted pilot, Gunner (NAP) Darrell E. Way, crashed astern of the carrier. Way and his two passengers, Ens. Harry A. Richards, Jr. (SC), USNR, and Storekeeper 1st Class C. R. Brinson, emerged unhurt and none the worse for their experience; the *Ranger* hoisted the lamed Duck on board before the watch was out.

Heavy rain squalls lashed Bermuda on 22 February, as the *Ranger* lay at anchor in berth 17, Shelly Bay, two boilers on the main steam line to enable the ship to get underway in an emergency. She stood out to sea a half-hour into the afternoon watch, and went to general quarters shortly afterwords. Over the next several days, the *Ranger*, operating as part of TG 2.7, in company with the heavy cruiser *Augusta* (CA-31), the light cruiser *Savannah*, and the destroyers *Wainwright* (DD-419), *Wilson* (DD-408) and *Lang*, participated in a "show of force" off the Vichy French island of Martinique, at one point steaming within 12½ miles of it.

While thus engaged, the *Ranger* conducted carrier qualification landings for the *Wasp*'s VF-72. Lieutenant (jg) Thomas C. Johnson, A-V(N), made a wheels-first landing in 72-F-1, which collapsed the gear at 1325 on 23 February; no less than eight minutes later, Lt. (jg) Robert W. Rynd collapsed 72-F-12's gear in like fashion. Two days later, Ens. William H. Longley, A-V(N), of VS-41, with Aviation Machinist's Mate 2d Class B. J. Dietrich in back, made a slightly fast gliding approach as he returned from a practice bombing hop. His SB2U-1 (BuNo 0757) hit the deck wheels first and bounced into the air without snagging a wire. Although headed toward the port side, Longley managed to manhandle the SB2U back to the centerline, where it stalled, the right wing tip, right wheel, prop and engine, and left wheel, hitting the deck in succession. The right side of the landing gear broke upon impact and the plane settled into a horizontal position. The impact of the crash distorted the right stub wing, crumpled both landing gear fairings, crumpled the right wing and landing flaps, sheared a half dozen bolts on the landing gear attachment fairings, damaged the left wheel and the cowl nose ring. The impact of the plane hitting the deck on its landing gear also blew both tires.[12] Those proved to be the only mishaps during the operations off Martinique, and, delayed in her return by high winds and rough seas, the *Ranger* dropped anchor in Murray's Anchorage a little over an hour into the afternoon watch on 4 March.

Underway during the forenoon watch on Friday, 13 March, the *Ranger* operated with the *Augusta* and the *Savannah* in TG 2.7, until returning to Murray's Anchorage on the 17th, anchoring a little over an hour and a quarter into the afternoon watch. She remained there only a short time, however, weighing anchor and standing out three-quarters of an hour into the first dog watch, setting course for Norfolk, in company with the *Wainwright*, *Wilson*, and *Lang*. The *Ranger* passed Cape Henry Light abeam on the morning of the 19th, and moored alongside Pier 7 soon thereafter.

After discharging gasoline at NOB Norfolk, the *Ranger* shifted to the Norfolk Navy Yard to begin a 15-day availability, putting over her mooring lines during the forenoon watch on 21 March. For the most part, hers was an uneventful stay, enlivened eight days into the work by calls to fire and rescue quarters during the first dog watch on 29 March, when the transport *Joseph Hewes* (AP-50), moored nearby, reported a leak that was flooding a fireroom. The *Ranger* provided 40 men, equipped with "electric submersible pumps, diving gear, suction line and pressure hose," to carry out damage control on board the troopship.

During her time in the yard, the *Ranger* received the installation of FD radars for her Mk. 33 directors, and thirty 20-millimeter Oerlikon machine guns (which replaced the .50-caliber Brownings) to provide "all around protection of the ship, concentrating the number of guns in sufficiently large groups to obtain a desired volume of fire from each group."[13] In addition, the yard accomplished the installation of splinter protection for the 20 millimeter, 1.1-inch, and 5-inch mounts, as well as for the 1.1-inch directors and clipping rooms, pilot house, and other vital spaces in the island (including fly control, air plot, and flag bridge), and power drives for the 1.1-inch mounts and directors, an auxiliary operating system for the airplane elevators, and removed weight to compensate not only for those alterations, but also for the allowance of heavier planes, in the future. The overhaul proceeded as planned, interrupted only briefly when a welder accidentally ignited cork insulation in the 1.1-inch clipping room aft of the island, on 2 April. Before the overhaul was completed, the *Ranger* served as the scene of the change of command, when Rear Adm. Ernest D. McWhorter relieved Rear Admiral Cook as ComAirLant and Commander, Task Force 22, on 6 April.

Emerging from the yard on 7 April, the *Ranger* proceeded to degauss and calibrate her degaussing equipment at Wolf Trap, Chesapeake Bay. She then returned to Pier 7 the following day to load ammunition, gasoline, fuel oil, and provisions, and embarked her assigned squadrons.

Fine detail shot of the *Ranger*'s island, showing details of the CXAM-1 radar, the tripod mast, the after Mk. 33 director with the new FD radar, and the 1.15-inch/.75 guns aft of the island, Norfolk, 11 April 1942. (NA, 19-N-32952)

At the same time that the *Ranger* had been in the yard, training proceeded apace for her squadrons based ashore, operations punctuated by the occasional mishap. Ensign Clyde A. Tucker, Jr., A-V(N), of VS-41, was making a field carrier practice landing on the afternoon of 3 April, with Seaman 2d Class B. F. Welch in back, when his SB2U-1 (BuNo 0736) stalled in the groove as he approached Monogram Field, and spun in from low altitude, crumpling both wings, damaging the right wheel, badly bending both propeller blades, and damaging the engine by its sudden stoppage in the crash. Investigators blamed the accident on Ensign Tucker's having the prop set in cruising pitch, instead of full low pitch, the latter giving the pilot more response to the LSO's signals.[14] Five days later, VF-41 was operating from Norfolk's East Field. Lieutenant (jg) Ernest W. Wood, Jr., cost the squadron one of its F4Fs when he exhibited what a trouble board deemed as "carelessness or negligence" in inadvertently making a wheels-up landing. "Woodie" Wood walked away unhurt, but the F4F-4 (BuNo 4078) caught fire and, with the exception of the tail assembly, burned completely.[15]

The *Ranger* sailed for Narragansett Bay on the morning of 13 April, in company with the destroyers *Hambleton* (DD-455), *Emmons* (DD-457), and *Ellyson* (DD-454). Her planes provided inner and outer antisubmarine patrols for the task group, and she conducted test landings of Grumman TBF-1 Avengers, the type of plane earmarked to replace the Douglas TBD-1 in her embarked torpedo squadron.

Fighting Forty-One suffered two mishaps during CAP recovery, during the first and second dog watches on the 13th. Ensign Charles V. "Chuck" August, A-V(N), made a normal approach, received a "high" signal just before the cut, but found himself "high and somewhat to starboard." August nosed the F4F over slightly, to try to catch a wire, but, just before his wheels touched the deck, he applied full throttle and dropped his left wing. August's right wing brushed the island and the Wildcat charged through two barriers. A trouble board not only faulted August's judgment and technique, but also leveled a quarter of the blame on the LSO, "who should not have cut such an inexperienced pilot in the position he did." August's F4F-4 (BuNo 4088) required extensive repairs.[16]

Ensign William H. "Pete" Bolt, Jr., A-V(N), who had logged 73.6 hours of flight time in the F4F in the previous three months, made, as August had, a normal approach. The LSO gave him "roger" and "low dip" signals, but, after receiving the cut, Bolt held his F4F-4 (BuNo 4090) off the deck and engaged number seven wire. The Wildcat's propeller, however, engaged the number three-A barrier, wrapping its cable around the prop hub and stopping the engine cold. Impact with the barrier badly dented the cowling, and the accident resulted in the loss of the aircraft's pitot tube and damage to its left wing surface.[17]

The *Ranger* reached Narragansett Bay the following afternoon and, after her planes had carried out the requisite patrols covering her arrival, transferred her air group ashore. The following day, her future employment came up at the highest levels of Allied planning, when she figured in a message sent by British Prime Minister Winston Churchill to President Roosevelt. "At present," Churchill lamented in the wake of the devastating Japanese carrier raids on Allied shipping in the Bay of Bengal on 5–6 and 9 April, "there seems to be no adequate restraint upon Japanese movements to the West." The "only way out of the immense perils which confront us," the Prime Minister continued, "would seem to be to build up as quickly as possible an ample force of modern capital ships and carriers in the Indian Ocean."[18]

To that end, Churchill asked Roosevelt to consider detaching the *Ranger* and the new battleship *North Carolina* (BB-55) from TF-22 to join Adm. Sir James Somerville's fleet. Failing that, Churchill suggested sending the *North Carolina* to Scapa Flow to join her sistership, the *Washington* (BB-56), permitting the British to send the battle cruiser HMS *Renown* to the Indian Ocean, and sending the *Ranger* directly to Capetown. The President's response of 16 April reflected Admiral King's unwillingness to mix U.S. and British ships. Noting that the British contemplated use of the *Ranger* "as a ferry boat" (the words King had used two months before), however, Roosevelt allowed that that was a task for which she was "best suited . . . as we are not proud of her compartmentation and her structural strength."[19]

The *Ranger* then shifted to NAS Quonset Point, Rhode Island, on the 17th, to participate in "Project 157," the ferrying of P-40s to Africa. Before the first P-40Es had reached Quonset, having been delayed by inclement weather en route, the *Ranger* managed to obtain one from a local squadron, to be hoisted on board to test the ship's handling equipment and to investigate the feasibility of overhead stowage. The Army Air Force provided five special hoisting slings that helped expedite the handling of the aircraft involved. In advance of the mission upon which the *Ranger* was about to embark, NAS Anacostia had provided Captain Harrill with information on the takeoff runs required by the P-40E under conditions of one-half ammunition allowance and 100 gallons of gasoline. Anacostia's experts recommended a takeoff run of 280 feet. Harrill, perhaps suspicious of the data provided, initiated his own comparative takeoff tests at Quonset, using a P-40 and an F4F-4.

The latter showed that a takeoff run of 390 feet against 25 knots of wind would be required—a full 110 feet more than that recommended by Anacostia.[20]

Consequently, two hours into the afternoon watch on 21 April, the *Ranger* began hoisting on board 68 P-40Es from the 33d Pursuit Squadron, an operation that consumed the next three and a half hours. In addition, the carrier welcomed Lt. Col. John E. Barr, USAAF, and 67 other pilots (only 3 of whom had ever taken off from a carrier before), and a 30-man maintenance detail of 18 mechanics, 4 armorers, and 8 radiomen, to serve as ground crew. The enlisted detail was placed under the guidance of a chief petty officer, augmented by 18 qualified plane captains, from the *Ranger* Air Group. After all of the P-40s had been embarked, the *Ranger* hoisted on board 4 SB2U-2s from her own air group.

Ranger men soon learned, however, that the Army people seemed to know a good deal about their mission and destination. Rear Admiral McWhorter, who would command TF 36 on the ferry mission, reflected later "that the Army did not observe the same rigid secrecy as was maintained by the Navy."[21] That same day, President Roosevelt sent a message to Prime Minister Churchill, telling him that the *Ranger* would be available "for further ferrying additional airplanes to India via Africa on its return from West Africa. To what extent and with what equipment it will be loaded will be determined after [the] present movement starts."[22]

Underway on the morning of 22 April, the *Ranger* sailed for the Gold Coast, in company with the heavy cruiser *Augusta* and five destroyers. During the first leg of the voyage, the *Augusta*'s floatplanes carried out the required air patrols; the report of an enemy submarine operating in its path on 23 April prompted the force to change course. The *Ranger* and her consorts only spotted one ship en route—the British freighter *Lobos* on the 24th. The experienced officers of the *Ranger*'s Air Department lectured the Army pilots on taxiing and takeoff procedures "and other applicable subjects," to prepare them to carry out their mission. In addition, there were daily conferences and instruction periods in navigation "and other problems incident to their task of ferrying the planes from the point of disembarkation to their ultimate destination."[23]

The *Ranger* reached Trinidad on the 28th and fueled that day from the British tanker *Servitor*. Standing out of the Gulf of Paria the following morning, under the watchful eyes of Trinidad-based Navy patrol planes, and the company increased by the addition of the oiler *Merrimack* (AO-37) to fuel the destroyers, the *Ranger*'s force, under the overall command of Rear Adm. Alexander Sharp, Commander, Task Force 22, who wore his flag in the *Augusta*, moved out into the Atlantic.

With their parent ship engaged in taking part in Project 157, her squadrons continued training from shore stations. Tragedy, however, struck on the afternoon of 30 April, in the hazy skies off Sandy Point, Block Island. As the *Ranger* group reassembled upon completing the first of a number of practice dive-bombing attacks, Ens. David L. Kauffman, A-V(N), of VS-41, with Lt. (jg) Howard Lapsley, A-V(S) in back, made a climbing left turn to rejoin a small group of planes flying in right echelon and turning to the left. Evidently, Kauffman failed to see a second group of five planes, also in right echelon formation and also circling to the left, at the same altitude. Kauffman turned close under the lead aircraft of the second group.

Just ahead, Ens. Frederick W. Tracey, A-V(N), with Aviation Radioman 3d Class J. C. Brown on board, was flying number three wing position of the second section of VS-42's first division, when Kauffman's Vindicator suddenly sheared off part of Tracey's right wing and empennage. Kauffman's SB2U-2 (BuNo 1365), shedding its right wing in the collision, immediately spun toward the waters off Sandy Point. Tracey's SB2U-1 (BuNo 0746) also went into an unrecoverable spin, but Tracey and Aviation Radioman 3d Class Brown parachuted to safety. Observers noted one of the occupants of Kauffman's SB2U get clear of the aircraft as it plunged toward the sea, but the parachute did not open, and the man plummeted to his death. Searchers only recovered Tracey and Brown, who both survived their immersion and returned to duty.[24]

The *Ranger*'s, passage was enlivened by a report of a large concentration of submarines operating 140 miles from the track of the task force on 7 May, but she reached her appointed fly-off point on the morning of the 10th, finding good-to-excellent operating conditions prevailing. She turned into the wind and launched her SB2Us, to provide antisubmarine screen during the launch, then began launching the first group of 12 P-40s at 0910. As soon as they effected a rendezvous, the P-40s headed for Accra, which at that point lay 82 miles away. Those who planned the flight favored a southwestern launch point, because, in the event of bad weather, all the pilots had to do was fly north to the coast, turn right, and follow the coastline to their destination.

The second group, of 20 planes, took off without incident, formed up, and headed for their destination at 0947, with the *Ranger* changing course to head back toward Accra, to facilitate the launch of the third group of 20 fighters. Bringing up aircraft from the hangar deck and respotting the flight deck consumed the interval of time between the launch of the second and third groups. Sending the third group off between 1041 and 1107, the *Ranger* encountered rain squalls immediately thereafter, which prompted delay in launch of the fourth group. The 1300 weather report from Accra, indicating favorable weather ahead, buoyed hopes for the launch of the rest of the planes. When the weather did clear long enough to permit launch at 1514, the fourth group of P-40s took off for their destination.

Five P-40s, however, either unable to start or having various engineering difficulties, remained behind. "Strenuous trouble shooting and repair work," however, allowed them to be declared "ready" to join the others already winging their way toward the coast of Africa. The *Ranger* thus turned into the wind and, at a launch point only 31 miles from Accra, launched the quintet of P-40s, completing the evolution at 1709. Directly afterwards, the *Ranger* and her consorts set course for home, tensely awaiting the pre-arranged message that would indicate the safe arrival of the Army fighters at their destination. At 1935, Lieutenant Colonel Barr radioed from Accra: "Cheerio Barr 157." All 68 P-40s had reached shore safely.[25]

The mission had not been thoroughly flawless, however: Keen Harrill observed subsequently that, despite the "many lectures on the subject, several Army pilots came dangerously close to hitting the water after take-off although there was about 35 knots of wind over the deck and long runs available." That prompted the *Ranger*'s captain to recommend that, in future operations of that type, Army pilots be thoroughly indoctrinated "in take-off technique until they can take off in the shortest possible run."[26]

Rear Adm. Ernest D. McWhorter (Commander Carriers, Atlantic) (foreground), with members of his staff, during a light moment on the *Ranger*'s flag bridge, 5 June 1942. Those present (L–R): Lt. Comdr. Ira E. Hobbs (assistant operations), Capt. John J. Ballentine (chief of staff), Comdr. Thomas B. Williamson (operations), and Lt. Comdr. John R. Ruhsenberger (communications). (NA, 80-G-20162)

The return portion of the voyage proved uneventful, until the night of 17 May, when the *Hambleton* and the *Ellyson* collided in a heavy rainstorm. Damage to the *Hambleton*'s bow prevented her from exceeding 12 knots, so, rather than hazard the task group at that speed, Rear Admiral Sharp ordered the *Macomb* (DD-458) to stand by her damaged sistership and that the two ships proceed independently. The *Ranger* and the *Augusta* and the remaining destroyers, accompanied by the *Merrimack*, which had replenished the force's fuel bunkers as needed during the voyage, reached Trinidad on 21 May. The *Hambleton* and the *Macomb* reached port the following day. NOB Trinidad people, assisted by appropriate ratings from the *Ranger*, carried out repairs on board the *Hambleton*, to allow her to proceed to San Juan.

The *Ranger* and her consorts sailed on the 23d, and reached Narragansett Bay on the 28th, the task force dissolved upon arrival. Admiral Royal E. Ingersoll, CinCLant, praised the mission as a difficult one "well executed."[27]

Shifting from her anchorage in Narragansett Bay to NAS Quonset Point on the 29th, the *Ranger* welcomed on board a new captain on the morning of 30 May, when Capt. Calvin T. Durgin relieved Capt. Harrill—the latter bound for temporary duty in BuAer in Washington, before traveling to become Air Officer for the Northwest Sea Frontier. "Cal" Durgin, USNA 1916, came to the *Ranger* from BuAer, where he had headed the bureau's flight division. After service in battleships and destroyers, Durgin reported to NAS Pensacola in September 1919 for aviation instruction. Designated as a naval aviator on 27 May 1920, he had

Two VT-4 Douglas TBD-1s, 4-T-6 and 4-T-7, sit on the flight deck, aft, with F4F-4s and SB2Us forward, Argentia, 18 June 1942. (NA, 80-G-14533)

served in a variety of sea and shore billets and in squadrons. He had served in the *Saratoga*, had assisted in fitting out the *Yorktown*, and had served as exec and commanding officer of the *Wright*.

A good captain can make or break a ship, but a good chaplain can also be a very positive force. The day after Cal Durgin relieved Keen Harrill as the *Ranger*'s captain, the ship received a new chaplain, Boston-born Lt. Joseph Timothy O'Callahan, who had recently finished a tour at NAS Pensacola. "After Pearl Harbor Day," O'Callahan wrote later, "most of my Pensacola Navy friends had gone to war in carriers. Eventually and happily, my orders to the *Ranger* had enabled me to join some of them." Indoctrinated into sea duty at Pensacola with the "seriocomic instructions" to "go aboard, face forward thus; on your right is starboard, the other side is port." Reporting on board the *Ranger* on the last day of May, however, O'Callahan, who had just turned 37 earlier in the month, found himself confronted by a hangar deck that appeared "so big and symmetrical I could not tell where was forward and where aft."[28]

Sadly, during the *Ranger*'s time at sea, Lt. Comdr. Gilbert C. Carpenter of VS-41 died in an aircraft accident on 18 May, while flying from Quonset Point to Norfolk. Approaching the wrong runway at NAS Norfolk, Carpenter received instructions from the tower not to land. At the controls of an SB2U-1 (BuNo 0758), the pilot maintained altitude at between 150 and 200 feet before apparently deciding to make an emergency landing. The SB2U touched down in normal landing attitude, but turned over on its back in the mud, trapping both Carpenter and his passenger, Aviation Machinist's Mate 1st Class R.L.C. Bernard in the overturned aircraft; both men asphyxiated before rescuers could reach them.[29] Lieutenant Comdr. Lamar P. "Pete" Carver, who had taken part in the Earhart search alongside the *Ranger*'s aircrew in 1937, became commanding officer of VS-41 soon thereafter.

Underway for Argentia, Newfoundland, the *Ranger* stood out of Narragansett Bay on the afternoon of 2 June and reached her destination on the morning of the 5th. She resumed flight operations within a week's time. On the morning of 10 June, during refresher landings, Lt. (jg) Woodie Wood was coming in low and slow; the LSO signaled "come on." The nose of 41-F-16 (BuNo 4092), however, swung to the left, momentarily blocking out the signal officer from his view. The F4F-4's tail hit the ramp in the vicinity of the LSO platform. Wood closed the throttle in an attempt to engage the arresting gear, but the Wildcat's hook came down outboard of it and continued up the deck, breaking three barrier stanchions, went over the side, and sank. Fortunately, the *Macomb* picked up Wood, who had suffered shock, submersion, a concussion, and slight bruises and abrasions. A trouble board faulted Wood for poor judgment and poor technique.[30]

A second VF-41 mishap occurred three days later, on 13 June, when Ens. Edmund J. Kelly, A-V(N), bringing in his F4F-4 (BuNo 4079) for a refresher landing, made his approach high and slow, and his Wildcat made an "extremely hard landing," because of a "lack of control necessary for a proper cushioned landing." During the resultant bounce, the arresting gear slammed the tail to the deck, causing a failure of the tail wheel assembly and buckling the fuselage. Those who analyzed the accident faulted Kelly for "poor technique," with 80% of the accident attributed to that lack of skill.[31]

16

"THERE IS A NEED FOR A CARRIER IN THE ATLANTIC"

At the time that the *Ranger* was training pilots, men elsewhere were pondering a role for her—in the Mediterranean. With Malta enduring repeated pounding by the *Luftwaffe* and the *Regia Aeronautica*, the British again sought help from the U.S. Navy. Twice that spring, the *Wasp* had ferried Supermarine Spitfire fighters within flying distance of that important British possession, operations that had prompted Winston Churchill's famous quip: "Who said a *Wasp* couldn't sting twice?" With the *Wasp* having sailed for the Pacific on 5 June, however, in the wake of the loss of the *Lexington* at Coral Sea on 8 May, the *Ranger* became the only U.S. fleet carrier in the Atlantic.

By mid-June, 1942, British naval strategists had come up with three plans concerning an imminent resupply run to Malta, to follow in the wake of the recent Operation Harpoon, in which heavy Axis air attacks had sunk four of the six supply ships (two of which had had U.S. Navy armed guard gunners defending them) that had been sent to the beleaguered isle, despite a strong naval escort. The covering force, which had included the aircraft carriers HMS *Argus* and HMS *Eagle*, had simply proved unable to impede Italian torpedo planes and German dive-bombers.

Under "Plan A," the British would ask that the U.S. Navy allow the *Ranger* and a screen of six destroyers to proceed directly to Gibraltar from the United States. There, the *Ranger* would then join the *Eagle*, and the two carriers would provide cover for the projected convoy, supposing that the two could field a force of between 52 and 64 modern fighters and between 12 and 24 torpedo bombers. That option ("Plan A") would allow the British to run a PQ convoy on 26 June and another in August.[1]

Under "Plan B," the *Ranger* and six destroyers would proceed directly to Scapa Flow, as the *Wasp* had done. There, the *Ranger* would transfer 24 folding-wing "Martlets" (as the British had christened the F4F-4 Wildcat), together with the pilots to fly them, to the British carrier HMS *Victorious*, freeing the latter to participate in the Malta mission. With the *Victorious* deployed to the Mediterranean, the *Ranger* would operate with the Home Fleet. Because the British were prepared to suggest that the Americans retain 12 Wildcats on board the *Ranger*, they planned to suggest that the *Ranger* bring "at least 40 folding Martlets so as to have a few to spare." With the *Ranger* thus holding down the proverbial fort, at Scapa Flow, the *Victorious* and the *Eagle* could operate at least 46 modern fighters and 9 torpedo bombers between them. The Allies allowed that Plan B would not interfere with running any PQ convoys, but depended upon the *Ranger* being available until the end of August 1942.[2]

"Plan C" involved use of only the *Victorious*, equipped with only Fairey Fulmar fighters, and the *Eagle*, but, unless the United States could provide the *Ranger* and six destroyers to operate out of Scapa Flow, deploying the *Victorious* to the Med would leave the Home Fleet without a single carrier. British naval planners found Plan C the least attractive of the three, because it provided very little fighter cover for the battleships HMS *Rodney* and HMS *Nelson* or the *Victorious* herself, not to mention the ships of the convoy that the covering force was supposed to protect.[3]

188

Admiral Sir Charles J. C. Little, head of the British Admiralty Delegation in Washington, met with Admiral King on 17 June and presented him with a message from the First Sea Lord. In response, King "enquired regarding the possibility of employing *Furious* on the duty proposed for *Ranger*." King soon received a memo from Rear Adm. Charles M. "Savvy" Cooke, Jr., his exceptionally able assistant chief of staff (plans), dealing with the British proposal to employ the *Ranger* in a Malta-related operation. Noting that the *Ranger* then had embarked an air group that consisted of a fighter squadron, one dive-bomber squadron (a second had been deployed on maneuvers at Fort Benning, Georgia), and a torpedo squadron, Cooke wrote that, if that carrier were used in the proposed operation, she would need to embark a second fighting squadron, which would have to be formed expressly for the purpose. Once formed, it would have to be put on board the *Ranger* with all of its equipment and support people, and that in itself would require that the ship be returned to Norfolk. "It seems probable," he wrote, "that the *Ranger* could not properly be ready for this movement before 1 July, at Norfolk." Noting that the British had asked for the *Ranger* to proceed to Scapa Flow as soon as possible with six destroyers, Cooke posited that the British carrier HMS *Furious*, recently refitted in the United States, "could be made available at Scapa as soon as the *Ranger*" could be.[4]

Cooke also noted that the *Ranger* was "of flimsy construction" and was thus "not fitted for the character of the operation contemplated." Scrutinizing the British request carefully, Admiral King's assistant chief of staff noticed that the ally had seemed "ambiguous," because the elimination of a Russia-bound PQ convoy in June would permit the British to cover a Malta operation without the *Ranger*. "If this is the case," Cooke observed, "the risk to the *Ranger* is being set up against the importance of carrying out the June convoy."[5]

Cooke noted "that the British have in the Indian Ocean three carriers, with armored decks, and with modern fighters, which are now rendering very little useful employment and which the British refuse to make available for employment in the Southwest Pacific—an area where the *Ranger* could be given very useful and active employment." Cook suggested that "the British reply to our request for employment of the British Fleet in the eastern Indian Ocean could well be returned...as a full answer to this request." More important, however, Cooke evinced decided skepticism and suspicion about the recent British proposals concerning the use of the only available U.S. fleet carrier. "Inevitably," he wrote warily, "if the *Ranger* is used in this operation and survives, additional requests for her use—in spite of the fact that the British now have seven carriers—will arise."[6]

Summing up, Cooke wrote that the *Ranger* was "not now ready to undertake this operation and cannot properly be made ready earlier than 1 July (at Norfolk)." He added that the *Ranger* was "not suited for this task, cannot be spared for this task," and noted that the British "have a number of carriers not now usefully employed which can be made available if the British consider the attending risk justified. The British refuse to use their carriers in areas where the *Ranger* is very much needed." Accordingly, Cooke suggested that a message be sent to the Admiralty:

> Thoroughly appreciate the great importance of getting supplies through to Malta. Regret however that *Ranger* cannot be made available due to the fact that there are now on board only three aircraft squadrons up to complement, that the *Ranger* is of flimsy construction entirely unsuited for this character of operation, and that there is need for her services on other duties in areas where it appears that British carriers cannot be made available.
>
> Suggest you consider the employment of Indian Ocean carriers to cover your Eastern Mediterranean Convoy. However, I take note of your view . . . that we must conserve our carriers and avoid bringing them up against strong shore based aircraft.[7]

Evidently, the proverbial great minds working in similar channels must have come into play, for the First Sea Lord had sent an urgent message the same day to Admiral Little, addressing Admiral King's suggestion to use the *Furious* in lieu of the *Ranger*, to which Cook had alluded in his memorandum. "Perhaps it will be thought," the First Sea Lord wrote, "that H.M.S. *Furious* might carry out duties for which we have asked U.S.S *Ranger*. Serious defects were found in alignment of *Furious*'s shaft which were not detected until her return to U.K. after refitting in U.S.A. Her defect will not be completed until 1st July and she will then have to work up as an operational carrier. She cannot therefore be available for operation proposed."[8]

The issue did not apparently end there, for, on 20 June, members of Admiral King's staff addressed the matter further. Savvy Cooke noted that the Japanese possessed at least four operable "medium to large" carriers and two small carriers, with one (the *Shōkaku*, badly damaged at Coral Sea in May) under repair. The enemy, Cooke noted, possessing the advantage of interior lines of communication and supply, could "rapidly concentrate carriers anywhere from the Kuriles to the Solomon[s]."[9]

"This," Cooke continued, "makes it essential for us to be able to concentrate two or three carriers simultaneously in the

Central Pacific (possibly the North Pacific) and in the South Pacific." Allowing for the necessity of overhauls and the possibility of damage, Cooke posited that "five carriers are needed in the Pacific to cope with the situation." Regarding American carriers, Cooke noted that the *Hornet* was to be ready "about 28 June," the *Enterprise* "about July 1," and the *Saratoga* "sometime during [the] week [of] June 21 to 28, and the *Wasp* ready in the Hawaiian area "about July 1."[10]

"There is a need for a carrier in the Atlantic," Cooke allowed, "but if the *Ranger* is retained in the Atlantic it will probably be diverted recurrently to meet British demands for employment." With the availability of the aircraft escort vessel *Charger* (AVG-30) in the Atlantic, and additional AVGs "to come out soon," as soon as they were converted from tanker hulls, Cooke recommended "that *Ranger* be removed to the Pacific immediately."[11]

Cooke's recommendation to keep the *Ranger* out of the British' clutches found a ready adherent in Rear Adm. Richard S. Edwards, King's deputy chief of staff. "The British have got into a jam in the Middle East," he observed, "largely as the result of a plan to concentrate virtually all aviation in [the] UK, which is an idea of debatable soundness.... It looks as though they intend to go on sacrificing their own Navy and such parts of ours as they can borrow to keep on with this scheme." Although admitting that his own knowledge of the Mediterranean situation was at best "superficial," Edwards wrote that "we should keep a carrier in the Atlantic to meet the German naval threat. But believing that if we attempt this course of action we will end up by turning over the vessel to the British Mediterranean Fleet, I concur in Cooke's recommendation to shift *Ranger* to the Pacific where, apparently, we can expect no help from the British."[12] King's Chief of Staff, Vice Adm. Russell Willson, added his comment across the bottom of Cooke's memorandum: "I concur, move be made as soon as present discussion of that vessel [*Ranger*] is cleared up."[13] King stood firm. The *Ranger* stayed in the U.S. Fleet and out of the Home Fleet, thus avoiding being sacrificed by an ally on the altar of expediency, at least for the time being. She would, however, soon be involved in ferrying planes again.

Departing Argentia during the first watch on 20 June, in company with the *Augusta* (Rear Admiral Sharp) and the destroyers *Corry* (DD-463), *Ellyson*, *Emmons*, *Hobson* (DD-464), and *Forrest* (DD-461), the *Ranger* set course for Quonset Point. The light cruiser *Juneau* (CL-52) joined up during the second dog watch the next day, "breaking all the rules of the [nautical] road," observed Seaman 2d Class Crochet, "traveling in close formation at high speed in heavy fog. Mission must be urgent as we have left at night & traveling at top speed back to [the] U.S."[14]

The *Ranger* anchored in Narragansett Bay during the first dog watch on 22 June, then got underway and moored alongside the pier at NAS Quonset Point early in the forenoon watch the following day. That same day, 23 June, Rear Admiral McWhorter relieved Alex Sharp as Commander, Task Force 22.

Transferring her squadrons ashore to NAS Quonset Point on the morning of 29 June, the *Ranger* completed loading 72 P-40Fs from the 57th Fighter Group (Lt. Col. Frank H. Mears, Jr., USAAF, commanding) and 4 of VS-42's SB2U-2s on the morning of 1 July, having embarked the USAAF ground crew (20 mechanics, 5 ordnancemen, and 5 communications specialists) the night before for security purposes. The *Ranger* had also embarked 74 pilots, all of whom had received indoctrination and instruction in carrier takeoff technique at Mitchell Field, Long Island, by an officer temporarily detached from the *Ranger*'s Air Department for the purpose. The carrier sailed that afternoon for Trinidad, on the first leg of her voyage to Africa and participation in Project 337.[15] Her escort included the *Augusta*, the *Juneau*, five destroyers, and the oiler *Housatonic* (AO-35). Two days later, on the 3d, the *Ranger* contacted a friendly patrol bomber, which sighted a submarine and dropped depth charges on it, some two miles off the group's port bow. The *Hobson* reported a submarine contact and dropped depth charges, too. The next day, the *Forrest*, her boilers and feed water salted-up, departed to effect repairs.

Grim evidence that U-boats had been wreaking destruction nearby soon materialized, when the *Ranger* and her consorts spotted a drifting life raft during the afternoon watch on 4 July. The *Corry* altered course and rescued what proved to be the only survivors of the American freighter *Ruth*, torpedoed and sunk by the *U-153* on 28 June, 100 miles north of Cape Maysi, Cuba. In a display of chivalry that would become more rare as the Battle of the Atlantic intensified, the *U-153* had rescued one of the four men and placed him on the raft with his three shipmates. The four, however, were all that remained of a crew of 34 souls. Lost with the merchantman had been the four Navy armed guard sailors.[16]

Reaching Trinidad without further incident on 6 July, the *Ranger* sailed two days later, the escort diminished by the detachment of the *Juneau*. Possible submarine contacts enlivened the 11th, when the *Forrest*, which had rejoined the task force on the 7th, reported a contact to starboard at 1908. The *Ranger* went to general quarters five minutes later, and the *Forrest* and the *Ellyson* made depth charge attacks in succession. The *Hobson* depth-charged a contact on the 17th, with no observable results.

The *Ranger* reached the launching point off the Gold Coast on the morning of 19 July, and turned into the

Forward end of the flight deck while en route to Africa, 18 July 1942, showing the "desert pink"-painted Curtiss P-40Fs. Note four SB2Us from the *Ranger* Air Group parked among the USAAF fighters, and heavy cruiser *Augusta* (CA-31) off the carrier's port bow. (NA, 80-G-12974)

wind and commenced launch at 0906. After putting aloft 72 P-40Fs in the space of a little under six hours, the carrier proceeded on the homeward leg of the voyage—one soon enlivened by submarine contacts on the 22d. That day, the *Corry*, the *Forrest*, and the *Hobson* all depth-charged contacts.

That same day, while making his approach to the carrier upon returning from a routine sector search and antisubmarine patrol, 24 year-old Lt. (jg) John E. Wagner, A-V(N), with Aviation Radioman 3d Class Robert N. Shaw, USNR, as his passenger, banked steeply to get in the groove. His SB2U-2 (BuNo 1382) apparently stalled, however, going into a low altitude spin from which the pilot could not recover. Wagner's Vindicator hit the water left-wingtip-first, then submerged for a moment before it bobbed to the surface, where it remained for only about a minute, then sank for good. The *Fitch* (DD-462) picked up the passenger, who had suffered a broken arm, but could not locate the pilot, who apparently had been knocked unconscious by the impact and could not exit the plane before it sank.[17]

Reaching Port of Spain, Trinidad, on 30 July, the *Ranger* stood out on the 31st, bound for Hampton Roads, which she reached on 5 August. During the mission, the *Ranger* bettered her timing of taking a tanker alongside and rigging all connections, accomplishing the work in one hour and 13 minutes with the *Housatonic*, compared to an hour and 39 minutes with the *Merrimack* on the previous trip.

As those entrusted with the execution of the recently completed ferry mission wrote the necessary reports citing lessons learned, others wrote as much as they could, security considerations in mind, to their loved ones. Upon his return to Norfolk, Seaman 1st Class George E. Biggs, Jr., of VS-41, wrote his mother in Suquamish, Washington. Biggs, the youngest of four children, had enlisted in the Navy in May 1941, and had just turned 20 years of age on 7 July.

"Who told you I got sick?" he wrote. "Well—Yes I did! This trip we had a little rough weather and I stayed on the rail for a whole day. But after ya get over it you feel swell and eat anything they throw at you." The "pay off" came in the first flight he had in one of the SB2Us embarked for the trip: "We did a little practice bombing," he continued, exhibiting the "unbeatable" sense of humor wherein "everything has its funny side," and he "urped all over the plane. Go ahead," he urged his mother with evident mock seriousness, "laugh!" He soon overcame the airsickness, adding confidently that "I'm getting so air minded even my ears are spreading out like wings." Later in his missive to his mother, he reflected:

"You get to thinking the darndest things while you fly. There isn't much to look at from a plane at sea. But it's always pretty to watch the ships all turning at once as if you were pulling a string and they were all tied to it. And then you can go up in to the clouds and watch them go by. Or, down close to the water and count fish swimming, they are easy to see under water from up a ways. Then you do a little bombing, straight down at 300 miles an hour. When he flips it over and starts down you swear you left your stomach somewhere behind. But when he pulls out your stomach comes back with a bang and your eyelids try to close and your head bends down as if some guy had just settled a trunk on your back. Yep, it's nice work but I'm not saying how long it would be before your hair turned gray, or fell out all together."[18]

During the *Ranger*'s time in the Norfolk Navy Yard, the ship's force and yard workmen had diligently continued their efforts to reduce weight. Captain Robert N. S. Baker, writing on behalf of the commandant of the yard, informed BuShips of the carrier's sterling work in trimming sails by some 200.5 tons! "This is really a remarkable 'score' for the past nine months of weight effort," an officer in BuShips wrote admiringly on 26 August, adding that the bureau had "already complimented the *Ranger* and the yard for their efforts."[19] Following voyage repairs and upkeep, the *Ranger* operated in lower Chesapeake Bay, running the degaussing range, calibrating her radio direction finders and compensating her compasses, in addition to training for, and firing, gunnery exercises.

While the *Ranger* had been at sea on Project 337, the usual shore-based training continued for her air group—routine work occasionally punctuated by mishaps. On 12 July, Lt. (jg) Robert R. Marks, A-V(N), of VS-42, made a normal landing at Quonset Point after a practice bombing flight in an SB2U-1 (BuNo 0739), but felt the slight crosswind from the left lifting his right wing. Erroneously believing that his left gear was not locked down he applied full throttle to get airborne. Swerving off the runway, Marks cut

The *Ranger* leaves Norfolk Navy Yard, 18 August 1942, freshly painted in Measure 12 (modified) camouflage. (NA, 19-N-32901)

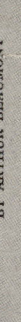

Canal Transit—U.S.S. Ranger

BY ARTHUR BEAUMONT

A President's Mission — U.S.S. Tuscaloosa

PRINTED BY LYNTON KISTLER, LOS ANGELES

the gun. The Vindicator, unable to clear the obstructions near the field, did a somersault. Marks's passenger, Aviation Machinist's Mate 2d Class H. F. Arthur, Jr., survived without a scratch; medical people treated Marks's scalp lacerations.[20]

Lieutenant Wallace A. Sherrill of VT-4, flying a TBF-1 (BuNo 00524), with Aviation Metalsmith 2d Class Joseph Karpiak on board, on 20 July, on a familiarization flight, joined a field carrier landing circle at Quonset, but did not land and took off straight up the runway. As he did so, however, his engine began to sputter, as the fuel system gave out. Over the end of the runway, the engine quit abruptly. Thus forced to land, Sherrill pushed the nose over and attempted a wheels-up landing; he tried to reach a golf course, but did not have enough altitude and ended up in a rockpile just short of a fairway. Sherrill suffered scalp and facial lacerations and possible internal head injuries; Karpiak suffered multiple contusions and a fracture of the first lumbar vertebrae, in the crash that resulted in the aircraft being stricken.[21]

The *Ranger* returned to Pier 7 at 1330 on 21 August, where she embarked VF-9, under Lt. Comdr. John Raby, for "its first taste of life at sea." The carrier then sailed for Narragansett Bay on the afternoon of 23 August, in company with the *Augusta* and five destroyers, arriving at Quonset Point the following morning, to begin refresher training.

Observers could see that one of "Captain Jack" Raby's junior pilots, Ens. George N. Trumpeter, A-V(N), was bringing in Nine-Fox-Eight, on 26 August, with his left wing down, as he took the LSO's cut. Exhibiting what a trouble board later considered bad judgment and poor technique, Trumpeter failed to bring the wing up, and his F4F-4

Ensign George N. Trumpeter, A-V(N)'s Nine-Fox-Eight, a Grumman F4F-4 (BuNo 03396), 26 August 1942, caught by the cross-deck pendant after a bad landing. (NA, 80-G-11800)

Lieutenant Ernest W. Wood, Jr., of VF-41, gives an organ recital, 1 September 1942, with his squadronmate Lt. (jg) Charles A. "Windy" Shields, A-V(N) (R), among the listeners. Wood's USNA classmates came to know "Woodie" as a "master pianist and organist," who was a "happy-go-lucky fellow with a heart of gold—always a true friend and ever the gentleman." (NA, 80-G-11807)

(BuNo 03396) landed on the port side of the flight deck at an angle to the centerline, headed for the side of the ship. Catching the number two wire, however, Trumpeter's Wildcat continued on over the port side, suspended by the cross-deck pendant. Trumpeter exited the aircraft without injury, but the necessity to enable the ship to recover the planes still airborne prompted the flight deck crew to consign Nine-Fox-Eight to the deep.[22]

The *Ranger* carried out flight operations again on the 27th, before poor flying conditions compelled her return to Quonset on the 29th. Underway once more on the 30th, the *Ranger* dropped anchor in Hampton Roads during the second dog watch on the last day of August. She shifted to Pier 7 during the forenoon watch on 1 September.

For most of September 1942, the *Ranger* conducted flight operations and gunnery drills in the waters of lower Chesapeake Bay. On 5 September, Ens. Michael R. Saska, A-V(N)'s F4F-4 (BuNo 03399), from VF-9, crashed into the bay upon takeoff, and, despite extensive dragging operations, efforts to recover the body of the 26-year-old former student at Pittsburgh's Carnegie Institute of Technology proved fruitless.[23]

Later that same day, Lt. (jg) Harold R. Keller, Jr., A-V(N), was bringing his SB2U-1 (BuNo 0768) in for a landing, when his plane's propeller locked in high pitch, giving him excessive speed for a carrier recovery. The Vindicator floated into number three barrier aft and number four, forward, the engine being torn free from the plane when it somersaulted

A grim Chief Shipfitter Jessie J. Wilborn, U.S. Navy Diver 2d Class, during the unsuccessful efforts to locate the body of Ens. Michael Saska of VF-9 after Saska's crash on 5 September 1942. (NA, 80-G-11804)

Both Lt. (jg) Keller and his passenger, Aviation Radioman 3d Class William T. Shackelford, having been safely extricated from their crashed SB2U-1, the flight deck crew prepares to right BuNo 0768. (NA, 80-G-14144)

over on its back. Fortunately, although the SB2U suffered damage beyond the capability of an overhaul, the flight deck crew extricated both Keller and Aviation Radioman 3d Class William T. Shackelford from the overturned Vindicator, without any serious injuries.[24]

While VF-9 had been practicing its trade at sea, VF-41 had been carrying out its training from shore bases. During an aerial gunnery hop near Woodleigh, North Carolina, on 28 September, Lt. Tag Grell was leading the second pair of a four-plane section, attempting to crossover to place all four planes of the section in right echelon formation. As Grell attempted the maneuver, however, he lost sight of the number two plane of the first pair and continued closing, until his F4F-4 (BuNo 02136) collided with that flown by Ens. Boyd N. Mayhew, A-V(N). Grell's propeller sliced off Mayhew's tail section. Mayhew bailed out of his tailless Wildcat (BuNo 5034), bruising a leg in so doing; Grell managed to maintain control of his plane and land safely at NAS Norfolk. The trouble board faulted Grell, a pilot of over two years' experience and 804.4 hours in the cockpit, for "carelessness." Mayhew's mount had crashed; Grell's Wildcat had suffered a flattened right wing leading edge, a dented left wing, a bent pitot tube, propeller blades bent and a torn and bent cowling nose ring, a cracked windshield, and broken cockpit hood.[25]

With VF-9, VF-41, and VS-41 embarked (the last-named squadron having only recently transitioned from the SB2U to the SBD), the *Ranger* sailed for Bermuda on 3 October, in company with the auxiliary aircraft carrier *Charger* (ACV-30) and her familiar escorts, the *Forrest*, the *Hobson*, the *Fitch*, and the *Corry*. Rear Admiral McWhorter and his staff, however, remained behind in Norfolk, as planning

Lieutenant Hugh D. "Danny" O'Neill, Jr., of VF-9, looks on from the cockpit of 9-F-21, as the *Ranger*'s deck crew prepares to remove his crashed F4F-4 (BuNo 11704) from the flight deck, 5 October 1942. (NA, 80-G-16949)

continued for the long-awaited and "much-discussed" second front.

Dispatch and officer messengers had brought the initial increments of material pertaining to the Operation codenamed Torch. "Soon it came in packages and rolls," Admiral McWhorter noted later, "finally an armored convoy arrived to deliver 3½ tons of papers, maps and photographs," all of which needed to be "segregated for distribution to the ships." Details changed daily, necessitating the "constant rewriting of the operation orders and the corollary annexes and appendices to the annexes."[26]

As Rear Admiral McWhorter and his staff wrestled with the reams of Torch-related paperwork, the *Ranger* and her consorts continued their passage toward Bermuda. Both VF-9 and VF-41 experienced trouble with a pitching deck during flight operations two days into the voyage, when Lt. Hugh D. "Danny" O'Neill, A-V(N) of VF-9, and Lt. (jg) Hubert T. "Hubie" Houston, A-V(N), of VF-41, both crashed upon landing. Trouble boards faulted both fliers for poor technique, and both F4F-4s, O'Neill's (BuNo 11704) and Houston's (BuNo 11747), required major overhauls.[27]

The *Ranger* reached Bermuda on 6 October, and launched 28 F4Fs, the CRAG's TBF-1, and 7 SBDs (3 SBDs to fly inner air patrol, until the ships entered the harbor) to land at Kindley Field. She spent the next four days and a fortnight at Base "Mike," interspersing training with in-port upkeep.

Rear Admiral McWhorter and his staff embarked in the new light cruiser *Cleveland* (CL-55) at Norfolk on 10 October, bringing with them the required paperwork for Torch, the "vast bulk" of which filled the warship's vault.[28] Their ship having been in commission for only four months, the *Cleveland*'s crew sensed that something big lay ahead, when all of the nonessential linoleum, furniture, and paint had been removed from her interior; "stripping ship," one cruiser sailor would write, "foretold the imminence of battle."[29] Escorted by the *Hobson*, the *Cleveland* set course for Bermuda.

On the same day that Rear Admiral McWhorter had sailed to rejoin his flagship, Ens. James M. Wilkerson, A-V(N), VF-9's assistant education officer, flying an aerial gunnery run one mile off Bermuda, inadvertently allowed his F4F-4 (BuNo 11702) to collide with the target. "Silky" Wilkerson immediately noticed a drop in oil pressure (the banner had struck his oil filter) as he headed for Kindley Field, and the engine failed. Wilkerson made a forced landing at sea: Although he was rescued promptly, the plane sank in deep water, beyond salvage.[30]

Rear Admiral McWhorter rejoined his flagship after the *Cleveland* reached Great Sound on 12 October. The *Ranger*'s and squadron intelligence officers soon got a look at the "sealed material that had been delivered to them. They went to work," the admiral noted, "searching for space to display the various maps, charts, and aerial photographs. They gave

VS-41 breaks in its new planes en route to Bermuda; SBD pilots dive-bomb a spar towed in the *Ranger*'s wake, as seen from the auxiliary aircraft carrier *Charger* (ACV-30), 5 October 1942. (NA, 80-G-19281)

lectures on history, geography, politics, native customs, communications, weather, all based on the information they received. That they did a good job was obvious," one observer later recounted, "especially when many of the pilots admitted that they knew the area better than their home towns."[31]

Training proceeded ahead. On 15 October, when the *Ranger* conducted flight operations, screened by the *Macomb*, the *Hobson*, and the *Hambleton*, Lt. (jg) Reuben H. "Rube" Denoff, A-V(N), VF-9's transportation officer, exhibited what a trouble board later criticized as poor technique. He engaged a wire, but his Wildcat (BuNo 11743) came down hard on deck. Rube Denoff's F4F-4 required a major engine overhaul in the wake of the mishap.[32]

During the forenoon watch on 21 October, the *Ranger* got underway and stood out. Accompanied by the auxiliary aircraft carriers *Suwanee* (ACV-27), *Sangamon* (ACV-26), and *Santee* (ACV-29), plus the *Cleveland* and nine destroyers, she then participated in a dress rehearsal for the air operations planned for Torch. "The carriers operated from the approximate relative positions that were called for in the [operations] plan, using the island for the coast of Morocco. Much was learned from this rehearsal," Rear Admiral McWhorter later disclosed, "but there was no time for another."[33]

In flight operations during the morning watch on 22 October, Ens. Christos E. Mikronis, A-V(N), of VF-41, made a normal approach, but, apparently bothered by the glare of the rising sun into which his landing course took him, landed "on the wheels." His F4F (BuNo 4090) bounced, then floated up the flight deck without engaging

Forty-One-Sail-Eight engages the *Ranger*'s number five wire during operations off Bermuda, 15 October 1942. (NA, 80-G-19624)

any of the cross-deck pendants. Mikronis's Wildcat penetrated two barriers before going over on its back at the third, suffering class B damage: sudden engine stoppage, bent propeller, power unit torn from the prop, buckled engine mounts, a left wing that had been cut into by the barrier wire, buckled firewall, upper longitudinal stringer, and demolished hood and windshield.[34] A little over an hour later, Ens. William J. Bonneau, A-V(N), VF-9's assistant materiel officer, failed to answer the LSO's signals and made a hard landing. His F4F-4 (BuNo 03398) required a major overhaul.[35]

On the morning of 25 October, the *Ranger*, wearing Rear Admiral McWhorter's flag as Commander, Task Group 34.2, stood out of Murray's Anchorage, in company with her task group. Lieutenant Malcolm T. "Mac" Wordell, VF-41's exec, later complained that the squadron left, having accomplished "unsatisfactory" training, because of the lack of facilities at that advanced base.[36] Unsatisfactory training or no, the time had come to set forth on the largest amphibious operation of the war. Seaman 2d Class Crochet's diary probably reflected the views of many in the *Ranger*'s ship's company when he had written a few days earlier: "Warships coming in every day. Something big coming up."[37]

One day out of Bermuda, Cal Durgin spoke to his officers in the wardroom. "I have a message that is of vital importance to you all," he began, "and I would like to have you listen carefully." After making sure that all present could hear him, he continued: "I am sure that it comes to you as no surprise that an operation against the enemy in which we are to participate is contemplated for the very near future; in fact we are now headed for this battle area and will make no more stops between here and that point." He apologized that more details could not have been disseminated, but "you . . . realize the reason why such action on my part was not possible."[38]

Durgin went on to explain that he had given the task of "assembling, sorting out, and analyzing the enormous amount of information, orders and instructions," to "eight or nine" officers who had stood no watches nor had any collateral duties. Their work, he added, would continue. "The rest of you will have plenty to do in preparing your men and the material for which you are responsible."[39]

The *Ranger*'s captain came to the point, confirming speculation. "The scene of our action," he explained, "as you may have guessed, will be along the African coast. Specifically French Morocca [sic]. The *Ranger* Air Group will attack air fields, gun batteries and enemy ships and airplanes and will furnish air protection to our landing force in and around Casablanca." After outlining the missions assigned to the four auxiliary aircraft carriers, he noted that all of the action described would take place before dawn. He went on to note that predawn amphibious landings would take place to capture and hold the western part of French Morocco. Simultaneous operations would take place along the shores of Algeria and Tunisia.[40]

"This is the start of the real second front of which there has been so much talk. You may wonder why we start against the Vichy French. . . . The answer is easy. The Vichy French ever since Laval has had control, have positively and definitely shown themselves to be friendly toward the Germans and unfriendly toward the United Nations. We know that they have permitted German and Italian submarines to use their ports . . . have forced French civilians to go to Germany to work in war munitions factories . . . have harbored enemy forces in their ports and in many other ways have given aid to our enemies. Our attack . . . is not with the object of gaining and holding territory . . . but to stop its being used by enemy forces. If the Vichy French do not attack us, we will not in any way harm them. We will, however, put an end to all Axis activities in French African territory."[41]

The advantages of hitting the Germans and Italians in Africa, Durgin explained to the assembled officers, were "many fold," beginning with the fact that it constituted the "most accessible and vulnerable flank of the Germans." The operations then contemplated would place the Allies "to the rear of [Field] Marshall [sic] Rommel's forces in North Africa and will make possible [the] complete liquidation of his forces" thus relieving the Allies of the "long and costly" Cape of Good Hope supply line and free shipping for use elsewhere against the Axis. It would complicate the German position on the continent by giving the Allies another place from which to invade Europe. It would perhaps force Italy out of the war and prevent a union between the Germans and the Japanese in the East or Near East. It would deprive the Axis of bases along the coast of Africa, and could eliminate Dakar as a possible base for German U-boats and surface raiders. "A second front at any point," Durgin continued, "will raise the morale of the subjugated people in Europe and lower the morale of the Axis countries." It would also relieve pressure on Russia and encourage its hard-pressed military.[42]

Durgin told his listening officers,

"You may remember I said when I first took command that we would have to work days and weeks and maybe many months and months getting ready for one big moment and that if we worked hard and prepared ourselves well we would be successful. I have been on this ship long enough to see, what a hard working, smooth running organization and efficient group of officers and men I have under me. I have no doubt that when we do strike we will be successful and will return to our homes filled with satisfaction in knowing that we have accomplished our mission in a manner that is a credit to our Country, our Navy and ourselves."[43]

"There are, of course, many things still to be done, and I want you to turn-to these last few days to put the finishing touches on your training programs. Make sure your gun crews, lookouts, and all watch standers are always on the alert, that all of you know the various silhouettes of airplanes and ships so that you can readily and definitely identify our own and enemy aircraft, and that you learn and teach all of your men all you possibly can about fire-fighting, damage control, and abandoning ship."[44]

Should any of them "be so unfortunate as to fall in[to] the hands of the enemy," he reminded them that all they were required to divulge was "name and rank." He urged them not to attempt to outsmart their captors, "because six or seven specially trained Gestapo agents can outsmart anyone of us."[45]

He went on to tell them that he would provide more information as he was permitted to, over the days that lay ahead. He charged his officers with holding close the information that they were bound for North Africa. "I shall tell the men over the general announcing system as much of this information as it is wise to do so at this time."[46]

Having already briefed the ship's and air group's officers, Capt. Calvin T. Durgin addresses the crew: "I expect great things," Durgin told his men, 26 October 1942, "because you have shown me that you can do great things." (NA, 80-G-30373)

"Last but not least," he told his listeners in the *Ranger*'s wardroom, "I want to tell you from the bottom of my heart that I am proud of you all. I expect great things because you have shown me that you can do great things. Good luck," he concluded, "and God bless you all."[47]

Later, as he had informed the wardroom, Durgin went on the general announcing system and told the crew that they would soon be involved in the second front. His talk mirrored that which he had given the officers, with the important exception that he did not divulge the objective. Telling the enlisted men where they were headed would come later.

The next day, Captain Durgin authorized his executive officer, Comdr. John Hoskins, to issue "*Ranger* War Communique No. 1" at 1930 on 27 October. "It is expected that our group of ships will rendezvous with many additional ships of our main body tomorrow evening," Hoskins reported during the second dog watch. "This main body consists of two battleships, many cruisers and destroyers, and a large number of transports. The *Ranger*'s position in the Cruising Disposition will be about seven or eight miles behind the guide of the main body." After telling the crew that the transports in the force were carrying "a large number of U.S. Army troops," he reported that the light cruiser *Cleveland* had intercepted a German code message. Although the message could not be deciphered, it indicated the presence of a U-boat or a surface ship, in their general area, then about 1,200 miles due west of the Azores. As to the ship's readiness for what lay ahead, "The Captain requested me to tell you that he has had excellent reports concerning the manner in which you are turning to in preparation for the Big Show," Hoskins told all hands, "and he is decidedly pleased with the proficient manner in which you responded to the Fire and Abandon Ship drills today." He then declared that that was the first of a series of such communiques that would be shared with the crew "as information becomes available."[48]

The *Ranger* steamed across the Atlantic, her course resembling "the track of a reeling drunk in the snow."[49] Her embarked aviators "studied the geography of French Morocco, the enemy and their equipment, and the specific mission that was to be ours." As Mac Wordell would later observe, "We did very little flying in those two weeks" that preceded Torch.[50] The pilots did, however, receive "every bit of information that was available" on where they were headed. "We had excellent maps of the region to study, also the economics of each place. We were able to utilize the approximately two weeks it took to get there with studies and quizzes, etc.," VS-41 pilots recalled later, "By the time we arrived, it was pretty familiar territory."[51]

"The day set for the rendezvous," an observer on board the *Ranger* wrote later, "was sunny with a slight mist on the horizon. Everybody strained their eyes to sight the convoy. At last, out of the haze loomed a ship, then another, and another, until there was no use counting them. We swung into our place in the formation with the signal lights blinking from halfway around the horizon."[52] Thus, late in the forenoon watch on 28 October, did the *Ranger* rendezvous with Task Force 34 (Rear Adm. H. Kent Hewitt), the main invasion convoy, and shaped course toward her objective.

"Now that we have joined up with our own main body and train," Johnnie Hoskins informed the *Ranger* one hour into the first dog watch on the 29th, "I will give you the cruising disposition: the disposition is circular in shape covering a front of about 24 miles and is about 26 miles deep. This covers a total sea area of 624 square miles, in order words, it covers an area over one half the size of the state of Rhode Island." After relating how the *Augusta* was serving as the guide for the formation, and the composition of the screen and the convoy (which included "many troop ships, cargo vessels," etc.), Hoskins informed the crew that, the next day, the carrier would fuel from "our old friend the *Merrimac*[k]." Telling the crew that a number of enemy submarines had been reported in the area of the Azores, which lay about 700 miles due east of the *Ranger*'s location that day, and that the ship had picked up radio bearings of strange vessels, the exec informed his listeners that "our planes have been directed to assume that all planes other than Allied aircraft are enemy and to destroy them." All of the foregoing, Hoskins concluded, had not been given "to alarm you, but to keep you informed and so that you may keep on the alert."[53]

"As you probably know," Hoskins informed the *Ranger* on 1 November, "we have now completed the refueling in this task force. Our Admiral told our Captain that he was well pleased with the *Ranger*'s refueling. We are all pleased with your work.... We are also delighted with the speed with which you are removing paint. In case of a bomb hit this excellent work you are doing may save the ship." Hoskins went on to tell his listeners about the force passing through a line of submarines between the Azores and the Cape Verde Islands, and warning all hands to "keep on the alert and do not smoke nor show lights on the weather decks after sunset." Then came the word many had been waiting for: "I can now tell you," the exec continued, "that this force is going to support a landing on the Atlantic Coast of French Morocco. The landing will be made by the U.S. Army troops with us and will be well covered by our planes and surface vessels. We are not trying to attack France or a French possession. Neither are we going to defeat the Axis powers and thereby liberate the French people who have been our friends throughout our history. We hope that the people of French Morocco will appreciate our intentions and join with us. However, if they are so completely under the domination of Germany as to offer resistance then we must overcome their resistance. If they do not resist they will not be harmed in any way." Hoskins then concluded the *Ranger* War Communique No. 3 with a recitation of the advantages of hitting the Germans and Italians in Africa, which reflected, verbatim, what Captain Durgin had shared confidentially with the *Ranger*'s wardroom six days earlier.[54]

During the second dog watch the following day, Rear Adm. McWhorter informed Cal Durgin that the "primary mission of all aircraft is to maintain control of the air." If circumstances revealed that the CAP maintained by the *Suwanee* proved inadequate, he authorized the *Ranger* to use her own planes in that role. He did not, however, authorize attacking objectives "further inland than those now assigned unless specifically directed" to do so. He desired the CRAG's TBF "reserved for special assignment."[55]

Although the goodly company of ships included four auxiliary aircraft carriers, converted oilers, the use of one, the *Chenango* (ACV-30), as a ferry solely for P-40 fighters earmarked to be put ashore once the landing force had secured a suitable field, rendered her unusable as a regular carrier. In addition, the ACVs being unable to make more than 19 knots meant that they "could not regain position if the wind was not dead ahead without a long pull." As Capt. Joseph J. "Jocko" Clark, commanding officer of the *Suwanee* put it, "We decided that it would be best not to operate [the ACVs] on the way across. So as to save our strength until we got [to North Africa]."[56]

Thus, with the conservation of the auxiliary aircraft carriers for the work that lay ahead, the lot fell to the *Ranger* to do most of the antisubmarine patrolling on the passage eastward. The fighters did little flying, but the dive-bombers alternated with the battleship- and cruiser-based floatplanes in antisubmarine patrols. On the morning of 3 November, the *Ranger* launched six SBDs, midway through the forenoon watch, for antisubmarine patrol and a photographic mission. Less than a half an hour into the flight, Lt. Gordon P. Chase,

Rear Admiral McWhorter (R) and his chief of staff, Capt. Ballentine, on the *Ranger*'s flag bridge en route to North Africa, 1 November 1942. (NA, 80-G-30209)

Ranger sailors remove paint from the overhead in a berthing compartment to reduce the danger of fire in the event of battle damage, ca. 1 November 1942. (NA, 80-G-30364)

A-V(N)'s SBD-3 (BuNo 06619), suffered engine failure. Chase deftly ditched 41-S-18 near the destroyers steaming on picket duty off the port side of the convoy, and the *Wilkes* (DD-441) soon rescued both Chase and his passenger, Chief Photographer's Mate Burton C. Abel, uninjured.[57]

As Lieutenant Chase and Chief Abel enjoyed the destroyermen's hospitality, preparations continued on board the ship that they had left behind, albeit without choice. As the American armada steamed determinedly toward its objective, some 350 miles west of Gibraltar, on 6 November, Commander Hoskins referred to the *Ranger*'s morning press news that told of the defeat of Field Marshal Erwin Rommel (in what history would record as the Battle of El Alamein), declaring that "the retreat is assuming more and more the aspects of a rout." Referring to the third communique (about the purpose of the landing in French Morocco), Hoskins explained that, "if our help is not needed in the destruction of General Rommel's forces," then the ship would be involved in one of the alternative plans. If that turned out to be the case, the exec continued, the crew would be so informed.[58]

"For several days our planes have been dropping leaflets in and broadcasting to occupied France," the messages contained therein assuring "the French people that our intentions toward them are entirely friendly" and "that we are on a mission which will eventually bring about their liberation from German oppression. We have reason to believe that our message to the French people is bearing fruit."[59]

"All that I have been telling you in this communque," Hoskins concluded, "is good news." However, he warned that "Rommel has retreated before and then staged a magnificent comeback." He also warned those who listened to the general announcing system on board the carrier "that enemy submarines

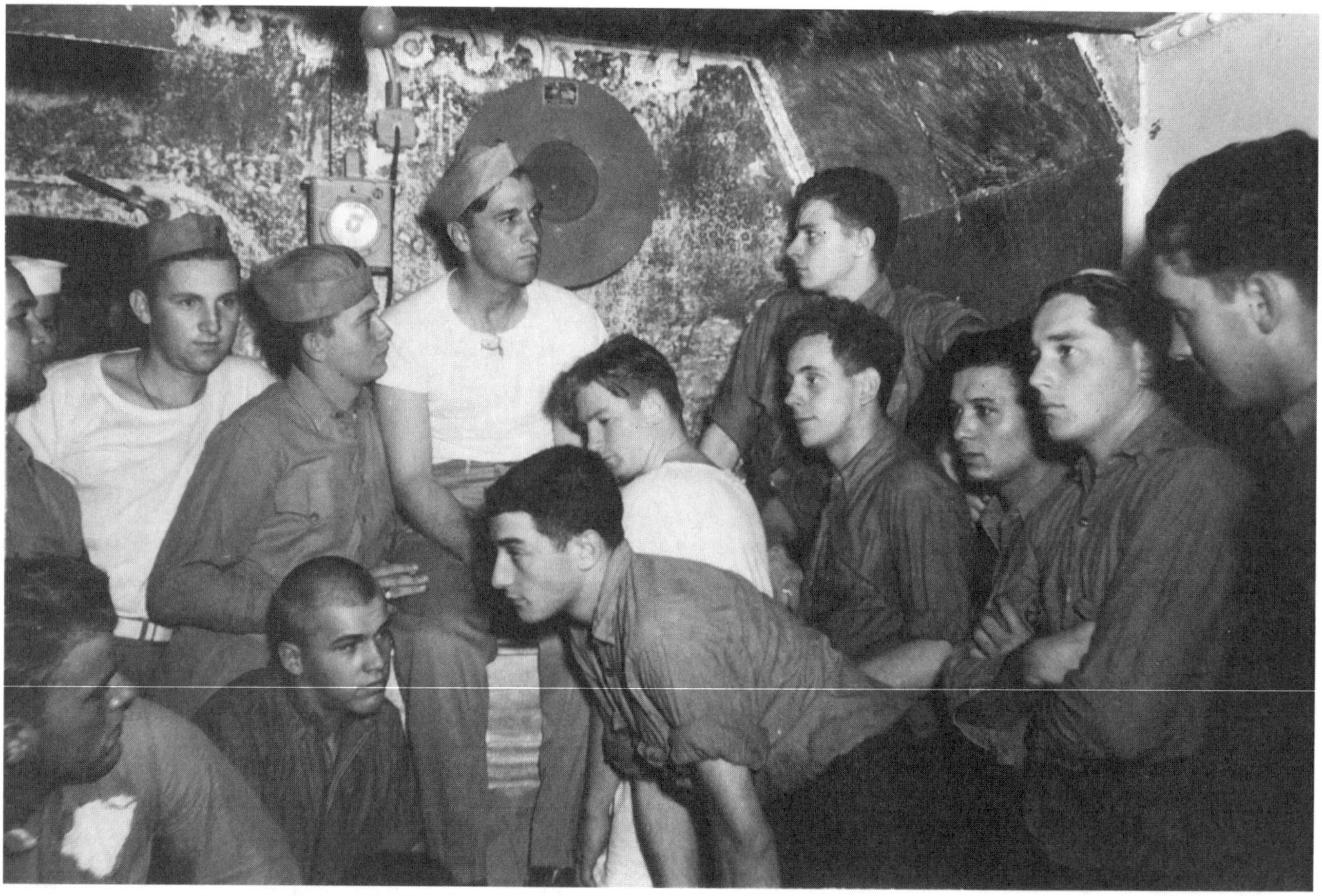

Sailors and Marines, the unpainted bulkhead behind them reflecting how their ship had been stripped for action, listen to one of Commander Hoskins's war communiques en route to North Africa. (NA, 80-G-30267)

Forty-One-Sail-Seven on inner air patrol over TF-34, 3 November 1942. (NA, 80-G-30216)

Lieutenant Gordon P. Chase, seen here with Aviation Radioman 2d Class R. J. Monahan, en route to North Africa, ca. November 1942. (NA, 80-G-31334)

Boresighting the guns, 3 November 1942. From the foreground: 9-F-20, 9-F-9, and 9-F-18; [41-F-]22, [41-F-]21 and [41-F-]25, showing the differences in the markings used by the *Ranger*'s two embarked F4F-equipped squadrons. VF-9 has retained the squadron number [9]-mission [F for fighter]-individual plane number; VF-41 uses only the individual plane number. Both squadrons display the yellow surround applied around the blue and white fuselage star. (NA, 80-G-30362)

"Fighting Nine in fighting regalia" on the eve of Torch before one of the squadron's planes, 9-F-13. Kneeling (L–R): Menard, Bardeen, Amesbury,* Wilhoite,* Martin, Denoff, and Childers; Standing (L–R): McWhorter, O'Neill, Toliver, Gerhardt, Onstott, Smith, Raby, Wilkerson, Bonneau, Winters, Franger, Feasley, Brooks, Micka,* and Vita. Photograph taken by Captain Durgin. *Indicates lost during Torch. (VF-9 Historical File, AvH)

VF-41's pilots pose in front of 9-F-13. (NA, 80-G-31230)

VS-41's pilots pose in front of 41-S-6. (NA, 80-G-31234)

are all around us . . . so we cannot relax our vigilance nor rest on our oars until we have decisively won this war and are alongside Pier 7 for a long recreation and leave period."⁶⁰

November 7th passed in anticipation. Commander Hoskins told the *Ranger*'s officers and men that the original plan would be followed, and that landings would commence in Algeria, as well as along the Atlantic Coast of French Morocco, with the focal point of the latter being Casablanca. "As we have told you before," Hoskins explained, "it is entirely possible that the French people will not oppose us but will welcome us and even join us." Acknowledging the sincere hope that that would be the case, he reminded his listeners that "campaigns are not won by hoping or wishful thinking.'" Although "hoping for the best," the *Ranger*'s exec added that "we are prepared for anything the opposition can dish out."⁶¹

After describing the *Ranger*'s mission, he related that the *Suwanee* would provide a CAP over the task group, the *Santee* (ACV-29) would be supporting the southernmost landings, and the *Sangamon* (ACV-26) the northernmost. Comparing the size of the Allied expeditionary force involved in Torch with the fabled Spanish Armada and the English force mustered to defeat it, the *Ranger*'s exec noted: "Our combined force is considerably larger than the entire total of the Spanish Armada plus the English fleet." Acknowledging that time did not permit him to provide those listening to his words with the "many details of our mission," he did assure them "that it was well planned. And I believe that we are just the people to carry out those plans, and make Mister Hitler sorry that he ever quit his house painting job. It is not only a privilege for us to be a part of this history making expedition but a very great honor," Hoskins concluded, "and I believe we will show the folks back home that we are worthy of that honor."⁶²

17

"WE COULD TAKE NO CHANCES"

General quarters, sounded throughout the *Ranger* at the end of the mid watch on 8 November, found all VF-41 pilots in their ready room. "Spirits were high," Mac Wordell wrote later, "the time had come." An "excellent esprit de corps" prevailed that morning, "and all pilots joined in the singing and the jokes, and the anticipation of enemy action," with the uncertainty of the sounding of "batter up" or "play ball" (familiar baseball terms employed as code words for conditions of readiness and imminent action) adding an element of suspense. As each pilot reached the room, he received the greeting: "Happy dog day." Captain Durgin and Lieutenant Commander Booth, individually greeted with a boisterous rendition of "For He's a Jolly Good Fellow" as they arrived, each "wished the boys luck." Chaplain O'Callahan's coming in temporarily silenced the gaiety, but, in addition to "wish[ing] the boys luck," as the captain and squadron commander had done, he "offered prayers for their safety."[1]

"Long before it was light," plane captains, in the blue-gray and light-gray camouflaged aircraft spotted on the flight deck, their blue and white fuselage stars outlined with a yellow surround for use as a recognition measure, started their engines, the blue exhaust flames bright against the darkness. French Morocco lay just over the horizon. Sunrise on 8 November found the wind blowing from the southwest at force one to two; there was a moderate sea with only slight swells. Weather conditions, observers noted, were excellent, except for surface haze near the shoreline.

"The main problem up to this time," Rear Admiral McWhorter reflected, "had been a psychological one. Was there going to be any fighting or wasn't there? The progress of the political offensive fluctuated from day to day. One day it seemed like the French were not going to resist, then word came that the Army and Air Forces would not oppose us, and then that the attitude of the French Navy was in doubt. Everyone hoped they would save their bullets for the Nazis, but French war-time psychology is completely inexplicable and we could take no chances."[2]

Less than an hour after the ship had gone to battle stations, she intercepted the order to "play ball" at Safi. At 0615 on 8 November, as the first streaks of dawn began to appear, the *Ranger* swung into the wind and commenced launching 18 F4F-4s from VF-9, under Captain Jack Raby, to proceed to the Rabat-Salé airport to attack the planes they found there—on the ground or in the air. Raby had orders not to attack, however, unless he received the signal to begin offensive action—"play ball"—at that location. Ten minutes after the first of Fighting Nine's F4F-4s had begun to take off, Rear Admiral McWhorter transmitted the order.[3]

FLIGHT A-1 (VF-9)

First Section

Lt. Comdr. John Raby	9-F-1
Ens. Marvin J. Franger, A-V(N)	
Lt. (jg) Gordon M. Braun, A-V(N)	9-F-25

Second Section

Lt. Kenan C. Childers
Ens. Louis A. Menard, A-V(N)
Lt. (jg) Harold E. Vita, A-V(N)
Ens. Charles W. Gerhardt, A-V(N)

Third Section

Lt. (jg) Stanton M. Amesbury,   9-F-24
  A-V(N)   (BuNo 11765)
Ens. James M. Wilkerson, A-V(N)

Five minutes later, at 0630, the flight deck officer motioned Fighting Nine's second division, led by VF-9's exec, Lt. Theodore H. "Pedro" Winters, Jr., forward. A short time later, the *Suwanee* launched eight F4Fs from VGF-27, under Lt. Comdr. Thomas K. Wright, to fly CAP over the *Ranger* and their own ship.

FLIGHT A-1(A), (VF-9)

First Section

Lt. Theodore H. Winters, Jr.
Ens. Thomas M. Wilhoite, A-V(N)
Lt. (jg) Mayo A. Hadden, Jr., A-V(N)
Lt. (jg) Armistead B. Smith, Jr., A-V(N)

Second Section

Lt. Edward Micka
Ens. Merle M. Hershey, A-V(N)
Ens. William J. Bonneau, A-V(N)
Ens. James E. Toliver, A-V(N)
Ens. Robert M. McGann, A-V(N)[4]

Soon after both divisions of fighters had gotten airborne, the flight deck crew had positioned VS-41's SBDs in the intricate and well-rehearsed flight deck ballet. Seventeen Dauntlesses began taking off soon afterwards, at 0635. Their mission: to attack submarines and capital ships in Casablanca harbor, "in that order of priority," reflecting the decision that Lt. Comdr. Pete Carver and his pilots had reached before takeoff. The first two divisions would dive on any sub they encountered, and the third would take on the *Jean Bart*, if it appeared that the French boats had already been knocked *hors de combat*.

FLIGHT A-2 (VS-41)

First Division

Lt. Comdr. Lamar P. Carver
   Aviation Chief Radioman Reginald A. Miner
Lt. (jg) Cyrus F. Weeks, A-V(N)
   Aviation Radioman 3d Class G. H. Perry
Lt. (jg) William H. Longley, A-V(N)
   Aviation Radioman 3d Class John G. Korecki
Lt. Cecil V. Johnson
   Aviation Radioman 2d Class Gerhard H. O. Kleiner
Lt. (jg) Robert H. Higley, A-V(N)
   Aviation Radioman 3d Class L. E. Colon
Lt. (jg) Clyde A. Tucker, Jr., A-V(N)
   Aviation Radioman 3d Class Lloyd E. Edens

Second Division

Lt. John M. DeVane, Jr.
   Aviation Radioman 1st Class William O. Haynes, Jr.
Lt. (jg) Woodie L. McVay, Jr., A-V(N)
   Aviation Radioman 2d Class Kenneth W. Jobe
Lt. (jg) Maxwell A. Eaton, A-V(N)
   Aviation Radioman 3d Class William T. Shackelford
Lt (jg) Horace R. White, A-V(N)
   Aviation Radioman 3d Class A. R. Smith
Lt. (jg) Robert L. Arthur, A-V(N)
   Aviation Radioman 3d Class Morris S. Waterson

Third Division

Lt. Ralph A. Embree
   Aviation Radioman 1st Class Joseph M. Eardley
Lt. (jg) Joseph P. Keigher, Jr., A-V(N)
   Aviation Radioman 3d Class J. J. Lankowicz
Lt. (jg) Clarence A. Twiddy, Jr., A-V(N)
   Aviation Radioman 3d Class R. E. O'Connor
Lt. (jg) Harold R. Keller, Jr., A-V(N)
   Aviation Radioman 2d Class A. W. Lorentzen
Lt. (jg) Ralph W. Ross, A-V(N)
   Aviation Radioman 3d Class L. J. Devine
Lt. (jg) John G. McReynolds, Jr., A-V(N)
   Aviation Radioman 3d Class Oscar I. Light

By the time Carver's flight had formed up, the battleship and heavy cruisers of the nearby covering force (TG 34.1) had launched nine floatplanes. The *Massachusetts* (BB-59) had put aloft two Vought OS2U-3s (for gunfire spotting), the *Tuscaloosa* had put up four Curtiss SOCs (two for antisubmarine patrol and two for spotting) and the *Wichita* three (two for spotting and one for antisubmarine patrol). They, too, headed toward their respective stations. On board the *Wilkes*, Gordon Chase, of VS-41, prepared to go into battle as an observer and "acting anti-aircraft control and identification officer."[5]

Scouting Forty-One's three divisions proceeded toward Casablanca, climbing en route to an altitude of 14,000 feet. As the pilots and radio-gunners prepared to perform their

Fighter squadron's ready room before dawn, 8 November 1942. VF-41's commanding officer, Lt. Comdr. Charles T. "Tommy" Booth, II, who, like others in the room, is wearing red goggles, so that he can acclimate his eyes to the predawn darkness topside, stands at the front of the room, hands thrust casually in his pockets. Beside him, his left foot propped on a chair arm, is Lt. (jg) Charles V. "Chuck" August, A-V(N), famed for his "Clark Gable" mustache. Lieutenant George H. "Spanky" Carter is turning in his chair just to left of center. Seated on the deck are Lt. John R. "Jawn" Sweeney, with Ens. Robert C. Cronin, A-V(N), immediately behind him, with Ens. Andrew B. Conner, A-V(N), and Lt. Walter F. "Wally" Madden, A-V(N). Seated in chair at left is Lt. Maynard M. "Bud" Furney, A-V(N); at lower right, Lt. (jg) Walter E. Laake, A-V(N). Before the day is out, August will be a POW; Carter will have been shot down, too, but will be at liberty until the following day. (NA, 80-G-30252)

mission, the French airfield at Casablanca stirred with preparations for battle. The general alert had sounded at 0530, as sirens wailed over the port with the appearance of a strange aircraft—most likely one of the Royal Air Force Hudsons from Gibraltar—dropping leaflets.

Commandant Georges Tricaud, the 41-year-old commanding officer of *Groupe de Chasse* II/5 "Lafayette," who had survived three bail-outs in the desperate Battle of France in 1940, informed his pilots that the Americans had arrived to attack the coast of Africa between Casablanca and Algiers. Tricaud, his men knew, suffered from intense back pain, inflammation of the sciatic nerve that "tortured" him; he needed to employ two canes just to walk. The moment had come, he told the younger pilots with his characteristic forthrightness, to face the adversary and defend *l'honneur de l'Empire*.[6] Ironically, the insignia (the profile of the head of a Sioux chief) painted on the fuselages of their American-built Curtiss Hawk 75's harked back to an earlier conflict when the Americans had come as friends, not enemies.

Another view of fighter pilots gathering in the ready room before dawn on 8 November; those present include many from flight A-4: front row (L–R): Lt. (jg) Arthur J. Cassidy, A-V(N) (VF-41's "Red Rippers" patch on his jacket), Lt. Keene G. "Kagey" Hammond (grinning broadly, with chartboard in lap), (Unidentified); Lt. (jg) Clyde C. Andrews, A-V(N). Lt. (jg) William H. "Pete" Bolt, A-V(N), is seated behind Cassidy. Standing in the back of the room are what appears to be an Army pilot (embarked to fly Piper L-4s ashore once a field had been secured), Lt. Mac Wordell of VF-41, Lt. Jake Onstott of VF-9, and Lt. Earle F. "Buster" Craig of VF-41, whose sweat-stained shirt reflects the poorly ventilated spaces in which they were meeting. Ens. Hamilton McWhorter, III, A-V(N), is at far right, seated (wearing flying helmet). (NA, 80-G-30253)

Two types of aircraft equipped GC II/5: the Curtiss Hawk 75A (export version of the U.S. Army Air Force's P-36) and the Dewoitine D.520. On charge on 8 November were 20 of the former and 12 of the latter. French pilots justifiably considered the Curtiss's light armament a handicap in air-to-air combat, but praised the plane's ruggedness, which had enabled many an aviator to survive engagements with German aircraft in the Battle of France. Additionally, the Hawk's Pratt and Whitney engine, a powerplant used not only in the H.75 fighter, but in the Martin 167 and Douglas DB-7 bombers, received high praise, more than one pilot commenting favorably on its running "like a clock."[7]

At 0640, GC II/5 put aloft a *patrouille double* of six H.75As: one section consisting of *Sous Lieutenant* Pierre Villaceque, *Adjudant-Chef* Delannoy, and *Sergent* René Lavie, the other of *Lieutenant* Tremolft, *Adjudant-Chef* Marcel Verrier, and *Sergent* Lucien Heme. *Commandant* Tricaud watched them take off, leaning grimly on his canes.

Meanwhile, back on board the *Ranger*, the purposeful movement of planes on the flight deck continued; soon, the first of 18 F4F-4s from VF-41, under the squadron commander, Lt. Comdr. Charles T. "Tommy" Booth, II, began rolling down the deck at 0700, bound for Cazes, to destroy any planes they found there—either on the ground or in the air. One by one, they banked away after clearing

Commandant Georges Tricaud, commander of *Groupe de Chasse* II/5 "Lafayette," who, along with his pilots, met the *Ranger*'s in combat on 8 November 1942. A man of action, he is seen here during his tour as *commandant* of GC I/6 (14 December 1939–16 August 1940) in the cockpit of a Bloch 152 fighter. He had earned his pilot's wings in 1921, and had fought with distinction in the Battle of France, being credited with three victories and the award of the *croix de guerre*. (*Service Historique de l'Armee de l'Air* via Mersky)

the bow ramp, wobbling perceptibly as the pilots cranked up the landing gear with the requisite 32 turns. For them, the French attitude was not an academic matter; if the French resisted, then they would have to meet force with force.

FLIGHT A-3 (VF-41)

First Section

Lt. Comdr. Charles T. Booth, II	[41-F-]1
Lt. (jg) Boyd N. Mayhew, A-V(N)	[41-F-]2
Lt. Theodore A. Grell	[41-F-]3
Lt. (jg) George M. Harris, Jr., A-V(N)	[41-F-]4

Second Section

Lt. Herold J. Weiler, Jr.	[41-F-]5
Lt. (jg) Dee Jones, A-V(N)	[41-F-]6
Lt. Ernest W. Wood, Jr.	[41-F-]7
Ens. Andrew B. Conner, A-V(N)	[41-F-]8
Lt. (jg) George E. Harris, A-V(N)	[41-F-]25
Ens. Christos E. Mikronis, A-V(N)	[41-F-]26 (BuNo 02023)

Third Section

Lt. George H. Carter	[41-F-]17 (BuNo 11703)
Lt. (jg) Charles V. August, A-V(N)	[41-F-]18 (BuNo 4094)
Lt. (jg) Edmund J. Kelly, A-V(N)	[41-F-]19
Lt. (jg) Walter E. Laake, A-V(N)	[41-F-]20

Fourth Section

Lt. Maynard M. Furney, A-V(N)	[41-F-]21
Lt. (jg) Charles A. Shields, A-V(N)	[41-F-]22 (BuNo 4087)
Lt. (jg) Edward N. Seiler, A-V(N)	[41-F-]23
Ens. Will "W" Taylor, A-V(N)	[41-F-]24

Vichy French-marked Dewoitine D.520 fighters, such as those faced by the *Ranger*'s F4F-4 pilots in November 1942. (*Service Historique de L'Armée de L'Air* Photo No. 83.175 via Lambert)

Flight A-3 rendezvoused over the *Ranger* at 5,000 feet and proceeded toward their objective—the airdrome at Cazes—in a gradual climb. Their route, however, took them too near the battleship *Massachusetts*. Shortly before Tommy Booth's troops had taken off, Lt. Carl R. Doerflinger, the *Massachusetts*'s senior aviator, had been preparing to spot his ship's main battery fire when he encountered two French fighters, most likely from GC II/5's *patrouille double*. Doerflinger flew his Vought OS2U-3 Kingfisher toward the ship. "Am coming in on starboard bow," he radioed, "with [a] couple hostile aircraft on my tail. Pick them off— I am the one in front."[8]

The *Massachusetts*'s five-inch mounts 1 and 3 barked soon thereafter. "Her barrage was quite good," Lieutenant Commander Booth wrote with professional detachment, as the battlewagon's gunfire apparently burst close enough to the *Ranger*'s climbing Wildcats to necessitate "a slight deviation from course to avoid it."[9] Lieutenant George H. "Spanky" Carter later extended begrudging praise, too, to U.S. Navy gunners: "Their fire was excellent and it is a miracle none of us were not knocked down."[10] Gordon Chase, however, on board the *Wilkes*, in the *Massachusetts*'s screen, observed that "the identification of aircraft by [the *Wilkes*'s] officers and men was nearly nil, although they told me they had studied and had lectures enumerable [*sic*] times prior to this engagement."[11]

While the OS2U pilots had been meeting opposition, and the *Ranger*'s fliers were encountering friendly fire, more French planes were taking off from Cazes: around 0700, that included *Lieutenants* Boudier and Fabre, and *Adjudant* de Montgolfier. Within 30 minutes, another three-plane patrol rose into the skies: *Lieutenants* Le Stum, Rubin, and François La Chaux. More pilots began to reach the field soon thereafter.

Carl Doerflinger had been fortunate to escape being shot down; his shipmate from the *Massachusetts*, Ens. Thomas A. Dougherty, A-V(N), however, suffered a different fate. *Sergent* Lavie of GC II/5's *patrouille double* crippled Dougherty's OS2U-3 (BuNo 5804), wounding Aviation Radioman 2d Class Robert C. Etheridge, his

Sous-Lieutenant Pierre Villaceque (L) and *Sergent* Andre LeGrande (R), Casablanca, July 1942. Note GC II/5's insignia harkening back to the Lafayette *Escadrille* of World War I, on the fuselage of the Hawk 75 that they are standing beside. (*Service Historique de L'Amée de L'Air* Photo No. B90/0260 via Lambert)

radio-gunner, and compelling Dougherty to make a rough landing off Casablanca and taxi in to the beach. There, French sailors manning a shore battery north of the harbor took them prisoner: Dougherty had wrenched his back in the landing, and Etheridge had suffered a bullet wound in his right calf and shrapnel wounds in the groin. The French transported the *Massachusetts*'s OS2U crew to naval headquarters.

Shortly after the *Ranger* had launched Tommy Booth's VF-41 flight, the carrier began putting aloft Flight A-4, eight F4F-4s from VF-41 and eight from VF-9. Under Mac Wordell, VF-41's exec, the mixed Fighting Forty-One/Fighting Nine group was to protect the troops going ashore at Fedala; they were to "attack and destroy any enemy aircraft in the air . . . any machine gun nests or local shore batteries firing on our boats or transports." Before leaving the ready room, Wordell had told his men to "stay together—not to separate." After wishing them all "Good hunting," he strode out confident that his men were well prepared for whatever lay ahead of them.[12]

FLIGHT A-4 (VF-41/VF-9) ("VF-49")

First Section (VF-41)

Lt. Malcolm T. Wordell	[41-F-]9
	(BuNo 11707)
Lt. (jg) Clyde C. Andrews, A-V(N)	[41-F-]10
Lt. Earle F. Craig	[41-F-]11
Lt. (jg) Hubert T. Houston, A-V(N)	[41-F-]12

Second Section (VF-41)

Lt. Keene G. Hammond	[41-F-]13
Lt. (jg) William H. Bolt, Jr. A-V(N)	[41-F-]14
Lt. (jg) Arthur J. Cassidy, A-V(N)	[41-F-]15
Ens. Philip S. Ball, Jr., A-V(N)	[41-F-]16

Third Section (VF-9)

Lt. Jacob W. Onstott	9-F-17
Ens. Hamilton McWhorter, III, A-V(N)	9-F-18
Lt. (jg) Charles L. Moutenot, A-V(N)	9-F-19
Ens. Burton L. Bardeen, A-V(N)	9-F-20

Fourth Section (VF-9)

Lt. Hugh D. O'Neill, A-V(N)	9-F-21
	(BuNo 11704)
Lt. (jg) Reuben H. Denoff, A-V(N)	9-F-22
Lt. (jg) Jack H. Sands, A-V(N)	9-F-23
Lt. (jg) Harrison Feasley, A-V(N)	9-F-24

At that time, Jack Raby's VF-9 flight was heading toward Rabat-Ville, which served as a base for the 26 Hawk 75s of GC I/5, the 18 Potez 29s, and 6 Farmans (F.222.2, F.223.3, and F.224 types) of GT I/15, and the 13 Liore et Olivier (LeO) 451s of GR I/22; Pedro Winters's flight was heading toward Rabat-Salé. Tommy Booth's "Red Rippers" were about to descend upon Cazes, where, by 0745, *Groupe de Chasse* II/5 "Lafayette" was as mobilized as it could be.

After Boudier's and Le Stum's patrols had taken off to join Villaceque's and Tremolft's, as more pilots arrived, they took off singly: *Capitaines* Robert Huvet (a veteran of the Battle of France, with six confirmed kills) and Elie Reyne, and *Lieutenant* Georges Ruchoux. Obviously unwilling to

Grumman F4F-4s, from what is most likely flight A-4 (no bombs slung beneath the wings) are warmed up for a dawn take-off on 8 November 1942. (NA, 80-G-30260)

send his pilots off to do something he would not do himself, *Commandant* Tricaud, although suffering from the excruciating sciatica, stiffly climbed into the cockpit of his plane and, as his men understood it, to set "a noble example," took off, too.

As VF-41 neared its objective, communication difficulties complicated what Tommy Booth thought should have been "an easy mission." As soon as he made a landfall, Booth tried to radio Weiler, Carter, and Furney, his section leaders. Poor communication, under what seemed ideal conditions, allowed him to raise only one of the three, and then only intermittently. Booth, unable to direct his section leaders, thus left each section "more or less on its own." Arriving over the target at 15,000 feet, Booth pushed over to strafe the airdrome, home to the H.75s and D.520s of GC II/5 and the 13 Douglas DB-7s from *Groupe de Bombardement* I/32, in accordance with the plan.

Each section, however, arrived from a different direction, because of the lack of communication. Woodie Wood, in Ham Weiler's second section, flamed Lt. Georges Ruchoux's Dewoitine. Ruchoux, wounded in one leg, bailed out of the crippled D.520. Wood later teamed up with Lt. (jg) George E. Harris, A-V(N), to flame a second Dewoitine. Wood later battled another long-nosed enemy fighter, most likely flown by the experienced ace, *Capitaine* Huvet, one of GC II/5's "most brilliant pilots."[13]

Ensign Mikronis, also from Ham Weiler's group, lost track of his section leader in the first dive; he strafed an antiaircraft gun, seeing one hit, then released his AN-M-54 incendiary bomb. He then strafed two of GB I/32's DB-7s and saw his bullets hole them. Frustratingly, however, the Douglases did not burn. Mikronis climbed in tight left spirals to clear the field, but soon encountered an H.75.[14]

In the ensuing dogfight, Mikronis managed to gain altitude on his adversary before antiaircraft fire scored a direct hit on his engine, which cut out immediately. Too low to bail out, he turned south of the airdrome to try for a forced landing. But, given a new lease on life, the H.75 pilot latched onto him, and the Frenchman squeezed off about five bursts. Seeing that Mikronis was helpless, however, the

Lieutenant George H. "Spanky" Carter in the cockpit of his F4F-4 (BuNo 11703), [41-F-]17, en route to North Africa; note miniature "Red Rippers" insignia beneath the cockpit sill. On the original print the pilot's name, *G. H. Carter*, can be seen arching over the VF-41 insignia. (NA, 80-G-31322)

Hawk pilot abruptly quit firing and flew wing on him for a time. Hit in the head and wounded by shrapnel, Mikronis, clinging doggedly to consciousness by sheer force of will, put his flaps down, but did not lower his landing gear. Turning away from the radio tower at the field at an altitude of between 150 and 200 feet, Mikronis passed out.[15]

Spanky Carter, leading the third section, having gotten "separated from the skipper" and been rendered incommunicado at about 0745, around the time the last French fighters had gotten aloft, noted the enemy planes over the south end of the Cazes airdrome 15 minutes later.[16] Chuck August, Carter's wingman, heard his flight leader (Booth) report the completion of his first attack, but Carter apparently did not. The plans called for each section to dive and strafe the field in succession, so Carter's radio being out of order meant that he did not hear the other section leaders (Booth and Weiler) report their completed attacks.[17]

After having waited about 15 minutes, Carter initiated the third section's attack, having become separated from one of his section, either Lieutenant (jg) Kelly or Lieutenant (jg) Laake, before pushing over. Carter strafed what he took to be the refueling area of the airdrome, sighting-in on a Douglas DB-7, then dropping his two AN-M-54 incendiaries. Frustratingly, he, too, observed no fires.[18]

Chuck August pushed over into his dive, but his cockpit enclosure, except for a six-inch circle in the center of the windshield, fogged over. Attacking from east to west, August encountered further difficulties when he opened fire. During the strafing run, the housing for the light bulb of the Mk. 8 bombsight fell out of position. August continued his strafing run, silencing an antiaircraft battery, but he had to hold the housing in place by hand as he did so. He dropped his pair of AN-M-54s, but soon became so heavily engaged that he never bothered to see the results of his drop, because, upon the completion of his strafing and bombing run, he and his section leader encountered trouble.[19]

Carter pulled up from his strafing run on the DB-7 to find about a dozen H.75s and D.520s deployed in a loose Lufbery circle over the south end of the airdrome, at an altitude of about 2,500 feet. He quickly fired at the first plane that came into his sights, an H.75, which dove into the ground and exploded upon impact. His wingman, too, although antiaircraft fire had hit his F4F-4 and caused his right landing gear to extend, almost immediately after completing his strafing and bombing run, engaged a "P-36." Overshooting with his first burst, August "shortened [the] lead" and raked his adversary, which "turned turtle, plunged to earth and burst into flames."[20]

In the desperate, unequal dogfight that unfolded, Carter had no time to savor his victory: an instant later, the sight of a French plane making a head-on approach confronted him. Carter's adversary fired and "struck my plane with a large number of bullets." The French pilot shot away [41-F-]17's elevator tab control, "evidently" punctured the vacuum tank for the flaps, and apparently ruptured the oil cooler or oil lines in the left wing. Losing power and hearing the sound of his engine making a "metallic clanking noise," Carter, turning tightly, broke off the fight as soon as he realized what was happening. He headed south along the coast with his manifold pressure "steadily decreasing."[21]

The enemy, however, was not about to let the 29-year-old North Dakotan contemplate his predicament unhindered. Soon after Carter had realized that his plane had been rendered *hors de combat*, he found himself again on the receiving end of more French gunfire, as an H.75 immediately slid in astern. He soon heard the "sharp smack as bullets struck the armor plate" behind him. His engine rapidly lost power, and he headed into the onshore breeze. Two miles offshore, he ran out of altitude.[22]

His shoulder straps adjusted tightly, Carter survived the water landing, made without flaps, with a "minimum of discomfort from the rapid deceleration." The Wildcat sank quickly, the water having risen over the cockpit as he exited his foundering fighter without a moment to spare. "As I bobbed to the surface," he said later, "the elevators disappeared in a welter of bubbles." The H.75 circled the scene once "and [its pilot] either did not see me or was decent enough not to strafe me in the water for he immediately headed back for Casablanca."[23]

Inflating one side of his life jacket, Carter made sure that his unopened rubber boat was firmly attached to his belt, then scanned the horizon. He soon spotted a small boat about two miles away. To lessen the prospect of being seen, he pulled off his white flying helmet and threw it away, and lifted the orange life jacket from around his neck. Pulling it down between his legs, he sat on it "and rode it like the rubber horses at a bathing beach," confident that his efforts had rendered him "quite invisible to any watchers" on shore.[24]

Soon after the H.75 pilot had eliminated Carter from the battle, Carter's wingman quickly encountered troubles of his own. Chuck August fired at an H.75 and a D.520, in quick succession and at close range (150–175 yards). He saw one of the French planes make "a convulsive movement into [a] stalled attitude while the other continued in its dive." A pair of H.75s on his tail, however, quickly drew his attention to matters closer at hand. "All attempts to outclimb or outmaneuver the tailing P-36's [sic] were futile," August later related, "and their bullets could be heard and felt to strike the fuselage and armor plate aft of the cockpit." In desperation, August pushed over into a dive, pulling out within 10 feet of the ground, whereupon Windy Shields showed up to divert the attackers.[25]

August then gained altitude and instituted a "full deflection high side attack" on a Hawk. August's .50-caliber fire soon flamed the Curtiss, which immediately burst into flames and began losing altitude. The pilot bailed out. August heard Shields's exhortations in his earphones: "Tally ho, good shot, good shot," as he gave chase to the remaining P-36.[26]

Ensign Mikronis, having landed miraculously, saw August's quarry bailing out, but had regained consciousness with no recollection of how he had descended and made his crash-landing. Mikronis also found himself disarmed and minus his flight gear, which had been taken from him. He was standing next to a farmhouse talking with a French farmer, some 150 yards away from his plane, which he had somehow put down without so much as a scratched wingtip. Doubtlessly bewildered, he later recalled seeing at least three other H.75s crash. He tried to return to his plane, but the farmer good-naturedly trained a gun on him and would not allow him to do so.[27]

After he washed his face with some water his captor had provided him, Mikronis found himself the object of curiosity of a small group of French people who gathered around. Taken into the house and put to bed, Mikronis made a second attempt to get back to his crashed Wildcat, but found that his captor had maintained an equal resolve: the Frenchman was not about to let him do so. An ambulance soon arrived with what Mikronis believed were unarmed Red Cross workers, one of whom produced a first aid kit, from which the pilot procured a battle dressing and applied it to his face wound. The worker then took the kit away from the American, and Mikronis was taken to the waiting ambulance.[28]

Chuck August had returned to Cazes and strafed what appeared to be parked D.520s, until he heard a call for help from another F4F pilot. August responded that he was right behind the two H.75s that were chasing a Wildcat, and summarily broke up their attack. He remained on the Curtiss' tails, and tried to get into a position below and astern. Each time he pulled up to fire, however, he lost distance and speed, and found himself in a stalling position.[29]

A glance at his gas gauge showed 60 gallons remaining, so he began to fly toward Mèdouina, the prearranged rendezvous point. Suddenly, his engine began making loud clanking noises and vibrated excessively. Then, abruptly, it quit. A quick inspection of his instruments showed fuel pressure zero (boosted to 15 pounds with the hurried use of the wobble pump), oil pressure zero, cylinder head temperature normal, and rpms, 1,000. Seeing the hilly and rocky nature of the terrain beneath him, August bailed out at about 1,100 feet, but hit his left thigh on the right horizontal stabilizer. The impact threw him into a spin. Recovering by spreading his arms and legs, he floated down in his parachute, making a heavy landing because he had not stopped swinging like a pendulum. Dragged on his back for a short distance, he collapsed his chute by pulling on the shrouds. He experienced some difficulty in disengaging his harness, inadvertently releasing the CO_2 in his life jacket as he did so.[30]

August then took stock of his situation, after he had folded his parachute. He noticed that 41-F-18 lay less than the length of a football field away, and that he had lost his ration bag and his wristwatch in his descent. He limped over to his battered Wildcat, very quickly joined by "two Frenchmen and a large number of Arabian men and women," who surrounded the smoking wreck. August made a hurried inspection. He found the right wheel sheared off at the draglink, the engine severed and lying about four feet ahead of the fuselage, and the left wing jammed over the crumpled cockpit, presenting an insurmountable obstacle to his retrieving his maps. He also noticed that the underside of the cowling and the nose section covering had been perforated by what looked like .40-caliber bullets; the after section of the fuselage and the tail section looked well-holed by .30-caliber slugs. He saw that gasoline from the demolished main tank had saturated the

Aviation Radioman 3d Class Morris S. Waterson scored hits on one attacking H.75 and drove off a second on 8 November with his .30-caliber machine guns. Here he turns down Aviation Machinist's Mate 1st Class R. M. Price's offer of $230.00 to trade places with him. Note faintly visible VF-41 "Top Hat" insignia on the SBD's fuselage, just below the forward cockpit enclosure. (NA, 80-G-30248)

accessory section of BuNo 4094, and the ground beneath it. "Chasing away the spectators," he resolutely drew the Very pistol from his belt and fired three times, igniting the volatile fuel. Crackling orange flames soon enveloped the Wildcat in a *Beau Geste*-like "Viking funeral" which, in view of the North African theater, seemed entirely fitting.[31]

Windy Shields, however, who had prolonged August's battle over Cazes but who had only postponed his being shot down in the end, suffered a similar fate. Bailing out, he landed on the edge of the field, where he was taken prisoner by the French. "Treated very well" by those who had captured him, he formed the impression that the French were fighting "only because of orders and possible fear of retribution."[32]

Jack Raby, meanwhile, arrived with his VF-9 flight in the vicinity of Rabat-Ville. Finding only average flying conditions and visibility fair, he observed what appeared to be only seven planes on the ground—four fighters and three bombers. Starting his first dive from 10,000 feet, Raby led his nine-plane flight in several strafing runs from north to east, before they joined up and made two more runs in the same direction. Raby reported "all aircraft destroyed." The French, however, had skillfully camouflaged and dispersed the aircraft at Rabat-Ville, and only suffered the loss of three H.75s. As Raby broke off the attack, he glanced toward Rabat-Salé. He could soon see that VF-9's second division, under Pedro Winters, had achieved some success.

Circling the field, Winters had found Rabat-Salé apparently unprepared for VF-9's arrival. "It was at once apparent," he later reported, "that the attack was a complete surprise; no evidence of activity and engine covers on planes." Circling even lower, he reported "no enemy resistance encountered." Soon thereafter, however, antiaircraft bursts dirtied the sky through which he had just flown. His radio inoperative and thus unable to pick up the "play ball" code, he immediately reported "batter up." He had counted what appeared to be four very large bombers—the Farmans—and "about ten" medium bombers—the LeO.451s, all well-dispersed. While the second section—Lieutenant Micka and Ensigns Hershey, Bonneau, and Toliver—assumed combat air patrol overhead, Winters led his section—himself, Ens. Willie Wilhoite, and Lts. (jg) Mike Hadden, Chick Smith, and Bob McGann, down to strafe. Attacking in a four-plane echelon line, weaving, they pursued their task thoroughly, none more enthusiastically and vigorously as Willie Wilhoite, who set at least three LeO.451s afire and machine-gunned several others.

After Winters's section had carried out five strafing runs, Micka's section joined in the attack when it became evident that no French aerial opposition had materialized. Moderate amounts of antiaircraft fire, from guns emplaced in front of the hangers facing the landing area, drew strafing fire that apparently silenced them, but not before a bullet had pierced the blower of "Oliver" Toliver's engine.

Upon arrival over Casablanca, Pete Carver soon saw that the support force ships had already begun shelling the harbor installations, and that a running surface engagement—most likely centering around the sortie of eight French boats of the Moroccan Submarine Flotilla—had developed offshore. Having determined his unit's plan of attack, Carver led VS-41's first division in a dive from 14,000 feet, picking as his target what looked like a nest of five to seven submarines at the foot of the *Jettie Delure*. The second division

The submarine *Gunnel* (SS-253), ca. August 1942. (NA, 19-LCM, Box 540)

Lieutenant (jg) Joseph P. Keigher, Jr. (R), with his radio-gunner, Aviation Radioman 3d Class J. J. Lankowitz, who inadvertently attacked the *Gunnel* off Casablanca on 8 November. (NA, 80-G-31341)

under Count DeVane soon followed. Heavy smoke from the guns in the harbor, and from the shell and bomb bursts, made damage assessment difficult, but the first two divisions scored two direct hits: Pete Carver scored one on the nest; nobody owned up to the other. Five TBF-1s from the *Suwanee*'s VGS-27, under Lt. Comdr. Milton A. Nation, bombed the nest as well, claiming one hit on a submarine and one on an "unidentified ship" moored across the pier from the battleship *Jean Bart*. A subsequent accounting noted the destruction of three submarines that morning: the *Oréade*, the *La Psyché*, and the *Amphitrite* all of which had been unable to put to sea.[33]

Ralph Embree, whose six-plane division had been orbiting at 17,000 feet, led VS-41's third division in a wide, diving turn, to attack along the fore and aft axis of the *Jean Bart*, pushing over at 10,000 feet. Pete Carver later gave Lieutenant (jg) Twiddy credit for a hit with his 500-pounder, but Twiddy's ordnance had, in fact, hit the edge of the dock near the battleship's bow. A second bomb struck the *Jean Bart*'s catapult. Intense antiaircraft fire, from guns along the jetties and from the *Jean Bart*'s batteries, peppered the sky over Casablanca harbor, holing three VS-41 planes.[34] The *Ranger*'s pilots had added to the damage wreaked upon the Vichy French capital ship, which had also been hit by five 16-inch shells from the *Massachusetts*. Down by the stern, the *Jean Bart* appeared out of the fight.

As Lt. (jg) Ross, from Embree's third division, recovered from his dive, two Dewoitine D.520s attacked. Aviation Radioman 3d Class Devine returned fire with his twin .30-calibers, forcing one of the long-nosed French fighters to flee with a holed cowling. Ross chased the second D.520, and forced its pilot to think better of challenging the SBD, as 30 rounds from Ross's fixed .50-calibers drove off the second adversary. Almost simultaneously, as Lt. (jg) Bob Arthur, tail-end charlie of Count DeVane's second division, tried to join up, two Hawks deployed to attack. One opened up at long range, holing Arthur's tail surfaces, but Aviation Radioman 3d Class Morris Waterson, who had turned down an offer of over $200 to allow someone to take his place that morning, got a burst into the first Curtiss's engine and cockpit. The first H.75 headed for a cloud, trailing a thin wisp of white smoke. Waterson quickly fired at the second, which banked away and broke off the pursuit.

As Ralph Embree was leading the third division back to the *Ranger* at 1,000 feet, and between 10 and 12 miles offshore, he sighted a submarine, around 0745, clearly visible below the broken clouds, which lay beneath them at 500 to 700 feet. Embree noted the boat heading to the northwest at what looked like full speed, away from Casablanca. As soon as he had sighted the sub, however, he observed her flashing the correct challenge for the day: "negat" [N] "as rapidly as possible with a small portable light which had a definite reddish color."[35]

Embree had Joe Eardley, his radioman, respond with the correct answer to the "negat" [N] challenge: "dog" [D]. By that time, Embree and his division had overtaken the sub, and were leaving her behind on their port quarter. Assessing her lines, appearance, and the correct challenge, Embree felt sure that the boat was American. Opting not to attack, he maintained a course to return to the *Ranger*. Embree proved correct, because the boat was the *Gunnel* (SS-253), which had been off Casablanca since about midway through the second dog watch on 4 November.

Lieutenant (jg) Joe Keigher, however, flying number two on Embree's wing, peeled off. Embree radioed Keigher several times; while other pilots later declared that they had heard their division leader's orders to leave the boat alone, Keigher claimed he had not. In any event, Keigher dove and opened up with his fixed guns as the boat hastily submerged. Recognition on each side proved woefully poor: the *Gunnel*, which had suffered no damage in the encounter, later described her tormentor as an "Army P-40." Once the VS-41 pilot left her alone, the *Gunnel* surfaced to watch the bombardment of Casablanca.[36]

As Carver's, DeVane's, and Embree's divisions returned to the *Ranger* between 0743 and 0800, they encountered antiaircraft fire over the American support force. "For the record," Pete Carver later observed, "the most accurate A/A fire encountered by the squadron was that thrown at them by our own naval vessels, particularly those acting as a screen for the U.S.S. *Massachusetts*."[37] After the recovery of VF-9 (flights A-1, A-1A) and VS-41 (A-2), the *Ranger*'s flight deck crews toiled purposefully to ready the next strike. As Rear Admiral McWhorter reflected later, it seemed that the pilots seldom left their planes between flights, and, if they did, "they would just have time to get to the ready-room and grab a cup of coffee while the intelligence officers interrogated them."[38]

18
"A 'RED RIPPER SPECIAL'"

Mac Wordell's "VF-49" flight had joined up and proceeded directly to Fedala. After a 25-minute flight, the 16 F4Fs arrived over the objective and circled, VF-41's sections at 9,000 feet and VF-9's at 10,000. Wordell saw the transports lying offshore, northeast of Fedala, and the landings were underway. He noted a fire burning at the bend of the Mellah River nearest the road that lay close by it, and saw a pall of smoke hanging over the dockyard area. Antiaircraft fire from the French guns seemed scattered and ineffective.

The VF-41 sections joined up as trained, but the VF-9 pilots under Jake Onstott seemed to be having trouble doing so. Wordell had enjoined them to stay in groups of four, and never less than in pairs. Onstott's "groups" seemed composed of four, three, and one—one VF-9 pilot even broke radio silence to ask for instructions, showing, in Wordell's professional estimation, "poor indoctrination."

Wordell formed his sections into a "large elliptical defensive circle with a four at each cardinal point over the landing area," at 8,000 feet. For the next half hour, flight A-4 circled, observing and reporting. They saw the landings proceeding, as the boats landed without trouble. Swooping down low to look for antiaircraft guns, Wordell found it "impossible to tell who was firing on whom." He "desperately needed communication with the ground forces" and tried unsuccessfully to contact other *Ranger* flights.

Around 0815, he impatiently radioed the *Ranger*, seeking "another mission . . . things were too quiet." After having spent a little less than an hour orbiting Fedala, and unable to see the guns that would occasionally shoot at his sections, with only 60 gallons of gas remaining, Wordell decided "to look for trouble" at about 0820. He took his section with him, and left Lt. Keene G. "Kagey" Hammond's VF-41 section and the two VF-9 sections, under Onstott and O'Neill, over Fedala.

While an impatient Mac Wordell had been seeking a mission, a column of French warships had begun to stand out of Casablanca harbor around 0800. *Contre-Amiral* Raymond Gervais de Lafond, who had just celebrated his 52d birthday eight days before, had been in command of the *2ème Escadre Légère* [Second Light Squadron] since April, and had been decorated for bravery in battling a superior force of British destroyers in the eastern Mediterranean in June 1941. With his flagship, the light cruiser *Primauguet*, undergoing last-minute machinery repairs, Gervais de Lafond shifted his flag to the destroyer leader *Milan* to lead the squadron to sea. One by one, the light-gray ships, each bearing prominent brick red alphanumeric pendant numbers on their hulls, unmoored and got underway: the *Albatros* (the *Milan*'s sistership) and the destroyers *Brestois* and *Boulonnais* of the 5th Division; and the *L'Alcyon*, *Fougueux*, and *Frondeur* of the 2d. As the warships stood out, the dark-robed chaplain of the *Primauguet* stood, heedless of the shells still falling upon the waterfront, "his arm raised in blessing on the ships and men," who now sallied forth, tricolors bravely flying, *sans* air cover and with wholly inadequate antiaircraft batteries, to determine the identity of the foe.

Contre-Amiral Raymond Gervais de Lafond, commander of the *2ème Escadre Légère* in its valiant effort to disrupt the landings off Fedala, 8 November 1942. Among his tours of sea duty in the interwar period had been two in command of gunboats and four in destroyers; among his shore assignments, he had been naval attaché in Rome between September 1936 and August 1939. (*Service Historique de la Marine* via Mersky)

Wordell soon found the trouble he'd been looking for: "a French naval force consisting of one CL [light cruiser] and one DL [destroyer leader] . . . and 4 DDs [destroyers]" standing out of Casablanca harbor in column, bones-in-teeth, setting a course toward the waters off Fedala. Wordell, heading southwesterly, "with plenty of throttle" over the beach at 8,000 feet, reported the sortie of the French warships and that he was going to strafe them.[1]

Originally, Wordell had hoped to use eight planes to strafe the French ships, but Kagey Hammond's second section lay too far behind. Reasoning that he was in a good position to attack at that moment, Wordell decided not to summon Hammond and thus delay the assault. He knew the difficulty of coordinating "an attack on such a swell target using the most favorable approach, and [he] figured the CLs [most likely the *Milan* and the *Albatros*] could wait until later." Wordell peeled off, full gun, out of the sun, and barrelled toward the French ships from astern. "The approach," he later recounted, "was exactly what I wanted, a 'Red Ripper Special'—down wind, down sun, parallel to the fore and aft axis, with a clear area to retire in, about 260 knots." Disregarding the "light cruisers," which he hoped to attack next, Wordell went down the column of destroyers, "pouring in the lead from all six guns," and having a "glorious feeling to see the tracers pour into those ships."[2]

The French sailors manning the antiaircraft guns on board the lead destroyer, standing to their weapons with very little in the way of protection, proved worthy adversaries. Bullets from below soon began thudding against Wordell's left wing; his gunsight failed, and some of his guns in that wing stopped firing. Followed by Andrews, Craig, and Houston, Wordell retired at full speed ahead of the Vichy men-of-war, parallel to their course and just above the waves. As soon as he had cleared the immediate vicinity of the ships, Wordell took stock of his situation. One slug had perforated his left oil cooler, and he was losing lubricant. The inboard gun in the left wing was "smoking badly around the ammunition can," and one of his M-2 cartridges had caught fire, producing (as he noted with subsequent understatement) "a little fun in the cockpit." Although the burning cartridges resulted in "no great trouble," Wordell later noted, "enough is enough."[3]

Wordell's wingman, Andy Andrews, had inspected his leader's aircraft and called him over the radio to tell him the trouble. Wordell's oil pressure began to drop, so he decided to aim for reach Fedala, thinking that the place must have been in American hands by that point. Knowing that he was going to have to force-land BuNo 11707, Wordell radioed Andrews to fly ahead and pick out a spot to land on. As it turned out, all three of his section remained formed up on him—Andrews, Craig, and Houston, along with Lieutenant (jg) Bolt from Hammond's second VF-41 section—and they circled the area, as Wordell settled for what looked like a suitable field, about two and a half miles from Fedala and three miles inland.

Having fired off the rest of his ammunition to lighten the plane, Wordell went through the checkoff list, then cut his switch, once he was headed into the wind and sure of reaching the field. Applying full right aileron and some right rudder kept his mount steady and prevented it from stalling off to the left, but Wordell soon found that his flaps would not work, so he had to make a bit faster landing, downhill, than he wanted to, at about 0830. After a short time, one wheel hit a rock and sheared off the drag links for both landing gears; the Wildcat slid roughly across the rocky pasture, on the right wheel and left wingtip, until it hit a shell hole and nosed up enough to bend one propeller blade. Wordell, thankful that his shoulder straps had prevented him from being injured in the crash-landing, heard Andy Andrews calling over the radio, asking if there was anything else he could do. "Yes. Go back and get those damn destroyers."[4]

Wordell knew that those instructions had not been necessary, for he knew that Andrews, former high school and college student body president, would know, intuitively, what to do. "I had always felt that my section was the best fighting four in the navy. At that moment," he later reflected, "I was positive of it."[5] As he prepared to secure his radio, Wordell heard Tommy Booth communicating with his wingman, Boyd Mayhew, as the battle continued. Wordell climbed out of the cockpit and waved at his three sectionmates, who circled him twice.

At about the same time that Mac Wordell was preparing to make his way toward Fedala, the four planes that had orbited him while he had landed in the rocky pasture returned to the work that they had begun. The French ships had changed course, turning seaward initially, then resuming their earlier course along the coast, *Contre-Amiral* (then-*Capitaine de Vaisseau*) Gervais de Lafond essentially replicating the tactics he had used successfully off Syria in June 1941. The sleek ships formed two columns abreast and steamed determinedly toward Fedala.

The first attack, pressed home from astern, had seen all four sections of the mixed VF-41/VF-9 flight leaving no ship unfired-upon. The next three attacks found flight A-4's F4Fs attacking from ahead of the two columns. Buster Craig assumed the reins of Wordell's first section; Kagey Hammond, the second; Jake Onstott, the third; and Danny O'Neill, the fourth. The section leaders each singled out two ships on which to concentrate their .50-caliber fire, and, whenever possible, took advantage of the sun and smoke.

Before the weight of the Wildcats' strafing began to tell, however, the French had managed to make their presence felt. *Contre-Amiral* Gervais de Lafond's flagship, the *Milan*, had opened fire at 0820, scoring a direct hit on a landing boat off Yellow beach, west of Cape Fedala; the *L'Alcyon*, *Fougueux*, and *Frondeur* opened up at 0835. Soon, the French destroyers were engaging the destroyers *Ludlow* and *Wilkes*, the latter with Scouting Forty-One's Lieutenant Chase and Chief Abel on board. The *Ludlow* managed to score a direct hit on the *Milan*, but suffered a direct hit below the waterline in return; soon, the two American destroyers were falling back.

Flight A-4, however, had done their work with devastating thoroughness: the strafers knocked out the *Brestois*'s antiaircraft battery; killed *Capitaine de Corvette* Charles Martinant de Preneuf, the commanding officer of the *Boulonnais*; severely wounded the gunnery officer of the *Albatros*; and wounded almost everyone—including *Contre-Amiral* Gervais de Lafond—on the *Milan*'s bridge, with only the destroyer's captain, *Capitaine de Frégate* François Costet, surviving the onslaught unhurt. By the time flight A-4 retired, low on ammunition and fuel, it looked like the leading two ships had been set afire, with a great deal of smoke coming from the "light cruiser's" bow, and large gouts of smoke were issuing from the two leading destroyers. Afterwards, the two light cruisers reversed their courses and stood back toward Casablanca; the destroyers "turned seaward, milled around," and later followed the heavier ships back to port. Those who assessed flight A-4's mission considered it 100% completed.

Mac Wordell's adventures ashore, however, were just beginning, far from the action that he had initiated in strafing the French warships. Moroccans came running excitedly from nearby huts, as it soon became apparent that American guns were shelling the field. Wordell breathed a sigh of relief when he discerned that none of the locals possessed weapons, then detonated the charge to destroy the plane's homing device. Being so near Fedala and friendly forces militated against his destroying his plane, so he cut away his escape kit and the canvas bag that contained water and food, disregarding the growing throng gathered around the blue-gray Wildcat. Working quickly, he emptied his chart board, destroying one confidential code sheet and stuffing the rest of those papers inside his shirtfront. After throwing his goggles, Mae West, and radio microphone into the cockpit and securing the battery switch, Wordell "closed the hood and proceeded to face the mob."

Seeing that "they seemed more puzzled than myself," Wordell "jabbered some French at them and ordered one of the biggest men in the crowd to guard the plane." A quick inspection had revealed "plenty of holes in the left horizontal stabilizer and a few holes in the left wing." All in all, his mount looked "in pretty good shape and should be salvaged if and when." That having been done, Wordell set out across the rocky field, charting a course for Fedala.

Part of the "mob" began to follow Wordell across the field, when suddenly a shell landed nearby; shrapnel hit some of the natives, who screamed, terrified at what had just happened. One piece of shrapnel had also hit Wordell in the left leg. Limping into M. Pierre Feugnet's wine shop near a fork in the nearby road, Wordell broke out the sulfanilamide from his first aid kit and dressed the wound, which, although not serious, bled upon being cleaned out. After putting on a sterile bandage, Wordell swallowed his sulfa pills with a rum chaser, the latter courtesy of his host, M. Feugnet. Feeling better about his situation, Wordell decided to move on and try to reach Fedala. As he looked outside, however, he soon caught his first glimpse of the enemy: Spahis, native cavalry.

Using his best Naval Academy French, Wordell, whom his classmates considered as having a radiant smile and ready with a cheerful word that won him many friends, tried to bribe the amiable shopkeeper to hide him. M. Feugnet seemed amenable to the idea, but the presence of the throng of excited neighbors nullified any notions of secrecy; the presence of an American Navy pilot would not remain a secret for long.

Soon, the commander of the Spahi troop detailed a corporal to collect Wordell from the wine shop. As Wordell later recounted it, the swarthy soldier "seemed a little puzzled—not knowing whether to shoot me, have a drink with me, or what," but finally decided to ask, politely, for the pilot's pistol. "Since he [the corporal] had so many comrades," Wordell obligingly agreed to hand it over, but asked for a receipt which M. Feugnet wrote out. The corporal "signed" it with a thumbprint.

As soon as his guard left with his pistol, Wordell hobbled into the kitchen and burned what papers he carried, then gave away "all the articles that would not be needed in my trip to come." In the meantime, many of the local citizenry had congregated in the shop, all talking excitedly of the events transpiring around them, an animated discussion accompanied by the rumble of artillery in the background, some of it, as Wordell noted, "pretty close." Only one

Vichy French destroyer leader *Milan*, her brick-red pendant number X III visible on her side, listing to starboard and aground off Roches Noires, 16 November 1942; her bridge was almost completely destroyed by the bombs and bullets eight days before, when she had served as *Contre-Amiral* Gervais de Lafond's flagship. (NA, 80-G-31610)

Frenchman seemed openly friendly, producing one of the leaflets that had been dropped earlier that day, prompting the pilot to reflect that the Allied propaganda seemed "too mild," for the French seemed used to the "bolder, stronger, German type."[6]

In the meantime, M. Feugnet produced some roast duck and red wine. As Wordell dined on that modest repast, the Spahi corporal returned and informed him that they were to go to Casablanca. Wordell, knowing that the place lay right on the Fedala–Casablanca road, tried to stall for time, hoping that the American advance would soon overtake them. Despite his best efforts, however, the captive VF-41 pilot soon found himself painfully mounting up behind his guard and setting out for Casablanca, with the corporal bringing up the rear. They stopped at the plane long enough for the Spahis "to strip out the M-2 pistol, the radio cords, my life jacket, and a few other pieces of equipment"; the parachute and rubber boat, Wordell suspected, "had already been taken by the natives." They began the trip to Casablanca, alternately walking and riding, the latter causing Wordell's leg wound to bleed. The Spahis, "openly anxious to get on" with the journey, allowed him to walk for short periods.[7]

The *Ranger*'s receiving an urgent appeal for fighter support to repel French strafing attacks on landing craft, and the report of the unremitting attempts by *Contre-Amiral* Gervais de Lafond's gallant destroyermen to disrupt the landings, prompted her turning into the wind at 0840 to begin launching 10 VF-9 Wildcats, five minutes after Ensign McGann of Fighting Nine, from flight A-1(A), running low on fuel, had landed on board the *Suwanee*. Four F4F-4s, under Jack Raby, were to proceed to Fedala, thence to Port Lyautey, and to destroy any enemy forces encountered. Six, under Casey Childers, would take up CAP over the carrier.

FLIGHT A-5 (VF-9)

Lt. Comdr. John Raby   9-F-1
Ens. Marvin J. Franger, A-V(N)
Lt. (jg) Gordon M. Braun, A-V(N)
Ens. Albert E. Martin, A-V(N)

FLIGHT A-5(A) (VF-9)

Lt. Kenan C. Childers
Lt. (jg) Harold E. Vita, A-V(N)
Ens. Louis A. Menard, A-V(N)
Ens. Ernest D. Brooks, A-V(N)
Ens. James M. Wilkerson, A-V(N)
Ens. Charles W. Gerhardt, A-V(N)

Soon after the last of the Grummans roared over the ramp and wobbled on their way, as their pilots cranked up the gear, 15 SBD-3s from VS-41 began taking off into the wind at 0845, to rain destruction on the *2ème Escadre Légère*.

FLIGHT A-6 (VS-41)

First Division

Lt. Comdr. Lamar P. Carver
    Aviation Chief Radioman Reginald A. Miner
Lt. (jg) William H. Longley, A-V(N)
    Aviation Radioman 3d Class John G. Korecki
Lt. Cecil V. Johnson
    Aviation Radioman 2d Class Gerhard H. O. Kleiner
Lt. (jg) Robert H. Higley, A-V(N)
    Aviation Radioman 3d Class L. E. Colon
Ens. Charles C. Bevis, Jr., A-V(N)
    Aviation Radioman 3d Class William T. Shackelford
Ens. Charles J. Duffy, A-V(N)
    Aviation Radioman 3d Class George E. Biggs, Jr.
Lt. John M. DeVane, Jr.
    Aviation Radioman 1st Class William O. Haynes, Jr.
Lt. (jg) Woodie L. McVay, Jr., A-V(N)
    Aviation Radioman 2d Class Kenneth W. Jobe
Ens. Donald E. Chapman, A-V(N)
    Aviation Radioman 3d Class J. J. Lankowicz

Second Division

Lt. Ralph A. Embree
    Aviation Radioman 1st Class Joseph M. Eardley
Ens. Arthur L. Warta, A-V(N)
    Aviation Radioman 3d Class R. E. O'Connor
Lt. (jg) Harold R. Keller, Jr., A-V(N)
    Aviation Radioman 2d Class A. W. Lorentzen
Ens. George F. Dalton, A-V(N)
    Aviation Radioman 2d Class Aubra T. Patterson
Lt. (jg) Horace R. White, A-V(N)
    Aviation Radioman 3d Class A. R. Smith
Ens. Thomas M. Hubbard, A-V(N)
    Aviation Radioman 3d Class R. L. Fenton

Soon after the last SBDs had taken off, lookouts spotted two trawlers flying the Spanish ensign, five miles off the task group's starboard bow. The presence of four Spanish trawlers about an hour later prompted the *Ranger*'s navigator, Comdr. Frank M. Adams, to warn the neutral ships, utilizing the special talents of Master Sgt. Enrique Marcos, USMC, one of the *Ranger*'s Marines, who found unique employment during the efforts to warn away the neutral fishing vessels. Frustrated by the fishermen's behavior, Commander Adams tried to communicate by pantomime—hand signals and gestures. Master Sergeant Marcos read a message to the fishermen via the powerful Bogen flight deck bullhorns: get out of the way; proceed to the south for two hours or be sunk.

During that time, possessing insufficient gasoline to reach the *Ranger*, Lieutenant Hammond, Lieutenants (jg) Andrews, Cassidy, and Bolt, and Ensign Ball from flight A-4 landed on board the *Suwanee*, beginning at 0915, where Andrews found that his F4F-4, 41-F-10, had taken one hit under the emergency gasoline tank and a second aft of the cockpit.[8] "After refueling and rearming and pursuant to instructions received from [the] *Ranger*," the *Suwanee* launched Hammond's flight to fly CAP over their home base.[9] Arriving back on board the *Ranger*, Jake Onstott observed that the French heavy antiaircraft fire was "not good," but the lighter guns "better aimed."[10]

Casey Childers would find CAP over the task force uneventful; Jack Raby took his section to Fedala, but, after observing no enemy forces there, proceeded up the coast to Port Lyautey. Patrolling that area, Raby and his section spotted what looked like a Liore et Olivier (LeO) 45 at 400 feet, three miles off the coast and flying north, heading on an opposite course.

Fighting Nine's Wildcats turned and came up from directly astern; Jack Raby opened up at 150 yards, aiming for the twin-tailed bomber's port engine. Soon, the .50-caliber slugs hit home, and the engine burst into flame. Marv Franger approached the target and fired at the starboard engine, setting that afire as well. During the early part of the engagement, the plane had flown a straight, undeviating course, while the gunner opened fire, holing Raby's F4F. The gallant gunner's efforts, however, proved fruitless, for

Master Sergeant Enrique Marcos, USMC (L), with Lt. (jg) Louis L. Bernard, USNR (R), on the *Ranger*'s signal bridge, preparing to broadcast warnings to Spanish fishing vessels off Casablanca. (NA, 80-G-30368)

Raby and Franger teamed up to shoot down the plane, which plummeted into the sea and exploded upon hitting the water. No one saw any parachutes. Regrettably, a post-battle reckoning would indicate that Raby and Franger's victim was, most likely, a Lockheed Hudson from Coastal Command No. 233 Squadron, one of five such aircraft engaged in dropping leaflets on Casablanca, four of which were lost during Torch.[11]

The 15-plane VS-41 force under Lieutenant Commander Carver had completed its rendezvous and proceeded to a point midway between Casablanca and Fedala. From his viewpoint at 16,000 feet, Carver could see a battle in progress: the *Augusta* and the light cruiser *Brooklyn* (CL-40), accompanied by the destroyer *Swanson* (DD-443) and the *Wilkes*, were engaging the *2ème Escadre Légère*. All French ships appeared to be "giving off large quantities of heavy smoke," thus making it "impossible to determine from the air whether this was due to fires set by our forces' shell fire or was being artificially created as a screen."

Carver selected a "CL" as his target—most likely the destroyer leader *Milan*—and led VS-41's first division to the attack. To make a head-on approach, Carver and his troops attacked crosswind from the west, diving to the east, gliding from altitudes that ranged from 16,000 to 12,000 feet and diving to 2,000 feet to release their ordnance. All planes pulled out in the teeth of heavy antiaircraft fire, at altitudes that ranged from 300 to 1,000 feet. Unfortunately, the first division scored no direct hits, with Carver's bomb hitting about 15 feet from the starboard beam; Ensign Duffy later described seeing his bomb hit the water near the ship's starboard bow.

Ralph Embree's second division did little better, attacking downwind, from 16,000 feet, on an approach course that took them abeam the target from the starboard quarter to the port bow. Pilots soon discovered that the winds at that altitude were proving stronger than anticipated, compelling them to release their ordnance from a higher altitude. Ensign Hubbard, the last man to dive, reported that Lieutenant (jg) White, who had preceded him in the attack, had scored a hit on the target's bow. Flight A-6 also had had to contend with fogging bombsights, windshields, and instruments. In addition, the heavy smoke tended to hide the targets from view, and the contrary winds blew the second division over their target.

In the meantime, the *Ranger* recovered 8 VF-41 fighters from those she had launched after 0700 and 10 from the mixed VF-9 and VF-41 flight. Upon VF-41's subsequent return to the ship, Tommy Booth assessed his mission as "100% successful," despite the communications difficulties that had plagued it. "The French pilots seemed to lack aggressiveness," he noted, "but they did attack. Planes engaged from 17,000 feet down to 50 ft, within a 10 miles radius of Cazes." Flying in groups of three at the outset, the French "did not stay together in combat," preferring to fight or avoid "individually in dog fight fashion."[12]

Although Mac Wordell's time as a prisoner of war was just beginning, Chuck August still enjoyed his liberty—at least for the time being. After having set fire to his Wildcat, August, a local Frenchman, and a Moroccan, who had brought back the pilot's rolled-up parachute at the Frenchman's bidding, walked to a farmer's house about two blocks away. Given two shots of brandy, August noted that it was about 1000 Moroccan time (an hour later than the time observed by the Americans). The farmer "readily produced" a map and August conveyed to him his need to get to Fedala as soon as possible.[13]

Soon thereafter, a French doctor "with his very attractive wife" appeared, checked the pilot's pulse, and gestured "thumbs up." No sooner had the physician and his pretty spouse arrived on the scene, but so, too, did a truck bearing men wearing uniforms of the *Armee de l'Air*. *Sous-Lieutenant* Villaceque (who had been wounded that morning in the aerial combat over his field, when a .50-caliber bullet had shattered his windshield), along with three armed guards, took August into custody at 0935. Confiscating the American's pistol and flight gear, Villaceque and the guards drove him to Cazes.[14]

Likewise ending up at Cazes, at least for a brief time, was Ensign Mikronis, who noticed Dewoitines dispersed under trees, and something, he could not see what, burning. After being taken to a dressing station, where medical people applied bandages to his wound, he found himself missing all of his possessions, including his identification tag. Deemed in good enough shape to travel, Mikronis found himself placed in a private automobile with two armed, but "very friendly," guards, who transported him to Casablanca.[15]

As Wordell, Mikronis, and August began their captivity at the hands of the Vichy French, Spanky Carter still remained at liberty, drifting offshore. After about an hour in the water, however, the former two-time trombone soloist with the University of North Dakota concert band began to experience a chill that prompted him to inflate his rubber boat. Crawling in, he bailed it out and "relaxed comfortably in the warm sunshine." After a few minutes, however, Carter could see that the current was taking him toward the beach a little faster than he would have wanted. He also noted that "numerous characters whose intentions at the time I could not fathom . . . were regarding me with a great deal of interest if not moreso." He then "broke out the little paddles" and began rowing to keep away from the beach.[16]

Ensign Andrew B. Conner, A-V(N), sitting on the cockpit sill of [41-F-] 17 en route to North Africa, was the first *Ranger* pilot to ditch on 8 November; he was picked up by the destroyer *Ellyson*. (NA, 80-G-31321)

For the destroyers operating with the *Ranger*, the movements of the carrier governed their evolutions as they maintained the antisubmarine screen and reoriented on each course change. They also stood ready to rescue downed pilots, if the occasion demanded. One of the *Ranger*'s consorts was the destroyer *Ellyson*, which reported a surfaced submarine on the *Ranger*'s starboard bow at 0925, but the sub dove quickly and disappeared from sight. At 0946, Ens. Andrew Conner of VF-41, from flight A-3, ditched [41-F-]8 1,500 yards on the *Ellyson*'s starboard beam. Lowering her motor whaleboat, the *Ellyson* picked up Conner from off the *Ranger*'s port beam and brought him on board.

At 0945, the *Ranger* had commenced putting flight A-7 aloft—seven F4F-4s from VF-9, led by Pedro Winters, to destroy enemy aircraft in the air and on the ground at the aerodrome at Port Lyautey:

FLIGHT A-7 (VF-9)

First Section

Lt. Theodore H. Winters, Jr.	9-F-9
Ens. Thomas M. Wilhoite, A-V(N)	9-F-10 (BuNo 02023)
Lt. (jg) Mayo A. Hadden, Jr., A-V(N)	
Lt. (jg) Armistead B. Smith, Jr., A-V(N)	

Second Section

Lt. Edward Micka
Ens. Merle M. Hershey, A-V(N)
Ens. William J. Bonneau, A-V(N)

Arriving over the objective, Winters could see what appeared to be seven D.520s being refueled. Starting the first dive at 10,000 feet, VF-9's exec led his two sections on a series of low, fast, strafing runs, using erratic approaches to prevent the Vichy gunners from drawing a bead on the weaving Wildcats. Making the first attack from a generally westerly direction, Winters and his men made subsequent runs from various points of the compass. Fighting Nine, however, did not get away unscathed. Halfway through the second strafing run, two pilots in the first division heard Willie Wilhoite call out "They got me," shortly before his F4F, 9-F-10 (BuNo 02023) banked to the left and flew out of sight. Pedro Winters suffered lacerations from fragments when his plane took a direct hit through the cockpit. French antiaircraft hit two other F4Fs, but flickering flames and rolling columns of smoke testified that flight A-7 had given better than it had received.[17]

The tempo of flight operations remained high. The *Ranger* recovered VS-41's flight A-6, after their attack on the French ships off Casablanca, at 1004, as well as an additional VF-41 Wildcat from the earlier VF-9/VF-41 flight. Moments later, reflecting the submarine-consciousness of the escorts, one of the screening cruiser's floatplanes dropped a depth charge on what appeared to be a submarine off the *Ranger*'s port quarter.

At about the same time that the *Ranger* was bringing Pete Carver's troops on board, after their attacks on the French destroyer leaders and destroyers, the light cruiser *Primauguet* sortied from Casablanca harbor to support them; almost simultaneously, the destroyer *Boulonnaise*, her steering casualty rectified, joined her divisionmates. The *Ranger* soon monitored a radio message telling of the light cruiser *Brooklyn* engaging the French ships, in concert with the *Augusta*. The *Massachusetts*, the *Wichita*, and the *Tuscaloosa* came up to assist.

Soon, the overwhelming gunfire of the heavier American ships began to tell. The *Fougueux* disappeared in a forest of green and white splashes at about 1000; her sistership, the *Frondeur*, turned to starboard and began zig-zagging. Inside a quarter of an hour, the French destroyers, covered by the *Primauguet*, altered course toward Casablanca. Fires broke out on board the *Milan* as she emerged from a similar grove of green splashes, having taken three direct hits below the waterline and at least two or three below her bridge. The *Brestois* and the *Boulonnaise* attempted a torpedo attack; the *Augusta* sank the *Boulonnaise* and, in concert with the *Brooklyn*, damaged her sistership, which soon began zig-zagging behind a smoke screen, with the *Alcyon* (the only undamaged French ship) and the *Frondeur* joining on her.

Mac Wordell, as he neared Casablanca, enjoyed a low-angle "bird's eye view" of the battle, discerning three "rather large French DD's, two of which were on fire. They were taking an awful lacing from the *Brooklyn*, the *Augusta*, and a few supporting DD's. The fall of shot was beautiful, with the colored dye, but too many were not close enough to suit me. The French DD's wiggled and squirmed but all in vain." The sight of four F4Fs passing low overhead in a sharp right-hand circle prompted him to wave his helmet in hopes of attracting their attention. Their pilots, however, were apparently watching the unfolding engagement.[18]

At 1015, the *Ranger* had recovered two F4F-4s from the *Suwanee*, part of a mixed VGF-27/VGF-28 flight under Lt. Sam L. Silber, A-V(N), which had been launched at the end of the morning watch and had flown CAP over the *Ranger* and their parent ship. The *Ranger* then commenced launching four VF-9 F4Fs, under Jake Onstott, and the two *Suwanee* Wildcats, for CAP over the ship at 1053.

FLIGHT A-8 (VF-9)

Lt. Jacob W. Onstott
Lt. Hugh D. O'Neill, Jr., A-V(N)
Lt. (jg) Reuben H. Denoff, A-V(N)
Lt. (jg) Harrison Feasley, A-V(N)

At 1055, the *Ranger* began launching flight A-9, under Fighting Forty-One's skipper, Tommy Booth. Their mission was to fly combat air patrol over Fedala, Rabat-Salé, and Port Lyautey, and to destroy any enemy aircraft encountered, whether they were in the air or on the ground, as well as any ground installations.

FLIGHT A-9 (VF-41)

Lt. Comdr. Charles T. Booth, II	[41-F-]1
Lt. (jg) Boyd N. Mayhew, A-V(N)	[41-F-]2
Lt. Theodore A. Grell	[41-F-]3
	(BuNo 02136)
Lt. (jg) George M. Harris, Jr., A-V(N)	[41-F-]4
Lt. Herold J. Weiler, Jr.	[41-F-]5
Lt. (jg) Dee Jones, A-V(N)	[41-F-]6
Lt. Ernest W. Wood, Jr.	[41-F-]7
Lt. Maynard M. Furney, A-V(N)	[41-F-]21
Ens. Robert C. Cronin, A-V(N)	[41-F-]25
Lt. Earle F. Craig	[41-F-]11
Lt. (jg) Hubert T. Houston, A-V(N)	[41-F-]12

Tommy Booth's troops proceeded to Port Lyautey via Fedala and Rabat-Salé, urged on by a radio message from the *Ranger*, which told of the flight being "badly needed" there. A little over a quarter of an hour later, the *Ranger* recovered four of the six F4Fs from the *Suwanee*'s VGF-30, which had originally been launched under Lt. Comdr. Michael P. "Bag" Bagdanovich for CAP over the *Sangamon* off Mehdia. After servicing the transient Wildcats, the *Ranger* launched them to fly another CAP mission.

In the meantime, Chuck August, courtesy of *Sous-Lieutenant* Villaceque, had reached Cazes, where the pilots from GC II/5 began questioning the American—less in the nature of an interrogation than in the spirit of genuine curiosity, one professional airman to another. They asked him what kind of an aircraft he had flown, how many pilots the Americans had lost. August, in turn, asked them how many planes they had sent up and how many had been lost.

"Eighteen planes had been sent up," Villaceque responded, "six had been seen to crash, four had returned, and eight are missing." One of the Vichy pilots chimed in that one of August's shipmates, Ensign Mikronis, "was in their informary with a bullet wound in his right cheek which was not serious." Taken thence to see the commanding officer of the station, August noticed "at least a dozen Dewoitine 520s [sat] parked in the north side of the east–west runway" and what appeared to be "many" military and commercial planes in a large hangar north of the east–west runway. There also appeared to be D.520s and H.75s in tents beside the runway.[19]

Once in the station commander's office, a room strewn with glass from shattered windows, August encountered a *Lieutenant* Maison, who served as the interpreter. The commander asked, through Maison, for August's name, rank, and serial number, then asked whether or not the British (for whom the French harbored a particularly virulent hatred, after Mers El-Kebir and Oran in the summer of 1940) had taken part in the operations. August assured them that the British had not, and no further questions on the attack ensued. At that point, someone asked August if he had any concealed weapons on his person.

"Are you referring to firearms?" August responded. "If so, the answer is no." The equivocal nature of August's answer, however, apparently made *Lieutenant* Maison nervous, for the French officer quickly broadened his definition of "weapon" and "promptly mentioned knives." August wordlessly pulled up his right trouser leg to reveal a 10-inch hunting knife in a scabbard attached to his leg. *Lieutenant* Maison, "rather annoyed," asked August: "Did you intend to stick it in my back when I wasn't looking?"[20]

August reflected later that the French officers at Cazes exhibited friendliness and courtesy throughout the entire time he was there, "frequently remarking in a regretful, rather than resentful manner [when referring to the events of the morning], 'This is bad, bad.'" At their request, he also joined them as their lunch guest at their mess, dining on "one boiled egg, sliced tomatoes, French bread, and two glasses of dry wine."[21]

At 1145, probably around the time that August was partaking of the modest repast with his French hosts, the *Ranger* began launching flight A-9(A), whose mission was to proceed to Port Lyautey and to seek out and destroy any resistance encountered.

FLIGHT A-9(A) (VF-9)

First Section

Lt. Comdr. John Raby
Ens. Marvin J. Franger, A-V(N)
Lt. (jg) Gordon M. Braun, A-V(N)   9-F-25 (BuNo 5206)
Ens. Albert E. Martin, A-V(N)

Second Section

Lt. Kenan C. Childers
Ens. Louis A. Menard, A-V(N)
Lt. (jg) Harold E. Vita, A-V(N)
Ens. Charles W. Gerhardt, A-V(N)

Third Section

Lt. (jg) Jack H. Sands, A-V(N)
Ens. Ernest D. Brooks, A-V(N)
Ens. Hamilton McWhorter, III, A-V(N)

19

"LOOKING FOR TARGETS OF OPPORTUNITY"

Having received word that several French naval vessels, including those previously attacked, were still in action, but proceeding toward the entrance of Casablanca harbor, the *Ranger* prepared flight A-10 to prevent those ships from getting into a position to bottle up the harbor, and began launch at 1053. To augment A-10, the *Ranger* launched one TBF-1, retained for special missions, flown by Comdr. "Bash" Overfield, CRAG, directly afterwards.

FLIGHT A-10 (VS-41)

First Division

Lt. Comdr. Lamar P. Carver   41-S-17 (BuNo 06620)
    Aviation Chief Radioman Reginald A. Miner
Lt. (jg) Cyrus F. Weeks, A-V(N)
    Aviation Radioman 3d Class C. H. Perry
Lt. (jg) Joseph P. Keigher, Jr., A-V(N)
    Aviation Radioman 3d Class J. J. Lankowitz
Lt. Cecil V. Johnson
    Aviation Radioman 2d Class Gerhard H. O. Kleiner
Lt. (jg) Ralph W. Ross, A-V(N)
    Aviation Radioman 3d Class L. J. Devine
Lt. John M. DeVane, Jr.
    Aviation Radioman 1st Class William O. Haynes, Jr.
Lt. (jg) John G. McReynolds, Jr., A-V(N)
    Aviation Radioman 3d Class Oscar I. Light
Lt. (jg) Maxwell A. Eaton, A-V(N)
    Aviation Radioman 3d Class William T. Shackelford

Second Division

Lt. Ralph A. Embree
    Aviation Radioman 1st Class Joseph M. Eardley
Lt. (jg) Clyde A. Tucker, Jr., A-V(N)
    Aviation Radioman 3d Class Lloyd E. Edens
Lt. Clarence A. Twiddy, Jr., A-V(N)
    Aviation Radioman 3d Class R. E. O'Connor
Lt. (jg) Horace R. White, A-V(N)
    Aviation Radioman 3d Class A. R. Smith
Lt. (jg) Robert L. Arthur, A-V(N)
    Aviation Radioman 3d Class Morris S. Waterson

FLIGHT A-11 (CRAG)

Lt. Comdr. David B. Overfield   C
    Aviation Radioman 1st Class Jack L. Aday
    Aviation Machinist's Mate 2d Class Reginald H. Miller

At 1100, the *Ranger* experienced her first operational loss of the day, when Pete Carver's SBD-3 lost power and crashed soon after leaving the ramp. The *Corry* sped to the scene and rescued Carver and Aviation Chief Radioman Miner, the radio-gunner, as their plane, 41-S-17 (BuNo 06620), sank. Fortunately, both men suffered only minor lacerations in the ditching.[1] Carver's loss elevated Ralph Embree to command of Scouting Forty-One.

The French warships that lay ahead of them had been badly mauled in the morning's action. Cruiser gunfire had damaged the *Milan*, the *Albatros*, the *Frondeur*, and the

Lieutenant Comdr. Lamar P. Carver (R), commanding officer of VS-41, and Aviation Chief Radioman Reginald A. Miner (L), his radio-gunner, en route to North Africa, ca. November 1942. (NA, 80-G-31347)

Primauguet. The *Milan* was beached initially near the *Jettie Delure*, then near Roches Noires; the *Primauguet* anchored off the latter, as well. The badly damaged *Brestois* anchored outside the harbor entrance off the *Jettie Delure*; the *Frondeur*, down by the stern, had managed to reach the inner harbor.[2] During that time, Mac Wordell and his Spahi guards had reached the outskirts of the city and saw two of the beached French destroyers off Roches Noires: "One was down by the stern pretty badly."[3]

Count DeVane assumed the lead of the first division and attacked the *Albatros*—the ship already having suffered two hits from the gunfire of the *Wichita* and the *Tuscaloosa*—pushing over at 13,000 feet toward the south, and along the destroyer leader's fore-and-aft axis. Of the seven pilots who dove, DeVane and Lieutenants (jg) Eaton and McReynolds, reported hits. The other four, Lieutenant Johnson and Lieutenants (jg) Weeks, Keigher, and Ross, all obtained near-misses. The *Albatros*, having taken at least two hits from the VS-41 attack, which flooded a fireroom and one engine room, pugnaciously engaged the *Augusta* and promptly received one hit from her larger adversary. She suffered at least 25 killed and 80 wounded of her 200-man complement.

Ralph Embree led the attack on the *Primauguet*, the light cruiser already having taken hits from the eight-inch guns of the *Augusta* and the six-inch of the *Brooklyn*, coming in from the north over Fedala. Pushing over at 12,000 feet, Embree's troops released their ordnance at 1,500 feet and retired seaward. Lieutenant (jg) Tucker claimed a

Vichy French destroyer *Albatros*, down by the bow and listing to port, tricolors still flying from the foremast and aft. Her third funnel has been destroyed. View taken 16 November 1942. (NA, 80-G-31611)

direct hit on the starboard bow; Lieutenant (jg) Arthur believed one of his two 100-pounders hit the target squarely. As VS-41's second division retired, strafing the other destroyers as they did so, the old light cruiser seemed to be a mass of flames and a shambles amidships. She was, however, still afloat, and, almost amazingly, some of her guns were still firing. Two of VS-41's planes came away holed by the antiaircraft fire, but not badly enough to render them unserviceable.

At 1130, Lt. (jg) Horace White, of VS-41's second division, spotted what appeared to be a group of four submarines, fully submerged, proceeding as a group a mile off shore and approximately midway between Casablanca and Fedala. White immediately radioed a report of what he had seen.

Lieutenant Commander Overfield had rendezvoused with the SBDs and proceeded to Fedala, climbing en route. Once Overfield reached the objective, he circled the area at 15,000 feet, then broke away from VS-41 and remained eastward of Fedala, so that he could utilize a down-sun approach on the target. He remained in the vicinity for about 20 minutes, endeavoring to locate the battery. About five to six miles north of Pont Blondin, the CRAG observed smoke puffs, but could discern no gun flashes. Assuming that to be his target, Overfield opened his bomb bay doors and approached from up-sun. He informed his crew to be ready to attack, but soon heard Aviation Machinist's Mate 2d Class Reginald H. "Buddy" Miller, manning his position in the TBF's belly, report that the four 500-pound bombs had fallen when the bomb bay doors had opened, thus leaving Overfield no ordnance to drop on the target.

At 1150, the *Ranger* launched a portion of flight A-12, the pilots having been entrusted with a threefold mission: CAP over the ship, destroy enemy bombers over Fedala, and destroy whatever enemy aircraft or warships were encountered. The *Suwanee* launched the other, consisting of four of the five pilots from flight A-4 (Hammond, Bolt, Cassidy, and Ball) who had been unable to reach the *Ranger* earlier that morning.[4]

FLIGHT A-12 (VF-41)

First Section (VF-41)

Lt. Keene G. Hammond
Lt. (jg) William H. Bolt, Jr., A-V(N)
Lt. (jg) Arthur J. Cassidy, A-V(N)
Ens. Philip S. Ball, Jr., A-V(N)

Second Section (VF-41/VF-9*)
(Asterisk indicates VF-9 pilot)

Lt. (jg) Edwin N. Seiler, A-V(N)
Ens. Will "W" Taylor, A-V(N)
Lt. (jg) Edmund J. Kelly, A-V(N)
Ens. James E. Toliver, A-V(N)*

Flight A-12 took up their CAP over the *Ranger*, but soon Kagey Hammond received orders to take his sections over to Fedala to destroy enemy bombers that had been reportedly attacking the troops landing there. Although Hammond found no French planes aloft, he did see them on the ground at Cazes, and soon led the attack on that aerodrome, diving from 6,500 feet and strafing in the east–west direction. Pulling up after their attack, the VF-41/VF-9 flight pushed over from 5,500 feet for a second run. Fire blossomed from five of the seven planes found there; of the seven that remained, two looked like they had already been destroyed. Satisfied that they had hit all of the machines on the field, Hammond noticed that there had only been three or four bursts of antiaircraft fire during their attack. Returning from their mission, Hammond and his troops dove from 5,000 feet and strafed a French destroyer, diagonally from the port quarter, but failed to slow her down as she doggedly continued toward the harbor entrance. The pilots noted negligible antiaircraft fire from the ship that they had attacked, the destroyer having also been in company with what looked like a destroyer and a light cruiser.

At high noon, the *Ranger* launched flight A-14 to proceed via Fedala to Port Lyautey and to destroy enemy forces resisting the landing of American troops. Soon thereafter, the *Suwanee* launched Ens. Bob McGann of VF-9 and two F4Fs from VGF-27, to fly CAP over the *Ranger*.

FLIGHT A-14 (VF-9)

Lt. Jacob W. Onstott
Lt. (jg) Reuben H. Denoff, A-V(N)
Lt. Hugh D. O'Neill, Jr., A-V(N)
Lt. (jg) Harrison Feasley, A-V(N)

Antiaircraft guns had fired at Tommy Booth's flight from positions surrounding Rabat-Salé, but generally the passage of the 11 VF-41 Wildcats had been without incident. They maintained an altitude of between 8,000 and 10,000 feet, and observed no enemy activity for about 30 minutes. After that half hour over Port Lyautey, Ham Weiler, of the second section, radioed his CO that he saw French guns firing upon the landing barges approaching Mehdia. Occasionally, antiaircraft fire came up at the flight, but it proved ineffectual. At about 1215, Booth led his flight on a strafing run on a battery about three miles west of Port Lyautey.

After silencing the French guns, VF-41 rendezvoused over Port Lyautey at 7,000 feet. Upon completion of their attacks, Tag Grell and Lieutenant (jg) Harris proceeded out to sea, trying to make the *Ranger*. Apparently, Grell's F4F had taken hits in the fuel system, for he signaled to Harris that he was out of gas, and soon ditched his Wildcat about 800 to 1,000 yards from some fishing smacks and about 10 miles from the *Ranger*. Harris saw Grell swimming toward those boats, with his life jacket inflated, and hastened to return to the ship, landing and relating the story of Grell's ditching. Thankfully, one of the ubiqitous fishing vessels plucked the downed pilot from the sea.

At 1300, another VF-9 flight, A-15, took off from the *Ranger* to fly protective cover over the landings continuing at Port Lyautey.

FLIGHT A-15 (VF-9)

Lt. Edward Micka
Lt. (jg) Mayo A. Hadden, Jr., A-V(N)
Ens. Merle M. Hershey, A-V(N)
Lt. (jg) Armistead B. Smith, Jr., A-V(N)

Jake Onstott, Rube Denoff, Danny O'Neill, and Jim Feasley, from flight A-14, observed no enemy forces at Fedala, but observed "two large and two small steamers and three small trawlers aground" in a cove 10 miles to the north of there. The vessels seen by the pilots were probably the ships of the Vichy French convoy encountered at 1241 by the minesweeper *Auk* (AM-57) and the destroyer *Tillman* (DD-641). The convoy escort, the surveying vessel *Estafette*, had defiantly refused to heave to and had bravely opened fire on the American ships. In the ensuing unequal contest, the *Tillman*'s heavier guns damaged the *Estafette* and forced her, along with three other ships in the convoy, aground.

Ranging up and down the beach, Onstott and his troops then returned to the skies over Fedala, "looking for targets

Port Lyautey, 11 November 1942; chartered merchant ship *Contessa* lies in the Wadi Sebou (upper right). (NA, 80-G-37241)

of opportunity." At altitudes ranging from 200 to 500 feet, they found themselves targets, as French antiaircraft guns scored hits on one Wildcat, before they flew out of range. En route back to the ship, Onstott noted three SOC floatplanes on the disengaged side of the *Massachusetts*, and three cruisers bombarding Casablanca.

Eddie Micka's flight A-15 encountered poor flying conditions—low ceiling, steady rain, and poor visibility—but no enemy forces. Fighting Nine's pilots did see, however, that the French batteries at Port Lyautey seemed to be quite active, drawing fire from one battleship, one heavy cruiser, and one destroyer. They also saw a pair of SOCs at 5,000 feet, spotting for a battleship and a cruiser. Picking out what appeared to be gun emplacements, Micka led his men in a strafing attack. He came away feeling that they had silenced coastal guns and an antiaircraft battery. From his vantage point, Micka saw that, although the landing forces appeared to be making good headway, they had not moved much beyond the beach.

Chuck August's imprisonment continued. Accompanied by an armed guard and a driver, August and *Lieutenant* Maison embarked in a small sedan and left Cazes for Casablanca at about 1245 (Moroccan time). En route, the French officer politely asked his prisoner if August would permit him to retain his hunting knife as a souvenir. August assented.[5]

In the meantime, Ensign Mikronis had reached Casablanca for interrogation at the *Marine National* headquarters. Two French officers questioned him, as did what appeared to be a German, who questioned him in English. Mikronis provided them with only name and rank. To the rest of the queries—where he was from, where he called home, if a convoy—had come via Gibraltar, and how many ships, planes, and troops were in the convoy—Mikronis only said: "I am not permitted to tell you." Silence greeted his replies. Mikronis's captors then produced his personal gear, examined it, and placed it in a bundle. They seemed the most curious about his fountain pen and the two packages of Life Saver candy, before they sent him to the nearby hospital, *sans* his gear, in the same car that had transported him from Cazes.[6]

Mikronis took note of his surroundings after the car broke down two blocks from the *Marine National* headquarters.

He saw craters blown in railroad tracks, and two railroad cars off the tracks, as if they had been toys rudely tossed aside by a wanton child. Workmen busily repaired holes in the streets. The concussion of exploding shells had blown out many windows. Within 5–10 minutes, Mikronis and his captors had resumed their drive through the streets of Casablanca to the hospital.[7]

Reports that the *Primauguet* still posed a threat, firing from a position directly outside the entrance to Casablanca harbor, prompted the dispatch of a dozen SBDs from VS-41 to deal with her. At 1308, soon after Eddie Micka had led his section toward Port Lyautey, the *Ranger* commenced launching flight A-16.

FLIGHT A-16 (VS-41)

First Division

Lt. Comdr. Ralph A. Embree
    Aviation Radioman 1st Class Joseph M. Eardley
Lt. (jg) William H. Longley, A-V(N)
    Aviation Radioman 3d Class John G. Korecki
Ens. Arthur L. Warta, A-V(N)   41-S-2
    Aviation Radioman 3d Class Aubra T. Patterson

Lt. (jg) Harold R. Keller, Jr., A-V(N)
    Aviation Radioman 2d Class A. W. Lorentzen
Ens. George F. Dalton, A-V(N)
    Aviation Radioman 2d Class R. J. Monahan
Ens. Thomas M. Hubbard, A-V(N)
    Aviation Radioman 2d Class R. L. Fenton

Lt. (jg) Woodie L. McVay, Jr., A-V(N)
    Aviation Radioman 2d Class Kenneth W. Jobe
Ens. Charles J. Duffy, A-V(N)   41-S-9
        (BuNo 06641)
    Aviation Radioman 3d Class George E. Biggs, Jr.

Second Division

Lt. Cecil V. Johnson
    Aviation Radioman 2d Class Gerhard H. O. Kleiner
Ens. Charles C. Bevis, Jr., A-V(N)
    Aviation Radioman 3d Class Oscar I. Light

Lt. (jg) Robert H. Higley, A-V(N)
    Aviation Radioman 3d Class L. E. Colon
Lt. (jg) Clyde A. Tucker, Jr., A-V(N)   41-S-6
        (BuNo 06630)
Aviation Radioman 3d Class Lloyd E. Edens

The necessity of conducting photographic reconnaissance of Casablanca harbor and the coast north to Port Lyautey prompted the dispatch of one F-56 20-inch camera-equipped F4F-4, flown by Lt. John R. "Jawn" Sweeney, one of the two trained photo-recon pilots in the squadron. His photo-configured F4F-4 carried four .50-caliber guns for its own protection, with 920 rounds (tracer, incendiary, and armor-piercing) of ammunition.

FLIGHT A-17 (VF-41)

Lt. John R. Sweeney   [41-F-]28

Tommy Booth and his remaining planes had patrolled the Port Lyautey area for 30 more minutes, before Ham Weiler signaled that he was low on gas. Consequently, he tried to reach the *Ranger* in company with Woodie Wood and Lieutenant (jg) Jones, but they soon discovered that they could not reach their home deck. Fortunately, the auxiliary aircraft carrier *Sangamon* was operating nearby, so the three VF-41 pilots landed on board her, returning later to their own deck after refueling. Tommy Booth returned to the *Ranger* at 1330, landing 15 minutes later. The exigencies of war permitted him little rest: less than an hour after Ralph Embree had led flight A-18 off on its mission, Booth took off in the lead of a group of 16 F4F-4s, (14 from his own squadron and 2 from VF-9), to bomb shore batteries at El Hank and "targets of opportunity." Takeoff began at 1400, each Wildcat loaded with 1,420 rounds of ammunition (20% tracer, 30% incendiary and 50% armor-piercing) per plane. Nine planes (the rest had no racks installed) carried two 100-pound demolition bombs.

FLIGHT A-18 (VF-41/VF-9*)

Lt. Comdr. Charles T. Booth, II
Lt. (jg) Boyd N. Mayhew, A-V(N)

Lt. Earle F. Craig
Lt. (jg) Hubert T. Houston, A-V(N)

Lt. Maynard M. Furney, A-V(N)
Lt. (jg) Walter E. Laake, A-V(N)

Lt. (jg) Clyde C. Andrews, A-V(N)
Ens. Burton L. Bardeen, A-V(N)*

Lt. Keene G. Hammond
Lt. (jg) William H. Bolt, Jr., A-V(N)

Lt. (jg) George M. Harris, Jr., A-V(N)
Ens. Philip S. Ball, Jr., A-V(N)

Lt. (jg) Edmund J. Kelly, A-V(N)
Lt. (jg) George E. Harris, A-V(N)

Ens. Will "W" Taylor, A-V(N)
Lt. (jg) Stanton M. Amesbury, A-V(N)*

Lieutenant Jawn Sweeney takes off on a photo-reconnaissance hop, 8 November 1942, flying Forty-One-Fox-Twenty-Eight. Note that his F4F-4 carries drop tanks, has only two .50-caliber machine guns in each wing instead of the usual three, and that the yellow surround obscures part of the plane's side number. (NA, 80-G-30311)

Jack Raby's troops had proceeded first to Fedala and, after observing no enemy activity there, flew up the coast to Port Lyautey, covering the beach. They overflew the aerodrome there, and observed no enemy aircraft or any other enemy forces. They then overflew the road to Petitjean, but saw no enemy forces there, either. Flying back to Rabat-Salé, VF-9 encountered some antiaircraft fire that proved ineffective.

Casey Childers's second section had flown at 8,000 feet, covering the other two sections that had been engaged in the active searching. From their Olympian vantage point, it seemed like the landings at Port Lyautey were meeting little French resistance. Jack Raby later submitted that it appeared that active resistance to the landing had either been destroyed or had ceased voluntarily between 1015 and 1215. Gordon Braun ran out of gas and glided to a smooth landing in the water 1,500 yards off the *Ellyson*'s starboard beam at 1423, and that destroyer lowered her motor whaleboat and welcomed a second *Ranger* pilot on board that day, Andy Conner having been the first. Although the first two sections managed to reach the *Ranger* safely, the last section, under Jack Sands—Sands, Doug Brooks, and Mac McWhorter—had to land on board the *Suwanee*, instead.

While VF-9's flight A-9(A) had been returning to their home base, Ralph Embree and his flight had been nearing Casablanca; they pushed over from seaward at 15,000 feet, releasing their bombs at 1,000 to 1,500. Lieutenants Embree and Johnson, and Ensign Duffy, each scored direct hits on the already battered *Primauguet*; Ensigns Bevis, Dalton, and Hubbard had near-misses. Each pilot strafed nearby destroyers after pull-out, but encountered heavy antiaircraft fire during and immediately following the attack. Four TBFs from the *Suwanee*'s VGF-27, led by Lt. Comdr. Milton A. Nation, added to the destruction wreaked on the French ships: Three scored one direct hit,

Sorting and annotating prints following a photo-reconnaissance mission. Note bare steel bulkheads, stanchions, and ventilation ducts which mutely testify to the extensive paint-stripping efforts carried out en route to North Africa. (NA, 80-G-30313)

one probable, and six near near-misses of twelve 325-pound depth charges dropped on a "CA" in Casablanca's outer harbor, one TBF scoring one hit and three near-misses on a "CL" or destroyer leader. The final attacks on the *Primauguet* wrecked the forward half of the ship; a direct hit on the bridge had killed nine officers, including her commanding officer, *Capitaine de Vasseau* Mercier, and the executive officer.

Embree noted that at least 10 of the 12 planes joined up after the attack, with the eleventh, Clyde Tucker's, lagging to the rear, but gaining. At that juncture, one of the VS-41 pilots spotted something in the water below, about 10 to 12 miles from shore, which at first glance and at a distance, resembled a submarine. Closer examination revealed the object to be a capsized SOC-1 (BuNo 9922) from the *Wichita*, which had been shot down by an H.75A earlier that morning. Embree could see that the battleship *Massachusetts* and two destroyers steamed nearby, on a course that would bring them near the plane. Fortunately, the SOC's pilot, Lt. Donald E. Anderson, A-V(N) (who had suffered a broken bone in his right arm from a French bullet) and Radioman 2d Class C. F. Duke had been rescued by a fishing vessel.

Embree led his flight down to low altitude, to circle and call attention to the downed plane, then reformed to return to the *Ranger*. A count soon thereafter, however, disclosed only eleven planes, with Ensign Duffy's 41-S-9 missing. Mickey Edens, Clyde Tucker's radio-gunner, had seen 41-S-9 pull out of its dive, but then had lost sight of it.[8]

Almost simultaneously, several pilots and radiomen noticed Aviation Radioman 3d Class Aubra T. "Pat" Patterson,

The Vichy French light cruiser *Primauguet*, beached and burned-out, November 1942. Note extensive fire damage, forward; the ship lost 90 killed, including her captain, and over 200 wounded (over half her complement) on 8 November. (AUTHOR)

Ensign Warta's radio-gunner in 41-S-2, who had volunteered to serve as a radioman on this and one previous mission (and who had only that morning turned down an offer of $230 to give up his place), slumped in his seat, facing aft. The young radioman's head had rolled to one side and his mouth appeared open. Embree immediately radioed Warta, told him of Patterson's plight, and instructed him to get back to the *Ranger* "as quickly as possible."

Consequently, Warta approached the ship and signaled for an emergency landing. "I saw a scout circling around," Lt. William A. Stuart, the *Ranger*'s LSO, later recounted, "and giving me the sign he had to get down." Bill Stuart brought him in, and, at 1425, the *Ranger* recovered Warta's SBD. A grim sight awaited those who looked into the after cockpit of 41-S-2 soon afterward: Pat Patterson was dead, his right leg shot off just above the knee.

A five-plane CAP from the *Suwanee* (four F4Fs from VGF-27 and one from VGF-28, under Lt. Jack A. Mahony, Jr.) covered the *Suwanee* and the *Ranger*, as the latter recovered the rest of flight A-21, between 1425 and 1435. As for Ensign Duffy and Bugs Biggs, his radio-gunner, no one ever saw 41-S-9 again.[9]

Chuck August's POW experience continued, as he arrived at the *Marine National* headquarters in Casablanca "for interrogation." For an hour, August stood in silence in the lobby of the building, under guard, before armed sailors then marched him a half block down the street to the *Marine National* Prison. There, his captors relieved him of his cigarettes, lighter, money, pocket knife, fountain pen, and "Allah Be Praised" booklet, but let him retain his identification tag and a silver wristlet. As his guards marched him to the door of a dark cell, August heard a voice from

Plane handlers push 41-S-9, an SBD-3 (BuNo 06641), past number two elevator, 8 November 1942. This aircraft would be lost, most likely to Vichy French antiaircraft fire, later that day. Note ordnanceman trundling bomb in right foreground, and .30-caliber Browning machine guns in the catwalk as added close-in defense. (NA, 80-G-30303)

within say in English: "Have a seat." The heavy oak door locked behind him, the VF-41 pilot found Tom Dougherty of the *Massachusetts*.[10]

August found that his cell measured about 4½ wide by 10 feet long, with a 15-foot ceiling. A six-inch square peephole in the door admitted some light, but not much came from the half-inch holes drilled in the boards that covered the barred window at the other end of the room. A platform of 3-by-12-inch planks, and one army blanket, was evidently to serve as a sleeping platform for the two men.[11]

One of August's shipmates, meanwhile, was busy. Jawn Sweeney, a man whom his USNA classmates considered to possess "unbounded" courage (a good quality to have when conducting unescorted photo reconnaissance missions), found good flying weather en route to his objective. Approaching the coast from the south of Ain Diab, he began taking photographs over Casablanca harbor at 21,000 feet, before he proceeded up the coast. After finding clouds covering the shoreline almost as far as Port Lyautey, Sweeney reversed course and took a reverse duplicate run of photos along the coast and through Casablanca, before he headed for home.

En route to El Hank and other targets of opportunity, VF-41's flight A-18 encountered two of the latter an hour into the mission, when Lieutenant (jg) Mayhew spotted the conning tower of a fully surfaced submarine roughly southeast by south, as he flew toward the coast. Soon thereafter, the VF-41 pilots saw a second boat. Assigning the targets by radio, Tommy Booth led his flight into a climbing turn. Pushing over into a 45-degree dive from 8,000 feet, from up-sun, Booth's and Furney's sections attacked one boat, Hammond's and Kelly's the second. Opening up with all six

Ensign Charles J. Duffy, A-V(N) (R), with Aviation Radioman 3d Class George E. "Bugs" Biggs, Jr., (L) his radio-gunner, standing on the wing of an SBD-3 (BuNo 06620), 41-S-17, ca. November 1942; both men would be lost in 41-S-9 on 8 November, each on his second mission of the day. Duffy, a 22-year-old New Yorker, had earned a physical education degree from Manhattan College in 1941, and played semipro baseball with the Allentown (Pennsylvania) Red Sox. (NA, 80-G-31327)

.50-calibers at a range of 800 yards, the pilots broke off 50 yards from their targets. Flight A-18 took both boats under fire simultaneously, one from dead ahead and the other on the beam. Painted black, with what appeared to be red numerals on their conning towers, both submersibles had not started crash-dives before the attacks started, enabling all but one of the F4Fs (seven strafed one boat and eight the other) to make strafing runs. Each of the Wildcats expended about 250 rounds (of the 1,420 carried). Stan Amesbury, one of the two VF-9 pilots on the mission, dropped one of his instantaneous-fused 100-pound demolition bombs 25 yards ahead of where the long, low, black conning tower disappeared beneath the sea; the bomb exploded ahead of the swirl about four seconds later.

Tommy Booth and his flight lingered in the area of the antisubmarine action for almost a quarter of an hour, seeing only a small oil slick in the wake of Amesbury's attack, before pushing on to undertake their mission to attack the French guns at El Hank. Flight A-18 reached its objective and the pilots dove from 12,000 feet, flying along an axis from north to south. Eight of the pilots whose planes carried bombs dropped 15 on the batteries, 3 of which hit inside the blast shelters around the guns; pilots only saw one or two other bombs explode. All of the F4F pilots strafed their targets, encountering only a small amount of antiaircraft fire.

VF-41's skipper observed that the antiaircraft batteries at Table d'Aoukacha were still firing, that a large amount of

Aviation Radioman 3d Class Aubra T. "Pat" Patterson (R), with Lt. (jg) Horace R. White, A-V(N), on the wing of 41-S-18, en route to North Africa. Patterson, mortally wounded in the course of his second mission on 8 November, died en route back to the *Ranger*. He was awarded a posthumous Silver Star. (NA, 80-G-31333)

antiaircraft fire came from near a stadium close to El Hank, and that ships in the harbor were still putting up a moderate amount of fire. In the outer harbor, he took note of a light cruiser, a destroyer leader, and two destroyers "lying to, ready to go out," and several ships in the harbor still burning. Booth's section strafed what he identified as a destroyer leader or light cruiser at anchor just outside Casablanca harbor. "The fire was well directed," he reported later, "it [is] believed that everything on deck was hit." Upon reflection later, Booth believed that, because of the speed with which such an attack could be made, fighter attacks on submarines "appear to be highly feasible."

Even as his shipmates continued to take the war to the enemy, one of the missing Red Rippers, Spanky Carter, kept up his efforts to evade capture. As he paddled, he noticed "a small French ship...moving slowly along the coast every mile or so for about a half hour at a time...," leading him to speculate that the vessel was sowing mines. "I was more than rewarded for my efforts," he recounted later, "when late in the afternoon as I paddled slowly past a point of land...rifle bullets began singing past my little boat." Redoubling his efforts, doubtless spurred on by the song of the bullets, and perhaps reflecting upon Winston Churchill's observation from the Boer War concerning nothing being more exhilarating than to be shot at without result, Carter breathed a sigh of relief when the firing ceased.[12]

To attack small craft operating outside Casablanca harbor, the *Ranger* soon put up flight A-19, a section of four

F4Fs, starting at 1515, followed presently by a section of five Wildcats to bomb and strafe gun emplacements at El Hank.

FLIGHT A-19 (VF-9)

Lt. Comdr. John Raby
Ens. James E. Toliver, A-V(N)

Lt. (jg) Charles L. Moutenot, A-V(N)
Ens. William J. Bonneau, A-V(N)

FLIGHT A-20 (VF-9)

Lt. Theodore H. Winters, Jr.
Ens. Louis A. Menard, A-V(N)
Lt. (jg) Harold E. Vita, A-V(N)
Ens. James M. Wilkerson, A-V(N)
Lt. (jg) Harrison Feasley, A-V(N)

Taking their departure, Raby led his section over Fedala and, after observing no enemy forces there, headed toward Casablanca, coming out of the sun over the harbor. He picked out four destroyers lying just north of the harbor, and led his men down to strafe them and drop 100-pound bombs. Raby, Moot Moutenot, Oliver Toliver, and Bill Bonneau each picked one ship to attack, pushing over into their dives at 14,000 feet. Making fast, weaving attacks, one plane per ship, the VF-9 pilots each dropped their two 100-pound bombs. Although he felt the flight had hit the destroyers "hard," Jack Raby could not determine the extent of the damage inflicted.

Pedro Winters's section reached its objective, and observed gun flashes from an antiaircraft emplacement one mile inland and at the edge of a racetrack. Pushing over into their dives at 16,000 feet, the VF-9 pilots made weaving approaches from the south, salvoing their 100-pounders. Recovering from their dives at 400 feet, Winters and his troops turned abruptly and carried out fast, flat strafing runs. Winters assessed the mission as successful, apparently silencing the guns, which they left covered with debris amidst no signs of life or movement.

There was movement in Chuck August's cell. For two hours he had been incarcerated, and, when a guard entered, August subjected him "to a storm of recriminations." Finally, the Frenchman permitted the pilot to have one of his own Chesterfields that had been confiscated. Once the guard had left, Dougherty, who had been a licensed embalmer and funeral director before the war, revealed a cartridge box filled with "Philip Morris cigarettes, several chocolate bars, a can of fish, and some wet packages of chewing gum." He also informed August that there was an American pilot in the next cell. August easily identified him when he heard a description: it was his squadronmate, Windy Shields.[13]

Soon after the *Ranger* had gotten VF-9's Wildcats aloft at 1530, she began launching flight A-21, consisting of three SBDs, to bomb coast defense batteries at the tip of Point El Hank.

FLIGHT A-21 (VS-41)

Lt. Ralph A. Embree
    Aviation Radioman 1st Class Joseph M. Eardley
Lt. (j.g.) Joseph P. Keigher, Jr., A-V(N)
    Aviation Radioman 3d Class J. J. Lankowitz
Lt. (jg) Ralph W. Ross, A-V(N)
    Aviation Radioman 3d Class L. L. Devine

Following Embree's three SBDs, Commander Overfield took off in his TBF-1, designated as flight A-21A, to bomb the French guns at the tip of El Hank.

FLIGHT A-21A (CRAG)

Comdr. David B. Overfield   C
    Aviation Radioman 1st Class Jack L. Aday
    Aviation Machinist's Mate 2d Class Reginald H. Miller

This was followed immediately by flight A-22: six SBDs slated to bomb the *Primauguet* off the entrance to Casablanca harbor. They carried out their attacks almost simultaneously with the F4Fs from Jack Raby's flight A-19.

FLIGHT A-22 (VS-41)

Lt. John M. DeVane, Jr.
    Aviation Radioman 1st Class William O. Haynes, Jr.
Lt. (jg) Maxwell A. Eaton, A-V(N)
    Aviation Radioman 3d Class William T. Shackelford
Lt. (jg) John G. McReynolds, Jr., A-V(N)
    Aviation Radioman 3d Class Oscar I. Light

Lt. (jg) Cyrus F. Weeks, A-V(N)
    Aviation Radioman 3d Class G. H. Perry
Ens. Donald E. Chapman, A-V(N)
    Aviation Radioman 3d Class R. L. Fenton
Lt. (jg) Clarence A. Twiddy, Jr., A-V(N)
    Aviation Radioman 3d Class R. E. O'Connor

Ralph Embree's three-plane section approached the target from along the coast, at 14,000 feet, coming out of the sun and from above a layer of clouds, gliding down to 10,000 feet. At that point, Embree and his two wingmen pushed over into steep dives and released their bombs at 1,500 feet, laying their ordnance in the immediate vicinity of the four gun sites. With bombs gone, the Scouting Forty-One flight retired to seaward, just above the water. Embree believed that all bombs had hit on target and the guns had been "severely damaged."

Commander Overfield had rendezvoused with Embree's scouts en route and proceeded to the target with them, arriving over El Hank at 14,000 feet. Breaking off, Overfield selected a four-gun battery at the tip of El Hank as his target and flew to a point 10 miles south of it to initiate a glide-bombing attack. Just after the last of the scouts had dropped his bomb, Overfield released his four 500-pound demolition bombs, beginning at 2,000 feet and concluding at 1,200. The first bomb hit and destroyed a building, the second and third straddled a gun emplacement and the fourth landed in the water.

The CRAG also noted heavy-caliber antiaircraft fire during the approach and retirement phase, but that it had been ineffective, because the gunners were not leading the target; the bursts always exploded behind his TBF. He soon had more pressing concerns, however, when he spotted eight H.75s approaching in a southerly direction, coming up on his starboard beam.

Apparently adopting the course of action that the best defense was a good offense, Overfield picked out the last H.75 as his target and started a run, but the fixed .30-caliber nose gun did not fire. At that, the Hawks turned and came up from astern; Overfield saw no tracers as he nosed down and gathered speed in an attempt to get away from the French fighters.

During his descent to escape the Curtisses, Overfield noticed "several enemy bombers" apparently making runs on the landing boats off the beachhead, northeast of Fedala. Because the Hawk 75s discontinued their pursuit of the CRAG when they were "about even with the beach," Overfield made a run on one of the Douglas DB-7s, but again experienced the frustration of his fixed gun not working. Whether or not the probably unexpected presence of a TBF had caused the French bombardiers to jettison their bombs too early, Overfield noticed that the DB-7s obtained only near-misses.

His bombs gone and his fixed gun obviously inoperative, Overfield returned to the *Ranger*, coming on board 20 minutes after the ship had recovered the last of Ralph Embree's flight. A check of the fixed .30-caliber Browning in the nose of the CRAG's assigned TBF yielded the discovery that a portion of a cartridge case had "lodged in the mechanism," thus rendering it *hors de combat*.

Count DeVane, meanwhile, led his flight inland behind Casablanca, approaching from 11,500 feet. Gliding down to 9,000, flight A-22 dove in succession from southeast to the northwest. DeVane had opted for that approach from the landward side to allow his pilots the whole length of the *Primauguet* for a target, which also meant that they did not have to fly at low altitude over the "many, and increasingly accurate" light antiaircraft batteries on the jetties.

DeVane, in the lead, scored a direct hit amidships, triggering a "terrific explosion [that] sent flame and debris to an estimated height of 1,000 feet." Jack Raby, nearby on a strafing mission (flight A-19), saw the blast and later reported it as "the most beautiful thing I've ever seen." Heavy smoke then obscured the target from view, which meant that none of the pilots that followed could see whether or not his bombs had hit squarely or were near-misses. Later assessments agreed that perhaps either, or both, Lieutenants (jg) Weeks and Twiddy had scored hits. As Lieutenant (jg) Eaton leveled out after his dive, his radioman, Bill Shackelford, strafed a destroyer with his flexible .30-calibers. All six planes returned to base, half of which had taken hits from the still potent antiaircraft fire.

From his vantage point on board the *Wilkes*, Gordon Chase observed that the ships operating off the Fedala–Casablanca area "never seemed to have any information on the operations being conducted by aircraft and vice versa." Information of that kind, Chase later posited, could be made available over the TBS "instead of the constant prattle of insignificant information which sounded like an old ladies' tea party." Later, as Chase looked on, the *Wilkes* silenced French guns on the northeast side of Cape Fedala.[14]

John Sweeney returned to the *Ranger* at 1545. Soon, the men in the ship's photographic laboratory were busy developing the film and printing the pictures of the areas over which Sweeney had flown.

With the ebb and flow of the day's activities, the *Ranger*'s crewmen toiling below—handling bombs and ammunition, standing the engine room watches and at damage control stations, as well as providing coffee, sandwiches, and hot meals—had been kept apprised. Lieutenant O'Callahan had broadcast a running commentary over *Ranger*'s loudspeaking system.[15]

At day's end, Rear Admiral McWhorter praised his flagship:

"The outstanding performance of the *Ranger* and *Ranger* Air Group on Sunday, November 8, 1942, surpasses any known achievement by a carrier and its air group. The cheerful and willing manner in which pilots took off on a total of 203 flights to engage the enemy on land, on sea and in the air in a single day constitutes a bright page in the history of the *Ranger*. The efficient handling of planes and ship by the officers and crew of the *Ranger* made this remarkable performance possible. Several men have made the extreme sacrifice in fighting our country's cause but our aircraft have made a major contribution to the successful landing by Army troops at Fedala and Port Lyautey. I take pleasure in saying 'Well Done' McWhorter."

Commander David B. Overfield, Commander *Ranger* Air Group (CRAG), November 1942, standing by the cockpit of the sole Grumman TBF-1 assigned to the ship at that time. The "C" marking on the inside of the wing section at bottom denotes the group commander's plane. (NA, 80-G-30330)

One of the cheerful and willing pilots to whom the admiral had extended praise contemplated his dank surroundings: Chuck August eyed his dinner—a chunk of bread, "a small piece of very bad beef," and a glass of water. He tasted the bread and the beef, but ate neither. He then asked to visit Windy Shields, who spoke a little French, and was able to procure two blankets. Giving his flying suit to Tom Dougherty, who was still clad in the wet clothes in which he had been captured, August roomed with Shields, the latter unfortunately suffering from a severe head cold. The two VF-41 pilots tried to sleep, but a guard interrupted their fitful slumber by shining a light on them every 15–20 minutes.[16]

At least Chuck August had been offered solid food. Ensign Mikronis had not even been given the option of turning down poor fare. He had arrived at the hospital earlier that day and had seen "a great number" of badly wounded Frenchmen. Yet, although the facility appeared full, the French gave him a private room. No further treatment, however, ensued. His bandages remained dirty and "the lack of facilities" seemed very apparent. After sleeping until late in the afternoon, he received only a liquid diet: wine, coffee, and tea. Apparently left at liberty within the hospital, however, he strolled around, curious, looking for other Americans. Finding none, and noting that the only guards in sight were those at the hospital's front gate, he turned in and, with nothing else to do, slept well.[17]

Mac Wordell had finally reached Casablanca, alertly assessing his surroundings, as he and his Spahi guards proceeded toward a French cavalry camp to the south of the city. As he later recounted, he "felt like Don Quixote and his party," greeting everyone in his best French, "seldom without some

The resilient Vichy French battery at El Hank, seen here on 11 November 1942. (NA, 80-G-37209)

degree of success." Eventually taken into the city in a civilian automobile, accompanied by the same Spahi corporal who had taken him prisoner earlier, to the headquarters of the *4th Bureau,* and introduced to a *Capitaine* Levaçon, Wordell saw only a few officers and men present that Sunday morning. After "introductions and wine" had been passed around, VF-41's exec noted that the junior officers seemed glad to see him, but their seniors, although not unfriendly, made no effort to interrogate him. "No one seemed much concerned with the war," he wrote later. "No one present spoke English, but I spoke enough French to learn where they were from and ask them how they felt about Americans." Learning his hosts' anxiety as to whether or not "any English were attacking," Wordell told them "they were all Americans who came to help them beat the Germans." He immediately began a one-man propaganda campaign directed at anyone with whom he would come in contact over the ensuing days. "I was so sold on the debt we owed Lafayette . . . I hardly knew of anyone else in the American Revolution unless it was Washington."[18]

Later, assailed by too many "misgivings" to sleep, Wordell relaxed and watched the increasingly busy routine at the *4th Bureau.* "I thought of home, the squadron, everything I held dear, and I thanked God I was still alive and not seriously hurt." His captors granted his request for a blanket as the night became chilly, and promised him medical care on the morrow. "I was not unhappy," he later reflected, "It appeared that the Americans were well installed in Fedala by now, and these people did not contest the invasion."[19]

At about midnight, a bone-weary Spanky Carter finally made his way ashore through the booming surf. The breakers tossed his boat violently, filling it with water but somehow not upsetting it. Although he "felt quite normal," Carter surprisingly found himself unsteady as he stepped onto dry land. His fingers too numb to turn the nut to deflate his rubber boat, he unsheathed his knife and stuck it into the craft's skin to hasten the deflation process. Once he had squeezed all of the air out of it, Carter rolled it up and began walking inland. Finding a dry spot somewhat shielded from the wind, he "dug a hole in the sand and buried myself like we used to do when kids. In this manner," he later wrote, "I spent the night."[20]

By day's end, the dramatic turn of events at Casablanca concerned Vice Adm. Karl Dönitz, commander of the *Kriegsmarine's* U-boat arm. Early that day, Dönitz had informed the Naval High Command of "large scale landing operations on the Moroccan Coast by the Americans." Treating the invasion of the Moroccan and Algerian coasts as a big venture "for which the enemy will need an enormous amount of supplies," Dönitz believed that U-boats could make serious inroads on Allied logistics, although he freely acknowledged that submarine operations were too late for the first landings.[21]

To enable his U-boats to reach the area as soon as possible, however, he directed eight then at sea—the *U-103, U-108, U-130, U-155, U-173, U-411, U-515,* and *U-572*—to proceed at high speed toward the coast of North Africa. He ordered an additional seven—the *U-86, U-91, U-185, U-510, U-511, U-519,* and *U-752*—to average 200 miles per day and steer for a grid coordinate off the coast of French Morocco. Although Dönitz knew that the first boats, even proceeding at top speed, would not reach the area until between 9 and 11 November, he believed that they could "work effectively against the subsequent follow-up landings and against the supply line."[22] He deemed "the Casablanca area, Safi and Port Lyautey" as the "most important harbors for flanking action." Dönitz realized, too, that his boats would have to carry out their attacks in waters less than 50 meters deep when attacking transports and warships, in the face of heavy air operations from Gibraltar, and in the face of "heavier destroyer and corvette patrols."[23] Nevertheless, the head of the German Navy's U-boat arm wrote, "Every attack in these shallow waters will demand great determination. But the importance of dislocating the enemy's supply lines calls for the boldest possible intervention."[24]

20

"MORALE DROPS QUICKLY BEFORE AN ENEMY WHO IS CLEARLY SUPERIOR"

Unloading at Fedala had gone slowly. Major Gen. George S. Patton, Jr., concerned about the pace at which it was proceeding, went directly to the beaches at dawn. "The beach was a mess," Patton later wrote in his diary, "and the officers were doing nothing." The general personally took charge to inspire the army shore parties, which seemed to exhibit neither energy nor resourcefulness in getting what had already been unloaded and landed off the beach, commandeering a boat to catch up with the tank lighters "and show them into the harbor."[1]

While the colorful and energetic Patton prowled about the beachhead, spurring on his lethargic logisticians, the officers and men of *Groupe de Chasse* II/5 "Lafayette" stirred well before dawn on 9 November. A diminished *patrouille double* ascended into the gray predawn skies, one section led by *Lieutenant* Rubin and consisting of himself, *Adjudant-chef* Gras, and *Sergent* Lavie, the other section consisting of *Lieutenant* Boudier and *Adjudant-chef* Marcel Verrier. They flew toward the beachhead at Fedala, where, despite heavy antiaircraft fire, they strafed empty landing barges and collections of supplies along the shoreline in the direction of Bouznika. Dispersed by the fog on the return flight, the men of the Lafayette squadron returned with three planes damaged.

A heavier French raid, however, was soon on its way to the skies over Fedala and Pont Blondin: 10 Le O 451s from GB II/23 and 2 Martin 167s from the French Navy's *Flotille* 3F, which had flown in from Meknès, joined by a trio of Douglas DB-7s from GB I/32, at Mèdouina. Fifteen H.75s from GC I/5—9 planes from the first squadron and 6 from the second—flew cover.

Rising before sun-up, Spanky Carter shook off as much of the sand as he could and, avoiding the main roads, began hiking through the countryside. He soon encountered a hospitable Moroccan who "insisted that I eat a couple of raw eggs and partake of a little of his bread and the barley water he fondly thought resembled coffee." After tasting some of the beverage and seeing his host's hopeful and expectant expression, however, Carter thanked him for his kindness and went on his way.[2]

Mac Wordell awakened to find much of the office work at the *4th Bureau* had ceased. He breakfasted on a piece of French bread and "some Ersatz coffee, mostly barley, without sugar or milk. It tasted good." Before the morning was out, he would be interrogated by his captors, but language difficulties intervened. Believing "an offense is the best defense," Wordell soon began to barrage the French with requests for "my belongings, some soap, a toothbrush, some medical care, and a bath." Nothing materialized, although he was allowed to get some fresh air and exercise on the roof of the *4th Bureau*. That would have to suffice for the moment.[3]

Scouting Forty-One got the ball rolling for the *Ranger* on the second day, when Ralph Embree led flight B-1 off at 0645, 20 minutes before sunrise.

Major General George S. Patton, Jr., unhappily surveys the beach at Fedala. (NA, 80-G-19802)

FLIGHT B-1 (VS-41)

Lt. Ralph A. Embree
    Aviation Radioman 1st Class Joseph M. Eardley
Lt. (jg) Joseph P. Keigher, Jr., A-V(N)
    Aviation Radioman 3d Class J. J. Lankowicz
Lt. (jg) Clarence A. Twiddy, Jr. A-V(N)
    Aviation Radioman 3d Class R E. O'Connor
Ens. Arthur D. Warta, A-V(N)
    Aviation Radioman 2d Class R. J. Monahan
Lt. (jg) William H. Longley, A-V(N)
    Aviation Radioman 3d Class John G. Korecki

Lt. (jg) John G. McReynolds, A-V(N)
Aviation Radioman 3d Class Oscar I. Light

Flight B-1 encountered fair flying weather, with visibility that stretched to between 5 and 10 miles. Flying beneath the cloud layer that stretched above them at 9,000 feet, the VS-41 SBDs reached the coast at Temara, then followed the coastline to Bouznika, Fedala, and Casablanca.

The *Ranger* soon put flight B-3 aloft: seven VF-41 F4Fs under Tommy Booth, to assume CAP over Port Lyautey:

FLIGHT B-3 (VF-41)

First Section

Lt. Comdr. Charles T. Booth, II
Lt. (jg) Boyd N. Mayhew, A-V(N)

Lt. (jg) Edmund J. Kelly, A-V(N)
Lt. (jg) Clyde C. Andrews, A-V(N)

Second Section

Lt. Herold J. Weiler, Jr.
Lt. (jg) Dee Jones, A-V(N)
Lt. Ernest W. Wood, Jr.

To provide CAP over the *Ranger*, the ship launched flight B-4 at 0652:

FLIGHT B-4 (VF-41)

First Section

Lt. Keene G. Hammond
Lt. (jg) William H. Bolt, Jr., A-V(N)

Lt. (jg) Arthur J. Cassidy, A-V(N)
Ens. Philip S. Ball, Jr., A-V(N)

Second Section

Lt. Maynard M. Furney, A-V(N)
Lt. (jg) George E. Harris, A-V(N)

Lt. (jg) Edwin N. Seiler, A-V(N)
Ens. Will "W" Taylor, A-V(N)

En route to Fedala, meanwhile, Ralph Embree saw three "large merchant vessels" aground, and three or four small craft lying just offshore between Temara and Bouznika. At Fedala, the airmen could see landing boats coming in without opposition, but that no large ships were yet using the harbor. Antiaircraft guns, firing from a position well inland from behind Table d'Aoukacha, betrayed the only sign of activity in or around the harbor area at Casablanca. Smoke, rising from a merchant ship moored at the eastern end of the *Mole du Commerce*, appeared to be "artificially created," rather than the result of damage. They could also see the battered *Primauguet* and the *Milan*, and the *Albatros* lying "at anchor or aground" east of the *Jettie Transversale*, all "obviously heavily damaged." What appeared to be a submarine lay moored alongside the *Jettie Delure*.

Seeing no targets below them worth expending ordnance on, Embree, known to his academy classmates to possess "alertness and imagination," retired from the skies over Casablanca and returned to the area where the antiaircraft battery had fired upon them earlier. Climbing to 10,000 feet, Embree led his flight inland and turned, to dive toward the sea. All but Lieutenant (jg) McReynolds dove on the battery, releasing their bombs at 1,200–1,300 feet. Embree, whose plane took two hits from antiaircraft fire during the attack, observed "a good pattern," which silenced the battery at least temporarily. McReynolds, who could not locate the target, glide-bombed the shore batteries at the Table d'Aoukacha, his bombs landing very near one of the heavy guns. Their bombs gone, flight B-1 turned to head for home.

Fighting Nine's flight B-2 began taking off at 0730, to take up CAP over Fedala, in the wake of GC II/5's dawn visit.

FLIGHT B-2 (VF-9)

First Section

Lt. Comdr. John Raby
Ens. Marvin J. Franger, A-V(N)

Lt. (jg) Harrison Feasley, A-V(N)
Ens. Albert E. Martin, A-V(N)

Second Section

Lt. Kenan C. Childers
Ens. Louis A. Menard, A-V(N)   9-F-15 (BuNo 11762)

Lt. (jg) Harold E. Vita, A-V(N)
Ens. Charles W. Gerhardt, A-V(N)   9-F-8 (BuNo 03461)

Tommy Booth's flight encountered slight antiaircraft fire when it arrived over Port Lyautey, VF-41's skipper noting "much vehicular activity" centered on a large red hangar at the aerodrome. He soon spied a column of between 30 and 40 trucks, spread out over 10 miles, driving east on the main road that led to the port, moving at about 30–40 miles per hour. The head of the heterogenous column (some trucks carrying only troops and several with machine guns mounted in the rear) was about three miles from the juncture of two main roads. At 0735, Booth radioed the *Ranger*:

I BELIEVE I SEE ENEMY TROOPS FROM THE EAST ON THE MAIN ROAD WILL YOU CONFIRM THIS SO I CAN IMMEDIATELY ATTACK[4]

To which the ship responded five minutes later:

DID TRUCKS HAVE ALLIED FRIENDLY MARKINGS, IF NOT ATTACK[5]

And added almost as a postscript at 0744:

IF TRUCKS DO NOT STOP SUDDENLY, ATTACK[6]

The trucks continuing to move soon prompted four of flight B-3's seven F4Fs to strafe the column, setting six or eight afire and forcing four to six of them into ditches alongside the road. The head of the column could still move, Booth noted, but the damage inflicted by the "Red Rippers" had blocked the road further back. Later, VF-41's skipper noted that the "column could have been completely destroyed" had not orders arrived over the radio ordering them to cease fire. Nevertheless, he observed later with professional pride that the "20% tracer, 30% incendiary and 50% armor piercing loadings" had proved "very effective."

Twenty minutes after Jack Raby had led flight B-2 off to carry out its mission, the *Ranger* received a report of a submarine contact, 1,500 yards on the port beam. The *Corry* and the *Ellyson* proceeded to the scene to depth-charge it, and the *Ranger* and the rest of her screen made an emergency turn to starboard and rang down full speed. Within five minutes' time, the carrier received a report of a formation of French bombers heading north, up the coast from Safi.

By the time Raby led his two 4-plane sections aloft, the weather had worsened to the point that visibility extended only about three miles, and the ceiling had dropped to 8,000 feet. When they arrived on station, Fighting Nine's skipper spotted what appeared to be 16 Hawk 75s just inland of Fedala, flying on a northerly heading at an altitude of 8,000–9,000 feet.

While Raby and VF-9 had been headed for Fedala, so, too, had the French. But the Vichy strike en route to the Fedala–Pont Blondin area encountered difficulties, undoubtedly inherent in marshalling a force from the decimated remnants of the French air assets in Morocco. In fact, the 30 planes winging their way toward the American beachhead at Fedala represented all of the available Vichy planes in that sector. The rendezvous point had been fixed at a point over land less than 30 kilometers from the American ships. A 15-minute delay in their arrival resulted. Attacking at the start of the forenoon watch, the mixed group of LeOs, Glenn Martins, and Douglases jettisoned their bombs and broke formation with the immediate arrival of VF-9's flight B-2. Observers to seaward in TG 34.9 counted what appeared to be about 60 bombs that did "little damage" to beaches Red-2 and Blue. Some of the bombers headed for the clouds.

On the beach, Major General Patton observed "some cases of fright" among his troops, as the result of the French bombing attack. Seeing that anxiety displayed, in addition to his having seen the somewhat slack attitude continuing to be exhibited by the shore parties, moved him to a "state of exasperated frustration." He saw one soldier, who had been helping to push a boat ashore, run up on the beach and, gibbering, assume the fetal position in the sand. "I kicked him in the arse with all my might and he jumped right up and went to work," Patton later wrote in his diary, "Some way to boost morale." He remained on the beach to see what he could do to move things along.[7]

Possessing a 1,000-foot altitude advantage, VF-9's octet pushed over and attacked the Hawk 75s covering the bombers, although the odds lay two-to-one in favor of the French. Raby made an above-rear approach and opened fire on what looked like the leader of GC I/5's second group, pressing the firing button at 150 yards. Raby saw tracers entering his quarry, but the Vichy pilot pulled up into a cloud and disappeared from view. Soon thereafter, VF-9's skipper passed through a cloud; upon emerging, he sighted a Curtiss only 75 yards away. Making a side approach, Raby cut loose with all six .50-calibers, hammering the Hawk's cockpit and engine. In a flash, the H.75 blew up and tumbled in flaming pieces to the ground. Raby's wingman, Marv Franger, carried out a head-on approach on an H.75, loosing a fearsome fusillade with all six .50s at point blank range. Al Martin made an underside approach on Franger's quarry, and fired, setting the Vichy fighter ablaze.

In the swirling dogfight, a Hawk latched onto Casey Childers's Wildcat, and Childers pushed over into a tight spiral and a controlled spin to shake off his pursuer. Coming out of the spin in a tight nose-high turn and cutting the gun at 1,000 feet, Childers spied an H.75 in his gunsight and opened fire with all six Brownings, at a range between 150 and 400 yards. The Hawk, trailing only a trace of black smoke, spun into the ground. Childers saw no parachute.

Flying number two on Childers, Lou Menard saw an attack developing by three Hawks. He broke off and made an overhead approach on the number three H.75, loosing a full barrage from the six .50-calibers. Hit in the cockpit and the fuselage aft, the Curtiss began shedding parts, then burst into flame before crashing into the ground. Flying in the number three position, Hal Vita spotted an H.75 coming out of the clouds on an opposite course. The French pilot made a climbing turn to port, but came within firing range (100–150 yards). Vita fired a full six-gun burst, hitting the Hawk's underside and setting the H.75 afire. The Vichy fighter, however, disappeared in the clouds.

As the action ended, Raby took stock of how his flight had fared with the French: he counted five Hawks downed

Glenn Martin 167A-3 bombers, 28 March 1941. (Peter Mersky)

and a further four damaged, at no cost to Fighting Nine. As the flight formed up to return to the *Ranger*, however, one of the pilots noticed that the right side of Charley Gerhardt's 9-F-8 glistened with oil. Shortly, Gerhardt peeled off at 7,000 feet and ditched in the Atlantic, just short of the *Ranger*, where the *Mayrant* picked him up at 0854.[8]

GC I/5, however, had suffered much in the "rapid and brutal encounter" over Fedala. *Lieutenants* LeBlanc and LeCalvet had been killed; *Adjudant-chef* Tesseraud (perhaps the victim of Lou Menard and Al Martin, or of Hal Vita) "very seriously burned." Damage to their H.75s had forced *Capitaine* Dugas and *Lieutenant* Flubeau to make forced landings. GC I/5's people mourned their slain, tended their wounded, and reflected that the morning's encounter had proved that not only did a Hawk turn less rapidly than a Wildcat, but the H.75 was slower and less heavily gunned than the F4F-4. Then, too, there was the melancholy fact that the French had had to fight Americans, former allies. As

Curtiss Hawk 75As from GC I/5, 1942. (Peter Mersky)

GC I/5's dispirited but candid diarist wrote in the groupe's *journal de marche*: "*Le moral tombe vite devant un adversaire nettement supérieur et que l'on considère difficilement comme un ennemi.*" [Morale drops quickly before an enemy who is clearly superior and whom one considers an enemy only with difficulty].⁹

The French pilots had fought bravely, as their sailors had the day before off Casablanca. Amidst the surreal nature of hostilities between two traditional allies, Spanky Carter, after his encounter with the Moroccan, was soon picked up by M. Jean Lagorce, a French civilian, who took him into his house, "a compact little place set in the middle of vineyards and what looked like fields devoted to extensive vegetable raising."¹⁰ Lagorce bathed Carter's feet in hot water, provided him with an "excellent" breakfast, and waxed "most emphatic about his friendship and admiration of the Americans." He also promised to arrange a ride, so that Carter could get to Fedala as early as possible.¹¹

One of M. Lagorce's neighbors, however, an Italian woman, "chanced to come in" and see the American in Lagorce's residence. Evidently, the neighbor's clearly Axis sentiments prompted her to inform the Vichy authorities of Carter's presence in the Frenchman's house, because, very promptly a French sailor, accompanied by a Moroccan rifleman, arrived and took Carter prisoner, leading him off to a local French naval station, the place from which he had been fired upon the previous afternoon. Soon, a car arrived from Casablanca, and Carter was on his way to captivity in the capital.¹²

At the same time that Jake Raby's VF-9 was tangling with GC I/5 over Fedala, the *Ranger* had been busily launching planes to undertake reconnaissance missions, flights B-5 and B-6, beginning at 0811:

FLIGHT B-5 (VF-41)

Lt. Walter F. Madden, A-V(N)

FLIGHT B-6 (VS-41)

Lt. (jg) Woodie L. McVay, A-V(N)
Aviation Radioman 2d Class Kenneth W. Jobe

Ensign Charles W. Gerhardt, A-V(N), flashes the "V" for victory sign, sitting atop the engine cowling of Spanky Carter's F4F-4 en route to North Africa. (NA, 80-G-31311)

Lt. (jg) Maxwell A. Eaton, A-V(N)
Aviation Radioman 3d Class William T. Shackelford

The planners for the day's operations had given Wally Madden, who, like John Sweeney, possessed training in photo reconnaissance, the mission of photographing the entrance to Casablanca harbor, the coastline, and the dock areas, the coastal gun batteries at El Hank, and the coastline as far north as possible. In addition, he was to reconnoiter the roads south of Casablanca. Woodie McVay and Max Eaton were to "reconnoitre and photograph anything of military significance on [the] road from Casablanca to Safi." Madden's recon-configured F4F carried four .50-caliber machine guns with 920 rounds (20% tracer, 30% incendiary, and 50% armor-piercing), in addition to the 20-inch F-56 camera. Each SBD carried 250 gallons of gasoline and a bomb load of one 500- and two 100-pounders.

Chuck August and Windy Shields awakened to a breakfast of bread and barley coffee. Initially, their need to relieve themselves prompted them to try to communicate that desire to their captors, who apparently knew no English. Eventually, the two VF-41 pilots resorted to pantomime to get their point across. Later, the French took August and Shields from their cell and put them in with Tom Dougherty; their captors then brought several U.S. army prisoners and put them in a large cell. The influx of POWs prompted the American pilots to clamor for transfer to a dispensary: August for his bruised thigh, Dougherty for his wrenched back, and Shields for his head cold and sprained ankle. The French, however, seemed deaf to the requests: the Americans' request for an interpreter encountered the same rebuff.[13]

After she had launched the two reconnaissance missions, the *Ranger* began a cycle of flight operations beginning at 0848; first off was flight B-7 for CAP over the beachhead at Fedala.

FLIGHT B-7 (VF-9)

First Section

Lt. Theodore H. Winters, Jr.
Ens. Merle M. Hershey, A-V(N)
Lt. (jg) Armistead B. Smith, Jr., A-V(N)

Second Section

Lt. Jacob W. Onstott
Lt. (jg) Reuben H. Denoff, A-V(N)

Lt. (jg) Charles L. Moutenot, A-V(N)
Ens. Burton L. Bardeen, A-V(N)

Soon afterward, the *Ranger* launched a three-plane patrol of F4Fs from VF-41, for CAP over the ship:

FLIGHT B-8 (VF-41)

Lt. Earle F. Craig
Lt. (jg) Walter E. Laake, A-V(N)
Lt. (jg) George M. Harris, A-V(N)

With the fighters gone, the *Ranger*'s flight deck crew then got a four-plane strike from Scouting Forty-One ready to support the troops at Fedala:

FLIGHT B-9 (VS-41)

Lt. John M. DeVane, Jr.
    Aviation Radioman 1st Class William O. Haynes, Jr.
Lt. (jg) Horace R. White, A-V(N)
    Aviation Radioman 3d Class A. R. Smith

Lt. (jg) Cyrus F. Weeks, A-V(N)
    Aviation Radioman 3d Class G. H. Perry
Lt. (jg) Robert L. Arthur, A-V(N)
    Aviation Radioman 3d Class Morris S. Waterson

Pedro Winters's flight, meanwhile, flew its protective patrol over the harbor area, over a 5- by 10-mile swath of island. At one point, Winters observed antiaircraft fire, and radioed his flight to "look for flashes on the ground."[14] The Fighting Nine flight subsequently observed no French forces, and saw that the American troops were meeting "no apparent opposition." Landing craft appeared to be using harbor facilities, and a large transport appeared to be entering the harbor. All bridges in the vicinity of Fedala seemed to be intact.

With the launch of Count DeVane's flight, the *Ranger* recovered the planes that had been out on missions since the morning watch: Tommy Booth's (B-3), Kagey Hammond's (B-4), and Ralph Embree's (B-1) flights. With the completion of that cycle, the flight deck crew busily carried out its work, preparing the next succession of flights for takeoff, beginning with flight B-10—eight F4F-4s, under Kagey Hammond—to take up CAP duty over their parent ship, which led off at 0947:

FLIGHT B-10 (VF-41)

First Section

Lt. Keene G. Hammond
Lt. (jg) William H. Bolt, A-V(N)

Lt. (jg) Arthur J. Cassidy, A-V(N)
Ens. Philip S. Ball, Jr., A-V(N)

Second Section

Lt. Maynard M. Furney, A-V(N)
Lt. (jg) George E. Harris, A-V(N)

Lt. (jg) Edward N. Seiler, A-V(N)
Ens. Will W. Taylor, A-V(N)

Soon thereafter, plane directors motioned flight B-11 into position, and an eight-plane VF-41 CAP/ground support mission began taking off, followed directly by an eight-plane VS-41 section (B-12), to support the ground forces at Fedala and to bomb targets of opportunity.

FLIGHT B-11 (VF-41)

First Section

Lt. Comdr. Charles T. Booth, II
Lt. (jg) Boyd N. Mayhew, A-V(N)

Lt. (jg) Edmund J. Kelly, A-V(N)
Lt. (jg) Clyde C. Andrews, A-V(N)

Second Section

Lt. Herold J. Weiler, Jr.
Lt. (jg) Dee Jones, A-V(N)

Lt. Ernest W. Wood, Jr.
Lt. (jg) Hubert T. Houston, A-V(N)

FLIGHT B-12 (VS-41)

First Division

Lt. Cecil V. Johnson
    Aviation Radioman 2d Class Gerhard H. O. Kleiner
Lt. (jg) Harold R. Keller, Jr., A-V(N)
    Aviation Radioman 2d Class A. W. Lorentzen
Lt. (jg) Clyde A. Tucker, Jr., A-V(N)
    Aviation Radioman 3d Class Lloyd E. Edens

Ens. George F. Dalton, A-V(N)
   Aviation Radioman 2d Class R. J. Monahan
Ens. Charles C. Bevis, Jr., A-V(N)
   Aviation Radioman 3d Class J. J. Lankowicz

Second Division

Lt. (jg) Robert H. Higley, A-V(N)
   Aviation Radioman 3d Class L. E. Colon
Lt. (jg) Ralph W. Ross, A-V(N)
   Aviation Radioman 3d Class L. J. Devine
Ens. Thomas M. Hubbard, A-V(N)
   Aviation Radioman 3d Class R. L. Fenton

During their hour aloft in the overcast skies over the task group, Buster Craig and his wingmen only saw U.S. surface and air forces. Theirs was a routine patrol. The *Ranger* began to take Craig and his wingmen on board at 0956, soon followed by Jack Raby's flight B-2. Lou Menard, from the latter group, made a high and fast approach when he returned to the *Ranger* and missed the arresting wires at 1006. His Wildcat, 9-F-15, floated into the barrier and swung into the island, wrecking BuNo 11762 "beyond ordinary repair."[15]

At about the same time that Lou Menard's Wildcat crashed into the barrier, Ensign Mikronis awoke from a good night's sleep in the hospital. Well-rested, Mikronis got up and walked into a nearby dressing room. He discovered that he was not, in fact, the only American there, because he soon made the acquaintance of Aviation Radioman 2d Class Robert C. Etheridge, late of USS *Massachusetts*'s aviation unit.[16]

Mikronis found the hospital attendants "friendly, and [they] did everything they could" to make the two navy fliers comfortable. Many of the "Arabs" evidenced a particular friendship and fondness for Etheridge, whose hair was cut short. The Moroccans had been prisoners of the Germans, they explained to the Americans, and had had their hair cut, too—they may have thought Etheridge a fellow

Lou Menard's 9-F-15 (BuNo 11762) after its barrier crash on 9 November. (NA, 80-G-30242)

former sufferer of German captivity. The French "Marines" encountered in the hospital, too, evidenced great friendliness for the Americans. Mikronis learned that at least five of them, having relatives languishing in German concentration camps, "wanted to fight with the Allies."[17]

The French medical people finally attended to Mikronis about 1100. They cut away his hair from his head wound and put on a fresh bandage. Finally given some solid food, Mikronis found it "very bad." Brown bread accompanied a "mush" made from dried split peas or lentils; there was also "a stew with meat in it." His captors also served him broth and coffee and wine. The French Marines picked oranges for Mikronis from a tree in the yard of the hospital, and gave him plenty of cigarettes. Later that day, he saw four captured U.S. soldiers and one sailor.[18] As Mikronis's situation was beginning to improve, and he saw that he was not the only American in the hospital in Casablanca, the war continued.

Count DeVane's flight circled the Casablanca–Fedala area for almost two hours. Given the mission of supporting the ground forces landing at the latter place, they had been assigned no specific targets. For its part, VS-41's reconnaissance flight encountered not much more exciting prospects. After skirting Casablanca, northwest of the harbor, McVay and Eaton reconnoitered the principal road to Mazagan; they saw no activity, and the town was quiet. One pilot saw a sign: "Welcome U.S.A.," which indicated the attitude of at least some of the local populace. Nearby, at the Mazagan airfield, the two VS-41 crews saw three Wildcats, one of which lay upside down. Proceeding down the coast to Safi, the two SBD crews observed American landing boats entering the harbor against no apparent opposition, and U.S. tanks and armored cars "were moving out of the town and appeared to command all approaches to a distance of several miles." East of the outskirts of town, a destroyed LeO 451 lay in a field.

As McVay and Eaton turned to clear Safi and return to Casablanca, however, they encountered a very low ceiling. Flying at altitudes ranging from 50 to 300 feet and unable to get into the clear, both pilots opted to climb over the clouds. In so doing, however, they became separated. McVay continued up the coast, overflying a heavy cloud formation before swinging out to sea and returning to the *Ranger* alone. Eaton flew on to Casablanca. Finding broken clouds that extended up to an altitude of 10,000 feet, however, he circled inland. As he did so, intermittent heavy-caliber antiaircraft fire spattered the sky. Eaton carefully noted the location of the bursts and took advantage of the cloud cover, while Shackelford photographed the harbor. Eaton then looked for a "target of opportunity" for the bombs they carried. Deciding to bomb the batteries at El Hank that had caused so much trouble since the beginning, he pushed over and dove on the northeasternmost gun emplacement. After leveling-off, he banked around to observe the result, and noted that "it appeared that the bombs had hit on or near the target." Having exhausted the supply of film, however, Shackelford could obtain no more photographs.

While Lieutenants (jg) McVay and Eaton had been undertaking their missions, Wally Madden took 53 photographs of Casablanca and El Hank from an altitude of 9,000 feet, then made one pass over Cazes, where he saw a pair of planes, which he identified as "possibly" Potezes. Descending to around 800 feet, Madden followed the road to Ber Rechid-Settat, and spotted a train consisting of an engine, a baggage car, three coaches, and 19 freight cars, on a branch line west of Settat. He also saw a second train—an engine, nine coaches, and a baggage car—north of Ber Rechid, heading for Casablanca. From his vantage point, he could see that neither train carried troops.

By that point on 9 November, the frequency with which the French had been able to carry out aerial harassment of the Fedala beachhead—particularly the efforts of *Lieutenant* Boudier of GC II/5—prompted Admiral Hewitt to signal Rear Admiral McWhorter:

FREQUENT STRAFING AND BOMBING OF FEDALA BEACHES EMPHASIZES NECESSITY OF FIGHTER PATROLS [in] THIS VICINITY X CAN YOU GET AT PLANES AT THEIR POSSIBLE SOURCE XX[19]

Soon thereafter, Wally Madden made two significant discoveries, one of which dealt with Commander Task Force 34's concerns about getting at the French aircraft "at their possible source." Madden had flown north to Mèdouina, where, arrayed on the road beneath him, he saw a military convoy. He radioed the *Ranger* immediately, reporting 19 troop-laden trucks, nine of which appeared to be towing artillery pieces, and 4 automobiles. Dispersed at the airfield nearby, Madden saw what looked like 5 Douglas DB-7s, 2 or 3 Martin 167s, and at least 15 fighters. He also saw trenches on the southwest side of the airport and what appeared to be light antiaircraft guns emplaced nearby. Having reported his find, Madden took a "few pictures" of the field and returned to El Hank. He began taking photographs again at that point, and continued doing so until he ran out of film just south of Rabat.

The *Suwanee* had put up 7 F4Fs (2 from VGS-30 and 5 from VGF-27), under Lt. James F. X. Fitzpatrick, Jr., for CAP over their home base and the *Ranger*: Tommy Booth's flight B-11 had taken up its CAP station in the overcast skies above Fedala in two 4-plane sections, one at 4,000 feet and the other at 8,000. Action came soon enough. After an army liaison officer reported that a lone French fighter had strafed the beach, Ham Weiler took his section down to be ready for any further enemy attempts to disrupt the ongoing landings.

Soon thereafter, Weiler's section spotted "a lone French fighter" and chased it out to sea. At an altitude of 4,000 feet, Woodie Wood caught up with the fleeing fighter and made a flat high-side attack from its starboard beam, commencing fire at 250 yards and ceasing at 75; six seconds' worth of .50-caliber fire proved enough, for the plane "burst into flames and fell into the sea" soon thereafter. No one saw a parachute.[20]

Johnny Johnson's flight encountered poor flying weather, in the form of rain and snow at 7,000 feet, and noted "nothing new of any particular interest" in the Fedala area. They saw a section of Grumman fighters circling the beachhead, while the landing boats continued to come ashore unopposed. They observed transports lying closer in, with boats and landing craft shuttling back and forth "at frequent intervals." The Scouting Forty-One aircrew could also see what appeared to be a transport or supply ship moored alongside a dock in the harbor proper.

A heavy antiaircraft battery fired at flight B-12 as it circled down toward Casablanca proper, the guns emplaced about a mile inland and about seven and a half miles southwest of Fedala. Johnson's division pushed over at 6,500 feet and attacked. The pilots released their bombs at 1,500 feet, and pulled out of their dives at 700. Although the poor visibility limited the ability to assess the damage inflicted, the returning pilots all testified that all bombs hit within 50 feet of the target. Aviation Radioman 3d Class Lankowicz strafed the ground installations as his pilot, Ensign Bevis, the tail-end charlie of Johnson's division, pulled out.

Lieutenant (jg) Higley's division circled overhead as Lieutenant Johnson's bombed the battery that had fired upon them. Convinced that that attack had silenced those particular guns, Higley led his division down across the city, "waiting for enemy batteries to open fire," as if taunting the Vichy gunners. For a time, it seemed that no one would accept VS-41's challenge, until about three miles east-southeast of El Hank, when black bursts smudged the sky "uncomfortably close for a few seconds," from a heavy antiaircraft gun battery. Higley pushed over at 9,000 feet, followed by Lieutenant (jg) Ross and Ensign Hubbard, and released at 1,900. All bombs appeared to hit near the objective, which convinced the three pilots that they had "wiped out" the battery.

About three-quarters of an hour before the end of the forenoon watch, the *Ranger* recovered Wally Madden, followed in succession by Pedro Winters's troops (B-7), Count DeVane's (B-9), and Johnny Johnson's (B-12). Wally Madden's flight having revealed not only the presence of aircraft dispersed at Mèdouina, but the convoy on the road to Casablanca, VF-9's and VS-41's deck crews serviced the next two strikes that the *Ranger* would be putting aloft to deal with that threat.

21

"EUCALYPTUS, BY THE SMELL"

Thus, at the start of the afternoon watch on 9 November, the ship began launching flight B-13:

FLIGHT B-13 (VF-9)

First Section

Lt. Comdr. John Raby
Ens. Marvin J. Franger, A-V(N) 9-F-2
Lt. (jg) Harrison Feasley, A-V(N)

Second Section

Lt. Hugh D. O'Neill, Jr., A-V(N)
Lt. (jg) Reuben H. Denoff, A-V(N)

Third Section

Lt. Theodore H. Winters, Jr.
Ens. James M. Wilkerson, A-V(N)

Lt. (jg) Mayo A. Hadden, Jr., A-V(N)
Lt. (jg) Armistead B. Smith, Jr., A-V(N)

Fourth Section

Lt. Edward Micka 9-F-13 (BuNo 11708)
Ens. Merle M. Hershey, A-V(N)

Ens. William J. Bonneau, A-V(N)
Ens. James E. Toliver, A-V(N)

Ten minutes later, four SBDs from VS-41 (flight B-14), under Ralph Embree, began taking off, having been given the mission of bombing and strafing enemy trucks and tanks near Rabat, and of scouting the area between Rabat and Port Lyautey:

FLIGHT B-14 (VS-41)

Lt. Ralph A. Embree 41-S-4 (BuNo 06627)
    Aviation Radioman 1st Class Joseph M. Eardley
Lt. (jg) Joseph P. Keigher, Jr., A-V(N)
    Aviation Radioman 3d Class J. J. Lankiewicz

Lt. (jg) John G. McReynolds, A-V(N)
    Aviation Radioman 3d Class Oscar I. Light
Ens. Donald E. Chapman, A-V(N)
    Aviation Radioman 2d Class Robert J. Monahan

About 20 minutes after the last of Ralph Embree's SBDs had cleared the bow ramp, the *Ranger* began bringing on board Kagey Hammond's flight B-10 and Tommy Booth's B-11. During the latter, Hubie Houston's guns accidentally discharged upon landing; fortunately, no one was hurt. The two-plane VS-41 photo reconnaissance flight returned subsequently, Woodie McVay and Max Eaton having made their way back separately: Eaton had returned to the *Ranger* with only 15 gallons of gasoline in his tanks.

Jack Raby and his flight, given the dual task of destroying enemy aircraft at Mèdouina and attacking an enemy force moving from Ber Rechid to Casablanca, found good flying weather, with visibility between 10 and 12 miles, as they headed for their objective, at 10,000 feet. Circling the field upon arrival, Raby and his flyers saw a row of what appeared to be at least 15 fighters in front of the hangars, and 5 or 6 medium bombers dispersed around the airdrome. Consequently, Raby led the first section down, strafing the field in a northerly direction, heading toward the hangars, making a fast, low attack in echelon line formation, as heavy antiaircraft and machine gun fire came up to meet them. Marv Franger's 9-F-2 took a direct hit from a machine gun bullet on the windshield, which cracked and frosted the glass for a radius of three inches, but failed to penetrate.

Pedro Winters's second division attacked on the heels of the first, Winters adopting a similar approach and tactical formation. As Jack Raby later noted, the Vichy planes being well dispersed made it necessary for small groups of two or three planes apiece to come in from various directions. The heavy antiaircraft fire accounted for no less than 12 hits on Mike Hadden's 9-F-11, with Hadden suffering a leg wound from a shell fragment.

On his fifth strafing run, Eddie Micka, leading VF-9's fourth section, came in fast and low, heading north, west of the hangars. Making a feint for the buildings, he banked 9-F-13 sharply to starboard and began strafing the DB-7s parked in front of the hangars. A previous attack, however, had set fire to one of the Douglases (No. 87) and, having been fully loaded with bombs and fuel, it exploded. Micka's Wildcat, at an altitude of only about 45 feet, flew directly into the debris thrust violently skyward. As *Capitaine* Fourniol, the pilot whose bombs had straddled the *Brooklyn* the day before, watched, Nine-Fox-Thirteen crashed into the ground, shedding its wings, with the fuselage and engine coming to rest about a half mile from the field. Both fuel tanks exploded; blown clear, they set fire to other parts of the wreckage.[1]

Men from GB I/32 immediately rushed to the wreck and retrieved Micka's half-charred corpse from 9-F-13's cockpit; they buried the dead pilot on the spot, the French airmen according him the military honors due a fallen foe. Micka's grave, *Capitaine* Fourniol noted, marked with a white cross to which had been affixed the fighter pilot's identification tag, lay about 500 meters north of the northern border of the field at Mèdouina, and 300 meters east of the Ber Rechid–Mèdouina–Casablanca highway.

Upon completion of the mission, Jack Raby radioed the ship:

WE DESTROYED ALL THE PLANES ON THE FIELD AT MÈDOUINA FIELD BUT ON THE ROAD SAW NO TROOPS[2]

At about the same time, Ralph Embree and his flight encountered fair flying weather, with visibility ranging between 10 and 20 miles. Broken clouds lay at 2,500 feet.

Lieutenant Eddie Micka poses astride the cockpit sill of Spanky Carter's F4F-4, en route to North Africa, November 1942. He would be killed in action a little over a week after the birth of the daughter that he would never see. (AUTHOR)

After closing the shoreline just above Mehdia, flight B-14 followed the main road northeast from Port Lyautey, looking for the reported large concentration of armored vehicles and troop-carrying trucks. Embree and his flyers looked in vain, finding "nothing of this nature" anywhere north or east of the city. Even the airport seemed to have been abandoned.

Banking to the south of Port Lyautey and out to the coast, the VS-41 flight discovered many tank tracks, and followed them. The trails led to what appeared to be eight American tanks, their tops painted yellow as a recognition measure, parked in a field five miles from the city, between the main coastal highway and the sea. A half mile to the south, Embree and his men sighted some 10 to 12 French tanks dispersed around an open field; they also observed 15 to 20 other motorized units attempting to hide beneath the cover afforded by trees along the main road. Embree and his flight made no attacks, since it seemed that there was no activity, and he reasoned that perhaps the French armor had either already surrendered or were about to do so.

Proceeding thence to Salé, Embree spotted "several French troop-carrying trucks" motionless, parked curbside on the town's main street. The approach of the SBDs dispersed the French soldiers. Reasoning that a bombing and strafing attack would have "endangered the civilian populace," Embree led his flight away from the town, circling and heading back toward Port Lyautey. A heavy antiaircraft battery near the Rabat-Salé airport opened fire on them, but the VS-41 flyers ignored it.

When about two-thirds of the way back to Port Lyautey, however, the VS-41 crews noticed that the trucks and armored cars previously in hiding appeared to be trying to sneak into the city. Consequently, Embree led the four SBDs in repeated glide-bombing and strafing attacks, strafing an armored car and a truck, bombing three tanks (destroying one and shaking up two with near-misses) and strafing and setting afire one tank. As the SBDs had deployed to attack, a group of soldiers, displaying what one VS-41 pilot called "just cold hard fighting courage," abandoned their truck and deployed what appeared to be a .30-caliber machine gun to fire back at the lead plane.[3] Don Chapman, flying wing on Embree, "nosed over and strafed the position, silencing the gun."

The aggressive Ralph Embree, meanwhile, intent on strafing a moving truck, was concentrating on his target, but failing to take note of the trees alongside the road. Forty-One-Sail-Four, with its bomb load still intact (and the 100-pounders known to be particularly sensitive) smashed head-on through some foliage ("eucalyptus, by the smell," Embree dead-panned upon returning to the *Ranger*), denting the underside of his SBD's cowling. "Although the plane was severely damaged," he noted matter-of-factly later, "it continued flying and was brought safely back to the ship."[4]

A little less than an hour and a half after the *Ranger* had put aloft Jack Raby's and Ralph Embree's sections, she turned into the wind and began launching four more flights; B-15, under Tommy Booth, to provide CAP over Fedala, B-16, under Count DeVane, to scout the Fedala–Casablanca–Mèdouina–Ber Rechid area; and B-17, a lone photo-reconnaissance F4F piloted by Jawn Sweeney.

The last of the four flights consisted of three Piper L-4 Cubs flown by Army pilots, for spotting duties from Fedala; they were to land at the racetrack near the city, with the field marked by a panel. To prevent any potential problems, Rear Admiral McWhorter signalled that the *Suwanee* advise her pilots that "three Army Tiger [*sic*] Cubs are taking off to land and operate at Fedala."[5]

FLIGHT B-15 (VF-41)

First Section

Lt. Comdr. Charles T. Booth, II
Lt. (jg) Boyd N. Mayhew, A-V(N)

Lt. Earle F. Craig
Lt. (jg) Hubert T. Houston, A-V(N)

Second Section

Lt. Keene G. Hammond
Lt. (jg) William H. Bolt, A-V(N)

Lt. (jg) Edward N. Seiler, A-V(N)
Ens. Robert C. Cronin, A-V(N)

FLIGHT B-16 (VS-41)

First Section

Lt. John M. DeVane, Jr.
    Aviation Radioman 1st Class William O. Haynes, Jr.
Lt. (jg) Clarence A. Twiddy, Jr., A-V(N)
    Aviation Radioman 3d Class R. E. O'Connor

Second Section

Lt. (jg) Cyrus F. Weeks, A-V(N)
    Aviation Radioman 3d Class G. H. Perry
Lt. (jg) William H. Longley, A-V(N)
    Aviation Radioman 3d Class John G. Korecki

FLIGHT B-17 (VF-41)

Lt. John R. Sweeney

FLIGHT "Q" (U.S. ARMY PIPER L-4s)

Capt. Ford A. Allcorn, USA   236389
    Capt. Brenton A. De Vall, USA

First Lt. John R. Shell, USA

Second Lt. William H. Butler, USA

A quarter of an hour into the flight, when flying just north of the river Nefifikh, DeVane looked back and saw what appeared to be a French Dewoitine 520 strafing the Fedala beaches from an altitude of about 50 feet. The flight leader immediately called attention to the activities of the brave Vichy pilot, advising the friendly fighters who were patrolling the area.

DeVane and his flight then continued up the coast to Bouznika, and there turned inland, taking a southeasterly course that brought them over Mèdouina. The VS-41 pilots and radio-gunners could see that the aerodrome had been

Lieutenant Ralph A. Embree and Aviation Radioman 1st Class Joseph M. Eardley, his radio-gunner, November 1942. (NA, 80-G-31339)

"thoroughly strafed," evidence to that thoroughness provided by the "charred wrecks of several enemy aircraft" on the ground. They also saw the "burned wreck of one of our Grumman fighters," possibly the charred carcass of Eddie Micka's 9-F-13, reflecting the fact that wreaking destruction upon the Vichy force had not been achieved without cost.

In looking over the field, however, DeVane and his section saw what appeared to be five "still relatively undamaged" D.520s. "This division therefore set about destroying these remaining enemy aircraft," a VS-41 chronicler matter-of-factly wrote later, "by a combined bombing and strafing attack." The SBD's fixed .50-calibers soon torched two of the Dewoitines, but the other three, "while obviously hit,"

refused to burn. Bill Longley released his entire bomb load, his 500-pounder from the displacing gear and the two 100-pounders from the wing racks, on the field. His section leader "had intended to let everything go," too, but for some reason DeVane could not get his 500-pounder to release.

DeVane and his flight continued on to Ber Richid, and thence north to Casablanca, seeing nothing en route. However, about one mile south of El Hank, the VS-41 flight took anti-aircraft fire from one of the still troublesome French batteries. DeVane gave permission for Weeks and Twiddy, who still retained their bombs, to attack. Without further ado, they did so, diving on the battery, releasing their ordnance, then retiring to seaward and returning directly to the ship. DeVane and

Lieutenant Embree's SBD-3 (BuNo 06627), 41-S-4, after encountering a eucalyptus tree on 9 November. (NA, 80-G-30288)

Longley continued to follow the main road toward Mazagan for about 25 miles. Seeing no signs of any enemy forces, the two pilots turned out to sea, with DeVane finally able to jettison his bomb into the ocean before the *Ranger* recovered him a quarter of an hour into the first dog watch.

In the meantime, the *Ranger*, CAP coverage provided in part by a portion of the five-plane flight commanded by Lt. Harry W. Harrison, Jr., A-V(N) (four F4Fs from VGS-30 and one from VGF-27), put aloft by the *Suwanee* a little over an hour into the afternoon watch, began another cycle of launches, beginning with a flight of eight F4Fs, under Ham Weiler, which had been put aloft in response to a dispatch that had been received from an army liaison officer at 1355:

ENEMY DRAWING IN INFANTRY AND TANKS REINFORCEMENTS WILL REQUIRE MUCH ASSISTANCE X BELIEVE SPITFIRE OR P40 WILL TURN THE TIDE

FLIGHT B-19 (VF-41)

First Section

Lt. Herold J. Weiler, Jr.
Lt. (jg) Walter E. Laake, A-V(N)

Lt. Ernest W. Wood, Jr.
Lt. (jg) George M. Harris, Jr., A-V(N)
Lt. (jg) Dee Jones, A-V(N)

Second Section

Lt. Maynard M. Furney, A-V(N)
Lt. (jg) George E. Harris, A-V(N)

Lt. (jg) Edmund J. Kelly, A-V(N)
Ens. Will "W" Taylor, A-V(N)

FLIGHT B-20 (VF-9)

First Section

Lt. Comdr. John Raby
Lt. (jg) Harold E. Vita, A-V(N)

Lt. Hugh D. O'Neill, Jr., A-V(N)
Lt. (jg) Stanton M. Amesbury, A-V(N)

Second Section

Lt. Jacob W. Onstott
Ens. Burton L. Bardeen, A-V(N)

Lt. (jg) Charles L. Moutenot, A-V(N)
Ens. Albert E. Martin, A-V(N)
Ens. William J. Bonneau, A-V(N)

FLIGHT B-21 (VS-41)

Lt. (jg) Horace R. White, A-V(N)
    Aviation Radioman 3d Class A. R. Smith

Captain Ford A. Allcorn, USA, prepares to take off in his Piper L-4 "Cub" (Serial Number 236389) around 1354 on 9 November 1942, with Capt. Brenton A. De Vall, USA, in back. Note personal name "Elizabeth" in script below the windshield. (NA, 80-G-30339)

Ens. Arthur L. Warta, A-V(N)
    Aviation Radioman 3d Class Morris S. Waterson
Lt. Cecil V. Johnson
    Aviation Radioman 2d Class Gerhard H. O. Kleiner
Lt. (jg) Robert H. Higley, A-V(N)
    Aviation Radioman 3d Class L. E. Colon
Lt. (jg) Clyde A. Tucker, Jr., A-V(N)
    Aviation Radioman 3d Class Lloyd E. Edens
Lt. (jg) Harold R. Keller, Jr., A-V(N)
    Aviation Radioman 2d Class A. W. Lorentzen

Taking off from the *Ranger* late in the afternoon watch, at 1455, Jack Raby led flight B-20 toward Port Lyautey, to support the advance of the troops in that sector. As Fighting Nine's sections headed for their objective, the *Suwanee* put aloft four F4Fs (two each from VGS-30 and VGF-28, under Lt. Comdr. Bag Bagdanovich), for CAP over their home base and the *Ranger*.

Raby's first section descended to between 500 and 1,000 feet and reconnoitered the road from Rabat to Port Lyautey, as well as the roads inland from the latter place, Jake Onstott's second section flew cover at 5,000 feet. Moderate antiaircraft fire, put up from guns at Rabat-Salé, spattered the scattered clouds as VF-9 flew by, showing that the French still possessed plenty of fight.

Having identified targets below—trucks and tanks on the roads stretching north from Port Lyautey and between that place and Petitjean—Raby led his flight down on fast and low strafing runs, in column formation, starting from a dive. Despite heavy antiaircraft and machine gun fire, Raby and his sectionmates shot up five trucks and a tank, setting one of the trucks afire. One of the VF-9 fliers observed several trucks parked in a grove 15 miles east of Rabat on the Rabat-Meknes road, which bore strange markings—what appeared to be large white squares and yellow crosses. Uncertain what the markings signified, VF-9's flight took no action.

Stan Amesbury, the tail-end charlie of the formation, failed to return. When his group recovered after the third or fourth strafing attack on the column on the Port Lyautey–Petitjean road, he was nowhere to be found. Amesbury had been about 400 yards behind the plane preceding him, but no one saw what befell him. However, when the pilot who had preceded Amesbury in the strafing run pulled up from his dive following his attack, there was an explosion behind him of sufficient force to buffet his plane.

Recovery operations proceeded apace, with the ship bringing on board Ham Weiler's and Jack Raby's sections, starting a little less than midway into the first dog watch. At 1723, a brief ceremony accompanied the remains of Aviation Radioman 3d Class Aubra T. Patterson being committed to the

The pilot of [41-F-]25 moves his F4F-4 up the deck on 9 November, while Army Piper L-4s (visible in distance) prepare to fly in to Fedala. A plane handler stands ready with a chock (R). Note row of full bomb carts (L) and an "Asbestos Joe" (a crewman in an asbestos suit) standing ready by the island. (NA, 80-G-30244)

deep in a solemn burial-at-sea ceremony. Ten minutes later, the ship recovered the last of her own aircraft for the day, bringing in flight B-21. Twenty minutes after that, she recovered three F4F-4s from the *Suwanee*'s VGF-27, part of Lt. Fitz Fitzpatrick's flight that had flown CAP over the *Sangamon*.

That afternoon, about the time that the *Ranger* had launched flight B-16, Chuck August's captors took him before an interpreter, a French naval commander, who asked him a number of questions: name and rank, the reason for attacking the French, and what kind of aircraft he had flown. The French officer also asked him what part the British had taken in the operation. August's outright refusal to answer that particular question prompted the interpreter to declare that "Vichy represented a policy or form of government peculiar to the French and not coupled with or controlled by the Nazis."

August then complained about their quarters and demanded "accommodations befitting an American officer." Told that the French had not expected to take prisoners, that no other quarters were available, and that he and his comrades would have to spend one more night in the jail, August asked for, and offered to pay for, medical treatment and for better food. In response, the French returned him to the large cell from which captive U.S. soldiers had been removed.[6]

Around 1400, the French had taken August, Windy Shields, and Tom Dougherty to the naval arsenal across the street from the admiralty headquarters. A fusillade of shots nearby greeted their arrival, at which time all of the French sailors in the vicinity stationed themselves with their rifles behind barricades. After the excitement passed, the same French officer who had questioned Chuck

August interrogated Windy Shields as well. Superficial medical treatment for the three pilots ensued at a naval infirmary.

Upon being returned to the naval prison, which they soon nicknamed the "Bastille," for the prison in Paris made famous by its destruction during the French Revolution, the three aviators encountered Spanky Carter, who was just being brought in. As August later recorded it, after learning of the others' experiences and the conditions under which they had been imprisoned, Carter, who by virtue of his rank was the senior prisoner of war, began protesting their treatment. A member of Phi Delta Phi, the legal fraternity at the University of North Dakota, Carter asserted their rights as prisoners and "strenuously demanded accommodations befitting officer prisoners of war" and insisted that they be permitted to go to the admiralty.

Carter, who later characterized his response to the others' telling him of conditions as "vigorous," soon found that his protests availed them nothing. A French naval officer simply asked them if they "were going to obey orders." The interpreter then ordered the pilots into a "filthy, dark, poorly ventilated" cell "not suitable for dogs," insisting that there were simply no more accommodations available for them. The French did, however, provide them with "several mattresses and more blankets," and bribes managed to persuade "a young friendly French lad" to obtain oranges and tangerines, on which the Americans subsisted "in lieu of bread and water." That night, the previous evening's experience fresh in his mind, Chuck August "threatened the guard with a fate worse than death if he dared flash his light even once." All hands were finally able to get some sleep.

Mac Wordell chafed at the busy-ness of the *4th Bureau* offices, where he was being held. He had not seen any U.S. Navy planes all day, and as a result had been "a little depressed." He had had a good meal prepared by a general's cook—cooked lentils, pork sausage, and red wine—but had still not received any medical care. As evening came on, his khaki shirt afforded little protection from the chill, so he borrowed a French tank officer's leather coat. Walking out onto the terrace to escape the "nightmare" that the office had become, his morale boosted slightly by using a French ruler as a swagger stick, he looked out over the partially blacked-out city. It was very quiet, and the cool evening air proved soothing. He tiredly strolled back inside and lay down on the mattress on the cement floor. Still not having bathed, Wordell itched so much, he recalled, "I don't believe that I slept at all."[7]

On board the *Ranger*, Commander Hoskins spoke to the crew, summarizing events up to that point, acknowledging the "excellent play by play" given by Chaplain O'Callahan the day before. "Up until we started this engagement," the exec began, "we had reasonable assurances that we would meet no opposition. However, as I told you before it is never safe to do wishful thinking. Fortunately for us, our high Command planned for the maximum resistance and it is well that they did so plan." Alluding to President Roosevelt's "friendly appeal" to the French, Hoskins noted that the "French saw fit to disregard [it] and have offered all the resistance in their power against not only a friendly nation but one which is doing everything possible to remove the German heel of oppression from the necks of the French people." He noted the resistance that the French were still putting up, observing, with a folksy baseball allusion that often flavored the exec's speech, that "since the French have seen fit not to play ball with us it has been unnecessarily costly for both sides." Alluding to the enemy's concentrating his undersea forces in the area, Hoskins urged his listeners to keep "a sharp lookout for submarines every minute he is on the topside." So far, he concluded, "our Squadrons and the ship's crew have done marvelous work and I have never read a message containing higher praise than our Admiral gave us yesterday. However," he added, again using another diamond analogy, "we must keep on hitting the ball if we are to successfully complete our mission and arrive safely at Pier 7."[8]

During the day, the U-boats directed to proceed toward the coast of French Morocco did so at their best speeds. Because of the modification of earlier orders, Operation Torch, which the Germans had not anticipated, greatly effected U-boat operations then underway. Depleted fuel supplies and long homeward voyages lay before most of the boats already deployed. Boats that had slipped through the heavily patrolled Straits of Gibraltar received a message from the Führer himself: "I expect a completely victorious operation." To the boats headed for the coast of French Morocco, Hitler waxed no less optimistic about success. He had exhorted his U-boat sailors to complete victory in the Mediterranean, and he also expected the same from the boats deployed to counter Torch. "I expect the same from boats off Morocco and Gibraltar. We must relentlessly carry out the Führer's will with our tested brutal methods of attack. The sinking of transports will have great significance for the American attack and the French defense."[9]

22

"WELL DONE, *RANGER*"

Two and a quarter hours into the morning watch on 10 November, the *Ranger* inaugurated flight operations for the day by launching four F4F-4s, under Casey Childers, at 0615 for CAP over the ship:

FLIGHT C-1 (VF-9)

Lt. Kenan C. Childers
Ens. Merle M. Hershey, A-V(N)

Lt. (jg) Mayo A. Hadden, Jr., A-V(N)
Lt. (jg) Armistead B. Smith, Jr., A-V(N)

Flight deck crews then spotted more VF-9 Wildcats on deck, to follow the first group launched for the CAP over the *Ranger*. The second group, Captain Jack Raby in the lead, began taking off to provide support for ground forces in the Fedala area. At about the same time, the *Suwanee* was turning into the wind and launching four F4F-4s from VGS-30, under Bag Bagdanovich, to augment Casey Childers's flight.

FLIGHT C-2 (VF-9)

First Section

Lt. Comdr. John Raby
Lt. (jg) Harold E. Vita, A-V(N)

Lt. Hugh D. O'Neill, Jr., A-V(N)
Lt. (jg) Reuben H. Denoff, A-V(N)

Second Section

Lt. Jacob W. Onstott
Ens. Hamilton McWhorter, III, A-V(N)

Lt. (jg) Charles L. Moutenot, A-V(N)
Ens. Burton L. Bardeen, A-V(N)

About three-quarters of an hour after putting VF-9's flight C-2 aloft, the *Ranger* put up a single SBD, to deliver messages to the *Augusta*, thus beginning another cycle of launchings at 0655:

FLIGHT C-3 (VS-41)

Lt. John M. DeVane, Jr.
    Aviation Radioman 1st Class William O. Haynes, Jr.

Although unsuccessful in his attempt to drop messages on board the flagship as planned, DeVane flew over to Fedala to carry out an antisubmarine patrol, encountering poor weather—a 400-foot ceiling, rain, and visibility extending only a quarter of a mile.

Soon after putting DeVane's single-plane flight into the air, Ralph Embree led off Flight C-4, to bomb coast defense positions near the lighthouse at El Hank:

FLIGHT C-4 (VS-41)

Lt. Ralph A. Embree
    Aviation Radioman 1st Class Joseph M. Eardley

Lt. (jg) William H. Longley, A-V(N)
  Aviation Radioman 3d Class John G. Korecki
Lt. (jg) Woodie L. McVay, Jr., A-V(N)
  Aviation Radioman 2d Class Kenneth W. Jobe
Lt. (jg) Horace R. White, A-V(N)
  Aviation Radioman 3d Class A. R. Smith
Ens. Arthur L. Warta, A-V(N)
  Aviation Radioman 3d Class R. E. O'Connor

As the skies began to lighten, the activity on the *Ranger*'s flight deck continued unabated. Once the roar of the SBDs' engines had subsided, as Ralph Embree's flight took off on its assigned missions, the deck crews brought up a trio of Wildcats from VF-41 for a reconnaissance mission of the area between Petitjean and Casablanca. Once that group had been put up, the ship brought that cycle of launches to a close with flight C-6, four F4F-4s, under Ham Weiler, to conduct CAP over the ship.

FLIGHT C-5 (VF-41)

Photographic

Lt. Walter F. Madden, A-V(N)

Escort

Lt. Earle F. Craig
Lt. (jg) Hubert T. Houston, A-V(N)

FLIGHT C-6 (VF-41)

Lt. Herold J. Weiler, Jr.
Lt. (jg) Dee Jones, A-V(N)

Lt. Ernest W. Wood, Jr.
Lt. (jg) Clyde C. Andrews, A-V(N)

Upon reaching their objective, Embree's troops encountered poor visibility and rain, which limited visibility to a mile, and a 100-foot cloud ceiling. With the low clouds militating against a dive-bombing attack, Embree deployed his half-dozen SBDs in a glide-bombing run "in order to remain on target." Antiaircraft fire began to blossom in the sky, from guns around the battery, as well as at the root of El Hank point. Embree returned to the ship believing that his flight had scored at least three good solid hits, one directly on a battery position, with three bombs missing the objective. On the return flight to the *Ranger*, the VS-41 airmen noticed two small fishing boats in the waters approximately five miles north of the ship. A quick investigation revealed "no evidence of radio antenna or radio gear."

Lieutenant Comdr. Jack Bandy led a mixed flight (three F4Fs from VGF-27, five from VGF-28 and two from VF-9) off the *Suwanee*, starting at 0825, to fly CAP over the *Ranger*, his old ship. To provide close air support for the troops near Fedala, the *Ranger* launched an eight-plane flight (C-7), beginning five minutes later. She then launched the three F4Fs from the *Suwanee*'s VGF-27, which had come on board late in the first dog watch the day before, to fly CAP over their own ship; they would eventually join up with Jack Bandy's for the return flight.

FLIGHT C-7 (VF-41)

First Section

Lt. Comdr. Charles T. Booth, II
Lt. (jg) Boyd N. Mayhew, A-V(N)

Lt. (jg) Edmund J. Kelly, A-V(N)
Lt. (jg) Walter E. Laake, A-V(N)

Second Section

Lt. Keene G. Hammond
Lt. (jg) William H. Bolt, Jr., A-V(N)

Lt. (jg) Arthur J. Cassidy, A-V(N)
Ens. Philip S. Ball, A-V(N)

FLIGHT C-8 (VGF-27)

Three F4F-4s

Beginning at 0839, the *Ranger* began recovery of the three flights that she had launched during the morning watch, bringing on board Casey Childers's CAP flight and Jack Raby's ground support group. Count DeVane had returned to the ship after an uneventful flight. Attempts to perform his drop on the *Augusta* had not been successful, and the antisubmarine patrol of the transport area yielded no evidence of submarine activity. When he returned to the ship, however, DeVane made a high approach and landed hard on his left wheel, bringing that particular recovery cycle to a close. His SBD-3 (BuNo 06628) required a major overhaul.[1]

In the meantime, at 0854, the *Suwanee* launched four TBF-1s from VGF-27, under Lt. Waller C. "Moe" Moore, Jr., to fly antisubmarine patrol over the transport area off Fedala. Circumstances, however, would soon dictate a change of mission. Ralph Embree's six-plane flight returned to the *Ranger* soon after Count DeVane's landing mishap and began coming on board at 0906. Having noted that the guns at El Hank appeared to be pointing toward the harbor area, and that the weather appeared to be moderating, Embree overflew the *Ranger* and dropped a message recommending that a return flight be sent back to the battery to silence the guns. The carrier had recovered three of Embree's six planes, however, when two torpedo wakes passed close astern and prompted her to execute an emergency turn to starboard and ring down emergency full speed ahead. Two additional torpedoes broached 100 yards astern, and narrowly missed the light cruiser *Cleveland*, steaming astern of the carrier. Jack Bandy's *Suwanee* CAP section aided in the search for the submarine.

The intrepid Vichy boat was most likely the *Tonnant*, which had endured two days of depth-chargings in attempts to attack the American ships. She had escaped Casablanca harbor on the morning of 8 November, under Lt. Pierre Corre, her executive officer, who had had to assume command after the ship's commanding officer had been killed en route to the ship during the bombardment of the port area. Lieutenant (jg) Arthur, who had been one of those not yet recovered, sighted the sub, but was unable to get off a contact report.

Soon after winding up the recovery of Embree's flight, the *Ranger* began bringing in Ham Weiler's CAP flight, which had sighted the ubiquitous Spanish fishing vessels in the area. Andy Andrews, in the landing circle, however, spotted a disturbance in the water on the port beam, about 500 yards from the ship and inside the destroyer screen. He received no direct reply, but a query for clarification: "What's that position again?" Andrews replied: "Directly astern." The *Corry* dropped depth charges, but could not obtain a sound contact. She eventually abandoned the search and rejoined the screen at 0936.

Tommy Booth's flight C-7 had, meanwhile, made contact with American forces in the vicinity of the Fedala–Rabat bridge that spanned the Cherrat River. The VF-41 sections saw two U.S. trucks and between 10 to 15 soldiers near the bridge, on the southwest bank of the river. Proceeding south, Booth and his men spotted "several unidentified tanks, scout cars, trucks, and motorcycles moving north on the road." Contact with a liaison officer soon yielded instructions to destroy "any vehicles in this vicinity not identified as friendly."

Booth and his pilots then moved up and down the road between Bouznika and the Nififikh River, strafing anything that moved, their .50-caliber gunfire stopping the column's movement, setting fire to a tank, two trucks, and three or four motorcycles; several light tanks burned for a few minutes at a time, before the VF-41 sections flew north to Rabat aerodrome. After observing no activity there, Booth radioed a report of the destruction wreaked on the column on the road to the liaison officer, and headed for home.

Less than an hour after the *Tonnant*'s attack had first interrupted flight operations, the *Ranger* recovered Lieutenant Craig and Lieutenant (jg) Houston from flight C-5. They had separated from Wally Madden early in their mission, Craig and Houston flying east to reexamine Mèdouina aerodrome. Finding two fighters on the ground that "didn't look to be completely destroyed," they strafed them until they were. Craig's recovery was not without incident: his F4F-4 went into the barrier, but without serious damage.

No sooner had she recovered Craig and Houston than the *Ranger* spotted a submarine periscope 2,000 yards on the starboard bow. She executed an emergency turn to port and again worked up to full speed. The *Ellyson*'s lookouts reported a periscope dead ahead; the destroyer surged to the attack and dropped a "full pattern depth charge with shallow settings at [the] position of [the] contact." She then regained her position ahead of the carrier, after conducting her attack; the *Hobson*, on the *Ranger*'s starboard quarter, dropped depth charges at the point of contact, with no observable results. The *Ranger* then directed Moe Moore's section of TBFs from the *Suwanee* to shift their antisubmarine patrol to the *Ranger*'s vicinity.

Wally Madden, separated from his escort, had reached Fedala, but encountered rain. Flying to El Hank, and thence to Rabat, in search of better weather, he continued on to Port Lyautey, where he managed to take some photographs. The occupants of a small truck traveling east to Port Lyautey abandoned their vehicle at his low-level approach; he then strafed it before continuing on. He flew on to Petitjean, where he encountered machine gun south of that place, and set course to return to the *Ranger*.

As the *Brooklyn* joined the task group, Cal Durgin had a signal sent to her commanding officer, Capt. Francis C. Denebrink: "Glad to have you with us. Submarines are after us. Keep your eyes open. Cal." From the *Brooklyn* came an answering signal: "Glad to be here. Our luck good so far. We've knocked them before and we can do it again. Denny."[2]

In between the exchange of pleasantries between captains, the *Ranger* put up a CAP flight over Fedala, with the pilots given the additional duty of attacking enemy forces on the roads in the vicinity, as well as any targets of opportunity. Flight C-9, consisting of eight F4F-4s from Fighting Nine, under Pedro Winters, began taking off at 1040. Inside a quarter of an hour, the *Suwanee* was putting up a five-plane flight (VGF-27), under Fitz Fitzpatrick, to fly CAP over the *Ranger*.

FLIGHT C-9 (VF-9)

First Section

Lt. Theodore H. Winters, Jr.
Ens. Merle M. Hershey, A-V(N)

Lt. (jg) Mayo A. Hadden, Jr., A-V(N)
Lt. (jg) Armistead B. Smith, Jr., A-V(N)

Second Section

Lt. Kenan C. Childers
Ens. Louis A. Menard, A-V(N)

Lt. (jg) John H. Sands, A-V(N)
Ens. James M. Wilkerson, A-V(N)

Shortly after Pedro Winters's sections had taken off and headed out on their mission, the *Ranger* recovered Tommy Booth's flight C-7, then Wally Madden, who returned to the ship over an hour after his escort. Shortly, however, events began to transpire that would involve a ship that the *Ranger*'s pilots had felt sure they had knocked out of the fight.

At 1120, the *Augusta* received word that what appeared to be two French "destroyers" had sortied from Casablanca and were shelling U.S. 7th Infantry positions near Roches Noires. Consequently, the heavy cruiser, accompanied by the destroyers *Tillman* and *Edison* (DD-439), altered course to engage what proved to be the second-class sloops (*avisos*) *Commandant Delage* and *La Gracieuse*, mindful of the French battery at El Hank still being operational (and thus staying out of range of its troublesome guns), but confident in aerial observers' reports that the *Jean Bart*, having been hit by bombs and 15-inch shells on 8 November, had been "gutted by fire." The *Augusta* opened up with her 8-inch guns at 1135, and soon straddled the *Commandant Delage* several times.

Unknown to the Americans, however, the *Jean Bart* was far from out of action. After the pounding that the *Massachusetts* had administered on 8 November, it was believed that the *Jean Bart* would cause no trouble. Although Herculean efforts had cleared the wreckage that had jammed her one main battery turret in train and allowed it to be restored to full capacity, it had been left the way it had appeared the day before, to create the impression that it was out of action. Soon, however, as the range, closed, the *Jean Bart*'s 15-inch rifles bellowed. Yellow-orange–dyed geysers of water leapt skyward alongside the *Augusta*, the spray falling upon the men on her flag bridge. Without further ado, the cruiser sped seaward to open the range, a bone in teeth. One of the *Jean Bart*'s projectiles landed ahead of the *Augusta*, the towering splash drenching almost the forward half of the ship. As Lt. Comdr. Allan G. Gaden, the *Augusta*'s communication officer later observed, "No hits [from the *Jean Bart*'s shells] were registered and we returned to the transport area feeling very fortunate that no damage had been sustained and indignant at the falsity of the report that the *Jean Bart* had been 'gutted by fire.' Admiral Hewitt then ordered a dive bombing attack on the *Jean Bart* by our carrier planes."[3]

In the meantime, in the course of their two-hour mission, Pedro Winters's flight encountered generally "very poor" flying conditions, with visibility ranging between three and five miles, with a 250-foot ceiling and rain. Patrolling over the beach and observing no enemy forces, and seeing that friendly forces met no apparent opposition, Fighting Nine's flight proceeded down the road to Rabat for 15 to 20 miles, before they encountered a column of trucks and what appeared to be ammunition carts, spread down the highway at a considerable interval, but in no particular concentration. Some sat parked alongside the road, some moving, some in the woods nearby. Those moving vehicles appeared to be heading north. Encountering light antiaircraft fire, Winters's flight, using a weaving approach, made fast strafing attacks, setting afire and destroying at least eight vehicles. Two of the trucks appeared to have been canopied, and bore camouflage, leading one observer to speculate that they may have been used for transporting troops.

The weather had abated slightly by the time the *Ranger*'s flight deck crew had spotted VF-9's next flight, C-10, to take up CAP over Fedala. At 1225, Jake Onstott began leading off C-10.

FLIGHT C-10 (VF-9)

First Section

Lt. Jacob W. Onstott
Ens. Hamilton McWhorter, III, A-V(N)

Lt. (jg) Harrison Feasley, A-V(N)
Ens. Robert M. McGann, A-V(N)

Second Section

Lt. Hugh D. O'Neill, Jr.,
Lt. (jg) Reuben H. Denoff, A-V(N)

Ens. William J. Bonneau, A-V(N)
Ens. James E. Toliver, A-V(N)

Directly afterwards the *Ranger* recovered Moe Moore's four TBF-1s from the *Suwanee*, low on fuel, which had been flying antisubmarine patrol in the *Ranger*'s vicinity after the *Tonnant* had disrupted flight operations during the forenoon watch. As the flight deck crew spotted the transient TBFs forward, the ship began recovering Pedro Winters's flight. She also brought in two of Jake Onstott's flight C-9 ahead of schedule: almost immediately after takeoff, Bill Bonneau had noticed his engine beginning to siphon oil.

Bonneau turned back to return to the ship, accompanied by Oliver Toliver, and landed at 1254.

Jake Onstott's six-plane flight thus proceeded to Fedala, encountering better weather than Pedro Winters' had; Onstott assessed it as fair, with visibility varying from 3 to 10 miles, and a ceiling that varied from 500 feet to unlimited. Making landfall at Rabat, C-10 patrolled down the road toward Fedala; from Rabat to the Cherrat River, the pilots observed "large numbers of burned trucks and equipment" along the roadway—most likely the victims of flight C-9's pilots earlier. Onstott and his fliers strafed a cavalry unit as they proceeded south, as well as trucks parked alongside the road, setting afire four vehicles. As they headed south to Fedala, they observed the remnants of the *Estafette* convoy beached north of that port; once they reached Fedala proper, they orbited the port at 4,000 feet, awaiting a reported inbound attack by enemy bombers that never materialized. The patrol had gone without incident, although two pilots later reported poor radio reception and another that both of his mid wing guns had gone out of commission.

To maintain the CAP, the *Suwanee* turned into the wind, an hour and a half into the afternoon watch. After putting aloft a five-plane flight (from VGF-28), under Lt. Howard L. Johnson, to patrol over their home base, the auxiliary aircraft carrier launched a mixed flight (one F4F from VGS-30, one from VGF-28, and three from VGF-27), under Sam Silber, to stand watch in the skies over the *Ranger*.

A short time later, as Silber's flight was winging its way to take up its station overhead, almost midway through the afternoon watch, in the wake of the *Jean Bart*'s demonstrating her still possessing fight, Admiral McWhorter issued the order to his flagship:

WHEN READY LAUNCH 9 VSB ARMED WITH 1,000 POUND BOMBS TO ATTACK JEAN BART X 8 VF TO STRAFE BATTERIES ON DOCKS AND STRAFE ENEMY DDS OUTSIDE HARBOR X LAUNCH 4 SUWANEE TBFS TO RETURN TO THAT SHIP X 8 VF FOR COMBAT AIR PATROL OVER FEDALA[4]

To carry out that directive, the *Ranger*'s flight deck crew spotted Moe Moore's 4 VGF-27 TBF-1s from the *Suwanee*, so that they could carry out an antisubmarine patrol off Fedala. Once the visiting TBFs had been put aloft, the *Ranger* began launching flight C-11—8 F4F-4s from VF-9, under Jack Raby—beginning at 1417. The pace of operations incident to Torch, however, had reduced the number of operational SBDs on board the *Ranger* to 12; F4Fs to 19.[5]

FLIGHT "N" (VGF-27)

Lt. Waller C. Moore, Jr. (4 TBF-1s)

FLIGHT C-11 (VF-9)

First Section

Lt. Comdr. John Raby
Ens. Marvin J. Franger, A-V(N)

Lt. (jg) Harold E. Vita, A-V(N)
Ens. Ernest D. Brooks, A-V(N)

Second Section

Lt. (jg) Charles L. Moutenot, A-V(N)
Ens. Albert E. Martin, A-V(N)

Ens. William J. Bonneau, A-V(N)
Ens. James E. Toliver, A-V(N)

Five minutes after the last Wildcat had wobbled aloft and begun heading toward Casablanca, the *Ranger* began launching a nine-plane strike from VS-41, to put the *Jean Bart* out of business for good.

FLIGHT C-12 (VS-41)

Lt. Ralph A. Embree
    Aviation Radioman 1st Class Joseph M. Eardley
Lt. (jg) Harold R. Keller, Jr., A-V(N)
    Aviation Radioman 2d Class A. W. Lorentzen
Lt. (jg) John G. McReynolds, A-V(N)
    Aviation Radioman 3d Class Oscar I. Light

Lt. John M. DeVane, Jr.
    Aviation Radioman 1st Class William O. Haynes, Jr.
Lt. (jg) Cyrus F. Weeks, A-V(N)
    Aviation Radioman 3d Class G. H. Perry
Lt. (jg) Clarence A. Twiddy, Jr., A-V(N)
    Aviation Radioman 3d Class R. E. O'Connor

Lt. Cecil V. Johnson
    Aviation Radioman 2d Class Gerhard H. O. Kleiner
Lt. (jg) Robert H. Higley, A-V(N)
    Aviation Radioman 3d Class L. E. Colon
Lt. (jg) Clyde A. Tucker, Jr., A-V(N)
    Aviation Radioman 3d Class Lloyd E. Edens

Because Count DeVane's drop of photographs on the *Augusta* had been unsuccessful, the *Ranger* turned into the wind five minutes after the last of Embree's troops had taken off to bomb the *Jean Bart*, to attempt a second photo-delivery run to the flagship. A little over a quarter of an hour after the launch of the sole SBD from VS-41, the

Three of the four TBF-1s from VGF-27, from the *Suwanee,* preparing to take off at 1420 on 10 November. Spotted immediately behind them on the flight deck are Jack Raby's VF-9 flight and VS-41 SBDs earmarked to attack the still troublesome *Jean Bart*. (NA, 80-G-30328)

Ranger recovered Jake Onstott's flight after its ground support mission.

FLIGHT C-13 (VS-41)

Lt. (jg) Horace R. White, A-V(N)
    Aviation Radioman 3d Class A. R. Smith

To ensure that trigger-happy gunners received the word, Admiral McWhorter had a dispatch sent to the *Augusta*:

ONE VSB WILL MAKE MESSAGE DROP ON MIGHTY [call sign for the *Augusta*] SOON X REQUEST YOU NOTIFY OTHER SHIPS[6]

Raby and his Fighting Nine contingent found flying conditions good over the objective, with 8–10 mile visibility and a ceiling of broken clouds at 4,000 and 9,000 feet, as they came in from the south of Casablanca at 14,000 feet. Raby and his three sectionmates broke off and dove on the *Jean Bart,* opening fire with their .50-calibers at 4,000 feet, in the teeth of heavy antiaircraft and machine gun fire. Simultaneously, Moot Moutenot and Al Martin began shooting up the gun emplacements on the *Jettie Delure;* Bill Bonneau and Oliver Toliver began doing the same to the antiaircraft guns at the base of the *Jettie Transversale.* Raby and his troops pulled out at 400 feet and raced to seaward.

No sooner had Jack Raby's eight Wildcats cleared the area than Ralph Embree led his nine SBDs, each with a 1,000-pound bomb with a 1/100-second delay fuse, down onto their unmistakeable target, which lay immobile, but still full of fight, beneath them. Embree and his men found the conditions "perfect for dive-bombing,"—good visibility and a large cumulus cloud at 8,000 feet, which cloaked their approach. Coming in from the east at 11,000 feet, Embree, in the lead, slanted down into a fast glide at that altitude, maintaining it until the altimeter read 8,000, when he pushed over into the dive.

Lieutenant (jg) Clyde A. Tucker, Jr., A-V(N), and Aviation Radioman 3d Class Lloyd E. "Mickey" Edens, his radio-gunner, November 1942. (NA, 80-G-31343)

Despite VF-9's strafing runs, however, light- and medium-caliber antiaircraft fire still continued to pepper the sky, as Scouting Forty-One dove on the *Jean Bart*. Embree's bomb landed in the water on the *Jean Bart*'s port beam, a very near miss; Keller's hit a warehouse on the pier. As Keller pulled out, however, he looked around to see McReynolds's bomb make a direct hit; debris and smoke soon obscured the battleship's bow. DeVane placed his bomb very near where McReynolds's had hit; Weeks and Twiddy put their 1,000-pounders between the warehouses off the *Jean Bart*'s starboard quarter. Johnson scored a direct hit "squarely on the starboard portion of the aft deck," which peeled back a section of that deck as if a giant can-opener had been taken to it. Higley's bomb struck just to the left of the after turret mount, inboard of the port rail,

and Tucker capped the attack with a hit on the stern. Jack Raby's pilots counted at least three or four direct hits.[7] Despite the damage wreaked by Scouting Forty-One, however, the *Jean Bart*'s 15-inch guns and fire control apparatus still remained functional.

Imprisoned nearby, Spanky Carter felt the entire building tremble, and large pieces of plaster fell from the ceiling with each explosion. During the raid, the four Americans learned that they were to be transferred again. They left their lunch uneaten. Taken outside to a promenade, the Americans observed a predominance of U.S.-made equipment, including Ford trucks and B.F. Goodrich tires. Subsequently, after about 90 minutes, the French told the VF-41 pilots to gather up their gear—they were being transferred to another prison. A strafing attack delayed the start of the

Second Section

Lt. Maynard M. Furney, A-V(N)
Lt. (jg) George E. Harris, A-V(N)

Lt. (jg) Edward N. Seiler, A-V(N)
Ens. Will "W" Taylor, A-V(N)

Five minutes after the first of Ham Weiler's sections had begun their takeoff runs, Jawn Sweeney took off to photograph Casablanca harbor, Mèdouina aerodrome, and the coast of French Morocco as far north as Port Lyautey.

FLIGHT C-15 (VF-41)

Lt. John R. Sweeney

Sweeney reached Casablanca at about 1535 and found a solid overcast prevailing at 10,000 feet over the city. Descending through the clouds, he found that the clouds extended down 6,000 feet before he emerged into the clear. He flew at 2,000 feet over the *Jean Bart*, observing "medium fire and heavy smoke" issuing from the damaged Vichy battleship and the adjacent dockyard area. Continuing north along the coast, he saw 15 American trucks headed south on the main road between Fedala and Casablanca, then overflew Fedala at 6,000 feet, where he saw neither antiaircraft fire nor any interference with the ongoing landings. Heading for Rabat-Salé, he saw four American tanks heading north on the road just outside of Fedala, and spotted two P-40s in the air nearby. Descending to 3,000 feet over Rabat-Salé, he saw neither activity nor flyable aircraft. As he flew along the coast north to Port Lyautey, he perceived "no hostile action" of any kind, but he noted several demolished French trucks on the road and six U.S. tanks headed east, about a mile east of his northernmost objective. He saw more P-40s on the ground at Port Lyautey, before he flew over Mèdouina at 8,000 feet and Cazes at 9,000, and returned to Casablanca and the *Jean Bart*, diving out of the overcast at 4,500 feet and finding that the ship still appeared to be on fire.

Flight C-11, returned to the *Ranger* at 1535, C-12 at 1540, the latter flying in a V formation. Each mission had taken an elapsed time of only an hour and a quarter. Despite the heavy antiaircraft fire encountered, only Marv Franger's F4F-4 suffered any damage. He counted four bullet holes clean through his wings and one through his engine. At 1545, Hal White (flight C-13) returned to the ship, thinking that he had failed to deliver his packages of photographs to the deck of the *Augusta*. He later learned, however, that one package had indeed been retrieved from the water, when the *Augusta* radioed the *Ranger*:

Lieutenant Cecil V. "Johnny" Johnson (R), one of 12 children (three brothers graduated from the Naval Academy) and Aviation Radioman 1st Class Gerhard W. O. Kleiner, his radio-gunner, en route to North Africa, November 1942. (NA, 80-G-31345)

movement, and, when the transfer actually began, Spanky Carter and his comrades found themselves in a bus that had, according to their captors, survived six strafing attacks—all of the glass had been shattered and both the roof and seats were filled with bullet holes.[8]

Some of the shipmates of the VF-41 pilots being moved to new locales were again taking to the air, to furnish CAP over the transports and landing forces at Fedala and to furnish ground support. Designated as flight C-15, the eight F4Fs began taking off at 1508. Shortly thereafter, the *Suwanee* launched four Wildcats from VGS-30 and two from VGF-28, under Lt. Harry W. Harrison, Jr., A-V(N), to furnish CAP over the *Ranger*.

FLIGHT C-15 (VF-41)

First Section

Lt. Herold J. Weiler, Jr.
Lt. (jg) Dee Jones, A-V(N)

Lt. Earle F. Craig
Ens. Robert C. Cronin, A-V(N)

Lieutenant (jg) John G. McReynolds, A-V(N) (L), pictured here with Aviation Radioman 3d Class Oscar I. Light, his radio-gunner, November 1942, scored a direct hit on the bow of the *Jean Bart* on 10 November. (NA, 80-G-31335)

MESSAGE DROP RECOVERED FROM WATER X THANK YOU.⁹

Ham Weiler's flight had rendezvoused over the ship at 2,000 feet, then set course for Fedala. Once they reached the objective, Weiler deployed four planes to patrol at 4,000 feet and four at 15,000. After an hour overhead and seeing no signs of enemy action, he radioed the Air Liaison officer and asked for a specific mission. The latter asked for a search of the main road between Casablanca and Rabat-Salé. Leaving Bud Furney's section to continue to patrol over Fedala, Weiler took his own along the road north from the Nefifikh River bridge, between 25 and 30 miles.

Still observed by Moe Moore's VGS-27 flight, Weiler's section flew in single-column formation at altitudes of between 50 to 100 feet, and outside of a line of trees that paralleled the road, and strafed armored cars, medium tanks, and trucks on the thoroughfare south of Bouznika; they also worked over what appeared to be an inactive camouflaged antiaircraft battery on the north bank of the Cherrat River. In response to Weiler's request that he do so, Bud Furney then took his section to search the roads leading to Fedala from the east. He and his men headed inland, sighting a burnt-out light tank, a burned motorcyle, and a burned armored car on the road to Bouznika, but no active enemy vehicles, troops, or emplacements.

Damage to Vichy French battleship *Jean Bart*'s starboard side, aft, as the result of the bomb dropped by Johnny Johnson on 10 November. (NA, 80-G-31605)

At about the same time that Ham Weiler was requesting a mission for his flight, the *Ranger* again turned into the wind for another cycle of flight operations. To carry out strafing attacks on the destroyers in Casablanca harbor, she launched five F4Fs from VF-9, under Pedro Winters, beginning at 1617:

FLIGHT C-17 (VF-9)

Lt. Theodore H. Winters, Jr.
Lt. Kenan C. Childers

Lt. (jg) Armistead B. Smith, Jr., A-V(N)
Ens. James M. Wilkerson, A-V(N)
Ens. Merle M. Hershey, A-V(N)

Soon thereafter, less than an hour after Ralph Embree had returned to the ship, he was preparing to go out again, as was his radio-gunner, Joe Eardley. Embree was to lead another flight, designated as C-18, which had been given a threefold mission: to bomb the antiaircraft batteries at the root of the *Jettie Transversale* and at the elbow of the *Jettie Delure;* to attack the shore batteries at El Hank, and to bomb the antiaircraft batteries adjoining the military garrison that lay immediately south of a cemetery southeast of El Hank. None of the pilots and radio-gunners who had flown the mission against the *Jean Bart* would go on this hop. Armorers affixed 1,000-pound bombs with 1/100-second delay fuses beneath the center section of each Dauntless.

FLIGHT C-18 (VS-41)

Mission No. 1

Lt. Ralph A. Embree
Aviation Radioman 1st Class Joseph M. Eardley

Damage to the *Jean Bart*'s starboard bow, 16 November 1942. (NA, 80-G-31601)

Lt. (jg) Maxwell A. Eaton, A-V(N)
 Aviation Radioman 3d Class William T. Shackelford

Mission No. 2

Lt. (jg) Horace R. White, A-V(N)
 Aviation Radioman 3d Class A. R. Smith
Lt. (jg) Robert L. Arthur, A-V(N)
 Aviation Radioman 3d Class Morris S. Waterson
Lt. (jg) Woodie L. McVay, A-V(N)
 Aviation Radioman 2d Class Kenneth W. Jobe
Lt. (jg) William H. Longley, A-V(N)
 Aviation Radioman 3d Class John G. Korecki
Ens. Donald E. Chapman, A-V(N)
 Aviation Radioman 2d Class R. J. Monahan

Mission No. 3

Lt. (jg) Joseph P. Keigher, Jr., A-V(N)
 Aviation Radioman 3d Class J. J. Lankowitz
Lt. (jg) Ralph W. Ross, A-V(N)
 Aviation Radioman 3d Class L. L. Devine

Pedro Winters's section accompanied Embree's SBDs, and, as the latter deployed to attack, the former pushed over and dove just ahead of them to strafe the ships in the harbor, the Wildcat pilots starting their glide from 17,000 feet, out of the sun. They opened fire at 3,000 feet. Winters, followed by Casey Childers and Chick Smith, flying in a loose column formation, weaving as they neared their target, attacked one destroyer; Silky Wilkerson and Merle Hershey similarly and simultaneously strafed another nearby destroyer. Each pilot fired about 600 rounds, as they raked the ships from stem to stern; ceasing fire at 500 feet, they peeled away in the face of light antiaircraft fire from the destroyers and heavy-to-light barrages from the shore batteries all along the coast. Two Wildcats returned to the ship holed.

The *Jean Bart* (center), her still-operable quadruple turret plainly visible, as seen during flight D-7, 11 November 1942. Note tremendous destruction (from bombs and shells) wreaked on the warehouse area near where she lay moored at Casablanca. (NA, 80-G-37188)

In the interim, Ralph Embree approached his target, the heavy antiaircraft battery at the root of the *Jettie Transversale*, from the southwest and down-sun, along with his wingman, Max Eaton. Unable to locate any major-caliber guns firing from that place, however, Embree shifted his sights to a destroyer at anchor outside the jetty. Making a steep dive from 11,000 feet, he released his 1,000-pounder at 1,200 feet, but he neither felt the detonation of the bomb, nor saw any splash in the water near the ship he had attacked. Later, upon return to the ship, he would note the intact arming wire that indicated that his bomb had been a dud.

Eaton, volunteering to make an unassisted attack on the "troublesome A/A emplacements" in the "elbow" of the *Jettie Delure*, opposite the eastern end of the *Mole du Commerce*, pushed over at 9,000 feet, at a 65-degree angle. Seeing that the antiaircraft batteries seemed to be concentrating on his commanding officer, Eaton released his 1,000-pounder at 2,000 feet, and retired to seaward. His bomb made a direct hit.

The attack cheered up Mac Wordell, who witnessed it from the *4th Bureau*'s headquarters roof. He had just enjoyed a long-delayed shave and a bath—in a general's bathroom no less—when "right out of the sun . . . came a co-ordinated attack by SBD's and F4F's. It was beautiful to behold." Empty shell casings fell around him, and "the bombs made a terrific noise." As he later observed, however, the most danger lay in the French antiaircraft fire, one piece of a nose fuse landing on the lower roof of the building in which he had been imprisoned. When the attack was over, he observed what appeared to be two columns of smoke rising into the sky over the port area.[10]

Ralph Embree's second section, led by Horace White, meantime, approached El Hank from the south, flying at 12,000 feet. Pushing over and diving from south to north, in line with the gun emplacements, the pilots opened their flaps at 7,000 feet and released their ordnance at 1,500, encountering only slight antiaircraft fire. White and Arthur aimed for the guns emplaced near the lighthouse at the point; the former's gunsight and windshield fogged up, so that White's bomb "fell far off target." Arthur's 1,000-pounder hit close to one emplacement. The four-gun battery near the tip of El Hank soon got the attention of the other three pilots, and, although they reported no direct hits, McVay, Longley, and Chapman all believed that their bombs had hit close to the guns.

Keigher and Ross wound up the attack by approaching their target—antiaircraft emplacements at the military garrison—from down-sun, at 13,000 feet. Diving at a 15-degree angle with no flaps, they reached 9,000 feet, when the batteries opened up. Both pilots then popped their flaps and pushed over into a steep dive, releasing their bombs at 1,500 feet and, like their squadronmates, retiring toward the sea. Both pilots' ordnance had landed close enough to the batteries to at least temporarily silence the guns.

Soon after the *Ranger* had put aloft flights C-17 and C-18, from the *Brooklyn*, in the screen, Captain Denebrink had a signal sent to Rear Admiral McWhorter, once Jack Raby's and Ralph Embree's flights had returned triumphantly from their mission over Casablanca: "*Brooklyn* sends congradulations [sic] on the splendid job yesterday and today particularly the shellacking you gave *Jean Bart*. The volume of traffic on *Ranger* deck today is something to observe. If the opportunity offers we will run interferrance [sic] for you with pleasure."[11]

In view of the *Jean Bart*'s having been returned to her limited operational capacity and having precipitated the air strike against her earlier that day, Admiral Hewitt signalled Admiral McWhorter:

IN VIEW CONTEMPLATED OPERATIONS DESIRE AS SOON AS PRACTICABLE PHOTOGRAPHIC OBSERVATIONS OF RESULTS ATTACK ON JEAN BART X[12]

Soon thereafter, Admiral McWhorter again paid tribute to his flagship in an internal dispatch, less than a half hour before the end of the first dog watch:

YOUR CONTINUED EFFICIENT AND EFFECTIVE OPERATIONS ARE AN INSPIRATION TO ALL X AGAIN WELL DONE RANGER AND RANGER AIR GROUP[13]

The admiral's message essentially capped the day's activity: his flagship began recovering the last four of her airborne flights beginning at 1715, bringing in Ham Weiler's CAP, Sweeney's single-plane photo reconnaissance mission, and Pedro Winters's strike mission. The *Ranger* began landing Ralph Embree's bombers starting at 1725, shortly before sunset.

The movement of the *Ranger*'s pilots who had been captured by the enemy had taken place: the French took Spanky Carter and the other pilots to the Hippodrome, where, turned over to French Army control, the captured aviators found some 47 or 48 U.S. Army MPs, one U.S. Navy enlisted man, and a number of British civilians who had "refused to pledge allegiance to the Vichy government." As Carter later recounted it, the French had "simply run the horses out and run the prisoners in," and the captives soon found that lice and fleas abounded. The major who had been placed in charge of the prisoners "carefully explained the unfortunate necessity of subjecting our officers to unpleasant conditions," and promised that change would be coming, and soon. Spaghetti, bread, wine, and almonds made up the fare for the evening, and the French provided the Americans with mattresses and blankets.[14] Mac Wordell, separated from his shipmates, had been cheered up by recalling "silly little things like (1) 'Home on the RANGER,' a song arrangement we [had] worked out in the squadron (2) 'Strip Polka' from our squadron juke box . . . (3) squadron catch words like 'salubrious,' 'the round man,' 'five by five,' 'caddy poem,' and its catch phrase 'was he ready yet?'" As the night wore on, he had heard talk of an armistice. "They threw in the sponge," he later wrote, "better late than never."[15]

During the second dog watch on 10 November, the *Ranger*'s lookouts sighted three white lights on the horizon on the port bow. Two minutes into the first watch, radar picked up contacts on the port bow, 5,990 yards away, but all objects faded from the screen at 2040. Lookouts spotted what they reported as a torpedo wake passing across the bow from starboard to port.

The mid watch on 11 November had passed quietly, and the *Ranger* soon began to stir for the day's operations. Shortly before the midpoint of the morning watch, however, Admiral Hewitt informed his force in an urgent plain-language dispatch:

CASABLANCA MAY CAPITULATE IN NEXT FEW HOURS X UPON RECEIPT OF PROPERLY AUTHENTICATED MESSAGE IN CLEAR QUOTE CEASE FIRING UNQUOTE CEASE ALL HOSTILE ACTION IN THAT AREA XX[16]

Consequently, Rear Admiral McWhorter outlined the missions for the morning in an internal dispatch to Cal Durgin:

WHEN READY LAUNCH FOLLOWING AIRCRAFT FOR MISSIONS ASSIGNED X (A) 12 VSB ARMED WITH 1000-POUND BOMBS DESTROY

BATTERIES AT CAMP MILITAIRE…0715 TO 0730 BATTERY AT FOOT OF JETTY [sic] TRANSVERSALE 0730 TO 0745 BATTERY AT FOOT OF MALE [sic] DU COMMERCE 0730 TO 0745 X (B) 12 VF ATTACK WITH GUNS DDS AND OTHER ENEMY NAVAL VESSELS FIRING ON OUR GROUND FORCES X (C) 12 VF DIVERT BY MACHINE GUN ATTACK ANY LIGHT BATTERIES FIRING ON OUR GROUND FORCES X (D) MAINTAIN AIR COMBAT PATROL OF 6 VF OVER CASABLANCA X ATTACK ONLY AIR TARGETS ATTACKS MUST BE MADE AT DESIGNATED TIME OR NOT AT ALL X ONLY DESIGNATED TARGETS ARE TO BE ATTACKED X (E) 1 VTB ANTI-SUBMARINE PATROL VICINITY RANGER X PILOTS BE ALERT FOR PLAIN LANGUAGE AUTHENTICATED MESSAGE QUOTE CEASE FIRING UNQUOTE IN WHICH CASE ALL HOSTILE ACTION CEASE IMMEDIATELY XX[17]

At the time that five Wildcats from the *Suwanee* (three F4Fs from VGS-30 and two from VGF-28), under Lt. Harry Harrison, were on their way to assume their CAP station overhead, the *Ranger* turned into the wind and soon began launching flight D-1, nine SBDs, under Ralph Embree, well before sunrise:

FLIGHT D-1 (VS-41)
First Division (Camp Militaire)

Lt. Ralph A. Embree
    Aviation Radioman 1st Class Joseph M. Eardley
Lt. (jg) Joseph P. Keigher, Jr., A-V(N)
    Aviation Radioman 3d Class J. J. Lankowicz

Second Division (Mole du Commerce)

Lt. (jg) Horace R. White, A-V(N)
    Aviation Radioman 3d Class A. R. Smith
Ens. Charles C. Bevis, Jr., A-V(N)
    Aviation Radioman 3d Class William T. Shackelford
Ens. Thomas M. Hubbard, A-V(N)
    Aviation Radioman 3d Class R. L. Fenton

Third Division (Jettie Transversale)

Lt. (jg) Woodie L. McVay, Jr., A-V(N)
    Aviation Radioman 3d Class Kenneth W. Jobe
Lt. (jg) Clarence A. Twiddy, Jr., A-V(N)
    Aviation Radioman 3d Class R. E. O'Connor
Lt. (jg) Robert H. Higley, A-V(N)
    Aviation Radioman 3d Class L. E. Colon
Lt. (jg) William H. Longley, A-V(N)
    Aviation Radioman 3d Class John G. Korecki

The *Ranger* then began putting up 12 F4Fs, under Tommy Booth, to strafe French naval vessels in Casablanca harbor, designated as flight D-4:

FLIGHT D-4 (VF-41)
First Section

Lt. Comdr. Charles T. Booth, II
Lt. (jg) Boyd N. Mayhew, A-V(N)

Lt. (jg) Edward N. Seiler, A-V(N)
Lt (jg) Walter E. Laake, A-V(N)

Second Section

Lt. Keene G. Hammond
Lt. (jg) William H. Bolt, Jr., A-V(N)

Lt. Earle F. Craig
Lt. (jg) Hubert T. Houston, A-V(N)

Third Section

Lt. Maynard M. Furney, A-V(N)
Ens. Philip S. Ball, A-V(N)

Lt. (jg) George E. Harris, A-V(N)
Ens. Will "W" Taylor, A-V(N)

To support ground forces around Casablanca, the *Ranger* began putting aloft flight D-5, beginning at 0645:

FLIGHT D-5 (VF-9)
First Section

Lt. Jacob W. Onstott
Ens. Marvin J. Franger, A-V(N)

Lt. (jg) Harrison Feasley, A-V(N)
Ens. Albert E. Martin, A-V(N)

Second Section

Lt. (jg) Charles L. Moutenot, A-V(N)
Ens. Burton L. Bardeen, A-V(N)

Third Section

Lt. (jg) Hugh D. O'Neill, Jr., A-V(N)
Lt. (jg) Reuben H. Denoff, A-V(N)

Lt. (jg) Jack H. Sands, A-V(N)
Ens. Ernest D. Brooks, A-V(N)

Fifteen minutes after Jake Onstott had led off flight D-5, Pedro Winters led off flight D-6, to take up CAP over Casablanca.

FLIGHT D-6 (VF-9)

First Section

Lt. Theodore H. Winters, Jr.
Ens. Robert M. McGann, A-V(N)
Lt. (jg) Armistead B. Smith, Jr., A-V(N)

Second Section

Lt. (jg) Mayo A. Hadden, Jr., A-V(N)
Ens. Merle M. Hershey, A-V(N)
Ens. William J. Bonneau, A-V(N)

The four flights of planes put aloft during the morning watch, however, soon found their missions changed, a little less than an hour before the end of that period of time, when the *Ranger* logged word of the awaited "cease fire" at 0704 and broadcast it to her airborne aircraft. After confirming the authenticity of the message, Ralph Embree ordered a return to the ship, two minutes later. "Enemy ceased firing," Seaman 2d Class Crochet later confided to his diary, "We launched patrols all day anyway—in case."[18]

In the event that events transpired to revert back to combat, Admiral Hewitt adjured his force:

BE READY RESUME HOSTILITIES AGAINST FRENCH NAVAL FORCES REPEAT NAVAL FORCES CASABLANCA AT SHORTEST NOTICE XX[19]

Embree and Keigher jettisoned their bombs and landed on board at 0755. Tommy Booth led his recalled flight back on board, beginning at 0757.

In the meantime, Cal Durgin, harkening back to their days at the Naval Academy, responded to Captain Denebrink's congratulatory message received early in the first dog watch the day before:

THANK YOU FOR YOUR KIND MESSAGE I AM PROUD OF THE BOYS TOO X NOW WE HOPE TO GO TO THE SOUTH PACIFIC AND WOULD LIKE TO HAVE YOU AS OUR BLOCKING BACK X IT IS LIKE OUR OLD LACROSSE DAYS TO HAVE YOU BEHIND ME X CONGRATULATIONS ON YOUR EXCELLENT WORK X CAL[20]

The *Ranger* then launched one camera-equipped F4F-4 from VF-41 and a pair of SBDs from VS-41, to conduct photo reconnaissance, the former to photograph the *Jean Bart* and Casablanca harbor and the landing areas between Fedala and Port Lyautey, and the latter to reconnoiter the coast between Casablanca and Port Lyautey. Designated as flight D-7, Wally Madden led off at 0827, followed by Johnny Johnson and Clyde Tucker at 0830.

FLIGHT D-7 (VF-41)

Lt. Walter F. Madden, A-V(N)

FLIGHT D-7 (VS-41)

Lt. Cecil V. Johnson   41-S-3
    Photographer's Mate 2d Class M. D. Mokos
Lt. (jg) Clyde A. Tucker, Jr., A-V(N)   41-S-5
    Photographer's Mate 2d Class William Wade

Soon after launching the sole F4F and the two SBDs, the *Ranger* brought that cycle of launches to a conclusion by putting aloft the CRAG's TBF-1 on an antisubmarine patrol around the ship:

FLIGHT D-8 (CRAG)

Comdr. David B. Overfield   C
    Aviation Radioman 1st Class Jack L. Aday
    Aviation Machinist's Mate 2d Class Reginald H. Miller

As Overfield proceeded out on his patrol, Admiral Hewitt signalled Rear Admiral McWhorter:

I COMMEND THE EXCELLENT WORK OF YOUR GROUP WHICH CONTRIBUTED SO GREATLY TO THE SUCCESS OF OPERATIONS X CONVEY MY CONGRATULATIONS TO OFFICERS AND MEN XX[21]

Inside a quarter of an hour, the *Suwanee* was launching a flight, under Bag Bagdanovich. Consisting of three F4Fs from VGS-27 and two from VGS-30, the *Suwanee*'s planes were to fly CAP over the *Ranger*.

Despite the message of congratulations, the cessation of hostilities with the Vichy French, and the maintenance of patrols "just in case," there still remained the matter of logistics. Obviously concerned over the U-boat menace, Rear Admiral McWhorter sent a dispatch to Admiral Hewitt noting that the *Ranger* and her accompanying cruiser would require fuel before reaching Bermuda, and could not fuel from an auxiliary aircraft carrier. To that end, he asked that a tanker accompany them 300 miles to fuel them at sea. He expressed his belief that the "present operating area [was] hazardous for fueling."[22]

About a half hour after the *Ranger* had launched the photo-reconnaissance flights, she put aloft an eight-plane CAP:

FLIGHT D-9 (VF-41)

First Section

Lt. Herold J. Weiler, Jr.
Lt. (jg) Dee Jones, A-V(N)

Lt. (jg) Arthur J. Cassidy, A-V(N)
Lt. (jg) Walter E. Laake, A-V(N)

Second Section

Lt. Ernest W. Wood, Jr.
Lt. (jg) Clyde C. Andrews, A-V(N)
Lt. (jg) Edmund J. Kelly, A-V(N)
Ens. Philip S. Ball, A-V(N)

Mac Wordell, meanwhile, only had thoughts of returning to an American unit. "All the French were too kind to me that morning," he recounted later, "Those who had been sincerely friendly before were very nearly swamped by those who wished to be friendly now. It made me a little sick to see how some of them could change face so fast." After the "usual ersatz breakfast," the French took him "down to meet George [Carter], Chuck [August], Windy [Shields], and Tom [Dougherty]." Wordell could not believe his eyes, thinking first that they must have come ashore to retrieve him. Then he learned how they, too, had been prisoners of the Vichy French—all except Spanky Carter—since 8 November.[23]

The *Ranger* began recovering Jake Onstott's flight starting at 0905, after a routine CAP; Pedro Winters and his pilots flew a CAP at 12,000 feet over the ship, before they began returning on board at 0915. Ralph Embree's remaining seven planes circled the carrier, until they, too, jettisoned their ordnance and landed on board, beginning at 0925.

Wally Madden, during the interval, found a 1,000-foot ceiling over Fedala and, as a consequence, flew to Casablanca. Finding clear weather there, he took three sets of aerial photographs of the harbor area: one at 8,000 feet, one at 7,000, and one at 6,000. Upon completion of his work and observing a clear area over Fedala, he flew there and shot photos of the harbor, the beaches, and part of the town, from 6,000 feet. Returning thence to Casablanca, Madden shot a final series of views from 12,000 feet, before he set course to head back to the ship, the carrier recovering him shortly before the end of the forenoon watch.

Johnson and Tucker overflew their designated areas while Madden was overflying those that had been assigned to him, and could see that all gun emplacements appeared to be intact at El Hank, and at Casablanca, three merchant ships lay partially sunk at the foot of the *Jettie Transversale*. It appeared that a direct hit had been made on the antiaircraft emplacements at the elbow of the *Jettie Delure*. Blown-out deck and side plating, and a large hole on her starboard quarter, testified to the fury of the attacks on the *Jean Bart*, and she appeared to have settled by the stern. Her sole main battery turret, however, was still defiantly undamaged.

Near the battered Vichy battleship, the VS-41 crews could see the scope of devastation on the *Mole du Commerce*, from the bombs and shells that had missed the target. Off Fedala, Johnson and Tucker and the photographers could see that the troop landings appeared to be "progressing rapidly," and mobile units appeared to be en route to Casablanca. At Port Lyautey, they counted about 40 P-40s that had been flown in from the *Chenango*, some (6–8) showing evidence of having been damaged upon landing. Throughout the flight, neither plane encountered any other aircraft or observed any hostile troops or active antiaircraft batteries. Both planes departed the skies over Casablanca at 1110.

The return flight to the *Ranger*, however, proved more exacting than the flight to the objective, because neither Mokos nor Wade, photographers by trade, could work the ZB gear in the rear cockpits of the two SBDs, and neither Johnson or Tucker had any success in getting their passengers to turn on the correct switches, so that neither could home in on the *Ranger*'s "hayrake" (YE antenna).

The necessity to lighten the planes to increase their time aloft prompted a momentary crisis for Photographer's Mate 2d Class Bill Wade, Lieutenant (jg) Tucker's passenger, when Tucker told him "he was having trouble finding the ship and that our fuel supply was getting low. He told me to throw out everything I could out of the rear cockpit to lighten the plane." Wade did as ordered, but hesitated at jettisoning the camera. "As I wrestled with this decision," he later recalled, "the term 'direct disobedience of orders' went through my mind." Then he recalled an instructor in photo school once being asked by a student what would happen if a camera was dropped from a plane. "No problem," the chief petty officer instructor had replied, "if you bring back the handles." Since the handles were an inseparable part of the camera, Wade would bring back the handles—and the camera to which they were attached.[24]

Both planes had working ADB sets, but so did about 20 other planes within a 50-mile radius. With neither 41-S-3 nor 41-S-5 having been recovered an hour and a half after they had left Casablanca, the *Ranger* instituted lost-plane procedures, but static and the "other innumerable ADBs" in the vicinity hindered communications between the ship and flight D-7. Fortunately, Johnson and Tucker spotted the ship at 1310, and brought their eventful return trip to a happy ending at 1335.[25]

Later that day, a quarter of an hour before the end of the forenoon watch, the *Ranger* launched an eight-plane division from VF-9, to fly a precautionary CAP over the ship, under Casey Childers. Patrolling overhead as CAP were four F4Fs from VGF-28, under Fitz Fitzpatrick, launched from the *Suwanee* at 1045.

Photographer's Mate 2d Class M. D. Mokos, Lt. Cecil V. Johnson's passenger on 11 November, gives a "thumbs up" to shipmates upon the return from the photo reconnaissance flight of that day. (NA, 80-G-30312)

FLIGHT D-10 (VF-9)

First Section

Lt. Kenan C. Childers
Ens. Louis A. Menard, A-V(N)

Lt. (jg) Harrison Feasley, A-V(N)
Ens. Ernest D. Brooks, A-V(N)

Second Section

Lt. (jg) John H. Sands, A-V(N)
Ens. James E. Toliver, A-V(N)

Lt. (jg) Harold E. Vita, A-V(N)
Ens. James M. Wilkerson, A-V(N)

Fifteen minutes before the end of the forenoon watch, the *Ranger* began launching four VS-41 SBDs to conduct inner-air and antisubmarine patrol near the ship, designating them as flight D-11:

FLIGHT D-11 (VS-41)

Lt. (jg) Harold R. Keller, Jr., A-V(N)
    Aviation Radioman 2d Class A. W. Lorentzen
Ens. George F. Dalton, A-V(N)
    Aviation Radioman 2d Class R. J. Monahan

Lt. (jg) Ralph W. Ross, A-V(N)
    Aviation Radioman 3d Class L. J. Devine
Ens. Donald E. Chapman, A-V(N)
    Aviation Radioman 3d Class J. A. Puryear

At the start of the afternoon watch, Admiral McWhorter directed that the *Ranger* maintain an antisubmarine patrol of two SBDs armed with depth bombs, over the transport area, from 1230 "until such time as will permit recovery by sunset."[26] Soon he modified his original order, directing that the ship maintain two SBDs with depth bombs on antisubmarine patrol and four F4Fs for CAP over the *Ranger*, send two SBDs armed with depth bombs for antisubmarine patrol over the transport area, and that the ship hold the remainder of the SBDs armed with 1,000-pound bombs "ready for special missions." He also added that "CRAG may be used in addition" to the SBDs, concluding with orders that all aircraft return to the ship in time to be recovered by sunset.[27]

Three hours later, at 1445, the *Ranger* began putting aloft four more SBDs from VS-41 (flight D-12). Two were to conduct antisubmarine patrol off Fedala and two near the ship. She also launched a fifth SBD (flight D-13), flown by Ralph Embree, to drop messages on board the *Augusta*, and the CRAG's TBF for an antisubmarine patrol. Overhead, as a CAP from the *Suwanee*, were four F4Fs from VGF-28 and two from VGS-30, under Bag Bagdanovich, leading his second CAP over the *Ranger* that day.

FLIGHT D-12 (VS-41)

Fedala Area

Lt. (jg) Cyrus F. Weeks, A-V(N)
    Aviation Radioman 3d Class G. H. Perry
Lt. (jg) William H. Longley, A-V(N)
    Aviation Radioman 3d Class John G. Korecki

Ranger Area

Ens. Arthur L. Warta, A-V(N)
    Aviation Radioman 3d Class R. E. O'Connor

Lt. (jg) John G. McReynolds, Jr., A-V(N)
Aviation Radioman 3d Class Oscar I. Light

FLIGHT D-13 (VS-41)

Lt. Ralph A. Embree
Aviation Radioman 1st Class Joseph M. Eardley

FLIGHT D-14 (CRAG)

Comdr. David B. Overfield   C
    Aviation Radioman 1st Class Jack L. Aday
    Aviation Machinist's Mate 2d Class Reginald H. Miller

D-12's Fedala section observed only a U.S. supply vessel clearing the docks for sea, and another moving into the harbor to unload. None of the landing boats they saw shuttling back and forth from the ships to the shore appeared to have been carrying troops, but they saw many carrying supplies into the beach. The *Ranger* section returned to the ship after an uneventful patrol. The carrier began recovering flight D-12 one hour into the first dog watch. Ralph Embree and Joe Eardley, having successfully completed their message drop to the *Augusta*, returned around the same time; the CRAG came on board last, winding up the day's flight operations shortly before sunset. Less than an hour later, the *Chenango* and the *Suwanee* joined the formation.

Although the armistice had stilled the French guns, the situation permitted no relaxation of vigilance as far as submarines were concerned, especially given the number of U-boats setting course for the coast of French Morocco. To emphasize that, Admiral Hewitt sent a dispatch to TF-34:

HOSTILITIES IN FRENCH MOROCCO HAVE CEASED X BE ESPECIALLY VIGILANT AGAINST AXIS SUBMARINES[28]

Midway through the first watch, Admiral McWhorter sent a dispatch to Admiral Hewitt, in the *Augusta*. He reported that the *Ranger*'s plane availability for antisubmarine patrol rested in nine SBDs, the *Suwanee*'s in seven TBFs. McWhorter, believing that number "insufficient for both carriers and transports," considered it "urgent that if [the] Army is not going to take over air operations the Navy take over the field [Port Lyautey] and operate PBYs from it." Until then, Commander, Task Group 34.2 concluded, "[we] will maintain maximum antisubmarine patrol with planes available."[29]

23

"YOU HAVE ALL DONE A GRAND JOB"

ComInCh's U-boat estimates for 12 November placed 98 in the Atlantic, including eight between Gibraltar and Casablanca, nine southbound and three northbound off Portugal. One of the *Ranger*'s lookouts had reported a flare dead astern 17 minutes into the mid watch on 12 November; at 0520, lookouts spotted a yellow flare on the starboard bow. Whether or not the flares signified enemy submarine activity, Admiral McWhorter reemphasized to Admiral Hewitt his concerns over that particular menace, early in the morning watch on 12 November, revisiting the subject of his dispatch the previous evening, when he sent a priority message to the flagship at 0546:

IF FIELD NOT AVAILABLE FOR PBYS SUGGEST INVESTIGATE USE OF RIVER LANDINGS AND TAKEOFFS X PBYS HAVE LONG ENDURANCE CARRY HEAVY BOMB LOADS AND ARE EQUIPPED WITH EXCELLENT RADAR AND I BELIEVE WILL GIVE YOU GOOD DAY AND NIGHT A/S PROTECTION X CONSIDER CARRIER BASED AIRCRAFT ENTIRELY INADEQUATE X RETENTION OF CARRIERS NOT CONSIDERED JUSTIFIED XX[1]

Admiral McWhorter had directed that, at dawn on 12 November, the *Ranger* launch and maintain four fighters for CAP over the ship. In addition, he directed that two SBDs, armed with depth bombs, be put aloft to patrol around the transports off Fedala and two, similiarly armed, around the ship. He ordered that the CRAG's TBF be utilized for antisubmarine patrol, in addition to any other SBDs "as available."[2] To that end, at well before dawn on 12 November, the *Ranger*'s flight deck crews began spotting flight E, under Moot Moutenot, at 0615, to conduct CAP over the ship. Beginning 20 minutes later, the ship commenced launch.

FLIGHT E (VF-9)

Lt. (jg) Charles L. Moutenot, A-V(N)
Ens. Marvin J. Franger, A-V(N)

Ens. Burton L. Bardeen, A-V(N)
Lt. (jg) Armistead B. Smith, Jr., A-V(N)

Two planes took up patrolling at 9,000 feet and two between 1,500 to 2,000. They sighted no enemy forces and encountered nothing other than routine. Soon after the last of the fighters had wobbled aloft, Commander Overfield took off for antisubmarine patrol, his Avenger armed with four 325-pound depth charges set to explode at a depth of 25 feet.

FLIGHT E-2A (CRAG)

Comdr. David B. Overfield   C
    Aviation Radioman 1st Class Jack L. Aday
    Aviation Machinist's Mate 2d Class Reginald H. Miller

Soon after Overfield's TBF-1 had lumbered down the deck and the CRAG had taken off to take up his patrol sector, the *Ranger* began launching four SBDs from VS-41, under Count DeVane, to carry out antisubmarine patrols, as well:

FLIGHT E-2 (VS-41)

Fedala Area

Lt. John M. DeVane, Jr.
    Aviation Radioman 1st Class William O. Haynes
Lt. (jg) Maxwell A. Eaton, A-V(N)
    Aviation Radioman 3d Class William O. Shackelford

Ranger Area

Lt. (jg) Joseph P. Keigher, Jr., A-V(N)
    Aviation Radioman 3d Class J. J. Lankowitz
Lt. (jg) Robert L. Arthur, A-V(N)
    Aviation Radioman 3d Class Morris S. Waterson

DeVane and Eaton found no submarines in their assigned sector, but beheld evidence that one had been at work, when they saw the *Hambleton*, which had been torpedoed by the *U-173* shortly before the end of the second dog watch the night before. They could clearly see the damage where the destroyer had been hit amidships on the port side.

At 0643, a lookout on board the *Ranger* spotted what appeared to be a periscope 1,800 yards off the starboard bow; the slip soon executed an emergency turn to port and rang down emergency full speed ahead, within sight of the African coast 18 miles distant. As the sun rose at 0701, the day dawned fair, an observer on board the *Brooklyn* noted, "another typical [northeasterly] trades day."[3]

For about an hour after sunrise, things remained quiet, until a second sighting stirred the task group to action at 0806, when lookouts reported a submarine lurking about 5,000 yards off the port quarter, near two Spanish fishing vessels off to the west. The *Ranger* opened fire. At 0812, a torpedo wake prompted the *Ranger* to execute another radical turn to port and emergency full ahead. The *Brooklyn*'s Captain Denebrink, however, disagreed with the assessment of the "torpedo wake."

At 0815, Joe Keigher and Bob Arthur picked up the radio traffic pertaining to the unfolding action. As Keigher neared the area at 1,300 feet, he perceived "what appeared to be a submarine about 30 feet below the surface." Making a power glide along the fore and aft axis of the sub, Keigher released his depth charge at 300 feet. No oil or debris appeared in the water after the explosion. Bob Arthur saw no submarine, but "being under the impression that the ship was firing on the fishing boats," made one strafing attack on the Spanish trawlers, expending 70 rounds of .50-caliber against the doubtlessly surprised fishermen. Because the *Ranger* had ceased fire, Arthur did likewise before he executed a second strafing run.

The destroyer *Woolsey* (DD-437), detached to investigate the trawlers, dropped an embarrassing barrage of four depth charges on a "fair" contact near the fishing vessels. The *Woolsey*'s boarding party's investigation of the first boat yielded no evidence of any "unneutral service" having been engaged in, and indicated "nothing out of order."[4] The Spanish vessels, four days out of Cadiz, proved to be the *Carbovi* and the *Manuel C. Friere*, their holds filled with only ice and fish. They reported having sighted neither submarines nor torpedo wakes. After her sailors had checked out the second boat, the *Woolsey* radioed the *Ranger* over the TBS:

BOTH FISHING VESSELS WERE APPARENTLY ALL RIGHT X NO RADIO ABOARD AND NO INDICATION OF ANY TOOLS FOR FUELING SUBMARINES[5]

At 0912, however, soon after the *Ranger* had received the *Woolsey*'s "weak and fading signal," the sighting of a periscope on the port bow compelled the carrier to make an emergency turn to port once more and to ring down full speed ahead. Having flown a semicircular patrol three miles in radius and at an altitude between 1,000 and 1,200 feet, Bash Overfield picked up the voice radio transmission from the *Ranger* that reported a submarine in the vicinity of the task group. The CRAG set course to conduct a search.

Further emergency course and speed changes ensued, when lookouts spotted a torpedo wake crossing the carrier's bow from port to starboard. The *Ellyson* did not spot the periscope, but her sound operator reported hearing a torpedo pass from port to starboard astern. As her captain later admitted, however, "all vessels were making high speeds and radical changes of course rendering sound gear useless. . . . It is possible that this torpedo report was false." The *Ellyson* did subsequently warn the *Ranger* of an approaching torpedo wake approaching the carrier's port bow at 0926.

Despite the necessity of taking evasive action, maintaining the CAP and antisubmarine patrols remained a high priority; beginning at 0930, the *Ranger* began putting aloft four F4F-4s from VF-41, under Ham Weiler, for CAP over the ship.

FLIGHT E-3 (VF-41)

Lt. Herold J. Weiler, Jr.
Lt. (jg) Boyd N. Mayhew, A-V(N)

Lt. Ernest W. Wood, Jr.
Ens. Will "W" Taylor, A-V(N)

Once the Wildcats had wobbled off to take up their CAP duties, the five SBDs designated as flight E-4, under Ralph Embree, began rolling down the deck toward the bow ramp. Embree and his men had been enjoined to be "particularly alert," because the sighting of an enemy sub earlier

The *Ranger*'s gunners fire at a suspected submarine, as Commander Overfield's CRAG TBF flies low in the background (R), 12 November 1942. (NA, 80-G-30305)

that morning had "tended to confirm our Command's belief that U-boats were being concentrated in the *Ranger*'s area."[6]

FLIGHT E-4 (VS-41)

Lt. Ralph A. Embree
    Aviation Radioman 1st Class Joseph M. Eardley
Lt. (jg) Robert H. Higley, A-V(N)
    Aviation Radioman 3d Class L. E. Colon
Ens. Charles C. Bevis, Jr., A-V(N)
    Aviation Radioman 3d Class Lloyd E. Edens
Ens. Thomas M. Hubbard, A-V(N)
    Aviation Radioman 3d Class R. L. Fenton
Ens. George F. Dalton, A-V(N)
    Aviation Radioman 3d Class J. A. Puryear

His search having proved unsuccessful, Commander Overfield returned to his patrol sector, but soon picked up another voice radio transmission, at about the time the *Ranger* was launching flight E-4, reporting a "disturbance" in the water about 2,000 yards away on the *Ranger*'s port quarter. After covering the designated spot, Overfield extended the search, but soon heard the order to return to the ship, preparatory to being recovered. At that instant, Overfield saw a feather wake below, with what appeared to be a periscope at its apex. Attacking immediately, the CRAG placed one of his 325-pound depth charges about 100 feet ahead of the apex of the feather wake, after the object had appeared for about 8–10 seconds, while he was in his dive. As he later reported, the "feather" "in no way resembled a breaking wave but rather was in the shape of a uniform elongated vee."

Having heard the *Ranger*'s radio traffic with her planes engaged in the attacks on the submarine, Count DeVane and Max Eaton had flown to the scene to assist. Eaton saw the CRAG's attack and sped to the spot. From 1,000 feet, he spotted what looked like the wake of a submarine conning tower, and impulsively dove and dropped his depth charge. Later, he reflected that he had possessed "insufficient evidence to make an attack." CRAG, meanwhile, returned to the ship, and the *Ranger* began recovering Count DeVane's flight E-2 and the CRAGs (E-2A), beginning at 0950.

Engine trouble had forced Charley Bevis to return to the ship, and the *Ranger* took him on board in an emergency forced landing at 1050. Almost simultaneously, the *Ellyson*, steaming at 32 knots to regain her station in the formation, after the unsuccessful submarine hunt, spotted a periscope about 600 yards dead ahead; reporting the contact, the destroyer dropped a "full pattern barrage with shallow settings," as she passed over the location. The *Ranger* altered course to starboard.

Up to that moment, VS-41's second antisubmarine patrol of the morning had been routine, a condition that was, however, changing rapidly. Ralph Embree saw the *Ellyson*, on the *Ranger*'s port quarter, dropping depth charges. Almost directly overhead at the time, Embree scrutinized the sea, but saw nothing suspicious. He started to fly around the *Ranger*'s stern, counterclockwise. The *Ranger* had no sooner altered course in response to the *Ellyson*'s report than the *Woolsey*, just ahead of the carrier, reported a periscope directly in her path. Again the *Ranger* maneuvered radically to starboard; while Embree, then a half mile off the carrier's starboard quarter, saw the *Woolsey* drop depth charges.

Embree saw the circular shock wave, then a "black bubbling disturbance" boil out of the *Woolsey*'s wake. Shortly afterward, he saw a "large white bubble of air and foam come to the surface" to a height of 100 feet, 90 degrees relative to the point at which the depth charge had exploded. Believing that the disturbance he witnessed in the water reflected the presence of a submarine, Embree pushed over from 1,500 feet and dropped his 325-pound depth charge "right on the patch." As he did so, he heard a radio report: "Submarine on starboard bow." The *Ranger*'s starboard batteries immediately opened fire on what appeared to be a periscope 600 yards away; this alerted Ham Weiler, who, on CAP, had seen oil slicks on the *Ranger*'s starboard bow, extending toward the formation, and he investigated them. Flying low, he observed nothing suspicious, until the carrier had opened fire on the feather wake. Weiler dove and strafed the wake.

As Embree pulled out of his dive, he looked back and saw the fan-shaped spray characteristic of an aerial depth charge explosion. He also saw "a great deal of tracers being shot in one direction" 5,000 yards off the *Ranger*'s port quarter. Climbing to 1,000 feet, Embree followed the line of tracers for a mile and a half, but saw nothing suspicious in the water. Doubling back toward the ship, he spotted an object beneath the water that appeared to be light green and about the size of "an upside down row boat." Embree told Eardley to throw out a smoke light when he waggled his wings. Passed in his dive by a pair of F4Fs (most likely Woodie Wood and Ensign Will Taylor), Embree rocked his wings, and Eardley threw out the smoke light as instructed. The device worked and began to emit smoke as Embree pulled out of his dive. Wood fired a full six-gun burst at what he later reported was a submarine, and the *Woolsey*

The *Ranger*'s gunfire intensifies during the battle on 12 November. (NA, 80-G-31720)

Curving wakes and shell splashes testify to evasive action on 12 November. (NA, 80-G-31719)

immediately turned, proceeding to the spot, and circled the smoking float, dropping depth charges. Ham Weiler spotted what appeared to be a feather wake on the *Ranger*'s port quarter, twice as far away as the first, and he strafed it.

Although other pilots in the flight had witnessed the attacks, they had done so from too far away to be able to lend assistance. A little over a half an hour later, however, at 1130, Aviation Radioman 3d Class Cy Colon, Lieutenant (jg) Higley's radio-gunner, spotted what appeared to be a feather wake two miles off the *Ranger*'s starboard quarter. Ham Weiler saw "a small wake" in that area, as did Will Taylor of VF-41, who later reported having seen "the full conning tower and the outline" of a submarine "apparently jumping out of the water as it let go a torpedo," as did Woodie Wood. Higley, meanwhile, pushed over and dropped his depth charge, before he circled and strafed the spot. Ensign Hubbard and Ens. Gerald A. Anderson, A-V(N), flying 8-CS-9, an SOC from the *Brooklyn*, which had been catapulted aloft shortly before sunrise for antisubmarine patrol, also attacked, dropping depth charges. As the *Ranger*'s task group stood to the westward, screened by the *Ellyson* and the *Woolsey*, the *Fitch* remained behind until the other ships were well clear, then bent on speed to rejoin.

Flight E-6—five SBDs from VS-41, under Lt. (jg) Clarence Twiddy—began rolling toward the *Ranger*'s bow ramp at 1210 for inner-air and antisubmarine patrol. A second VS-41 antisubmarine patrol, of four planes, took off soon thereafter.[7]

FLIGHT E-6 (VS-41)

Lt. (jg) Clarence A. Twiddy, Jr., A-V(N)
    Aviation Radioman 3d Class R. E. O'Connor

Ens. Arthur L. Warta, A-V(N)
 Aviation Radioman 3d Class Oscar I. Light
Lt. (jg) Ralph W. Ross, A-V(N)
 Aviation Radioman 3d Class L. J. Devine
Ens. Donald E. Chapman, A-V(N)
 Aviation Radioman 2d Class R. J. Monahan
Lt. (jg) Harold R. Keller, Jr., A-V(N)
 Aviation Radioman 2d Class A. W. Lorentzen

Having launched the last antisubmarine patrols for the day early in the afternoon watch, the *Ranger* recovered Ham Weiler's (E-3) and Ralph Embree's (E-4) flights, without further incident. Although both Lieutenant (jg) Higley's and Ensign Hubbard's depth charges had been properly armed, as attested by the arming wires brought back, neither had exploded.

Shortly after takeoff from the *Ranger*, three of the five pilots in flight E-6 spotted what appeared to be an oil slick, about a quarter-mile across. It bore 15 degrees one mile out from the ship, but those who saw it detected neither oil nor air bubbles rising within it.

Twenty-five minutes after launching flight E-6, the *Ranger*, in company with the *Suwanee*, the *Brooklyn*, the *Cleveland*, and five destroyers, formed a cruising disposition and began steering toward home, "thus closing," a VS-41 observer wrote later, "this phase in the battle for North Africa." After the VS-41 antisubmarine flights had spotted nothing else of interest for the remainder of the patrol, the *Ranger* began bringing them on board at 1525.

As the *Ranger* and her consorts shaped course for home, Ensign Mikronis, back in Casablanca, was busy. He had remained in hospital, recuperating from being wounded the first day, and, during his time there, had observed that the morale of the wounded U.S. soldiers there had been excellent. He had also made the acquaintance of some officers of a British merchantman that had been torpedoed in September. Around noon on the 12th, Capt. T. Donald McCarthy, a U.S. Army medical officer, arrived with a staff of two, and promised Mikronis that he would be evacuated as soon as possible. In the meantime, Mikronis helped McCarthy obtain the names of all of the Americans in the hospital, and later assisted him in the burial of 26 American Army and 2 U.S. Navy fatalities who had been kept in the hospital morgue. Full military honors accompanied the interments, and both American and British consuls in Casablanca attended the funeral; the French provided coffins, crosses, and burial lots.[8]

Mikronis's work, however, had kept him from obtaining dinner. He had spent part of that time in a U.S. Army truck driving through the streets of recently occupied Casablanca; most of the people he encountered waved at him. Lost, however, he had to ask a French pilot for the directions to Fedala. Obtaining them, he eventually reached an evacuation center located midway between Casablanca and Fedala, a house well equipped with U.S. hospital gear. Sent on to Fedala, his original destination, he managed to dine on some broth at an Army unit he passed on the way.[9]

Eventually sent to the transport *Tasker H. Bliss* (AP-42) off Fedala, Mikronis embarked in a boat and set off. Perhaps because of his head injuries, however, he soon forgot the name of the ship. The boat coxswain thus set course for the cargo ship *Arcturus* (AK-18). Although Mikronis recalled his original destination halfway into the trip, his boat had apparently gone so far that turning around and retracing the route to the ship to which he was supposed to have gone would have consumed too much time. A medical officer met Mikronis upon his arrival on board the *Arcturus*, and took him to see the captain. Soon given toilet articles, clothing, and a special diet of soft foods, he was given a bath and put to bed. Awakened later at the sound of the general alarm, he got up, dressed, and headed topside.[10]

Mikronis's memory lapse proved providential. *Kapitänleutnant* Ernst Kals, the decorated 37-year-old commanding officer of the *U-130*, one of the boats diverted to North African waters, had boldly penetrated the transport screen off Fedala. "My intention," Kals later explained in his war diary, was "to go inshore till I reached the 15 fathom line and then to proceed along the coast to the Fedala roadstead and attack. The patrols will hardly expect a U-boat to approach so close inshore." The *U-130* had grazed the bottom during the approach, and proceeded "with great caution on account of [the] completely unruffled sea." Kals, utilizing the periscope only for glimpses of the ships, "fired four single torpedoes from [the] bow tubes," then turned and fired one from one of the stern tubes. In a very short time, the *Hugh L. Scott* (AP-43), the *Edward Rutledge* (AP-52), and Ensign Mikronis's original destination, the *Tasker H. Bliss*, shuddered, in quick succession, with the impact of torpedo detonations. Reasoning that patrolling escorts would likely expect him to make for deep water to the north and northwest, Kals crept along the 10-fathom curve and escaped "without any difficulty."[11]

Although the U-boats had achieved some success, the Atlantic Fleet's carriers that had participated in Torch had emerged unscathed, having achieved success in the vital task of close air support. Two days into the homeward-bound voyage, Admiral McWhorter sent a dispatch to the ships in company:

WE ARE HOMEWARD BOUND X OUR SCREEN IS VERY THIN X THE UTMOST ALERTNESS BY ALL

HANDS WILL BE REQUIRED TO GET US THROUGH SAFELY X YOU HAVE ALL DONE A GRAND JOB—DON'T RELAX NOW[12]

Three days later, the Admiral sent another dispatch to his task group:

WE HAVE TAKEN PART IN THE PRELIMINARY STAGES OF AN OPERATION WHICH WILL REQUIRE MANY PASSAGES THROUGH SUBMARINE INFESTED WATERS X THE SUCCESS OF OUR CAUSES REQUIRES THAT INFORMATION REGARDING OUR MOVEMENTS NOT LEAK OUT TO THE ENEMY X COMMANDING OFFICERS WILL TAKE APPROPRIATE STEPS TO SEE THAT OFFICERS AND MEN OF THEIR COMMANDS COMPLY WITH STANDING INSTRUCTIONS OF CINCLANT NOT TO DISCUSS WHERE THEY HAVE BEEN WHAT THEY HAVE BEEN DOING OR WHAT THEY HAVE SEEN[13]

The *Ranger* reached Port Royal Bay, Bermuda, nine days later. She sailed thence, on the afternoon of 22 November, with a different company of consorts, finally anchoring in Hampton Roads on the morning of the 24th. The next morning, she shifted to the familiar Pier 7 for upkeep.

The *Ranger* resumed flight operations in Chesapeake Bay on 10 December, evolutions that included qualifying pilots from VGS-28. On 11 December, Lt. (jg) George F. Hardman, A-V(N), with Aviation Radioman 3d Class Roland O. Jackson on board, exhibited poor technique and made an off-center landing, his left wheel going off the waterway on the port side after having snagged a wire. His TBF-1 (BuNo 00582) required a major overhaul. The following morning, Ens. Nelson R. Charles, A-V(N), with Aviation Radioman 2d Class Robert H. Jaeger in back, replicated his shipmate's off-center landing of the afternoon before, but his TBF-1 (BuNo 01770) rolled over onto the stacks. It, too, required a major overhaul in the wake of the class B damage sustained.[14]

Bringing that stint of operations to a close on the afternoon of the 12th, the *Ranger* returned to Pier 7 on the morning of the 14th, and shifted to the Norfolk Navy Yard on the afternoon of the 16th. There she remained, receiving a drydocking and repairs and alterations, through the end of 1942.

24

"WE ARE TOO VALUABLE AS A STRIKING FORCE"

Torch had seen the *Ranger* operating two augmented fighting squadrons and a scouting squadron, because of her specific mission; now, the reequipping of her assigned torpedo squadron continued apace. Sadly, tragedy dogged its days before the year was out, at a time when celebration, even when muted by the war, rather than mourning, was more common.

Lieutenant (jg) William Y. Bailey, A-V(N), ferrying a TBF-1 (BuNo 00676) from Norfolk to Quonset Point on the day before Christmas, dropped out of a four-plane formation as the flight passed over Norton, Connecticut, at 1,500 feet, early in the second dog watch. A layer of overcast at 2,500 feet obscured the moon, and none of the other three pilots saw Bailey again. The report of an unidentified aircraft three hours later, at a point approximately 40 miles from where the other pilots in the flight last saw Bailey, provided a clue to his fate. More evidence came to hand late the following day, about six to seven miles east-southeast of Faulkner Island, in the waters between New Haven and Saybrook, Connecticut.[1]

When hostilities engulfed the United States, the Coast Guard swelled its numbers with the acquisition of pleasure craft to be used for district patrol duties. One such boat, a 38-footer given only the prosaic identification number *CGR-1996*, while on patrol out of Eaton's Neck, Long Island, during the second dog watch on Christmas Day, came across some flotsam and an oil slick. The Coast Guardsmen recovered "blueprints, fur-lined overshoes, gloves, 4 green cans used to hold oxygen, some instructions on Grumman aircraft and [a] piece of a packing box with the white label that bore the legend TBF SBI-06076 [*sic*]," which bore testimony to what had most likely transpired in the darkness the night before.[2]

The trouble board investigating the disappearance of Lt. (jg) Bailey and his aircraft speculated (because neither pilot nor plane was ever found) that Bailey had left formation when his fuel ran out in one tank. Shifting to another, and regaining suction, at a lower altitude, prompted the pilot to try to reorient himself as to where he was in the darkness. The board believed that Bailey had flown for another three hours until fuel exhaustion forced him to make a water landing. Having had a purportedly defective life jacket, the 23-year-old Ohioan had been unable to extract the rubber boat and drowned, in the cold wintry darkness, alone, on Christmas eve.

The need to go on with the war effort, to continue training, often meant little time for mourning tragedies like that which had befallen Lt. (jg) Bailey. Continuing on meant that the business of repairs and alterations proceeded unabated. For those on board a ship undergoing a yard overhaul, there is seldom time for quiet reflection, and not even the ship's captain could escape the tumult.

"You were certainly lucky to get off the ship before we went into overhaul," Cal Durgin wrote to his former exec, Johnnie Hoskins, from Norfolk. "It was the damnedest horror I have ever seen. The Navy Yard workmen came in two hundred strong with chipping hammers to chip off the paint in officers' quarters, hangar deck and every place.

They worked twenty-four hours a day, driving all the officers to eat at the Officers' Club and also to sleep there when they did not have the duty. I hope that I never shall have to see the ship go through that again.... It just about drove one nuts to stay aboard [*sic*] for more than an hour or two at the time." When all was said and done, however, Durgin praised the workmen for their having done "a damn good job."[3]

Shifting back to NOB Norfolk on 6 January 1943, the *Ranger* got underway to resume training on the 8th, with the *Tuscaloosa*, the oiler *Chicopee* (AO-34), and five destroyers. She operated in the Atlantic through the third week of January, sailing thence to North Africa to ferry the air echelon of the 325th Fighter Group—75 P-40s strong—diverted from the Ninth Air Force to Cazes on 19 January, launching all of the Curtiss fighters between 0846 and 1218.

Returning from a routine patrol flight a half hour into the first dog watch that same day, Lt. (jg) Mervin T. Knight, A-V(N), with Aviation Ordnanceman 3d Class Andy McSary, Jr., and Ordnanceman 2d Class Ashton C. Starke, USNR, on board, with four Mk. 17 depth bombs slung in the bomb bay, made a hard, "slight wheels landing followed by [the] tail coming down," which buckled the Avenger's fuselage. BuNo 06074 required a major overhaul, including realignment of the fuselage.[4]

One of the screening destroyers, the *Corry*, sighted what she thought was a submarine and promptly attacked what proved to be a whale on 23 January. Seventeen minutes into

Electrician's Mate 3d Class R. A. Royer (L) checks the temperature of a generator bearing (L); Electrician's Mate 2d Class A. A. Michette (R) watches the gauges on the generator distribution board, as he communicates by telephone with the after dynamo electrician, to ensure a balanced load between the forward and after dynamos, January 1943. (NA, 80-G-36674)

"A tense moment during takeoff," as a P-40 roars down the flight deck toward the bow ramp, 19 January 1943. (NA, 80-G-34283)

the afternoon watch that day, the *Ranger* launched a TBF-1 (BuNo 06075), piloted by Lt. (jg) George W. O'Mary, A-V(N). Unfortunately, although O'Mary's takeoff run looked normal, he apparently lost directional control of the Avenger, and 4-T-4 swerved off the flight deck over the port gun gallery and into the sea. Because it only required movement of one-half to three-quarters of an inch to arm and release the depth bombs carried in the Avenger's bomb bay, those who investigated the crash surmised that the impact of the TBF-1's hitting the water abruptly armed its ordnance. Although O'Mary's two crewmen—Aviation Radioman 2d Class William E. Pyne and Photographer 1st Class George W. Lightfoot—floated free of the sinking TBF, to be rescued by the *Ellyson*, one or more of the Avenger's bomb load exploded before the plane even had time to sink beneath the surface, killing the pilot instantly.[5]

Investigators adjudged O'Mary's accident as 100% pilot error (judgment and technique), but another TBF mishap occurred on 25 January that did not involve any lack of judgment and technique on the part of a pilot. Lt. (jg) Wendell S. Koozer, A-V(N), with Aviation Radioman 3d Class B. L. Jacobs and Aviation Machinist's Mate 2d Class P. J. Blanos on board, made a normal landing and engaged number two wire. After the tail hook had pulled out about three feet of wire, the hook came loose; thus freed, the Avenger charged up the deck, crashing into number one barrier, the after clipping house, and the island, in succession, rupturing the steam line to the whistle and siren. Although the pilot and turret gunner emerged unhurt for the experience, the radioman, Jacobs, required treatment for a "nasal hemorrhage."[6]

Those who looked into the accident attributed it 100% to material—the arresting hook, the entire assembly having

*Ranger*men look over Lt. (jg) Wendell Koozer's TBF-1 (BuNo 06073), [4-T-]1, after it had crashed into the after clipping room and the island, when the arrestor hook mechanism carried away, 25 January 1943. Koozer's radioman, Aviation Radioman 3d Class Jacobs, suffered a bloody nose in the crash. (NA, 80-G-34450)

been pulled free. Koozer had made three successful landings just prior to the crash, and had had his wings for a little over a year. The TBF-1 (BuNo 06073) required a major overhaul, after having the right wing outer panel demolished, the inner panel demolished and misaligned, as well as the engine damaged.

Cal Durgin grew restive at the lack of action for his ship, which had, in his estimation, more than proved her worth. "Things are getting along swimmingly," he wrote to Johnnie Hoskins on 28 January, and "We are quite fortunate in having a trip such as we are now making to shake-down after such a hectic overhaul. I hope, however, that we will not have to continue doing this for the rest of the war. We are too valuable as a striking force to be kept at this chore much longer."[7]

Returning to NOB Norfolk on 30 January, the *Ranger* then underwent further repairs and alterations at Norfolk Navy Yard (1–7 February), before she resumed operating in lower Chesapeake Bay. She trained her squadrons and fired day and night gunnery exercises with her 5-inch and newly installed 40-millimeter (the latter having replaced the 1.1-inch guns) batteries.

During the course of simulated attacks on the ship on 9 February, Lieutenant (jg) Knight, who had survived the landing mishap in BuNo 06074 on 19 January, was piloting a TBF-1 (BuNo 06217), making a simulated torpedo attack at an altitude of 75 feet. Simultaneously, a Wildcat from VF-4 had just completed a "strafing" run on the *Ranger* and was on a collision course with Knight's Avenger at the same altitude. Apparently, Knight saw the F4F at the last instant and instinctively shoved the stick forward to avoid a midair collision, before he may have even been aware of the danger. His TBF-1 slammed into Chesapeake Bay at 1606 and sank immediately, taking Knight, Seaman 1st Class Arthur G. Whitten, and Ordnanceman 2d Class Ashton Starke (who, like his pilot, had survived the deck landing accident in the depth bomb-armed Avenger on 19 January) with it. A Coast Guard cutter immediately left a buoy to mark where 4-T-4 sank and retrieved floating gear. The tragedy led to a trouble board's recommendation that "simulated strafing attacks not be ordered while other aircraft are operating at low altitudes in the immediate vicinity of the ship." Neither the Commander, *Ranger* Air Group, nor Commander, Air Force, Atlantic Fleet, however, concurred. The prosecution of intense training for war needed to be maintained.[8]

Mishaps with green pilots continued. The next day, during the afternoon watch, Ens. Harlan C. McFadden, A-V(N) proved slow in answering a wave-off. His TBF-1 (BuNo 00618) lumbered over the side of the flight deck, hitting the after port gun gallery and splashing into the water. As the Avenger sank, the plane guard rescued Ensign McFadden and his sole passenger, Aviation Machinist's Mate 2d Class R. W. T. Landry.[9]

Returning to the NOB on the afternoon of 11 February, the *Ranger* then fueled, provisioned, and hoisted on board another group of USAAF fighters to be ferried to North Africa. She sailed on the 14th. Reaching the flying-off point on 24 February, the *Ranger* launched the 75 P-40Ls, between 0853 and 1141, in six groups, interspersing that with the launching and recovery of TBFs for inner air patrol over the task force. Having completed the ferry mission that morning, the carrier and her consorts set course to return to Hampton Roads.

Shortly before the end of the afternoon watch on 26 February, Ens. R. W. Labyak, A-V(N), on antisubmarine patrol, with Aviation Machinist's Mate 3d Class R. A. Tremblay as his turret gunner and Aviation Radioman 3d Class A. Beard, Jr., as the bomber-radioman, spotted a surfaced U-boat, with its conning tower awash in the choppy sea, about five miles ahead. Labyak signalled his wingman, Ens. G. W. Bolt (whose crew included Aviation Machinist's Mate 2d Class P. J. Blanos as bomber and Aviation Radioman 3d Class Charles W. Barr as turret gunner/radioman), to starboard, to follow him, and pushed over into a power glide on a reciprocal course to the submarine. Apparently, the submarine spotted the planes, for she quickly crash-dived. About 30 seconds after the boat had disappeared, Labyak released his two 325-pound Mk. 19 depth charges, at an altitude of 200 feet, one 400 feet and the other 375 feet ahead of the swirling water where the boat submerged. The exploding bombs blew holes in the underside of the TBF. Ensign Bolt's attack soon thereafter yielded no result. Both planes returned to the *Ranger* to refuel and rearm. A subsequent search found nothing.[10]

In assessing the attacks, Rear Adm. Alva Bernhard, Commander, Task Force 22, believed that one of the nose fuses of Ensign Labyak's bomb may have been inadvertently armed, leading to its exploding upon impact with the water; although he considered Labyak's attack satisfactorily executed, the length of time between submergence of the U-boat and when the bombs were dropped made the prospect of damage to the submarine limited. The Atlantic Fleet Anti-Submarine Warfare Officer's criticism proved stern: "It is realized," he wrote, "that carrier aircraft squadrons are called upon to perform many tasks other than ASW [anti-submarine warfare]. It is considered, however, that if they are to be employed on ASW missions, the indoctrination of their personnel in the principles of that type of warfare must be sufficiently thorough to insure their taking action when contact with an enemy submarine is made."[11]

During the passage back to the United States, Ens. Ralph R. "Andy" Anderson, A-V(N), flying a TBF-1 (BuNo 06253), with Aviation Machinist's Mates 3d Class Donald L. King and John H. Holden on board, attempted to execute a wave-off while being recovered during the afternoon watch on 2 March, but did so at the instant of his hook's snagging a wire. The tethered TBF bounced heavily over the port side and came to rest upside down atop the first two stacks. It required a major overhaul in the wake of the mishap.[12] That same day, the *Hobson* rescued 46 survivors (three of whom were women) from the torpedoed steamship *St. Margaret*.

The *Ranger* reached Hampton Roads on 6 March. After taking on fuel, stores, and provisions, she sailed for Narragansett Bay shortly after midday on the 9th, and moored at NAS Quonset Point the following afternoon, to resume the process of taking on supplies and embarking Air Group Four. Underway on the afternoon of 12 March, the carrier, screened by the destroyers *Rodman*, *Fitch*, *Corry*, and *Hobson*, carried out training off the eastern seaboard.

Less than a quarter of an hour into flight operations during the morning watch on 13 March, Ens. Albert J. Baldwin, A-V(N), sat in the cockpit of his F4F-4 (BuNo 12040), ready to take off on a routine CAP flight. Opening his throttle, he noticed the manifold pressure and rpms as satisfactory, and indicated to the flight deck officer his readiness to take off. The latter gave him the "go" signal, at which point Baldwin released his brakes and started down

Crewmen gingerly extract the bombs from Ens. Andy Anderson's TBF-1 (BuNo 06253), [4-T-]7, as it rests atop the first two stacks on the port side, after Anderson had attempted to execute a wave-off, 2 March 1943. (NA, 80-G-50051)

the deck. Onlookers, however, noticed a sharp decrease in rpms as Baldwin's Wildcat reached "a distance equal to about two-thirds of the take off run," and as the pilot opened his wing flaps to assist him in getting aloft. The F4F-4 crossed the deck from starboard to port, and "mushed" off the flight deck from the port bow, with the Wildcat not yet up to flying speed. Flying in a level attitude, BuNo 12040 hit the water about 100 yards ahead and slightly to port of the *Ranger*. Once again true to the firm's nickname (Grumman "Iron Works"), the F4F-4 sank quickly. Fortunately, Baldwin freed himself from the cockpit of his sinking mount, and the *Hobson* picked him up soon thereafter.[13]

The trouble board faulted Baldwin, who had won his wings in 1942, for carelessness or negligence. Before taking off, all pilots had been warned to observe the check-off list and the ordinary precautions one followed when taking off from a carrier, with special attention being accorded propeller settings and tightening up the friction discs before they took off. In the aftermath of Baldwin's mishap on 13 March, all pilots were again cautioned to tighten throttle friction discs before takeoff.

Such problems did not figure in the mishap that occurred a little over six hours later, during the forenoon watch, when another VF-41 pilot experienced difficulty, this time in coming on board. Lieutenant Woodie Wood tried to "cushion" his landing and ended up floating into the barrier. His F4F-4 (BuNo 11701) and engine required a major overhaul before it was fit to fly again.[14]

During the afternoon watch on 15 March, Lt. (jg) Chuck August crashed on landing. A trouble board later faulted August's coming in with his tail slightly high. The

Ensign Albert J. Baldwin swims away from his sinking F4F-4 (BuNo 12040), [4-F-]13, on 13 March 1943; the destroyer *Hobson* picked him up a short time later. (NA, 80-G-60040)

hook bounced over the arresting wires and August's F4F-4 (BuNo 11705) crashed into the barrier. As in the case of Woodie Wood just two days earlier, both plane and powerplant would require a major overhaul.[15]

The *Ranger* returned to Quonset Point on the 16th; the following morning, all hands mustered at quarters at 0830, and Capt. Gordon Rowe, USNA 1918, relieved Cal Durgin as the *Ranger*'s commanding officer. Durgin had been promoted to flag rank a little over a fortnight earlier and had been given the post of Commander, Fleet Air, Quonset Point. Formerly Keen Harrill's exec in the *Wright*, Gordon Rowe had been serving, at the American entry into hostilities, as Commander, Patrol Wing Four; he then served on temporary duty with Patrol Wing Two in the Fourteenth Naval District, before moving on to command NAS Palmyra Island. Subsequently, he served as air officer on the staff of the Commander, Hawaiian Sea Frontier.

"I, of course, was very much disappointed to have to give up my ship," Cal Durgin reflected to Rear Adm. William H. P. Blandy, Chief of the Bureau of Ordnance on 6 April, "but I don't guess one can hope to be a skipper forever. I probably should be satisfied with the broad stripe in place of being captain of the good old *Ranger*."[16] To another friend, Capt. Kenneth B. Bragg, at Great Lakes, Durgin expressed similar thoughts on 18 April: "I regretted very much giving up my command as I was happier in that ship than I ever have been before. I had it for almost a year, and while we did not have a great deal of active contact with the enemy we did do a job that we feel sure had a great effect on the war effort being made in Europe."[17]

Cal Durgin's old ship continued training out in the Narragansett Bay–Quonset Point area. Thus far, the deck landing accidents that had occurred had been instructive, but had been mostly free of tragedy. That changed with brutal abruptness during the first dog watch on 20 March, shortly after the *Ranger* had turned into the wind and begun recovering aircraft. The first plane to approach, 42-B-8, crashed into the sea as the pilot, Lt. (jg) Prince H. Gordon, A-V(N), lost control.

Buffeted by the choppy sea as he extricated himself from the sinking Dauntless, Gordon, his mouth severely cut upon impact (he had lost six teeth), and suffering from shock and immersion, soon discovered that only one of the two CO_2 cartridges in his life jacket worked; the other had been improperly installed. Nevertheless, he swam over to Aviation Radioman 2d Class C. P. Triche (both of whose CO_2 cartridges had been punctured, but failed to work as they were supposed to), and kept his passenger afloat. Although a boat from the *Hobson* (her second rescue in a week) picked up both men within 15 minutes, all efforts to revive Triche on board ship failed.[18]

The litany of deck landing accidents, part and parcel of a dangerous and demanding profession, continued. Ensign Howard F. Edwards, A-V(N), was bringing in his F4F-4 (BuNo 12000), the day after Lt. (jg) Gordon's mishap. Failing to answer a wave-off, Edwards floated into the barrier. Although the plane itself required only minor repairs, the impact of the landing caused the trouble board to assess the damage to the powerplant as requiring a major overhaul to restore it to operational status.[19]

On the morning of 24 March, the *Ranger* sailed for Casco Bay, Maine, and conducted carrier qualifications en route: each day's evolutions, over the three days that followed, were marred by at least one mishap. Lieutenant (jg) Laurence L. "Ham" Hamrick, A-V(N)'s TBF-1, [4-T-]1

Ensign Harlan McFadden's TBF-1 (BuNo 05922), after it almost ended up in a 40-millimeter quad gun tub, 25 March 1943. (NA, 80-G-60045)

(BuNo 06253), going into the gallery at 1400 and coming to rest against 40-millimeter mount number five and on top of the three 20-millimeter mounts just abaft that gun. Unlike the accident that occurred on 2 March, in which the same plane had required a major overhaul, this time there was no fixing the battered Avenger: it had been damaged beyond repair.[20]

The next day, Ens. Harlan McFadden of VT-4, with Aviation Radioman 3d Class Shelton E. Garner and Aviation Ordnanceman 3d Class Charles P. Jackson, Jr., on board, made a hard landing in BuNo 05922, and his Avenger ended up nearly rampaging into the 40-millimeter quad mount aft of the island. The TBF required a major overhaul before it could be flown again.[21] The same day, Buster Craig, of VF-41, crashed when he landed on his left wheel in the vicinity of number four wire. Missing the cross-deck pendant, the F4F-4 (BuNo 11995) fouled the barrier and crashed into the island. Craig's mount, like McFadden's, required a major overhaul.[22]

Early in the afternoon watch on 26 March, Windy Shields made what appeared to be a textbook landing, until wires number five and nine broke. Shields suffered no injury in the mishap, but his F4F-4, BuNo 11997, required a major overhaul.[23] During the afternoon watch, a little over three hours later, Lt. Cy Weeks of VB-41, with Aviation Radioman 3d Class Herbert C. Meredith, USNR, in back, made a wheels-first landing that caused his SBD-3 (BuNo 06666) to bounce into the air after it had snagged a wire. The Dauntless required major work before it could be returned to operational service.[24]

Arriving at Casco Bay during the forenoon watch on 28 March, the *Ranger* took on fuel, provisions, and stores, before weighing anchor during the forenoon watch on 30 March, to proceed to the Boston Navy Yard. En route, the *Ranger* carried out flight operations, and exercised at avoiding simulated air and torpedo attacks. She turned into the wind at 1525 to launch planes—25 F4Fs, 4 SBDs, and 1 TBF—to fly to Quonset Point. Leading the flight was Lt. Mac Wordell of VF-41.

As the planes warmed up on deck and made ready for the flight, the pilots were to be shown two blackboards. One was to read: "Land at Squantum and obtain Quonset weather"; the other gave the bearing and distance to Squantum. Inexplicably, the first was never shown the departing pilots. Mac Wordell, thus not knowing he was to proceed first to NAS Squantum, set a direct course to Quonset Point.[25]

Within an hour of departure, however, Wordell's formation began to break up as it encountered bad weather. Entering thick clouds at 1620, the pilots soon found themselves in zero visibility conditions extending from 200 to 7,000 feet, with icing conditions. Ten minutes after the formation broke up in the storm, Lt. Tag Grell's F4F-4 (BuNo 12196) went into a steep dive. Unable to recover, Grell bailed out at 175 feet in the swirling snow, but did not get a chance to pull the ripcord of his parachute, because the airfoil balance of the rudder tore open his parachute pack when he hit it upon leaving the aircraft. The Wildcat crashed to total destruction 150 yards away, and Grell landed in a tree, suffering lacerations of his left hip and left great toe, and contusions about his face.[26]

Lieutenant Kagey Hammond and Lt. (jg)s Chuck August and Dee Jones flew as far as New Paltz, New York, where Hammond went in wheels-up, his F4F-4 (BuNo 12186) taking minor damage; August did likewise and his mount, BuNo 12143, also suffered minor damage. Jones, however, found himself upside down when his Wildcat nosed over on its back. His plane (BuNo 12179) required a major overhaul.[27]

Although 20 of the F4Fs finally reached safe havens at various fields near Quonset Point, and the sole TBF landed without incident, only 3 of the 4 SBDs made it down safely. Lieutenant Lykes M. Boykin, A-V(N) of VB-42 had, immediately after takeoff, sought to fully lock the alternate air control in the "alternate" position, but found that it would not do so without his having to use his right hand to try to and lock it as often as he could. The throttle sticking in the cruising position, accompanied by the engine's running rough and losing power, soon betrayed the first signs of icing. Boykin loosened the throttle and moved it, and the mixture control, back and forth, causing an engine backfire in an attempt to blow the ice out of the carburetor. The engine smoothed out for a time, and Boykin encountered no trouble for about a quarter of an hour, but the engine began running rough again and losing power. Boykin tried to use the same techniques to clear the carburetor, up until the last possible moment, when a water landing loomed before him.[28]

All efforts having proved for naught, Boykin ditched his SBD-4 (BuNo 06826) off Swampscott, Massachusetts, the "summer resort and fashionable residential suburb of Boston," noted for the excellence of its fishing grounds. Fortunately, neither Boykin nor his passenger, Aviation Radioman 2d Class H. H. Reed, suffered any injuries in the mishap, which a trouble board concluded had occurred as the result of an "undetermined" cause or causes. Although fishermen off Swampscott had often enjoyed a fine catch, having little trouble filling their nets or lobster pots, salvagers trying to locate Boykin's SBD could not find the downed plane, thus frustrating attempts to determine exactly what had gone wrong.[29]

Lieutenant (jg) Arthur Cassidy, A-V(N), seen here ca. early November 1942, disappeared during the ill-fated ferry flight of 30 March 1943. (NA, 80-G-31316)

All hands were finally accounted for except one: Lt. Arthur Cassidy, a veteran of the "Red Rippers" Torch operations. The 24-year-old New Yorker and holder of a B.A. from Fordham University who had received his wings on 21 June 1941, Cassidy had been last seen in the vicinity of the city of Attleboro, Massachusetts. The details of what happened to him in the swirling snow of the last day of March 1943 will never be known for certain: neither Cassidy nor his Wildcat (BuNo 11740) was ever found.[30]

An investigation into the accident subsequently found that launching the flight had been fully justified in view of the "military exigencies" involved. The board deemed the lack of information about the weather that lay in the path of the flight, and the unsatisfactory radio communications, as "undoubtedly contributory causes." In light of the facts of the case, those who looked into the incident recommended (*a*) that the combined duties of the aerological officer and the communication officer on board the *Ranger* be "divested from the same officer as soon as practicable, resulting in a separate aerological officer and a separate communication officer each skilled in his particular branch of the service," (*b*) "that the internal organization of Air Plot aboard [*sic*] the *Ranger* be revamped to the end that it will be impossible for pilots to fail to receive last minute instructions, and (*c*) that accelerated training be continued to the end that carrier and attached group may be brought to the highest state of operating perfection possible, ready to carry out war missions under conditions much more severe than experienced to date."[31]

As part of her air group was experiencing that harrowing time, the *Ranger* reached her destination during the first dog watch on 30 March. She moored to the starboard side of the Commonwealth Pier of the South Boston Navy Yard, and set in-port routine soon after the first line had been made fast to the dock. The *Ranger* then underwent a brief period of repairs and alterations, until 2 April, when she sailed for Argentia.

Gremlins, however, still seemed to dog the *Ranger*'s air group, in the wake of the eventful flight to Quonset Point a few days earlier. During the afternoon watch on the day of departure for Argentia, Lt. George C. Simmons made a hard, wheels-first landing, buckling the fuselage of his SBD-4 (BuNo 10516); only minutes later Lt. Allen H. Thurwachter, A-V(N), did the same thing. His SBD-4 (BuNo 06827) and Simmons's required major overhauls.³²

The *Ranger* and her consorts reached Argentia without further incident, during the forenoon watch on 5 April. She remained there for over a week, taking on fuel and provisions, with her men performing routine upkeep and voyage repairs. The Air Group remained on board during the duration of the time in port. Then during the forenoon watch on 13 April, the *Ranger* stood out of Placentia Bay for sea.

As the *Ranger* returned from that stint of underway training, tragedy claimed another Torch veteran. Max Eaton, of VB-41, who had just turned 28 years old a little over a month before, took off in an SBD-4 (BuNo 06897) during the forenoon watch on 17 April, on a practice bombing hop, with Aviation Radioman 3d Class Bill Shackelford on board. Eaton, cruising in formation, was circling the ship about three miles out with three other planes, when his engine abruptly quit. Shackelford later

The *Ranger* at Placentia Bay, 10 April 1943. (NA, 80-G-66775)

Looking aft over the snow-covered flight deck, showing Dauntlesses, Wildcats, and Avengers of Air Group 4; visible in the background are the heavy cruisers *Augusta* (foreground) and *Tuscaloosa* (background), April 1943. (NA, 80-G-66802)

speculated that Eaton had tried to switch gasoline tanks, but that the engine failed to catch. Seeing the inevitable result, Eaton, when the altimeter reached about 1,000 feet, called out to Shackelford to stand by for a water landing. The plane being without power meant that the pilot had to land with his flaps still retracted. The SBD landed "hard" at about 0845.[33]

"Mr. Eaton got out of the plane before I did," Shackelford later recounted, "so he tried to get the life raft, but the plane went down too fast." Shackelford had emerged from the after cockpit, but had not had time to help his pilot extract the raft from its stowage. Eaton had had good reason to make haste to break out the rubber boat: he could not swim. Shackelford, as the SBD disappeared in a welter of bubbles, heard Eaton calling out for him. The radioman swam over to his pilot, who clung to him in the cold water, with waves breaking over both of them, for almost 20 minutes. Attempts to inflate Eaton's life jacket, either by CO_2 or by mouth, proved unsuccessful. Eaton then spied his parachute, which had floated free from the sinking plane. He released Shackelford and clutched the chute as a life preserver.[34]

The heavy seas hampered efforts to locate the struggling men, either from a ship or from an airplane. Leaving the formation to proceed to the scene of the crash, the destroyer *Forrest* finally spotted the survivors, stopped all engines and lowered her motor whaleboat at 0940. Shackelford found himself floating about 30 feet from Eaton, as the *Forrest* closed in on them; the radioman heard his pilot bravely yell "not to worry." In the rough sea that had a temperature of only about 34°F, however, Shackelford tried

Lieutenant (jg) Max Eaton and Aviation Radioman 3d Class William T. Shackelford, ca. early November 1942. (NA, 80-G-31338)

to swim over to talk to Eaton, but, when the enlisted man put up his head out of the water, he saw his pilot lose his grasp on the parachute and sink. As he lapsed into unconsciousness, Shackelford last saw Eaton "about four feet under water in a balled up position."[35]

Her whaleboat crew having rescued the unconscious radioman and retrieved the parachute upon which Eaton had so desperately staked his survival, the *Forrest* recovered her boat soon thereafter. Shackelford responded to treatment on board ship, as the destroyer continued searching for Eaton for two hours. Abandoning the effort five minutes before the end of the forenoon watch, the *Forrest* then rejoined the formation.

Later, during the afternoon watch, Ens. Gerald M. Barnett, A-V(N), obeyed all of the LSO's signals and came in for what appeared to be a normal landing. His hook, however, bounced, and his TBF-1 (BuNo 06303) soon took major damage when it struck the barrier. There were, fortunately, no casualties among the three-man crew: Barnett, Aviation Machinist's Mate 2d Class Thomas R. Sims, and Aviation Ordnanceman 2d Class Russell H. Bertucci.[36]

As the result of Lt. (jg) Eaton's death on 17 April (as well as, undoubtedly, that of Aviation Radioman Triche on 20 March), Rear Adm. Bernard directed Capt. Rowe "to the need for thorough indoctrination of all pilots in the emergency forced landing procedure and the necessity for more

Ceremony honoring *Ranger* plank owners (who had served in the ship since she had been commissioned in 1934) (L–R) Chief Water Tender R. T. Bradley, Chief Machinist's Mate E. W. Lovejoy, Chief Electrician's Mate D. A. Erickson, Chief Water Tender A. G. Shinty, and Machinist J. M. Dunn, Placentia Bay, 27 April 1943. (NA, 80-G-66804)

determined efforts to insure the proper functioning of life jackets."[37]

The next day, the *Ranger* moored to buoy P-5 at NOB Argentia. While the ship took on fuel, stores, and provisions, her air group operated from NAS Argentia and lived on board ship. At the time that the *Ranger* had been operating from Argentia, the *U-404*, under *Kapitänleutnant* Otto von Bülow, was stalking a convoy on 25 April. The 31-year-old von Bülow, who had commanded the *U-404* since 6 August 1941, and who held the Knight's Cross, identified an aircraft carrier—which he identified as "possibly" the *Ranger*—and escorting vessels, and attacked, firing five torpedoes. Four explosions followed and the Germans felt "several very heavy vibrations," as they made off on the surface. They presumed that their quarry sank, as "no air or surface defense" ensued. Although decorated for his feat (Oak Leaves to his Knight's Cross, authorized the day after the successful attack on the "*Ranger*"), von Bülow's "sinking" of the *Ranger* proved wishful thinking. His target was in fact the British escort carrier HMS *Biter*, and the explosions were only those of his torpedoes exploding at the end of their run. Reports of the *Ranger*'s demise, to paraphrase Mark Twain, proved to be greatly exaggerated.[38] Fifteen minutes into the forenoon watch on 26 April, the ship that *Kapitänleutnant* von Bülow had "sunk" got underway to conduct flight operations and gunnery exercises in Placentia Bay, accompanied by the *Ellyson*, the *Emmons*, and the *Fitch*.

Lieutenant Joseph T. O'Callahan (ChC), the *Ranger*'s chaplain, looks on as Lt. Robinson H. Dorion (MC), and Lt. (jg) Volkert B. Veeder censor Mother's Day V-mail, refreshed in their labors by the popular soft drink Coca-Cola, 3 May 1943. (NA, 80-G-66816)

During the afternoon watch on 28 April, the *Ranger* fired an antiaircraft practice and steered appropriate courses to launch and recover aircraft. One mishap marred the otherwise smooth evolutions that day, when Lt. (jg) George Harris of VF-41 was coming on board at 1522. His F4F-4 (BuNo 12158) landed on top of number two wire. The tail hook, failing to snag a pendant, bounced; the unbridled Wildcat floated over the wires and into the barriers, eventually ending up against the island, forward. A major overhaul lay in that fighter's immediate future.[39]

Eventually completing the recovery of her air group very early in the first dog watch, the *Ranger* stood into the swept channel, mooring to the familiar buoy P-5. The ship remained there, taking on fuel and provisions, into mid-May 1943. During that period, six F4Fs, six SBDs, and three TBFs from CVG-4 based ashore at NAS Argentia; the remainder stayed on board ship.

During the fixed gunnery phase of individual battle practice being fired by VF-41 on 4 May, Dee Jones, another Torch veteran, made an overhead run on a sleeve being towed at 6,000 feet, from an altitude of 7,500. Observers noted that Jones made a normal approach and a normal firing run from a vertical attitude, but made a slight turn, apparently to avoid fouling the sleeve. Jones effected a partial recovery, but soon entered into a tight spiral. He appeared to try a second recovery at about 3,500 feet, but at 1,000 feet he pulled out rapidly from the spiral. Briefly, his Wildcat could be seen in a "momentarily normal flight attitude," until it "appeared to disintegrate" and splashed in Argentia Sound in several pieces. The trouble board posited that Jones had apparently blacked out, because he did not exit the F4F.[40]

A little over a week later, Lt. (jg) John P. Featheringill, A-V(N), took off from Argentia on 12 May, at the controls of one of six VB-42 SBD-4s (BuNo 06920) that were basing ashore, with Aviation Radioman 3d Class James R. Butler, USNR, in the after cockpit. Featheringill was to carry out a training flight of an hour's duration. He was to dive-bomb a rock target in Placentia Bay and follow that with a radio beam orientation drill. Prior to this familiarization flight, the 25-year-old Kansan had been warned, twice, about making low pullouts on dive-bombing runs. Featheringill pushed over into a dive from which he did not recover. No one saw the actual crash, but a search later recovered Featheringill's body. No trace, however, was ever found of the aircraft or of James Butler. Investigators ruled the cause "undetermined or doubtful."[41]

25
"I AM FED UP WITH THIS PLACE"

Argentia, with its fog (not to mention the fatal accidents that had befallen the air group there), inspired less than favorable comment as to its suitability as an operating area. "I am fed up with this place," Gordon Rowe complained to Cal Durgin on 14 May. "When the weather turns good we do not have the escorts available and if they do show up in sufficient numbers we become fog bound. Of course, we came up here expecting and hoping to get into a fight but the rats stay in their holes and we ought to move to sunnier climes if we are to do a lot of first class training."[1]

The weather proved a natural hindrance to training, but pilot errors continued to plague CVG-4. Ens. Robert S. Fuller, A-V(N), took off from NAS Argentia during the afternoon watch on 17 May for field carrier landing practice (FCLP). As Fuller made his second approach for a landing, he allowed the SBD-4 (BuNo 06812) to go into a nose-high left turn, just before the LSO picked him up on the approach. Fuller's Dauntless fell off on its left wing and crashed just short of the runway, crumpling the wings, breaking the fuselage at the rear cockpit, and sheering off the wheels and landing gear. The impact of the crash threw the pilot forward, and Fuller suffered a compound skull fracture, which resulted in his initially being diagnosed as being in critical condition. His passenger, Aviation Machinist's Mate 2d Class J. F. Harrison, emerged from the mishap with a small laceration of his right cheek. Those who evaluated the crash noted that, for some reason, Fuller had not been wearing the shoulder harness with which the SBD was equipped; they posited that that particular piece of gear would have minimized his injuries.[2]

Returning to sea to conduct flight operations and train in repelling torpedo attacks, on 29 May, the *Ranger* steamed on a recovery course, as Lt. (jg) Hubie Houston, who had won his wings six days before Pearl Harbor, and who had just completed a tactics hop, came in fast. The LSO gave him the "cut" signal, but the F4F's hook failed to engage the wire, and the Wildcat (BuNo 12002) floated into the barrier. Its forward progress thus arrested abruptly, the F4F nosed over on its back. Houston suffered a concussion; flight deck crews hauled the wrecked Wildcat below with a badly damaged engine, propeller, vertical fin of the empennage, and a crushed cockpit enclosure. Those who assessed the damage also could see that both wings would require a major overhaul. Commenting on the accident, the LSO remarked that it was not unusual for an F4F, when landing in a three-point attitude on the deck, to skip wires.[3]

Training in night operations continued while the ship remained in port, moored at buoy P-5 in Placentia Sound. During the period that the *Ranger* lay at P-5 (14–19 June, inclusive), she based 15 planes ashore. Among them was a TBF-1 (BuNo 06378) piloted by Ens. Gerald W. "Jerry" Thomas, A-V(N), during the afternoon watch on 17 June, for field carrier landing practice. Thomas made a normal takeoff from NAS Argentia, without flaps. Once airborne, he retracted his landing gear. At an altitude of about 100 feet, however, the engine sputtered and misfired. Thomas quickly sized up the situation. If he continued his take off

Fine shot of SBD-3s from VB-41 or VB-42 in formation above the clouds over Argentia, ca. May 1943. (NA, 80-G-79102)

with a balky engine, he would have run the risk of not being able to clear the rock-crushing plant that he knew to be in his path, and then of proceeding out over the bay, risking a water landing. Jerry Thomas chose to cut his engine, and landed, wheels-up. The impact of the crash demolished the bomb bay doors, tore some of the metal skin off the fuselage aft of the bomb bay "over an area about 42" long by 12" wide," and bent and twisted all three propeller blades. The engine, after investigation, proved to be undamaged.[4]

The trouble board could not agree on a cause for the mishap on 17 June, but expressed doubt that a successful landing, with wheels down, could have been made under the circumstances confronting Ens. Thomas. "Although the engine turned up satisfactorily subsequent to the crash," the board judged, "in view of the obstructions in the take off path...the pilot exercised good judgment in electing to land." Subsequently, as Jerry Thomas confided to his journal, the TBF-1 was "sold to the supply officer, NAS Argentia, for the total price of $1 and a new plane was issued to Torpedo Squadron Four."[5]

Night added an additional element of danger to carrier landings—evolutions which by nature have enough hazards of their own—a fact amply demonstrated on board the *Ranger* during an overcast mid watch on 21 June. Lieutenant John L. Erickson, making his first night qualification landing, made a slightly fast approach. He managed to snag the fifth or sixth cross-deck pendant, but, after pulling out 30 feet of wire, the hook parted. Thus unhindered, the SBD-4 (BuNo 06808) headed straight up the centerline, clearing two barriers that had been lowered before crashing into the third. A postaccident inspection revealed that the hook had parted at the weld that joined the "fish hook" to the shaft. Investigators declared that, because that was the second known failure of that type, probably caused by improper welding practices, the area adjacent to the weld should be left unpainted, so that the appliance could be inspected visually after each landing. Erickson's SBD-4 required an engine change, as well as changing the left landing gear oleo strut. Damage to the left wing resulted in its being changed.[6]

One hour later, with the sea moderate, the moon nearly full, and with scattered clouds and good visibility conditions prevailing, Ens. Hartwell R. Hawkins, A-V(N), a little under two months shy of 20 years old, who had conducted four field carrier landing practices during the preceding week and who had been adjudged ready to qualify on board ship, brought in his F4F-4 (BuNo 03464), to conduct his first qualifying landing. With his F4F weighing 7,500 pounds, all guns loaded, a main tank with 60 gallons and a full reserve tank, Hawkins showed what was later judged to be poor technique and poor judgment, coming in fast on his approach. After receiving the cut, Hawkins's Wildcat floated until its right wing hit the island, the F4F swinging violently to starboard just at the instant its hook snagged the last cross-deck pendant. It crashed through the first barrier and slammed into the island, head-on, badly damaging both wings and the engine, wrinkling the fuselage, and breaking loose the tail structure. The trouble board that investigated the mishap, however, leveled half of the blame on the LSO, "only in that inherent and unavoidable limitations to judging speed at night" caused him to give the "cut" signal faster than he would otherwise do.[7]

Less than two hours later, at the start of the morning watch, Lt. Harold Keller came in to the groove for a night qualification landing, and, after receiving the cut from the LSO, floated up the deck and crashed into a barrier, nosing up and receiving enough damage to warrant a major overhaul. Unlike Erickson's landing, for which the arresting appliance on the aircraft received the full blame, investigators believed Keller's had stemmed from 75% poor judgment and 25% poor technique. Fortunately, none of the incidents on 21 June resulted in any injuries to the pilots involved.[8]

A trouble board had faulted the LSO for his decision when he gave Ens. Hawkins the cut during night qualifications on 21 June, and it did the same with the LSO two days later. Lieutenant (jg) Walt Laake, of VF-41, was bringing in his F4F-4 (BuNo 11950) for his first night qualification landing, with the sea moderate, the sky overcast, and visibility unrestricted, after having demonstrated, during FCLP the preceding week, his fitness to land on board ship. As in Hawkins's case, Laake's Wildcat carried its full ammunition allowance, 60 gallons of fuel in the main tank, and a full reserve tank. "Fast" at the cut, Laake's Wildcat touched down near number three cross-deck pendant. The tail hook, however, did not engage the wire, and the F4F charged up the deck and fouled the first barrier, where it nosed up and want over onto its back. The cockpit enclosure crumpled, crushing Laake's right hand. Once again, flight deck crews found themselves unfouling the deck of a battered Wildcat, like Hawkins's a few days before, with a damaged engine, propeller, and tail structure.[9]

Night qualification work, with all of its inherent hazards, continued. Early in the mid watch on 24 June, Ens. Graydon D. Wright, A-V(N), was making a slow approach in one of VT-4's TBF-1s (BuNo 06303). The LSO, however, detected Wright's settling to ramp level or below and drifting off to the right of the groove that all pilots followed—hopefully—to a safe landing on board, and signalled "wave-off." On being wavedoff, however, close aboard, Wright pulled the nose up, but soon had big trouble on his hands, as the TBF stalled and its left wing slanted down. The Avenger crossed the port corner of the flight deck in a vertical bank, continued rolling, lifting the port wing clear of the deck, then went over the side in an inverted dive and splashed close aboard to port, at about a 45–50 degree angle. Wright held full throttle until the crash. Onlookers noted that the Avenger stayed afloat for about 10 seconds, a small fire breaking out aft.[10]

"[Wright] landed with his wheels sticking straight up in that cold, cold water," then-Lt. (jg) Leonard L. "Ham" Hamrick later recounted, "We all thought that was all for G.W." Wright, however, although having suffered facial lacerations and shock, managed to get clear of the sinking Avenger; a plane guard destroyer rescued him inside a quarter of an hour.[11] Those who looked into the circumstances surrounding Wright's accident laid the blame to "personnel error." Investigators faulted not only the pilot for his slow approach and radical wave-off technique, but the LSO for waving off Wright too late. Despite that combination of factors, the trouble board doubted that a "less violent maneuver at that time would have cleared the ramp," anyway.[12]

The board also declared that the advent of the Avenger had "introduced a slight change in the basic technique of carrier landings" with that type of plane. The difficulty experienced by pilots in climbing near the ramp, and the TBF's poor maneuverability at slow speed and full throttle, indicated "the desirability of making a power glide approach rather than a constant altitude power drag up the groove." By contrast, the "high, slowly settling approach allowed ample margin for wave-offs, gives a better view of the deck,

Rear Admiral Bernhard, accompanied by Capt. Gordon Rowe, the carrier's commanding officer, inspects the *Ranger*'s mess decks, 16 June 1943. (NA, 80-G-391595)

and better control of the plane during the approach." Tests showed that pilots who had utilized that tactic in landing had experienced no difficulty day or night in ridding themselves of the excess altitude "by dropping the nose slightly and recovering for a normal tail-down landing."[13]

In addition, the board also "most strongly" recommended that the Advance Carrier Training Group (ACTG) change its training regimen for TBF pilots. Instead of a 75-knot (indicated) "drag around a square pattern," those who looked into what had happened in Ensign Wright's case suggested that a "smooth turning, 80-knot power glide, as actually used afloat." The 75-knot (indicated) speed equaled 64 knots true—only one knot above "power-off stalling speed." The method as taught in the ACTG gave TBF pilots very little margin for mistakes.[14]

Later that same day, during the first dog watch, Lt. Comdr. Spanky Carter, VF-41's exec, came in high and fast, upon returning from a routine tactics hop. Seeing the LSO's cut, Carter dove for the deck. His F4F-4 (BuNo 11956) struck wheels-first, and crashed through the number one barrier, stopping the engine suddenly, damaging both wings, bending and tearing the engine cowling, cracking the engine's nose section, and tearing the propeller cuffs. Carter walked away from the accident unhurt, but a trouble board cited pilot error as the cause, faulting judgment and technique.[15]

In the aftermath of "G.W." Wright's accident of 24 June, some of his squadronmates visited him in the hospital and found him sitting up in bed, his face bandaged, smoking a cigarette. "I have things all arranged," he confided to his

Ensigns Howard F. "Eddie" Edwards (VF-4), Ralph R. "Andy" Anderson (VT-4), Charles R. "Hoppy" Hopson (VF-4), and Lt. (jg) Dee Jones (VF-4) (L–R) relax over cards in the wardroom, while Lt. Homer H. "Hutch" Hutcheson, VT-4's exec, looks over Ensign Hopson's hand, ca. May 1943. (NA, 80-G-79124)

Ensigns Clifford M. White (L) and Hartwell R. Hawkins (R) (with "Mae West" over his shoulder), from VF-4, peruse *Colliers* and *Life*, respectively, ca. May 1943. The wardroom magazine rack (R) contains issues of other popular periodicals of the day, including *The New Yorker*, *Time*, and *Click*. (NA, 80-G-79125)

VB-4 radio-gunners, in flight gear, relax while a shipmate strums a guitar, June 1943, in this photo that reveals how cramped the berthing areas had become by this point in the ship's life. (NA, 80-G-79127)

friends, "There are five nurses here who cook us steaks and bring the rest of the food and we will have a party. You guys bring a few bottles of booze and come at seven." His friends followed his directions, and they all "had a grand party that night—all in his hospital room."[16]

Although Cal Durgin had moved on, he still harbored affection and concern for his old command. "I wish you would get the Padre [O'Callahan] working on the people with whom he has the most influence to get the *Ranger* down here," he wrote to Lt. Comdr. Everett M. Bessie, (MC) USNR, the *Ranger*'s senior medical officer, on 25 June. "The summer is just in full swing now and I am sure the officers and men would enjoy themselves in these parts. I have told everybody with whom I came in contact that the *Ranger* should be brought back to a decent part of the world where it can get some good operations in. So far I have not had much luck but still don't believe that ComInCh will keep you up there indefinitely. He certainly must know that the squadrons are not getting much training and that the morale of officers and men is not improving."[17]

Bessie, responding to his former commanding officer's suggestion about Chaplain O'Callahan's working the divine chain of command about getting the *Ranger* sent to warmer climes, wrote that "Not only do we have the Padre, but every one else from the Captain down, working on bringing about your suggestion." The "last word we had from CinCLant," heard on board the *Ranger* was, however, "that we were here 'for strategical reasons' so I guess that's that. We're all trying to get used to it."[18]

For the first three days of July 1943, the *Ranger*, serving as flagship for Commander TG 22, remained moored in the familiar waters of berth P-5 in Placentia Sound; 15 aircraft based ashore, carrying out day and night training. Underway again during the forenoon watch on Independence Day, the *Ranger* sailed in company with the *Augusta,* and the *Tuscaloosa*; five destroyers, the *Forrest* and the *Hobson*; and the new *Fletcher*-class destroyers *Kidd* (DD-661), *Isherwood* (DD-520), and *Bell* (DD-587). The carrier's air group practiced touch-and-go landings.

Turning into the wind and launching her air group shortly before the end of the morning watch, the *Ranger* then launched her F4Fs as a combat air patrol. A little over an hour into the forenoon watch, CVG-4 began mock attacks on the task group, in a drill executed with such skill that CTG 22 gave the *Ranger* a "Well Done" on its "Excellent coordinated attack."

During the course of the day, Lt. (jg) John Iarrobino had flown one of VB-41's SBD-3s (BuNo 06634), and had reported a hard landing, when it had landed left-wheel first. The inspecting crew looked over the aircraft, but only noted the obvious damage: a blown left tire. Subsequently, Lt. Daniel K. Weitzenfeld took off in the same plane with Aviation Radioman 2d Class J. J. Kunze in back. Danny Weitzenfeld soon found, however, that his left wheel would neither fully retract nor fully extend. When he came in for a landing at the conclusion of his flight, 41-B-13 hit the deck and bounced, the impact apparently jarring the

Lieutenant Danny Weitzenfeld's SBD-3 (BuNo 06634), 41-B-13, after its left wheel fully extended and locked in place upon landing, 5 July 1943. Weitzenfeld and his passenger, Aviation Radioman 2d Class J. J. Kunze look on (foreground), and a corpsman (center), his first aid bag over his shoulder, stands by, his assistance fortunately not required. (NA, 80-G-79108)

damaged wheel down into the locked position. A second inspection revealed the left stub wing buckled and torn at the landing gear strut mounting, with the skin on the underside of the wing buckled, too.[19]

The *Ranger* lay on a 24-hour sailing notice, moored to the familiar buoy P-5 in Argentia Sound on 7 July, retaining all but 15 aircraft from CVG-4 on board. Over the next few days, the 15 based ashore at NAS Argentia conducted training flights. On the afternoon of 13 July, Ens. Emmet Parkerson, Jr., A-V(N), of VB-42, took off, with Aviation Radioman 2d Class L. E. Colon in the after cockpit, for a familiarization flight in an SBD-4 (BuNo 06808). Parkerson put his gear down and made a normal landing on the runway. After rolling between 1,500 to 1,700 feet, he swerved to the left to turn off the runway. Unfortunately, although he had his gear control lever in the down position, Parkerson had not turned his landing check-off list so that a warning horn would sound if the gear were not locked down. The turning movement collapsed the left wheel, and the SBD slid along on its belly for about 50 feet, tearing the bomb displacing gear from the firewall, buckling the right wing, bending and tearing the flaps, and denting and tearing the left wing where it joined the stub wing. Damage to the engine had ensued, as it stopped suddenly when the plane collapsed onto its belly. The trouble board subsequently blamed the accident entirely on "pilot error," citing "carelessness" as the cause.[20]

That same afternoon, Lt. George C. Simmons of VB-41, with Aviation Radioman 3d Class C. Kozek in back, had led a cross-country hop to Torbay, Newfoundland, where the control tower people had instructed him to land on what proved to be a crosswind runway. Half-completing his landing run, Simmons felt his plane beginning to swerve to the right. With a weak left brake, he could not prevent his

Forty-Two-Baker-Twelve being struck below, August 1943. (NA, 80-G-79110)

As the war progressed, markings on the planes changed; this view illustrates how individual plane numbers on the tail make their appearance, and fuselage markings disappear. Soon, the blue/white star on the fuselage will have white bars added, and the insignia will be outlined in red. Although the markings have changed, the motive power for spotting planes—manpower—has not. (NA, 80-G-79112)

SBD-4 (BuNo 10778) from ground-looping into loose rock along the runway proper, resulting in a blown tire and a damaged wheel rim. With a new wheel and tire flown to Torbay, Simmons took off to return to Argentia, but soon discovered that he could not lower the left wheel. Coming in on one wheel, Simmons landed without further incident, but BuNo 10778 required repairs to the bent left and center landing flaps, the Mk. 43 miniature bomb rack, and the propeller blades. Those who assessed the cause of the accident blamed it upon the landing gear.[21]

During night carrier landing practice on 18 July, Lt. (jg) Dean S. Laird, A-V(N), with two years' flying experience and a clear record, made a normal approach, but crossed the ramp fast and high. After mistakenly reading the LSO's wave-off signal as one to land, Diz Laird landed; consequently, his F4F-4 (BuNo 11951) floated over the barrier and nosed over on its back. Laird suffered a mild concussion in the mishap, and his Wildcat took class B damage that required a major overhaul.

After a brief respite from 18 to 20 July, the *Ranger* got underway less than an hour into the forenoon watch on the latter day, passing through the gate in the net defenses of Placentia Sound and going to general quarters for leaving port. She then conducted SRBP runs, using one of her escorting destroyers as her target. During night refresher landings, being conducted in good weather and with a calm to moderate sea, during the first watch Lt. Johnny Johnson, with Aviation Radioman 2d Class Cy Colon in the rear seat, came up the groove "somewhat high and fast."

Although Lt. Francis V. Kenney, A-V(N), the LSO, could see that Johnson was "still slightly high and fast," he nevertheless gave him the "cut" sign. Johnson caught the number seven wire, which failed to stop the charging Dauntless from engaging the barrier wires with its prop, causing a sudden stoppage of the engine and bending the prop blades. The trouble board, in apportioning blame for the damage to the SBD-4 (BuNo 06866), divided it equally between Johnny Johnson, for his poor technique, and Kenney, for not exercising better judgment and waving off Johnson when he should have.[22]

Once the deck had been cleared of the lamed Dauntless, as the watch changed, the *Ranger* continued the night flight operations, still in company with the *Forrest*, the *Hobson*, and the *Corry*. Only a short time before the night training evolutions were to begin, Lt. Comdr. George O. "Otto" Klinsmann, who had been commanding officer of VB-42 since 28 October 1942, had lectured his pilots on "safe techniques" for such operations. He urged them, above all else, when taking off: "Keep cool. Don't lose your orientation." The *Ranger* turned into the wind, 11 minutes into the mid watch, and, 5 minutes later, Otto Klinsmann, in the cockpit of 42-B-1 (BuNo 10774), released his brakes and pushed the throttle forward.[23]

Torpedo Squadron 4 pilots on board the *Ranger*, 22 July 1943, in front of 4-T-4, a Grumman TBF-1 (BuNo 06302). Front (L–R): Ens. George D. Walker, Ens. Robert F. "Bob" Ruth, Lt. (jg) Page P. Stephens, Ens. Felix E. Ward, Ens. Wilbur S. "Souz" Souza, Ens. Gerald M. "Buck" Barnett; middle row (L–R): Lt. (jg) Louis G. Gardemal, Lt. J. Welsh Harriss, Lt. Richard Claytor, A-V(S), Lt. Comdr. David W. "Woot" Taylor, Jr. (commanding officer), Lt. Homer H. "Hutch" Hutcheson (executive officer), Lt. (jg) George W. Bolt; rear row (L–R): Lt. (jg) John H. "Johnnie" Palmer, Lt. (jg) Laurence L. "Ham" Hamrick, Lt. (jg) Ralph R. "Andy" Anderson, Lt. (jg) Robert E. "Burt" Trexler, Ens. Gerald W. "Jerry" Thomas. (NA, 80-G-76054)

Enlisted aircrew from VT-4 pose in front of [4-T-]4, 22 July 1943. (NA, 80-G-76079)

Ensign Gerald Thomas, not scheduled to fly that night, stood among those who watched as Forty-Two-Baker-One roared, full-throttle, down the flight deck. "About the time Otto popped his flaps," Thomas later recalled, "the plane started bouncing off toward the starboard [side] before it became airborne." Klinsmann's plane crashed off the *Ranger*'s starboard bow. Fortunately, the *Forrest* picked up Klinsmann and Aviation Chief Radioman Elmer M. Rogers, his radio-gunner, within eight minutes of their impromptu dip, and soon the carrier turned into the wind and resumed launching VB-42's 12 SBDs. When questioned the next morning as to what had happened, Klinsmann admitted: "I lost my orientation."[24]

Returning to the berth P-5, Placentia Sound, the *Ranger* there received orders, at the start of the second dog watch on 23 July, to be prepared to get underway at the start of the forenoon watch on the 24th. Accordingly, the ship began to embark the 15 planes that had been shore-based, via lighters.

An hour before the end of the morning watch on 24 July, the *Ranger* received the order to get underway at 1230, just five and a half hours away. For the duration of the morning and forenoon watches, the *Ranger* completed lightering her shore-based aircraft, embarked her hospital patients that had been under treatment ashore, and completed the other required preparations that accompanied her departure. Sailing at 1222, eight minutes ahead of schedule, the *Ranger* proceeded out of Argentia harbor, and cleared the swept channel, sailing in company with the *Tuscaloosa* and the destroyers *Forrest*, *Hobson*, *Corry*, and *Isherwood*.

During the first dog watch that day, Ens. Louis K. Lepp, A-V(N), of VF-41, returned from a routine tactics hop and made a normal approach to the ship. Receiving the cut from the LSO, Lepp erred in judgment, however, when he observed that he seemed slightly to port of the deck, and accordingly dropped the right wing and the nose to position himself better for the landing. Unfortunately, those techniques proved unsuccessful, and Ensign Lepp's F4F-4 (BuNo 12042) crashed onto the deck, damaging the engine by the sudden stoppage, bending the prop, damaging the right wing, and tearing out the right landing gear oleo and the gear mount.[25]

Following that mishap, the voyage to Boston proceeded uneventfully, until the morning of 26 July. On routine antisubmarine patrol during the forenoon watch, Ens. Gerald E. Grimes, A-V(N), became lost. With their radio receiver out of commission, Grimes and Aviation Radioman 1st Class Julius C. Theis could not get a bearing on the ship, which had the lost SBD-4 on her radar screen, bearing 038 degrees (T), only 23 miles away. Unable to either contact the ship or to find her, Grimes and Theis encountered worsening weather, visibility lessening to a mile, with a ceiling ranging from 500 to 1,500 feet, sometimes down to sea level, with intermittant rain. Heading for the nearest land, Grimes found the coast of Nova Scotia. With visibility dropping to three-quarters of a mile and a ceiling of 300 feet, and with only a small amount of gas remaining, he made a power landing in Ketch Harbor, Nova Scotia, in 15 feet of water. Breaking out the rubber boat, Grimes and Aviation Radioman Theis paddled to shore. With the help of a local Royal Canadian Air Force unit, the industrious Ens. Grimes succeeded in salvaging the SBD-4 (BuNo 10785) 53 hours later, "and had it prepared and crated for shipment." The trouble board apportioned equal blame for the mishap to pilot error and weather.[26]

Four-Tare-Three (L) and 4-T-4 (R) fly low near the camouflaged British passenger liner *Queen Mary* as she steams toward Halifax with Prime Minister Churchill embarked, 9 August 1943. (NA, 80-G-81442)

The next day, 27 July, the *Ranger* arrived at the South Boston Navy Yard Annex. After carrying out such voyage repairs and alterations permitted by her being on 48-hour sailing notice, the carrier got underway during the forenoon watch on 5 August. Under orders to sortie at 0900, the ship cast off all lines at 0845 and got underway, 15 minutes ahead of schedule. She proceeded out to sea, and at 1040 began recovering her air group, an evolution she had to interrupt immediately, when she changed course to avoid the fishing vessel *Lobster*.

The voyage to Halifax in company with the *Tuscaloosa* and the destroyers *Forrest, Corry, Hobson, Isherwood, Bell, Luce* (DD-522), and *Hale* (DD-642) (the last four ships being detached prior to arrival, to operate independently) proceeded, for the most part, uneventfully. The *Ranger* began conducting flight operations during the forenoon watch on 9 August, and continued them into the afternoon. Her planes covered the arrival of the liner *Queen Mary* and her important passenger, Prime Minister Winston Churchill, who, "despite wartime censorship" found that word of his reaching Halifax had spread in advance, with a "large and enthusiastic crowd" on hand to welcome him when he set foot ashore. Tarrying briefly at Quebec, Churchill would then visit President Roosevelt at Hyde Park, before the President and the Prime Minister and their respective advisors would return to Quebec for a major conference on war strategy.[27]

Providing cover for the arrival of one of the key Allied leaders or no, flight operations, with their attendant hazards, continued. During the forenoon watch that day, two barrier crashes occurred on board the *Ranger* in a little over a half hour. In the first, Lieutenant (jg) Harris encountered the barrier in his F4F-4 at 1122, but walked away unhurt. In the second, Ens. Grimes, who had made the water landing at Ketch Harbor back in July, made a normal approach, but received a slightly high cut from the LSO. Grimes, with Aviation Radioman 3d Class Earl F. Flanigan on board, engaged number eight wire, which the SBD-5 (BuNo 28609) pulled into number three barrier, the top cable of the barrier wrapping itself around the propeller. A trouble board assessed responsibility for the major damage to the aircraft as 100% "pilot error" (judgment and technique). In Grimes's defense, however, the board noted that his commanding officer had said that the pilot "had not made a carrier landing for [a] relatively long time."[28]

As the *Ranger* neared Halifax, during the second dog watch on 9 August, the visibility dropped to zero. The ship stopped all engines and anchored in the channel, and began sounding fog signals as she paused in her passage. She then embarked her pilot and got underway once more, steaming various courses and speeds to conform to the channel. Three-quarters of an hour into the first watch, the *Ranger* dropped anchor in 12 fathoms of water, and after shifting the watch from the bridge to the quarterdeck, the *Ranger* set in-port routine.

The "strategical reasons" that Doc Bessie alluded to back in early July in his letter to the *Ranger*'s old skipper soon dictated the ship's next destination. To offset the dispatch of the battleships *South Dakota* (BB-59) and *Alabama* (BB-58) to the Pacific—the two had been operating with the British Home Fleet for a time, because of the Royal Navy's concern with the powerful German surface squadron formed around the battleship *Tirpitz* (sistership of the ill-fated *Bismarck*), the battle cruiser *Scharnhorst* and the armored ship ("pocket battleship") *Lützow* (ex-*Deutschland*), then based in Norwegian waters—the *Ranger*, along with her old heavy cruiser consorts, the *Augusta* and the *Tuscaloosa*, were sent to take the place of the battleships. The British (as they had longingly looked forward to "borrowing" her in the dark days of the summer of 1942) particularly welcomed the *Ranger*, since deploying the more modern HMS *Illustrious* to the Mediterranean left the venerable HMS *Furious* as the Home Fleet's sole carrier.

26

"THE OLD SHIP CAME ACROSS IN GOOD STYLE"

The orders governing the *Ranger*'s joining the Home Fleet did not permit her to linger long in Halifax. She took on fuel, provisions, and aviation gasoline during her stay. Initially, she had received orders to assume a two-hour notice for sailing on 11 August; those were amended to call for her to sortie at 0900 on the 11th. Consequently, the *Ranger* sailed for the Orkney Islands as scheduled, and reached Scapa Flow on the afternoon of the 19th. She immediately commenced fueling, provisioning, and converting to British naval procedure (including embarking four British signalmen) for all communications, and began training soon thereafter.

CVG-4's pilots soon began operating from Royal Naval Air Station (RNAS) Hatston, when not embarked in the *Ranger*. Before long, the first mishap occurred during the first dog watch on 21 August, when Ens. Hartwell R. Hawkins returned from a routine tactics flight. Under favorable weather conditions, he made a normal approach, but, when about four feet off the runway, he dropped his right wing. He simultaneously applied the throttle to take a voluntary wave-off but, as the Wildcat clawed for altitude, its left wing tip caught the turf. Hawkins's F4F-4 (BuNo 12209) cartwheeled, the impact of the crash severing the engine from the rest of the aircraft at the firewall. The damage to the wings, fuselage, and tail assembly, however, prompted those who surveyed the wrecked Wildcat to recommend that the plane be deemed damaged beyond repair and stricken. Hawkins walked away from the crash uninjured.[1]

Flying out to the *Ranger* late in the mid watch on 26 August, returning from temporary duty ashore, Lt. Ed Seiler made a normal, albeit slightly fast, approach. The LSO, with the average relative wind force over the deck about 25 knots, gave Seiler the cut, but the pilot landed wheels-first. Consequently, his F4F-4 (BuNo 11953) became airborne once more, and floated into, and crashed through, barriers one and two. As the Wildcat tore through the latter, flames broke out at the fuel line that had been severed in the contact with it, and enveloped the F4F's accessory section. Prompt action by the *Ranger*'s flight deck firefighters, however, prevented the blaze from spreading. Seiler's F4F suffered damage ranging from the usual stoppage of the engine that came with a deck crash to damaged propeller blades, the entire landing gear carried away, the main fuel tank and electric fuel pump destroyed, the cowling and fuselage beneath the main tank bent, and the left wing tip and pitot tube damaged. Unlike the other more recent accidents that had befallen VF-4, the trouble board only faulted Seiler 75% pilot error. The rest of the damage had been incurred because of the structure of the barriers that had arrested the theretofore unbridled passage of Seiler's aircraft up the deck.[2]

Underway during the morning watch on 27 August, the *Ranger* participated in exercise CN with elements of the Home Fleet that day, evolutions that included streaming and recovering her paravanes and the usual flight operations. One minor mishap marred the day, occurring late in the afternoon watch, when Ens. Emmet Parkerson, with

323

Aviation Radioman 3d Class C. W. Nelson in back, made a normal approach at 1530 and received a slightly "high" cut by the LSO. Parkerson nosed the SBD-5 over, but pulled back on the stick, holding the Dauntless off the deck until the port wing stalled into the flight deck, damaging the port wing, port bottom flap, and aileron and stabilizer tip beyond repair. The crash also damaged the plane's port elevator, but inflicted no damage to the SBD's engine. The trouble board attributed the blame solely to Parkerson, dividing it equally between judgment and technique.[3] The ensign had only 15.1 hours flight time in SBD-5s over the past three months, and his carelessness had resulted in damage to another Dauntless on 13 July.

Admiral Sir Bruce Fraser, Commander in Chief, Home Fleet, came on board during the forenoon watch on 31 August, with the *Ranger* breaking the CinC's flag in place of CTG 112.1's. The admiral spent the balance of the day watching flight operations—evolutions marred by three deck crashes: the first occurring during the forenoon watch, when Buster Craig made a "fast and slightly skidding approach." After seeing the LSO signal "cut," Craig dropped his right wing. The F4F-4 (BuNo 12153) skidded across the deck, struck the after 40-millimeter gun (mount V) and ended up in the starboard catwalk. Craig suffered a cut and bruised left knee in the accident, but BuNo 12153 proved beyond repair.[4]

During the afternoon watch, Lt. (jg) Chuck August's F4F-4 (BuNo 11927), 4-F-5, crashed on deck at 1547; August suffered injuries in the accident: severe scalp lacerations and a mild concussion. Once the flight deck crew cleared away the damaged fighter with its bent propeller, engine damaged by the sudden stoppage, both wings damaged, fuselage wrinkled, and tail bent badly, the *Ranger* resumed recovery operations five minutes before the beginning of the first dog watch.[5]

No sooner had the ship begun bringing planes back on board again when Lt. George Simmons, of VB-4, made a normal approach, but took the cut while still turning into the groove. Consequently, Simmons "never quite straightened out" and his SBD engaged the number one cross-deck pendant, but continued across the deck from starboard to port, dropping its port wheel into the catwalk. Postcrash assessment revealed the engine damaged by the sudden stoppage, propeller hub threads sheared, propeller blades bent and twisted, and the center and port bottom flaps damaged beyond repair. Again, the trouble board cited "pilot error" as the underlying reason for the accident (judgment and technique), but neither Simmons nor Aviation Radioman 3d Class Colon, the veteran back-seater, suffered any injuries. Crashes seemed to be becoming "old hat" to Cy Colon, who had experienced a landing accident on 13 July and a barrier crash a week later.[6]

Later that day, after launching half of her air group to base ashore, the *Ranger* returned to the waters of Scapa Flow, dropping anchor, during the second dog watch, in Berth B-1, with 17 fathoms of water beneath her keel. A little over a quarter of an hour after the *Ranger* had dropped anchor, then secured her main engines, Admiral Fraser left the ship.

The *Ranger* resumed training on 2 September, clearing Scapa Flow during the morning watch, standing out in company with her familiar escorts, the *Forrest*, the *Hobson*, and the *Corry*. The ship carried out a full schedule of training that day, sounding "torpedo defense" stations for gunnery practice with her 20-millimeter batteries. Later that day, the *Ranger* conducted short-range tracking runs, and carried out flight operations.

Given that the *Ranger* had been operating in waters "where the danger of attack by submarine [was] ever present," Captain Rowe, after consultation with the ships' officers concerned, decided that his ship needed two damage control stations, rather than one, given the proximity of central station to gasoline tanks and bomb stowage. In the event of a torpedo hit, the people in central station as it existed faced two choices: being burned out or flooded out. To that end, the ship's force added a few telephone plugs at frames 35 and 107 on the third deck. Because the ship was engaged in actual operations in U-boat-infested waters, Rowe deemed "any delay in putting the new stations into effect . . . pointless." Additionally, because the *Ranger* was the only ship of her kind, the internal reorganization (rather than an actual "alteration") that the captain investigated was applicable to his ship only. Experience and training showed the new stations very effective, providing closer contact with repair parties, decentralizing damage control people, and allowing "greater elasticity in handling casualties."[7]

The *Ranger*'s training in the Orkneys occupied her for the rest of the month of September, her air group interspersing their operations between the ship and RNAS Hatston. Ensign Harry L. Dunn, A-V(N), of VB-4, took off on 8 September for routine FCLP in an SBD-5 (BuNo 28709). He made one landing without incident, and took off with flaps and wheels down. Reaching an altitude of 100 feet, however, Dunn felt his SBD's engine vibrating. Having had only 15.1 hours of cockpit time in SBDs in the last three months, Dunn reduced rpm and manifold pressure, in an attempt to lessen the vibrations. He then increased manifold pressure and air speed to attempt to raise his flaps.

Despite his best efforts, however, the engine began losing power, emitting profuse amounts of bluish smoke. Unable to keep the plane in flight, Dunn pulled up his wheels and landed in a stubble field. The SBD would need a major overhaul.[8]

Underway during the forenoon watch on 16 September, the *Ranger* stood out in company with the *Corry*, the *Hobson*, and the *Forrest*. One day out, VF-4's Lt. Kagey Hammond took off during the afternoon watch, for a routine training hop. Hammond made what looked like a good approach, but strong winds and heavy seas combined to give the *Ranger* an abnormal pitching motion. Given a "fast" signal by the LSO, Hammond throttled back; pulling back on the stick, he eased up the F4F-4's nose. After receiving the cut, however, Hammond's Wildcat appeared to stall. The right wing dropped and the plane hit the deck wheels-first. Besides the usual damage to the engine caused by the sudden stoppage of the propeller, both landing gear sprockets tore loose from the firewall, leaving a hole there; the main fuel tank was damaged, necessitating a tank change, and the right counter balance broken. The resulting trouble board considered that Hammond had overcorrected for the fast signal, and the F4F-4 (BuNo 11957) proved "abnormally slow" when he received the cut.[9]

As she had done the previous month, the *Ranger* covered the movements of the British Prime Minister, as Churchill, embarked in the battle cruiser HMS *Renown*, returned to his country following the conferences with President Roosevelt at Quebec. On 18 September, the *Ranger* received the signal from the *Renown* during the first dog watch:

Five TBF-1s from VT-4, hooks down, prepare to enter the landing circle, 9 September 1943. Note unique markings: individual plane number in white, ahead of the red-outlined fuselage star, as well as the repeating of the number ahead of the forward edge of the wing root and at the tip of the fin. The individual plane number was also repeated on a fourth location, beneath the lower lip of the engine cowling, in black. (NA, 80-G-81441)

Captain Gordon Rowe introduces Secretary of the Navy Frank Knox to Lt. Comdr. George O. Klinsmann, commanding officer of VB-4, during the Secretary's visit to the *Ranger* at Scapa Flow, 21 September 1943. Lieutenant Comdr. David W. "Woot" Taylor, Jr., son of a distinguished San Francisco newspaperman (Knox's long-time profession) and commanding officer of VT-4, waits at left. At far left stands Lt. Comdr. George W. R. Nicholl, Royal Navy liaison officer on board the *Ranger*. (NA, 80-G-88078)

CTG 112.1 FROM PRIME MINISTER CHURCHILL X PLEASE ACCEPT MY THANKS FOR YOUR ESCORT AND I SHOULD BE GRATEFUL IF YOU WILL CONVEY MY APPRECIATION TO U S SHIPS IN COMPANY X IT IS ALWAYS A PLEASURE TO ME TO BE UNDER THE ESCORT OF THE U S NAVY XX[10]

The *Ranger* anchored in Scapa Flow midway through the forenoon watch on 19 September, and logged the arrival the following day of Secretary of the Navy Frank Knox, accompanied by Adm. Harold R. Stark, Commander Naval Forces, Europe, in the destroyer *Fitch*, after their passage from Thurso, Scotland. Admiral Stark visited the *Ranger* that same day, 20 September. The Secretary of the Navy visited the carrier the following morning, coming on board a half hour into the forenoon watch and departing at 0905.

During the month of September 1943, a daring raid by British midget submarines succeeded in immobilizing the *Tirpitz*, and the *Lützow* sailed from her base at Altenfjord for the Baltic for a refit. Although the latter managed to reach her destination unscathed, evidence indicates that British plans to attack the pocket battleship, while she was en route, twice would have involved the *Ranger* or her planes. First, Adm. Fraser contemplated sending the *Ranger* to a point that would allow her to launch CVG-4 to attack the *Lützow* off Stadlandet, Norway, on 27 September and, failing that, that VF-4 Wildcats would escort an attack force on 28 September—neither of which came to pass.[11]

Circumstances did not permit the *Ranger* having a hand in the destruction of one of the *Kriegsmarine's* two pocket battleships, but she did take part in an offensive operation made possible by the immobilization of the *Tirpitz*. Consequently, on 2 October, the *Ranger*, wearing Rear Adm. Olaf M. Hustvedt's flag, stood out of Scapa Flow during the forenoon watch, in company with the British battleships HMS *Duke of York* (Admiral Fraser embarked) and HMS *Anson*, the heavy cruiser *Tuscaloosa*, and the British light cruiser HMS *Belfast*. Ten destroyers (five that flew the Stars and Stripes and five the White Ensign) rounded out the goodly complement. TF-121 proceeded to carry out Operation Leader, an attack by the *Ranger's* air group "on shipping targets in the Norwegian leads off Bodø and in the stretch 90 miles to the south of it with the following alternative military targets: shipping and oil tanks in the harbor of Bodø, the Bodø aerodrome, and the radar and D/F [direction finding] station at Rost."[12]

During the morning watch on 4 October, the carrier's men went to general quarters at 0544, but the *Ranger* turned into the wind at 0600, only to encounter a near dead calm. The inadequacy of the *Ranger's* designed speed compelled her to spend nearly 20 minutes searching for enough wind over the deck ("chasing the catspaws," as Admiral Fraser described it), to allow her to launch planes. At times, the ship's changes of course, in the condition of light airs then prevailing, meant that the screening ships were out of position to protect her, a condition of affairs that prompted emphasis later on the carrier serving as guide during actual flight operations. Admiral Fraser attributed the *Ranger's* occasionally being unprotected as "chiefly due to some of the Commanding Officers failing correctly to appreciate a difficult and rapidly changing situation."[13]

VB-4's officers pose in front of a pair of VT-4's TBF-1s (4-T-2 at right), Scapa Flow, 1 October 1943. (NA, 80-G-88059)

Finally, at 0618, she began launching planes, starting with a four-plane CAP and an inner antisubmarine patrol of two SBDs; throughout the day, the *Ranger* rotated those patrols as needed.

ANTISUBMARINE PATROL (VB-4)

Lt. (jg) Leo R. Norman, A-V(N)   [4-B-]18
    Aviation Radioman 3d Class J. C. Brilhart
Lt. (jg) Darrell E. Way   [4-B-]4
    Aviation Radioman 3d Class G. C. Ellis

Commander Bill Stuart's efficient flight deck crews then spotted the planes of the Northern Attack Group, consisting of 20 SBD-5s, under Otto Klinsmann, and 8 F4F-4s, under Lt. Comdr. Charles L. Moore, Jr., VF-4's commanding officer. The weather forecast for the day had resulted in the reduction in bomb loads, for 6 of the 20 Dauntlesses, from 1,000-pound bombs to 500-pounders. On board Lt. Stratton's 4-B-7, in Klinsmann's division, rode Lt. Odd Dahm of the Royal Norwegian Navy, "who was thoroughly familiar with the area," to help designate "proper shipping targets as only ships directly serving the enemy." Those who planned Leader, utilizing simple but effective terrain models, and the briefings by the Norwegian officers, took great care "to avoid willful damage to the local passenger and cargo ships serving a friendly people."[14]

Completing the launch without incident after 15 minutes, the northern attack group completed its rendezvous and took departure from the ship at 0640. Despite having only 31 knots of wind over the deck, none of the SBD pilots experienced any difficulties getting aloft.

NORTHERN ATTACK GROUP

VB-4 (*indicates photographer)

First Division

Lt Comdr. George O. Klinsmann   [4-B-]1
    Aviation Chief Radioman Elmer M. Rogers
Lt. Cyrus F. Weeks, A-V(N)   [4-B-]10
    Aviation Radioman 3d Class Herbert C. Meredith, USNR
Lt. Henry T. Stratton, A-V(N)   [4-B-]7
    Lt. Odd Dahm (Norwegian)
Lt (jg) Ralph W. Ross, A-V(N)   [4-B-]20
    Aviation Radioman 3d Class L. L. Devine

Second Division

Lt. Joe L. Bettinger, Jr.   [4-B-]17
    Aviation Radioman 1st Class Robert N. Shaw*
Lt. (jg) John G. McReynolds, Jr., A-V(N)   [4-B-]2
    Aviation Radioman 1st Class Wilbert C. Parrish
Lt. (jg) William H. Longley, A-V(N)   [4-B-]5
    (BuNo 28731)
    Aviation Radioman 2d Class Lloyd E. Edens
Lt. (jg) Charles G. Hendricks, Jr., A-V(N)   [4-B-]22
    [Keefe]

Third Division

Lt. Harold R. Keller, Jr., A-V(N)   [4-B-]9
    Aviation Radioman 2d Class William T. Shackelford*
Lt. (jg) Charles R. Breckheimer, A-V(N)   [4-B-]6
    [Branson]
Lt. Lykes M. Boykin, A-V(N)   [4-B-]13
    Aviation Radioman 2d Class Henry H. Reed
Lt. (jg) Sumner R. Davis, A-V(N)   [4-B-]15
    (BuNo 28636)
    Aviation Radioman 2d Class Donald W. McCarley, USNR

Fourth Division

Lt. Cecil V. Johnson   [4-B-]11
    Aviation Chief Radioman Joseph Eardley*
Lt. Clyde A. Tucker, Jr., A-V(N)   [4-B-]19
    (BuNo 11011)
    Aviation Radioman 2d Class Stephen D. Bakran
Lt. Richard W. Phillips   [4-B-]23
    Aviation Radioman 2d Class J. J. Lankowitz
Lt. (jg) William E. Dill, A-V(N)   [4-B-]14
    Aviation Radioman 2d Class L. J. Blier

Fifth Division

Lt. Gordon P. Chase   [4-B-]3
    Aviation Radioman 2d Class A. W. Lorentzen
Lt. (jg) Prince H. Gordon, A-V(N)   [4-B-]29
    Aviation Radioman 2d Class Morris S. Waterson
Lt. Daniel K. Weitzenfeld   [4-B-]21
    Aviation Radioman 2d Class Kenneth W. Jobe
Lt. George C. Simmons   [4-B-]27
    Aviation Radioman 3d Class L. E. Colon

VF-4 STRIKE ESCORT

Lt. Comdr. Charles L. Moore, Jr.   [4-F-]1
    (BuNo 11957)
[Wingman unknown]
Lt. (jg) George M. Harris, Jr.   [4-F-]7
Ens. Louis K. Lepp, A-V(N)

Lt. Earle F. Craig
Ens. Lawrence A. Hensley, A-V(N)

Lt. (jg) Boyd N. Mayhew
Lt. (jg) Clifford M. White, A-V(N)

Otto Klinsmann deployed his squadron in five 4-plane divisions, with two 2-plane sections in each, planning to attack by sections. Lieutenant Comdr. Charlie Moore's F4Fs flanked the SBD formation, one 4-plane section on each side. They headed for the Norwegian coast at altitudes that ranged between 50 and 100 feet.

At 0654, less than a quarter of an hour after the northern attack group had taken its departure, the *Ranger* launched two F4Fs to augment the CAP, followed by the southern attack group—10 TBF-1s and a 6-plane escort of F4Fs, under Comdr. Joseph A. Ruddy, Jr., Commander, Carrier Air Group 4. The Avengers leading the purposeful procession down the deck, their bomb bays each containing four

Lieutenant Comdr. Joseph A. Ruddy, Jr., seen here on board the auxiliary aircraft carrier *Santee* (ACV-29) in November 1942, led (as a commander) the *Ranger*'s CVG-4 in the Bodø raid. Photograph taken by Lt. Comdr. Horace Bristol, USNR. (NA, 80-G-469663)

500-pounders. To better enable them to tell friend from foe, a Royal Norwegian Air Force lieutenant, Lt. Kirsebom, rode in Ruddy's Avenger; Kirsebom possessed very recent experience in the area, gained as a navigator on board PBYs.

Ruddy, an All-American water polo player at the Naval Academy (USNA 1930), had come to the *Ranger* from command of Escort Scouting Squadron (VGS) 29; he had earned the Navy Cross during Torch, flying from the *Santee*. Known for his "spontaneous humor and quick wit," the habit of "looking out for the bright side of life" was not enough for him, a classmate wrote warmly, "he wanted to reach out a helping hand to those in a rut."[15] Well over half of the men under his command in Carrier Air Group 4, then winging their way toward a stark and forbidding shore to seek out enemy shipping between Sandnessjøen and Bodø, had never seen combat.

None of the TBFs carried torpedoes. Planners deemed the one- to one-and-a-half-mile width of the leads, as well as the resulting restrictions on approaching a target in the leads to enable a torpedo to be used, as factors militating against their use. Additionally, torpedoes would not prove appropriate for use against land targets should no ships be found. Admiral Fraser concurred in the decision to arm the Avengers with bombs to enable them to attack either sea or land targets.

SOUTHERN ATTACK GROUP

VT-4

Comdr. Joseph A. Ruddy, Jr.
(Commander, CAG-4)   C
    Lt. H. Kirsebom (Royal Norwegian Air Force)
    Aviation Chief Radioman Jack L. Aday
    Aviation Ordnanceman 2d Class R. L. Barfield
Lt. (jg) Laurence L. Hamrick, A-V(N)   [4-T-]3
    Aviation Radioman 2d Class Charles W. Barr
    Aviation Radioman 1st Class J. T. Rushing
Lt. Comdr. David W. Taylor, Jr. (CO, VT-4)   [4-T-]1
    Aviation Chief Radioman Henry Karsemeyer, USNR
    Aviation Chief Machinist's Mate G. W. Lightfoot
Ens. Felix E. Ward, Jr., A-V(N)   [4-T-]2
    Aviation Radioman 3d Class Donald M. Applegate
    Aviation Machinist's Mate 3d Class Donald L. King
Lt. (jg) John H. Palmer, A-V(N)   [4-T-] 4
    (BuNo 06302)
    Aviation Radio Technician 1st Class Joseph L. Zalom, USNR
    Aviation Machinist's Mate 1st Class Reginald L. Miller
Ens. Robert F. Ruth, A-V(N)   [4-T-]5
    Aviation Radioman 2d Class R. G. Walsh
    Aviation Chief Metalsmith 3d Class M. W. Richardson
Lt. Homer H. Hutcheson (XO, VT-4)   [4-T-]6
    Aviation Radioman 1st Class C. J. Lacy
    Aviation Machinist's Mate 1st Class P. J. Blanos
Ens. Gerald M. Barnett, A-V(N)   [4-T-]7
    Aviation Radioman 2d Class C. B. Bowman
    Aviation Machinist's Mate 1st Class B. M. Dalton
Lt. (jg) Robert E. Trexler, A-V(N)   [4-T-]8
    Aviation Radioman 1st Class Reuben F. Gray, USNR
    Aviation Machinist's Mate 1st Class H. D. Youmans
Ens. Gerald W. Thomas, A-V(N)   [4-T-] 9
    (BuNo 06136)
    Aviation Ordnanceman 2d Class Charles P. Jackson, Jr.
    Aviation Radioman 2d Class Shelton E. Garner

VF-4 STRIKE ESCORT

Lt. Comdr. George H. Carter	[4-F-]13
Lt. (jg) Will "W" Taylor, A-V(N)	[4-F-]10
Lt. Edward M. Seiler	[4-F-]26
Lt (jg) Clyde C. Andrews, A-V(N)	[4-F-]11
Lt. (jg) Keene G. Hammond	[4-F-]20
Lt. (jg) Robert C. Cronin, A-V(N)	[4-F-]22

The northern group, made landfall on Myken Light, which lay 18 miles from the area earmarked to be searched. Commencing a slow climb to 1,500 feet, about 10 miles in from the lighthouse and approaching the leads, Otto Klinsmann detached Lt. Gordon Chase's fifth division to search an alternative channel, accompanied by one section of Wildcats; he and the other four divisions continued to fly to northeastward.

Soon, Chase's division spotted the 8,056-ton German cargo steamer *La Plata*, formerly of the *Hamburg-Südamerikanische Dampfschiffahrts Gesellschaft*, at 0724, about a half mile south of Aamno. Charlie Moore led in his section and strafed the *La Plata*, reducing her antiaircraft fire. Moore's F4F-4 (BuNo 11957) took hits in each of the first two strafing attacks, one shell exploding in the baggage compartment and causing extensive fragment damage to the after fuselage. Despite his cockpit filling with smoke, Moore grimly pressed home his runs, so that the bombers that followed would meet less resistance.

Chase and Gordon made mast-head bombing attacks at 200 knots; one pilot strafed the ship with his fixed .50-calibers, putting the forward antiaircraft gun out of action. Going "in very close," Gordon later recounted to debriefers, "so close in fact, I had to pull up severely to miss [the]

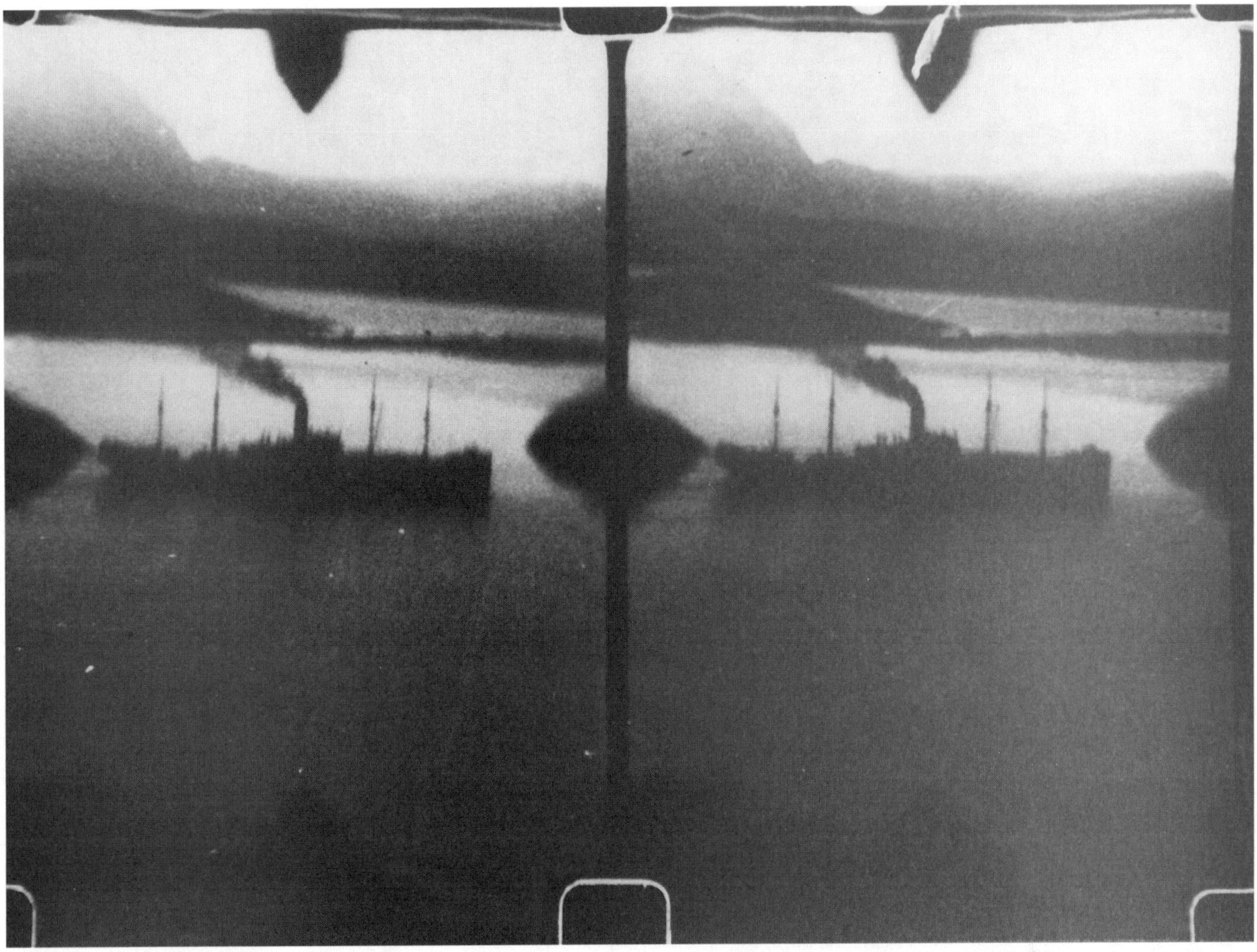

Gun camera stills from [4-F-]1, of German freighter *La Plata*, as Lt. Comdr. Charles F. Moore, Jr., VF-4's CO, begins his first strafing run, 4 October 1943. (NA, 80-G-201239)

The after fuselage of Charlie Moore's F4F-4 (BuNo 11957), showing the fragment damage. (NA, 80-G-201175)

German tanker *Schleswig*, burning astern. (NA, 80-G-201026)

foremast," he pulled out at 60 feet.¹⁶ Considering the *La Plata* already seriously damaged by the first two pilots' attacks, Weitzenfeld and Simmons retained their ordnance for other targets. VB-4's fifth division then rejoined the main force.

Klinsmann's main flight continued resolutely up the leads; three Norwegian fishing vessels heading north in Fuglo Fjord, and a small Norwegian coastal cargo and passenger vessel heading south near Fuglo, passed unmolested beneath the gaze of the pilots and the radio-gunners in the planes that bore the stars and bars. Because of the thorough indoctrination received beforehand, the Americans encountered no difficulty identifying local landmarks.

Then a convoy hove into sight, consisting of what appeared to be a "5,000-ton motor vessel," a *Löwe*-class torpedo boat, and the 10,243-ton tanker *Schleswig*.¹⁷ The port section of F4Fs strafed the lead ship, and the starboard strafed the escort ship. Lieutenants (jg) Mayhew and White carried out repeated low-level strafing attacks on all three vessels. Klinsmann and Weeks then pushed over from 1,000 feet into a glide-bombing approach, pulling out at 75 feet and releasing their bombs at 200 knots. Klinsmann's bomb passed over his target, but Weeks's made a direct hit on the motor vessel just aft of its stack. Fire and smoke indicated that part of the side of the ship seemed to have been blown out. When last seen, the vessel was "proceeding at reduced speed, smoking slightly and turning in to beach" herself.¹⁸

Johnny Johnson's section followed the fighters in and attacked the *Schleswig*. Although the fighters' strafing reduced its volume, antiaircraft fire from all ships continued at the attacking SBDs as they pushed over into their glides, strafing on the way down. Johnson's SBD-5 took a small-caliber explosive shell hit that punched a four-inch hole in the top skin of the starboard wing just outboard of the auxiliary

Douglas SBD-5 (BuNo 11011), Lt. Clyde Tucker's [4-B-]19 in foreground, as VB-4 looks for targets in the leads, 4 October 1943. (NA, 80-G-201064)

gasoline tank, which fortunately did not adversely affect the controls. Lieutenant Clyde Tucker's SBD-5 (BuNo 11011) was on fire: Aviation Radioman 2d Class Stephen D. Bakran, Tucker's radio-gunner, still fired his twin .30-caliber guns as the Dauntless, glided toward the water in a 30 degree dive and splashed into the cold waters of the fjord. Neither Johnson nor Tucker had correctly estimated the speed of the target, however, and their ordnance splashed between 80 and 20 feet of the tanker's stern. In Johnson's second section, Dick Phillips' plane took a 40-millimeter hit on the right stabilizer, which holed the fin and rudder, and a same caliber hit on the left wing, which nicked, but did not puncture, the gasoline tank. Fragments pierced the upper skin of the wing.[19]

Klinsmann's second section, Stratton and Ross, and Weitzenfeld and Simmons, the two pilots who had retained their bomb loads intact after the initial attack on the *La Plata*, went after the *Schleswig*, on the heels of fighter strafing. In the teeth of increasing antiaircraft fire, the pilots had varying success: one accidental drop, one dud, followed by two direct hits with 500-pounders, one aft and one under the stern. Down by the stern and afire, the *Schleswig* set course for shallow water.

Antiaircraft fire, however, had hit George Simmons's Dauntless, perforating the radio compartment aft of Aviation Radioman 3d Class Cy Colon, severing the right rudder cable and damaging the battery, IFF equipment, and radar.

Clearing the way for the bombers had proved no easy matter. Antiaircraft fire hit Lieutenant (jg) Harris's F4F-4, wounding him and knocking out his electrical systems. Harris's wingman, Ensign Lepp, could see that the his plane was in a bad way: 4-F-7's landing gear hung down. Lepp guessed—correctly, as it turned out—that Harris was dazed and severely wounded and that his compass and radio were gone. Harris needed help. Although Lepp's own radio was not functioning, the 23-year-old Illinois native, University of Illinois Class of '41, stuck with Harris, motioning that he should follow him. Over a hundred miles of cold ocean lay between the two Wildcat pilots and the *Ranger*.

Communication difficulties vexed Otto Klinsmann, too. After the first attack, Klinsmann's radio failed. A delay thus ensued, until he could make contact via VHF with one of the division leaders. Relaying instructions via that medium, Klinsmann directed the divisions that had unexpended

Splash marks where Lieutenant Tucker's SBD-5 crashed a mile and a half off Bodø. (NA, 80-G-201056)

ordnance to attack the shipping in Bodø harbor proper. He directed the six planes with empty racks to the original point of departure.

The remaining SBDs attacked the four ships in Bodø harbor, after the fighters had swept in. Despite the efforts of the Wildcat pilots, the SBDs encountered a "considerable volume of accurate A/A . . . by shore installations all around [the] harbor and [a] small volume from [the] ships."[20] Each of the four SBD sections picked out a separate target, releasing their ordnance at altitudes from 50 to 125 feet and strafing the ships on the way in. Otto Klinsmann's division, bombs already gone, circled near Bodø, drawing fire.

The first section attacked the 2,711-ton steamer *Malaga* from the northwest, from the starboard quarter, obtaining one very near miss, and inflicting minor damage from a "dud" bomb. The second section attacked its target from the east, flying port to starboard, coming away claiming one hit on the bow and a near-miss amidships and leaving her afire amidships. The next section came in from the northwest, attacking from the starboard quarter, but scoring no hits. Planes attacking the ships in Bodø proper sank the 2,719-ton steamer *Rabat* and forced the beaching of the 1,536-ton steamer *Kaguir* in the inner harbor.

The damage had not, however, been wreaked without cost. The last section had come in from the southwest. Lieutenant Boykin's SBD-5 took three 20-millimeter hits on the starboard wing, several hits on the port elevator and horizontal stabilizer, and one hit on the starboard horizontal stabilizer. The last plane over the target took fatal damage, as Tucker's had.

Lieutenant (jg) Sumner R. Davis, A-V(N), Boykin's wingman, believed that his plane had taken a hit in his engine, as his oil pressure began to drop; white smoke issued from beneath the cowling. Davis signalled Boykin that he was losing oil pressure. About 12 miles west of Bodø, Davis made what observers called an "excellent forced landing" near Prestoya, a small island in the Helligvaer group; both he and Aviation Radioman 2d Class

Lieutenant Harold Keller (4-B-9) leads Lt. (jg) Charles Breckheimer (4-B-6) in glide-bombing the *Malaga* off Bodø. (NA, 80-G-201053)

Donald W. McCarley, USNR, his radio-gunner, exited the sinking SBD-5 (BuNo 28636), extracted the life raft from its compartment, and shoved off. Both gave their circling shipmates overhead the "thumbs up" sign.

Rescue came quickly. A Norwegian fisherman, Odd Karlsen, and his father, engaged in their livelihood at the time of the raid, picked up the two chilled Americans about 20 minutes later and took them to their home on Helligvaer. One of the townspeople, Morten Gryt, summoned because he spoke English, sadly explained to Davis and Mac McCarley, however, that the prospects were slim for the Americans hiding from the occupying Germans on the small islands and escaping to Sweden. "The Germans had seen the crash and had lookouts almost everywhere," the younger Karlsen later explained, "there was little we could do."[21] Faced with those discouraging prospects, Davis gave his watch and ring to Gryt. Later that day, the Germans indeed picked them up as prisoners-of-war and took them to Bodø.[22]

Joe Ruddy's group, meanwhile, completed its rendezvous at 0708, at an altitude of 500 feet, with Spanky Carter's F4Fs riding shotgun on the Avengers, four dispersed on the port side of the formation and two to starboard. Upon taking departure from the ship, Ruddy took the group down to 100 feet above the waves. After proceeding at 160 knots (indicated air speed) toward a point that lay two miles north of Yuterholm, the group ascended to 1,800 feet, entering the leads to look for targets. No clouds cloaked their attack, as the formation spread out. Several small fishing vessels and a ferry plied the waters below, unmolested.

German guns at Fagerviken, most likely those of the *Marineartillerieabteilung* 510, opened up as Ruddy's group

German freighter *Malaga* is straddled during the Bodø raid. Previous captions of this ship being identified as the *Saar* are inaccurate, because comparison with contemporary recognition drawings shows this vessel clearly to be the *Malaga*. (NA, 80-G-201051)

charged in, still in formation. Flak hit Four-Tare-Four's right wing tank and the TBF-1 (BuNo 06302), flown by Lt. (jg) John H. "Johnnie" Palmer, A-V(N), slanted toward the water. Palmer called for Aviation Radio Technician 1st Class Joseph L. Zalom, USNR, and Aviation Machinist's Mate 1st Class Buddy Miller (the latter a Torch veteran), to bail out, but received no answer.

Woot Taylor saw Palmer's burning TBF losing altitude and immediately radioed the pilot, telling all hands to jump. Observers saw Palmer exit the Avenger and land in the water offshore, but his two crewmen (who were perhaps, as Palmer later speculated, already dead, having been killed by a shell that had gone through the back of the plane) did not or had been unable to. Palmer extricated himself from his chute and struck out through the cold water. Hailing some fishermen failed to get results,

and, when he reached land, he soon found himself walking into a German antiaircraft gun position and being captured.[23]

Spanky Carter and his VF-4 pilots strafed the 4,991-ton Norwegian steamship *Topeka*, shooting her up fore and aft and abeam, opening up at a distance of about 2,000 feet from the ship, in "skillfully executed and daringly pressed home" attacks. Return fire from the ship seemed to be small-caliber and "in fairly large volume: but neither accurate nor effective."[24] Despite that assessment, Ed Seiler's F4F took an explosive shell that badly damaged the fuselage and destroyed his compass.

Woot Taylor began his run at masthead height, aiming at the highest bridge structure; in the plane's tunnel compartment, Aviation Chief Radioman Karsemeyer, working with precision born of training, set up the bombing panel and

Gun camera stills from Lt. (jg) Will "W" Taylor's [4-F-]10 showing the Norwegian freighter *Topeka* being strafed. (NA, 80-G-201243)

The *Topeka*, as seen from Lt. Comdr. "Woot" Taylor's [4-T-]1 at the instant of release. (NA, 80-G-201108)

A massive explosion rocks the *Topeka*. (NA, 80-G-201001)

arming levers, in spite of the radical maneuvers in which his pilot was engaged. Taylor scored three hits on the *Topeka* and one near-miss, the hits triggering a series of violent explosions; the attack left six of her antiaircraft crew dead, four wounded. Raging fires began to consume the ship as her crew ran her aground. Ensign Ward aimed at the second highest bridge structure, making his attack through the flak that prompted Aviation Radioman 3d Class Don Applegate to reflect later: "Boy! Could those Germans shoot!"[25] Having lost his wingman and section leader, Johnnie Palmer, at the outset of the antiaircraft fire, Ens. Robert F. Ruth attached himself to Taylor's section, and attacked the *Topeka*, too, scoring a direct hit and adding further to the destruction wreaked on the ship. All three TBF pilots engaged in violent jinking during retirement.

Lieutenant Hutch Hutcheson, VT-4's exec, picked out the 687-ton engines-aft Norwegian passenger and cargo steamer *Vaagan*, a ship that the fighters had not strafed. He made a mast-head attack, followed by his wingman, Ens. Buck Barnett. The two pilots straddled the *Vaagan* with five 500-pounders, then returned to strafe her with their single .30-caliber fixed guns, silencing what appeared to be the ship's antiaircraft battery of two 7.9-millimeter machine guns. As Hutcheson and Barnett retired, they could see their victim listing and down by the stern, the crew abandoning the vessel, which later sank from the pounding administered by the brace of 500-pound general purpose bombs.

The German transport ferry *MFP-231*, chugging north, alone, on a line between Tomma and Handneso, soon found herself under attack from three pilots who identified her as an 800-ton barge-type tanker. Lieutenant (jg) Robert E. Trexler strafed her and bombed her as well. Her gunners stood to their weapons, however, defending her with the tenacity of a man-of-war, and put a bullet through 4-T-8, slightly wounding Aviation Radioman 1st Class Reuben J. Gray. Several geysers of spray erupted around the

Tossed about like a toy boat by the explosion of 500-pound general purpose bombs close aboard, the Norwegian steamer *Vaagan* begins to sink. (NA, 80-G-201005)

MFP-231 from near-misses, two of which had been dropped by Ham Hamrick, in 4-T-3, and the auxiliary vessel eventually ran aground in the bay of Valla, her crew abandoning ship.

Jerry Thomas, in 4-T-9, scored a hit amidships, after the *MFP-231* had stopped, wounding two crewmen, but the antiaircraft fire from the feisty ferry had taken out a cylinder from Thomas's engine. His troubles soon multiplied as he heard Aviation Radioman 2d Class Shelton Garner, his turret gunner, shout, "We're on fire!" Instinctively pulling back on the stick to gain altitude, Thomas picked up his intercom microphone and responded: "Bail out!" With the TBF at an altitude of about 800 feet, he slid back the hatch, unfastened his safety belt and started to climb out of the cockpit.[26]

Thomas, however, had never bailed out before. Thus having providentially failed to unplug his headset, he heard Garner's anxious voice: "Don't jump, don't jump. Jackson's popped his chute in the plane and he can't get out."[27] Aviation Ordnanceman 2d Class Charles Jackson, his bombardier, had inadvertently pulled the "D"-ring on his parachute, spilling the contents inside the cramped confines of the belly of 4-T-9. Trapped by a silk cocoon of his own making, Jackson would not have stood a chance of getting free before the plane crashed. Consequently, Jerry Thomas settled back into his bucket seat and instructed Garner and Jackson to strap themselves in.

In the meantime, Joe Ruddy had picked out the biggest ship, the cargo steamer *La Plata*. Ed Seiler and Andy Andrews each strafed the ship, twice. Aviation Chief Radioman Aday, Ruddy's bombardier, in the tunnel of the jinking Avenger, went about his task; and the group commander scored a direct hit forward. Ham Hamrick added a second that started a fire on board. The *La Plata*, badly damaged, headed for shore and beached herself in the shallows.

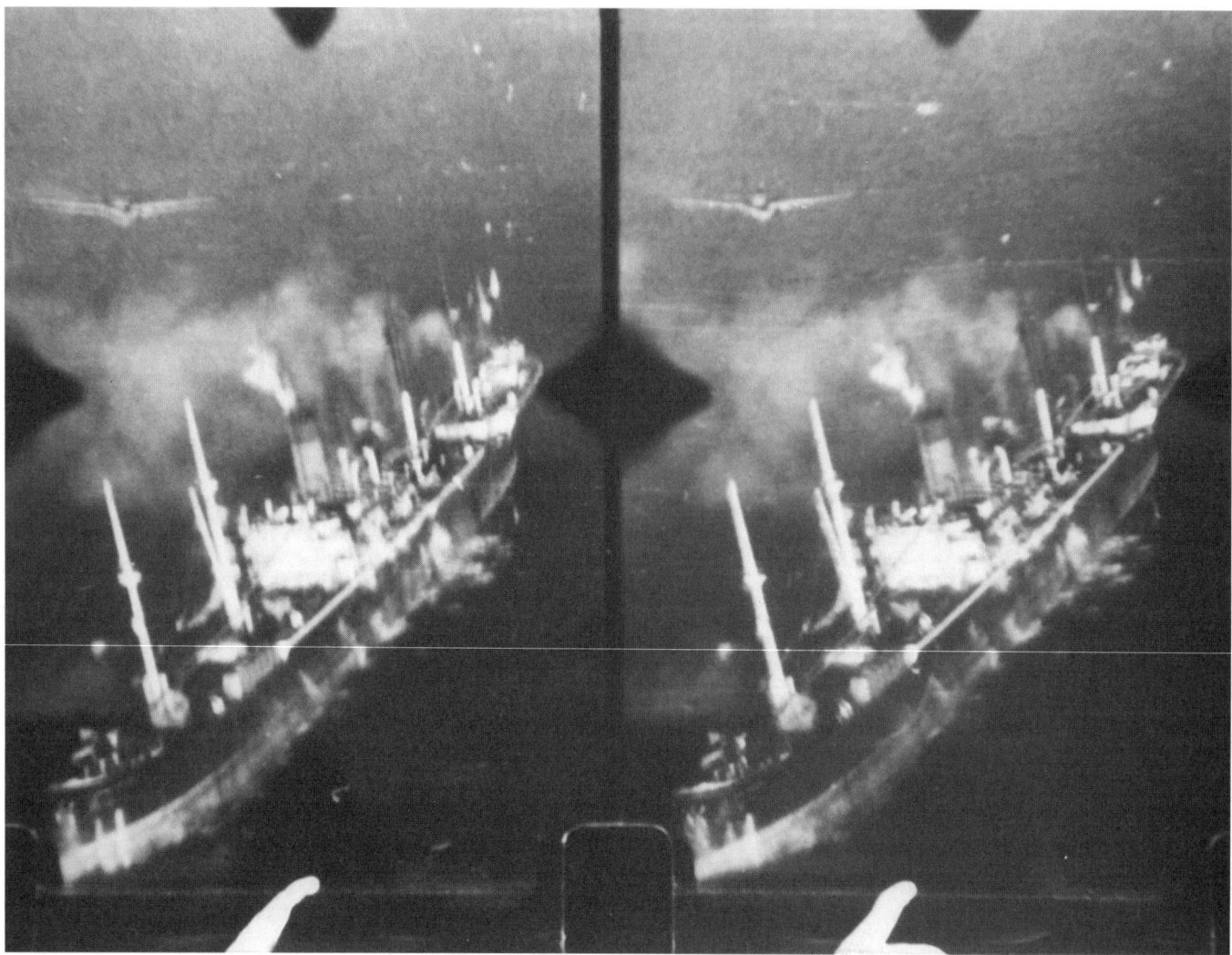

Gun camera stills from [4-F-]10, as Lt. (jg) William "W" Taylor strafes the *La Plata*; note another F4F over the embattled German ship, illustrating the mast-head height of the attack. (NA, 80-G-201246)

Spanky Carter, Will Taylor, Kagey Hammond, and Bob Cronin strafed the 4,300-ton troop transport *Skramstad*, whose funnel still bore a red band with a white "K" upon it, the markings of the shipping line to which she had belonged before the war, A. F. Klaveness and Company of Oslo. Joe Ruddy scored a direct hit on her, as well, as did Ham Hamrick. The *Skramstad* had had 834 soldiers on board when CVG-4's onslaught began; the attacks left 200 dead and 15 seriously wounded, and the vessel in a sinking condition.

The steamer *Kerkplein* with 1,551 prisoners on board, had taken two bomb hits that killed 13 men and seriously wounded 17 of her crew, disabled her steering and forced her to be towed into Bodø Roads. Of the unfortunate prisoners (perhaps Russians, from the eastern front), 14 died and 29 suffered serious wounds. The Germans counted a further nine as missing. Machine gun fire had slightly damaged the 1,367-ton steamer *Ibis*.

Choosing a water landing over setting down on a strange and rocky shoreline, Jerry Thomas started setting his TBF down toward a small island. Planning to make a wheels-up, full-stall landing, he soon realized that, from some point, anti-aircraft fire was becoming hotter. Shoving the throttle forward, he steered 4-T-9 toward the open sea, jinking as much as possible to avoid any further damage than he had already received. Two miles offshore, he eased back on the stick to try gain altitude, the TBF still trailing a thin stream of white smoke. Expecting tell-tale signs of trouble—red lights among his instruments—Thomas checked his panel, but found everything normal. Momentarily relieved of that concern, he began concentrating on how best to reach the *Ranger*.

Thomas remembered from the briefing before takeoff that a man could expect to live 15 minutes in the cold sea, 20 at most. Neutral Sweden lay 90 miles away; the *Ranger* 100. Opting to head for the neutral country, Thomas told his crew what lay ahead, and began climbing to 5,000 feet. In the distance, the sight of the snow-covered mountains did not provide a comforting vista. With all other *Ranger* planes gone from the area, however, German guns opened up on the only one that remained—4-T-9. "OK," Thomas thought, "forget Sweden."[28]

Chopping back the throttle to save his engine, Thomas pulled out his plotting board, only to experience a sinking feeling that he did not know precisely where the *Ranger* was, nor what heading he needed to take to find her. Looking around, he suddenly spied another TBF off to the south. As he tried to approach the other Avenger to join up, however, his squadronmate, perhaps remembering the briefing about what German fighters ("up to nine" Messerschmitt Bf-109s or Bf-110s had been based at Bodø "from time to time") could be encountered in those regions, cautiously shied away from a rendezvous, leaving Thomas on his own once more. Running out of options, he guessed on a heading and hoped for the best, using dead reckoning without a precise Point Option. It was, he later wrote from the comfortable perspective of hindsight, "a sure formula for disaster."[29]

Jerry Thomas soon spotted several more TBFs, who had less compunction about allowing him to join up, perhaps feeling that safety lay in numbers, and he thankfully joined them. Although circumstances had seen radio silence broken by that point, Thomas still did not open up in clear. He signalled to one of the other pilots and pointed to his own engine. His squadronmate flew around 4-T-9 and gave Thomas a "thumbs up." The 24-year-old ensign from Small, Idaho, wondered, how could that engine still run and continue to smoke like it was? Watching his instruments and listening for any change in the sound of the engine in front of him, Thomas noted that oil had almost completely covered his cockpit canopy. Sliding open the hatch, he reached out into the slipstream with his left hand to try and clear the windshield. After only succeeding in smearing the oil around and almost breaking his arm in the slipstream, Thomas enjoyed the increased visibility with the open hatch "but the cold air made me shiver."[30]

Lieutenant (jg) George Harris brings in his damaged F4F-4 after the strike on Bodø. (NA, 80-G-201193)

Crane truck removes Lt. Harris's Wildcat from the flight deck after its landing gear had collapsed upon landing. Note hole in plexiglass sliding canopy. (NA, 80-G-201177)

After putting aloft a relief CAP (eight F4Fs) and an antisubmarine patrol (two SBDs), beginning at 0846, the *Ranger* recovered the northern group. The wounded George Harris, guided back by Ensign Lepp's expert navigation over 140 miles, brought in 4-F-7, but, when he landed at 0852, his landing gear collapsed. Harris was quickly admitted to sick bay for treatment of a laceration of his neck, a contusion of his right hand, a gunshot wound in his left thigh, and multiple abrasions and contusions.

Steadying into the wind an hour into the forenoon watch, the *Ranger* then recovered the southern attack group. Jerry Thomas had managed to nurse 4-T-9 back to the ship, his oil pressure decreasing. Unable to follow the LSO's signals through the oil-covered windshield, but able to see, marginally, out the right side of the cockpit, he "placed the island of the ship where I thought it should line up with the flight deck. I chopped the throttle, pulled the stick into my lap to stall the plane, and hoped for the best." His hook caught a cross-deck pendant as the TBF hit the barrier and his wing brushed the island. While the plane handlers converged on BuNo 06136, Thomas and his crew exited it. Commander Bill Stuart, the flight deck officer, however, grabbed Thomas and administered a swift verbal reprimand for the latter's ignoring a wave-off and for temporarily fouling the deck. Shaking the irate air officer's hand loose from his flight suit, Thomas went below, fully expecting a court martial.[31] After Burt Trexler landed on board, the *Ranger*'s medical people soon attended to Aviation Radioman Gray, giving him 5 cc. of tetanus antitoxin and dressing his wound, to enable him to return to duty.

Meanwhile, Lt. (jg) Diz Laird, having waited impatiently in VF-4's ready room as the strikes against the German shipping had unfolded, had offered eagerly to man the spare Wildcat "for any launch when his division was not scheduled" to fly. As Laird later explained it, the *Ranger*'s lively qualities influenced his decision, too: "She rolled a lot, and I felt better in the air."[32]

Thus, after the *Ranger* rotated the CAP and the antisubmarine patrol, less than an hour before the end of the forenoon watch, early in the next watch, between 1327 and 1330, she launched seven F4Fs (one flown by Diz Laird) for a combat air patrol. Eight had been readied for that particular mission, but one, given a "down," proved unable to take off. Additionally, the *Ranger* put aloft another pair of SBDs to continue the antisubmarine patrols.

COMBAT AIR PATROL (VF-4)

Lt. Earle F. Craig
Lt. (jg) Boyd N. Mayhew, A-V(N)
Lt. (jg) Dean S. Laird, A-V(N)
Ens. Laurence A. Hensley, A-V(N)

Lt. Edward N. Seiler
Lt. (jg) Charles R. Hopson, A-V(N)   [4-F-]16
                                     (BuNo 11852)
Ens. Thomas J. Graham, A-V(N)

Less than a half hour after the last Wildcat had wobbled aloft from her flight deck, at 1355, the *Ranger*'s radar pinpointed the location of the three planes (two Junkers JU-88s and one Heinkel HE-115) ordered aloft by Air Commander, Lofoten [Islands]. Accordingly, Lt. Frank C. Sherrard, D-V(G), the *Ranger*'s fighter direction officer (FDO), whom Diz Laird later praised as "the best [FDO] I ever worked with," vectored Buster Craig's division out 340 degrees, and then 190 degrees, to intercept the first contact about 22 miles from the ship.[33]

The JU-88D-1 (WNr 1682) (4N+EH) of the first staffel of *Fernaufklarungs Gruppe* [long range reconnaissance group] 22, piloted by *Leutnant* Johannes Hoss, transmitted a contact report telling of sighting 17 warships, including a carrier, steaming south in grid square AF 2671. *Leutnant* Hoss, using the natural cover it afforded, ducked in and out of the cloud formations at an altitude of 3,000 feet. Boyd Mayhew, flying 3,000 feet above the JU-88, executed a high-side attack, firing a full burst from full to half deflection, setting the Junkers's port engine afire. Diz Laird obtained hits in a similarly conducted attack, in the face of return fire from a dorsal gun position.[34]

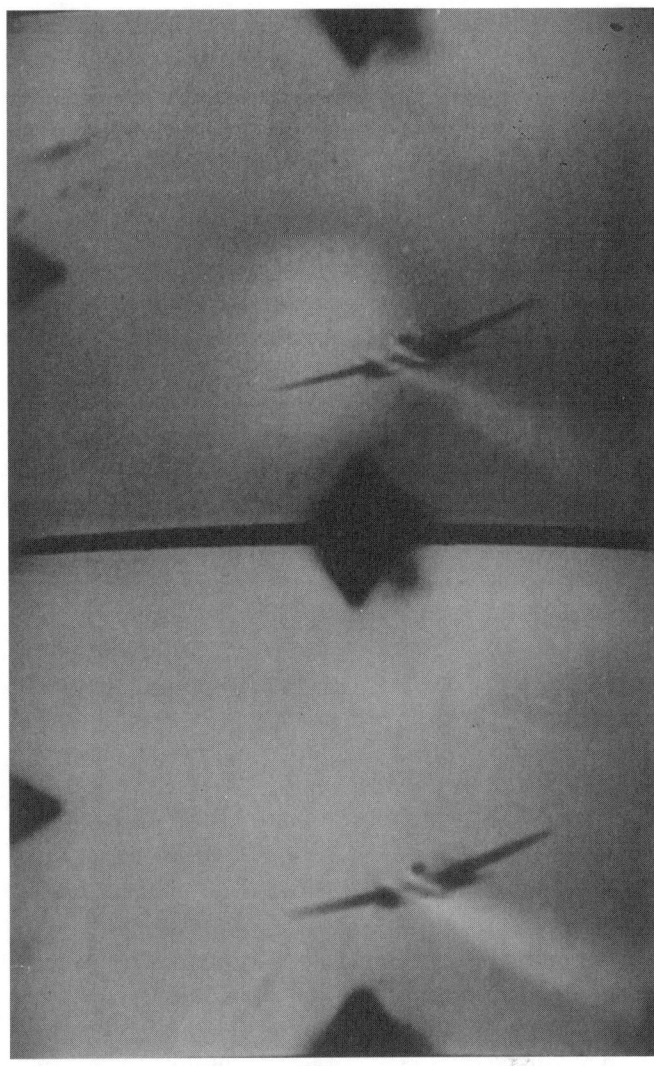

Gun camera stills from 4-F-27 showing the Junkers JU-88D-1 (WNr 1682) (4N+EH) of the first *staffel* of *Fernaufklarungs Gruppe* [long range reconnaissance group] 22 beginning to catch fire. (AUTHOR)

Mayhew then made a high-side run on the JU-88's starboard side, and Laird was on the port. *Leutnant* Hoss ducked the mortally wounded Junkers into another cloud, and the two Wildcat pilots prepared to intercept the German when he emerged. They would soon see, however, that their combined attacks had splashed the first snooper, the JU-88 plunging into the sea, leaving a ring of fire on the sea below. Neither Mayhew nor Laird saw any survivors in the water: lost with 4N+EH were *Leutnant* Hoss, *Feldwebel* Otto Blasig (observer), *Uffizier* Alfons Fischer (gunner), and *Obergefreiter* Friedrich Krieger (radio operator).[35]

At 1410, shortly after she had recovered the two SBDs from the last antisubmarine patrol of the day, Lieutenant Sherrard tried to direct Ed Seiler's three-plane division toward a second contact. Seiler, however, with an inoperative transmitter, could not acknowledge the vector, leading the ship to redirect Buster Craig's division toward the fresh contact. On a vector of 113 degrees, just 13 miles from the ship, a Heinkel HE-115B (WNr 1866) floatplane (K6+MH) of the first *staffel* of *Küstenflieger Gruppe* [coastal patrol group] 406, piloted by *Oberfeldwebel* Friedhelm Schulz, flying 200 feet above the waves, came into view. *Oberfeldwebel* Schulz may have seen the approaching Wildcats, because he put the floatplane into a 180 degree turn.[36]

Buster Craig set the Heinkel's port engine afire on his first pass: It began to trail a thin banner of smoke as *Feldwebel* Heinz Geyer, the radio operator, returned fire. Boyd Mayhew, Ens. Hensley, and Diz Laird then attacked in quick succession, flames visible from the port nacelle, as Laird made his pass. The VF-4 pilots were beginning a second attack when the Heinkel crashed, disintegrating upon impact with the unyielding sea. Ed Seiler, circling the HE-115's wreckage a few moments later, however, saw three men in the water, one obviously badly wounded, because of the crimson pool that surrounded him. Plagued by radio failure, however, Seiler tried to communicate with his wingman, but the latter could not understand his hand signals to send a message to the ship. *Hauptmann* Christian Fischer (observer), *Oberfeldwebel* Schulz and *Feldwebel* Geyer were, like the crew of the Junkers shot down a short time before, never recovered.

The only casualty to the CAP occurred upon its return to the ship. In response to the LSO's cut, Lt. (jg) Hoppy Hopson made a "very erratic landing well to the port side of the flight deck center line" at 1449. Hopson's hook engaged the number three wire, but, because 4-F-16 had touched down well on the port side of the deck, the tail swung violently inboard. The wrenching motion caused the arrestor hook carriage roller shaft to shear off and the hook and hook assembly to come loose from the tail. BuNo 11852 charged onward and somersaulted over the port side, damaging four 20-millimeter mounts in the gallery as it did so. Number 16 hit the water tail-first and sank in 10 seconds. Fortunately, Hopson freed himself from the sinking Wildcat and inflated his rubber raft. The British destroyer HMS *Scourge* rescued him unharmed.[37]

In Leader, some 60% of the *Ranger*'s aircrew flew combat for the first time, led by some of the veterans—Joe Ruddy, Spanky Carter, Johnny Johnson, Clyde Tucker, Cy Weeks, to name a few—who had flown against the Vichy French. "As a result," observed Gordon Rowe, his mostly tyro pilots exhibited "an undue eagerness to expend ammunition against the first targets that showed up." In the future, he did not doubt that his aviators would show more

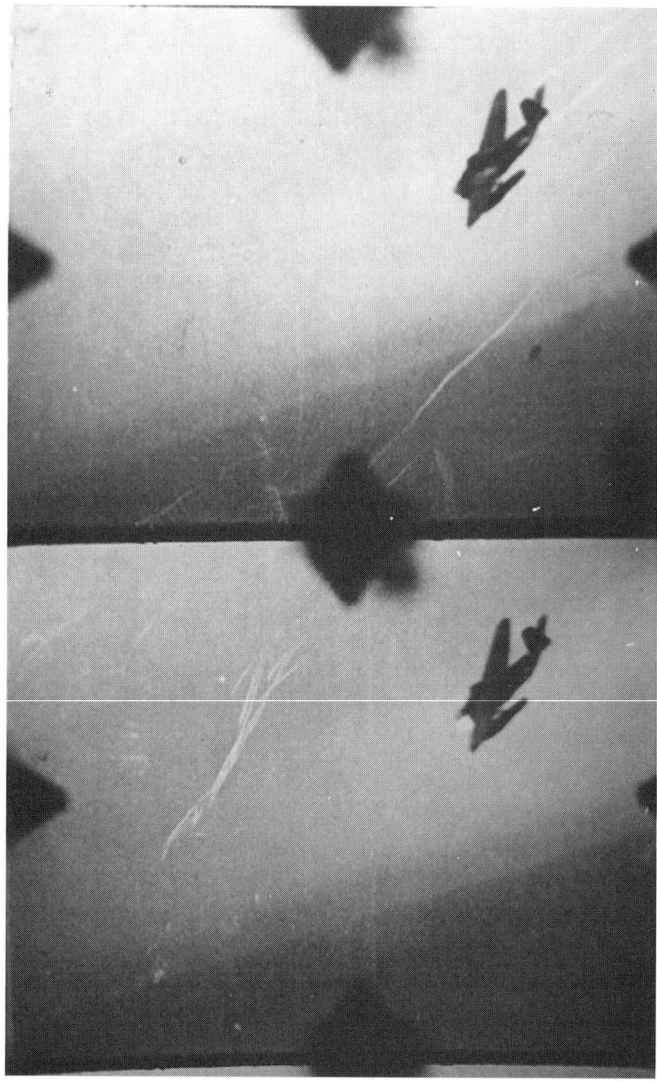

Gun camera stills from 4-F-27 showing the Heinkel HE-115B (WNr 1866) floatplane (K6+MH) of the first *staffel* of *Küstenflieger Gruppe* [coastal patrol group] 406 trying to take evasive action. (NA, 80-G-201258)

caution in expending ammunition. Although observing that that premature use of bombs and bullets caused "several fine targets" to be passed up, Rowe noted that the loss of three of the *Ranger*'s planes to antiaircraft fire, and the "mute testimony of bullet ridden [*sic*] planes upon [their] return to the ship" reflected the fact that "the pilots drove home their attacks in accordance with the best traditions of the service and all credit is due to [them] for their splendid work in inflicting so much damage on the enemy."[38]

Admiral Fraser praised the *Ranger*'s air group: "The conduct of the striking force," he wrote, "in the face of considerable flak opposition was extremely satisfactory." The *Ranger*'s conduct of flight operations during Leader likewise

Lieutenant (jg) Boyd N. Mayhew in his F4F-4, upon return to the *Ranger* following the action in which he assisted in shooting down a Junkers JU-88D-1 and a Heinkel HE-115B, 4 October 1943. (NA, 80-G-201198)

elicited his commendation, as did the work of the CAP. "Not the least satisfactory feature of this operation," the British flag officer concluded in that regard, "was the instant destruction by [the] *Ranger*'s combat air patrol of two out of three snoopers who attempted to locate and shadow the fleet." He also commented on the "most satisfactory" degree of mutual understanding and cooperation between the U.S. and Royal Navies in the Home Fleet, and "the desire of all in the Task Force to meet the enemy at the earliest possible moment" impressed him.[39]

In his postmortem of the attack, Rowe also suggested that SB2Cs and F6Fs replace the SBDs and F4Fs that equipped CVG-4. Noting that the newer plane types weighed more, the *Ranger*'s captain posited that the contemplated addition of blisters to the ship's hull might provide the necessary stability to permit operation of the heavier aircraft. He recommended that the necessary alterations be accomplished "when and if the ship can be spared." "We should not ask our pilots to fight in obsolete aircraft," Rowe declared, "when better types are available and provision can be made for their use."[40] Rear Adm. Hustvedt seconded Captain Rowe's suggestion that the SBD-5s and F4F-4s be replaced "as soon as newer types can be allocated."[41] No one seemed to have any qualms about the TBF, however; Joe Ruddy asserted: "The Avenger is definitely the plane for this type of work."[42]

"We learned much," Commander, CVG-4 admitted later. He believed that Leader had been an "excellent training exercise." That the operation had a salutary effect on all concerned prompted him to conclude: "We went in as many boys and came out as many men."[43]

As Joe Ruddy had surmised, because of a lack of offshore reconnaissance, the attack by the *Ranger*'s comparatively inexperienced, but aggressive, aircrew had indeed come as a "complete surprise" to the Germans, and the *Ranger*'s CVG-4 had inflicted "appreciable" damage on the enemy.[44] "The amount of shipping encountered," Rear Adm. Hustvedt later wrote, "was substantially greater than that which was expected," a discovery that prompted Adm. Fraser to observe: "the number of targets . . . was far greater than I had dared to hope."[45] Leader vexed the German naval high command. Admiral Northern Waters feared a repetition of similar surprise attacks until the days became short, because no reconnaissance of coastal waters was being carried out. Such a strike would endanger submarines and their bases, that flag officer concluded glumly, as well as ships carrying supplies, ore, and men, because of the "small number of our escort forces and inadequate anti-aircraft defense."[46]

"Every operation against the enemy," Rear Adm. Hustvedt observed in a sobering perspective on Leader, "serves also as training in preparation for future operations. In order to realize fully the training benefits . . . we must analyze our successes and our mistakes critically with a view toward holding the technique which leads to the one and eliminating the causes of the other." His analysis of Leader indicated that "further training and more thorough attention to detail" would yield "substantially better results." He noted that the percentage of bomb hits was only about 21%, which, "even considering the limited opportunity which the Air Group had had to train at masthead bombing," was "somewhat disappointing." Training had stressed the possible value of bombs dropping short and the total wastefulness of "overs," but approximately 75% of the misses had been "overs." VT-4 squadron doctrine had dictated that bomb racks be checked to determine if all bombs had been expended: the fact that five bombs had been brought back on board reflected the fact that doctrine had not been followed. Stoppages had occurred in about 12% of the fixed guns of the F4Fs, a figure that "improved gun maintenance and inspection of ammunition" would remedy.[47]

"The damage inflicted on the enemy . . . was considerable," Hustvedt concluded, "and the outcome regarded by British naval authorities as being highly successful." The *Ranger*'s air group had "derived most valuable experience" from Leader, something "sure to be reflected by still greater effectiveness in future operations." In the operation just concluded, "in which they have played the leading roles, the *Ranger* and her Air Group have brought much credit to themselves and to the United States Navy."[48]

The *Ranger*'s skipper modestly agreed. "At long last," Gordon Rowe wrote to Cal Durgin, "the *Ranger* has again had a little action. Yesterday we raided the Norwegian coast and believe we did considerable damage to German shipping in the leads. It was a gamble whether or not we would find any enemy shipping present and as it turned out they ran out of bombs and ammunition." The weather expectations compelled glide-bombing, he wrote, but "when it was all over the SBD pilots stated that they would prefer dive bombing." He went on to note the loss of three planes, the lack of aerial opposition, the destruction of the two snoopers, and that preliminary investigations indicated that .50-caliber strafing "did not seriously affect the enemy merchant ships or silence their gun crews; the 1,000 pound G.P. [general purpose] bombs with five seconds delay [fuses] did not blow the enemy merchant ships to pieces and that the German flak was very accurate."[49]

"It was certainly kind of you to take time out," Cal Durgin responded, when the man who had relieved him had informed him of the *Ranger*'s role in Leader, "and write to me in regard to your recent operations. I truly appreciate your thoughtfulness—you know I am going to be interested in what the old *Ranger* does as long as I am around. From all accounts the old ship came across in good style . . . I am proud of you but terribly envious to think that I wasn't on the bridge during the fracas." Durgin told his successor that he had shared his letter with "all the *Ranger* sailors in this area, of which there are many, and they are just as proud as I am."[50]

27

"*RANGER* COULD BE MADE INTO AN EXCELLENT TRAINING SHIP"

Securing from flight operations a little less than three-quarters of an hour into the second dog watch on 4 October, the *Ranger* and her consorts set course to return to Scapa Flow. During the forenoon watch, her engine room reported the main condensate pumps out of commission, limiting her top speed to 23 knots. She nevertheless maintained an active schedule of flight operations, putting up a CAP that Frank Sherrard twice vectored out in search of an unidentified plane without success. Eventually, however, the stranger proved to be a Catalina.

Released during the morning watch on 6 October to proceed independently with the *Hobson*, the *Corry*, and the *Fitch*, the *Ranger* sounded flight quarters at 0600, and steamed into the wind less than an hour later to begin launching her air group. Ultimately, her planes flown ashore to Hatston, the *Ranger* dropped anchor in berth B-1, with 17 fathoms of water beneath her keel, greeted with three cheers from the assembled Royal Navy ships in Scapa Flow.

On the morning of 9 October, a flight of six F4F-4s from VF-4 took off from Hatston for gunnery exercises under Lt. Buster Craig. The pilots found excellent visibility conditions and an unlimited ceiling. Flying at 6,000 feet, until the arrival of a plane towing the target for the morning's practice, Craig initiated fighter tactical exercises. The first pair of F4Fs maneuvered through a loop with the other pairs following.

As he recovered from the loop at 0925, however, Lt. (jg) Bob Cronin, leader of the third section, flying BuNo 12106, overtook and collided with the trailing number two plane, flown by Ens. Ivan C. Johnson, Jr., A-V(N). Cronin's propeller sliced off the empennage of Johnson's Wildcat (BuNo 11955) and both F4Fs tumbled into the waters below. No one saw any parachutes, and a search soon thereafter, by a Royal Navy amphibian and a crash boat, yielded only a USN-type seat raft and part of a USN chute. A trouble board cited pilot error on Cronin's part, but it also faulted Buster Craig for his "initiating a loop in the formation then being flown," and thus assigned 50% of the responsibility for the collision, the crash, and the resulting loss of two pilots and two planes, upon him. ComAirForLant directed Captain Rowe "to take disciplinary action" in Craig's case.[1]

During the time that the *Ranger* lay at anchor at Scapa Flow, Captain Rowe contemplated his ship's capabilities to carry out her mission, and signed a recommendation that the ship be given a comprehensive refit and modernization. He pulled no punches in stating the reasons why he felt it necessary: "It has been recognized repeatedly," he wrote on 13 October, "that this vessel has low stability, is weak structurally and has virtually no protection against underwater attack"—all deficiencies that lay in her original design. Additionally, as he had noted in the internal reorganization accomplished in September, a torpedo hit near the present gasoline tanks or bomb stowage, or the near-miss by a bomb, could trigger "uncontrollable fires and explosions." The *Ranger*'s low structural strength prompted a limitation on her displacement to 20,600 tons (20,300 in winter in the North Atlantic), a limitation that reduced her fuel

Lieutenant Kagey Hammond inspects .50-caliber ammunition before Seaman 2d Class W. Q. Hase and Aviation Ordnanceman 3d Class G. H. Hampton load it into the magazine that will be installed in his Wildcat's wing, 5 October 1943. The day before, three link jams, one belt jam, two extractor failures and one charging cable jam had vexed VF-4's pilots in the southern attack group. (NA, 80-G-201178)

capacity "considerably below 95% capacity on an even keel." Under optimum conditions, Rowe explained, "the ship cruises with a large group of empty oil tanks on the starboard side, which further reduces its ability to withstand damage in the event of a hit on the starboard side." On top of that, as he had noted in his postmortem on Leader, the ship's air group "is comprised in part of obsolescent planes and replacement with a full group of modern planes will introduce further weights into the ship."[2]

To that end, Rowe emphasized to BuShips that plans to improve the *Ranger*'s protection had already been proposed and planned by the addition of blisters and the relocation of gasoline stowage on board. Rowe judged the "installation of blisters . . . to be of the utmost importance and . . . will vastly improve the ability of the vessel to overcome its other limitations." The carrier's captain also reiterated the need for the ship to receive a combat information center (CIC) and also a deck edge elevator to replace the present number two elevator. Pointing out that damage from tugs and from heaving up the anchors had already caused some leakage forward, Rowe emphasized the need to strengthen that part of the ship. He declared that "vital military operations might easily suffer adverse effects if this vessel were unable to operate at necessary speeds due to a failure of this bow at a critical time." Summing up, the *Ranger*'s commanding officer considered that "a comprehensive refit and modernization would enhance the value of the ship to a very great extent." He therefore recommended that "such a modernization be authorized as soon as possible as soon as strategic conditions permit and that a study of all alterations be made with a view towards inclusion into one modernization project."[3]

Modernization for the *Ranger*, however, if it was approved, would have to come in the future. Current operations continued, and the prevailing strategic situation did not permit any interruption in her operations with the Home Fleet. While the *Ranger* had been operating out of Scapa Flow in early September, the German Navy had sortied from its Norwegian lair, and, in Operation *Zitronella*, the battleships *Tirpitz* and *Scharnhorst*, supported by ten destroyers, bombarded Spitsbergen on the 7th of the month. A landing party wrecked the Allied installations there, and the shelling destroyed the village; the Norwegian garrison had taken to the mountains as the Germans retired.

Over the ensuing weeks, however, the Norwegians had begun rebuilding the base at Spitsbergen. To assist in the reconstruction and restoration, the *Ranger*'s old consorts, *Tuscaloosa* and *Fitch*, and three British destroyers—HMS *Onslaught*, HMS *Orwell*, and HMS *Oribi*—were to proceed to the island to deliver stores, embark the survivors of the original garrison, and land fresh troops. To provide cover, a strong force built around the *Ranger*, British battleship HMS *Anson*, the British heavy cruiser HMS *Norfolk*, and three British destroyers, (two Canadian, and one American [the *Corry*]), sailed from Scapa Flow during the afternoon watch on 14 October. The *Ranger* went to flight quarters 15 minutes into the first dog watch to recover CVG-4, finally bringing the last plane on board at 1937, securing from flight quarters eight minutes later.

Earlier that afternoon, before the force sailed, Ens. Gerald Grimes, with Aviation Machinist's Mate 2d Class J. S. Dunn in back, took off from Hatston in an SBD-5 (BuNo 28765), for a tactics hop. As soon as the SBD became airborne, Grimes pulled his wheels up, but smelled smoke from what he thought was an electrical fire in his cockpit. Opting for an emergency landing, Grimes put down his flaps, but did not lower the landing gear. The field control officer in the tower tried to warn Grimes by radio and red Very star that his gear was not down. Grimes neither heard nor saw the danger signals and made a wheels-up landing. A subsequent examination revealed no fire of any sort had occurred on board the aircraft.[4]

The *Ranger* put into Akureyi, Iceland, during the afternoon watch on 15 October, and remained there for almost a day, sailing the next afternoon. The carrier operated in the Greenland and Norwegian seas with the Home Fleet, supporting Operation FQ, with the *Tuscaloosa* and her escorting destroyers accomplishing their mission successfully on the 19th. That same day, during recovery operations, an F4F-4 landed hard and its guns discharged; fortunately, no casualties ensued.

The *Ranger* returned to Scapa Flow on the 22d. For its part, Torpedo Four had provided antisubmarine coverage, conducting two-thirds of its operations "between the Arctic Circle and the 76th parallel, in conditions of poor visibility and sea-level icing." Woot Taylor commended his men for performing their duty "with such precision and dispatch as to earn a 'Well Done'" from British and American flag officers alike, in spite of "unfavorable weather, the freezing seas, the wet and icy flight deck, and the full load of depth bombs carried."[5] But the work had not been accomplished without cost: during flight operations on 22 October, Aviation Machinist's Mate 3d Class Edward L. Laundrigan tripped and fell into the path of a taxiing TBF. Laundrigan died of the injuries he suffered when the eight-ton airplane ran over him.

Having completed that stint with the Home Fleet, the *Ranger* proceeded to the Royal Naval Dockyard at Rosyth, Scotland. Passing beneath the Firth of Forth Bridge on the

Commander John R. Van Nagell, Rear Adm. Olaf M. Hustvedt, Capt. Walter F. Boone, and Capt. Rowe on the flag bridge, bundled in parkas and gloves, while en route to the Firth of Forth, 25 October 1943. (NA, 80-G0-201191)

morning of 25 October, she anchored that day, shifting to drydock number one three days later, for hull repairs, as workmen welded the crack in the stem casing, concern for which had motivated Captain Rowe's addressing the need to strengthen that part of the ship in his 13 October letter to BuShips. With the *Ranger* at Rosyth, half of her officers and men enjoyed a well-deserved leave. Undocked during the afternoon watch on 3 November, the *Ranger* sailed for Scapa Flow the next afternoon.

Standing in toward Pentland Firth during the mid watch on 5 November, the *Ranger* steamed past numerous drifters and small vessels, burning her side lights and running lights, as necessary, to steer clear of them. Operating in Pentland Firth during the forenoon watch, the carrier then recovered her brood, without incident, during that time, and dropped anchor in the familiar berth B-1 at 1247 on the 5th.

Underway shortly before the end of the morning watch on 7 November, the *Ranger* went to flight quarters as she stood out, joining the *Forrest* and the *Corry* and the Canadian destroyer HMCS *Iroquois*, once outside of Scapa Flow. The ship exercised at torpedo defense drills and exercised her 40- and 20-millimeter guns during the forenoon watch. Subsequently conducting flight operations during the afternoon, launching planes to carry out a mock attack on the ship, the *Ranger* reprised torpedo defense drills, before turning into the wind to recover her brood.

After taking part in the mock strafing attacks, Ens. Lawrence Hensley came up the groove in a manner that concerned the LSO, who gave him two violent "come on" signals before giving him a wave-off. In trying to answer the wave-off, however, Hensley firewalled the throttle, but to no avail. The F4F-4 (BuNo 12001) settled, engaging the number two crossdeck pendant; the pilot felt the hook engage the wire, so cut his throttle. The plane managed to stay in flight long enough to clear the flight deck, but ended up on the port stacks.[6]

Before the *Ranger* would conclude flight operations that afternoon, steaming through the slight ground swells off the Orkneys, two more mishaps, both involving Bombing

Four, occurred. Lieutenant (jg) Darrell Way of VB-4, flying an SBD-5 (BuNo 28605), with Aviation Radioman 3d Class G. C. Ellis in back, took the LSO's cut, but second-guessed him. Believing that he was coming in high, Way dove for the deck. The impact of the Dauntless's landing drove the left wheel strut into the wing stub, buckling the fuselage and blowing the right tire.[7] A little over a half an hour later, Ens. Gus B. Baker, flying the same SBD-5 that Ens. Grimes had landed, wheels-up, at Hatston on 14 October, landed slightly fast, gliding unbridled up the deck, until engaging number eight wire. Although BuNo 28765 went into the barrier, nicking the propeller blades, bending the engine cowling, and damaging the radar antennae, neither Baker nor Aviation Radioman 3d Class A. J. D. Black, Jr., his radio-gunner, suffered any injuries.[8]

In the meantime, Captain Rowe's request that the *Ranger* receive a thorough refit and modernization had reached the next stop on its way up the chain of command. Rear Adm. Gerald F. Bogan, Commander Fleet Air, Norfolk, assessed the recommendation, observing the existing facts-of-life about the *Ranger*: she was highly vulnerable, particularly to a torpedo, because of inadequate longitudinal strength, lack of torpedo bulkheads, outboard gasoline stowage, bomb stowage inboard of gasoline, and a low margin of stability. A single torpedo hit, Bogan observed, would "probably" prove fatal, and there was a "strong likelihood that a torpedo hit amidships would cause the vessel to break in two," because of her lack of longitudinal strength. The admiral also recounted the ship's inadequacy from the standpoints of slow elevators with inadequate capacity, a flight deck not strong enough to handle modern planes, inadequate CIC facilities, insufficient ready room accommodations, and lack of a catapult. After addressing weight compensation matters concerning blisters, flight deck strengthening, and modern planes, the admiral recommended replacing the 5-inch battery with four additional 40-millimeter quads. Because of the *Ranger*'s deficiencies, however, Bogan recommended, on 9 November, that "she be made available at the earliest practicable date for such time as may be necessary for the addition of blisters, rearrangement of gasoline stowage, modification of armament, and the completion of other vital alterations which weight considerations will permit. The withdrawal from service for this period and for this purpose," Commander Fleet Air, Norfolk, concluded, "is excellent insurance for *Ranger*'s continued combatant service."[9] The *Ranger*'s former captain, Vice Admiral Bellinger, on whose desk Captain Rowe's request next landed, having accumulated Commander Fleet Air, Norfolk's endorsement en route, concurred. "It is strongly recommended," he wrote, "that all reasonable measures be taken at the earliest practicable date to modernize the *Ranger* from the standpoint of underwater protection and ability to operate modern airplanes."[10]

As those concerned with the *Ranger*'s future contemplated those matters, on board the ship, scuttlebutt soon indicated a return to the Norwegian waters, perhaps to even attack the *Tirpitz*, which had lain immobilized at its lair in Altenfjord after the attack by British midget submarines. Jerry Thomas of Torpedo Four confided to his journal on 9 November of a post-poker game discussion of "the much-anticipated air raid on Norway. We are to carry torpedoes this time instead of bombs. Fighter opposition is expected and AA fire will be more severe than on October 4. Should get underway tomorrow."[11]

Shortly before the end of the afternoon watch on 10 November, the *Ranger* did in fact get underway, shifting outside the antitorpedo baffles, and anchored in the open waters of Scapa Flow, preparatory to a night sortie. The operation in which the *Ranger* was to participate, however, was called off before the time came to sail, prompting "disappointment among many pilots today.... The Norwegian operation has been cancelled." Consequently, the *Ranger* returned to berth B-1 during the afternoon watch on 11 November, the significance of the day not lost on one observer: "Armistice Day for World War I and here we are in the midst of another war between Nations." The *Ranger* remained at anchor on the 12th, conditions proving unsuitable for flight operations.

The weather abated the next day, however, and the *Ranger*, in company with the *Fitch*, *Forrest*, and *Corry*, put to sea during the forenoon watch. She carried out flight operations off Scapa Flow, launching two groups of planes for tactical exercises, before exercising at torpedo defense quarters during the forenoon watch.

A little less than a half hour into the afternoon watch, the *Ranger* began bringing her brood on board amidst worsening weather, squalls, and a rough sea. Only three minutes into the evolution, Ens. Hartwell Hawkins made a skidding approach through the squalls in his F4F-4P (BuNo 5160), trying for the pitching and rolling deck. In the practiced gaze of the LSO, the 20-year-old Texan was flying on the starboard side of the groove, left wing down, headed on a course that would take him slightly across the deck. As the *Ranger* rolled to starboard in the heavy sea, the deck rose to meet the incoming Wildcat. Hawkins landed hard on number three elevator, slightly to port of the centerline, the impact collapsing the Grumman's narrow-track landing gear. Skidding on its belly, the F4F-4P shed its tail hook and veered toward the edge of the flight deck. The fuselage and left wing brushed four of the five 20-millimeter

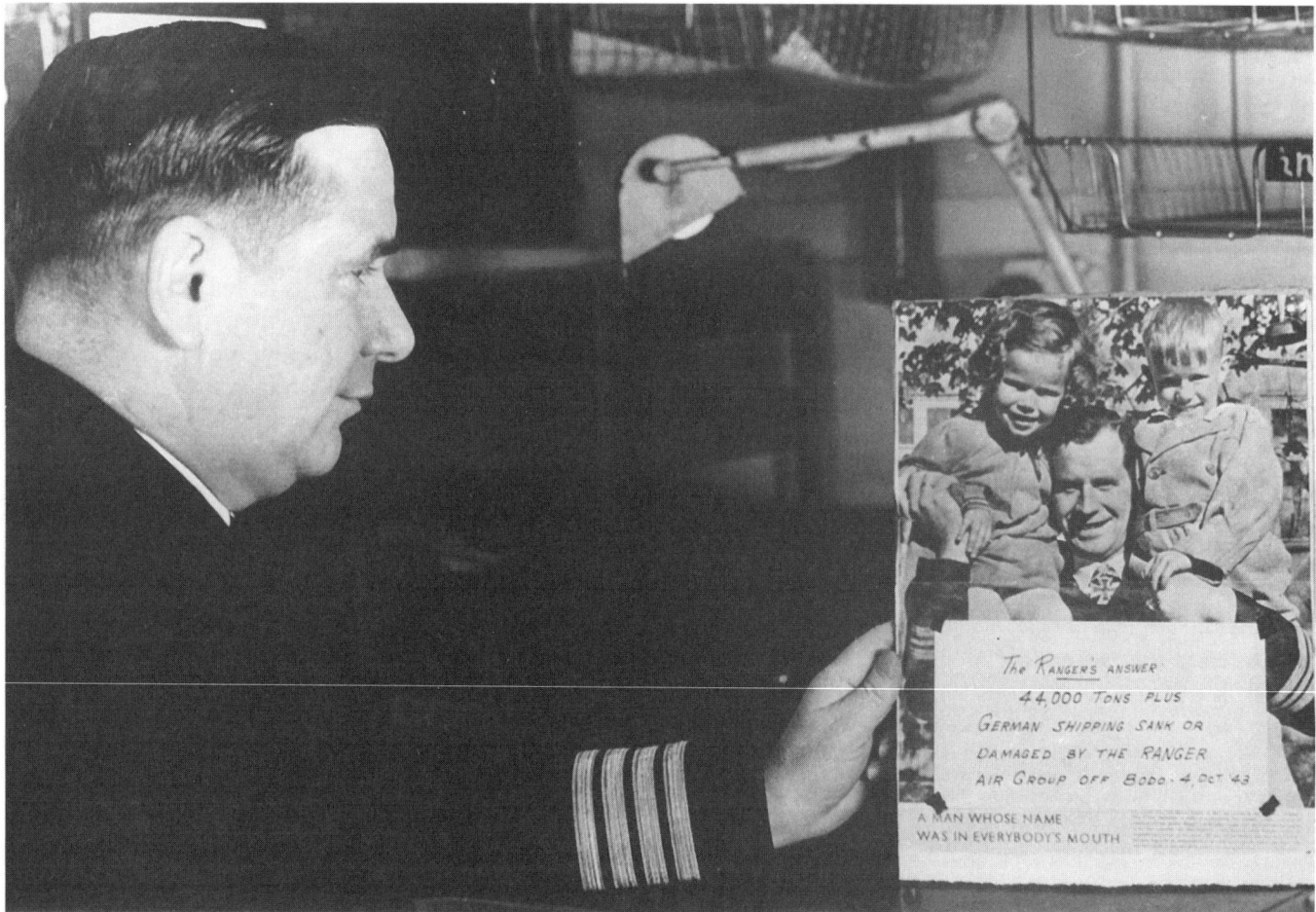

A bemused Capt. Rowe looks at a German propaganda photo showing *Kapitänleutnant* Otto von Bülow ("a man whose name was in everybody's mouth" for his "sinking" the *Ranger*) with the decorated U-boat commander's children. Taped to the photo is a piece of paper with the words: "THE *RANGER'S* ANSWER: 44,000 TONS PLUS GERMAN SHIPPING SUNK OR DAMAGED BY THE RANGER AIR GROUP OFF BODØ—4 OCT '43." (AUTHOR)

mounts in the port catwalk, before the Wildcat, hookless and brakeless, slid over the side just aft of number one barrier and splashed, nose-first, alongside, as the *Ranger* swept past.[12]

Hawkins's body floated to the surface some 300 yards astern. Recovery operations for the rest of the air group continued, while the *Corry* retrieved the unconscious Hawkins about 18 minutes later. In accordance with orders sent to her at 1416, the destroyer sped back to Scapa Flow. Artificial respiration, however, proved unavailing, and the medical officer declared Hawkins dead several hours later. The trouble board assessed a number of factors in trying to determine what had happened: it noted 15% "miscellaneous" conditions, because of the state of the sea, but it assessed 85% as "pilot error." Hawkins's own errors in judgment (50%) and technique (35%) had proved fatal.[13]

After flying off the air group to Hatston, the *Ranger* passed through the outer gate at Scapa Flow a little over a quarter of an hour into the first dog watch on the 13th. She dropped anchor in berth B-1 soon thereafter, securing her main and steering engines and five of her six boilers, leaving only boiler number one in use for auxiliary purposes. Heavy weather, with squalls and a northerly gale, prevailed over the next few days.

Captain Rowe's letter recommending modernizing the *Ranger*, meanwhile, had reached CinCLant. The reception, however, proved lukewarm. "In view of the progress made in the CV program and in the absence of knowledge of planned requirements, present or future, in carriers in the various theaters of war," CinCLant expressed himself "unable to recommend approval or disapproval of the alterations requested." In her present condition, the *Ranger* "cannot be considered a first line carrier." Citing the fact

VF-4 officers, November 1943. First row (L–R): Lt. George M. Harris, Jr., Lt. Edwin N. Seiler, Lt. Edward F. "Buster" Craig, Lt. Richard Claytor, A-V(S), Lt. Comdr. Charles L. Moore, Jr. (commanding officer), Lt. Keane G. "Kagey" Hammond, Lt. Robert B. Johnston, Lt. Charles C. "Andy" Andrews, Lt. Charles A. "Windy" Shields, Lt. William H. "Pete" Bolt, Jr. Second row: Lt. (jg) Lloyd H. Launder, Jr., Ens. Louis K. Lepp, Ens. Robert G. Nicholson, Lt. (jg) Dean S. "Diz" Laird, Lt. (jg) Will "W" Taylor, Lt. (jg) Richard W. Callen; Lt. (jg) Clifford M. White, Ens. Howard F. "Eddie" Edwards, Lt. Hubert T. "Hubie" Houston, Lt. (jg) Charles R. "Hoppy" Hopson. Third row: Ens. Laurence A. Hensley, Ens. Charles L. Martin, II, Ens. Warren A. Brown, Ens. Robert S. Kelley, Ens. Thomas J. Graham, Ens. Frank A. Garrigan, Jr., Ens. Chauncey G. Welton, Ens. Ferrell D. Sears, Ens. George R. Gilbert, Ens. Robert F. Grant. (NA, 80-G-201174)

that, even if she were modified, she would still be handicapped by her low speed, militating against "her inclusion in a task force of modern CV's," CinCLant believed that, "if the needs for war were not too pressing, [the] *Ranger* could be made into an excellent training ship. In that case, a brief overhaul would be sufficient. If, on the other hand, it is decided that she is to be used in action against the enemy, it would then be well worth while to provide additional underwater protection and other modifications," such as her captain had recommended.[14]

That same day, as her limitations and her future continued to be contemplated on up the Atlantic chain of command, the *Ranger* recovered CVG-4 during the forenoon watch on the 16th. Rumors persisted of a Norwegian raid ("Looks like I'll pack a torpedo against the Germans yet," Jerry Thomas wrote), as the ship anchored later in the watch, again in berth B-1, but she remained there only until the next afternoon, when she again got underway to launch 40 planes to return to Hatston, before she returned to anchor.[15] Underway again the following morning, in company with the *Capps* (DD-550) and the British destroyers HMS *Obdurate* and HMS *Venus*, the *Ranger* conducted exercises with the British submarine HMS *Thrasher*, before returning to port during the first dog watch. The *Ranger* subsequently recovered her air group during the fore- and afternoon watches on the 21st.

In company with the *Augusta* and the *Capps* and the British destroyers HMS *Ashanti*, HMS *Musketeer*, HMS *Matchless* and HMS *Obdurate*, the *Ranger* departed Scapa Flow on 22 November, leaving "for good," wrote Signalman 3d Class Crochet in his diary.[16] The next day, the task force encountered heavy seas that cracked windows in the secondary conning station beneath the *Ranger's* flight deck, forward, and pounded her hull so badly that a split seam admitted a gallon of water per hour. "This is the roughest sea I have ever seen," Jerry Thomas confided to his journal, "This old ship bashes into the waves and shudders . . . even split a seam . . . water over the forecastle and flight deck . . . sure wish I was back on the farm. . . ."[17]

The *Ranger* reached Hvalfjordur, Iceland, two days later, reverting to American signal procedures again. As the ship got underway on the morning of 26 November, in the prevailing icy conditions and heavy seas, however, she lost one of VF-4's F4F-4s (BuNo 03433) over the side, as well as Aviation Machinist's Mate 3d Class James D. Westmoreland, Jr., a plane captain who was in the cockpit. The bad weather militated against Westmoreland's being rescued. He would be the final fatality incurred during the *Ranger's* tour with the Home Fleet.

Returning to the U.S. Fleet on the day of her departure from Iceland, she sailed as part of TF-68, in company with the *Augusta* and the *Tuscaloosa* and the destroyers *Forrest*, *Fitch*, *Corry*, *Capps*, and *Hobson*. Cheers rang out and resounded throughout the ship, greeting the news over the general announcing system that day that the ship was due in Boston on 3 December. The task force encountered rough weather twice, on 28 November and 1 December, during the passage.

The *Ranger* maintained a continuous antisubmarine patrol on 2 December, from the morning into the afternoon watches. As she recovered her combat air patrol during the latter period, Ens. Howard F. "Eddie" Edwards, A-V(N), made a normal approach, but, when he took the LSO's cut, nosed his F4F-4 (BuNo 11956) down. Landing on its wheels, the Wildcat bounced up the deck and floated into the barrier. Edwards suffered no injuries in the mishap, but his plane required a complete overhaul.

On 2 and 3 December, the *Ranger* launched her air group to base at Quonset Point. An hour and a quarter into the forenoon watch on the latter day, she moored "amid cheers and confusion" at the South Boston Navy Yard, to commence upkeep and an overhaul that kept her yard-bound into 1944.[18]

As the *Ranger* lay in yard hands, on 18 December 1943, Admiral King, as CNO/ComInCh, asked the Chief of the Bureau of Ships to prepare detailed plans and to collect and prefabricate the materials necessary to modernize the *Ranger's* underwater protection and her ability to operate modern aircraft. He noted, however, that "in view of the time required for preparation, the availability of the subject vessel . . . will be determined at a later date."[19]

BuShips subsequently informed CNO/ComInCh that plan work had been completed concerning the installation of blisters and that the steel for the actual job would be obtained from Navy warehouse stock and the February 1944 rollings at several steel mills. With the Norfolk Navy Yard estimating one month for prefabrication, delivery of the steel in March would allow plenty of time to prepare for the installation to go forward in April. The same situation applied to the fabrication of the gasoline saddle tanks. As to the modifications to the existing elevators, BuShips informed CNO that the plans had been developed utilizing equipment originally procured for installation in the *Lexington* and *Wasp*, but which was not used because both ships had been lost in 1942. Other items of work upon which BuShips reported included a deck-edge elevator, a flight deck catapult, projected replacement of the 5-inch/25 battery with 5-inch/38s, a new CIC, rearrangement of radar and radio antennae, replacement of emergency power supply batteries with diesel generators, and "miscellaneous outstanding Shipalts [shipboard alterations]" that would be tackled when the ship became available. BuShips promised that the preparation of plans and assembly of material could be completed by 10 April.[20]

Within a week of BuShips' memo to the CNO, BuAer weighed in on the *Ranger's* modernization, by noting the increased use of catapults by carriers, and recommendations from the Pacific area that suggested the installation of two bow catapults in all CVs. Given the *Ranger's* speed limitations, BuAer considered the installation of two catapults as "particularly desirable if they can be accommodated."[21]

BuOrd likewise weighed in on the modernization as it involved the ship's battery. In view of a proposal to remove the 5-inch/25s and substitute additional 40-millimeter mounts, but CNO's not contemplating that measure, BuOrd suggested an increase of "not less than four, and preferably six, 40mm twin mounts." The bureau also recommended provision for "ready service aircraft machine

Captain Rowe (L) congratulates Seaman 1st Class Marion M. Reynolds (C) during an awards ceremony before the assembled ship's company, 22 November 1943; while Seaman 2d Class Merle B. Rothe and Quartermaster 3d Class Robert E. Walsh, USNR (R) look on. Rowe commended all three men for their alertness in spotting the only German aircraft that got close enough to the task force during Operation Leader, resulting in the CAP's splashing both. (NA, 80-G-201202)

gun ammunition, bomb, and torpedo stowage with a view towards decreasing the time required for airplane rearming operations, within the limits of prescribed safety precautions." It also advocated the study and provision of adequate facilities "to permit expeditious handling from below decks magazines and stowage spaces to hangar and flight deck[s]."[22]

Because of the ship's extensive operations in northern waters, Captain Rowe recommended subsequently, on 30 December, that the *Ranger* and her air group be sent to Trinidad to train—strategic considerations permitting—until the Norfolk Navy Yard was ready to commence the ship's modernization overhaul. Those who scheduled the *Ranger*'s operations, however, did not place Trinidad in her schedule—northern climes would continue to remain her area of operations. Departing Boston on the afternoon of 2 January 1944, the *Ranger* reached Narragansett Bay the following morning.

The *Ranger* operated out of Quonset Point, going to sea for four-day stretches of day and night operations with CVG-4, through the second week of April—evolutions sometimes interrupted by snow and high winds. As was often the case, the occasional mishap punctuated the routine. Ensign Vincent Rusbosin, A-V(N), of VB-4, with Aviation Radioman 2d Class W. R. H. Campbell, USNR, on board, brought in his SBD-5 (BuNo 28660) and took the cut after a normal approach. As he came up the deck, however, he dropped the right wing, throwing the plane into a skid and causing a hard one-wheel landing. As Rusbosin's mount engaged the cross-deck pendant, the right wheel buckled: a major overhaul lay in BuNo 28660's future. Ensign Earl J. Nicolini, A-V(N), of VF-4, flying out to the ship from Quonset Point, made a normal approach and executed all of the signals the LSO had given him while coming up the groove. After getting the cut, however, Nicolini held off and ended up floating into the barrier. Before his F4F-4 (BuNo 11996) could be flown again, it required a replacement of the left and right drag links, a new propeller, and an engine change. The resulting trouble board faulted Nicolini's technique. Negligence characterized Lt. (jg) Marshal P. Deputy, Jr., A-V(N)'s mishap that same day: he made a normal landing, but, while taxiing up the deck, attempted to pull up his flaps. He accidentally pulled the wheel control as well as the flaps, and both sides of the landing gear retracted, first the left, then the right, damaging both wings, landing flaps, ailerons, and wing bomb racks beyond repair, puncturing the starboard auxiliary gas tank and destroying both radar antennae.

Misfortune seemed to dog CVG-4 ashore as well as afloat: two days after the rash of flight deck miscues on 9 January, Ens. Warren A. Brown, A-V(N), took off in an F4F-4 (BuNo 11863), to tow a target for aerial gunnery practice on the 11th. Receiving clearance from the Quonset Point tower, Brown released his brakes and started to taxi. He had not, however, noticed a Grumman J2F-5 coming in for a landing ahead of him. When the Duck suddenly materialized in his path, Brown skidded to the left to clear it. Already on the left side of the runway, however, the young pilot, who had received his wings on New Year's Day 1943, and who up to that point had had a clear accident record, swerved into a snow bank. A major overhaul lay in store for BuNo 11863.

"Miss Fortune" returned to the *Ranger* and her aviators on 16 January, with a vengeance. Lieutenant (jg) William E. Dill, A-V(N), with Aviation Chief Machinist's Mate A. S. Reagan on board, brought his SBD-5 (BuNo 28811) in for a landing at 1525. When his tail hook caught the wire, the sudden impact jarred loose a miniature practice bomb from his rack and it bounced forward into the propeller, bending one blade beyond the capability of the ship's force to fix.[23] Five minutes later, Lt. (jg) Jack F. Radford, A-V(N), with Ens. Billy N. Kinder, A-V(N), in back, climbed as he approached the ramp, took a "high" cut and dove for the deck; failing to recover in time, Radford's SBD-5 (BuNo 28800) made a hard, wheels-first landing, buckling both sides of the fuselage.[24] At 1640, Lt. Charles Breckheimer, A-V(N), with Aviation Machinist's Mate 2d Class J. C. Brown on board, made an approach that the LSO adjudged normal but slightly fast, but received the cut nevertheless. Breckheimer's SBD-5 (BuNo 29090), however, caught the number seven wire, which he pulled out until he hit the barrier. Those who analyzed the accident judged that the flight deck crew had failed to lower the barrier in time to prevent irreparable damage to one propeller blade.[25] Only five minutes later, Ens. Francis Moses, A-V(N), brought in his SBD-5 (BuNo 28949), with Aviation Radioman 2d Class G. C. Ellis in back, in what looked like a normal approach. Moses climbed as he reached the ramp, however, and, as a result, lost sight of the LSO. Thinking that he was too slow to take a wave-off, the pilot decided to dive for the deck and cut the throttle. Making a "very hard landing," Moses's poor judgment and technique resulted in a major overhaul for BuNo 28949.[26]

The next day, Ens. Billy Kinder, who had been Jack Radford's passenger in a hard landing the day before, made a normal but slightly fast approach, 15 minutes into the forenoon watch on 17 January, and took the cut. Kinder's SBD-5 (BuNo 29041) caught number six wire, but the flight deck crew had not dropped number one barrier in time, so that, at the run-out, the Dauntless fouled it.

Neither Kinder nor his passenger, Aviation Radioman 3d Class R. W. Humphrey, suffered any injuries in the mishap, which the trouble board lay firmly upon Kinder's judgment and technique.[27]

Just over a month later, the *Ranger* suffered her first fatality of 1944, a little over an hour into the mid watch of 20 February, losing the recently promoted and newly married Lt. (jg) Eddie Edwards. Edwards had made a normal but slightly fast approach for a night recovery, but made a wheels-first landing after getting the cut. As the General Motors FM-2 (BuNo 16367) bounced, Edwards applied the throttle to attempt to take a wave-off. The Wildcat's right wing struck the radio antenna and the bridge structure, however, then crashed on deck forward of the barrier and fell over the starboard side into the sea. The *Ellyson* searched unsuccessfully for Edwards. The *Ranger* returned to her moorings at NAS Quonset Point at 1705 on the 20th. Two hours into the afternoon watch the following day, the *Ranger* held a memorial service on the hangar deck for the lost pilot. A trouble board later adjudged the crash the results of poor judgment, technique, and "disobedience."

On 23 February, the *Ranger* exercised with night fighter squadrons VF(N)-77, -78, and -79, as well as her CVG-4. During one period of operational exercises with the latter, on 28 February, after the *Macomb* had intercepted high-frequency direction-finder signals from what was believed to be a U-boat, the carrier launched 20 SBD-5s, each armed with a Mk. 47 depth charge, in what proved to be a negative search.

Underway from Quonset Point 20 minutes into the forenoon watch on 5 March, the *Ranger* put to sea with the *Hambleton*, the *Ellyson*, and the *Macomb*. The carrier exercised her batteries during that watch. She later conducted flight operations—principally qualification and refresher landings—from the afternoon watch into the first watch. During the first dog watch, Ens. Joseph F. Moore, A-V(N), from VF(N)-79, brought in his F6F-3N (BuNo 40896) and took the cut to land, but held off; his tail hook caught the last wire, but the night fighter Hellcat encountered the barrier before coming to a stop.

During the second dog watch, Lt. (jg) Rusbosin, of VB-4, engaged number three wire in his SBD-5 (BuNo 36154) and, after being cleared from the gear, taxied forward. The hook dropped, however, and snagged number four wire. The LSO, meanwhile, had brought Ens. Donald A. Henry, A-V(N), into the cut position to land. Henry's TBF-1C (BuNo 47921) came up the groove without a hitch, but the LSO gave Henry a late wave-off; Henry tried to answer the signal, turning left and gunning the engine, but the Wright R-2600-8 Cyclone responded slowly. His tailhook caught number three wire, the one just vacated by Rusbosin, as Henry managed to line up with the deck and land well on the port side. The TBF-1C's right wing struck the canopy and propeller of Rusbosin's SBD, and the right landing gear strut and prop hit the Dauntless's port wing. Fortunately, no one in either plane—Rusbosin in the SBD and Ens. Henry and Aviation Radioman 3d Class E. A. Shirley in the TBF—was hurt in the mishap, which a trouble board blamed solely on the LSO and those who had been designated to inform him, in a timely fashion, of the status of the deck. "Don landed an Avenger on a Dauntless in the gear," Jerry Thomas later wrote, "tore both planes up."

The night's excitement, however, was not over yet. Lt. (jg) Warren Brown made a high approach, to the right of the centerline, a half hour before the end of the second dog watch. The LSO wagged "cut," but Brown hesitated to put the FM-2 (BuNo 16397) down on the deck, until it engaged number eight wire on the starboard side of the flight deck. As the plane continued the run-out, it struck the after 40-millimeter clipping house; before it could be returned to service, it required the change of the right wing, the engine, and the propeller. The trouble board faulted Brown's judgment and technique.

After a stint of operations with planes from both CVG-80 and CVG-4, between 9 and 12 March, the *Ranger* exercised with the *Ellyson*, the *Hambleton*, and the *Macomb*, on the 14th and 15th. Then, following upkeep and overhaul at NAS Quonset Point, the carrier brought on board CVG-4 and sailed on the 26th to resume training. Planes from her embarked air group carried out a simulated night attack on the *Augusta* and the *Tuscaloosa* on the 27th.

During a scouting mission on 28 March, a VB-4 flight was flying just below a layer of overcast that extended from 200 to 1,100 feet. The leader signalled Ens. Richard K. Allender, A-V(N), that the flight would climb above the cloud cover; putting his plane on autopilot, the leader began to ascend as indicated. At an altitude of 650 feet, the leader saw the 19-year-old Ens. Allender's 4-B-29 go into a steep left, nose-down turn, crossing behind the leader. Before Allender disappeared from view at about 300 feet, he was still in the diving attitude. A search over the next few days yielded no sign of the SBD-5 (BuNo 54127) or of Allender nor of his passenger, Aviation Radioman 3d Class Edward J. McMenamin, USNR.[28] "Ens[ign] All[e]nder got vertigo [the supposition of the trouble board, given the circumstances of Allender's disappearance] in a cloud and was last seen spiraling down in his plane. The Avengers and Dauntlesses spent the remainder of the day searching for survivors or wreckage," but, as Jerry Thomas noted later, "No luck."[29]

Firefighters deal with the crash of Lt. Reuben F. Peterson A-V(N)'s, Grumman F6F-5N (BuNo 40831), 25 February 1944. (NA, 80-G-223214)

By the end of March 1944, as the *Ranger* was continuing her operations out of Quonset Point, BuShips was once again addressing the issue of her modernization which had been contemplated, from recommendation to endorsements up the chain of command, since early October of the previous year. "With manpower shortages staring us in the face," one BuShips officer wrote in early March, "and if we must keep one carrier in the [the Atlantic] I would like to raise [the] question of [the] conversion of *Ranger*—[the work] force will come from repairs or new *Essex* class [carriers] building."[30] To accomplish the modernization, BuShips estimated, would require 1,600,000 man-hours. More important, however, refitting the *Ranger* would interfere with the construction of the *Shangri-La* (CV-38), which had been scheduled for commissioning in mid-September 1944, and the *Lake Champlain* (CV-39), slated to enter service in mid-November. The latter, Rear Adm. Edward L. Cochrane, Chief of BuShips, pointed out, had already suffered through the efforts to keep the *Shangri-La* on schedule, and to provide enough manpower for urgent repair work, "of which there is always a considerable load at the Norfolk Navy Yard." Furthermore, Cochrane pointed out in a memorandum to the CNO, "the manpower situation has reached the point at which it is no longer possible to cover additional work by taking more men. It is only by extreme measures that the present numerical strength of the yard force can be maintained. The yard's productive strength is diminished continually by dilution of less skilled and less capable recruits."[31]

That was not all. Cochrane assumed that work on the *Ranger* would be accomplished "at the expense of at least

The *Ranger*, with the destroyers *Ellyson* (DD-454) (L) and *Macomb* (DD-458) (R) moored alongside to port, shares Pier 1, NAS Quonset Point, with the heavy cruiser *Tuscaloosa* (L), 28 March 1944. Note style of number 4 painted on the carrier's flight deck. (NA, 80-G-394586)

one of the new first-line carriers [such as the *Essex*-class *Shangri-La* and *Lake Champlain*] which would otherwise be completed only shortly after the *Ranger*'s refit will be completed." Even acknowledging that the new carriers would require shakedown and training, the Chief of BuShips noted, however, that their readiness for operations would be "scarcely comparable" to the *Ranger*, because the latter would, even after modernization, "still be far from a first-line carrier." Cochrane pulled no punches as he sought confirmation of the decision to carry on the refitting and modernizing of the *Ranger* at Norfolk. "This is a question of major alterations to a relatively old carrier of basic inherent deficiencies of speed and protection against all forms of attack," he concluded, "versus the completion of first-line carriers of full effectiveness."[32]

A week later, Vice Adm. Frederick J. Horne, Vice Chief of Naval Operations, who had once flown his flag in the *Ranger*, boiled down the essentials of the modernization request: install blisters, modernize elevators, install catapults, and strengthen the flight deck. Modernizing the CIC, improving the battery, modernizing and relocating gasoline stowage, installing longitudinal bulkheads and overhauling her machinery, improvements that could improve the *Ranger*'s efficiency, as well as improve her ability to withstand damage, could all be accomplished concurrently. However, Horne noted, the work would only result in a carrier capable of handling 70 planes with a "moderately high protection against underwater damage, but limited to a maximum speed of about 28 knots." That work not being accomplished would limit the *Ranger* to operating planes no longer in front-line carrier service. Outstanding alterations and repairs to the bow would require a "considerable amount of Navy Yard work," which could, "in view of the time, labor, and material required," delay the completion of the *Shangri-La* and the *Lake Champlain*, as the BuShips' chief had pointed out. In view of "the fact that the modernization [of the *Ranger*] will not result in a first-line carrier," Horne suggested "that a review of the desirability of undertaking the work is in order at this time," and asked ComInCh to confirm whether or not the *Ranger* would, in fact, be modernized.[33]

Less than a fortnight later, on 6 April, CNO informed BuShips that the *Ranger*'s modernization would not be undertaken "at this time," but that Norfolk Navy Yard would nonetheless continue the planning and prefabrication of material for the *Ranger*'s overhaul, but "not to delay" the completion of the *Shangri-La* and the *Lake Champlain*. CNO also directed that the *Ranger* "be scheduled for [a] limited early overhaul which will fit her for training purposes," as had been suggested by CinCLant in November 1943. CNO finally directed that the *Ranger*'s "eventual modernization . . . be undertaken when it will cause less serious interference with other work."[34]

As her fate was being decided in Washington, the *Ranger* continued training pilots. After winding up training VF(N)-79, VT-44, and VF-7 on 1 April, she put to sea with CVG-4, VF(N)-78, and VF-7 embarked, with the *Macomb* and the *Ellyson* as plane guards, during the forenoon watch on 3 April. The *Ellyson* reported a sound contact at 1218 and developed it, making three runs with depth charges beginning at 1245, but attained no visible results. Group training then proceeded according to schedule, between the afternoon and first watches. During that time, the *Upshur* (DD-144) joined the screen.

Unhappily, during the first watch on 3 April, Lt. (jg) John R. "Jack" Fulnecky failed to answer the LSO's "low" and "come-on" signals, and, although he apparently tried to execute a voluntary wave-off, he settled down onto the deck at 2136. Four-Baker-Sixteen caught the number one wire and went over the side. The SBD-5 (BuNo 36907) briefly hung suspended by the tailhook until the latter broke, with the Dauntless plunging into the water. Both Fulnecky and his passenger, Aviation Radioman 2d Class A. A. Burns, exited 4-B-16, but for some reason Fulnecky did not inflate his life jacket. Burns had inflated only one side, but could not reach the other toggle—he had fastened the cord against the cylinder with a rubber band to avoid accidental inflation. Burns tried to help the pilot, but Fulnecky told him that they both could not be supported by only one side of one jacket. They both started swimming toward the *Macomb* as she approached them, but they became separated. Helpless onlookers saw Fulnecky sink out of sight; the *Macomb* rescued Burns.[35]

"It was Jack Fulnecky's turn tonight," Jerry Thomas later reflected bitterly in his journal, "Happy-Go-Lucky 'Ful'— just married—well liked—good aviator. He has been on this tub 14 months now and never had any trouble. I was in the air when it happened. Bad wave-off—caught a wire and over the side—throttle full on. Radioman picked up but not Jack. As the other pilots got down they asked who it was this time. When they were told it was Big Jack, the principle [*sic*] expression was 'G*d D*mn!' I can name 19 pilots lost since I got aboard the *Ranger*," he wrote, "only one in action—two captured. The rest were operational accidents. No wonder the air group is p.o.'d."[36]

Flight operations continued the following day between 0730 and 2050, evolutions not carried out without a certain amount of zest for at least one Bombing Four pilot: "Leo Norman [was] almost added to the list [of lost pilots] when he caught an F6F slipstream and almost went in on his back." During the afternoon watch, the *Ranger*'s 5-inch batteries and control stations got in some work, expending 43 rounds of ammunition in a gunnery shoot. On 5 April, after detaching the *Ellyson* to proceed independently, the *Ranger*, with the *Macomb* and the *Upshur* in company, continued her work with CVG-4, VF(N)-78, and VF-7, winding up those evolutions at the end of the forenoon watch that day, when she dispatched all aircraft to resume shore-based status. She herself fired a gunnery exercise that afternoon, with the *Greer* and the *Tarbell* (DD-142) reporting for duty, before mooring at Pier 1, NAS Quonset Point.

Underway again on 7 April, this time with CVG-4, VT-301, and VF-78 embarked, the *Ranger* sailed in company with the *Upshur*, the *Tarbell*, and the *Greer*. After firing an antiaircraft firing exercise for her 5-inch, 40-millimeter, and 20-millimeter batteries during the forenoon watch, the carrier exercised VT-301 in qualification landings during the afternoon and first dog watches, before hazy conditions compelled cancellation of CVG-4's planned carrier work-ups.

The following day (8 April) she received orders detaching her and Destroyer Division (DesDiv) 61 (less the *Lea*) from TF-22 and directing them to report to Commander TF-28 (Commander Fleet Air, Norfolk) for duty with that force. The *Ranger* exercised her embarked squadrons in carrier landings on that day and the next, before steering a course to return to Narragansett Bay.

On the last full day of that training cycle, Captain Rowe signed a lengthy confidential letter to BuShips addressing modifications to certain compartments. Although some of the changes concerned storerooms and fresh water capacity, Rowe suggested, in view of the proposed installation of a deck-edge elevator to replace the current number two elevator, that 150 additional berths and 50 lockers be installed in the vacated number two elevator pit "to provide a berth for each member of the present complement of the ship,

The *Ranger*'s LSO (lower right) waves off a Hellcat pilot during carrier qualifications in early April 1944. (NA, 80-G-230368)

staff, and squadrons, and 10% of the locker requirements." At the present time, the *Ranger*'s captain explained, "as many as three hundred men are berthed on the mess decks. Due to the nature of operations and the fact that air operations usually require very early and late meals for a portion of the crew, this entails very uncomfortable living conditions for the men concerned, many of whom stand arduous watches." Additionally, to provide berths for all the officers on board, it had been necessary to install a large bunkroom in one compartment, six berths in one passageway and two in another, with the latter "very congested and uncomfortable." The heavy traffic on that particular deck, which included handling stores, made it very difficult for the young officers berthed there, from both the ship and her embarked squadrons, "to obtain sufficient rest." Additionally, facilities for "reading, writing, studying and for proper stowage of uniforms and winter clothing are non-existent."[37]

Going to flight quarters at 0545 on 10 April, the *Ranger* launched a two-plane antisubmarine patrol, before sending the rest of her embarked planes in to NAS Quonset Point to resume shore-based status. Delayed, herself, from arriving at Quonset Point, because of a heavy fog blanketing Narragansett Bay, she finally put over her lines to the familiar pier 1 at 1847. Later that day, orders came through directing the *Ranger*, along with DesDiv 61 (less the *Lea*) to report to Commander Fleet Air, Norfolk (Commander TG-28.1), "for duty as a training carrier task unit to be temporarily assigned to [Commander Fleet Air, Quonset] for use as necessary to coordinate the training of all carrier squadrons, with emphasis on carrier qualifications." The following day, 11 April, the ship held memorial services for Jack Fulnecky.

Although she reported for duty with TG-28.1, by dispatch, on the 11th to begin her training assignment, the *Ranger* received word on 12 April that ComInCh had directed CinCLant to make her available to ferry a "maximum load" of Army planes from New York to Casablanca, in company with the escort carrier *Card* (CVE-11) "on or about 24 April." Directed to transfer the majority of her air department men to Carrier Aircraft Service Unit (CASU) 22, which had been established at Quonset Point on 1 January 1943 to "re-equip and support the shore based operations of carrier air groups, during which operations the group must be maintained and operated at its maximum military efficiency," as well as to remove all bombs and gasoline, the *Ranger*, accompanied by the *Uphsur*, the *Greer*, and the *Tarbell*, conducted training with CVG-4 and VF(N)-79, before having to cut short the scheduled exercises out of Narragansett Bay because of the report of a U-boat operating in the vicinity.[38]

Entering the swept channel into Narragansett Bay on the afternoon of 14 April, the *Ranger* moored at Pier 1 and began discharging gasoline, a process that continued into the mid watch on 15 April. Later, she unloaded bombs and torpedoes, a task that occurred during the forenoon and afternoon watches and the better part of the first and second dog watches on the 15th. In addition, that same day she transferred the three officers and 136 enlisted men from the carrier *Ticonderoga* (CV-14), who had been on board for temporary duty, to the Naval Training Station, Newport, Rhode Island. While at Quonset Point, she also received word that CVG-4 was to be re-formed there by 1 May, as a spare air group, equipped with 36 fighters, 36 scout-bombers, and 18 torpedo planes. If needed, the *Ranger* would embark "the most advanced CVG on [the] East Coast."

"Air Group 4 has been detached from the USS *Ranger*," Jerry Thomas wrote in his diary on 16 April, "to move to Fort Devens, Mass[achusetts] to be enlarged to a 90 plane outfit. Lunch aboard the *Ranger* was probably my last meal on that Flat Top. I'm leaving with some vivid memories, centering around hazardous day and night carrier landings, rough seas, foul weather, crap games, bull sessions, good friends, Argentia, Scapa Flow, Iceland, London, Edinburgh and the Norwegian Coast. She's a great ship," he concluded affectionately, "cussed and loved by many—but always a welcome sight to the Naval Aviator coming up the groove."[39]

On the day that the *Ranger* began off-loading all spare parts for FM-2s, SBDs, and TBFs, the ship held quarters for muster, at which Captain Rowe presented awards to the officers and men from CVG-4 who had been commended for action against the enemy during the Bodø strike the previous October. Commander Joe Ruddy received the Distinguished Flying Cross; Otto Klinsmann, Cy Weeks, Bob Ruth, and Jerry Thomas all received Air Medals; and Aviation Radioman 1st Class Reuben Gray received the Purple Heart. One hour after the awards ceremony, the ship began detaching 17 air department officers and 419 enlisted men.

The following afternoon, escorted by the *Tarbell*, the *Upshur*, and the *Greer*, the *Ranger* sailed for New York. She reached Staten Island the following morning, and the following day commenced loading twin-boom Lockheed P-38 fighters; the three venerable destroyers that had accompanied her were detached to operate with the escort carrier *Kasaan Bay* (CVE-69). On the day the *Ranger* completed loading the 76 Lightnings (22 April), Capt. Arthur Gavin relieved Capt. Rowe as commanding officer.

The *Ranger*'s new captain had enlisted in the Navy during World War I, after graduating from the University of

One of 76 Lockheed P-38 Lightnings is lowered to the *Ranger*'s flight deck, as the ship lies alongside Pier 13, Staten Island, in preparation for being ferried to Casablanca, 21 April 1944. (NA, 80-G-230384)

Wisconsin and, while stationed at NAS Pensacola, was appointed an ensign in the Naval Reserve Force. Designated as a naval aviator on 14 September 1918, Gavin transferred to the regular Navy in 1919, and advanced in the naval aviation community over the next two decades, serving in a succession of shipboard aviation units, interspersed with duty at shore stations. Highlighting his career was his winning the Schiff Trophy in 1927, when he set an endurance record of 37 hours aloft. Among his tours of sea duty had been successive ones as navigator and air officer of the seaplane tender *Langley*. He came to the *Ranger* from NAS Jacksonville, where he had served as commandant from 7 August 1943 to 17 April 1944. Gavin would be the *Ranger*'s only captain who had not graduated from the Naval Academy.

The *Ranger* embarked 41 Army officers, 57 naval officers, and four French Navy officers and 20 ratings, and 423 U.S. Navy enlisted men on the 23d, and sailed the following afternoon, as part of TG-27.1, in company with the *Card* and the destroyer escorts *Otter* (DE-210), *Stern* (DE-187), *O'Neill* (DE-188), *Solar* (DE-221), and *Robert I. Paine* (DE-578). She reached her destination on the early evening of 4 May and moored to the *Mole du Commerce,* where her bombers had damaged the *Jean Bart* in November 1942. Completing the off-loading of her cargo and disembarking her passengers the following day, she took on board seven Bell P-39 Airacobras for transportation back to the United States, and an additional two P-39s, nine Curtiss P-40s, and one P-38 for transportation, on the 6th. She embarked passengers on the 7th, including six German prisoners-of-war who purportedly expressed surprise when learning of their transport's identity—after all, had not the *Ranger* been sunk by *U-404*? Two French naval officers and 34 ratings, 87 U.S. navy sailors, and 26 Army officers and 22 enlisted men would ride the ship back to the states.

The *Ranger* sailed for home on the afternoon of 7 May. She refueled one of her escorts, the *Robert I. Paine*, on 10 May, as that ship was detached to join a "hunter-killer" group formed around the escort carrier *Block Island* (CVE-21) off the Cape Verdes. The *Ranger* reached Pier 14, Staten Island, during the first dog watch on 16 May, to disembark her passengers and off-load the mixed cargo of Army aircraft. The *Ranger* was to have taken part in a second ferry mission to Casablanca, but her place was taken by two CVEs and she was directed to proceed to Hampton Roads, where she was to conduct not only night fighter training, but carrier qualifications.

Underway for Norfolk a half hour into the afternoon watch on 18 May, in company with the *Greer* and the *Tarbell*, the *Ranger* reached NOB Norfolk the following morning and commenced unloading ammunition alongside Pier 5. Shifting to the Norfolk Navy Yard the following afternoon, she commenced a limited modernization overhaul that lasted well into June. During that period of work, completion of which had been delayed because of the priority assigned the completion of the ammunition ship *Mount Hood* (AE-11), the *Ranger*'s flight deck was strengthened, she received one Type H, Mk. 2, Mod. 1 catapult, an SM-1 radar, and an SC radar that replaced the CXAM-1 with which she had been fitted, and a CIC adjudged sufficient for night fighter interceptor training. Concluding postrepair trials on 8 July, the *Ranger* shifted to NOB Norfolk on the 9th. She loaded bombs the following day, and sailed, in company with the new destroyers *Blue* (DD-744) and *DeHaven* (DD-727) and the destroyer escort *McCoy Reynolds* (DE-440), on the afternoon of the 11th.

En route to Panama, the *Ranger* lost a man overboard early in the afternoon watch on 14 July, when Seaman 2d Class John F. Wilkinson fell from the fantail at 1210. The *Ranger* steered various course and speeds in an attempt to recover him, and, although the *DeHaven* lingered in the vicinity for at least an hour, searching, Wilkinson was never recovered. The ship held memorial services for the lost sailor the following afternoon.

Upon arriving in Limon Bay on the morning of 16 July, the *McCoy Reynolds* detached for temporary duty with the Panama Sea Frontier forces; the *Ranger* transited the Panama Canal later that day. She embarked 454 Army passengers on the 17th and sailed for San Diego the following morning, in company with the *Blue* and the *DeHaven*. The three ships were designated as TG 12.8. Generally, although two false submarine contacts enlivened the voyage on 20 July, the passage to San Diego unfolded uneventfully, with the *Ranger* refueling her two escorts on the 22d.

In Chesapeake Bay, 6 July 1944, displaying her new measure 33 (Design 1-A) camouflage and her new silhouette, altered by the removal of her Mk. 33 gun directors. Colors are Pale Gray (5-P), Haze Gray (5-H), Ocean Gray (5-O), and Dull Black. Decks are Deck Blue (20-B). (NA, 80-G-236719)

En route to San Diego, the *Ranger* refuels the destroyer *De Haven* (DD-727), 22 July 1944. (NA, 80-G-245745)

On the day of her scheduled arrival, 25 July, the *Ranger* received word that an attack group of marine aircraft, as well as planes from CVG-84, would carry out a simulated attack on TG 12.8, preceded by a search group of Consolidated PB4Ys from VB-117. The *Ranger* was to tow a target spar and, along with her escorts, take evasive action. At 0440, the *Ranger*'s radar picked up two of the incoming PB4Ys 59 miles distant, reporting her position. The *Ranger* went to general quarters at 0530, as the shadowing bombers continued to transmit position reports, and the *Blue* and the *DeHaven* assumed their screening positions five minutes later. At 0838, the radar picked up the inbound attack, 65 miles distant and closing. Marine F4Us made one simulated strafing run at 0943, following that up with strafing runs with tracers at the towed target. CVG-84, troubled during their search by a solid overcast (as well as by the evasive actions of the task group), located the task group at 1028, and the latter's F6Fs, SB2Cs, and TBFs delivered a "well coordinated attack" on the group, with the Hellcat pilots strafing the towed target as the marine Corsair pilots had done, and the Helldiver and Avenger pilots dropping miniature practice bombs upon it. All planes rendezvoused and soon returned to base. The *Ranger* moored at NAS San Diego at the end of the first dog watch.

Disembarking the passengers who had ridden the ship from Balboa on the 26th, the *Ranger* commenced taking on fuel, embarking more passengers, and loading VF(N)-102's 15 F6F-5Ns, and 6 TBM-1Cs, and an additional F6F-5P, 15 Curtiss SB2C-3Cs, 14 General Motors TBM-1Cs, 11 Vought F4Us, and 28 Goodyear FG-1s, for transport to Pearl Harbor. After embarking additional passengers on the 28th, the carrier sailed for Hawaiian waters later the same day, in company with the *DeHaven* and the *Blue*, mooring alongside Ford Island on the afternoon of 3 August. It marked the first time that the ship had ever been inside Pearl Harbor proper: her previous operations in Hawaiian waters, the last of which had been in 1938, had occurred before dredging operations permitted carriers to enter its confines. Three days later, Rear Adm. Matthias B. Gardner embarked in the *Ranger*, and the next day broke his flag as ComCarDiv 11, the carrier division established solely for the training of pilots.

Soon thereafter, the *Ranger* began operating from Pearl. Preceded by the destroyer escorts *Stafford* (DE-411) and *Gendreau* (DE-639), the carrier stood out an hour before the end of the morning watch on 9 August. She then conducted antiaircraft gunnery exercises, along with carrier air group qualification and refresher training of CVG-100—activated on 1 April 1944 as the first replacement pilot unit (it would grow into the first carrier replacement training group)—and CVG-44 accomplishing 98 landings and 78 launchings with the two groups.

The following day, after he had made a normal carrier landing at 0945, Ens. Frank B. McNulty, Jr., A-V(N), of VT-100, began to take off. As onlookers watched helplessly, however, his TBM-1C (BuNo 25179) swerved sharply to the left and skidded off the deck without airspeed, damaging three 20-millimeter guns in the port-side gun gallery, as it lumbered over them. The Avenger then crashed against the *Ranger*'s side and plunged into the Pacific. McNulty, who had suffered multiple fractures of the cervical vertebrae in the crash, managed to escape from the aircraft and inflate his life jacket, but made no attempt to reach for the life ring thrown from the deck. The *Stafford* soon retrieved him from the water; he recovered, but then lost consciousness. Two hours of artificial respiration failed to revive him.[40]

During the afternoon watch, Ens. D. T. Williams, A-V(N), from VF-44, reported empty fuel tanks and nonfunctioning landing gear. The *Ranger* had been unable to establish radio communication with him, but Williams managed to make an emergency forced landing in his F6F-3 (BuNo 42433). The *Gendreau* recovered the pilot, who had suffered only minor injuries in the crash.

The rest of the *Ranger*'s first stint of training in Hawaiian waters proceeded uneventfully, with the ship accomplishing 251 launchings and 251 landings with planes from the two embarked groups on the 11th and 26 landings and 46 launchings the following day, with the ship entering Pearl Harbor during the afternoon watch and mooring at berth Fox 5.

Returning to sea on the 15th, preceded by the destroyer *Howorth* (DD-592), the *Ranger* carried out gunnery exercises and conducted qualification and refresher landings for CVG-3 and CVG-100. Early in the first dog watch, Ens. Rex W. Stoney, A-V(N), of the latter group, made a bad landing and went over the side. The *Howorth* promptly plucked him from the sea, with only minor injuries.

Less than three-quarters of an hour after the end of the mid watch on 16 August, planes from the Night Aircraft Carrier Training Unit (NACTU), Barber's Point, carried out a simulated predawn attack on TG 19.4—the *Ranger* and the *Howorth*—before the carrier resumed her air training work, conducting 138 landings and 131 landings. The routine continued into the following day, 17 August, with the destroyer *Haraden* (DD-585) joining the escort screen soon after the end of the mid watch. As in the previous day, seven planes from the NACTU conducted a simulated attack on the task group.

Tragedy stalked VF-3's recovery operations during the forenoon watch on 17 August. At 0814, Lt. Samuel Solberger,

While an honor guard of marines presents arms, the ship's band plays appropriate music, and Lt. Robert M. Perry, Chaplain Corps, stands ready to conduct the memorial service, pallbearers carry the remains of the late Lt. Carlos R. McKee, A-V(N), and Seaman 2d Class Clayton O. Craft, USNR, 17 August 1944. (NA, 80-G-245748)

A-V(N), flying an F6F-5 (BuNo 58484), overshot during his landing attempt and, after missing all barriers, crashed into the seven fighters spotted forward. Among the latter was an F6F-5 (BuNo 58592) that had just been landed by Lt. Carlos R. McKee, A-V(N). Solberger's Hellcat crashed into McKee's, the impact pushing the entire armor plate and seat assembly forward, crushing McKee in the cockpit and killing him instantly. Seaman 2d Class Clayton O. Craft, USNR, one of the *Ranger*'s flight deck crew, who was in the process of placing chocks beneath the wheels of one of the planes forward, was struck by the propeller of Solberger's F6F, amputating his left leg at the thigh. Craft died of his injuries within a half hour. Both McKee and Craft were buried at sea with appropriate ceremony during the first dog watch.[41]

The relentless and unremitting pace of wartime training, however, left little time for sentimentality. Operations continued. Planes from the NACTU carried out another simulated attack just after the mid watch on the 18th, employing "window." The *Ranger*'s SM-1 radar, however, easily recognized the distinctive pattern, and the planes' burning running lights as they approached allowed them to be spotted. Captain Gavin later hypothesized that had the "attackers" not used running lights, visual fire control methods would not have been effective.

Later that day, Ens. Harold H. Stevens, A-V(N), of VT-3, was returning to the *Ranger* from an antisubmarine patrol in a TBM-1C (BuNo 45462), with Aviation Ordnanceman 2d Class Harry E. Haney as tunnelman and Aviation

Radioman 2d Class Ben S. Hatten, USNR, as turretman. Stevens turned into the groove in preparation to landing on board, but the Avenger's engine failed. Stevens set the Avenger down into the water in what observers deemed an "excellent" water landing about 200 feet astern of the ship. The plane sank nose first and its depth charges exploded as the plane sank. Fortunately, the crew had abandoned the aircraft and gotten on their backs, which lessened the injuries sustained. The *Howorth* rescued all three men; only Hatten suffered a minor laceration of his left elbow and chest pains from the blast effect of the depth charges. A trouble board later blamed the accident on the fuel system, recommending that the fuel gage be redesigned by eliminating the selector switch, to enable the pilot to read the fuel capacity in all tanks without changing the selector setting. That was accomplished in later models of the TBM.[42]

During the course of the continuing air operations on the 19th, the *Ranger*, early in the morning watch, welcomed Capt. Theodore R. Frederick, Rear Admiral Gardner's chief of staff, who reported on board by plane. For Ted Frederick, this proved a homecoming of sorts: he had served in the *Ranger* during her early days and had accomplished the ship's 1,000th landing, in April 1935. After exercising her 20- and 40-millimeter batteries, the *Ranger* returned to Pearl Harbor, mooring in berth F-2 during the afternoon watch.

Sortieing from F-2 on 24 August and preceded by the destroyer escorts *Richard W. Suesens* (DE-342) and one of her former consorts from the voyage from Norfolk to the Panama Canal Zone (the *McCoy Reynolds*), the *Ranger* again conducted gunnery excercises. "Twenty millimeter gunners are improving with each practice," Captain Gavin later told his men, "and 40-millimeter loading crews are becoming very proficient. The new and inexperienced men which we started with in July have now become a creditable anti-aircraft battery."

Unhappily, although the gunnery drills with which the ship started the day had gone well, refresher training for CVG-11 did not. Commander George T. McCutchan, the air group commander, piloting an F6F-3 (BuNo 40248), made a high and fast landing at 1427. He leveled off too high and failed to engage any of the cross-deck pendants. His Hellcat drifted to starboard, struck the mast with its right wing, scraping off a radio antenna, signal halliards, a signal searchlight, a long glass, and brushing the fly control station; part of the long glass hit and slightly injured a signalman on the bridge. The F6F-3 then dropped to number one elevator and cartwheeled over the side, its fuselage breaking in half at right angles just aft of the cockpit, sinking immediately. Observers did not see the pilot, most likely unconscious from the impact of the crash, emerge from the aircraft. The search by one of the plane guards failed to recover the 33-year-old McCutchan, a naval aviator since 12 May 1937, who was married and the father of two children.

The remainder of CVG-11's landings, however, proceeded without incident over ensuing days, with the group making 150 launchings and 175 landings on 25 August, 105 landings and 145 launchings on the 26th, and 179 landings and 177 launchings on the 27th. During that period of flight operations, the ship also participated in a night fighter director exercise designed to confuse lookouts and to conceal attacking planes. Two of three attempted deceptions succeeded in their intent: the releasing of parachute flares after passing the ship, to reduce the effect of ships' gunfire pursuing the attacking planes; and float flares dropping between a half mile and a mile from the ship on one side of the formation, to confuse the ship and form a silhouette. Releasing a parachute flare a mile from the ship, however, to confuse the ship, did not prove successful, because the light of the flare illuminated the underwing surfaces of attacking aircraft.

During the morning watch on 28 August, the *Ranger* came under a simulated attack, with the attackers using window. The carrier's radar operators managed to track the planes through the affected areas, however, distinguishing between the window and the aircraft. On the SC-3 radar, the 40-degree sector, 10–16 miles out, the window managed to effectively obscure the targets. All told, Captain Gavin considered the exercise successful in familiarizing Frank Sherrard's CIC people with the affects of window.

The *Ranger* sortied from berth Fox-10 shortly after 0800 on 1 September, preceded by her escorts, the destroyers *Gansevoort* (DD-608), *Coghlan* (DD-606), and *Fanning* (DD-385). She conducted gunnery exercises, then conducted day air training operations with CVLG(N)-42, preparing it for night evolutions, accomplishing 77 landings and 48 launchings over the remainder of the day, logging only one barrier crash, with no injuries. Training continued the following day, with CVLG(N)-42 and a return visit by CVLG-44. The *Ranger* conducted night and day qualifications with the latter group, as well as with CVG-11; CVG-3 returned to conduct further training on the 4th. The last-named group conducted both day and night training on the 5th, accomplishing the ship's 47,000th landing during that time.

Training resumed on the 9th, with day operations for CVG(N)-90, CVLG(N)-42, and NACTU, logging 57 landings and 28 launchings. Ensign Edwin R. Jones of CVG(N)-90, piloting an F6F-3 (BuNo 42324), caught the

Alongside Ford Island, moored in Berth Fox-10, September 1944, as seen from the escort carrier *Altamaha* (CVE-18). (NA, 80-G-286222)

number one wire, but the hook pulled out, allowing the Hellcat to float up the deck, crash through the number four barrier, and plunge over the side into the water. The plane sank, but the *Fanning* promptly picked up Jones, who had suffered a slight head laceration in the crash.[43]

The *Ranger* conducted operations with CVG(N)-90, CVLG(N)-42, and NACTU through the morning watch on 11 September, then brought on board CVG-100 for day air operations, logging 117 landings and 137 launchings. At 1427 that day, however, Ens. Marion B. White landed on board, but mistook the "taxi" signal for "take off." Seeing White's F6F (BuNo 41465) charging up the deck, Aviation Machinist's Mate 2d Class Ambrose I. Schitter, USNR, and Aviation Machinist's Mate 3d Class William J. Whitney, members of the flight deck crew, instinctively tried to dodge the oncoming Hellcat. Tragically, their bid for safety took them both into the idling propeller of an FM-2 Wildcat, which killed both men instantly. A third man, Aviation Machinist's Mate 2d Class E. L. Tumilovich, suffered slight injuries in the mishap.[44]

After a brief in-port period (11–13 September), the *Ranger* stood out an hour before the end of the morning watch on 14 September, preceded by the *Fanning* and the *Caldwell* (DD-605). She conducted antiaircraft gunnery exercises during the forenoon watch, before she carried out air group qualification and refresher training for CVG-81, accomplishing 138 landings and 108 launchings, with only two barrier crashes. As re-spot operations proceeded during the second dog watch, an Avenger rolled off the port corner of the after end of the flight deck. Fortunately, no one was on board the plane at the time.

CVG-4 returned to its old ship the following day, joining CVG-81 in accomplishing 224 landings and 220 launchings, with only one barrier crash. At 1036 on the 15th, Lt. H. D. Sellar, A-V(N), of VF-81, after reporting an oil leak, suffered engine failure. He made a water landing in his F6F-3 (BuNo 42131), which sank irretrievably into the depths, but the *Fanning* logged her second rescue of a *Ranger* pilot inside a week's time, when she picked up Sellar, none the worse for his ditching. Later that day, the *Edwards* (DD-619) replaced the *Fanning*.

CVG-4 continued its training operations off the *Ranger* on the 16th, accomplishing 58 landings and 88 launchings, with only one barrier crash, before the ship returned to Pearl, mooring alongside pier Fox-9 at 1707. She would remain there until the 19th. On the latter date, on the other side of the country, the issue of her modernization was at last decided—with Olympian finality—at ComInCh headquarters. In a simple, one-paragraph memorandum for the Vice Chief of Naval Operations, Admiral King declared:

"The *Ranger* will not be modernized. Dispose materials collected and fabricated to best use."[45]

Preceded by the destroyer escorts *Tabberer* (DE-418) and *Melvin R. Nawman* (DE-416), the *Ranger* conducted more antiaircraft gunnery exercises that morning, before resuming air training operations—this time with VC-82 and CVG-4. She logged 99 landings, 93 launchings, and one barrier crash. During the afternoon watch, at 1409, Ens. M. McKinney, A-V(N), of VC-82, spun in aft of the ramp during his approach to the groove. Although his FM-2 (BuNo 16763) sank to the bottom of the Pacific, McKinney was rescued by the plane guard, unhurt.

Over the next three days, the *Ranger* continued operations with her old air group (CVG-4) and CVG-81, before she returned to Pearl on the 22d for a three-day respite, before beginning the process over again, going to sea with CVG-100 on 25 September, accompanied, as during the previous stint, by the *Tabberer* and the *Melvin R. Nawman*. She logged one serious mishap on 27 September, when Lt. Paul A. Quarnberg, A-V(N), of VF-100, was making his third pass, with his fuel mixture control set at full-rich. When he received a wave-off from the LSO, he abruptly added the throttle. The engine began to belch thick black smoke, however, as the F6F-3 (BuNo 42513) lost flying speed and crashed astern, as the motor cut out. The *Ranger*'s plane guard again came to the rescue, picking up Quarnberg unhurt soon thereafter. The *Ranger* returned to Pearl during the afternoon watch on 28 September, mooring to Fox-10 at 1539; she remained there for the balance of the month.

The pace remained relentless for the *Ranger* as the month of October began, when she sailed from Pearl, steaming out in the wake of the *Saratoga*, the destroyer *Meade* (DD-602) and the destroyer escorts *Tabberer*, *Melvin R. Nawman*, *Howard F. Clark* (DE-539), and *Oliver Mitchell* (DE-417). After the *Saratoga* and the two latter DE's broke off to operate independently, the *Ranger* began operating VC-82 and VC-83, conducting both day and night qualifications. CVG-3 operated from the *Ranger* on the 2d, CVG-4 on the 3d and 4th, CVG-81 on the 4th and 5th. After the *Saratoga* and her two consorts rejoined the formation during the morning watch on 5 October, the task group returned to Pearl that afternoon. The *Ranger* returned to sea on the 8th, operating CVG(N)-90 on that day and the next, and CVLG(N)-42 on the 9th and 10th before putting back into port on the latter date.

Rear Admiral Gardner shifted his flag to the *Ranger*'s old running-mate *Saratoga* on 11 October, and two days later the *Ranger* sailed for San Diego, where she arrived on the 19th. Shifting to NAS Alameda, joined en route by the

Ensign Tilman E. Pool, USNR, in the cockpit of his F6F-3 (BuNo 41820), in which he had made the *Ranger*'s 50,000th landing at 0912, 28 October 1944. Pool, flying from the carrier *Hornet* (CV-12), would go on to win three Distinguished Flying Crosses and five Air Medals in the closing stages of the Pacific War, and would participate in the attack on the Japanese battleship *Yamato* off Okinawa on 7 April 1945. (NA, 80-G-286481)

Captain Arthur Gavin congratulates Ensign Pool on achieving the ship's milestone 50,000th landing, 28 October 1944, as Comdr. Joe Ruddy, the *Ranger*'s air officer, and Comdr. Frank M. Hammitt, the carrier's exec, look on. (NA, 80-G-286482)

destroyer *McFarland* (DD-237), the *Ranger* resumed her training routine in the waters off Southern California, where she had begun them nearly a decade before—starting with CVG-6 and CVG-17—on 24 October, the *McFarland* serving as her plane guard. She conducted operations with those two groups on that day and the next, returning to Alameda early in the second dog watch on the 25th.

Although bad weather and sea conditions combined to prevent flight operations on the 26th, the *Ranger* resumed them the following morning, and maintained them, operating CVG-17, for that day and the next. On the latter date, 28 October, Ens. Jack Garrett, USNR, came in high and fast, and, at the LSO's cut signal, dipped for the deck at 0830. His excessive speed, however, resulted in his F6F-3 (BuNo 70061) bouncing, before it caught a wire. Too late to dip and snag another pendant, Garrett nosed his Hellcat into the barrier, bending the propeller, tearing the left wingtip, and twisting the fuselage forward of the firewall.[46]

At 0917, the *Ranger* logged a milestone, when Ens. Tilman E. Pool, USNR, brought in his F6F-3 (BuNo 41820) for the ship's 50,000th landing. Before the forenoon watch was over, however, that particular plane suffered severe damage in the hands of another pilot, when Ens. Bernard A. Smith, USNR, made his approach too close abeam. As he took the LSO's cut, Smith was in a steep bank; he tried to line himself up with the center of the deck, but ended up putting the Hellcat into a violent right skid. Instead of a cross-deck pendant, Smith's tailhook snagged one of the brackets that held the wire off the deck; the unyielding bracket tore off the tail of the fighter just ahead of the stabilizer. The F6F came to rest on the number two elevator, pointing toward the starboard quarter.[47]

The cake that commemorated the 50,000th landing, the handiwork of Baker 1st Class H. Ponsell. (NA, 80-G-286484)

VF-17's travails continued, when Ens. C. W. McAdoo, USNR, preparing to take off, received the signal from the fly one officer to turn up to full power. McAdoo, however, did not have the stick pulled all the way back when he did so, nosing the F6F-3 (BuNo 41118) over and bending the prop. Later that day, Ens. Murray Winfield, USNR, made a good approach, but ducked for the deck upon getting the LSO's cut. The Hellcat touched down between the wires and bounced free of them; Winfield nosed over the F6F-3 (BuNo 40563), but was unable to catch a cross-deck pendant. His right wing hit a 40-millimeter mount, before going into the barrier and coming to an abrupt stop against the island, breaking the prop, shearing off the right wing, damaging the landing gear, and twisting the fuselage halfway between the cockpit and the vertical stabilizer.[48]

After a brief in-port respite (29–30 October) at Alameda, the *Ranger* returned to sea, again with the *McFarland* as plane guard, and qualified and refreshed CVG-6 (the bomber squadron of that air group commanded by Lt. Comdr. Gordon Chase, who had served on detached nonflying duty in the *Wilkes* during Torch) on 31 October and 2 November. Following that period of training, the ship underwent a period of upkeep alongside the carrier pier at Alameda, during which time her number two 40-millimeter mount was replaced.

Shifting to NAS San Diego in company with the *McFarland* on 13 November, the *Ranger* resumed day air training operations with CVLG-33, accomplishing 101 landings, with only one barrier crash that day. After continuing her work with that group the following day, the carrier flew it off to NAS Livermore, California, before she set course for NAS San Diego, arriving there on 15 November.

The *Ranger* sortied the following day with six fighters from CVLG-30 and all of CVG-12, logging 242 day landings, with only one clip-house crash. After launching five of the CVLG-30 fighters to land at North Island, the *Ranger* operated CVG-12 over the next two days. For some pilots of VF-12, it must have seemed like déjà vu, because Lts. Rube Denoff, Hal Vita, Armistead B. Smith, Hamilton McWhorter, Lou Menard, Oliver Toliver, and Lane Bardeen—Torch veterans all—had served in VF-9.

Not all of VF-12's operations, however, went off without a hitch. At 0730 on 17 November, Ens. Archer B. Campbell, USNR, as he took off, applied his left brake to align his F6F-3 (BuNo 40977) with the flight deck. In so doing, he swerved to the left so far that, even after applying right rudder, he could not correct his passage up the deck. He passed over the port bow, striking the first four 20-millimeter mounts. Remaining airborne after striking the splinter shields of those guns, Campbell made a successful emergency landing, although his Hellcat suffered class B damage in the process.[49]

The next day, Ens. James C. Nash, USNR, qualifying on board the *Ranger* and flying an F6F-3 (BuNo 70601), took a late cut while high in the groove, and ended up overshooting the arrestor cables and crashing into the barriers at 0940. A trouble board faulted Nash's understandable inexperience in carrier work, and added that all pilots had been instructed to take "prompt, entire cut-off of throttle when instructed by [the landing] signal officer." Ens. Hugh E. Smith, USNR, later experienced difficulty of another sort, when he taxied up the deck too fast with the throttle on; applying the brakes under those conditions resulted in Smith's F6F-3 (BuNo 42945) nosing up, breaking off eight inches of each propeller blade. Ensign Nash, bringing in another F6F-3 (BuNo 41271) at 1155, took his second late cut of the morning, high in the groove, and overshot the arresting gear, again going into the barrier, bending and breaking both landing gear fairings, springing the engine mount downward, bending the prop blades, and bending the nose cowling and air cooler flaps. As in the previous incident, Nash received the admonition to take the cut promptly.[50]

The *Ranger* operated CVG-12 planes for a second stint (20–23 November), at the conclusion of which the ship launched the group to fly to its base at NAS Ream Field. During the day on 23 November, the destroyer-seaplane tender *William B. Preston* (AVD-7) joined the formation to operate as plane guard. The Ranger reached NAS San Diego on the 24th and remained there until the 27th, when she returned to sea to conduct training with VT-12, VF-12 and the night fighters assigned to the latter squadron, in addition to VF-84 pilots as well. Winding up her training of the CVG-12 units on 28 November, she operated CVG-84 units, including qualifying the Corsair-equipped VF-84, the squadron using the new Brewster F3A and Vought F4U-1D models. "The landing characteristics of the new Corsairs," Captain Gavin wrote, "appear to be excellent; the new oleo struts have reduced the bounce to a minimum. It seems to be an excellent carrier-based aircraft."

Even so, not all went smoothly. On 1 December, Lt. (jg) Leo G. Adrian, USNR, of VB-84, took a wave-off and made a tight turn, but spun into the water, suffering minor chest injuries and lacerations of his hands and legs in the crash. The *McFarland* rescued him. The next day, while *William B. Preston* plane-guarded, the carrier continued qualifying CVG-84—not without incident for the group's Corsair pilots. In the course of the 193 landings that occurred that day, Ens. Stephen Komar, USNR, made a very hard one in his F4U-1D (BuNo 57791), wrecking the fuselage ahead of the cockpit; Ens. Francis B. Phillips, USNR, a quarter of an hour later, received a wave-off after the LSO saw him coming in low and slow, but he caught number one wire anyway and ended up in the port catwalk. Subsequent trouble boards faulted Komar for technique, but apportioned the blame in the latter case 75% to Ensign Phillips and 25% to the LSO, Lt. George H. Budde, for his error in judgment.

During December, the *Ranger* qualified CVG-84, CVG-12, and VT-98, and a succession of Marine Corps fighting squadrons: VMF-112, VMF-511, VMF-512, VMO-351, VMF-123, VMF-221, and VMF-451, achieving a per diem record on 8 December, when she logged 326 day landings. On 12 December 1944, the *Ranger* became a flagship once more, when Rear Adm. William K. Harrill, Commander, Fleet Air, West Coast—the *Ranger*'s first wartime commanding officer—temporarily shifted his flag to his old command from the escort carrier *Makassar Strait* (CVE-91), as she put to sea to conduct day air training operations.

In the interim between his leaving the *Ranger* and returning as a flag officer, Harrill had been air officer of the Northwest Sea Frontier, had commanded NAS Seattle, served as Commander, Fleet Air Alameda, and as Commander, Fleet Air, West Coast, the last-named post for the first three months of 1944. He returned to sea, as Commander Carrier Division One, and commanded a fast carrier task group, earning the Legion of Merit for directing attacks on Japanese bases at Guam, Rota, Iwo Jima, and Chichi Jima, before an emergency appendectomy sidelined him in July 1944.

On the day that Admiral Harrill broke his flag in his old command, the *Ranger* operated three Corsair-equipped

Vought F4U-1D from VF-84 about to touch down, 1 December 1944; the hookman waits to disengage the Corsair's tailhook from the cross-deck pendant and another F4U prepares to slip into the groove (NA, 80-G-294114)

USMC squadrons: VMF-123, VMF-221, and VMF-451. During the course of the 97 landings accomplished that day, 2d Lt. J. K. Shannon suffered minor lacerations of his scalp and left knee, when his F4U-1D went over on its back after a hard landing. The carrier operated those same squadrons the next two full days, before she returned to North Island on the morning of 15 December.

Underway again the following morning, in company with the *William B. Preston*, the *Ranger* resumed her acquaintance with CVG-12, accomplishing 214 day landings, one search problem, and a fighter direction exercise. Machinery casualties, however, compelled the *William B. Preston* to return to port after the conclusion of the day's schedule, her place taken the next day by her sistership, the *Childs* (AVD-1).

Although the *Ranger* logged no barrier crashes on the 17th, Ens. Russell I. Morgan, USNR, crashed on takeoff that day. Although Morgan's F6F-3 (BuNo 42945) sank irretrievably into 2,200 fathoms of water, the *Childs* rescued the pilot uninjured. Two VB-12 pilots experienced problems of a different nature, when they proved unable to locate the ship while returning from a search problem. The *Ranger* vectored them to a safe landing at Goleta field, Santa Barbara, California. Fog hampered flight operations the following day.

On 19 December, CVG-12 prepared for its night qualifications. Its pilots carried out 130 day landings with no crashes, but, after sundown, it proved a different matter, as CVG-12 accomplished 53 night landings between the second dog watch and early in the mid watch. It was, as

Curtiss SB2C-3 Helldiver from VB-84 prepares to descend for a landing, 1 December 1944, during CVG-84's carrier qualifications off the California coast. (NA, 80-G-294115)

Captain Gavin later admitted, "one of the most unsuccessful night operations experienced by the USS *Ranger* in night qualification," something attributed to the "haze . . . which tended to blot out the horizon."

VF-12 alone suffered four crashes during that period, the first occurring at 2150, when Ens. William T. McAdams, USNR, took a delayed cut. His F6F-3's tailhook engaged the number seven wire, but the Hellcat (BuNo 43004) went into the barrier, badly bending the nose cowling, bending and scarring the propeller blades, and damaging the engine by the sudden stoppage. Soon thereafter, Ens. Joseph Mangieri, USNR, held off taking the LSO's cut and ended up snagging number nine wire; his F6F-3 (BuNo 41182) charged forward with enough force to end up in number three barrier, bending the prop blades and damaging the engine.[51]

Later in the same watch, Ens. Charles O. McDaniel, USNR, lost sight of the ship's lights, after the moon had gone down and caused a radical change in visibility. McDaniel switched to instruments, but apparently suffered vertigo during the crosswind leg of his approach and flew into the water at 2258. The auxiliary vessel *Kennison* (AG-83) rescued McDaniel unhurt, but the F6F-3 (BuNo 42777) sank out of sight in 1,800 fathoms.[52]

A little less than an hour later, Ens. Sanford W. Brock, USNR, took the LSO's cut, but failed to bring his F6F-3 (BuNo 42818) down onto the deck. The Hellcat floated over the arrestor cables and struck the barrier. As the F6F lurched forward and began to turn over, Brock placed his left hand in front of his face; as the four-ton plane went onto its back, mashing the windshield and cockpit hood

Steaming off the California coast with planes of CVG-84 spotted forward, 1 December 1944. (80-G-294111)

and breaking the gunsight, the weight of the overturned fighter caught the fingers of his left hand between the windshield and the deck, causing the loss of the tips of all except the index finger. Fortunately, Brock had cinched his shoulder harness tight, saving him from further injury, in an accident a trouble board reported as 100% "pilot error" (poor technique).[53] Brock's injuries in time led to his detachment from the squadron.

VF-12's misfortunes continued the following day: during refresher landings during the afternoon watch, Lt. Carleton E. Tobey, USNR, took a high cut to the port side of the groove and overshot the arresting cables. His F6F-3 (BuNo 40458) then slammed into the third and fourth barriers, folding one landing gear leg back into the wing, bending and breaking all propeller blades, badly wrinkling and springing the right stub wing, and breaking the right wing from leading to trailing edges. The trouble board faulted Tobey's technique: he had held off, had been high, and had not lined up his approach.[54]

A cycle of troubles for VF-12 continued during night qualification evolutions, during the first watch on 20 December, beginning when a signalman inadvertently motioned a plane astern of the F6F-3 (BuNo 42989) flown by Lt. (jg) James K. Steel, USNR, into a takeoff spot at 2040: the propeller of the plane astern of Steel's tore off the rudder and damaged both elevators.[55]

A more serious mishap, a sobering reminder of the dangerous occupation engaged in by naval aviators, occurred a little over an hour later, when Ens. Frederick A. Hittel, USNR, radioed the *Ranger* at 2152, reporting engine trouble and requesting an emergency landing. As Hittel's F6F-3 (BuNo 42969) entered the crosswind leg of the approach, observers heard his engine stop. The Hellcat slanted abruptly toward the water and crashed off the *Ranger*'s port quarter, sinking in 1,940 fathoms of water. A search of the area by the *Childs* and the *Kennison* failed to locate any trace of Ensign Hittel, who apparently went down with the plane.[56]

Moments after Hittel's F6F-3 crashed, the ship brought in Lt. James N. Lemon, USNR, of VB-12, who received the LSO's cut and made what looked like a good landing. His tailhook, however, failed to snag a wire, and the SB2C-3 (BuNo 19639) hit the barrier, breaking the left wheel oleo strut and causing engine damage by the sudden stoppage.[57]

After conducting further operations with CVG-12, the *Ranger* paused in her labors over Christmas, spending 23–26 December moored at Pier Fox, NAS San Diego, before she got underway on the latter date to resume day and night work with CVG-12, winding that up during the mid watch on 27 December. She then hosted CVG-98, a replacement air group, for the balance of December, although, at one point, VT-98's unreadiness for night operations caused their qualification landings to be cancelled on the 28th.

On 29 December, CVG-98's planes, flying in relays from North Island, conducted simulated approaches on the ship, but made no landings. Ensign Leonard H. Plog, USNR, of VB-98, made a successful approach in his SB2C-3 (BuNo 18707) and, after taking the waveoff from the LSO, proceeded upwind of the *Ranger*. When his Wright Cyclone, however, began to cut out, Plog turned on the emergency fuel pump and called the ship, telling her that he was in trouble. He acknowledged having plenty of gas, and expressed the belief that the engine would run properly after he had engaged the emergency pump. A few seconds later, however, the Wright cut out entirely, forcing Plog to make a wheels-up landing in the water, where the *McFarland* came to his rescue and picked him up.[58]

28

"SHE DIDN'T NEED HEADLINES TO BE A GREAT SHIP"

At the time that the *Ranger* was engaged in the vital business of training men to take the war to the enemy from the decks of an aircraft carrier, those who contemplated such matters came to decry the inadequacy of carrier qualification training as it was then being conducted. The lack of skill in landing, as evidenced by the new squadrons and pilots joining the fleet in the forward areas, was adversely affecting air operations. Furthermore, the lack of training in night operations imposed tactical restrictions on the operations that could be flown against the enemy. Consequently, in December 1944, Vice Adm. George D. Murray, Commander Air Force, Pacific Fleet, recommended to Adm. Chester W. Nimitz, the Commander in Chief, Pacific Fleet and Pacific Ocean Areas, that a carrier training squadron, composed of two divisions, be formed expressly for the purpose of providing intensive carrier qualification training to air groups and squadrons bound for the forward areas. Murray went on to recommend that one division be based in Hawaiian waters and the other on the West Coast. Such suggestions found fertile ground, leading to the establishment, effective 1 January 1945, of the Carrier Training Squadron, Pacific Fleet. Three days later, Rear Adm. Ralph E. Jennings received his orders to assume command of CarDiv 12.[1]

For the *Ranger*, the year began with a continuation of the routine that had marked her life during previous months. Over the next few months, each cycle of training operations would begin with the slow procession of tractors and planes that would work its way through the streets of North Island toward the pier to which the ship lay moored. As the cavalcade progressed haltingly toward the ship, the public address system on board the carrier would pass the word: "Air Department is to stand by to receive aircraft." One by one, the ship's airplane crane hoisted Hellcats, Avengers, Wildcats, and Helldivers on board, after which the flight deck crews would spot about a dozen on deck for the next day's evolutions. The rest sat below on the hangar deck as spares. The new pilots, with a sprinkling of older combat-experienced lieutenants (jg) or lieutenants to ride herd on them, then came on board over the brow, some awkwardly saluting the colors of a man-of-war for the first time. Inspection of the ship by the newcomers would follow, after which they would eat dinner, see a movie, and get to bed early, to prepare themselves for the business of the morrow.

Designated as the flagship for CarDiv 12, the *Ranger* departed San Diego on 8 January 1945, in company with her old consort, the *McFarland*, bound for Alameda. The *Ranger* logged 28 day landings with CVEG-24 during the afternoon watch that day. The following morning, as the carrier resumed operations with CVEG-24, Lt. Darwin S. Costley, USNR, caught number three wire in his F6F (BuNo 65955), but the purchase cable parted and the Grumman went over the side into 22 fathoms. The *McFarland* recovered Costley uninjured.

After catapulting CVEG-24's planes during the forenoon watch on 10 January, the *Ranger* moored to the carrier pier at Alameda at 1504, but remained there only until the forenoon watch on the 11th, when she returned to the business of carrier qualifications, standing out in company with the *Lawrence* (DD-250). Over the next three days, the *Ranger* qualified pilots of VBF-87, VOC-2, and VC-7. She logged 423 landings, with only four major and four minor barrier crashes; bad weather and heavy seas delayed operations on the 12th. Excessive tailhook bounce resulted in two FM-2s from VOC-2 being sent ashore to North Island to have those items of equipment readjusted.

The day after Rear Admiral Jennings broke his flag as ComCarDiv 12 in the escort carrier *Commencement Bay* (CVE-105), at San Diego, the *Ranger* returned to North Island on the morning of 15 January. There, Capt. Douglass P. Johnson relieved Captain Gavin as commanding officer at 1100. The *Ranger's* new captain had attended Missouri Military Academy and Westminster College, before attending the Naval Academy, and graduated with the USNA Class of 1920. Known to his classmates as "Johnnie," "Dippy" (for his first two initials), or "The Man," Johnson graduated in 1919, because of the accelerated nature of the training during the World War. After initial service in battleships and cruisers, he served in a succession of destroyers, before he served in the battleship *Nevada* (BB-36) and seaplane tender *Wright*.

Designated a naval aviator the day after Christmas of 1922, Johnson instructed at the Naval Academy, and then took part in the developing and testing of the Mark 11 bombsight at the Naval Proving Grounds at Dahlgren, Virginia. Returning to the fleet in 1928, Johnson flew torpedo planes, patrol planes, and battleship-based scout planes. He commanded VT-6, in the air group of the new carrier *Enterprise*, and served as that carrier's air officer from 19 April 1939 to 29 May 1940. Service at the Naval Examining Board followed, after which time he toiled in BuAer. Detached from Washington duty on 8 September 1942, Johnson, having received promotion to commander in July 1941, fitted out, then commanded, Patrol Wing Six, a tour of duty that lasted until his detachment, on 22 November 1943, to report to the new escort carrier *Fanshaw Bay* (CVE-70), then building at the Kaiser yards in Vancouver. A little less than a year later, when a powerful Japanese surface force fell upon the vulnerable CVEs off Samar, during the Battle for Leyte Gulf, Johnson maneuvered the *Fanshaw Bay* with consummate skill "to avoid crippling blows from an enemy surface force vastly superior in numbers, armor, firepower and speed." For his heroism and mastery of his ship during that battle, Johnson was awarded the Navy Cross.

Standing out in company with the *Lawrence* on 16 January, the *Ranger* conducted day training with VOC-2, VC-7, and VC-63, logging 230 landings, but the day also saw the first fatality for the *Ranger* for 1945. At 1404, Lt. Bert F. Walker, flying Z-17, an FM-2 (BuNo 74363), lost flying speed while turning into the groove. The tall-tailed Wildcat spun into 670 fathoms; the *Lawrence*, steaming to attempt rescue, spotted Walker face-down and sinking, but could not reach the scene in time.

Before mooring to the carrier pier at Alameda on the 17th, the *Ranger* accomplished 159 landings with pilots of VOC-2, VC-7, and VC-63. Only the latter squadron did not complete its training, because of a lack of time. Sailing the next day, in company with the *McFarland*, the carrier conducted 195 landings with CVG-5; she accomplished 218 on 19 January, including logging the milestone 58,000th. Two minor barrier crashes resulted in no injuries, and one F4U-1D, the pilot turning up the engine, jumped out of its chocks and chewed up the wing of another Corsair.

Accidents kept the *Ranger's* plane guard busy. During the forenoon watch on the 19th, Lt. (jg) Lloyd J. Milligan, USNR, of VT-5, making a refresher landing in a TBM-3 (BuNo 68698), held off after getting the LSO's cut. Consequently, his Avenger charged through two barriers and careened over the port side. Milligan emerged from the plane unhurt, inflated his rubber boat, and the *McFarland* picked him up less than 15 minutes after he had gone into the water.

Later, during the first dog watch on the 19th, Lt. (jg) Nathan P. Crawford, USNR's SB2C-4 (BuNo 20650) floated up the deck and engaged the forward barriers, on his fourth landing of the day, nosing up and bending all four propeller blades. Crawford's VB-5 squadronmate, Lt. Jack M. Hestilow, USNR, flying an SB2C-4 (BuNo 20268), on his third of six required landings for that flight, took the cut. He ducked for the deck, but failed to land tailwheel first, causing the Helldiver to bounce. Thinking he was still airborne, Hestilow tried to get back down. Because his wheels were already on the deck, the pilot's urgent maneuvers only raised the tail higher; the plane then charged through two barriers, swerved to port, and ended up in the water. The *McFarland* fished Hestilow out of the water in seven minutes.[2]

The next day, 2d Lt. J. E. Stout, USMCR, piloting an F4U-1D, suffered the amputation of a portion of the little finger of his left hand, when his Corsair turned over in the only barrier crash. Apparently, Stout had neglected to keep his hand in the cockpit when the bent-wing Vought turned over.

During the course of conducting 248 day landings and five group rendezvous and break-ups, the *Ranger* logged one major crash on the 21st. Ensign George E. Young, USNR, of VB-5, got the LSO's cut, but veered off to the port side of the flight deck. He caught a wire, but swerved into the catwalk. Young's SB2C-4 (BuNo 20504) suffered class C damage to the aircraft and class B to the engine, resulting from the latter's sudden stoppage.[3]

Before the *Ranger* dropped anchor in San Francisco Bay late in the afternoon of 22 January, she accomplished 74 landings that day, before she detached the *McFarland*. During the first dog watch on the 23d, the *Ranger* shifted to the carrier pier at Alameda, where, the next day, Coxswain John A. Campbell, a member of a working party, tripped on a line while guiding a loaded salmon board. He fell onto a lighter moored alongside, then caromed off into the water, face down and unconscious. Seaman 1st Class Edward J. Gross acted with what a witness described as "uncanny speed and without thought of his own welfare," immediately diving into the narrow strip of water between the ship and the lighter. Providentially, Campbell's body rose to the surface, and Gross turned his shipmate's face upward, out of the water, and sailors on the lighter quickly passed Gross a line to secure around Campbell. Men on board the *Ranger* passed down a salmon board from the hangar deck and hauled both men on board, and soon bore Campbell to sick bay, where the ship's medical people diagnosed a "moderate brain concussion and exposure" and retained him for treatment. Captain Johnson, in recommending Gross for the Silver Life Saving Medal, stressed that "if Gross had not been in the water at the time Campbell first came to the surface, face down and unconscious, Campbell would have drowned. Campbell, unconscious, was obviously helpless and only through the initiative and heroic action on the part of Gross did he manage to survive."[4]

The *Ranger* resumed day air refresher training operations on 26 January, sailing in company with the *McFarland*, to qualify CVEG-40 and VF-5. After a flawless stint (147 landings with no crashes), she launched CVEG-40 to return to its base. She bettered her routine the following

Seaman 1st Class Edward J. Gross (L) and Boatswain's Mate 2d Class John A. Campbell relax on the wing of a General Motors FM-2 Wildcat, ca. March 1945. For saving Campbell's life on 24 January 1945, Gross received the Navy and Marine Corps Medal. (NA, 80-G-337995)

day, logging 167 landings for VF-5 (including the ship's milestone 59,000th) without incident, before catapulting the squadron to return to its base. She returned to the carrier pier at Alameda the next day.

Heavy swells retarded operations when the *Ranger* returned to sea on the 29th, with CVG-1 embarked, for qualifications. With the *McFarland* operating as plane guard, the carrier accomplished 87 landings. As could be expected in the business of training and refreshing pilots, all did not go smoothly. During VBF-1's qualifications, Ens. Vincent L. Landau, USNR, failed to get his tail down when he landed his F4U-1D (BuNo 82296) at 1440, resulting in his hook catching the number nine wire. The Corsair went into the barrier, with consequent damage, leading to Landau's receiving instruction. Later in the day, Lt. Bruce E. Ponton, USNR, brought in his F4U-1D (BuNo 82363) too fast, bouncing and crashing into the island and barrier. Because he had not held the stick all the way aft when landing on board, Ponton received instructions to do that the next time.[5]

The next day, however, the *Ranger* set a new record when she recorded 369 landings in a single day, and, although two major and two minor barrier crashes occurred during that time, no injuries ensued. Ensign Robert J. Speckman, USNR, took a late wave-off in bringing in his F4U-1D (BuNo 82365) during the afternoon watch on 30 January. In getting away, Speckman's Corsair struck the LSO's windscreen with his left flap, partially locking the aileron. A trouble board cited "pilot error" as the cause of the accident.[6] The *Ranger* only logged nine landings the following day, with heavy weather severely curtailing operations.

Low visibility and heavy swells combined to hamper flight operations on 1 February. Late in the forenoon watch, Ens. Leonard L. Hieber, USNR, of VB-1, took a wave-off. Hieber's Helldiver (an SB2C-4, BuNo 19914) suddenly lost power about 200 yards ahead of the ship, at an altitude of 50 feet. Hieber put S-110, its engine smoking, into the water. Soon thereafter, the *McFarland* rescued him none the worse for wear, except for a few bruises.[7]

The *Ranger* launched CVG-1 to return to its base, as the morning watch drew to a close on 2 February, completing the evolution 20 minutes into the forenoon watch. That having been accomplished, the ship anchored in San Francisco Bay. She returned to sea the next morning, with CVG-1, again in company with the *McFarland*, and spent the next few days engaged in qualifying CVG-1 pilots. The carrier logged her 60,000th landing on 5 February.

At 0839 that day, Lt. George Damaskos (A1) USNR, 26 years old, a veteran pilot who had earned an air medal for pressing home an attack on Japanese installations in the Bonins on 4 July 1944, while serving in VB-1, taxied his SB2C-4 (BuNo 18805) out of the spot on the starboard side; the plane director motioned him forward about 20 feet, so that the wings could be spread and the pitot tube cover removed. Damaskos applied his brakes at the director's "stop" signal, but failed to close the throttle. His wheels locked; the Helldiver continued forward, unchecked. As the *Ranger* rolled to port in the seaway, the SB2C skidded from starboard to port, crashing over the catwalk into the stacks with wheels still locked, then plunged into 2,200 fathoms on its back. The *McFarland* and a blimp searched the area without success.

Captain Johnson, inspecting the flight deck immediately after Lieutenant Damaskos's accident, deemed the flight deck condition normal. Consequently, he recommended that blame for the mishap be assessed as 90% pilot error and 5% each to a rolling flight deck and moisture. Those who analyzed the accident in BuAer, however, considered the tragedy to be entirely the fault of the *Ranger*'s flight deck officer and his crew. "Grease and oil," BuAer declared with Olympian finality, "must be removed from [the] deck." In the wake of the accident of 5 February, recommendations were made to remove grease and oil from the flight deck to ensure safe taxiing conditions; for the chock puller to follow the plane to its takeoff spot and be ready to chock the plane at any time an emergency arises, and that plane handlers, when directing aircraft on a wet deck, should exercise special caution.[8]

Lieutenant Richard B. Eason, USNR, of VBF-1 took his cut from the LSO, but dove for the deck shortly before the end of the forenoon watch on 5 February. Consequently, his F4U-1D (BuNo 82360) hit the deck very hard, smashing the tail wheel structure. The film of grease and oil on the flight deck, however, when coupled with a rolling ship, spelled trouble again—although not with tragic consequences—about 10 minutes after Eason's mishap. Ensign Bain S. Allen, USNR, flying an SB2C-4 (BuNo 20678), took the cut from the LSO. His Helldiver landed on the port side of the flight deck and swerved into the catwalk. Investigators later leveled part of the blame for the accident on the inexperience of the pilot, but also faulted the LSO for his giving Allen the cut, although he was in a bad position to do so, being lined up with the port side of the deck. "[The] LSO should try to have planes in better positions before giving cuts," one observer recommended, "especially in cases where pilots are trying to qualify." BuAer analysts ultimately assessed the blame for Ensign Allen's mishap to pilot error (50%), as well as "other personnel" (in this case, the LSO) (25%) and "miscellaneous" (grease and oil on the rolling deck) (25%).

Later, Ens. David L. Ayres, USNR, brought in his F4U-1D (BuNo 82365) (the same Corsair in which Ensign Speckman had experienced his mishap less than a week before) a little past the mid point in the afternoon watch. Waved off, Ayres banked sharply, but his port wing hit the ramp. The bent-wing bird went over the side, out of control, and cartwheeled into the water, breaking up on impact. Neither lookouts on board the *Ranger* nor men on board the *McFarland* saw Ayres emerge, as the broken Corsair sank out of sight into 2,160 fathoms.[9]

The *Ranger* returned to San Francisco Bay during the forenoon watch on the 6th, and shifted to the carrier pier at Alameda the next afternoon. Underway again on 8 February, again in company with the *McFarland*, during the second dog watch, she was to conduct day training operations en route to San Diego. She took to sea the remnants of CVG-1 and VC-63, along with two other composite squadrons, VC-33 and VC-41. She accomplished 257 landings on 9 February, launching VBF-1 and VF-1 to return to their shore bases, logged the same number of landings on the 10th, and returned all groups to their shore bases on the 11th. She brought that stint of training to an end when she moored at NAS San Diego during the forenoon watch on 12 February.

The *Ranger* returned to sea two days later, this time with CVLG-49 and a marine squadron, with the *McFarland* again along as plane guard. She logged 140 landings on 14 February, before worsening weather forced her to vector 9 airborne F6Fs to San Nicholas Island, about three-quarters of an hour into the second dog watch. Worsening weather to the southwest also closed in the escort carrier *Block Island* (CVE-106), which was operating Marine Carrier Air Group 1. The *Ranger* aided in locating and vectoring 12 planes from the *Block Island* to safety at San Nicholas, although 7 crashed in the foul weather. Eight Marine aviators died.[10]

The pace of operations, however, continued unabated. The next day, 15 February, proved busy, as the *Ranger* carried out 227 landings, including her 61,000th. She recovered the 7 F6Fs sent to San Nicholas, and sent out a 12-plane search that scoured the sea for signs of the *Block Island*'s lost planes, until she received word that all had been accounted for. And, as had happened at other times in the *Ranger*'s career, Marine aviators sometimes had just as much trouble as their Navy counterparts in bringing their planes on board. Captain R. H. Ross, USMCR, of VMF-351, dipped the nose of his F4U-1D (BuNo 57178), after taking the cut, and ended up in the barrier. Fifteen minutes later, Maj. C. B. Brewer, USMC, of the Headquarters and Service Squadron of Marine Aircraft Service Group 48, landed his F4U-1C (BuNo 82289) in a skid, shearing off the entire tailwheel assembly. Still later, 2d Lt. F. T. Watts, USMCR, of VMF-512 took a late cut and engaged the number eight wire in his F4U-1D (BuNo 57281). He ended up in the barrier, too. Subsequently, the *Ranger*'s air officer grounded both Captain Ross and 2d Lieutenant Watts "for further training in field carrier landings," but concluded that further experience would correct Major Brewer's technique (the LSO had noted two previous "unusually hard" landings that day).[11]

"Miss Fortune" resumed her acquaintance with the leathernecks the next morning. Second Lt. Edward C. Groves, USMCR, of VMF-512, landed his F4U-1D (BuNo 57293) hard, nosing over, with the stress of the landing buckling the fuselage.[12] That proved to be the only mishap over an 11-hour span, in which the *Ranger* accomplished 324 landings and 57 catapult shots that day. The following day, she wound up that stint of operations, returning CVEG-49 and the Marines to their respective home bases, before she herself returned to Pier Fox at San Diego.

The *Ranger*, with the *McFarland* and the *Hulbert* in company, operated VB-98 and VT-98 between 20 and 22 February, conducting day refresher and night qualification training off San Clemente Island. During the mid watch on 21 February, Ens. Raymond P. Duffin, USNR, of VB-98, making his first night carrier landing, came over the *Ranger*'s ramp "a little fast," but, after receiving the LSO's cut, held off landing and crashed into the barrier. The SB2C-4 (BuNo 20415) nosed up, the engine broke loose from its mounts, and the Helldiver caught fire. Duffin exited the plane without injury, but BuNo 20415 burned for almost 20 minutes, until the flight deck crew extinguished the blaze.[13]

Later that same day, during the first watch, Duffin, flying another SB2C-4 (BuNo 20468), took the cut and settled the Helldiver onto the deck in what "should have been a good landing." Gremlins, however, seemed to be dogging the determined Ensign Duffin that day: his tailhook failed to engage either the number three or number four wires. The SB2C bounced into the barrier, where the engine tore loose from the rest of the plane in the impact of the crash, and, in what must have triggered an eerie feeling of déjà vu on Duffin's part, caught fire. This time, however, the *Ranger*'s flight deck crew needed only five minutes to gain the upper hand. Duffin again exited his burning bomber unscathed.[14]

The ensuing trouble board noted Duffin's poor technique and lack of experience in the first instance, deeming the accident 100% pilot error, but wrote of an error in judgment and lack of experience, coupled with the failure of the arresting device, in the second. "Accidents of this nature will happen during night carrier qualifications," the board allowed in the first instance, and recommended that sand bags be placed in the SB2C-4's rear seat during carrier qualifications, believing "that many of the barrier crashes that have occurred in this plane could have been prevented if the normal weight had been provided for the rear seat."[15] In the wake of the third SB2C crash of the day on 21 February, when Lieutenant (jg) Donald L. Dunklee, USNR's mount, BuNo 19836, went into a barrier, the trouble board reprised its recommendation to put a sand bag in the rear cockpit.[16]

After a brief respite alongside North Island, the *Ranger* returned to sea on the morning of 24 February, in company with the *McFarland* and the destroyer seaplane tender *Childs*, this time with VBF-98 embarked for day refresher and night qualification flights. That day, she logged her 62,000th landing, which occurred among the 49 night landings. The following day, 25 February, the *Ranger* recovered Lt. (jg) Howard A. Barron, in a successful night emergency recovery; an inspection of the engine of Barron's Hellcat revealed only two bolts were holding on one cylinder to the crankcase.

Significantly, a short exercise conducted during a period of full moonlight by the *Ranger* operations in February demonstrated the practicability of giving each pilot the two required night landings under carefully controlled and fully favorable conditions. From that point on, CarDiv 12 continued the practice of qualifying the maximum number of pilots in nocturnal operations. The success of those operations on board the *Ranger*, together with the "eventual necessity for nearly all pilots to land aboard [sic] at night" prompted Rear Admiral Jennings to insist upon planning the operations of CarDiv 11, operating out of Pearl, so that each pilot could have at least two night landings under his belt before he left for combat duty in the forward areas.[17]

The *Ranger*, with CVEG-98 and VF-49 embarked, returned to sea during the afternoon watch on 1 March, again in company with the *McFarland* and the *Childs*. VF-49's operations proceeded flawlessly during the first and second dog watches the first day out, and only one minor barrier crash marred CVG-98's evolutions on 2 March, in which the *Ranger* logged 182 landings.

During the course of the 301 landings logged on 3 March, Ens. Elmer L. Kearns of VBF-98 made a bad landing: his F4U-1D crashed into the barrier and somersaulted onto its back. Kearns suffered an intercranial injury and abrasion of his right elbow in the mishap; the *Ranger*'s medical people retained him in sick bay for observation.

Two of Ensign Kearns' shipmates in VBF-98, Ens. John C. Kugler, USNR, and Lt. Edward W. Austermuehle, flying F4U-1Ds (BuNos 82238 and 82258, respectively), figured in the minor deck crashes that the *Ranger* logged the following day, during her 199 landing evolutions. In each case, recommendations ensued to provide pilots with more practice ashore before they were sent them to sea.[18]

The relentless march of training continued over the days that followed, as the *Ranger* carried out 329 landings on the 5th (including the ship's 63,000th), 264 on the 6th, and 137 on the 7th before she returned to Pier Fox at NAS San Diego during the first watch on 7 March. During that time, both the *McFarland* and the *Childs* accompanied her at the outset; the former had to return to port with a sick man on 4 March, then relieved the *Childs* of plane guard duties the following morning.

Returning to sea on 10 March in company with the destroyer *Stormes* (DD-780), the *Ranger* operated CVLG-32 remnants and VBF-2 during the afternoon and the first and second dog watches, logging 136 landings with no crashes, and 48 catapult shots.

The following morning saw Ens. Avery Thatcher, Jr., USNR, of VF-32, come in "rather high and a bit fast," an hour and a half into the forenoon watch and, in answering the LSO's cut, landed hard on his wheels. His F6F-3 (BuNo 66234) bounced, clearing two barriers and hitting a third. Swerving to starboard, Thatcher's Hellcat crashed into the island and lurched to a stop, resting partially in the catwalk, with a broken prop and with both wings and landing gear damaged.[19]

Ensign Thatcher emerged from his battered Hellcat without injury, but providence seemed absent when 21-year-old Ens. Milton G. Alberts, USNR, of VBF-2, came in, in his F4U-1D (BuNo 57649), about two hours after the VF-32 pilot's barrier crash. Alberts approached the ship at a slow speed, prompting the LSO to wig-wag "come on" repeatedly. When Alberts seemed unresponsive, the LSO immediately waved him off. Instead of adding throttle before the maneuver, however, Alberts pulled his Corsair's nose up, causing the F4U to begin to spin to the left, and the plane crashed low against the port side of the ramp. The fuselage broke aft of the cockpit and fell into the water, disappearing into 830 fathoms inside of 15 seconds. A one-hour search recovered neither plane nor pilot.[20]

As the Pacific war had progressed toward its third anniversary, and the *Ranger* had been training pilots, attacks by Japanese planes, whose pilots approached at wave-top level, then climbed to initiate diving kamikaze attacks with devastating effect, had prompted desperate measures to combat them. Radars mounted on the mastheads of ships could only detect the inbound raiders at ranges between 30 and 35 miles, and picket patrols of planes or ships could only identify the inbound enemy visually. Although the suicide plane threat, from October 1944 on had prompted the study of "airborne early warning," the genesis of the concept lay in the efforts, initiated in 1942, to develop a radar-relay system, to allow task force commanders to obtain information beyond the range of shipboard radars.[21]

Although established in June 1942, with research conducted principally by the Massachusetts Insitute of Technology-Radiation Laboratory (MIT-RL), progress on the radar-relay project, designated as NA-112, moved along slowly. Eventually, BuAer's Comdr. Lloyd V. Berkner, Head of Research and Development of Electronics Material, advocated work on putting radar aloft in a plane would provide optimum warning capability. Consequently, Project NA-178 came into being, eventually evolving into Project Cadillac (for the mountain in Maine, site of early avionics testing for the system—not for the automobile). Soon, ComInCh accorded work on a system that could detect a single low-flying plane up to reliable ranges at 65 miles, or groups of six or more at reliable ranges of up to 125, and to pick up ships the size of destroyers at reliable ranges of 200, and to present that information to a shipboard information center the "highest priority... in order to increase the effective search and intercept range of the Fleet."[22]

Airborne early warning (AEW) allowed early detection of enemy ships and low-flying planes far beyond the horizon of existing shipboard radar sets, by utilizing a high-powered microwave radar in a carrier-based plane that could transmit the information back to a ship by a radar relay. A plane flying at an altitude of 5,000 feet could search within a 100-mile radius out to the horizon of the plane, not of the ship. Flying at 20,000 feet permitted the airborne radar-equipped aircraft to extend the plane's horizon to 200 miles and search an area of 125,000 square miles. The method also allowed the extension of communications and IFF (identification, friend or foe). Work on a "roomy and robust airframe" to accommodate the MIT-RL-designed APS-20 radar soon proceeded apace, with General Motors-produced Avengers (TBMs), a "combat tested [and] . . . readily available" aircraft.[23]

After the *Ranger* wound up a stint of carrier qualifications on 12 March, logging 166 landings (including the ship's 64,000th), and, flying off VBF-2 to its base, she returned to North Island, arriving during the afternoon watch on 13 March. The *Ranger*'s respite alongside Pier Fox proved brief, however; she soon shifted to the Naval Repair Base, San Diego, early in the first dog watch, mooring alongside Pier 5 to commence a 10-day limited availability, to permit installation of shipborne equipment and maintenance facilities for AEW gear—approximately six tons of equipment that required compensatory weight removal. In keeping with the priority ComInCh had assigned the project, and the future importance of AEW to the postwar fleet, OpNav desired that the installation of the gear in the *Ranger* "simulate, as nearly as practicable, the installation to go into the CV9 [*Essex*] Class carriers."[24]

Returning to Pier Fox on 25 March, following that period of yard work, the *Ranger* sailed during the forenoon watch two days later, in company with the *McFarland* and the *Childs,* to conduct day qualification and refresher training

Grumman TBM-3W, such as those used during tests of Cadillac equipment. (AUTHOR)

with CVG-98, operations she conducted for the balance of the month, embarking "remnants" of VBF-14 and VF-2 on 31 March. The following day, Ens. C. S. Rouillard, USNR, of VF-2, flying an F6F-5 (BuNo 70628), took the cut, but made a skidding landing. Although he had snagged number four wire, Rouillard's tailhook pulled out and the Hellcat went over the side into the water. Although the Grumman sank in 300 fathoms, the *McFarland* picked up Rouillard uninjured. Later that day, Lt. (jg) K. G. Harris, USNR, flying an SB2C-4E (BuNo 65110), took the cut, but, when, he dropped the nose, saw that he was off center, on the port side of the deck. Banking right to line up on the centerline, he held off too long and ended up in the barrier.[25]

Winding up her operations with VF-2 on 3 April, the *Ranger* qualified VC-5 pilots on 4 and 5 April, and embarked CVG-98 on 9 April. A little over a half hour into the afternoon watch, in one of the 37 catapult launchings accomplished that day, Ens. Kenneth J. Carr, USNR, suffered engine failure six minutes after launch; he made a slightly nose-down landing in a very rough sea. His F4U-1D (BuNo 82254) sank in about 15 seconds in 120 fathoms, carrying Carr with it. The *Childs* immediately searched the area without success, aided later by a blimp.

Carrier qualifications the following day saw Ens. Victor C. Ideus, USNR, of VB-98, take the cut, at 1145. Ideus, who had been instructed about keeping the tail down after landing, failed to do so. Consequently, his SB2C-4E (BuNo 19827) missed all of the cross-deck pendants and crashed into the barrier, causing damage to the prop and the engine. The resulting trouble board faulted pilot error in the young flier's judgment and technique.[26]

Pilot error of a different sort figured in another VB-98 mishap the next morning, when Ens. Irwin E. Melton, USNR, thoroughly indoctrinated in the LSO's signals, received the cut, but missed the first four wires. Melton disobeyed standing orders, however, and opted to try to take off, thus giving himself a wave-off. Going beyond the first barrier, he tried to keep his SB2C-4E off the deck, but ended up shearing off the starboard landing gear on the forward gun tub. Managing to keep BuNo 20097 flying, the young pilot recovered just above the wavetops and regained a safe flying altitude, finally making an emergency landing without injury to himself. When in doubt, Melton was later told, try to hit the barrier at the center of the deck to minimize damage to the plane.[27] Disciplinary action followed.

The *Ranger* next qualified CVG-14 pilots in midmonth, operating with the *Hulbert* and the *Ballard*. Operations with that group did not proceed wholly without incident, being hampered by bad weather on 18 and 19 April. On 20 April, Ens. F. D. Frazer, USNR, responded to the LSO's high and fast signals and took the cut at the ramp. Nosing over, Frazer made a wheels-first landing: The SB2C-4 (BuNo 19862) bounced over the wires and into the barrier, taking damage to engine, prop, wings, landing gear, and control surfaces. The trouble board faulted the pilot for his inexperience and poor technique, but also blamed a part of the accident on the LSO, for giving Frazer the cut when he had been in a poor position to receive it.[28]

CVG-98 returned to the *Ranger* for more seasoning on 26 April. Outside of the occasional deck crashes, deemed major or minor, depending upon the circumstances, operations proceeded mostly without incident. On the afternoon of 28 April, however, a 10-plane flight took off from Los Alamitos, California, to fly out to the *Ranger* for night qualifications. An experienced pilot, Lt. (jg) Nathan Marx, USNR, was flying in a two-plane section when he developed engine trouble about 25 miles from San Nicolas Island and turned back toward San Nicolas. His wingman, Ensign Patterson, followed, advising the division leader as to the situation, and last saw Marx's SB2C-4 flying into a dense bank of fog. A subsequent search failed to locate any trace of the SB2C-4 (BuNo 19838) or of Lt. (jg) Marx or his passenger, Ensign Melton, the pilot who had managed to keep his plane under control and make a safe landing after giving himself the waveoff, a little over a fortnight before. The subsequent investigation submitted that the dense fog into which Marx had flown had prevented a successful ditching, and the Helldiver had crashed, killing pilot and passenger.[29] The bad weather in the vicinity of the ship resulted in night operations being cancelled.

Two days later, Ens. Harvey R. Collins, Jr., USNR, coming on board during the morning watch, took the LSO's cut, but, although he had been warned repeatedly to "fly the plane to [the] center of the deck after [the] cut," he continued up the starboard side, catching number seven wire. Unfortunately, the run-out of the pendant permitted Collins's SB2C-4 (BuNo 20476) to hit the island with enough force to twist the fuselage, so that it broke aft of the second cockpit, and cracked at the pilot's cockpit, and tore both wings loose. A trouble board faulted the pilot's technique and judgment in an accident that resulted in class A damage.[30]

The *Ranger*'s participation in the Cadillac tests proceeded apace during May, as did further carrier qualification trials for the Ryan XFR-1 Fireball, an interceptor fighter designed for operation from escort carriers, and the "first application of jet propulsion to Navy fighters with four .50-caliber guns."[31] On 3 May, the *Ranger* logged 306 landings, 13 catapult shots, 11 XFR-1 landings, and 1 Cadillac flight.

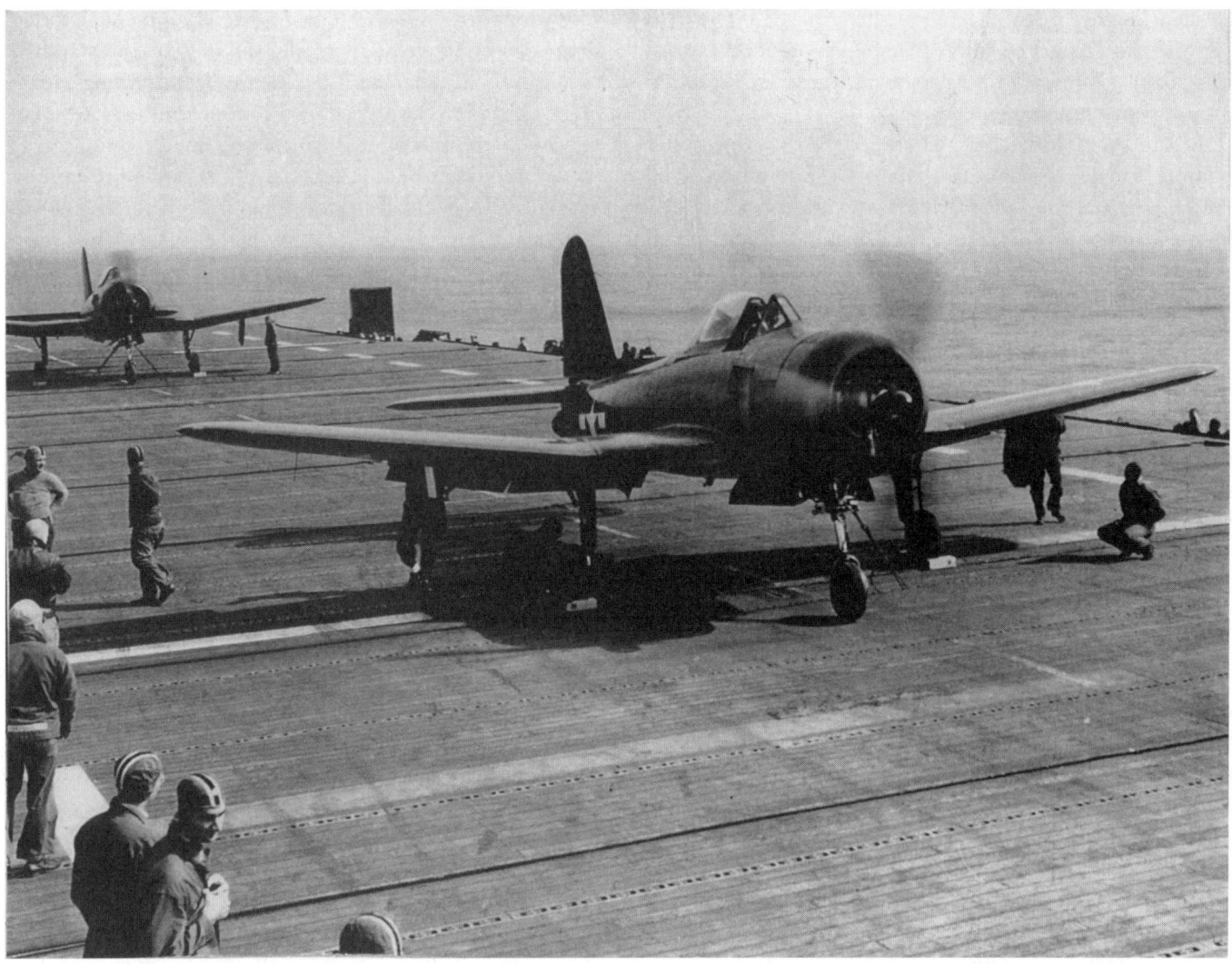

Two Ryan FR-1 Fireballs warm up aft on the flight deck during carrier trials, May 1945. (NA, 80-G-1053774)

Pilots who flew the revolutionary new fighter, which had undergone its initial carrier trials on board the escort carrier *Charger* (CVE-30), found it to be "easily flyable with no unusual characteristics in normal flight," and noted that forward engine power settings approximated that of the FM-2 Wildcat. With the jet turbine in operation, fliers found that the Fireball displayed "unusually high performance," especially in the area of rate of climb, and found that it could climb over 5,000 feet per minute, as well as in straight and level flight. Although fliers found the Fireball "extremely easy to land, with "no bounce tendencies at around 80 knots," they did not like the "feel" of the plane at low speeds, reporting that the controls tended to tighten up and that it was hard to maintain a turn.[32] Flight deck crews found the plane easy to spot on the deck—much more readily than conventional aircraft: with the center of gravity aft on the Fireball, the handling crew could pull the tail down and wheel the XFR-1 around as if it were a two-wheeled dolly.

Even as the *Ranger* was participating in significant research and development, her own ability to perform continued to come under scrutiny, with an eye toward better her capabilities. To improve the *Ranger's* stability and to advance the ship's weight removal program, Captain Johnson recommended that the splinter shields and that part of the forward and after 5-inch gun platforms that constituted an overhang outboard of the ship's hull structure, be removed. Johnson reasoned that, because the guns had been removed, removal of the platforms upon which the weapons had been installed would result in the reduction of some 37 tons. "This alteration," Johnson declared, "increases the power of survival and performance of the ship under various forms of attack or other hazards to which it might be exposed and will permit accomplishment of many highly desirable minor alterations," and would improve the *Ranger*'s stability "in anticipation of heavy topside loading present during missions involving ferrying planes, personnel, and equipment."[33]

Before such work could be undertaken, however, her training operations continued unabated. Accompanied by the *Hulbert* and the *Ballard*, the *Ranger* next operated VC-68 on 7 and 8 May, the latter day's operations punctuated by Ens. William A. J. Fredette, USNR, making a normal approach, but slightly low and to the right of the groove. Waved off, Fredette quickly—too quickly, as it turned out—applied full throttle, only to have the TBM-3E (BuNo 85858) settle, and go over the side. A subsequent trouble board not only faulted the pilot, who later qualified successfully, but also the LSO for not giving him a wave-off much sooner, before being in a quandry of whether to wave him off or give him the cut.[34]

The *Ranger* operated CVG-98 between 10 and 13 May, interspersing that group's work with Cadillac flights, again plane-guarded by the *Hulbert* and the *Ballard*. Ensign J. K. Thompson of VT-98 made a bad landing on 10 May: His TBM-3E (BuNo 56122) ended up crashing into the after end of the island, in a mishap that a trouble board later attributed partly to the LSO's giving him the cut when he should have waved him off. Ensign A. G. Stamm, USNR, reprised Thompson's mistake the next day, when he, too, made a bad landing and ended up with his TBM-3E (BuNo 86177) in the island. In Stamm's case, however, the trouble board leveled all of the blame on his poor technique.[35]

Even the Cadillac aircraft were not immune from mishaps. Lieutenant Comdr. Hildreth V. Anderson, USNR, who had been officer-in-charge of the radome section of the Naval Aircraft Factory between October 1942 and April 1944, noticing raw gasoline spurting all over the cockpit from the left side and oil streaming out of the engine cowling, reported a fuel and oil leak soon after takeoff during the first dog watch on 12 May. Making a normal downwind approach, Anderson began to lose altitude. As he shaped a straight course for the stern, his APS-20-equipped TBM-3W (BuNo 22857) began to sag toward the water; the LSO persistently signalled "low" and "slow." About 300 yards astern, the big-bellied Avenger, at about 35 feet altitude, spun to the left and crashed into the water in an almost inverted attitude. Anderson suffered a concussion, abrasions, and lacerations in the crash; his passengers, Lts. John L. Friesberg and Donald H. Smith, USNR, both survived uninjured.

Anderson's crash, however, proved the exception to the rule. Cadillac test flights continued into mid-June. "Much of the data from these early tests aboard the *Ranger* . . . proved very promising" for the project. The equipment detected single-plane targets at twice the distance of the standard mast-mounted radar, and it picked up approaching multi-plane formations at ranges "two to four times greater than previously feasible, while [it increased] the detection range of surface vessels by a factor of six." Those improvements "in radar range and detection times," by themselves, justified further development of AEW planes.[36] The application of Cadillac planes "eventually revolutionized naval warfare. By lifting a search radar into the air, the task force commander could now see all radar contacts within attacking radius and could pursue options to engage them. No longer . . . dependent on the visual search patterns of patrol or search aircraft. One AEW radar could track several contacts by itself without being susceptible to weather or cloud formations." Heartened by the success of Cadillac, the Navy continued its work on AEW concepts in the postwar period.[37] As she had done in other areas earlier in her career—cold weather operations and the development of director-controlled antiaircraft gunnery in carriers—the *Ranger* had performed an important role.

In the meantime, despite her advancing age, the *Ranger* continued to be exemplary. Four hundred and eighty landings recorded on 15 May 1945 set a record, prompting Rear Adm. Alfred E. Montgomery, on 23 May, to accord his old ship special recognition, as he commended her "consistently excellent performance." Records of that nature, Montgomery wrote, "are achieved by good organization, persistent hard work, and capable leadership. The paramount mission of the USS *Ranger* is to produce large numbers of well-trained carrier pilots in the shortest possible time. The USS *Ranger* has conclusively demonstrated her ability to fulfill this mission to utmost satisfaction and has thereby made a direct and indispensable contribution to the training effort." That having been written, Admiral Montgomery concluded with "Well done, *Ranger*."[38]

That was not to say, however, that such work proceeded flawlessly: the barrier crashes (both major and minor) and hard landings continued as part and parcel of training pilots to perform their demanding trade. Among the units the *Ranger* embarked, as the spring and summer went on, was CVG-18, which had been reformed in the wake of its successful war operations on board the *Intrepid* (CV-11). VF-18 went on board the *Ranger* for carrier qualifications on 22 May. VB-18 followed on 27 June. VBF-18 returned to San Diego, meanwhile, and devoted the ensuing weeks to field carrier landing practice, interspersing "bounce drill" with navigation, fighter direction, and tactics. Such training yielded dividends. Embarking in the *Ranger* on 14 July, the last of CVG-18's squadrons to go to sea for carrier

Captain Douglass P. Johnson (C) congratulates Maj. Francis E. Pierce, Jr., USMC (R), who has just made the 75,000th landing, 14 July 1945. Pierce held the Navy Cross for heroism in aerial combat off New Georgia in January 1943; his father had won a Navy Cross in Nicaragua in 1928. Commander Glenn W. Okerson (L), the air officer, won the Bronze Star for heroism as flight deck officer in the *Natoma Bay* (CVE-62) off Samar, the same battle in which Captain Johnson had commanded the *Fanshaw Bay* (CVE-70). (NA, 80-G-337998)

qualifications, VBF-18 "disembarked [on 16 July] with the finest record of any squadron on board that ship," conducting flawless landing operations (only a blown tire as the plane pushers took an F6F back to the elevator, after completing the last flight of the day, marred an otherwise perfect stint), but breaking the "speed record for qualifying pilots with 72 landings in 60 minutes." The squadron would have bettered its own mark, its historian later crowed, "when one flight made 60 landings in 45 minutes" (a pace that would have allowed 80 landings per hour), "but the flight had only 60 landings to make."³⁹

V-J Day, 14 August 1945, the day President Harry Truman announced the cessation of hostilities with Japan, found the *Ranger* moored to Pier Fox, NAS San Diego. Even though the war was over, the *Ranger* resumed her training operations one week later, on 21 August. Indicative of the coming demobilization, in the aftermath of the end of the conflict, the Navy's point system allowed the first draft of 33 men from the *Ranger* on 29 August to be eligible for their discharge to return to civilian life.

Early in the forenoon watch on 5 September, Ens. James M. Cady, USNR, of VBF-80, had made two successful landings during carrier landing practice (six the previous day), but he took an incomplete "cut" sign from the LSO, held off, then floated into the barrier. His FG-1D Corsair (BuNo 92109) consequently caught number two barrier with its wheels and flipped over, Ensign Cady receiving minor contusions about the head and face. The mishap resulted in a broken fuselage, tail section, and cockpit enclosure for his plane, as well as an engine damaged by the sudden stoppage.⁴⁰

How much longer would the *Ranger* train pilots? An informal board, convened on 7 September on postwar naval aviation training, had recommended that all carrier qualifications be conducted at Pensacola. Rear Adm. Charles A. Pownall, Chief of the Naval Air Training Command, believed that the *Ranger* could be "most advantageously and economically employed" in connection with carrier qualifications with North American SNJ aircraft. He believed her to be "ideally adapted [for] such duty," citing her "ample deck space, [the] relative lack of deck obstructions, fast deck operations." In addition, the *Ranger* held a speed advantage over a CVE, was of light draft, was maneuverable, and was economical to operate. All of the foregoing factors, he believed, tended to "increase safety of operations, insure continuity of training, [and the] availability of ship and aircraft." In addition, Pownall considered "early familiarization with [a] fleet type CV...highly desirable for all trainees." He believed that Pensacola could handle the *Ranger*, and thus requested "strongly" that ComInCh consider assigning the ship to the Training Command, when released from "present duties."

By the end of September, Captain Johnson had finally received a response to his alteration request dated 3 May. Although ComAirPac, ComServPac, and BuOrd had all weighed in, approving the request, BuShips turned it down, because "it is indicated that the U.S.S. *Ranger* will not be a unit of the post war fleet." The proverbial handwriting was on the wall.[41]

The *Ranger* sailed an hour into the forenoon watch on 27 September, in company with the *Breckenridge* (DD-148) and the *Childs*, to conduct day qualification landings with CVG-18 and CVEG-41. In addition, the *Ranger* also embarked Mayor Knox of San Diego and 17 news correspondents, to witness carrier operations of the FR-1s. During the afternoon watch and into the second dog watch, the carrier conducted flawless flight operations, logging 114 landings with no crashes. For Bombing Fighter Squadron (VBF) 18, however, poor weather conditions had resulted in full qualification for 22 of the 28 pilots that had gone to sea, and in partial qualification for the other 6. "Considering the small amount of time the pilots had in the [Grumman] F8F[-1]," VBF-18's chronicler wrote, "the results were quite gratifying as no planes were in any way damaged."[42]

Departing San Diego, with CVG-18 embarked (the F8F-1-equipped VBF-18 and VF-18; the TBM-equipped VT-18, and a planeless VB-18), on 30 September, in company with the *Hulbert* and the *McFarland* ("two DE's [*sic*] of ancient origin," a VBF-18 passenger wrote later, "so progress was very slow"[43]). Only one mishap marred the voyage, on 4 October, when Lt. (jg) Edwin Stouffer, Jr., USNR, of VF-18, in his second carrier landing in a Bearcat, dipped the nose after taking the LSO's cut. To prevent landing on his wheels, however, Stouffer pulled back the stick completely, resulting in his F8F-1 (BuNo 94829) hitting tail first (breaking the tailwheel assembly), but engaging number seven wire. The impact of the rough landing buckled both sides of the fuselage, and wrinkled both wings. The resulting trouble board faulted the pilot's judgment (60%), as well as his poor technique (40%).[44]

After detaching the *Hulbert* and the *McFarland* (the latter developed a slow leak in one boiler and had to slow to 12 knots, a little after the end of the mid watch on 8 October), the *Ranger* reached Balboa on 9 October. The local USO conducted historical tours during the day, and "various night clubs offered numerous forms of entertainment" in Panama City at night. Underway again a little less than three-quarters of an hour into the morning watch on 11 October, the *Ranger* transited the Panama Canal at the head of Task Force 11, and proceeded independently for New Orleans, her passengers aware of their destination for the first time. "The trip through the Panama Canal was outstanding," Lt. Comdr. George W. Bishop, Jr., USNR, CVG-18's administrative officer, reflected, "with the Air Group admiring seamanship at its best, as the *Ranger* continued on its [her] way with at times a centimeter of clearance to the good."[45] The *Ranger* proved to be a good host as well, as one member of VB-18 observed graciously: "The conditions aboard [*sic*] the *Ranger* were very conducive to a pleasurable trip."[46]

Launching 45 Grumman F8F-1 Bearcats (VBF-18 and VF-18) and 15 TBM-1C Avengers (VT-18) on the afternoon of the 15th, to fly into NAS New Orleans, when she had reached a point approximately 100 miles from the Crescent City, the *Ranger* reached her destination the following afternoon, mooring to the Bienville Street dock. Despite the limited facilities for aircraft maintenance, CVG-18 and the NAS people prepared the group for the scheduled Navy Day air show on 27 October. The local press received the exhibition of flying "with great enthusiasm," and the squadron's "groundlings," reported "a like feeling on the part of the populace," as the F8Fs and TBMs flew "V", columns, and capped the show with a simulated attack on the carrier.[47] Open for general visiting during the 20–28 October period, the *Ranger* hosted 102,739 visitors, 24,728 of them on Navy Day alone.

With the detachment at New Orleans of 157 officers and 113 men of CVG-18 on 29 October, the *Ranger* departed New Orleans for Pensacola the following morning, launching Lt. John Paskoski, Ralph H. Beatle, and Raymond G. Clemons in three F8Fs that afternoon to fly to NAS New Orleans, flying them off while she was underway in the Mississippi, in what Lieutenant Commander Bishop "believed to be the first Navy carrier take-off from a river."[48] Securing from flight quarters at 1325, the *Ranger* dismissed

Transiting the Panama Canal for the last time, 11 October 1945. (NA, 80-G-360552)

the Coast Guard patrol boat *CG-83492*, her plane guard, soon thereafter.

CVG-18, too, took leave of New Orleans, bound for Norfolk, the ground support people traveling by train, the rest flying the group's planes to its new base. "Perhaps the old French city was left behind," Lieutenant Commander Bishop recollected, "but as we looked out the coach windows, the memories returned: The Court of Two Sisters, Antoine's, Arnaud's, The Fountain Lounge of the Roosevelt, O'Brien's, The Old Absinthe House, The French Quarter, New Orleans' sea food, and coffee, and ------- .' By this time the Air Group could be taken for The New Orleans Chamber of Commerce in uniform."[49] "Fully exposed to southern hospitality," VBF-18's people had attended "many parties, dances and luncheons" during the course of their visit to the Crescent City.[50]

Reaching Pensacola on 31 October, the *Ranger* underwent a material inspection on 2 November, to determine her suitability for carrier qualification training. Three days later, Commodore Lester T. Hundt, Commander Naval Air Training Bases, Pensacola, came on board to look over the ship, as did Rear Admiral Pownall, who had enthusiastically backed the ship's assignment to the Training Command.

The material inspection, conducted for the most part by officers from the escort carrier *Guadalcanal* (CVE-60), revealed that the condition of the *Ranger*'s main condensers limited her to 20 knots. It also revealed that the flight deck planking in a considerable portion of the landing area had been worn to one-half the original thickness; the resultant wood softening and flaking had been responsible for a number of instances of hook failure during landings. In addition, one compartment, A601-W, had a leak necessitating the application of a cement-filled box patch. Leakage around the rudder post indicated the advisability of an early drydocking.

Consequently, Rear Admiral Pownall reported to CinCLant that Captain Johnson had estimated that the *Ranger* could be operated successfully for about two months before Navy yard repairs became imperative, and that her present condition limited her to SNJ landings only. In view of the carrier qualification program carried out from NAS Pensacola, the survey considered comprehensive repairs "well suited" for the ship. Pownall recommended that the *Ranger* be given an early Navy Yard availability, because carrier qualification requirements would soon be intensified, when the carrier qualification training unit at Saufley Field would commence operations about mid-January 1946, under the new syllabus.

Because of Charleston Naval Shipyard's recent request of CinCLant to have structural work assigned to it, Capt. Hugh P. Webster, speaking for CinCLant, called Capt. Benjamin P. Ward, the yard's production officer, on the afternoon of 9 November, and asked if it could handle the *Ranger*'s overhaul. Webster added that the carrier required a drydocking, however, as well as renewal of her flight deck. Ward stated that the yard "would like very much to have" the *Ranger* job, but the size of Charleston's largest drydock, 622 feet in length, meant that all work except drydocking could be accomplished, because the *Ranger*'s 769-foot length could not be accommodated there. Captain Webster countered that would not prove economical, since the *Ranger*'s schedule did not permit her to be shifted from one yard to another.[51] The following day, CinCLant ordered that the *Ranger* be directed to proceed to the Philadelphia Naval Shipyard for availability, and that the *Guadalcanal* remain at Pensacola until the *Ranger* returned.

Consequently, the *Ranger* sailed for Philadelphia on the morning of 13 November. Diverted to Norfolk while en route, to discharge aviation gasoline, the ship carried out that task on the 17th and 18th, proceeding on the latter date for her original destination. She arrived at the Philadelphia Naval Shipyard on the afternoon of the 19th. In view of the *Ranger*'s age, BuShips believed that "extensive redecking [was] not warranted." Plenty of Douglas Fir planking existed to be used for any "patch jobs" that might be required.[52] Additionally, the yard received authorization to remove the 40-millimeter foundation and the clipping room at frame 107, starboard side.

Indications are that the CNO contemplated expending the *Ranger* as a target in Operation Crossroads, the atomic bomb tests at Bikini atoll: A message of 14 November specified not only that end for the old pioneer, but that, upon release from active duty, she would be assigned to Commandant, 14th Naval District for "care and preservation."

During her time at Philadelphia, the *Ranger* went into drydock. On the day she entered drydock number three, on 7 December 1945, she received two visitors. A little over an hour into the afternoon watch, Rear Adm. Edwin D. Foster (SC), and Capt. John Hoskins came on board. They stayed for over an hour. Foster had been the first staff officer assigned to the ship, and he was her supply officer when she had been placed in commission in 1934; Hoskins had commanded VS-42 (including its operations in the *Lexington* during the Earhart search). He had served in succession as assistant air officer, air officer, and exec. Ordered to the small carrier *Princeton* (CVL-23) in September 1944, he was to have relieved Capt. William H. Buracker, but the Battle of Leyte Gulf intervened. Hoskins had lost a foot when the *Princeton* was hit by a Japanese bomb, but, animated by determination to obtain another sea command, had an artificial foot fitted and surmounted his handicap. "Hell, Admiral," he once complained to Adm. William F. Halsey, Jr., "the Navy doesn't expect a man to think with his feet. That blast didn't knock off my head."[53] Hoskins eventually triumphed in his bid to go to sea again. On 15 November, a little over three weeks before he visited the carrier he had once called "the best ship in the Navy," he read his orders to command the new *Essex*-class carrier *Princeton* (CV-37) at the Philadelphia Naval Shipyard.

As the *Ranger*'s future employment apparently hung in the balance, New Year's Day 1946 saw her moored at the naval base at Philadelphia. On 5 January, the ship's Marine detachment, two officers and 54 enlisted men, under Maj. William H. Enfield, USMC, was transferred to the Marine Barracks at the yard, for further transportation to the Marine Barracks at the Norfolk Naval Shipyard (formerly the Norfolk Navy Yard), to be disbanded. Two days later, Rear Adm. Cal Durgin visited his old ship, unofficially.

The *Ranger* stood down the Delaware River on 14 January on the initial leg of her return voyage to Florida. Pausing briefly at Norfolk en route (15–18 January), the carrier reached Pensacola on the 22d, to relieve the *Guadalcanal* as planned. That same day, a CNO message specified that the small carrier *Independence* (CVL-22) would replace the *Ranger* in Crossroads. Spared from nuclear destruction and having had her training role thus assured, the *Ranger*—despite a four-month layoff and the loss of many trained men through the demobilization that followed the conclusion of hostilities—resumed qualifying carrier pilots in SNJ-5Cs on 30 January, with a trio of plane guard destroyers: the *Gearing* (DD-710), the *Eugene A. Greene* (DD-711), and the *Gyatt* (DD-712).

The *Ranger* broke the flag of Rear Adm. Joseph J. "Jocko" Clark, Chief of Naval Air Basic Training, early in the first dog watch on 13 March, along with a party of dignitaries from Corpus Christi, Texas. The ship sailed the following morning, to conduct carrier qualifications, with the ship logging her 82,000th landing with a marine pilot, Second Lt. J. G. Stradley, USMCR. That same day, Ens. H. W. McWhorter tried to take a wave-off, but his SNJ-5C (BuNo 51950) crashed into the flight deck and went over the port side, aft. The *Ranger* immediately rang down left full rudder and ceased flight operations temporarily, and rang down her engines back two-thirds. Meanwhile, the *Gearing* picked up McWhorter and soon reported his condition to be good. After detaching the *Gearing* to return to port with the injured aviator, the *Ranger* resumed flight operations, eventually securing from flight quarters during the first dog watch.

After disembarking Rear Admiral Clark and his guests at 0852 on 15 March, the *Ranger* got underway, in low visibility conditions, to return to the NAS dock, assisted by the tug *Nellie*. Mr. G. T. Oldmixon, the civilian pilot embarked at 1307, conned the ship by radar and by referring to the whistle signals and searchlights from ships moored alongside the dock. Eventually, the carrier put out her lines at

1426, mooring starboard-side-to. She again hosted Rear Admiral Clark and a party of dignitaries the following month (10–12 April). She logged her 85,000th landing on 18 April.

The following day, 19 April, while returning to port, the *Ranger* ran aground after she changed course to avoid a private cabin cruiser, the *Patricia,* at 1340. She embarked a pilot at 1400, and a succession of ships, ranging from a seaplane wrecking derrick to the tug *Nellie* and the small seaplane tender *Absecon* (AVP-23) turned to free her from her predicament. By using her engines, the ship managed to get clear and finish her movement to the NAS dock. By month's end, Aviation Ordnanceman 1st Class Russell H. Bertucci would earn a commendation for "alertness and proficiency in performance of duty," when defective wiring caused as fire in a flight deck tractor on 29 April.

Lieutenant (jg) Billie C. Spell exerts body English to bring in a Hellcat. (Emil Buehler Aviation History Library)

Grumman TBM (BuNo 53091), its tail shattered, hangs over the port side over the waters of the Gulf of Mexico, 29 April 1946. Lieutenant Fletcher H. Burnham (USNA 1944) the pilot, survived the crash uninjured. (Emil Buehler Aviation History Library)

Captain George A. Dussault, USNA 1923, relieved Johnnie Johnson as commanding officer at 1936, on 1 May 1946. Known to his classmates as "Goat," Dussault, like most of his contemporaries, initially served in a battleship, the *Wyoming* (BB-32). Receiving his wings in May 1926, his first aviation duties found him in Observation Squadron One of Aircraft Squadrons, Battle Force. Later, he served as junior aviator of the battleship *West Virginia* (BB-48); while in VT-2B in the *Saratoga*, he received a commendation for his work during the Long Beach, California, earthquake in 1933. He served as flight instructor at Pensacola before he returned to VT-2B, the squadron serving in both the *Lexington* and the *Saratoga*. After serving as exec of the auxiliary aircraft carrier (later escort carrier) *Barnes* (ACV-20), Dussault commanded that ship as she participated in the Gilbert Islands operation in 1943. He received the Legion of Merit for his service as personnel officer on the staff of Commander, Air Force, Pacific Fleet, from 1 June 1944 to 1 September 1945 (serving successively under a former *Ranger* exec, Rear Admiral Pownall, and a former commanding officer, Vice Admiral Montgomery), his citation specifically praising his administrative ability and his establishment of reclassification centers that screened returning men from the war zones, to assign them duties for which they were best suited.

Over the weeks that followed, the *Ranger* operated SNJ-5Cs, FG-1s, F6F-3s, TBM-3s, and SB2C-4s. Given the fact

Grumman TBM (BuNo 8514) loses power at the ramp as Lieutenant (jg) Spell, the LSO, watches helplessly on 1 May 1946. The *Warrington* rescued Ens. W. K. Palmore, uninjured, a short time later. (Emil Buehler Aviation History Library)

that the ship had lost so many experienced sailors in the postwar standdown, Captain Dussault considered it "fortunate that under the circumstances there have been no serious accidents." She performed a mission of mercy, when, during the morning watch on 7 May, she brought on board Seaman 1st Class L. F. Piselli from the cargo ship *Newcastle Victory* (AK-233), for treatment of a perineal abcess. On 9 May, the *Ranger* hosted Vice Adm. Jorge Martins, the Brazilian Minister of Marine, and Rear Adm. Frank D. Wagner. Less than a week later, the lack of plane guards caused a temporary suspension of the *Ranger*'s operations.

The *Ranger* embarked the first group of ensigns from Aviation Indoctrination Training Class of 1947 for instruction, on 17 June. Rear Admiral Clark and a party of prominent civilians from Houston, Texas, came on board on 26 June and witnessed carrier operations the following day, before they disembarked. On 23 July, Adm. Aaron S. Merrill and a party of visiting civilians from New Orleans came on board the ship to observe operations; between 11 and 13 August, 80 civilians from the Dixie-Land Chamber of Commerce visited the ship and watched her men at work. Captain William H. Sinton, Chief of Naval Air Training Bases, with a party of guests in tow, visited the *Ranger* on 19 August.

Captain George A. Dussault, ca. February 1945. (NA, 80-G-300740)

As the *Ranger* turns to port, into the wind, six North American SNJ-5Cs prepare to take off, while onlookers watch from the signal bridge in foreground. (Emil Buehler Aviation History Library)

Tragedy occurred during this period as well, a sad punctuation to a period of otherwise routine operations, when Ens. Singleton W. Mason, Jr., (D)L, USNR, apparently lost power on takeoff for Saufley Field, on 14 August. His SNJ-5C (BuNo 51761), side number R-13, crashed and sank. Despite a 45-minute search by planes and plane guards, the 23-year-old Kansas City, Missouri, native was not recovered. He would be the *Ranger*'s final fatality.

The *Ranger*'s program of training carrier pilots was soon drawing to a close, as the aging flattop operated in the twilight of her career; she recorded her 92,000th landing on 27 August. Two days later, in the gathering dusk of 29 August, a Goodyear FG-1D Corsair flew up the groove, took the LSO's cut, and dropped onto the flight deck—the *Ranger*'s 92,262d, and final, landing.[54] "Flight quarters," secured at 1805, would never again ring out through the ship. Relieved of her training duties by the small carrier *Saipan* (CVL-48) (whose commanding officer, Capt. John G. Crommelin, had been exec of the *Ranger*'s VB-3 in 1939)—which would take her projected place in "showing the flag" at the Pensacola

Interstate Fair in October—the *Ranger* left Pensacola in her wake for the last time, when she stood out of the Naval Anchorage Area, Pensacola Bay, at 0920 on 3 September.

She ultimately stood into NOB Norfolk, where her commissioned service had begun, on 7 September and, after steaming the last of her 436,221 miles, moored to the port side of Pier 3 early in the first dog watch. There, on 1 October, Comdr. Ray Davis, the exec, relieved Captain Dussault, and thus became the *Ranger*'s final commanding officer. "Jeff" Davis, USNA 1933, earned his wings on 6 March 1941, and assisted in fitting out VS-8 of the *Hornet* Air Group, later participating in the Battle of Midway and earning the Distinguished Flying Cross for his participation in attacks on fleeing Japanese cruisers and destroyers on 5 June 1942, the second day of the battle. The end of the war in the Pacific had seen Davis commanding a carrier air group.

Midway through the forenoon watch on 18 October 1946, the *Ranger*'s crew assembled for quarters and the carrier was decommissioned, Lt. Comdr. William C. Lauritzen assuming custody for the naval shipyard. During the ceremony, Chief Water Tender Harry A. Ferguson, the last remaining *Ranger* plank owner, received a set of colors and the commissioning pennant. With the detachment of the remaining officers and the transferring of the last enlisted men to the 5th Naval District, Ens. David W. Wright, USNR, wrote beneath the last entry in the *Ranger*'s log: "Secured all watches and wrote FINIS to the glorious career of this gallant ship."

The *Ranger* was stricken from the Naval Vessel Register less than a fortnight later, on 29 October. A little less than two months after that, shortly before Christmas of 1946, the Navy announced that the ship would be "sold for conversion or scrap," and that salvageable material on board included "airplane elevators, refrigeration plants, cranes, and galley, laundry, and shoe shop equipment."[55] It also advised that those interested in her could inspect her at Hawkins Point, Maryland, where she had been taken. The Navy Material and Redistribution and Disposal Administration, headquartered at the New York Naval Shipyard, accepted bids until 14 January 1947. Ultimately, the Sun Shipbuilding and Drydock Company of Chester, Pennsylvania, secured the ship on 31 January 1947, for $259,000.00, and subsequently broke her up for scrap. Navy curatorial records list fewer than a dozen items from the *Ranger* in its inventory of artifacts, including a commemorative plaque, a builder's plaque, a bell, two antiaircraft gunnery trophies, and five athletic trophies. A model of the ship can be seen in the Navy Museum at the Washington Navy Yard.

Chaplain O'Callahan justly won praise for his heroism on board the *Franklin* (CV-13) in 1945, but he remem-

Commander Ray Davis, the *Ranger*'s last commanding officer. (AUTHOR)

bered the *Ranger*, the first carrier to which he had been assigned (31 May 1942–6 December 1944), with warmth and reverence. "The spirit of the *Ranger*," he wrote in his autobiography, *I Was Chaplain on the Franklin*, "was superb." She derived greatness from her people, from seaman to captain. "Seldom did the *Ranger* make headlines," he continued, "and her praises are not sung in Navy folklore, as is the case with other carriers. However dangerous her war duty, it was not as spectacular as were the assignments of other ships. But she didn't need headlines to be a great ship."[56] Her performance off North Africa and Norway had been workmanlike and professional. "Now the *Ranger* has long since been decommissioned and sold for scrap, and the public does not know about the lonesome vacuum in the hearts of those who were her crew. Yet in a sense the *Ranger* participated in the glories of the newer carriers. I believe that every first-line carrier built during the war received a large complement of *Ranger*-trained men. If the new ships had the old carrier spirit," O'Callahan posited, "this was derived at least in part from her simple greatness."[57] A fitting epitath indeed. She had been, in the context of her times, a "very valuable ship."

NOTES

INTRODUCTION
1. Gunnar Bernstein, quoted in Gerald W. Thomas, "Supplements to *Torpedo Squadron Four: A Cockpit View of World War II.*" Privately Published, 1990.

Chapter 1: "I CHRISTEN THEE *RANGER*"
1. Sadly, within three months of Rear Admiral Moffett's attending the *Ranger*'s christening at Newport News, he perished in the crash of the rigid airship *Akron* (ZRS-1) off the coast of New Jersey. Moffett's death proved particularly devastating to the Bureau of Aeronautics which he had headed since its creation in 1922. The Navy's aviation community mourned Moffett's loss; Rear Adm. Ernest J. King became bureau chief, and naval aviation carried on.
2. *New York Times*, 26 February 1933, 15.
3. Ibid.
4. *Army & Navy Journal*, 4 March 1933, 545.
5. The design of the *Ranger* could be the subject of a book in itself, given the hearings and studies on the subject. Unless otherwise noted, those portions of this operational history are derived from "History of Design of Aircraft Carrier #4" (photocopy in author's files), General Board Hearing, "Characteristics for 13,800-ton Aircraft Carrier," 9 March 1928 (Microfilm Mic A-127, Reel 7, Navy Department Library); and Norman Friedman, *U.S. Aircraft Carriers: An Illustrated Design History* (Annapolis: Naval Institute Press, 1983), 57–77.
6. Enclosure (A) to Memorandum, Senior Member Present, General Board to Secretary of the Navy, 1 November 1927, General Board No. 420-5 (Serial No. 1362).
7. U.S. Congress, 70th Congess, H.R. 11526, "An Act to Authorize the Construction of Certain Naval Vessels and for Other Purposes."
8. The first *Ranger* had been the first man-of-war to hoist the new national American flag and the first to receive an official salute rendered to it by the French at Quiberon Bay on 14 February 1778. On 23 April 1778, the *Ranger* met and soundly defeated the British sloop of war *Drake* in the Irish Channel, capturing her formidable adversary after a bitter and bloody fight. Ultimately, the British captured the *Ranger* at the fall of Charleston in 1780. The second *Ranger* was a small schooner (1814–16), the third a 14-gun brig acquired in 1814 and attached to Commodore Isaac Chauncey's squadron on Lake Ontario in the War of 1812. The fourth *Ranger*, an iron-hulled gunboat with auxiliary sails, served actively on a succession of foreign stations until loaned to the state of Massachusetts as a school ship in 1909. She was renamed *Rockport* in 1917 (and *Nantucket* in 1918) to clear the name *Ranger* for assignment to a battle cruiser authorized in the naval expansion act of 29 August 1916. Originally named *Lexington* (Battle Cruiser No. 4) on 30 October 1917, the ship that was to have been the fifth *Ranger* was given the latter name on 10 December 1917. Her keel was laid down on 23 June 1921 at Newport News. Before the year was out, however, the conference that would decide the fate of the *Ranger* began in Washington, and with the signing of the 1922 Washington Treaty, work came to a halt on 8 February 1923. The Navy cancelled the contract for her construction on 17 August, and sold the incomplete ship "as is, where is," to the Steel Scrap Company of Philadelphia, Pennsylvania, for $10,666.66 on 8 November. Two days later, the Navy struck the name *Ranger* from the Navy List. The Bureau of Construction and Repair reported "scrapping completed" by mid-November of 1924.
9. *The Ranger* [ship's newspaper] 1, no. 1 (24 August 1934): 1–8.
10. Edwin D. Foster, "Cafeteria Afloat," *U.S. Naval Institute Proceedings*, January 1937.

Chapter 2: "SET THE WATCH!"

1. Captain Bristol's biography is derived from material in his biographical file in Officer Biography Files, Box 69, OA; the 1906 *Lucky Bag* (U.S. Naval Academy yearbook); Joseph J. Clark, with Clark G. Reynolds, *Carrier Admiral* (New York: David McKay, 1968), 79 (hereinafter Clark, *Carrier Admiral*); and Patrick Abbazia, *Mr. Roosevelt's Navy: The Private War of the U.S. Atlantic Fleet, 1939–1942* (Annapolis: Naval Institute Press, 1975), 143.
2. The account of the formation of the ship's Marine detachment and the description of some of its people comes from *The Ranger* 1, no. 1 (24 August 1934): 5; Gaynor Pearson (a private 1st class in the ship's Marine detachment), "The Rambling Ranger," In *The Leatherneck* 17, no. 6 (June 1934): 19, and 17, no. 8 (August 1934), 15.
3. Unless otherwise indicated, the ship's activities that are recounted in the narrative have been derived from the deck log of the U.S.S. *Ranger* (CV-4), which begins on 4 June 1934 and ends on 18 October 1946 (hereinafter, *Ranger* Deck Log, with the appropriate date).
4. *The Ranger* 1, no. 1 (24 August 1934), 1; also Gaynor Pearson, "The Rambling Ranger," *The Leatherneck* 17, no. 8 (August 1934): 15.
5. *Ranger* Deck Log, 21 June 1934.
6. *The Ranger* 1, no. 1 (24 August 1934): 8.
7. Ibid.
8. Pearson, "The Rambling Ranger," *The Leatherneck* 17, no. 8 (August 1934): 15.
9. *Bureau of Aeronautics Newsletter*, no. 333. (1 August 1934): 7.
10. Ibid.
11. "Statement of Lieutenant (junior grade) J. G. Burgess Regarding Crash of F4B-4 Airplane, Number 9030 (5-B-9) on 23 July, 1934" in "VB Squadron FIVE-B Aircraft Trouble Report on F4B-4 Airplane No. A-9030 dated 24 July 1934" with endorsements, in VF4B-4/L11-1 File, vol. 4, (Records of the Bureau of Aeronautics) RG-72 Box 4918, NARA, Washington, D.C.
12. Ibid. Burgess's philosophical reflections are contained in the *Bureau of Aeronautics Newsletter*, no. 334 (15 August 1934): 5. Jack Burgess would die in a plane crash at Milsap, Texas, on 2 February 1935.
13. *Bureau of Aeronautics Newsletter*, no. 335 (1 September 1934): 7.
14. Ibid., 8.
15. "VS Squadron ONE-B Aircraft Trouble Report on SU-4 Airplane No. A-9419 dated 9 August, 1934," in VSU4/L11-1 files, vol. 2, RG-72, Box 5485, NARA, Washington, D.C.
16. Ibid. Upon his return to NAS Hampton Roads, Hopping failed his Schneider Index Test ("a numerical expression of an individual's circulatory efficiency," which had proved "very valuable in checking up on the physical fitness of the aviators"). Found to have a fever, Hopping was placed on the sick list. Reference to the Schneider Index can be found in U.S. Navy, Bureau of Navigation, *Handbook of the Hospital Corps, United States Navy, 1930* (Washington, D.C. GPO, 1930), 586.
17. Unless otherwise indicated, the description of the planning of the *Ranger*'s shakedown cruise is derived from the letter of Secretary of the Navy Claude A. Swanson to Sen. Gerald P. Nye, 2 March 1935, printed in Seventy-Fourth Congress, First Session, *Hearings before [the] Subcommittee of House Committee on Appropriations in Charge of [the] Navy Department Appropriation Bill for 1936* (Washington, D.C.: GPO, 1935), 86–88.
18. Entry for Edmund Weyman Strother in the 1908 *Lucky Bag*.
19. *The Ranger* 1, no. 1 (24 August 1934): 1.

Chapter 3: "THE JOB IS A DIPLOMATIC ONE"

1. *The Ranger* 1, no. 2 (31 August 1934): 3.
2. *The Ranger* 1, no. 1 (24 August 1934): 3–6.
3. Ibid., 1–8.
4. Ibid., 2.
5. Ibid., 1.
6. Ibid., 2–8.
7. Ibid., 2.
8. *The Ranger* 1, no. 2 (31 August 1934): 1.
9. Ibid., 1.
10. *The Ranger* 1, no. 3 (8 September 1934): 4.
11. *The Ranger* 1, no. 5 (22 September 1934): 1.
12. Ibid., 1–4.
13. "As far as meat is concerned," writes Russell H. FitzGibbon of such a feast in neighboring Uruguay, "one of the best treats to be had . . . is at an *asado*. The *asado* is an institution. It is cousin to a barbecue but done up with all the finesse and variety that only a meat-loving and -producing land can supply. The meat may be lamb or it may be beef. The iron grill is tilted at an angle over the slow fire and the savory aroma merely whets an appetite that was good to begin with." Russell H. FitzGibbon, *Uruguay: Portrait of a Democracy* (New Brunswick, NJ: Rutgers University Press, 1954), 64. "Space does not permit an adequate description," one *Ranger* sailor later observed of an *asado*. "Ask someone who went, and when he has taken an hour to tell you about it, double his description and you may have some idea of what it was all about." *The Ranger* 1, no. 4 (15 September 1934): 4.
14. Lester R. Schulz, "Montevideo," in *The Ranger Rolls Down to Rio: Being an Account of the Shakedown Cruise of the U.S.S. Ranger to Rio de Janeiro, Buenos Aires, and Montevideo, 17 August–5 October 1934*, Privately Published, 1934.
15. Ltr, Secretary of the Navy, Claude A. Swanson to Sen. Gerald P. Nye, 2 March 1935, op. cit.
16. Lieutenant Gen. Lewis J. Fields, USMC (Retired) Oral History Transcript, 32–33. Fields, born in Wicomico County, MD, would be awarded a commission as a 2d lieutenant on 25 June 1935, would earn a Bronze Star for his service in command of the 11th Marines at Cape Gloucester in 1943, and would eventually command the First Marine Division in Vietnam in 1965.
17. *Bureau of Aeronautics Newsletter* no. 338 (15 October 1934): 4–5.
18. *Bureau of Aeronautics Newsletter* no. 339 (1 November 1934): 7.
19. Ibid., 6.

20. *Bureau of Aeronautics Newsletter* no. 1 (1 April 1935): 6.
21. *Bureau of Aeronautics Newsletter* no. 344 (15 January 1935): 5.
22. *Bureau of Aeronautics Newsletter* no. 350 (15 April 1935): 9.
23. Aircraft Accident Report (hereinafter AAR) for BF2C-1 (BuNo 9588), 28 March 1935, on Aircraft Accident Report Microfilm (hereinafter AARM), Reel 2, AvH, NHC.
24. AAR for BF2C-1 (BuNo 9512), 28 March 1935, AARM Reel 2, AvH.
25. This summary of Admiral Butler's career up to 1935 is derived from the biographical material in his folder in Officer Biography Files, Box 86, OA.
26. *Bureau of Aeronautics Newsletter* no. 1 (1 April 1935): 7–8.
27. AAR for BG-1 (BuNo 9506), 23 April 1935, AARM Reel 2, AvH. The term "nose up" actually described a plane's digging its nose downward into the deck, a mishap that usually resulted in damage to propellers, cowlings, and (because of sudden stoppage) engines.
28. AAR for BF2C-1 (BuNo 9592), 24 April 1935, AARM Reel 2, AvH. Eventually, Vosseller would serve as the *Ranger*'s LSO (see Chapter XIII).

Chapter 4: "SHE WILL PROVE HERSELF A VERY VALUABLE SHIP"

1. Commander in Chief, United States Fleet, to Chief of Naval Operations, Subj: Fleet Problem XVI—Report on, 15 September 1935, 12. The subsequent critique pointed to the "absolute necessity of prompt, energetic and continuous effort, utilizing to the fullest practicable extent all available means, to meet a submarine threat," and to the value of an "adequate inshore and offshore patrol, working in coordination with the Fleet," for such operations. Commander in Chief, United States Fleet, to Chief of Naval Operations, Subj: Fleet Problem XVI—Report on, 15 September 1935, 10, copy in author's files.
2. Commander Aircraft, Battle Force, to Commander in Chief, U.S. Fleet (Commander White Main Body), Subj: Fleet Problem XVI, Phase II, report on, 28 May 1935,
3. "Remarks by Vice Admiral H. V. Butler, USN, at Critique on Fleet Problem XVI," in Enclosure "F" to Cincus Serial 5179 of 15 September 1935, "Critique of Fleet Problem Sixteen Held at San Diego, California, 15 June 1935," 35, Records Relating to United States Navy Fleet Problems I to XXII, 1923–1941, National Archives Microfilm Publication M964, Reel 18.
4. Lieutenant (jg) H. T. Johnson, U.S. Navy, to Trouble Board, Subj: Statement in regard to fire in BG-1 Airplane #9508 on 6 May, 1935, in VBG-1/L11-1 file, 5-1-35 to 9-30-35, RG-72, Box 4833, NARA, Washington, D.C.; also AAR for BG-1 (BuNo 9508) on AARM Reel 2, AvH.
5. Ibid.
6. Ibid.
7. Ibid.
8. Commander Aircraft, Battle Force, to Chief of the Bureau of Aeronautics, Subj: VB Squadron Three-B Aircraft Trouble Report on BG-1 Airplane No. A-9508, dated 1 May 1935 [*sic*], 7 June 1935, in VBG-1/L11-1 file, RG-72, Box 4833, NARA, Washington, D.C.
9. AAR for BF2C-1 (BuNo 9607), 8 May 1935, AARM Reel 2, AvH.
10. Aircraft Trouble Report on SU-4 Airplane No. 9426, dated 21 May, 1935, in VSU-4/L11-1 files, Vol. 2, RG-72, Box 5485, NARA, Washington, D.C. On the route sheet, one officer back in BuAer in Washington penciled "Apparently SU's will bounce too if they hit just right." See also AAR for SU-1 (BuNo 9426), 19 May 1935 in AARM Reel 2, AvH.
11. Landing Signal Officer to Trouble Board, Subj: Damage to SU-4 airplane No. 9424, in VSU-1/L11-1 file, vol. 2, RG-72, Box 5485, NARA, Washington, D.C.; also AAR for SU-1 (BuNo 9424), 21 May 1935, AARM Reel 2, AvH.
12. Commanding Officer [*Ranger*] to the Chief of the Bureau of Aeronautics, 2d Endorsement to Trouble Report on SU-4 Airplane #9428, dated 22 May, 1935—VS Squadron 1-B, in VSU-4/L11-1 file, Vol. 2, RG-72, Box 5485, NARA, Washington, D.C.
13. AAR for PM-1 (BuNo 8295), 21 May 1936, AARM Reel 2, AvH.
14. "Remarks of Admiral Laning at Critique of Fleet Problem Sixteen" in Enclosure "F" to Cincus Serial 5179 of 15 September 1935, "Critique of Fleet Problem Sixteen Held at San Diego, California, 15 June 1935," 31, op.cit.
15. "Remarks by Vice Admiral H. V. Butler, USN, at Critique on Fleet Problem XVI," in Enclosure "F" to Cincus Serial 5179 of 15 September 1935, "Critique of Fleet Problem Sixteen Held at San Diego, California, 15 June 1935," 35, op.cit.
16. Ibid., 37.
17. Ibid., 37–38.
18. Ibid., 35.
19. "Annual Report of the Commander in Chief, United States Fleet for the Fiscal Year, 1935," contained in "Annual Reports of Fleets and Task Forces of the U.S. Navy, 1920–1941," National Archives Microfilm Publication M971, Reel 10. Admiral Reeves's comments on the *Ranger* are found on pp. 18–19.
20. Ibid., 17–18.
21. AAR for JF-1 (BuNo 9438), 9 July 1935, AARM Reel 2, AvH.
22. AAR for O3U-1 (BuNo 8574). 14 August 1935, AARM Reel 2, AvH.
23. "Ltr, Sullivan, Hobart B., R.M.1c, U.S. Navy, to Trouble Board, Subj: Statement Concerning damage to SU-4 plane Bu. No. 9414, 19 September 1935," in "VS Squadron One-B Aircraft Trouble Report on SU-4 Airplane No. A-9414, dated 25 September 1935," in VSU4/L11-1 files, vol. 2, Box 5485, RG-72, NARA, Washington; see also AAR for SU-4 (BuNo 9414), 19 September 1935, in AARM Reel 2, AvH.
24. William D. Leahy "Diary" (hereinafter Leahy Diary), 4 October 1935.
25. "Aircraft Trouble Report" concerning damage to BG-1 BuNo 9548 in VBG-1/F42-1 to VBG-1/L11-1 Vol. 3, RG-72, Box 4833. When the report of the mishap reached Washington and

BuAer's Engineering Branch, Lt. John B. Pearson, Jr., Construction Corps, whimsically wrote "Generals Beware!" on the route sheet. Another officer appended the comment: "The general is OK. He still travels by air and likes it." As for the airplane, the *Ranger*'s air department people replaced the blades and the plane was flown to North Island. See also AAR for BG-1 (BuNo 9548), 4 November 1935, AARM Reel 2, AvH.

26. AAR for BG-1 (BuNo 9536), 4 November 1935, AARM Reel 2, AvH.
27. AAR for BG-1 (BuNo 9534), 4 November 1935, AARM Reel 2, AvH.
28. AAR for F2F-1 (BuNo 9654), 14 November 1935, AARM Reel 2, AvH.
29. AAR for TG-2 (BuNo A-8702), 2 January 1936, AARM Reel 3, AvH.
30. AAR for BM-2 (BuNo 9174), 6 January 1936, AARM Reel 3, AvH.
31. AAR for F2F-1 (BuNo 9651), 7 January 1936, AARM Reel 3, AvH.
32. AAR for F2F-1 (BuNo 9650), 8 January 1936, AARM Reel 3, AvH.
33. AAR for F2F-1 (BuNo 9664), 8 January 1936, AARM Reel 3, AvH.
34. "Additional Sheet to VF Squadron Three-B Trouble Report of 9 January 1936, on F2F-1 Airplane Number 9651," in VF2F-1/L11-1 files, Box 4876, RG-72, NARA, Washington, D.C.
35. Commander, VF Squadron Three-B to Chief of the Bureau of Aeronautics, Subj: VF Squadron 3-B Trouble Report on F2F-1 Airplane No. 9650, 13 January 1936, in VF2F-1/L11-1 vols. 5–6, Box 4876, op.cit.
36. "Commanding Officer [USS *Ranger*] to Chief of the Bureau of Aeronautics, Subj: VF Squadron 3-B Trouble Report on F2F-1 Airplane No. 9650," 26 February 1936, in VF2F-1/L11-1 Vol. 5/Vol. 6, Box 4876, NARA, Washington, D.C.
37. Commander Aircraft, Battle Force, to Chief of the Bureau of Aeronautics, Subj: VF Squadron 3-B Trouble Report on F2F-1 Airplane No. 9650 of 9 January 1936, dated. 10 March 1936, in VF2F-1/L11-1 vols. 5–6, Box 4876, NARA, Washington, D.C.

Chapter 5: "A VERY GOOD TIME WAS HAD BY ALL"

1. Rear Adm. George Van Deurs, Biographical File, Officer Biography Files, Box 655, OA.
2. Embarked planes included O3U-3s (BuNos 9167, 9168, and 9300), JF-1s (BuNos 9443 and 9454), SBU-1s (BuNos 9769, 9770, and 9771), F2F-1s (BuNos 9658, 9659, 9660, 9661, 9662, and 9663), BG-1s (BuNos 9494, 9504, 9505, 9513, 9514, and 9520) and BF2C-1s (BuNos 9599, 9607, and 9612).
3. Unless otherwise noted, the *Ranger*'s special operations in Alaskan waters are derived from "Report of Cold Weather Carrier Operations in Alaskan Waters, USS *Ranger*, 13 January to 19 February 1936," Commander Aircraft, Pacific, Records of Fleet and Operating Forces, RG-313, Box 2530, NARA, College Park, MD, the ship's deck logs for the time period, and *The CV-4* 2, no. 17 or 27 (25 January 1936); 2 no. 18 (1 February 1936); and 2 no. 19 (8 February 1936).
4. AAR for BG-1 (BuNo 9505), 17 January 1936, AARM Reel 3, AvH.
5. AAR for BG-1 (BuNo 9504), 17 January 1936, AARM Reel 3, AvH.
6. Prior to the Cold Weather Cruise, then-Vice Admiral Pownall recollected later in an oral history, "I told Mary [his wife]—please if there was a safe way to get me a half gallon of whiskey—which she did. [Captain] Bristol had the same idea. And the medical officer of the ship thought we ought to have whiskey. So we had whiskey; it was all under the medical department. We were prepared. . . . Kids would get wringing wet in the boat[s]. The doctor would put them to bed and give them eggs and a drink of whiskey. That was the standard procedure, whether they were pilots or enlisted boys. . . . It worked pretty good." Charles A. Pownall, *The Reminiscences of Vice Admiral Charles A. Pownall, U.S. Navy (Retired)*, Annapolis: U.S. Naval Institute, 1989.
7. C. H. Channing, "Grewingk Glacier," *The CV-4* 2, no. 19 (8 February 1936): 1–2.
8. Ibid., 3.
9. Commanding Officer [USS *Lea*] to Commander Destroyers, Battle Force. Subj: Plane guard duty in Alaskan Waters; Report on, 24 February 1936, Annex A of "Report of Cold Weather Carrier Operations in Alaskan Waters, USS *Ranger*, 13 January to 19 February 1936," Commander Aircraft, Pacific, RG-313, Box 2530, NARA, College Park, MD.
10. "USS *Ranger* Aircraft Trouble Report on SBU-1 Airplane No. 9771, 12 February 1936, VSBU-1/L11-1 vol. 1 file, RG-72, NARA, Washington, DC; also AAR for SBU-1 (BuNo 9771), 10 February 1936, AARM Reel 3, AvH.
11. "Report of Cold Weather Carrier Operations in Alaskan Waters, USS *Ranger*, 13 January to 19 February 1936," Commander Aircraft, Pacific, RG-313, op.cit.
12. Ibid.
13. Ibid.
14. Ibid.
15. Ibid.
16. AAR for SU-4 (BuNo 9428), 28 February 1936, AARM Reel 3, AvH.
17. AAR for F2F-1 (BuNo 9651), 31 March 1936; Hale's aspirations for a naval career are contained in his *Lucky Bag* entry.
18. *Bureau of Aeronautics Newsletter* 13, no. 27, (1 June 1936): 4–5.
19. 1932 *Lucky Bag*, 158.
20. AAR for SBU-1 (BuNo 9776), 26 April 1936, AARM Reel 3, AvH.
21. Ibid., 3.
22. *Bureau of Aeronautics Newsletter* 13, no. 32 (15 August 1936): 6.
23. AAR for BM-1 (BuNo 8885), 28 April 1936, AARM Reel 3, AvH.
24. AAR for SBU-1 (BuNo 9805), 28 April 1936, AARM Reel 3, AvH.
25. AAR for SBU-1 (BuNo 9811), 4 May 1936, AARM Reel 3, AvH
26. AAR for F2F-1 (BuNo 9649), 6 May 1936, AARM Reel 3, AvH; also *Bureau of Aeronautics Newsletter* 13, no. 29 (1 July 1936): 7.

27. AAR for SBU-1 (BuNo 9771), 6 May 1936, AARM Reel 3, AvH.
28. Unless otherwise noted, the narrative concerning the crash of BuNo 9454 is derived from "Aircraft Trouble Report" for JF-1 (BuNo 9454) in RG-72, VJF-1/L11-1 File, vol. 3, Box 4995, NARA, Washington, DC. See also AAR for JF-1 (BuNo 9454), AARM Reel 3, AvH. The JF-1 had been one of the two embarked in the *Ranger* during the work of the Cold Weather Test Detachment earlier that year.
29. *Bureau of Aeronautics Newsletter* 13, no. 29 (1 July 1936): 3.
30. AAR for SBU-1 (BuNo 9776), 17 May 1936, AARM Reel 3, AvH.
31. Leahy Diary, 20 May 1936.
32. AAR for BM-2 (BuNo 9184), 26 May 1936, AARM Reel 3, AvH.
33. Leahy Diary, 6 June 1936.
34. Commander in Chief, United States Fleet, to Chief of Naval Operations, Subj: Communications; Fleet Problem XVII, 14 June 1936, in Records Relating to United States Navy Fleet Problems I to XXII, 1923–1941, National Archives Microfilm Publication M964, Reel 21.
35. *The CV-4* 3 no. 2 (13 June 1936): 1.
36. 1910 *Lucky Bag*, 176.

Chapter 6: "HAVE REACHED A MARVELOUS EFFICIENCY"

1. 1910 *Lucky Bag*, 176.
2. George Van Deurs Papers, Naval Historical Foundation, Washington, D.C.
3. 1907 *Lucky Bag*, 25.
4. *Bureau of Aeronautics Newsletter* 13, no. 31 (1 August 1936): 3–4.
5. Ibid, 3.
6. *Bureau of Aeronautics Newsletter* 13, no. 32 (15 August 1936): 6.
7. *Bureau of Aeronautics Newsletter* 13, no. 31 (1 August 1936): 4.
8. *Bureau of Aeronautics Newsletter* 13, no. 33 (1 September 1936): 5.
9. *Bureau of Aeronautics Newsletter* 13, no. 30 (15 July 1936): 3.
10. Ibid.
11. *Bureau of Aeronautics Newsletter* 13, no. 31 (1 August 1936): 2.
12. *Bureau of Aeronautics Newsletter* 13, no. 30 (15 July 1936): 3.
13. *Bureau of Aeronautics Newsletter* 13, no. 31 (1 August 1936): 5.
14. Lieutenant (jg) M. T. Evans, U.S. Navy to Senior Member, Trouble Board, Subj: "Statement in regard to Crash of Airplane No. 9650 on 4 August 1936," 6 August 1936. In VF2F-1 Files, LF2F-1/L11-1 vols. 6–7, RG-72, Box 4876, NARA, Washington, D.C.; see also AAR for F2F-1 (BuNo 9650), 4 August 1936, AARM Reel 3, AvH.
15. AAR for F2F-1 (BuNo 9665), 31 August 1936, in AARM Reel 3, AvH.
16. Ltr, ComAirBatFor to Chief of BuAer, 14 October 1936, Second Endorsement to VF Squadron Three-B Aircraft Trouble Report on F2F-1 Airplane No. 9665, dated 8 Sept., 1936, RG-72, NARA, Washington, D.C.
17. *Bureau of Aeronautics Newsletter* 13, no. 32 (15 August 1936): 7.
18. *Bureau of Aeronautics Newsletter* 13, no. 34 (15 September 1936): 5.
19. AAR for F2F-1 (BuNo 9648), 5 September 1936, in AARM Reel 3, AvH.
20. Ltr, Commander Aircraft, Battle Force, to Commanding Officer, VF Squadron Three-B, Subj: National Air Races—Excellent Performance of Duty by Officers and Men of VF Squadron Three-B, 11 September 1936, copy provided to the author by Dr. Steve Ewing; original in the possession of the Flatley family.
21. *Bureau of Aeronautics Newsletter* 13, no. 35 (1 October 1936): 8–9.
22. AAR for F2F-1 (BuNo 9645), 8 September 1936, AARM Reel 3, AvH.
23. *The CV-4* 3, no. 15, 1–3.
24. *Bureau of Aeronautics Newsletter* 13, no. 37 (1 November 1936): 16.
25. AAR for SBU-1 (BuNo 9776), 1 October 1936, AARM Reel 3, AvH.
26. AAR for F2F-1 (BuNo 9655), 1 October 1936, AARM Reel 3, AvH.
27. AAR for BM-1 (BuNo 8879), 1 October 1936, AARM Reel 3, AvH.
28. *Bureau of Aeronautics Newsletter* 13, no. 36 (15 October 1936): 16.
29. AAR for O3U-6 (BuNo 9734), 2 October 1936, AARM Reel 3, AvH.
30. AAR for F4B-4 (BuNo 9041), 2 October 1936, AARM Reel 3, AvH.
31. "Weekly Carrier Operation Report, USS *Ranger*" for inclusive dates 5 to 10 October 1936; copy provided to the author by James T. Rindt.
32. AAR for F2F-1 (BuNo 9667), 21 October 1936, AARM Reel 3, AvH.
33. AAR for F3F-1 (BuNo 0220), 23 October 1936, AARM Reel 3, AvH.
34. AAR for F3F-1 (BuNo 0228), 10 November 1936, AARM Reel 3, AvH.
35. AAR for F3F-1 (BuNo 0221), 10 November 1936, AARM Reel 3, AvH. The grade of aviation cadet had been established on 15 April 1935, with the Aviation Cadet Act, which set up a pilot training program that allowed qualified applicants to undergo one year of flight training, enjoy the benefits of pay, uniform gratuities and insurance, and would enable them to be commissioned as ensigns (U.S. Navy) or second lieutenants (U.S. Marine Corps), after three additional years of active duty. Roy A. Grossnick, ed., *United States Naval Aviation 1910–1995* (Washington: Naval Historical Center, 1997), 89.
36. AAR for F3F-1 (BuNo 0228), 11 November 1936, AARM Reel 3, AvH.
37. Leahy Diary, 19 November 1936. Leahy, as Chief of the Bureau of Ordnance, with the rank of rear admiral, had been involved at one point in the design of the *Ranger*, having participated in the General Board hearing that discussed "Characteristics for [the] 13,800 Ton Aircraft Carrier" on 9 March 1928.

38. AAR for SBU-1 (BuNo 9810), 17 November 1936, AARM Reel 3, AvH.
39. AAR for SBU-1 (BuNo 9185), 17 November 1936, AARM Reel 3, AvH.
40. Leahy Diary, 19 November 1936.
41. AAR for BM-2 (BuNo 9174), 7 December 1936, AARM Reel 3, AvH; see also *Army and Navy Journal,* 12 December 1936, 316.
42. AAR for F2F-1 (BuNo 9659), 7 December 1936, AARM Reel 3, AvH.
43. AAR for F2F-1 (BuNo 9663), 7 December 1936, AARM Reel 3, AvH.
44. Patrick N. L. Bellinger, "Memoirs," mss., 277–278, Command File, Individual Personnel, OA.
45. *American Weekly,* 11 November 1936, quoted in Ralph G. Martin, *The Woman He Loved,* New York: Simon and Schuster, 1973, 382–383. This refutes Bellinger's recollection that Spencer made no statement in response to media queries.
46. Michael Bloch, ed., in *Wallis and Edward, Letters 1931–1937: The Intimate Correspondence of the Duke and Duchess of Windsor,* New York: Summit Books, 1986, however, describes Spencer as a "moody alcoholic, brutal and sadistic . . . suffering from pathological jealousy." Spencer would never return to the *Ranger.* He would be officially detached from the ship in September 1937, and, after a tour of duty at Headquarters, 12th Naval District, retired by reason of physical disability on 1 June 1939. He died of coronary thrombosis, 29 May 1950. Montgomery's becoming exec is recounted in *The CV-4* 3, no. 23 (Saturday, 5 December 1936): 1.

Chapter 7: "WHEN A SHIP BREAKS INTO THE MOVIES"

1. Lieutenant (jg) Dimmick's mid watch rhyme on 1 January 1937 was the only time that verse was employed in this fashion in the *Ranger*'s log during her commissioned service (1934–46).
2. AAR for F3F-1 (BuNo 0217), 13 January 1937, AARM Reel 3, AvH.
3. Rear Adm. Herschel A. House Biographical File, Officer Biography Files, Box 315, OA; also 1930 *Lucky Bag,* 168, and Richard Lamparski, *Whatever Happened To . . . ?* (New York: Crown Publishers, 1974), 148–149.
4. AAR for SBU-1 (BuNo 9801), 14 January 1937, AARM Reel 3, AvH. Pete Hall would ultimately be lost in the *Liscome Bay* (CVE-56), 25 November 1943.
5. AAR for SBU-1 (BuNo 9804), 18 January 1937, AARM Reel 3, AvH.
6. AAR for SBU-1 (BuNo 9801), 19 January 1937, AARM Reel 3, AvH.
7. AAR for SBU-1 (BuNo 9807), 20 January 1937, AARM Reel 3, AvH.
8. AAR for BM-2 (BuNo 9185), 20 January 1937, AARM Reel 3, AvH.
9. AAR for F2F-1 (BuNo 9643), 21 January 1937, AARM Reel 3, AvH.
10. AAR for SBU-1 (BuNo 9804), 21 January 1937, AARM Reel 3, AvH.
11. *Bureau of Aeronautics Newsletter* 13, no. 44 (15 February 1937): 10.
12. Unless otherwise noted, the adventures of Lieutenant (jg)s McClure and Jung and Aviation Cadet Loomis are found in Lt. (jg) William H. McClure to VF Squadron Three-B Trouble Board, "Flight of Aircraft of VF Squadron Three-B on 30 January, 1937, and subsequent crash of F2F-1 Airplane No. 9654," 1 February 1937; Lt. (jg) Karl E. Jung, to Commander, VF Squadron Three-B, "Statement in regard to extended flight on 30 January, 1937," 1 February 1937, and Aviation Cadet R. C. Loomis, USNR, to Commander, VF Squadron Three-B, "Statement in regard to extended flight on 30 January, 1937," 1 February 1937," enclosures to "Aircraft Trouble Report on F2F-1 Airplane No. 9654 (VF-3B) dated 2 February 1937," in VF2F-1/L11-1 files, Vol. 7/Vol.8, Box 4876, RG-72, NARA. See also AAR for F2F-1 (BuNo 9654), AARM Reel 3, AvH.
13. The brief description of Kramer is found in Gwendolyn Wright, intro., *The WPA Guide to California: The Federal Writer's Project Guide to 1930s California,* New York: Pantheon Books, 1984, 605.
14. Ibid., 422.
15. "Additional Sheet No. I to VF-3B Trouble Report on F2F-1 Airplane No. 9654, dated 2 Feb., 1937," "Aircraft Trouble Report on F2F-1 Airplane No. 9654 (VF-3B), dated 2 February 1937," in VF2F-1/L11-1 files, vol. 7–8, Box 4876, op.cit.
16. Commanding Officer, USS *Ranger* (CV-4) to Chief of BuAer, 18 February 1937, second endorsement to Aircraft Trouble Report on F2F-1 Airplane, BuNo 9654 (V.F. Squadron Three-B), dated 2 February 1937, op.cit.
17. AAR for F3F-1 (BuNo 0252), 8 February 1937, AARM Reel 3, AvH.
18. AAR for SBU-1 (BuNo 9811), 8 February 1937, AARM Reel 3, AvH.
19. AAR for F3F-1 (BuNo 0223), 10 February 1937, AARM Reel 3, AvH.
20. AAR for BM-1 (BuNo 8881), 12 February 1937, AARM Reel 3, AvH.
21. "Memorandum for Navy Department Motion Picture Board," Subj: "Screenplay titled 'Wings Over Honolulu'—Comments on script of," 31 December 1936, copy provided to the author by Dr. Lawrence Suid. The "Massie Case" of 1932 involved the murder of a Hawaiian by sailors in Honolulu. The local population (quite rightly) viewed the verdict in the case more lenient than warranted.
22. "*Ranger* on Location," *The CV-4,* 3, no. 34 (27 February 1937): 1.
23. Ibid., 3. A "versatile stage and screen director," Potter "worked with a variety of genres but proved to be at his best with comedy material," writes Ephraim Katz, *The Film Encyclopedia* (New York: Harper and Row, 1979), 925. Potter later directed such motion pictures as *Mr. Lucky* and *Mr. Blandings Builds His Dream House.*
24. *New York Times,* 29 May 1937.

25. AAR for SBU-1 (BuNo 9809), 24 February 1937, AARM Reel 3, AvH.
26. *Bureau of Aeronautics Newsletter* 13, no. 47 (1 April 1937) 10.
27. *The Bull Horn* 1, no. 1 (12 March 1937).
28. AAR for F2F-1 (BuNo 9645), 24 March 1937, AARM Reel 3, AvH.
29. U.S. Fleet Operation Order No. 6-37, 17 March 1937, and Annex Baker to same ("General Plan of 'U.S. Fleet' for Minor Joint Army and Navy Exercises, 23–25, April 1937," in "Records Relating to United States Navy Fleet Problems I to XXII, 1923–1941," National Archives Microfilm Publication M964, Reel 22.
30. AAR for SBU-1 (BuNo 9805), 23 April 1937, AARM Reel 3, AvH.
31. Lieutenant (jg) D. W. Shumway, U.S. Navy, to Senior Member Trouble Board. Subj: Damage to tail surfaces of SBU-1 airplane #9832, 26 April 1937; also Lt. A. Soucek, U.S. Navy, Flight Deck Officer, to VS Squadron One-B Trouble Board, Subj: Damage to SBU-1 Airplane, Bureau Bull. Number 9832—statement in regard to, 28 April 1937; in Aircraft Trouble Report on SBU-1 Airplane, Bureau Bull. Number 9832, VS Squadron One-B, in VSBU-1/L11-1 files, 7, Box 5406, RG-72, NARA, Washington, D.C.
32. *Bureau of Aeronautics Newsletter* 13, no. 52 (15 June 1937): 7–8.
33. Ibid. Over four years later, another naval aviator would see a "brilliant sun burst into the eastern sky." That aviator was Comdr. Fuchida Mitsuo, leader of the Japanese attack on the Pacific Fleet at Pearl Harbor on 7 December 1941. Fuchida Mitsuo, "I Led the Air Attack on Pearl Harbor," *U.S. Naval Institute Proceedings* 78, no. 9 (September 1952): 946.
34. Ltr, Capt. P. N. L. Bellinger, U.S. Navy, Commanding, USS *Ranger* to Commander Aircraft, Battle Force, Subj: Request authority for son to take passage on USS *Ranger* from San Francisco to San Diego, California, 26 April 1937, P. N. L. Bellinger Papers, "Official Correspondence," 1932–1940, Folder 4, Box 1, ArH, NHC.

Chapter 8: "BRING BACK AMELIA AND FRED!"

1. AARs for J2F-1s (BuNo 0176 and BuNo 0172), 2 May 1937, AARM Reel 3, AvH.
2. Ibid., see also *Bureau of Aeronautics Newsletter* 13, no. 52, (15 June 1937): 7.
3. Patrick N. L. Bellinger Autobiographical Manuscript (hereinafter Bellinger MSS), 280, AvH, NHC. Unless otherwise indicated, the exchanges of 7 May 1937, during Fleet Problem XVIII, between Captain Bellinger and Rear Admiral King, are from this source.
4. Unless otherwise specified, the account of the activities of the *Ranger* and her squadrons during Fleet Problem XVIII is drawn from the following: Commander Aircraft, Base Force (Commander White Air Force) to Commander in Chief, U.S. Fleet, Subj: Track Charts—Narrative of Events, White Air Force, Fleet Problem XVIII, 12 May 1937; Assistant Umpire USS *Ranger* to Commander in Chief, United States Fleet, Subj: Umpire Report on Fleet Problem XVIII, n.d.; Assistant Umpire, USS *Saratoga*, to Commander in Chief, United States Fleet, Subj: Fleet Problem XVIII—USS *Saratoga* Assistant Umpire's Report of, 10 May 1937; and Ship's Umpire, USS *Lexington*, to Commander in Chief, United States Fleet, Subj: Summary of Damage Assessed *Lexington* Incident to Fleet Problem XVIII, 8 May 1937 (all on Reel 23), also Commander Aircraft, Main Body, Black Fleet (Commander Aircraft, Battle Force), Subj: Chronological Resume of Operations of Aircraft, Main Body, Black Fleet, during Fleet Problem XVIII, 11 May 1937; all in "Records Relating to United States Navy Fleet Problems I to XXII, 1923–1941," National Archives Microfilm Publication M964, Reel 22.
5. Assistant Umpire, USS *Saratoga*, to Commander in Chief, United States Fleet, Subj: Fleet Problem XVIII—USS *Saratoga* Assistant Umpire's Report of, 10 May 1937, "Records Relating to United States Navy Fleet Problems I to XXII, 1923–1941," National Archives Microfilm Publication M964, Reel 23.
6. Commander Aircraft, Main Body, Black Fleet (Commander Aircraft, Battle Force), Subject: Chronological Resume of Operations of Aircraft, Main Body, Black Fleet, during Fleet Problem XVIII, 11 May 1937, in "Records Relating to United States Navy Fleet Problems I to XXII, 1923–1941," National Archives Microfilm Publication M964, Reel 22.
7. Ibid.
8. AAR for F3F-1 (BuNo 0225), 7 May 1937, AARM Reel 3, AvH.
9. Ship Umpire, USS *Holland* to Commander in Chief, United States Fleet, Subj: Summary of damage assessed against the USS *Holland* and AP6, Fleet Problem XVIII, 9 May 1937, "Records Relating to United States Navy Fleet Problems I to XXII, 1923–1941," National Archives Microfilm Publication M964, Reel 23.
10. AAR for SBU-1 (BuNo 9779), 7 May 1937, AARM Reel 3, AvH.
11. "Although greatly interested in the way [the] *Ranger* was operated," one historian has written of this particular cruise, "King kept to his flag bridge, for he subscribed heartily to Admiral [Henry T.] Mayo's view that flag officers must never interfere in the management of their flagships." Ernest J. King and Walter Muir Whitehill, *Fleet Admiral King: A Naval Record* (New York: W.W. Norton, 1952), 274.
12. *Bureau of Aeronautics Newsletter* 13, no. 52, 8.
13. AAR for BM-1 (BuNo 8885), 25 May 1937, AARM Reel 3, AvH.
14. AAR for SBU-1 (BuNo 9800), 25 May 1937, AARM Reel 3, AvH.
15. *Bureau of Aeronautics Newsletter* 13, no. 53 (1 July 1937); 6.
16. AAR for SBU-1 (BuNo 9799), 28 May 1937, AARM Reel 3, AvH.
17. In later years, Pat Bellinger would look back on his time in the *Ranger*, which had been "the most comfortable ship I ever served on," with a great deal of affection. "An Admiral once told me," he writes, "that the best job in the Navy that anyone could have was Commanding Officer of a good ship. I began to get this point of view [while commanding the *Ranger*]" and retained it for many years throughout his service at flag rank. Bellinger MSS, AvH, op.cit., 277.

18. 1906 *Lucky Bag*, 113; also "Vice Admiral John Sidney McCain, United States Navy, Deceased" [biographical summary], typescript copy in author's files.
19. AARs for F3F-1 (BuNo 0216), F2F-1 (BuNo 9631), and F2F-1 (BuNo 9633), all 17 June 1937, AARM Reel 3, AvH.
20. AAR for SBU-1 (BuNo 9808), 21 June 1937, AARM Reel 3, AvH.
21. Commander Aircraft, Battle Force, to Commander in Chief, United States Fleet, Subj: Comments and Recommendations—Fleet Problem XVIII, 4 June 1937, "Records Relating to United States Navy Fleet Problems I to XXII, 1923–1941," National Archives Microfilm Publication M964, Reel 23.
22. Ibid.
23. Ibid.
24. Commander Battle Force (Commander Black Fleet, Fleet Problem XVIII) to Commander in Chief, United States Fleet, Subj: Comments and Recommendations on Fleet Problem XVIII, 23 June 1937, "Records Relating to United States Navy Fleet Problems I to XXII, 1923–1941," National Archives Microfilm Publication M964, Reel 23.
25. Ibid.
26. Ibid.
27. Ibid.
28. Bureau of Aeronautics Newsletter 13, no. 54 (15 July 1937): 9.
29. AAR for BG-1 (BuNo 9504), 30 June 1937, AARM Reel 3, AvH.
30. Ibid., 7.
31. "Narrative of Earhart Search," Annex B to Commander, *Lexington* Group, to Commandant, Fourteenth Naval District, Subj: Report of Earhart Search, forwarding, 20 July 1937, Microfilm Copy in NHC OA. Hereinafter "Narrative of Earhart Search," with the appropriate page.
32. "Narrative of Earhart Search," 1.
33. Bureau of Aeronautics Newsletter 13, no. 55 (1 August 1937): 8.
34. Captain Jonathan Stuart Dowell, U.S. Navy. Re: Service of, Nav-327-OF, dated 17 November 1937, Officer Biography Files, Box 166, OA. Information about Dowell's Naval Academy days comes from *The Lucky Bag* for 1905, 50. Captain Dowell's embarking in the *Lexington* is recorded in USS *Lexington* (CV-2) Deck Log (hereinafter *Lexington* Deck log), 4 July 1937, Records of the Bureau of Naval Personnel, RG-24, NARA, Washington, D.C.
35. Those numbers of the *Ranger*'s planes indicate only the planes embarked on board the *Lexington*; it did not constitute the entire squadron. The *Monthly Report, Status of Naval Aircraft*, for July 31, 1937, lists 19 BG-1s (1 over the authorized operating strength) on "actual strength" for VB-4, 18 SBU-1s for VS-41 and 10 SU-4s and 3 SBU-1s (5 under strength) for VS-42. U.S. Navy, Bureau of Aeronautics, *Monthly Report, Status of Naval Aircraft*, July 31, 1937, AVH, NHC. Ironically, two of the *Ranger*'s pilots had had the occasion, while on an extended flight over Route "A," to inspect Earhart's Electra earlier in the spring of 1937 (*Bureau of Aeronautics Newsletter* 13, no. 47 (1 April 1937): 10.

36. *Bureau of Aeronautics Newsletter* 13, no. 56 (15 August 1937): 7.
37. Ltr,, Comdr. Donald A. Lovelace, Jr., USN (Ret) to RJC, 9 October 2000.
38. Francis D. Foley, "Why the Navy Didn't Find Amelia" [letter to the editor], *Naval Institute Proceedings*, April 1993, 29–30. Foley was a lieutenant (jg) in VS-42.
39. Ibid.
40. AAR for BM-2 (BuNo 9170), 13 July 1937, AARM Reel 3, AvH.
41. "60 Planes at Sea Hunt Miss Earhart," *New York Times*, 14 July 1937, 3.
42. Ibid.
43. "Narrative of Earhart Search," 8.
44. "Earhart Seekers Endure Fierce Sun," *New York Times*, 15 July 1937, 6.
45. "Narrative of Earhart Search," 9.
46. "Aircraft Trouble Report" for BG-1 (BuNo 9508), 19 July 1937, in VBG-1/L11-1 files, vols. 9–10, Box 4835, RG-72, NARA, Washington, D.C.; see also AAR for BG-1 (BuNo 9508), 17 July 1937, AARM Reel 3, AvH.
47. AAR for SBU-1 (BuNo 9798), 17 July 1937, AARM Reel 3, AvH.
48. *Lexington* Deck Log, 20 July 1937.
49. "Report of Earhart Search Operations, 3–18 July 1937," Annex D to Commander, *Lexington* Group, to Commandant, Fourteenth Naval District, Subj: Report of Earhart Search, forwarding, 20 July 1937, op.cit.

Chapter 9: "AN EVERLASTING REMEMBRANCE OF ADMIRATION AND FRIENDSHIP"

1. *Bureau of Aeronautics Newsletter* 13, no. 55 (1 August 1937): 10.
2. Martin Cole, "Red Airmen to California," *American Aviation Historical Society Journal*, Summer 1968, 103–111.
3. AAR for SU-4 (BuNo 9419), 16 July 1937, AARM Reel 3, AvH.
4. Commander, Scouting Squadron Forty-Two to Commander Aircraft, Battle Force, Subj: Statement regarding orders given to Lt. (jg) C. M. Campbell, USN, pilot of SBU-1 Airplane No. 9770, 3 August 1937, in VSBU-1/L11-1 files, vol. 9, RG-72, Box 5406, NARA, Washington, D.C.
5. U.S. Navy, *Report of Gunnery Exercises, 1936–1937*, FTP-165 (Washington: GPO, 1937), Chapter 3, 1. Hereinafter *RGE, 1936–1937*.
6. Ibid., 10.
7. Ibid., 10–11.
8. Ibid., 8.
9. Rear Adm. Timothy J. O'Brien, USN (Ret) biographical material, in Officer Biography Files, Box 480, OA. The ship won the trophy again the following year.
10. *RGE, 1936–1937*, 26.
11. AAR for F4B-4 (BuNo 9253), 26 July 1937, AARM Reel 3, AvH.
12. AARs for BFC-2 (BuNo 9332 and BuNo 9333), 26 July 1937, AARM Reel 3, AvH.

13. AARs for TG-2s (BuNos 8725 and 8715), 26 July 1937, AARM Reel 3, AvH.
14. AAR for BFC-2s (BuNos 9274 and 9338), 26 July 1937, AARM Reel 3, AvH.
15. AAR for BG-1 (BuNo 9510), 27 July 1937, AARM Reel 3, AvH.
16. AAR for BG-1 (BuNo 9538), 27 July 1937, AARM Reel 3, AvH.
17. Ibid.
18. AARs for BG-1s (BuNos 9506 and 9507), 28 July 1937, AARM Reel 3, AvH.
19. AAR for BM-1 (BuNo 8879), 29 July 1937, AARM Reel 3, AvH.
20. *Bureau of Aeronautics Newsletter* no.58 (15 September 1937): 18; see also AAR for TG-2 (BuNo 8713), 3 August 1937, AARM Reel 3, AvH.
21. AARs for F3F-1s (BuNos 0220 and 0236), 18 August 1937, AARM Reel 3, AvH.
22. AAR for BG-1 (BuNo 9511), 19 August 1937, AARM Reel 3, AvH. Moss later flew with Pan American Airways; copilot of the Martin 130 *Philippine Clipper*, he survived the bombing of the PanAir facility at Wake Island on 8 December 1941, to fly the clipper out to safety later that day.
23. Unless otherwise indicated, the reconstruction of the collision on the morning of 25 August 1937 is based upon: "Statement of Lt. (jg) W. C. Fortune, U.S. Navy, Regarding Collision Between 3-S-1 and 2-MF-1, SBU-1 #9765 and F3F-1 #0251, 27 August 1937; McDANIEL, J. R., RM3c, U.S. Navy to Commanding Officer, U.S. Naval Hospital, San Diego, California, Subj: Statement Regarding Crash of SBU-1 Airplane [on] 25 August 1937; and Statement of Captain Lawson H. M. Sanderson, U.S.M.C., 26 August 1937, all enclosures to "Aircraft Trouble Report" for SBU-1 (BuNo 9765) in VSBU-1/L11-1 Files, vol. 9., Box 5406, RG-72, NARA, Washington, D.C.; see also AARs for SBU-1 (BuNo 9765) and F3F-1 (BuNo 0251), 25 August 1937, AARM Reel 3, AvH.
24. AARs for SBU-1s (BuNos 9763 and 9798), 3 September 1937, AARM Reel 3, AvH.
25. *Bureau of Aeronautics Newsletter* 13, no. 61 (1 November 1937): 7–8.
26. "Aircraft Trouble Report on SBU-1 Airplane, Bureau No. 9759, VS Squadron Forty-Two, USS *Ranger*," 8 September 1937, in VSBU-1/L11-1 files, Vol. 10, Box 5408, RG-72.
27. "The Cruise of the *Ranger* to Peru, A Souvenir of the Goodwill Cruise, 4 September–5 October 1937," privately printed, 1937.
28. "Aircraft Trouble Report on SBU-1 Airplane, Bureau No. 9777, VS Squadron Forty-Two, USS *Ranger*," 14 September 1937, in VSBU-1/L11-1 files, Vol. 10, Box 5408, op.cit.
29. "Aviation Cadet Lane A. Hurst, USNR, to Aircraft Trouble Board, Subj: Crash of SBU-1 Airplane No. 9777, report on," 14 September 1937, in VSBU-1/L11-1 files, vol. 10, Ibid.
30. "Landing Signal Officer to Trouble Board, VS Squadron 42, Subj: Crash of SBU-1 Airplane, Bureau No. 9777, Aviation Cadet L. A. Hurst, USNR, Pilot, 14 September 1937," 14 September 1937, in VSBU-1/L11-1 files, vol. 10, Ibid.
31. *Bureau of Aeronautics Newsletter* 13, no. 61, 8.
32. C. Addison Pound, "USS *Ranger* (CV-4) Cruise to Lima, Peru, September 4–October 5, 1937," copy in author's possession.
33. *Bureau of Aeronautics Newsletter* 13, no. 61, 9.
34. Ltr, General Oscar R. Benavides to President Franklin D. Roosevelt, 28 September 1937, translation.
35. AAR for BG-1 (BuNo 9502), 2 October 1937, AARM Reel 3, AvH.
36. "Aircraft Trouble Report" concerning the loss of SBU-1 (BuNo 9804), VSBU-1/L11-1 files, vol. 10, RG-72, Box 5408, NARA, Washington, D.C.
37. "Statement of Evans, C. L., RM2c, USN, regarding crash of SBU-1 Airplane Bureau Number 9804 on 4 October, 1937," in "Aircraft Trouble Report" concerning the loss of SBU-1 (BuNo 9804), VSBU-1/L11-1 files, op.cit.
38. "Aircraft Trouble Report" concerning the loss of SBU-1 (BuNo 9804), VSBU-1/L11-1 files, Vol. 10, RG-72, Box 5408, NARA, Washington, D.C.; see also AAR for SBU-1 (BuNo 9804), 4 October 1937, AARM Reel 3, AvH.
39. Statement of Lt. J. F. Schumacher, U.S. Navy, regarding crash of SBU-1 Airplane, Bureau Number 9804, on 4 October, 1937, in "Aircraft Trouble Report" concerning the loss of SBU-1 (BuNo 9804), op.cit.

Chapter 10: "THE OFFICERS AND MEN KNOW THEIR BUSINESS"

1. *Bureau of Aeronautics Newsletter* no. 66 (15 January 1938): 8.
2. Ibid.
3. Lieutenant (jg) W. C. Fortune, U.S. Navy, to Aircraft Trouble Board, Subj: Damage to SBU-1 Airplane No. 9783 on 17 March, 1938—statement regarding, 17 March 1938, in VSBU-1/L11-1 file, vol. 12, Box 5408, RG-72; see also AAR for SBU-1 (BuNo 9783), 17 March 1938, AARM Reel 3, AvH.
4. "Aircraft Trouble Report on SBU-1 Airplane No. 9805, Av Cadet E. [sic] A. Jaeger, USNR, Pilot," dated 18 March 1938, in VSBU-1/L11-1 file, vol. 12, RG-72; pertinent statements contained therein include ltr, Aviation Cadet T. A. Jaeger, USNR, to Aircraft Trouble Board, "Damage to SBU-1 Airplane No. 9805 on 17 March, 1938—Statement regarding," dated 17 March 1938, and Landing Signal Officer [Lt. E. A. Hannegan] to Trouble Board, VS Squadron 42, "Crash of SBU-1 Airplane No. 9805, Aviation Cadet E. [sic] A. Jaeger, USNR Pilot, on 17 March 1938."
5. AAR for SBU-1 (BuNo 9790), 17 March 1938, AARM Reel 3, AvH; see also Lt. (jg) C. B. Lanman, U.S. Navy to Trouble Board, Subj: Damage to SBU-1 Airplane No. 9790, 17 March 1938, and Lt. C. L. Lee, U.S. Navy, to Trouble Board, Scouting Squadron Forty-One, Subject: SBU-1 Airplane No. 9790, statement in regards to damage of, 24 March 1938, in VSBU-1/L11-1 files, vol. 12, Box 5408, RG-72.
6. Aviation Cadet R. C. Santee, U.S.N.R., to Aircraft Trouble Board, Subj: Damage to SBU-1 Airplane No. 9799 on 17 March 1938—Statement regarding, 17 March 1938, in VSBU-1/L11-1 file, vol. 12, Box 5408, RG-72.

7. Lieutenant (jg) G. R. Luker, U.S. Navy, to Trouble Board, Subj: Damage to SBU-1 Airplane No. 9759 on 17 March 1938; Lt. (jg) L. M. Stevens, U.S. Navy, to Trouble Board, Subj: Damage to SBU-1 Airplane No. 9795, on 17 March, 1938, 20 March 1938; and Aviation Cadet J. M. Leslie, U.S.N.R., to Trouble Board, Subj: Damage to SBU-1 Airplane No. 9766 on 17 March, 1938, 20 March 1938; all contained in VSBU-1/L11-1 files, vol. 12, Box 5408, RG-72.
8. Lieutenant Commander J. M. Hoskins, U.S. Navy, to Trouble Board, Subj: Pilot's Statement in Regard to Crash of SBU-1 Airplane No. 9764, 18 March 1938, in VSBU-1/L11-1 file, vol. 11, Box 5408, RG-72.
9. Ltr, Adm. Claude C. Bloch to Adm. Harry E. Yarnell, 16 April 1938, in Claude C. Bloch Papers, General Correspondence, 1926–1942, Container 4, Library of Congress Manuscript Division, Washington, D.C., hereinafter Bloch Papers, LCMD.
10. Ltr, Adm. Claude C. Bloch to Adm. William D. Leahy, 29 April 1938, Container 2, Bloch Papers, LCMD.
11. Commander Aircraft, Battle Force, to Commanding Officer, Aircraft Two, FMF, Subj: Performance of Duty of Aircraft Two, Fleet Marine Force, 28 May 1938, copy in Aircraft Two File, Reference Section, Marine Corps Historical Center, Washington, D.C.
12. "Weekly Carrier Operation Report," 1 July 1938, copy provided the author by James T. Rindt. The Navy ultimately adopted the plane. Built by the Naval Aircraft Factory and designated as the SBN-1, it served primarily as a training aircraft, equipping Torpedo Squadron (VT) 8 of the *Hornet* (CV-8) Air Group in 1941.
13. Ltr, King to Arthur B. Cook, 7 July 1938, King Papers, LCMD.
14. AAR for TBD-1 (BuNo 0309), 13 July 1938, AARM Reel 3, AvH.
15. Delmar S. Fahrney, *The History of Pilotless Aircraft and Guided Missiles*, undated mss., World War II Command File, OA. Hereinafter Fahrney.
16. [Aviation Cadet A. L. Gurney, USNR] "Statement," 24 August 1938, in Aircraft Trouble Report dated 23 August 1938 on SBU-1 Airplane No. 9759, R-1535-82 Engine No. 1419, Assigned to Scouting Squadron Forty-One, in VSBU-1/L11-1 files, Vol. 10, RG-72.
17. Ibid.
18. [Lt. (jg) J. M. Wright, USN] "Statement," 23 August 1938, in Aircraft Trouble Report, dated 23 August 1938, on SBU-1 Airplane No. 9759, R-1535-82 Engine No. 1419, Assigned to Scouting Squadron Forty-One, op.cit.; see also AAR for SBU-1 (BuNo 9759), 22 August 1938, AARM Reel 3, AvH.
19. AAR for BG-1 (BuNo 9534), 23 August 1938, AARM Reel 3, AvH.
20. Officer in Charge, Project DOG, to Chief of BuAer, 26 August 1938, quoted in Fahrney, 233.
21. Captain McCain's comments are quoted in Fahrney, 236–237.
22. Ibid., 238.
23. Rear Adm. Arthur B. Cook, Chief of the Bureau of Aeronautics, quoted in Fahrney, 240.
24. Fahrney, 236.
25. AAR for SBU-1 (BuNo 9750), 25 August 1938, AARM Reel 3, AvH.
26. AAR for F3F-1 (BuNo 0216) and SBC-3 (BuNo 0571), 2 September 1938, AARM Reel 3, AvH.
27. Additional AAR for F3F-1 (BuNo 0216), 2 September 1938, AARM Reel 3, AvH.
28. Unless otherwise indicated, the account of the loss of Aviation Cadet Jaeger's SBU-1 is from the "Aircraft Trouble Report, dated 30 November 1938, on SBU-1 Airplane No. 9780 Assigned to Scouting Squadron Forty-two," in VSBU-1/L11-1 file, Vol. 13, RG-72, Box 5408. Principal documents include the statements by Lieutenant (jg) Moore and Radiomen 1st Class Herndon and Hogge, and the Second Endorsement on the report by Capt. John S. McCain, the *Ranger*'s commanding officer.
29. Aviation Cadet H.W. Crews. U.S.N.R., to Aircraft Trouble Board, Subject: Statement in regard to damage to SBU-1 #9756, 17 December, 1938, in VSBU-1/L11-1 files, vol. 13, Box 5408, RG-72, NARA, Washington, D.C. See also AAR for SBU-1 (BuNo 9756), 17 December 1938, AARM Reel 3, AvH.
30. Bureau of Aeronautics Newsletter no. 91 (1 February 1939): 4.

Chapter 11: "THE PROBABILITY OF AIR ATTACK ON CARRIERS"

1. *Bureau of Aeronautics Newsletter* no. 92 (15 February 1939): 8.
2. Ibid.
3. USS *Ranger* Weekly Carrier Operation Reports, 5–7 January 1939 and 9–12 January 1939, courtesy of James T. Rindt.
4. AAR for F3F-1 (BuNo 0217), 10 January 1939, AARM Reel 4, AvH.
5. *Bureau of Aeronautics Newsletter* no. 92 (15 February 1939): 9.
6. Ibid.
7. Subsequently, Comdr. Genda Minoru, of the Imperial Japanese Navy, saw the sight of four U.S. carriers steaming in column in what may have been a newsreel. "Why should we have trouble in gathering planes in the air," he thought afterwards, "if we concentrate our carriers?" Such a concentration enabled the Japanese to launch a devastatingly successful surprise attack on the U.S. Pacific Fleet at Pearl Harbor on 7 December 1941. Gordon W. Prange, *At Dawn We Slept: The Untold Story of Pearl Harbor* (New York: McGraw Hill, 1981), 24.
8. *The Bull Horn*, 4 February 1939, 4.
9. Ibid.
10. AAR for SB2U-1 (BuNo 0743), 14 February 1939, AARM Reel 4, AvH.
11. Unless otherwise specified, the operations of the *Ranger* during Fleet Problem XX are derived from "Records Relating to United States Navy Fleet Problems I to XXII, 1923-1941," National Archives Microfilm Publication M964, Reels 26–28.
12. AAR for SBU-1 (BuNo 9806), 24 February 1939, AARM Reel 4, AvH.
13. AAR for SB2U-1 (BuNo 0744), 25 February 1939, AARM Reel 4, AvH.
14. AARs for SBU-1s (BuNos 9763 and 9793), 26 February 1939, AARM Reel 4, AvH.

15. Commanding Officer, USS *Ranger*, to Commander in Chief, U.S. Fleet, Subj: Fleet Problem XX, Comments and Recommendations, CV4/A16-3/FPXX Serial 087 of 31 March 1939, "Records Relating to United States Navy Fleet Problems I to XXII, 1923–1941," National Archives Microfilm Publication M964, Reel 26.
16. Quoted in Commanding Officer, USS *Ranger*, to Commander in Chief, U.S. Fleet, Subj: Fleet Problem XX, Comments and Recommendations, CV4/A16-3/FPXX Serial 087 of 31 March 1939, "Records Relating to United States Navy Fleet Problems I to XXII, 1923–1941," National Archives Microfilm Publication M964, Reel 26.
17. Commanding Officer, USS *Ranger*, to Commander in Chief, U.S. Fleet, Subj: Fleet Problem XX, Comments and Recommendations, CV4/A16-3/FPXX Serial 087 of 31 March 1939, op.cit.
18. AAR for SB2U-1 (BuNo 0737), 27 February 1939, AARM Reel 4, AvH.
19. AAR for SBU-1 (BuNo 9809), 11 March 1939, AARM Reel 4, AvH.
20. AAR for SB2U-1 (BuNo 0739), 11 March 1939, AARM Reel 4, AvH.
21. *Bureau of Aeronautics Newsletter* no. 106 (15 September 1939): 10.
22. Ltr, Rear Adm. Alfred W. Johnson to Adm. Claude C. Bloch, 29 May 1939, Bloch Papers, LCMD.
23. Commanding Officer, USS *Ranger* (CV-4) to Chief of Naval Operations, Subj: Dry docking–USS *Ranger* (CV-4), Serial CV-4/S19-1 Ser 032 of 2 March 1940, RG-19, Bureau of Ships Confidential Correspondence C-CV4 #1, to 12/31/40, Box 707, NARA, College Park, MD. Subsequent inspection by ship's divers revealed that large patches of the plastic paint, some between 5 and 18 inches in diameter, were flaking off, because of the way in which the paint had been applied.
24. "Report on the Fitness of Officers" covering the period 1 April to 31 July 1926, in Ralph F. Wood, "Orders File," Emil Buehler Naval Aviation Library, Pensacola, FL. Wood's service biography is contained in Officer Biography Files, Box 699, OA.
25. "Memorandum for Admiral Nimitz, Subj: Rear Admiral Ralph Wood," 1 August 1944, in the correspondence of Fleet Admiral Nimitz with Fleet Admiral King, 1942–1945, Series XIII, Folder 19, Personal Papers Collection, OA.
26. Fortunately, as far as the *Ranger* was concerned, Commander Aircraft, Battle Force, normally the ship's type commander, delegated the turn-in and replacement of planes to Commander, Atlantic Squadron, thus allowing the smooth provision of overhauled aircraft to keep the air group up to strength.
27. AAR for J2F-1 (BuNo 0169), 29 June 1939, AARM Reel 4, AvH.
28. AAR for SB2U-1 (BuNo 0743), 13 July 1939, AARM Reel 4, AvH.
29. AAR for SBU-1 (BuNo 9771), 14 July 1939, AARM Reel 4, AvH.
30. AAR for SB2U-1 (BuNo 0731), 27 July 1939, AARM Reel 4, AvH.
31. AARs for SBU-1s (BuNos 9754 and 9807), 7 August 1939 and 11 August 1939, respectively, AARM Reel 4, AvH.
32. AAR for JRS-1 (BuNo 1054), 31 August 1939, AARM Reel 4, AvH.
33. AAR for SB2U-1 (BuNo 0776), 31 August 1939, AARM Reel 4, AvH.
34. *Bureau of Navigation Bulletin*, no. 280 (20 April 1940): 1.

CHAPTER 12: "RANGER HAS TAKEN THE NECESSARY CHANGES IN ITS STRIDE"

1. AAR for SBU-1 (BuNo 9811), 5 September 1939, AARM Reel 4, AvH.
2. AAR for F3F-1 (BuNo 0217), 6 September 1939, AARM Reel 4, AvH.
3. Ltr, Adm. Harold R. Stark to Adm. Claude C. Bloch, 30 October 1939, Bloch Papers, LCMD.
4. USS *Ranger*, "Weekly Carrier Operation Report," 28 November–3 December, 1939, courtesy of James T. Rindt.
5. "Telephone conversation between Admiral Ghormley and Comdr. J. L. Holloway, Chief of Staff, COMATRON, 3:20 P.M., 30 November, 1939" in "Telephone Conversations, 30 Nov[ember]–31 Dec[ember] 1939" file, World War II Command File, Box 217, OA. There are two versions of the Ghormley–Holloway conversation in file: one the verbatim transcript and the other a smooth, much-edited version. I have used the former, because it precusily reflects what was actually said.
6. *The Bull Horn* 3, no. 36 (9 December 1939): 3.
7. *The Bull Horn*
8. AAR for SB2U-2 (BuNo 1358), 4 January 1940, AARM Reel 4, AvH. Unfortunately, Joe Evans, who hailed from the little mining town of Shamokin, Pennsylvania, died in the crash of the same plane (BuNo 1358) off Guantanamo Bay, Cuba, while operating from the *Wasp* on 9 July 1940. Seaman 2d Class H. W. Reeder also perished in the crash.
9. AAR for BG-1 (BuNo 9501), 9 January 1940, AARM Reel 4, AvH.
10. AAR for F3F-1 (BuNo 0253), 15 January 1940, AARM Reel 4, AvH.
11. AARs for BG-1s (BuNo 9506 and 9534), 16 January 1940, AARM Reel 4, AvH.
12. AAR for SB2U-2 F2F-1 (BuNo 9673), 16 January 1940, AARM Reel 4, AvH.
13. AAR for SBU-1 (BuNo 9817) and SB2U-2 (BuNo 1360), 16 January 1940, AARM, Reel 4, AvH.
14. AARs for F3F-1s (BuNos 0263 and 0229), 17 January and 18 January 1940, respectively, AARM Reel 4, AvH.
15. AAR for SB2U-1 (BuNo 0745), 8 February 1940, AARM Reel 4, AvH.
16. AAR for SBU-1 (BuNo 9775), 13 February 1940, AARM, Reel 4, AvH.
17. AAR for SB2U-1 (BuNo 0746), 16 February 1940, AARM Reel 4, AvH.

18. AAR for F3F-1 (BuNo 0261), 27 February 1940, AARM Reel 4, AvH.
19. AAR for SB2U-2 (BuNo 1373), 4 March 1940, AARM Reel 4, AvH.
20. AAR for F3F-1 (BuNo 0257), 6 March 1940, AARM Reel 4, AvH.
21. AAR for F3F-1 (BuNo 0219), 7 March 1940, AARM Reel 4, AvH.
22. AAR for F3F-1 (BuNo 0242), 19 March 1940, AARM Reel 4, AvH.
23. AAR for F3F-1 (BuNo 0227), 1 April 1940, AARM Reel 4, AvH.
24. AAR for SBU-1 (BuNo 9812), 10 April 1940, AARM Reel 4, AvH.
25. AAR for F3F-1 (BuNo 0227), 10 April 1940, AARM Reel 4, AvH.
26. AARs for F3F-1s (BuNos 0259 and 0220), 8 and 10 May 1940, respectively, AARM Reel 4, AvH.
27. AAR for F3F-1 (BuNo 0262), 21 May 1940, AARM Reel 4, AvH.
28. AAR for F3F-1 (BuNo 0227), 1 April 1940, AARM Reel 4, AvH.

Chapter 13: "SPREADING THE BUTTER A LITTLE THIN"

1. Commandant, Norfolk Navy Yard to Chief of Naval Operations, Serial CV4/S7/S19(2-MOH) 7850 of 7 March 1940, Subj: USS *Ranger* (CV-4)—Dry docking; Commander Aircraft, Battle Force to Chief of Naval Operations, Subj: USS *Ranger* (CV-4)—Dry docking, Serial S19/CV4/23-He/FF2-3 (0356) of 30 March 1940 (Third endorsement to *Ranger* CV-4/S-19-1 (032) of 2 March 1940), op.cit.; Commander in Chief, U.S. Fleet, to Chief of Naval Operations, Subj: USS *Ranger* (CV-4)—Dry docking, Serial S19/S7/0590 of 8 April 1940; and Bureau of Construction and Repair and Bureau of Engineering to Commanding Officer, USS *Ranger*, Subj: USS *Ranger* (CV-4)—Drydocking During Restricted Availability Period, 3 June–1 July 1940, Serial C-CV4/S19(5-2-MCV) of 18 May 1940, in RG-19, Bureau of Ships Confidential Correspondence C-CV4 #1, to 12/31/40, Box 707, NARA, College Park, MD.
2. "Memorandum for Admiral Nimitz, Subj: Rear Admiral Ralph Wood," 1 August 1944, op.cit.
3. AAR for SB2U-1 (BuNo 0245), 10 June 1940, AARM Reel 4, AvH.
4. AAR for F3F-1 (BuNo 0238), 13 June 1940, AARM Reel 4, AvH.
5. AAR for SBC-3 (BuNo 0508), 14 June 1940, AARM Reel 4, AvH.
6. AAR for SB2U-1 (BuNo 0736), 25 June 1940, AARM Reel 4, AvH.
7. "Annual Report of Commander Atlantic Squadron [Rear Adm. Hayne Ellis], for the Period July 1, 1939 to June 30, 1940," in World War II Command File, "Fleets, Asiatic Fleet, Atlantic Squadron, Atlantic Fleet, Annual Reports—Instructions," 6, Box 225, OA.
8. U.S. Navy, *Report of Gunnery Exercises, U.S. Navy, 1939–1940* [FTP-203], Chapter 3, 1 (Washington: GPO, 1940).
9. AAR for SB2U-1 (BuNo 0750), 5 August 1940, AARM Reel 4, AvH.
10. AAR for SB2U-1 (BuNo 0746), 22 August 1940, AARM Reel 4, AvH.
11. AAR for SBU-1 (BuNo 9751), 5 September 1940, AARM Reel 4, AvH.
12. AAR for F3F-1 (BuNo 0219), 5 September 1940, AARM Reel 4, AvH.
13. AAR for F3F-1 (BuNo 0452), 20 September 1940, AARM Reel 4, AvH.
14. AAR for J2F-4 (BuNo 1652), 11 October 1940, AARM Reel 4, AvH.
15. Conf. Ltr, Commanding Officer, USS *Ranger* (CV-4) to Chief, Bureau of Ships, L9-3/S16-5 (1780) of 28 November 1940, Subj: USS *Ranger* (CV-4)—Alteration Request #21-40. Rear Admiral Cook's endorsement: Conf. Ltr, Commander Aircraft, Patrol Force, to Chief of the Bureau of Ships, L9-3(035) of 3 December 1940, Subj: USS *Ranger* (CV-4)—Alteration Request #21-40 (Replace or redesign the *Ranger* aircraft elevators, #1, #2, and #3 to operate at a speed commensurate with that obtainable in recent aircraft carrier design). The type commander, Vice Adm. William F. Halsey, Jr., Commander Aircraft, Battle Force, likewise concurred in Conf. Ltr, Commander Aircraft, Battle Force to Chief of the Bureau of Ships, L9-3/CV4/23-Rh/FF2-3 (027) of 8 January 1941, Subj: USS *Ranger* (CV-4)—Alteration Request #21-40 (Replace or redesign the *Ranger* aircraft elevators, #1, #2, and #3 to operate at a speed commensurate with that obtainable in recent aircraft carrier design) in RG-19, BuShips Confidential Correspondence C-CV-4 #4, to 6/19/41, Box 707, NARA, College Park, MD.
16. AAR for J2F-1 (BuNo 0187), 18 January 1941, AARM Reel 4, AvH.
17. AAR for BG-1 (BuNo 9514), 23 January 1941, AARM Reel 4, AvH.
18. AAR for F4F-3 (BuNo 1863), 29 January 1941, AARM Reel 4, AvH.
19. *Bureau of Aeronautics Newsletter* no. 141 (1 March 1941): 11–12.
20. Ibid.
21. Ibid.
22. Commander in Chief, U.S. Atlantic Fleet, Report, 1 July 1940–30 June 1941.
23. Lieutenant Comdr. E. C. Parker, U.S. Navy to Senior Member, Trouble Board, Subj: Pilots statement in regard to accident to F4F-3 airplane number 1865 on 12 February 1941, 13 February 1941, in VF4F-3/L11-1 vols. 1–2 to February 28, 1941, Box 4930, RG-72 Records of the Bureau of Aeronautics, NARA, Washington, D.C.; see also AAR for F4F-3 (BuNo 1865), 12 February 1941, AARM Reel 4, AvH.
24. Ensign W. F. Madden, A-V(N), USNR to Senior Member, Trouble Board, Subject: "Pilot[']s statement in regard to accident to

F4F-3 airplane number 1854 on 12 February, 1941" (hereinafter Madden) in VF4F-3/L11-1 vols. 1–2 to February 28, 1941, Box 4930, RG-72 Records of the Bureau of Aeronautics, NARA, Washington, D.C.; see also AAR for F4F-3 (BuNo 1854), 12 February 1941, AARM Reel 4, AvH.
25. Landing Signal Officer [Lt. J. O. Vosseller] to Trouble Board, Subj: Aircraft Trouble Report of F4F-3 Airplane Bureau no. 1854, February 13, 1941 (hereinafter Vosseller), in VF4F-3/L11-1 vols. 1– 2 to February 28, 1941, Box 4930, RG-72 Records of the Bureau of Aeronautics, NARA, Washington, D.C.
26. Madden.
27. Vosseller.
28. Commanding Officer [USS *Ranger*] to Chief of the Bureau of Aeronautics, Subj: Aircraft Trouble Report regarding damage on F4F-3 airplane BuNo 1854, dated 12 February, 1941, in VF4F-3/L11-1 vols. 1–2 to February 28, 1941, Box 4930, op.cit.
29. AAR for F4F-3 (BuNo 1859), 22 February 1941, AARM Reel 4, AvH.
30. [Memorandum] "Ocean Escort in Western Atlantic" [April 1941], *Pearl Harbor Attack Hearings*, Part 16, 2162–2163. Hereinafter PHA. Anglo-American concern over the commerce-raiding operations of the *Scharnhorst* and *Gneisenau* proved well-founded: on 15–16 March, the two battle cruisers sank 13 ships of a dispersed westbound convoy. The two ships concluded Operation *Berlin* by arriving safely at Brest, France, on 22 March. Between them, they sank 115,622 tons of shipping.
31. "Good cure for nonchalance," Lt. Comdr. William A. Evans, of BuAer's Flight Division, later observed on the routing sheet covering Bull's adventures, "I'm surprised to find it considered O.K. to dive any plane with [the] hood part way open." VF4F-3/L11-1 File.
32. Ltr, Rear Adm. Arthur B. Cook to Adm. Ernest J. King, 17 March 1941, Atlantic Fleet "C" Miscellaneous File, Box 8, King Papers, LCMD.
33. "Contract 58853—SB2U-2," handwritten notes, Naval Air Systems Command (NavAir) Collection, Box 33, AvH. "Wheel horse" = "a person who works especially hard and steadily in any enterprise."
34. AAR for F4F-3 (BuNo 2530), 22 March 1941, AARM Reel 4, AvH.
35. AAR for F4F-3 (BuNo 2521), 24 March 1941, AARM Reel 4, AvH; see also 1938 *Lucky Bag*, 125.
36. [Lieutenant Junius W. Millard, USNR] Memorandum for File, 31 March 1941, Subj: Trip to Norfolk Navy Yard, 27–28 March 1941, in RG-19, BuShips Confidential Correspondence C-CV-4 #4, to 6/19/41, Box 707, NARA, College Park, MD.
37. Ibid.
38. Ibid.
39. Ibid.
40. "Memorandum for the President," March 20, 1941, in Samuel Eliot Morison Papers, Series III, vol. 1 (60), NHC, OA.
41. AAR for F4F-3 (BuNo 2533), 3 April 1941, AARM Reel 4, AvH.
42. AAR for F4F-3 (BuNo 1886), 11 April 1941, AARM Reel 4, AvH.
43. "Ocean Escort in Western Atlantic," *PHA* 16, 2163. The *Yorktown* (see below) would be transferred to the Atlantic, instead of the preferred *Lexington*.
44. Ltr, Adm. Harold R. Stark to Adm. Husband E. Kimmel, 4 April 1941, *PHA* 16, 2161.
45. Ibid.
46. Msg, CNO to CinCPacFlt, 7 April 1941, Subj: Transfer of Units from the Pacific Fleet to the Atlantic Fleet, *PHA* 11, 5503.
47. Christman died in aerial combat in China, 23 January 1942; Petach during a strafing mission, 10 July 1942. Hill and Rector both became "aces" with the 14th Air Force, Hill with seven kills (six aerial, one ground) and Rector with nine (four aerial, five ground). Wanda Cornelius and Thayne Short, *Ding Hao: America's Air War in China, 1937–1945* (Gretna: Pelican, 1980).
48. AARs for F4F-3s (BuNos 2524 and 2536), 15 April 1941, AARM Reel 5, AvH.
49. Ltr, Adm. Harold R. Stark to Adm. Husband E. Kimmel, 19 April 1941, *PHA* 16, 2164.
50. Commander Aircraft, Atlantic Fleet [Rear Adm. Arthur B. Cook] "Rough Draft" n.d. [16 May 1941], Flag Files [xerox copy in author's files]. Captain Montgomery later observed that "one liberty every three weeks is not sufficient to maintain contentment of personnel." Commanding Officer [Capt. Alfred E. Montgomery] to Commander Task Force Two [Commander Aircraft, Atlantic Fleet], Subj: Patrol Operations, 9–23 May, 1941," Serial CV4/A4-3(3) of 24 May 1941; xerox copy in author's files.
51. Ibid.
52. Ibid.
53. Ibid.
54. Ibid.
55. Commanding Officer [Capt. Alfred E. Montgomery] to Commander Task Force Two (Commander Aircraft, Atlantic Fleet), Subj: Patrol Operations, 9–23 May, 1941," op.cit.
56. The three *Ranger* squadrons operated alongside the TBD-1-equipped VT-5, which, alone of the *Yorktown* squadrons, remained in its parent ship. All told, airplane hours for the 31 May–12 June cruise in the *Yorktown* totalled 1,279.8 hr, as the task group (TG 1) steamed 4,550 miles. Commander, Task Force Two to Chief of Naval Operations, Subj: Surface Patrol Tasks Executed by Task Groups of Task Force Two, during period 26 April to 30 August, 1941, Serial 00111 of 9 September 1941.
57. Clark, *Carrier Admiral*, 79.
58. Commanding Officer [Capt. Alfred E. Montgomery] to Commander Task Force Two (Commander Aircraft, Atlantic Fleet), Subj: Patrol Operations, 9–23 May, 1941," op.cit
59. Ibid.
60. AAR for F4F-3 (BuNo 2528), 22 May 1941, AARM Reel 5, AvH.
61. AAR for F4F-3 (BuNo 1862), 28 May 1941, AARM Reel 5, AvH.
62. "Aircraft Trouble Report," in VBT-1/L11-1, vol. 9–10, Dec.1, 1940 to Dec. 31, 1942 file, RG-72, Box 4850, NARA, Washington, D.C.

63. "Trouble Report, BT-1 type airplane, BuNo 0610 of 5 June, 1941" in VBT-1/L11-1, vol. 9–10, Dec.1, 1940 to Dec. 31, 1942 file, RG-72, Box 4850, NARA, Washington, D.C.
64. Conf. Ltr, Commandant, Norfolk Navy Yard to Chief of Naval Operations, CV4/S83(1-MP-6/19), Serial 779, 9 June 1941, in RG-19, BuShips Confidential Correspondence C-CV4 #4, to 6/19/41, Box 707, NARA, College Park, MD.

Chapter 14: "WITH CONTAGIOUS ENTHUSIASM"

1. AAR for SB2U-3 (BuNo 2082), 18 June 1941, AARM Reel 4, AvH.
2. AARs for SBC-4s (BuNos 1313 and 1816), 25 June 1941, AARM Reel 5, AvH.
3. AAR for F4F-3 (BuNo 1853), 26 June 1941, AARM Reel 5, AvH.
4. AAR for F4F-3 (BuNo 1879), 26 June 1941, AARM Reel 5, AvH. The colorful Red Bassett, an unforgettable squadron "character," later died in aerial combat in the Battle of Midway, 4 June 1942, trying to protect Torpedo Squadron Three in its charge toward the Japanese carrier force.
5. AAR for SB2U-2 (BuNo 1346), 27 June 1941, AARM Reel 4, AvH.
6. AAR for F4F-3 (BuNo 3955), 30 June 1941, AARM Reel 5, AvH.
7. AAR for SB2U-1 (BuNo 0749), 7 July 1941, AARM Reel 33, AvH.
8. AAR for F4F-3 (BuNo 1870), 16 July 1941, AARM Reel 13, AvH.
9. AAR for SB2U-2 (BuNo 1348), 19 July 1941, AARM Reel 33, AvH.
10. AAR for SB2U-1 (BuNo 0774), 28 July 1941, AARM Reel 33, AvH.
11. AAR for SB2U-1 (BuNo 0759), 30 July 1941, AARM Reel 33, AvH.
12. Conf. Ltr, Commander Aircraft, Atlantic Fleet to Chief of Naval Operations, Ser S75-3(X023), Subj: Torpedoes—Maintenance and Stowage on USS *Ranger* (CV-4) and USS *Wasp* (CV-7), 25 August 1941, in RG-19, Bureau of Ships Confidential Correspondence C-CV4 #3, to 11/31/41, Box 708, NARA, College Park, MD. Of the four scouting squadrons whose authorized operating strength included TBD-1s, only two were actually operating them around that time: VS-42 in the *Ranger* and VS-71 in the *Wasp*. Bureau of Aeronautics, *Status of Naval Aircraft*, 30 August 1941, AvH.
13. Conf. Ltr, Commander in Chief, United States Atlantic Fleet to Chief of Naval Operations, S75/(0929), Subj: Torpedoes—Maintenance and Stowage on USS *Ranger* (CV-4) and USS *Wasp* (CV-7), 2 September 1941, First Endorsement to Conf. Ltr, Commander Aircraft, Atlantic Fleet to Chief of Naval Operations, Ser S75-3(X023), 25 August 1941, op.cit., in RG-19, Bureau of Ships Confidential Correspondence C-CV4 #1, to 11/31/41, Box 708, NARA, College Park, MD. Chief of Naval Operations' approval of the alteration came on 17 October 1941, to be "accomplished at an early date." The time lag in approving the inclusion of torpedo maintenance and stowage facilities in the *Ranger* meant that the work to modify the ship's dope shop (made irrelevant by newer aircraft entering service with metal, instead of fabric-covered wings) into torpedo stowage could not be accomplished during the July–September 1941 overhaul, as originally hoped.
14. Quoted in Ltr, Chief of Naval Operations to Commanding General, First Marine Aircraft Wing FMF [Fleet Marine Force], Subj: Lt. Col. Louis E. Woods, U.S. Marine Corps—Letter of Commendation, 27 October 1941, Louis E. Woods Papers (PC-228), Folder 50, November–December 1941, Marine Corps Historical Center Personal Papers Section, Washington, D.C.
15. Quoted in Chief of Naval Operations to Major General Commandant, Subj: Louisiana Army Maneuvers, Report on, 3 December 1941, in RG-127, War Plans Section Records (copy in author's files).
16. Conf. Ltr, Chief of the Bureau of Ships to Commanding Officer, USS *Ranger*, C-CV4/S81(S12), C-CV4/S29, 10 September 1941, Subj: USS *Ranger* (CV-4)—Splinter Protection, in RG-19, Bureau of Ships Confidential Correspondence C-CV4 #3, to 11/31/41, Box 708, NARA, College Park, MD. Additionally, the delivery of 15-pound special treatment steel (STS) was "long overdue" anyway.
17. Unless otherwise noted, the difficulties involved in the July–September 1941 overhaul are from Conf. Ltr, Commandant, Norfolk Navy Yard to Chief of Naval Operations, CV4/L9-3(1-MP), Serial 1878, 30 October 1941, Subj: Norfolk Navy Yard Delay of Vessels of the Atlantic Fleet—USS *Ranger*—Overhaul Scheduled to Terminate September 15, 1941, in RG-19, Bureau of Ships Confidential Correspondence C-CV4 #4, to 12/31/41, Box 708, NARA, College Park, MD.
18. Ibid.
19. Ernest L. Crochet, Diary, 21 September 1941; hereinafter Crochet Diary, with the appropriate date.
20. Bureau of Aeronautics, *Status of Naval Aircraft*, 30 September 1941, lists VF-41 as having on actual strength 16 F4F-3s; VS-41, 14 SB2U-1 and 2 SB2U-2s, and VS-42, 12 SB2U-1s, 4 SB2U-2s, and 3 TBD-1s. The embarked utility unit had on board 2 SOC-1s and 1 J2F-3, AvH.
21. AAR for SB2U-1 (BuNo 0747), 3 October 1941, AARM Reel 33, AvH.
22. AAR for SB2U-1 (BuNo 0763), 3 October 1941, AARM Reel 33, AvH.
23. "Notes on 5th Sea Lord's Visit," Assistant Secretary of the Navy for Air Artemus Gates received these comments on 29 October, and passed a copy along to Adm. Husband E. Kimmel, the Commander in Chief of the U.S. Pacific Fleet. "I want [Vice Adm. William F.] Halsey and [Rear Adm. Patrick N. L.] Bellinger to read this when they come over here next time. [Captain Arthur C.] Davis see that they do so." Gates passed a copy along to Admiral King for his perusal, too. King read Lyster's comments "with much interest," but believed that "he [Lyster] did not have sufficient time to familiarize himself with certain

facts—and so has expressed erroneous conclusions in some instances..." Memorandum, Adm. E. J. King to Mr. Gates, 10 November 1941, Ernest J. King Papers, Series I, Box 1, OA.
24. Lieutenant Comdr. J. S. McClure, U.S. Navy, "Memorandum for File, Subj: Land-plane Facilities at Bermuda—Report on," 14 October 1941, Enclosure (A) to Commander Aircraft, Atlantic Fleet, to Commander in Chief, U.S. Atlantic Fleet, Subj: Landplane Facilities at Bermuda, File No. A4-3, Serial 0522 of 29 October 1941, copy in author's files.
25. Ibid.
26. Ibid.
27. AAR for F4F-3 (BuNo 2538), 22 October 1941, AARM Reel 13, AvH.
28. Commander Aircraft, Atlantic Fleet, to Commander in Chief, U.S. Atlantic Fleet, Subj: Landplane Facilities at Bermuda, File No. A4-3, Serial 0522 of 29 October 1941, op.cit.
29. Conf. Msg, COMAIRLANT to BUSHIPS, 300319 CR 0548 of 30 October 1941; Conf Msg, BUSHIPS to COMAIRLANT, 312226CR070 of 31 October 1941 confirmed "shipments being arranged." RG-19, Bureau of Ships Confidential Correspondence C-CV4 #3, to 11/31/41, Box 708, NARA, College Park, MD.
30. Conf. Ltr, Commanding Officer, USS *Ranger* (CV-4) to Chief of the Bureau of Ships, Serial CV4/S19 (0157), Subj: USS *Ranger* (CV-4)—Stain and Marking Paint for Flight Deck, 7 November 1941, in RG-19, BuShips Confidential Correspondence C-CV4 #4, to 12/31/41, Box 708, NARA, College Park, MD.
31. Conf. Ltr, Naval Research Laboratory to Bureau of Ships, C-F42-1/69H, Subj: Radio—USS *Ranger*—Model YE Installation, 14 November 1941, in RG-19, Bureau of Ships Confidential Correspondence C-CV4 #3, to 11/31/41, Box 708, NARA, College Park, MD.
32. AAR for SB2U-1 (BuNo 0756), 17 November 1941, AARM Reel 33, AvH.
33. Conf. Ltr, Commanding Officer, USS *Ranger* (CV-4) to Commandant, Norfolk Navy Yard, Serial CV4/S19 (0170), Subj: Low Visibility Deck Stain—Norfolk Formula No. L-81-3m, 19 November 1941, in RG-19, BuShips Confidential Correspondence C-CV4 #4, to 12/31/41, Box 708, NARA, College Park, MD.
34. Conf. Ltr, Commander Aircraft, Atlantic Fleet, to Chief of the Bureau of Ships, Serial S19 (0567), Subj: USS *Ranger* (CV-4)—Stain and Marking Paint for Flight Deck, 24 November 1941, First Endorsement to Conf. Ltr, Commanding Officer, USS *Ranger* (CV-4) to Chief of the Bureau of Ships, Serial CV4/S19 (0157), Subj: USS *Ranger* (CV-4)—Stain and Marking Paint for Flight Deck, 7 November 1941, op.cit., in RG-19, BuShips Confidential Correspondence C-CV4 #4, to 12/31/41, Box 708, NARA, College Park, MD.
35. AAR for SB2U-1 (BuNo 0757), 21 November 1941, AARM Reel 33, AvH.
36. Ensign Donald H. Dorris, Diary, 27 November 1941, quoted in Donald Hugh Dorris, *A Log of the Vincennes* (Louisville: Standard Printing, 1947), 126.
37. AAR for SB2U-1 (BuNo 0754), 28 November 1941, AARM Reel 33, AvH.
38. Ibid.
39. Commander Task Group 14.4 [Rear Adm. Arthur B. Cook] to Commander in Chief, U.S. Atlantic Fleet, Subj: Investigation of Suspicious Vessel Reported by SSFJ [radio call sign] WOLFE, 11 December 1941. Copy in author's files.
40. Ibid.
41. "McDonald Awaited Change in Course," *Navy Times*, 8 December 1971, 1.

Chapter 15: "OUR ONLY STRIKING FORCE AGAINST RAIDERS"

1. Conf Ltr, Commanding Officer, USS *Ranger* (CV-4) to Chief of the Bureau of Ships, Subj: USS *Ranger* (CV-4)—Weight Compensation for splinter protection, 20-mm guns, and other outstanding ready and contemplated alterations, Serial CV4/S29/S81-4 (019) of 10 February 1942, in RG-19, Bureau of Ships Confidential Correspondence, C-CV4 #5 to 5/30/42, Box 708, NARA College Park, MD.
2. AAR for SB2U-1 (BuNo 0743), 11 December 1941, AARM Reel 33, AvH.
3. VF-42 remained in the *Yorktown* into late May 1942, especially distinguishing itself in the Battle of the Coral Sea, 4–8 May 1942; later, an experienced cadre of VF-42 pilots, supported by VF-42's maintenance people, became amalgamated into VF-3 and participated in the Battle of Midway, 4–6 June 1942. See Robert J. Cressman, *That Gallant Ship: USS Yorktown (CV-5)* (Missoula: Pictorial Histories, 1985).
4. Kenneth Poolman, *Escort Carrier, 1941–1945: An Account of British Escort Carriers in Trade Protection* (London: Ian Allen, 1972), 30.
5. AARs for F4F-3s (BuNos 3862 and 2518), 24 and 28 December 1941, respectively, AARM Reel 13, AvH. Hessel's biographical sketch: 1937 *Lucky Bag*, 232.
6. AAR for F4F-3 (BuNo 3863), 28 January 1942, AARM Reel 13, AvH.
7. AAR for SB2U-1 (BuNo 0726), 4 February 1942, AARM Reel 33, AvH.
8. AAR for SB2U-1 (BuNo 0751), 5 February 1942, AARM Reel 33, AvH.
9. Conf. Ltr, Commanding Officer, USS *Ranger* (CV-4) to Chief of the Bureau of Ships, Subj: USS *Ranger* (CV-4)—Weight Compensation for splinter protection, 20-mm guns, and other outstanding ready and contemplated alterations, Serial CV4/S29/S81-4 (019) of 10 February 1942, op.cit.
10. Memorandum for the President, Subj: Use of Carrier to Transport P-40 Planes from the United States to Australia or the Netherlands East Indies to Fly-away, February 12, 1942, King Papers, Series I (1918–1942), February 1942 file, Box 1, OA.
11. Ibid. Eventually, this mission was given to the seaplane tender *Langley* (AV-3), once the Navy's first aircraft carrier, but she was bombed by Japanese land attack planes from the Takao *Kōkūtai*

[Air Group] 75 miles south of Tjilatjap, Java, on 27 February 1942, and abandoned. She and her cargo of 32 P-40s were lost. The Japanese invaded Java on 28 February; the Dutch surrendered on 9 March.

12. AAR for SB2U-1 (BuNo 0757), 25 February 1942, AARM Reel 33, AvH.
13. Conf. Ltr, Chief of the Bureau of Ships to Chief of Naval Operations, Serial C-CV4/S74 (S12), 2 February 1942, Subj: USS *Ranger* (CV-4)—Proposed Rearrangement of Close-In Armament, in RG-19 Bureau of Ships Confidential Correspondence, C-CV4#5 to 5/30/42, Box 708, NARA College Park, MD. BuShips regarded the installation of a heavy antiaircraft battery justifiable: "*Ranger*'s resistance to damage has always been unsatisfactory," an officer in BuShips wrote on 13 December 1942, "She is subject to serious unsymmetrical flooding. . . . Her only chance is to avoid being hit, for which reason I consider this tremendous armament justified." Route sheet comments, C-CV4/S74 of 13 December 1942, in RG-19, Bureau of Ships Confidential Correspondence, C-CV4#6 to 12/28/42, Box 708, NARA College Park, MD.
14. AAR for SB2U-1 (BuNo 0736), 3 April 1942, AARM Reel 33, AvH.
15. AAR for F4F-4 (BuNo 4078), 8 April 1942, AARM Reel 13, AvH.
16. AAR for F4F-4 (BuNo 4088), 13 April 1942, AARM Reel 13, AvH.
17. AAR for F4F-4 (BuNo 4090), 13 April 1942, AARM Reel 13, AvH.
18. Warren Kimball, ed., *Churchill & Roosevelt: The Complete Correspondence*, I, *Alliance Emerging, October 1933–November 1942* (Princeton: Princeton University Press, 1984), 453.
19. Ibid., 455.
20. Commanding Officer [USS *Ranger*] to Commander Carriers, Atlantic Fleet, Subj: Project 157, Report on, n.d., Enclosure (E) to Commander Task Force Thirty-Six to Commander in Chief, U.S. Atlantic Fleet, Subj: Transportation of U.S. Army P-40-E Aircraft from Naval Air Station, Quonsett [sic] Point, R.I., to Accra, Gold Coast, Africa. May 30, 1942, Cinclant, Oct 21, 1942–Dec 12, 1942, Box #2, OA [Now at NARA, College Park, MD].
21. Commander Task Force Thirty-Six to Commander in Chief, U.S. Atlantic Fleet, Subj: Transportation of U.S. Army P-40-E Aircraft from Naval Air Station, Quonsett [sic] Point, Rhode Island, to Accra, Gold Coast, Africa. May 30, 1942, op.cit.
22. Kimball, op. cit., 464.
23. Back in Washington, Gen. Henry H. "Hap" Arnold, chief of the Army Air Force, apparently suggested using the planes that the *Ranger* was transporting to attack Vichy French aircraft in Dahomey. Brigadier Gen. Vivian Dykes, in his diary, condemned Arnold's plan as "a crackpot scheme," and the British members of the joint staff prevailed upon General George Marshall "to boom the idea off." The attack was not carried out. Alex Danchev, *Establishing the Anglo-American Alliance: The Second World War Diaries of Brigadier Vivian Dykes* (London: Brassey's [UK]), 1990.
24. AARs for SB2U-1 (BuNo 0746) and SB2U-2 (BuNo 1365), 30 April 1942, AARM Reel 33, AvH.
25. Commander Task Force Thirty-Six to Commander in Chief, U.S. Atlantic Fleet, Subj: Transportation of U.S. Army P-40-E Aircraft from Naval Air Station, Quonsett [sic] Point, Rhode Island, to Accra, Gold Coast, Africa. May 30, 1942, op.cit.
26. Commanding Officer [USS *Ranger*] to Commander Carriers, Atlantic Fleet, Subject: Project 157, Report on, n.d., op.cit.
27. Commander in Chief, United States Atlantic Fleet, to Commander in Chief, United States Fleet, Subj: Report on Transportation of U.S. Army P-40-E Aircraft from Naval Air Station, Quonset Point, Rhode Island, To Accra, Gold Coast, Africa, 5 June 1942, Cinclant, Oct 21, 1942–Dec 12, 1942, Box #2, OA [Now at NARA, College Park, MD].
28. Joseph T. O'Callahan, *I Was Chaplain on the Franklin* (New York: MacMillan,1956), 4.
29. AAR for SB2U-1 (BuNo 0758), 18 May 1942, AARM Reel 33, AvH.
30. AAR for F4F-4 (BuNo 4092), 10 June 1942, AARM Reel 13, AvH.
31. AAR for F4F-4 (BuNo 4079), 13 June 1942, AARM Reel 13, AvH.

Chapter 16: "THERE IS A NEED FOR A CARRIER IN THE ATLANTIC"

1. "Malta Convoy" [Memorandum], n.d., Charles M. Cooke Naval Career Office File, Military Operations and Planning—European Theater, vol. 1, April 25, 1942–September 29, 1942. Box 21, Charles M. Cooke Papers, Hoover Institution Archives. Hereinafter Cooke Papers.
2. Ibid.
3. Ibid.
4. Memorandum for [the] Commander in Chief, Subj: Proposal for Employment of *Ranger* in Malta Operation, June 18, 1942, Cooke Papers.
5. Ibid.
6. Ibid.
7. Ibid.
8. Ltr, Adm. Sir Charles J. C. Little to Adm. Ernest J. King, 18th June, 1942, Cooke Papers.
9. Memorandum for [the] Commander in Chief, Subj: Carrier Situation, June 20, 1942, Cooke Papers.
10. Ibid.
11. Ibid.
12. Memorandum, From: Deputy Chief of Staff to: Admiral King, 20 June [1942], Cooke Papers.
13. Willson Marginalia on Memorandum for [the] Commander in Chief, Subj: Carrier Situation, June 20, 1942, Cooke Papers, op.cit.
14. Crochet Diary, 20 June 1942.
15. Commander in Chief, United States Atlantic Fleet, to Commander in Chief, United States Fleet, Subj: Transportation of U.S. Army P-40-F Aircraft from Naval Air Station, Quonset Point,

Rhode Island, to Accra, Gold Coast, Africa (Army Project 337–Heath), 19 September 1942, in Cinclant, Oct. 21, 1942–Dec. 12, 1942, Box 2 (now at NARA College Park, MD).

16. Memorandum for File, Subj: Summary of Statements of SS *Ruth*, U.S. Cargo Vessel, 3588 G.T., owned by A. H. Bull Steamship Company, Chartered to Isthmian Steamship Company, July 18, 1942, in Summary of Survivors Statements, June 1942, in World War II Command File, CNO—Intelligence, Summary of Survivor Statements, Jun 1942–Mar 1943, Box 185, OA.

17. AAR for SB2U-2 (BuNo 1382), 22 July 1942, AARM Reel 33, AvH. Wagner, a Knoxville, Tennessee, native, had been promoted to lieutenant (jg) 16 June 1942. "Transcript of Naval Service of Lieutenant (Junior Grade) John Eaton Wagner, A-V(N), U.S. Naval Reserve, Deceased," 19 August 1942, in Officer Biography Files, Box 662, OA.

18. Seaman George E. Biggs, Jr., to Mrs. George E. Biggs, 6 August 1942 [completed 7 August, postmarked 8 August], copy provided by Eugene Rowley, George Biggs's nephew, to RJC, June 2001. The reference to his sense of humor is from e-mail ltr, Mrs. Amy McQuade (one of Biggs's sisters) to RJC, 28 June 2001.

19. Conf. Ltr, Commandant, Norfolk Navy Yard, to Chief of the Bureau of Ships, CV4/S29(4-MDH) Serial 4189 of 24 August 1942, Subj: USS *Ranger* (CV-4)—Weight Changes, in RG-19, Bureau of Ships Confidential Correspondence, C-CV4#6 to 12/28/42, Box 708, NARA, College Park, MD.

20. AAR for SB2U-1 (BuNo 0739), 12 July 1942, AARM Reel 33, AvH.

21. AAR for TBF-1 (BuNo 00524), 20 July 1942, AARM Reel 33, AvH.

22. AAR for F4F-4 (BuNo 03396), 26 August 1942, AARM Reel 13, AvH.

23. AAR for F4F-4 (BuNo 03399), 5 September 1942, AARM Reel 13, AvH.

24. AAR for SB2U-1 (BuNo 0768), 5 September 1942, AARM Reel 33, AvH.

25. AARs for F4F-4s (BuNos 02136 and 5034), 28 September 1942, AARM Reel 13, AvH.

26. "Narrative Report on Torch Operation by Commander Task Group Thirty-Four Point Two," Enclosure (A) to Commander, Task Group Thirty-Four Point Two to Commander Task Force Thirty-Four, Subj: Reports on Torch Operation, 3 December 1942. Hereinafter TG 34.2 Narrative Report.

27. AARs for F4F-4s (BuNos 11704 and 11747), 5 October 1942, AARM Reel 13, AvH.

28. TG 34.2 Narrative Report.

29. "History of the U.S.S. *Cleveland*," USS *Cleveland* (CL-55) Ship History File, SH.

30. AAR for F4F-4 (BuNo 11702), 10 October 1942, AARM Reel 13, AvH.

31. TG 34.2 Narrative Report.

32. AAR for F4F-4 (BuNo 11743), 15 October 1942, AARM Reel 13, AvH.

33. TG 34.2 Narrative Report.

34. AAR for F4F-4 (BuNo 4090), 22 October 1942, AARM Reel 13, AvH.

35. AAR for F4F-4 (BuNo 03398), 22 October 1942, AARM Reel 13, AvH.

36. Lieutenant Malcolm T. Wordell, "Report on 'Torch' Operations by Lieutenant M. T. Wordell, USN," Enclosure (A) to Commander, Fighting Squadron Forty One to Commander Carriers, Atlantic Fleet, Subj: Narrative reports of Naval Aviators taken prisoners of war during recent operations, December 17, 1942, CNO Flag Files, Box 53 (hereinafter Wordell).

37. Crochet Diary, 20 October 1942.

38. "Talk Given to Wardroom Officers by Captain Calvin T. Durgin, Commanding USS *Ranger*," October 26, 1942, Box 7, Speech File, Vice Admiral Calvin T. Durgin Papers, Personal Papers Collection, NHC, OA; hereinafter Durgin Papers.

39. Ibid.
40. Ibid.
41. Ibid.
42. Ibid.
43. Ibid.
44. Ibid.
45. Ibid.
46. Ibid.
47. Ibid.

48. *Ranger* War Communique No.1, October 27, 1942, Durgin Papers.

49. TG 34.2 Narrative Report.

50. Wordell.

51. Excerpts from Interview of Lt. Comdr. C. T. Booth, USN, and Lt. M. T. Wordell, USN (Commanding Officer and Executive Officer of VF Squadron 41) in the Bureau of Aeronautics, 4 December 1942, 1.

52. TG 34.2 Narrative Report.

53. *Ranger* War Communique No. 2, October 29, 1942, Durgin Papers.

54. *Ranger* War Communique No. 3, November 1, 1942, Durgin Papers.

55. Internal msg (021818) CTG 34.2 to *Ranger*, 2 November 1942, Torch Despatches, Box 6, Durgin Papers (hereinafter Torch Despatches).

56. Interview of Capt. J. J. Clark, USN, USS *Suwannee* [*sic*] in the Bureau of Aeronautics, 27 November 1942, 1. This is the same "Jocko" Clark whom Rear Admiral Cook had often irritated by comparing the way things were done in the *Yorktown* and the *Ranger*.

57. AAR for SBD-3 (BuNo 06619), 3 November 1942, AARM Reel 22, AvH; also War Diary, Commander Carriers, Atlantic Fleet, 3 November 1942. They would later embark in the destroyer *Fitch*, via the high-speed minesweeper *Hogan* (DMS-6), on 12 November. Commander Aircraft, Atlantic Fleet, Tactical Dispatch 120720 of 12 November 1942, Torch Despatches.

58. *Ranger* War Communique No. 4, n.d. [6 November 1942], Durgin Papers.

59. Ibid.

60. Ibid.
61. *Ranger* War Communique No. 5, n.d. [7 November 1942], Durgin Papers.
62. Ibid.

Chapter 17: "WE COULD TAKE NO CHANCES"
1. Wordell.
2. TG 34.2 Narrative Report.
3. Unless otherwise noted, the narrative for Operation Torch is drawn from the *Ranger*'s War Diary for 8–12 November 1942, and the Action Report, USS *Ranger* (CV-4) Serial 0177 of 7 December 1942, which contains the individual reports of each numbered flight. Tactical organizations are drawn from the individual squadron reports contained therein. All war diaries and action reports consulted for this chapter are now held by the National Archives and Records Administration's College Park, MD, facility, in Record Group (RG) 38, Records of the Office of the Chief of Naval Operations, Records Relating to Naval Activity During World War II. For the operations of the *Suwanee*, which provided combat air patrols for herself and for the *Ranger*, the *Suwanee*'s War Diary is the source (RG-38, NARA, College Park, MD, World War II War Diaries, Box 1490).
4. Ensign McGann's name is not on the flight schedule recorded in the *Ranger* reports for 8 November 1942, but he is mentioned in the war diary of the *Suwanee* for that day. The *Ranger*'s war diary mentions 18 VF-9 planes taking off, yet the reports for A-1 and A-1(A) only mention 17 planes. McGann's makes 18.
5. Captain Gordon P. Chase, USN (Ret.), Officer Biography File, Box 105, OA. His being given that specific task to perform most likely reflected the fact that among his previous tours of duty had been one at the Naval Photo School at NAS Pensacola, between December 1941 and April 1942.
6. *Journal de Marche du G.C. II/5 "Lafayette" Pendant L'Operation Torch*, copy provided by John Lambert.
7. J. Cuny, "Hawk 75 In French Service," *American Aviation Historical Society Journal*, 11, no. 1 (Spring 1966); 22. Hereinafter Cuny, "Hawk 75 In French Service."
8. Commanding Officer, USS *Massachusetts* (BB-59) to Commander TG 34.1, Subj: Report of engagement with *Jean Bart*, shore batteries, and vessels of the French Fleet on November 8, 1942, off Casablanca, French Morocco, November 13, 1942.
9. Scouting Squadron Forty-One (USS *Ranger*), Detailed Report of Action, November 8 to 12 1942 (inclusive), Flight No. A-2, 4.
10. Unless otherwise indicated, the experiences of Lieutenant Carter are derived from "Report of Lieutenant G. H. Carter, reported missing after first attack on Cazes Airdrome on November 8, 1942." Enclosure (B) to Wordell; hereinafter Carter.
11. Lt. Gordon P. Chase, USNR, to Commander Destroyer Division Twenty Six, Via: Commander, Scouting Squadron Forty One, Ser VS 41/A16-3 of December 10, 1942, Subj: "Report, Aircraft—ship coordination at Casablanca–Fedala, French Morocco," hereinafter Chase.
12. Wordell.
13. Christian J. Ehrengardt and Christopher F. Shores, *L'Aviation de Vichy Au Combat*, 128; also *Journal de Marche du G.C. II/5 "Lafayette" Pendant L'Operation Torch*, op.cit.
14. Unless otherwise specified, Ensign Mikronis's experiences are drawn from "Report of Ensign E.C. Mikronis reported missing after first attack on Cazes Airdrome on November 8, 1942." Enclosure (E) to Wordell, op.cit. Hereinafter Mikronis.
15. Mikronis.
16. Carter.
17. Unless otherwise noted, Lieutenant (jg) August's experiences are drawn from "Report of Lt (jg) C. V. August, USNR, missing after first attack on Caxes [sic] Airdrome, November 8, 1942." Enclosure (C) to Wordell, op.cit.; hereinafter August.
18. Carter.
19. August.
20. August.
21. Carter.
22. Ibid.
23. Ibid.
24. Ibid.
25. August.
26. Ibid.
27. Mikronis.
28. Ibid.
29. August.
30. Ibid.
31. Ibid.
32. Unless otherwise noted, Lieutenant (jg) Shields's experiences are derived from "Report of Lieutenant (jg) C. A. Shields, USNR, reported missing after first attack on Cazes Airdrome on November 8, 1942." Enclosure (D) to Wordell, op.cit.; hereinafter Shields.
33. The heavy cruiser *Tuscaloosa* (CA-37) shelled the submarine berthing area between 0705 and 0719, before she shifted her 8-inch fire to French shore batteries at Table d'Aoukacha. The "unidentified ship" claimed by VGS-27 was most likely the 10,000-ton passenger vessel *Lipari* (1922) of the *Chargeurs Réunis, Compagnie Francaise de Navigation À Vapeur*, which had her back broken in the bombing of 8 November.
34. Damage to *Jean Bart* is derived from "French Account of Naval Actions, Nov. 8–10, 1942," Enclosure (F) to Commander, Task Force Thirty-Four, to Commander in Chief, United States Atlantic Fleet, Subj: Torch Operation, preliminary report of, 28 November 1942, in Admiral H. Kent Hewitt Papers, Series II: Subject File, A–L, "Casablanca," Box, OA. Hereinafter French Account.
35. Embree's report is quoted in Scouting Squadron Forty-One (USS *Ranger*), Detailed Report of Action, November 8 to 12 1942 (inclusive), Flight No. A-2, op.cit.
36. Ibid.; ironically, Lt. Comdr. John S. McCain, Jr., the son of the *Ranger*'s third commanding officer, is the *Gunnel*'s commanding officer.
37. Scouting Squadron Forty-One (USS *Ranger*), Detailed Report of Action, November 8 to 12 1942 (inclusive), Flight No. A-2, op.cit.
38. TG 34.2 Narrative Report.

Chapter 18: "A 'RED RIPPER SPECIAL'"

1. Wordell's initial count of six ships is accurate; of the seven destroyer leaders and destroyers that sortied, one of the latter, the *Boulonnais*, suffered steering gear problems en route, which forced her to lag behind.
2. Wordell.
3. Wordell.
4. Wordell.
5. Wordell.
6. Wordell.
7. Ibid.
8. Andrews, "Flight Report Form," 8 November 1942, in "VF 49" (an unofficial contraction of VF-41 and VF-9) action report file, Box 454, "VF 46 ACA Rpts to VF 51 5-29-44."
9. USS *Suwanee* (ACV-27) War Diary, 8 November 1942, RG-38, Records of the Office of the Chief of Naval Operations, WW II War Diaries, *Sutton* to *Suwanee*.
10. Onstott, "Flight Report Form," 8 November 1942, in "VF 49" action report file, op.cit.
11. Andrew Hendrie, "A Converted Airliner at War: The Lockheed Hudson Aircraft as Operated by Coastal Command, Royal Air Force," *Aerospace Historian*, 31, no. 4 (Winter/December 1984).
12. Fighting Squadron Forty-One, "Report of Flight A-3."
13. August.
14. August. *Sous-Lieutenant* Villaceque's facial injuries reflected the Hawk 75's lack of an armored windshield. One French aviation historian [Cuny, "Hawk 75 In French Service," 22] later surmised that that not only allowed pilots to suffer physical harm, but had "a psychological affect [sic] forcing premature breaks in combat."
15. Mikronis.
16. Carter.
17. Wilhoite was not the only VF-9 pilot to die that day. Lieutenant (jg) George N. Trumpeter, A-V(N), on temporary duty with the *Santee's* VGF-29, reported an oil leak at 0910 on 8 November and left formation. He attempted to land on the beach some 16 miles south of Casablanca. "Due to the rolling sand dunes or an exceptionally hard landing," however, Trumpeter's F4F-4 (BuNo 11767), 29-GF-A, bounced about 600 yards before turning over on its back, killing the pilot, who was buried by the Army at the European cemetery in Casablanca. Ltr, Commander Sea Frontier Forces, Western Task Force to Commander Amphibious Force, Subj: Report of Crashed Airplanes, CCSFWTF/L11-3 Serial 135 of December 6, 1942, copy in author's files.
18. Wordell.
19. August.
20. Ibid.
21. Ibid.

Chapter 19: "LOOKING FOR TARGETS OF OPPORTUNITY"

1. AAR for SBD-3 (BuNo 06620), 8 November 1942, AARM Reel 22, AvH. See also USS *Corry* (DD-463) War Diary, 8 November 1942, RG-38, World War II War Diaries, Box 761.
2. That afternoon, the French colonial sloop *La Grandiere* and the second-class sloops *Commandant Delage* and *La Gracieuse* sortied and picked up survivors from the ships sunk that morning; carrier-based aircraft later damaged the *La Grandiere*. That night, the *Frondeur* sank between the Phosphate Quay and the *Mole du Commerce*; the *Brestois* capsized and sank around midnight near the *Jettie Delure*.
3. Wordell.
4. Apparently, Andy Andrews's F4F-4 had not yet been repaired in time for him to take off.
5. August.
6. Mikronis.
7. Ibid.
8. Ltr, Mrs. [Alice] Wilson to Mrs. George E. Biggs, [29 January 1943], courtesy of Eugene Rowley.
9. A post-Torch accounting showed that no French pilot claimed to have shot down an SBD in aerial combat, making it most likely that Duffy and Biggs fell victim to antiaircraft fire.
10. August.
11. Ibid.
12. Carter.
13. August.
14. The "constant prattle of insignificant information" over the TBS on 8 November had been like that that had provoked Rear Adm. Robert E. Giffen, in the *Massachusetts*, to signal his force on 27 October while en route to French Morocco: "The amount of useless chatter over the TBS at night is disgraceful and sounds more like a Chinese laundry at New Years than a fleet going to the wars. We are not training broadcasters. Protective screen not at fault but a word to the wise is sufficient." Cruiser Division 7 War Diary, 27 October 1942, RG-38.
15. "Narrative Report of Torch Operations."
16. August.
17. Mikronis.
18. Wordell.
19. Ibid.
20. Carter.
21. *Kriegstagebuch der Befehlshaber der Unterseeboote* (KTB/BdU) [War Diary of the Commander in Chief, Submarines], 8 November 1942, NHC, OA.
22. Karl Dönitz, transl. R. H. Stevens [and David Woodward] *Memoirs: Ten Years and Twenty Days* (Annapolis: Naval Institute Press, 1990), 279. Hereinafter Dönitz.
23. *Kriegstagebuch der Befehlshaber der Unterseeboote*, 8 November 1942, op.cit.
24. Dönitz, 280.

Chapter 20: "MORALE DROPS QUICKLY BEFORE AN ENEMY WHO IS CLEARLY SUPERIOR"

1. Martin Blumenson, ed., *The Patton Papers, 1940–1945* (Boston: Houghton Mifflin, 1974), 108. Hereinafter Blumenson.
2. Carter.

3. Wordell.
4. Excerpt from 6290 kcs . . . log . . . 19 November 1942, Torch Dispatches.
5. Ibid.
6. Ibid.
7. Blumenson, 108.
8. AAR for F4F-3 (BuNo 03461), 9 November 1942, AARM Reel 13, AvH.
9. Translation of GCI/5's *journal de marche* provided by John Lambert.
10. M. T. Wordell and E. N. Seiler, *"Wildcats" Over Casablanca* (Boston: Little, Brown, 1943), 275. Hereinafter Wordell and Seiler.
11. Carter.
12. Ibid. The gender of M. Lagorce's neighbor is from Wordell and Seiler, 275.
13. August and Shields.
14. Excerpt from 6290 Log Radio One, 0959, 9 November 1942, Torch Dispatches.
15. AAR for F4F-4 (BuNo 11762), 9 November 1942, AARM Reel 13, AvH.
16. Mikronis.
17. Ibid.
18. Ibid.
19. Msg, CTF 34 to CTG 34.2, 091056 of 9 November 1942, Torch Dispatches.
20. Unfortunately, a postarmistice accounting revealed no French fighter aircraft lost under those circumstances that day. Christian J. Ehrengardt and Christopher F. Shores speculate in *L'Aviation de Vichy Au Combat* (144) that Woodie Wood's victim was most likely the unarmed Supermarine Spitfire piloted by Flight Lieutenant Brennan, from the Gibraltar-based RAF No. 544 Squadron, on a reconnaissance mission over the Moroccan coast between Casablanca and Marrakech.

Chapter 21: "EUCALYPTUS, BY THE SMELL"

1. Ltr, *Captaine* Fourniol of G.B. 1/32 to the Colonel, Commandant of American Aviation at Casablanca, 14 November 1942, Enclosure (C) to Wordell, op.cit.
2. Msg, Teaspoon [*Ranger*] V [from] 901 [9-F-1], 9 November 1942, Torch Dispatches.
3. Wordell and Seiler, 127.
4. AAR for SBD-3 (BuNo 06627), 9 November 1942, AARM Reel 22, AvH.
5. Msg, CTG 34.2 to *Suwannee* [sic], Torch Dispatches.
6. August.
7. Wordell.
8. "War Communique No. 6," November 9, 1942, Durgin Papers.
9. *Kriegstagebuch der Befehlshaber der Unterseeboote* (KTB/BdU) [War Diary of the Commander in Chief, Submarines], 9 November 1942.

Chapter 22: "WELL DONE, *RANGER*"

1. AAR for SBD-3 (BuNo 06628), 10 November 1942, AARM Reel 22, AvH.
2. Tactical Despatches 101036 and 101042, Torch Dispatches.
3. USS *Augusta* (CA-31) War Diary, 10 November 1942, RG-38.
4. Internal msg, CTG 34.2 to *Ranger*, 101354 of 10 November 1942, Torch Dispatches.
5. Handwritten note on CTG 34.2 to *Ranger*, 101354 of 10 November 1942, Ibid.
6. Msg, CTG 34.2 to CTF 34, 101422 of 10 November 1942, Torch Dispatches.
7. Apparently, the returning pilots waxed optimistic over their success, because Admiral McWhorter signalled the *Augusta*: SEVEN 1,000-POUND HITS OUT OF NINE REPORTED ON JEAN BART X REGRET ONE NEAR MISS IN WATER AND ONE ON DOCKS. Msg, TG 34.2 to *Augusta*, 101610 of 10 November 1942, Torch Dispatches.
8. Carter.
9. Msg, CTF 34 to CTG 34.2 1509 of 10 November 1942, Torch Dispatches.
10. Wordell.
11. Tactical Dispatch 101623, Torch Dispatches.
12. Msg, TF 34 to CTG 34.2, 101722 of 10 November 1942, Torch Dispatches.
13. Internal msg, CTG 34.2 to *Ranger* 101740 of 10 November 1942, Torch Dispatches.
14. Carter.
15. Wordell.
16. Msg, CTF-34 to TF-34, 0550 of 11 November 1942, Torch Dispatches.
17. Internal msg, CTG 34.2 to *Ranger*, 110631 of 11 November 1942, Torch Dispatches.
18. Crochet Diary, 11 November 1942.
19. Msg, CTF-34 to CTG 34.2 [et al.], 110726 of 11 November 1942, Torch Dispatches.
20. Msg, *Ranger* to *Brooklyn* 110735 of 11 November 1942, Torch Dispatches.
21. Msg, CTF-34 to CTG-34.2, 110828 of 11 November 1942, Torch Dispatches.
22. Msg, CTG-34.2 to CTF-34, 110839 of 11 November 1942, Torch Dispatches.
23. Wordell. All but Tom Dougherty embarked in the *Chenango* for passage back to the United States, but not before Wordell had made strenuous efforts to retrieve his aircraft, during which he visited Pierre Feugnet and his family to thank them for their kindness on 8 November.
24. Bill Wade, "Bring Back the Handles," Air Group 4 Web Site. (http://www.airgroup4.com)
25. Internal Dispatch 111754, 11 November 1942, Torch Dispatches.
26. Internal Msg, CTG 34.2 to *Ranger*, 11 November 1942, Torch Dispatches.

27. Internal Msg, CTG 34.2 to *Ranger*, 111236 of 11 November 1942, Torch Dispatches.
28. Msg, CTF 34 to TF 34, 111918 of 11 November 1942, Torch Dispatches.
29. Msg, CTG 34.2 to CTF 34, 112219, of 11 November 1942, Torch Dispatches.

Chapter 23: "YOU HAVE ALL DONE A GRAND JOB"

1. Msg, CTG 34.2 to CTF 34, 120546 of 12 November 1942, Torch Dispatches.
2. Internal Dispatch, CTG 34.2 to *Ranger*, 12 November 1942, Torch Dispatches.
3. USS *Brooklyn* (CL-40) War Diary, 12 November 1942, RG-38.
4. Commander Aircraft, Atlantic Fleet, Tactical Dispatch, November 12, 1942, Torch Dispatches; see also USS *Woolsey* (DD-437) War Diary, 12 November 1942, RG 38, World War II War Diaries, *Woolsey* to *Woolsey*, Box 1582.
5. Ibid.
6. Report of Flight No. E-4, November 12, 1942.
7. VS-41's accumulated reports for the operations of 9–12 November do not contain any mention of the composition of this second patrol.
8. Mikronis.
9. Mikronis.
10. Mikronis.
11. *U-130* War Diary quoted in Dönitz, 280. The *Hugh L. Scott* sank during the night, the *Edward Rutledge* at 1848; the *Tasker H. Bliss* burned until 0230 the next morning. Commander, TG 34.9 to Commander TF 34, Subj: Operation Torch—Report on, November 30, 1942. Enclosure (C) notes the efficiency of the three ships lost that night: *Edward Rutledge* was "fairly well trained," but the *Hugh L. Scott* and the *Tasker H. Bliss* were "partially and hastily converted [and] totally inexperienced in Amphibious Operations." A brief biography of Kals appears in Rainer Busch and Hans-Joachim Röll, *German U-Boat Commanders of World War II: A Biographical Dictionary*, London: Greenhill Books/Annapolis: Naval Institute Press, 1999. Hereinafter Busch and Röll.
12. Msg, ComTaskGroup 34.2 to Ships in Company, 140808, November 14, 1942, Torch Dispatches.
13. Msg, CTG 34.2 to TG 34.2, 180923, 17 November 1942, Torch Dispatches.
14. AARs for TBF-1s (BuNos 00582 and 01770), 11 and 12 December, AARM Reel 33, AvH.

Chapter 24: "WE ARE TOO VALUABLE AS A STRIKING FORCE"

1. AAR for TBF-1 (BuNo 00676), 24 December 1942, AARM Reel 33, AvH.
2. Eastern Sea Frontier War Diary, Enemy Action and Distress Diary, Mic A-143, Reel 4, NDL.
3. Captain Calvin T. Durgin to Capt. John M. Hoskins, 28 January 1943, Correspondence Files, 1943, E-H, Durgin Papers.
4. AAR for TBF-1 (BuNo 06074), 19 January 1943, AARM Reel 33, AvH.
5. AAR for TBF-1 (BuNo 06075), 23 January 1943, AARM Reel 33, AvH.
6. AAR for TBF-1 (BuNo 06073), 25 January 1943, AARM Reel 33, AvH.
7. Captain Calvin T. Durgin to Capt. John M. Hoskins, 28 January 1943, op.cit. "Your stay in the Navy Yard must have been very hectic. However, I can't agree with you that I am lucky to be off the ship, even to have missed that. The way I feel now is that I would be willing to undergo [al]most any ordeal in order to get out of this Navy Department and back on the RANGER . . . *the best ship in the Navy* [Hoskins's emphasis]." Captain John M. Hoskins to Durgin, February 10, 1943, Correspondence Files, E-H, 1943, Durgin Papers.
8. AAR for TBF-1 (BuNo 06217), 9 February 1943, AARM Reel 33, AvH.
9. AAR for TBF-1 (BuNo 00618), 10 February 1943, AARM Reel 33, AvH.
10. Reports of "Antisubmarine Action by Aircraft" filed by Ens. R. W. Labyak and G. W. Bolt of VT-4.
11. Atlantic Fleet Anti-Submarine Warfare Officer to Commander in Chief, U.S. Atlantic Fleet, Subj: VT-4 Anti-Submarine Action by Aircraft Report, dated 26 February 1943, analysis of, 30 March 1943. The U-boat may have been the *U-521*, a Type IXC boat whose presence is recorded (grid square DG 90) in proximity to where Ensigns Labyak and Bolt attacked on 26 February. The *U-521* (*Kapitänleutnant* Klaus Bargsten) had reported a faulty port diesel engine that limited her speed to 11 knots.
12. AAR for TBF-1 (BuNo 06253), 2 March 1943, AARM Reel 33, AvH.
13. AAR for F4F-4 (BuNo 12040), 13 March 1943, AARM Reel 13, AvH.
14. AAR for F4F-4 (BuNo 11701), 13 March 1943, AARM Reel 13, AvH.
15. AAR for F4F-4 (BuNo 11705), 15 March 1943, AARM Reel 13, AvH.
16. Rear Adm. Calvin T. Durgin to Rear Adm. William H. P. Blandy, 6 April 1943, Correspondence Files, 1943, A–D, Durgin Papers.
17. Rear Adm. Calvin T. Durgin to Capt. Kenneth B. Bragg, 18 April 1943, Correspondence Files, 1943, A–D, Durgin Papers.
18. Citation for Lieutenant (jg) Gordon's Letter of Commendation, Awards Cards, OA.
19. AAR for F4F-4 (BuNo 12000), 21 March 1943, AARM Reel 13, AvH.
20. AAR for TBF-1 (BuNo 06253), 24 March 1943, AARM Reel 33, AvH.
21. AAR for TBF-1 (BuNo 05922), 25 March 1943, AARM Reel 33, AvH.
22. AAR for F4F-4 (BuNo 11995), 25 March 1943, AARM Reel 13, AvH.
23. AAR for F4F-4 (BuNo 11997), 26 March 1943, AARM Reel 13, AvH.
24. AAR for SBD-3 (BuNo 06666), 26 March 1943, AARM Reel 22, AvH.

25. AAR for F4F-4 (BuNo 11740), 30 March 1943, AARM Reel 13, AvH.
26. AAR for F4F-4 (BuNo 12196), 30 March 1943, AARM Reel 13, AvH.
27. AARs for F4F-4s (BuNos 12143, 12179, and 12186), 30 March 1943, AARM Reel 13, AvH.
28. AAR for SBD-4 (BuNo 06826), 30 March 1943, AARM Reel 22, AvH.
29. Ibid. Swampscott's fishing grounds: Federal Writer's Project, *Massachusetts: A Guide to Its Places and People*, (Boston: Houghton Mifflin, 1937), 423.
30. AAR for F4F-4 (BuNo 11740), 30 March 1943, op.cit.
31. AAR for F4F-4 (BuNo 11740), 30 March 1943, op.cit.
32. AARs for SBD-4s (BuNos 10516 and BuNo 06827), 2 April 1943, AARM Reel 22, AvH.
33. AAR for SBD-4 (BuNo 06897), 17 April 1943, AARM Reel 22, AvH.
34. Ibid.; see also USS *Forrest* (DD-461) War Diary, 17 April 1943, RG-38, Box 867, NARA, College Park, MD.
35. Ibid.
36. AAR for TBF-1 (BuNo 06303), 17 April 1943, AARM Reel 33, AvH.
37. AAR for SBD-4 (BuNo 06897), 17 April 1943, op.cit.
38. Von Bülow's biography: Busch and Röll, 43. See also Jurgen Röhwer, *Axis Submarine Successes, 1939–1945* (Annapolis: Naval Institute Press, 1983), 163.
39. AAR for F4F-4 (BuNo 12158), 28 April 1943, AARM Reel 13, AvH.
40. AAR for F4F-4 (BuNo 11853), 4 May 1943, AARM Reel 13, AvH.
41. AAR for SBD-4 (BuNo 06920), 12 May 1943, AARM Reel 22, AvH.

Chapter 25: "I AM FED UP WITH THIS PLACE"
1. Ltr, Capt. Gordon Rowe to Rear Adm. Calvin S. Durgin, 14 May 1943, Box 1, 1943, R–Z folder, Durgin Papers, OA.
2. AAR for SBD-4 (BuNo 06812), 17 May 1943, AARM Reel 22, AvH.
3. AAR for F4F-4 (BuNo 12002), 29 May 1943, AARM Reel 13, AvH.
4. AAR for TBF-1 (BuNo 06378), 17 June 1943, AARM Reel 33, AvH.
5. Gerald W. Thomas, *Torpedo Squadron Four: A Cockpit View of World War II*, Privately Published, 1990. Hereinafter Thomas, *Torpedo Squadron Four*.
6. AAR for SBD-4 (BuNo 06808), 21 June 1943, AARM Reel 22, AvH.
7. AAR for F4F-4 (BuNo 03464), 21 June 1943, AARM Reel 13, AvH.
8. AAR for SBD-4 (BuNo 06824), 21 June 1943, AARM Reel 22, AvH.
9. AAR for F4F-4 (BuNo 11950), 23 June 1943, AARM Reel 13, AvH.
10. AAR for TBF-1 (BuNo 06303), 24 June 1943, AARM Reel 33, AvH.
11. Ibid.; see also Lawrence L. Hamrick, "Memories," Air Group 4 Web Site.
12. Ibid.
13. Ibid.
14. Ibid.
15. AAR for F4F-4 (BuNo 11956), 24 June 1943, AARM Reel 13, AvH.
16. Page P. Stephens, "The Best Section in Torpedo Four," Air Group 4 Web Site.
17. Rear Adm. Calvin T. Durgin to Lt. Comdr. E. M. Bessie, [MC] USNR, 25 June 1943, Correspondence Files, 1943, A–D, Durgin Papers.
18. Lieutenant Comdr. Everett M. Bessie, MC, USNR to Rear Adm. Calvin T. Durgin, 3 July 1943, Correspondence Files, 1943, A–D, Durgin Papers.
19. AAR for SBD-3 (BuNo 06634), 6 July 1943, AARM Reel 22, AvH.
20. AAR for SBD-4 (BuNo 06808), 13 July 1943, AARM Reel 22, AvH.
21. AAR for SBD-4 (BuNo 10778), 13 July 1943, AARM Reel 22, AvH.
22. AAR for SBD-4 (BuNo 06866), 20 July 1943, AARM Reel 22, AvH.
23. Thomas, *Torpedo Squadron Four*, 18.
24. Ibid.
25. AAR for F4F-4 (BuNo 12042), 24 July 1943, AARM Reel 13, AvH.
26. AAR for SBD-4 (BuNo 10785), 26 July 1943, AARM Reel 22, AvH.
27. Loewenheim, Francis C., Harold D. Langley, and Manfred Jonas, eds., *Roosevelt and Churchill: Their Secret Wartime Correspondence* (New York: Saturday Review Press/E.P. Dutton, 1975), 365. Among the results of the "First Quebec Conference" was a "blueprint for the cross-channel attack" that would be named Overlord, which would ultimately be carried out on 6 June 1944.
28. AAR for SBD-5 (BuNo 28609), 9 August 1943, AARM Reel 22, AvH.

Chapter 26: "THE OLD SHIP CAME ACROSS IN GOOD STYLE"
1. AAR for F4F-4 (BuNo 12209), 21 August 1943, AARM Reel 13, AvH.
2. AAR for F4F-4 (BuNo 11953), 26 August 1943, AARM Reel 13, AvH.
3. AAR for SBD-5 (BuNo 28659), 27 August 1943, AARM Reel 22, AvH.
4. AAR for F4F-4 (BuNo 12153), 31 August 1943, AARM Reel 13, AvH.
5. AAR for F4F-4 (BuNo 11927), 31 August 1943, AARM Reel 13, AvH.

6. AAR for SBD-5 (BuNo 11011), 31 August 1943, AARM Reel 22, AvH.
7. Conf. Ltr, Commanding Officer to Chief of Bureau of Ships, CV4/S88 Serial 076 of 17 November 1943, Subj: USS *Ranger* (CV-4)—Relocation of Damage Control Station, in RG-19, Bureau of Ships Confidential Correpondence, C-CV 4#8, Box 707, NARA, College Park, MD. BuShips subsequently approved the *Ranger*'s internal reorganization: "The Bureau notes that the rearrangement has been tested in operation over a period of three months . . . and it has been found capable of performing any tasks on which the previous single station had been capable." Conf. Ltr, BuShips to Commanding Officer, USS *Ranger*, Subj: USS *Ranger* (CV-4)—Damage Control Stations, Relocations of, C-CV4/S88 (812), 21 December 1943, in RG-19, Bureau of Ships Confidential Correpondence, C-CV 4#8, Box 707, NARA, College Park, MD, op.cit.
8. AAR for SBD-5 (BuNo 28709), 8 September 1943, AARM Reel 22, AvH.
9. AAR for F4F-4 (BuNo 11957), 17 September 1943, AARM Reel 13, AvH.
10. Quoted in appendix to Crochet Diary.
11. Stephen W. Roskill, *The War at Sea: 1939–1945, Vol. III, The Offensive, Part I, 1st June 1943–31st May 1944* (London: Her Majesty's Stationery Office, 1960), 70–71.
12. Commander in Chief, Home Fleet to The Secretary of the Admiralty, No. 1610/H.F. 01325/150 of 31st October 1943, Subj: Operation Leader—Summary of USS *Ranger*'s Air Operations, in Action Report, Commander, U.S. Naval Forces in Europe, Serial 001037 of 30 November 1943, Subj: Operation Leader—Summary of USS *Ranger*'s Air Operations.
13. Ibid.
14. Carrier Air Group Four, Aircraft Action Report No. 1-43, 4 October 1943. Stuart was later awarded a Bronze Star in 1946 for conducting the operations of the *Ranger*'s flight deck during the March–December 1943 time period, so "as to bring forth creditable remarks by the Commander in Chief, British Home Fleet, and also as a result of such efficient work, heavy damaging blows were struck against the enemy off Bodø, Norway, on 4 October 1943." Stuart, William A., Comdr., USN, Recommendation for Letter of Commendation (Ribbon), Awards Cards, OA.
15. 1930 *Lucky Bag*, 267. Ruddy was not only a champion intercollegiate water polo player, but, a classmate explained, "during the summer months he would be on the main deck aft slinging a mean pair of [boxing] gloves around in the manner of his Irish ancestors."
16. Ibid.
17. The *Ranger*'s action reports refer to the ship as the *Rigmor*; she was, in fact, the *Schleswig*, formerly the Norwegian tanker *Austvanger*. Walter Lohmann and Hans H. Hildebrand, *Die Deutsche Kriegsmarine, 1939–1945*, Vol. 1, (Bad Neuheim: Verlag Hans-Henning Podzun, 1964), 57. The *Sleipner*-class torpedo boat reported was one of four former Norwegian coastal destroyers (*Sleipner* herself had escaped to the Allies) captured in 1940: *Lowe* (ex-*Gyller*), Kapitänleutnant Prüfe; *Leopard* (ex-*Balder*), Kapitänleutnant Bethge; *Panther* (ex-*Odin*), Kapitänleutnant Friedrich Meier; and *Tiger* (ex-*Tor*), Oberleutnant zur See Nose; Lohmann and Hildebrand, 54. All four ships were serving as torpedo recovery boats for the 27th U-boat flotilla. Erich Gröner, *German Warships, 1815–1945, Volume One: Major Surface Vessels*, (Annapolis: Naval Institute Press, 1990), 216–217.
18. Carrier Air Group Four, Aircraft Action Report No. 1-43, 4 October 1943, op.cit.
19. Illustrative of the tragedies of war, Clyde and Clara Tucker's son would never see his father. Tucker's radio-gunner Stephen Bakran, of Croatian descent, had turned 20 on 23 August; one of 11 children, he had excelled in football and baseball in high school. He enlisted on 27 June 1941 and underwent basic training at Great Lakes, Illinois. Bakran's mother took his loss hard. "It was very devastating for her," his sister Elizabeth once related, "and we believe that she died [in 1946] of a broken heart." Biographical material provided to the author by Rudy Bakran, Stephen's brother, in November 2001.
20. Ibid.
21. Gerald W. Thomas, "USS *Ranger* Veterans Return to Norway," Air Group 4 Web Site.
22. Newspaper articles, *Nordlands Framtid*, Bodø, and *Nordlandsposten*, Bodø, 2 October 1993. Both Davis and McCarley survived their imprisonment. The Germans imprisoned Davis in Oslo soon thereafter. After 10 days' solitary confinement, Davis was transferred to *Stalag Luft* 1, where, for five weeks, his captors neither allowed him to shower nor to change his clothes. For six months, he received neither mail nor Red Cross packages. Davis remained in Nazi hands for 19½ months, shedding 40 pounds in prison, before liberation in 1945. When Odd Karlsen met Davis at Bodø airport in 1993, the latter embraced his rescuer of 50 years before. "You saved my life," Davis said. "I will never forget that." Elsa Gryt, Morten's widow, returned Davis's ring and watch to him on 4 October 1993.
23. Johnnie Palmer soon found himself on his way to captivity in Oslo. After a week there, he was taken to Frankfurt, where a week of interrogations and incarceration on bread and water ensued. Subsequently, his captors transferred him to *Stalag Luft* 3. "I was the only Navy guy in this camp," Palmer later recalled, "and I found people ignored me completely . . . they thought I was a German plant because nobody could identify me for about two weeks." How could Palmer have been off the *Ranger*, incredulous fellow POWs asked, when a German newspaper showed that she had been sunk. "Of course I told them I was off the *Ranger*," Palmer later recounted, "and they didn't believe me. They believed the newspaper."
24. Carrier Air Group Four, Aircraft Action Report No. 2-43, 4 October 1943. See also Seiler, Edwin Norton, Lieut., USNR, Recommendation for Air Medal, Awards Cards, OA.
25. Donald M. Applegate, "Norway to Tokyo," Air Group 4 Web Site.
26. Thomas, *Torpedo Squadron Four*, 7.
27. Ibid., 7.

28. Ibid, 8.
29. Ibid.
30. Ibid.
31. Ibid., 8–9.
32. Barrett Tillman, "Dean S. 'Diz' Laird," ["Where are They Now?"], *The Hook* 21, no. 4 (Winter 1993): 10–11.
33. Carrier Air Group Four, Aircraft Action Report No. 3-43, 4 October 1943. See also Tillman, "Dean S. 'Diz' Laird," op.cit.
34. Carrier Air Group Four, Aircraft Action Report No. 3-43, 4 October 1943, op.cit.; as to the identity of the aircraft and its crew: Genst.Gen.Qu.6 Abt. (Stat.), 7950/43:169—07.10.43 (microfilm) courtesy of James L. Perry, Jr., and James C. Sawruk.
35. Ibid.
36. Identity of the aircraft and its crew: Genst.Gen.Qu.6 Abt. (Stat.), 7950/43:170—07.10.43 courtesy of James L. Perry, Jr., and James C. Sawruk.
37. AAR for F4F-4 (BuNo 11852) of 4 October 1943, in AARM Reel 13, AvH.
38. Commanding Officer, USS *Ranger* (CV-4), to Commander in Chief, U.S. Atlantic Fleet, Subj: Operation Leader—Report of, Ser CV4/A16-3 (0201) of 9 October 1943.
39. Commander in Chief, Home Fleet to The Secretary of the Admiralty, No. 1610/H.F. 01325/150 of 31st October 1943, Subj: Operation Leader—Summary of USS *Ranger*'s Air Operations, op.cit.
40. Commanding Officer, USS *Ranger* (CV-4), to Commander in Chief, U.S. Atlantic Fleet, Subj: Operation Leader—Report of, op.cit.
41. Commander Task Force One Two One to Commander in Chief, United States Fleet, File No. A16-3 Serial 0216 of 18 October 1943, First Endorsement to Commanding Officer, USS *Ranger* (CV-4), to Commander in Chief, U.S. Atlantic Fleet, Subj: Operation Leader—Report of.
42. Commander Carrier Air Group Four's Remarks Concerning Operation "Leader," n.d.
43. Ibid.
44. War Diary of the German Naval Staff (Operations Division), Part A, October 1943, 42, TM-100-I, Mic 212, Reel 9, NDL.
45. Commander Task Force One Two One to Commander in Chief, United States Fleet, File No. A16-3 Serial 0216 of 18 October 1943, First Endorsement to Commanding Officer, USS *Ranger* (CV-4), to Commander in Chief, U.S. Atlantic Fleet, Subj: Operation Leader—Report of, op. cit.; see also Commander in Chief, Home Fleet to The Secretary of the Admiralty, No. 1610/H.F. 01325/150 of 31st October 1943, Subj: Operation Leader—Summary of USS *Ranger*'s Air Operations, op.cit.
46. War Diary of the German Naval Staff (Operations Division), Part A, October 1943, 61, TM-100-I, Mic 212, Reel 9, NDL.
47. Commander Task Force One Two One to Commander in Chief, United States Fleet, File No. A16-3 Serial 0216 of 18 October 1943, First Endorsement to Commanding Officer, USS *Ranger* (CV-4), to Commander in Chief, U.S. Atlantic Fleet, Subj: Operation Leader—Report of, op.cit.
48. Ibid. One former *Ranger* skipper—Vice Adm. Patrick N. L. Bellinger, Commander, Air Force, Atlantic Fleet—expressed pleasure with the outcome of Leader. "Considering that this action was the first of its kind for many of the pilots," he wrote, "the results were favorable."
49. Capt. Gordon Rowe to Rear Adm. Calvin T. Durgin, 5 October 1943, Box 1, 1943 Correspondence File (R–Z), Durgin Papers.
50. Rear Adm. Calvin T. Durgin to Capt. Gordon Rowe, 24 October 1943, Box 1, 1943 Correspondence File (R–Z), Durgin Papers. Durgin, undoubtedly remembering the post-Torch overhaul at Norfolk, added: "I figure it is about time for you to be coming back to this side of the world for an overhaul. This they will probably due in the middle of January or some other very cold month and the Navy Yard workmen will tear up the old ship to make life doubly difficult in the Yard. They either ought to send you home right now or let you bask in the sunlight of Bermuda before making you go through the ordeal of a winter in the Navy Yard."

Chapter 27: *"RANGER* COULD BE MADE INTO AN EXCELLENT TRAINING SHIP"

1. AARs for F4F-4s (BuNos 12106 and 11955), 9 October 1943, AARM Reel 13, AvH.
2. Conf. Ltr, Commanding Officer, USS *Ranger* (CV-4) to Chief of the Bureau of Ships, CV4/S1 Ser 215 of 13 October 1943, Subj: USS *Ranger* (CV-4)—Recommending a comprehensive Re-fit and Modernization, in RG-19, Bureau of Ships Confidential Correspondence, C-CV4#9 to 5/30/44, Box 709, NARA, College Park, MD.
3. Conf. Ltr, Commanding Officer, USS *Ranger* (CV-4) to Chief of the Bureau of Ships, CV4/S1 Ser 215 of 13 October 1943, Subj: USS *Ranger* (CV-4)—Recommending a comprehensive Re-fit and Modernization, in RG-19, Bureau of Ships Confidential Correspondence, C-CV4#9 to 5/30/44, Box 709, NARA, College Park, MD.
4. AAR for SBD-5 (BuNo 28765), 14 October 1943, AARM Reel 22, AvH.
5. Quoted in Thomas, *Torpedo Squadron Four*, 29.
6. AAR for F4F-4 (BuNo 12001), 7 November 1943, AARM Reel 13, AvH.
7. AAR for SBD-5 (BuNo 28605), 7 November 1943, AARM Reel 22, AvH.
8. AAR for SBD-5 (BuNo 28765), 7 November 1943, AARM Reel 22, AvH.
9. Conf. Ltr, Commander Fleet Air, Norfolk, to Chief of the Bureau of Ships, FF13-2(1)/CV4/S1 of 9 November 1943, Subj: USS *Ranger* (CV4)—Recommending a Comprehensive Refit and Modernization, 1st Endorsement to CO, *Ranger* Conf. Ltr, CV4/S1 Serial 90215 of 13 October 1943, op.cit., in RG-19, Bureau of Ships Confidential Correspondence, C-CV4#9 to 5/30/44, Box 709, NARA, College Park, MD. The arrangement of gasoline stowage in the preliminary plans would have given the *Ranger* the gasoline capacity equivalent to that of an *Essex*-class carrier. ComFAir, Norfolk, however, did not consider the need for that large a capacity to justify the increased vulnerability.

See Conf. Ltr, Commander Fleet Air, Norfolk, to Chief, Bureau of Ships, FF13-2(1)/CV4/S15, Subj: USS *Ranger* (CV4)—Preliminary Plans for Installation of Blisters—Comment Regarding, 12 November 1943, 1st Endorsement to CO *Ranger* Conf. Ltr CV4/S15 Serial 0183 of 11 September 1943, in RG-19, Bureau of Ships Confidential Correspondence, C-CV4#8 to 12/27/43, Box 709, NARA, College Park, MD.

10. Conf. Ltr, Commander Air Force, Atlantic Fleet, to Chief of the Bureau of Ships, FF13-2/CV4/S1 of 14 November 1943, Subj: USS *Ranger* (CV-4)—Recommending a comprehensive Refit and Modernization, 2d Endorsement to CO, *Ranger* Conf. Ltr, CV4/S1 Serial 90215 of 13 October 1943, op.cit., in RG-19, Bureau of Ships Confidential Correspondence, C-CV4#9 to 5/30/44, Box 709, NARA, College Park, MD.
11. Thomas, *Torpedo Squadron Four*, 30.
12. AAR for F4F-4 P (BuNo 5160), 13 November 1943, AARM Reel 13, AvH.
13. Ibid.
14. Conf. Ltr, Commander in Chief, United States Atlantic Fleet, to Chief of the Bureau of Ships, 17 November 1943, Subj: USS *Ranger* (CV-4)—Recommending a comprehensive Refit and Modernization, in RG-19, Bureau of Ships Confidential Correspondence, C-CV4#9 to 5/30/44, Box 709, NARA, College Park, MD.
15. Thomas, *Torpedo Squadron Four*, 30.
16. Crochet Diary, 22 November 1943.
17. Ibid, 32.
18. Thomas, *Torpedo Squadron Four*, 32.
19. Memorandum Endorsement for Vice CNO, Subj: USS *Ranger* (CV-4)—Refit and Modernization of, FF1/S1-1(CV) Serial 04222, 18 December 1943, in RG-19, Bureau of Ships Confidential Correspondence, C-CV4#9 to 5/30/44, Box 709, NARA, College Park, MD.
20. Memo, BuShips to Chief of Naval Operations, Subj: USS *Ranger* (CV-4)—Refit and Modernization of, 19 January 1944, in RG-19, Bureau of Ships Confidential Correspondence, C-CV4#9 to 5/30/44, Box 709, NARA, College Park, MD.
21. Conf. Ltr, Chief, BuAer, to Chief of Naval Operations, Subj: USS *Ranger* (CV-4)—Installation of Flight Deck Catapult, 25 January 1944, in RG-19, Bureau of Ships Confidential Correspondence, C-CV4#9 to 5/30/44, Box 709, NARA, College Park, MD.
22. Conf. Ltr, Chief of the Bureau of Ordnance to the Chief of Naval Operations, Subj: USS *Ranger* (CV-4)—Refit and Modernization of—Recommendations for Improvement of A.A. Armament, CV4/S74 of 29 January 1944, in RG-19, Bureau of Ships Confidential Correspondence, C-CV4#9 to 5/30/44, Box 709, NARA, College Park, MD.
23. AAR for SBD-5 (BuNo 28811), 16 January 1944, AARM Reel 22, AvH.
24. AAR for SBD-5 (BuNo 28800), 16 January 1944, AARM Reel 22, AvH.
25. AAR for SBD-5 (BuNo 29090), 16 January 1944, AARM Reel 22, AvH.
26. AAR for SBD-5 (BuNo 28949), 16 January 1944, AARM Reel 22, AvH.
27. AAR for SBD-5 (BuNo 29041), 17 January 1944, AARM Reel 22, AvH.
28. AAR for SBD-5 (BuNo 54127), 28 March 1944, AARM Reel 22, AvH.
29. Thomas, *Torpedo Squadron Four*, 37.
30. Route sheet comments [serial 0212193, file C-CV4/L9], ca 8 March 1944, in RG-19, Bureau of Ships Confidential Correspondence, C-CV4#9 to 5/30/44, Box 709, NARA, College Park, MD.
31. Conf. Ltr, Chief of the Bureau of Ships to the Chief of Naval Operations, C-CV4/L9(100), Subj: USS *Ranger* (CV-4)—Refit and Modernization of, 20 March 1944, in RG-19, Bureau of Ships Confidential Correspondence, C-CV4#9 to 5/30/44, Box 709, NARA, College Park, MD.
32. Ibid. The *Randolph* (CV-15) was to be delivered at Norfolk for outfitting and post-delivery work. "If the *Ranger* is late," one BuShips officer wrote, "as she may well be, she might interfere with three CVs. I think it is a mistake to do the *Ranger* at this time and place—indeed, to do it at all." Route sheet comments, in above file.
33. Memorandum Endorsement to Commander in Chief, U.S. Fleet and Chief of Naval Operations, Subj: USS *Ranger* (CV-4)—Refit and Modernization of, Op-23-V-DC (SC)S1-1/CV4 Serial 01767823, 27 March 1944, in RG-19, Bureau of Ships Confidential Correspondence, C-CV4#9 to 5/30/44, Box 709, NARA, College Park, MD.
34. Conf. Ltr, Chief of Naval Operations to Chief of the Bureau of Ships, Subj: USS *Ranger* (CV-4)—Refit and Modernization of, Op-23-V-DC(SC)S1-1/CV4 Serial 0197323 of 6 April 1944, in RG-19, Bureau of Ships Confidential Correspondence, C-CV4#9 to 5/30/44, Box 709, NARA, College Park, MD.
35. AAR for SBD-5 (BuNo 36907), 3 April 1944, AARM Reel 22, AvH.
36. Ibid, 37; see also Gerald W. Thomas, "Preparing for Combat in the Pacific," Air Group 4 Web Site.
37. Conf Ltr, CO, *Ranger* (CV-4) to Chief of Bureau of Ships C-CV4/L9-3(1)/S30/S33 serial 072 dated 9 April 1944 in RG-19, Bureau of Ships Confidential Correspondence, C-CV4#9 to 5/30/44, Box 709, NARA, College Park, MD. Additional concerns addressed by Captain Rowe included the poor drainage from the flight deck, which frequently resulted in "large quantities of water . . . cascading on to the hangar deck," with consequently "large amounts of water that collect throughout the hangar space when it rains"; Ibid.
38. "History of Carrier Aircraft Service Unit 22, 1 Jan[uary] 1943–31 Dec[ember] 1944," AvH, NHC. CASU-22's first commanding officer was Lt. Comdr. Wallace A. Sherrill, who had commanded VT-4 in 1942.
39. Gerald W. Thomas "Preparing for Combat in the Pacific," Air Group 4 Web Site.
40. AAR for TBM-1C (BuNo 25179), 10 August 1944, AARM Reel 30, AvH.

41. Commanding Officer, USS *Ranger* (CV-4) to Chief of Bureau of Medicine and Surgery, Subj: Report of Casualties, CV-4/P6-2 OFF16/LSS/hhm of 21 August 1944; Commanding Officer, Fighting Squadron Three to Chief of Bureau of Medicine and Surgery, Subj: Report of Casualties, 21 August 1944, and, Medical Officer, USS *Ranger* (CV-4) to Chief of Bureau of Medicine and Surgery, Subj: Disposition of remains, report of, 19 August 1944. BuPers Casualty Files (OA), copies in author's files. Other F6F-3s (in addition to BuNos 58484 and 58592) listed as damaged in the accident: BuNos 58536, 58556, and 58474.
42. AAR for TBM-1C (BuNo 45462), 18 August 1944, AARM Reel 30, AvH.
43. AAR for F6F-3 (BuNo 42324), 9 September 1944, AARM Reel 6, AvH.
44. Ltrs, CO *Ranger* (CV-4) to Chief of Bureau of Medicine and Surgery, Subj: Report of Casualties, CV-4/P6-2, OFF 16/LSS/hhm, 13 September 1944, BuPers Casualty files, op.cit.
45. Commander in Chief, United States Fleet, Conf. Memorandum for Vice Chief of Naval Operations, Subj: USS *Ranger* (CV-4)—Refit and Modernization of, FF1/S1-1(CV) Serial 03244, 19 September 1944, in RG-19, Bureau of Ships Confidential Correspondence, C-CV4#9 to 5/30/44, Box 709, NARA, College Park, MD.
46. AAR for F6F-3 (BuNo 70061), 28 October 1944, AARM Reel 6, AvH.
47. AAR for F6F-3 (BuNo 41820), 28 October 1944, AARM Reel 6, AvH.
48. AARs for F6F-3s (BuNos 41118 and 40563), 28 October 1944, AARM Reel 6, AvH.
49. AAR for F6F-3 (BuNo 40977), 17 November 1944, AARM Reel 6, AvH.
50. AARs for F6F-3s (BuNos 70601, 42945, and 41271), 17 November 1944, AARM Reel 6.
51. AARs for F6F-3s (BuNos 43004 and 41182), 19 December 1944, AARM Reel 6, AvH.
52. AAR for F6F-3 (BuNo 42777), 19 December 1944, AARM Reel 6, AvH.
53. AAR for F6F-3 (BuNo 42818), 19 December 1944, AARM Reel 6, AvH.
54. AAR for F6F-3 (BuNo 40458), 20 December 1944, AARM Reel 6, AvH.
55. AAR for F6F-3 (BuNo 42989), 20 December 1944, AARM Reel 6, AvH.
56. AAR for F6F-3 (BuNo 42969), 20 December 1944, AARM Reel 6, AvH.
57. AAR for SB2C-3 (BuNo 19639), 20 December 1944, AARM Reel 29, AvH.
58. AAR for SB2C-3 (BuNo 18707), 29 December 1944, AARM Reel 29, AvH.

Chapter 28: "SHE DIDN'T NEED HEADLINES TO BE A GREAT SHIP"

1. "The History of [the] Carrier Training Squadron, Pacific Fleet," in CarTrainRon, Pacific Fleet, Aviation History File, Box 152, AvH. The ships assigned to the division: CarDiv 11: the *Saratoga*, the *Tripoli* (CVE-64), the *Kasaan Bay* (CVE-69), and the *Makassar Strait* (CVE-91); CarDiv 12: the *Ranger*, the *Takanis Bay* (CVE-89), the *Matanikau* (CVE-101), and *Commencement Bay*. The names of the ships reflected the evolution of carrier-naming policy, beginning with the traditional "battles" from the past to battles of the then-present conflict (*Matanikau*) and "bays in Alaska." Rear Admiral Jennings's operations officer was Comdr. Tommy Booth, formerly VF-41's commanding officer during Torch.
2. AAR for SB2C-4 (BuNo 20268), 19 January 1945, AARM Reel 29, AvH.
3. AAR for SB2C-4 (BuNo 20504), 21 January 1945, AARM Reel 29, AvH.
4. Citation for award of Silver Life Saving Medal for Seaman 1st Class Edward J. Gross. Awards Cards, OA. Eventually, in ceremonies before the ship's company on 30 May, Captain Johnson awarded Seaman 1st Class Gross the Navy and Marine Corps Medal for his selfless heroism in saving Coxswain Campbell's life.
5. AARs for F4U-1Ds (BuNos 82296 and 82363), 29 January 1945, AARM Reel 9, AvH.
6. AAR for F4U-1D (BuNo 82365), 30 January 1945, AARM Reel 9, AvH.
7. AAR for SB2C-4 (BuNo 19914), 1 February 1945, AARM Reel 29, AvH.
8. AAR for SB2C-4 (BuNo 18805), 5 February 1945, AARM Reel 29, AvH.
9. AARs for F4U-1Ds (BuNos 82296 and 82363), 29 January 1945, AARM Reel 9, AvH.
10. Among the Marine aviators lost was Maj. Robert W. Vaupell, a survivor of the Battle of Midway.
11. AARs for F4U-1Ds (BuNos 57178, 82289, and 57281), 15 January 1945, AARM Reel 9, AvH.
12. AARs for F4U-1D (BuNo 57293), 16 January 1945, AARM Reel 9, AvH.
13. AAR for SB2C-4 (BuNo 20415), 21 February 1945, AARM Reel 29, AvH.
14. AAR for SB2C-4 (BuNo 20468), 21 February 1945, AARM Reel 29, AvH.
15. AARs for SB2C-4s (BuNos 20415 and 20468), Ibid., and op.cit.
16. AAR for SB2C-4 (BuNo 19836), 21 February 1945, AARM Reel 29, AvH.
17. "The History of [the] Carrier Training Squadron, Pacific Fleet," op.cit.
18. AARs for F4U-1Ds (BuNos 82238 and 82258), 4 March 1945, AARM Reel 9, AvH.
19. AAR for F6F-3 (BuNo 66234), 11 March 1945, AARM Reel 7, AvH.
20. AARs for F4U-1D (BuNo 57649), 11 March 1945, AARM Reel 9, AvH.
21. Edwin Leigh Armistead, "Naval Airborne Early Warning, 1945–1985," MA Thesis, Old Dominion University, December 1993. Copy in NDL.
22. Chief of Naval Operations to Chief of the Bureau of Ships, Subj: USS *Ranger* (CV-4)—AEW Installation, 9 February 1945, in

RG-19, Bureau of Ships Confidential Correspondence, 1940–1945, C-CV4#11 from 1/8/45, Box 709, NARA, College Park, MD.
23. Armistead, "Naval Airborne Early Warning, 1945–1985," 18.
24. Ibid. Apparently, a similar installation had been contemplated for the *Saratoga*, but operational commitments resulted in the *Sara* being unavailable. Chief of Naval Operations to Chief of the Bureau of Ships, Subj: USS *Ranger* (CV-4)—AEW Installation, 9 February 1945, op.cit. The *Saratoga* had been pulled from training duty and deployed as a night carrier. She participated in strikes on Tokyo (16–17 February 1945), which were carried out in support of Operation Detachment, the invasion of Iwo Jima.
25. AAR for SB2C-4E (BuNo 65110), 1 April 1945, AARM Reel 29, AvH.
26. AAR for SB2C-4E (BuNo 19827), 10 April 1945, AARM Reel 29, AvH.
27. AAR for SB2C-4E (BuNo 20097), 11 April 1945, AARM Reel 29, AvH.
28. AAR for SB2C-4 (BuNo 19862), 19 April 1945, AARM Reel 29, AvH.
29. AAR for SB2C-4 (BuNo 19838), 28 April 1945, AARM Reel 29, AvH.
30. AAR for SB2C-4 (BuNo 20476), 30 April 1945, AARM Reel 29, AvH.
31. XFR-1, FR-1 Fireball (Ryan) folder, Naval Air Systems Command Collection, Box 20, AvH.
32. Quarterly History of Fleet Air Command, West Coast, to 1 March 1945, dated 13 March 1945, in Aviation History Files, Fleet Air Wings, "Fairwest," Box 24, AvH, 7–8.
33. Commanding Officer to Chief of the Bureau of Ships, Subj: USS *Ranger* (CV-4)—Alteration Request Number 10-45, CV-4/L9-3(1)/S12 OF12/Soc, 3 May 1945, in RG-19, Bureau of Ships Confidential Correspondence, 1940–1945, C-CV4#11 from 1/8/45, Box 709, NARA, College Park, MD.
34. AAR for TBM-3E (BuNo 85858), 8 May 1945, AARM Reel 30, AvH.
35. AARs for TBM-3Es (BuNo 86122 and 86177), 10 and 11 May 1945, AARM Reel 30, AvH.
36. Edwin Leigh Armistead, *Grease Pencils and Flourescent Bananas: The History of Airborne Early Warning Aircraft*, (Virginia Beach: Privately Published, 1999), 7.
37. Armistead, "Naval Airborne Early Warning, 1945–1985," 22.
38. Commander Fleet Air, West Coast, to Commanding Officer, USS *Ranger*, Subj: Commendatory performance of USS *Ranger*, 23 May 1945, attached to Quarterly Historical Report of the USS *Ranger* for the first two quarters of 1945, 18 July 1945, in World War II Command File, Individual Ships, OA.
39. "War History of Bomber Fighter Squadron Eighteen," 19 November 1945, VBF-1—VBF-18, Box 62, AvH.
40. AAR for FG-1D (BuNo 92108), 5 September 1945, AARM Reel 13, AvH.
41. BuShips to CO, USS *Ranger*, Subj: USS *Ranger* (CV-4)—Alteration Request No. 10-45, Action on, 20 September 1945. RG-19, Bureau of Ships Confidential Correspondence, 1940–1945, C-CV4 #11 from 1/8/45, Box 709, NARA, College Park, MD.
42. "War History of Bomber Fighter Squadron Eighteen for period of 2 September 1945 through 31 March 1946," 6 May 1946, AvH. Hereinafter VBF-18 War History.
43. Ibid.
44. AAR for F8F-1 (BuNo 94829), 4 October 1945, AARM Reel 12, AvH.
45. "History—Air Group Eighteen—For Period 3 September 1945 to 31 March 1946," 13 May 1946, Aviation History, CAG-18 thru CAG-35, Box 12, AvH. Hereinafter CVG-18 History.
46. "War History for the Period 2 September 1945 to 31 March 1946, inclusive, in the case of Bombing Squadron Eighteen—Forwarding of," 9 May 1946, Aviation Commands, 1941–1952, VB-14—VB-20, Box 59, AvH.
47. CVG-18 History, op.cit.
48. Ibid.
49. Ibid.
50. VBF-18 War History.
51. "Conformation of Telephone Conversation" CV-4/L9-3 (N-O) of 13 November 1945, in CV 4, Vol. 18, Box 707, RG-19, Records of the Bureau of Ships, General Correspondence, NARA, College Park, MD.
52. Route Sheet comments, dated 19 November 1945, in CV 4, Vol. 18, Box 707, op.cit.
53. "Our Peg-Leg Admiral," *Life*, 14 August 1950, 77.
54. The ship's log does not record the name of the pilot who flew the aircraft.
55. "Aircraft Carrier USS *Ranger* To Be Sold for Conversion or Scrap," Press Release dated 19 December 1946 in USS *Ranger* (CV-4) Ship File, World War II Command File, OA.
56. O'Callahan, 4.
57. Ibid., 5. The Navy did not forget the name: it was assigned to a *Forrestal* (CVA-59)-class attack carrier, CVA-61. Laid down at Newport News on 2 August 1954 and launched on 29 September 1956, the next *Ranger* was commissioned on 10 August 1957. Her first commanding officer was Capt. Charles T. Booth, II, who had commanded VF-41 during Operation Torch. This *Ranger* continued the traditions of accomplishment established by the first carrier built as such from the keel up, through the Vietnam War.

BIBLIOGRAPHY

The primary sources for this book are the deck logs of the USS *Ranger* (CV-4), which, for the 1934–40 period, are held in RG-24, Records of the Bureau of Navigation, National Archives and Records Administration (NARA), Washington, D.C., and those for the 1941–45 period in RG-24, Records of the Bureau of Naval Personnel (ex-Bureau of Navigation), National Archives and Records Service, College Park, Maryland. Access to the log for 1946 was, at the time that research was conducted for the book, conducted through the Ships' Histories Branch, Naval Historical Center (NHC). Other primary sources are the *Ranger*'s war diary and action reports, which are held by the NARA's College Park facility, in RG-38. Small collections of material on the *Ranger* exist at the NHC's Ships Histories Branch (Ships' Names and Sponsor and Ship Source files), Operational Archives (World War II Command Files, Officer Biography Files, and Awards Citations), and the Aviation History Branch and Archives (individual squadron histories, historical files on aircraft, aircraft accident reports). Originals of the latter, many of which contain photographs of the wrecked planes, are held by the NARA at their Washington, D.C., and College Park, Md, branches, in the records of the Bureau of Aeronautics (RG-72). Copies of all materials used in this book will ultimately be placed in the Ships History Branch of the Naval Historical Center.

PRIMARY DOCUMENTS

USS *Ranger* (CV-4) Deck Logs, 4 June 1934–18 October 1946 (RG-24). NARA.

USS *Ranger* (CV-4) War Diary (RG-38). NARA.

USS *Ranger* (CV-4) Action Reports (RG-38). NARA.

U.S. Navy Ship/Aviation Squadron War Diaries. World War II (RG-38), NARA, College Park.

Records of the Bureau of Aeronautics (RG-72), NARA.

Records of the Bureau of Construction and Repair/Bureau of Ships (RG-19), NARA.

Records Relating to U.S. Navy Fleet Problems I–XXII (NARA Microfilm Publication M964).

Annual Reports of Fleets and Task Forces of the U.S. Navy, 1920–1941 (NARA Microfilm Publication M971).

USS *Ranger* (CV-4) Marine Detachment Muster Rolls, MCHC.

Aircraft Accident Reports, AVH, NHC.

Status of Naval Aircraft, AVH, NHC.

War Diary, Eastern Sea Frontier, 1942–1944, Microfilm A-143, NDL, NHC.

World War II Command File, OA, NHC.

ORAL HISTORY TRANSCRIPTS

Fields, Lewis J., Oral History Transcript, MCHC

Pownall, Charles A. *The Reminiscences of Vice Admiral Charles A. Pownall, U.S. Navy (Retired)*. Annapolis: U.S. Naval Institute, 1989.

PARTICIPANTS

Rudy Bakran (brother of the late Aviation Radioman 2d Class Stephen D. Bakran)

Ernest Crochet (Ship's Company)

Lloyd Edens (VS-41, VB-4)

Mrs. Amy McQuade (sister of the late Aviation Radioman 3d Class George E. Biggs, Jr.)

Eugene Rowley (nephew of the late Aviation Radioman 3d Class George E. Biggs, Jr.)

Gerald W. Thomas (VT-4)
Clifford M. White (VF-4)

PERSONAL PAPERS COLLECTIONS

Patrick N. L. Bellinger, AvH, NHC
Claude C. Bloch, LCMD
Charles M. Cooke, HIA
Calvin T. Durgin, OA, NHC
Ernest J. King, LCMD

PUBLISHED SOURCES
Books and Monographs

Abbazia, Patrick. *Mr. Roosevelt's Navy: The Private War of the U.S. Atlantic Fleet, 1939–1942.* Annapolis: Naval Institute Press, 1975.

Auphan, Paul, and Jacques Mordal. Translated by A. C. J. Sabalot, *The French Navy in World War II.* Annapolis: Naval Institute Press, 1959.

Baker, Marcus. *Geographic Dictionary of Alaska*, 2d ed. Washington: GPO, 1906.

Bloch, Michael, ed., *Wallis and Edward, Letters, 1931–1937: The Intimate Correspondence of the Duke and Duchess of Windsor.* New York: Summit Books, 1986.

Blumenson, Martin. *The Patton Papers, 1940–1945.* Boston: Houghton Mifflin, 1974.

Burns, James McGregor. *Roosevelt: The Soldier of Freedom.* New York: Harcourt Brace Jovanovich, 1970.

Busch, Rainer, and Hans-Joachim Röll, *German U-Boat Commanders of World War II.* London: Greenhill Books/Annapolis: Naval Institute Press, 1999.

Cornelius, Wanda, and Thayne Short. *Ding Hao: America's Air War in China, 1937–1945.* Gretna: Pelican, 1980.

Cressman, Robert J. *That Gallant Ship: USS Yorktown (CV-5).* Missoula: Pictorial Histories Publishing Co., 1985.

Danchev, Alex. *Establishing the Anglo-American Alliance: The Second World War Diaries of Brigadier Vivian Dykes.* London: Brassey's (UK), 1990.

Dönitz, Karl, transl. R. H. Stevens (and David Woodward). *Memoirs: Ten Years and Twenty Days.* Annapolis: Naval Institute Press, 1990.

Fern, Henry S. *Argentina.* Washington, D.C.: Frederick A. Praeger, 1969.

Fitzgibbon, Russell H., *Uruguay: Portrait of a Democracy.* Brunswick: Rutgers University Press, 1954.

Friedman, Norman. *Aircraft Carriers: An Illustrated Design History.* Annapolis: Naval Institute Press, 1983.

Goldstein, Donald M., and Katherine V. Dillon. *Amelia: A Life of the Aviation Legend.* Washington, D.C.: Batsford-Brassey, 1997.

Grossnick, Roy A., ed. *United States Naval Aviation 1910–1995.* Washington, D.C.: Naval Historical Center, 1997.

Jenkins, E. H. *A History of the French Navy: From Its Beginnings to the Present Day.* Annapolis: Naval Institute Press, 1974.

Katz, Ephraim. *The Film Encyclopedia*, New York: Harper and Row, 1979.

Kimball, Warren F. ed. *Churchill & Roosevelt: The Complete Correspondence.* Vol. 1, *Alliance Emerging, October 1933–November 1942.* Princeton: Princeton University Press, 1984.

King, Ernest J., and Walter Muir Whitehill. *Fleet Admiral King: A Naval Record*, New York: W.W. Norton, 1952.

Lamparski, Richard, *Whatever Became Of . . . ?* New York: Crown Publishers, 1974.

Loewenheim, Francis L., Harold D. Langley, and Manfred Jonas, eds. *Roosevelt and Churchill: Their Secret Wartime Correspondence.* New York: Saturday Review Press/E. P. Dutton, 1975.

Loewenstein, Karl. *Brazil Under Vargas.* New York: MacMillan, 1942.

Martin, Ralph G. *The Woman He Loved.* New York: Simon and Schuster, 1973.

O'Callahan, Joseph T. *I Was Chaplain on the Franklin*, New York: MacMillan, 1956.

Peterson, Harold F. *Argentina and the United States, 1810–1960*, State University of New York, 1964.

Poolman, Kenneth. *Escort Carrier, 1941–1945: An Account of British Escort Carriers in Trade Protection.* London: Ian Allen, 1972.

Prange, Gordon W. *At Dawn We Slept: The Untold Story of Pearl Harbor.* New York: McGraw Hill. 1981.

Ranger, USS. *The Ranger Rolls Down to Rio: Being an Account of the Shakedown Cruise of the U.S.S.* Ranger *to Rio de Janeiro, Buenos Aires, and Montevideo, 17 August–5 October 1934.* Privately published, 1934.

Röhwer, Jurgen. *Axis Submarine Successes, 1939–1945.* Annapolis: Naval Institute Press, 1983.

Roskill, Stephen W. *The War at Sea: 1939–1945.* Vol. III, *The Offensive, Part I, 1st June 1943–31st May 1944.* London: Her Majesty's Stationery Office, 1960.

Schurz, William L. *Latin America: A Descriptive Survey.* New York: E. P. Dutton, 1941.

Smith, T. Lynn, ed. *Brazil: Portrait of Half a Continent.* New York: Dryden Press, 1951.

Thomas, Gerald W. *Torpedo Squadron Four: A Cockpit View of World War II.* Privately Published, 1990.

U.S. Congress, Seventy-Fourth Congress, First Session. *Hearings Before [the] Subcommittee of House Committee on Appropriations in Charge of [the] Navy Department Appropriation Bill for 1936.* Washington, D.C.: GPO, 1935.

———, Seventy-Ninth Congress, First Session. *Hearings Before the Joint Committee on the Investigation of the Pearl Harbor Attack.* 39 parts. Washington: GPO, 1946.

U.S. Navy, Bureau of Navigation. *Handbook of the Hospital Corps, United States Navy, 1930.* Washington, D.C.: GPO, 1930.

Whitaker, Arthur P. *The United States and Argentina.* Cambridge: Harvard University Press, 1954.

Wright, Gwendolyn. Introduction, *The WPA Guide to California: The Federal Writer's Project Guide to 1930s California.* New York: Pantheon Books, 1984.

PERIODICAL AND JOURNAL ARTICLES

Cole, Martin. "Red Airmen to California." *American Aviation Historical Society Journal*, Summer 1968, 103–111.

Cuny, J. "Hawk 75 in French Service." *American Aviation Historical Society Journal* 11, no. 1, Spring 1966, 13–30.

Foley, Francis D. "Why the Navy Didn't Find Amelia" [letter to the editor]. *U.S. Naval Institute Proceedings*, April 1993, 29–30.

Foster, Edwin D. "Cafeteria Afloat." *U.S. Naval Institute Proceedings*, January 1937 (19–24).

Fuchida, Mitsuo. "I Led the Air Attack on Pearl Harbor." *U.S. Naval Institute Proceedings*, September 1952, 939–952.

Hendrie, Andrew. "A Converted Airliner at War: The Lockheed Hudson Aircraft as Operated by Coastal Command, Royal Air Force." *Aerospace Historian* 31 no. 4, Winter/December 1984, 234–242.

Lanius, Charles. "How It Feels to Fight Your Friends." *The Saturday Evening Post* 215, no. 46, May 15, 1943.

SHIP'S NEWSPAPERS

The Ranger
The CV-4
The Bull Horn

PERIODICALS

The Leatherneck
Bureau of Aeronautics Newsletter
The Army and Navy Journal
New York Times

INDEX

A
ABC-1 Staff Agreement, 148
Abel, Chief Photographer's Mate Burton C., 203, 224
Absecon (AVP-23), 393
Adams, Comdr. Frank M., 226
Adams, Secretary of the Navy Charles Francis, 3, *4,* 5, 12
Aday, Aviation Chief Radioman Jack L. (VT-4, CRAG), 232, 244, 282, 285, 286, 330, 339
Admiral Graf Spee (German armored ship), 131
Adrian, Lt. (jg) Leo G., USNR (VB-84), 374
Advance Carrier Training Group (ACTG), 313
Africa, North, 200, *202, 205, 229, 233, 243, 261, 275,* 291, 294
Airborne early warning (AEW), xiv, 385, 388
Alabama (BB-58), 322
Alameda, 373, 374, 379, 381
Albania, 125
Albatros (French destroyer leader), 222, 223, 224, 232, *234,* 251
Albert, Aerographer 3d Class J. F., 23
Alberts, Ens. Milton G., USNR (VBF-2), 384
Albores (Argentine boxer), 23
Alcyon (French destroyer), 230
Alexander, Lt. Stanley M., 147
Algeria, 200
Algiers, 210
Alice (U.S. tug), *161*
Allcorn, Capt. Ford A., USA, 262, *265*
Allegheny (AT-19), *13*
Allen, Ens. Bain S., USNR (VBF-1), 382
Allender, Ens. Richard K., A-V(N) (VB-4), 357
Almond, James (Yard workman), 25
Altamaha (CVE-18), *369*
Altenfjord, 351
America. See West Point (AP-23)
Amesbury, Lt. (jg) Stanton M., A-V(N) (VF-9), *206,* 209, 237, 242, 264, 265
Amphitrite (French submarine), 220

Amrine, Aviation Cadet Horace F., USNR (VS-41), 94, 95, 100
Anchor Point, 46
Anderson, Ens. Gerald A., A-V(N), 290
Anderson, Lt. Comdr. Hildreth V., USNR, 388
Anderson, Lt. Donald E., A-V(N) (VS-41), 239
Anderson, Lt. Guy J. (VS-42), 162
Anderson, Lt. (jg) Howard T. E., 99
Anderson, Lt. (jg) Ralph R. "Andy," A-V(N) (VT-4), 297, *298, 313, 319*
Anderson, Radioman 1st Class J. A., 141
Anderson, Seaman 1st Class F. C., USNR, 156
Andrews, Aviation Machinist's 1st Class J. L., 78
Andrews, Lt. Charles C. "Andy" (VF-4), 223, 224, 227, 339, *353*
Andrews, Lt. (jg) Clyde C., A-V(N) (VF-41), *211,* 214, 237, 251, 256, 269, 283, 330
AN-M-54 incendary, 216, 217
Anson, HMS (British battleship), 327, 349
Applegate, Aviation Radioman 3d Class Donald M. (VT-4), 330, 338
Arbes, Ens. James D., A-V(N) (VB-4), 123, 141, 144
Archer, HMS (British auxiliary aircraft carrier), 162, 177
Arctic Circle, xiii, xiv
Arcturus (AK-18), 291
Argentina, xiii, 16, 23
Argonne (AG-31), 81
Argus, HMS (British aircraft carrier), 188
Arthur, Lt. (jg) Robert L., A-V(N) (VS-41), 209, 221, 232, *234,* 256, 270, 278, 279, 280, 287
Arthur, Lt. Samuel H., 13, 15
Artigas, Uruguayan patriot Jose Gervasio, 23
"Asbetos Joe," *266*
Ashanti, HMS (British destroyer), 354
Ashford, Lt. (jg) William H. (VB-3B), 44, *50*
Asmus, Aviation Ordnanceman 1st Class D. F. (VF-4), 140
Astoria (CA-34), 120, 121
Atlantic Fleet, 143, 144, 148
Atlantic Squadron, 141

August, Lt. (jg) Charles V. "Chuck," A-V(N) (VF-41), 183, *210,* 212, 216, 218, 228, 231, 236, 240, 241, 244, 246, 255, 266, 267, 283, 298, 299, 301, 324
Augusta (CA-31), 181, 184, 186, 190, *191,* 228, 230, 268, 269, 271, 272, 273, 275, 285, *304,* 322, 354, 357
Auk (AM-57), 235
Austermuehle, Lt. Edward W., 384
Avocet (AVP-4), 88
Ayres, Ens. David L., USNR, 383
Azores, 201, 202

B

Badger (DD-126), 131
Bagdanovich, Lt. Comdr. Michael P. "Bag," 231, 265, 282, 284
Bailey, Lt. (jg) William Y, A-V(N), 293
Baird, Lt. Abraham L., 142
Baker, Capt. Robert N. S., 147, 192
Baker, Ens. Gus B. (VB-4), 351
Baker, Seaman 1st Class R. F., 53
Bakersfield, 71
Bakran, Aviation Radioman 2d Class Stephen D. (VB-4), 328, 333
Baldwin, Ens. Albert J., A-V(N), 297, 298, 299, *299*
Ball, Ens. Philip S., Jr., A-V(N) (VF-41), 214, 227, 234, 235, 237, 251, 256, 269, 281, 283
Ballard (AVD-10), 386, 388
Ballentine, Capt. John J., *164, 185, 202*
Bamber, Aviation Machinist's Mate J. (VT-3), 98
Bandy, Lt. Comdr. Jack I. (VF-4), 140, 145, 269, 270
Barbados, 123, *124,* 125
Barber's Point, 77
Bardeen, Lt. Burton L., A-V(N) (VF-9, VF-12), *206,* 214, 237, 256, 264, 268, 281, 286, 374
Barfield, Aviation Ordnanceman 2d Class R. L. (VT-4), 330
Barlau, Fireman 2d Class M. M., 37
Barner, Lt. Comdr. James D., 10, *25,* 27
Barnes, Aviation Machinist's Mate 3d Class Lloyd M. (VB-1B), 66
Barnes (ACV-20), 394
Barnett, Ens. Gerald M. "Buck," A-V(N) (VT-4), 305, *319,* 330, 338
Barr, Aviation Radioman 2d Class Charles W. (VT-4), 297, 330
Barr, Lt. Col. John E., USAAF, 184, 185
Barracuda (SS-163), 30, 32
Barren Island, 45
Barron, Lt. (jg) Howard A., 384
Barry (DD-248), 9
Bartlett, Aviation Chief Machinist's Mate Jerry F., 31
Bassett, Ens. Edgar R. "Red," A-V(N) (VF-41), 157
Beal, Radioman 1st Class Glen M., 81
Beard, Aviation Radioman 3d Class A., Jr., 297
Beard, Lt. Comdr. Jefferson D., 147, 148, *154*
Beary, Capt. Donald B., 172
Beatle, Ralph H., 390
Becker, C. F. (Associated Oil Company), 44
Belfast, HMS (British light cruiser), 327
Bell (DD-587), 316, 322
Bellinger, Capt. Patrick N. L., 57, 62, 64, 66, *67,* 71, *72,* 73, *74,* 77, 79, 80, 82, 83, 96, 139, 351
Bellinger, Frederick Wells, 77
Bell P-39 Airacobra, 363
Benavides, Gen. Oscar R. (President of Peru), 104, *104*
Bermuda, 149, 150, 151, 153, 155, 158, 161, 163, 164, 165, 178, *179, 180,* 181, *198,* 199, *199*
Bernard, Aviation Machinist's Mate 1st Class R. L. C. (VS-41), 187
Bernard, Lt. (jg) Louis L., USNR, 227
Berner, Lt. Warren K., 39
Bernhard, Rear Adm. Alva, 297, 305, *312*

Bertucci, Aviation Ordnanceman 1st Class Russell H., 305, 393
Bessie, Lt. Comdr. Everett M., (MC) USNR, 315
Bethlehem Shipbuilding Corporation, 5
Bettinger, Lt. Joe L., Jr. (VB-4), 328
Betts, Lt. (jg) Sherman W. "Sherry" (VB-1B), 63
Bevis, Ens. Charles C., Jr., A-V(N) (VS-41), 226, 237, 238, 257, 259, 281, 288, 289
Biggs, Aviation Radioman 3d Class George E., Jr. "Bugs" (VS-41), 192, 226, 237, 240, *242*
Bikini atoll, 392
Birdseye, Clarence, 6
Bishop, Lt. Comdr. George W., Jr., USNR (CVG-18), 390, 391
Bisson, Capt. Robert O., USMC (VMS-1), 142, 143
Biter, HMS (British escort aircraft carrier), 306
Black, Aviation Radioman 3d Class A. J. D. (VB-4), 351
Black, Seaman 1st Class J. A., 127
Blakely, Vice Adm. Charles A., 139
Blakemore, Radioman 2d Class G. P., 178
Blandy, Rear Adm. William H. P., 299
Blanos, Aviation Machinist's Mate 1st Class P. J. (VT-4), 295, 297, 330
Blasig, *Feldwebel* Otto (observer), 343
Blazer, Radioman 2d Class D. W. (VS-1B), 83
Bledsoe, Radioman 2d Class K. M. (VS-41), 91
Blenman, Lt. (jg) Charles, Jr. (VS-41), 125
Blessman, Lt. Edward M., 128
Blier, Aviation Radioman 2d Class L. J. (VB-4), 328
Bloch, Adm. Claude C., CinCUS, 84, 85, 111
Block Island (CVE-106), 184, 364, 383
Blue Bell (U.S. water taxi), 37
Blue (DD-744), 364
"Boar's Head" insignia, *110*
Bodø, xiii, 327, 330, 334, *334,* 335, *335, 336,* 340, 341, *341*
Boeing F4B-4:
  BuNo 9253, 96
  BuNo A-9030, 10, 11, *16, 17,* 23
  BuNo A-9041, 63
  general, 51
Bogan, Rear Adm. Gerald F., 351
Bolivia, 21, 23
Bolt, Lt. (jg) George W., 297, *319*
Bolt, Lt. William H., Jr. "Pete," A-V(N) (VF-41), 183, *211,* 214, 223, 227, 234, 235, 237, 251, 256, 262, 269, 281, *353*
Bombing Fighting Squadrons:
  VBF-1, 382, 383
  VBF-2, 384, 385
  VBF-14, 386
  VBF-18, 388, 389, 390
  VBF-87, 380
  VBF-98, 384
Bombing Squadrons:
  VB-1B, *37,* 41, 42, *50, 52,* 63, 64, 66, 69, 80, 81, 82, 83, 85, 99
  VB-2, 41, 96, 111
  VB-2B, 81
  VB-3, 97, 117, 118, 119, 121, 122, 125, 127, 134, 161, 209, 226, 232, *233,* 396
  VB-3B, 12, *17,* 23, 24, 25, 26, 29, 31, 32, *32,* 44, *50, 51,* 80, 85
  VB-4, 85, 87, 89, *89,* 91, *91, 93,* 98, 99, 103, *103,* 104, 106, *108, 110,* 113, 115, 117, 123, 128, 129, 131, 132, *136,* 140, 141, 143, 144, 156, 171, 172, 179, 180, 181, 183, 191, *196,* 202, 203, *205,* 209, 213, *218,* 220, *220,* 221, 224, 226, 232, 233, 237, 238, 239, 244, 245, 250, 251, 254, 255, 256, 257, 259, 260, 262, 263, *263,* 264, 265, 268, 269, 272, 274, *274, 275, 276,* 277, *277,* 278, 280, 281, 282, 283, 284, *284,* 285, 287, 288, 291, 301, 303, 304,

305, *305,* 308, *315,* 316, *316,* 317, 318, 319, 320, 324, 325, *326, 327,* 328, 329, 330, 332, 333, *333,* 334, *334,* 335, *335,* 344, 351, 356, 357, 362, 373, 394
VB-4B, 85
VB-4M, 40
VB-5, 123, 151, 380, 381
VB-5B, 10, 11, 12, 13, *16, 17,* 18, 23, 24, *25,* 26, 27, 28, 29, 32, 35, 38, 39, *50,* 51, 80
VB-7, 131, 132, 133, 134, 135
VB-18, 390
VB-41, 303, *310,* 316, 317, 318, 324, 328, 332, 333
VB-42, 301, 308, *310,* 317, 319, 320, *326,* 328, 329, 330, 332, 333, 334, 362
VB-84, 374, *376*
VB-98, 378, 383, 386
VB-117, 366
Bonita (SS-165), 30, 32
Bonneau, Ens. William J., A-V(N) (VF-9), 199, *206,* 209, 219, 230, 244, 260, 264, 271, 272, 273, 282
Boone, Capt. Walter F., *350*
Booth, Lt. Comdr. Charles T., II "Tommy" (VF-41), 208, *210,* 211, 212, 213, 214, 215, 216, 224, 228, 230, 231, 235, 237, 241, 242, 243, 251, 252, 256, 258, 260, 262, 269, 270, 271, 281, 282
Boudier, Lt., 213, 214, 249, 258
Boulonnaise (French destroyer) 222, 224, 230
"Bouncing Girl." *See* Great Lakes XBG-1
Bowman, Aviation Radioman 2d Class C. B. (VT-4), 330
Boxer Rebellion, 3
Boyd, Ens. Alfred I., A-V(N) (VF-4), 134, 135
Boykin, Lt. Lykes M., A-V(N) (VB-42), 301, 328, 334
Bradley, Aviation Chief Ordnanceman C. T. (VB-4), 141
Bradley, Chief Water Tender R. T., *306*
Bragg, Capt. Kenneth B., 299
Brand, Lt. John W. C. "Jack", 37, *50,* 58, 78, 83
Brandenburger, Lt. Harry A., 35
Brassfield, Aviation Cadet Arthur J., USNR (VS-42), 128
Braun, Lt. (jg) Gordon M., A-V(N) (VF-9), 226, 231, 238
Brazil, xiii, 8, 15, 16, 19, 21
Breckenridge (DD-148), 390
Breckheimer, Lt. (jg) Charles R., A-V(N) (VB-4), 328, *335*
Bremerton, *107*
Brestois (French destroyer), 222, 230
Brewer, Maj. C. B., USMC, 383
Brewster F3A, 374
Brewster XSBA-1, 111
Bridge (AF-1), 41
Briggs, Ens. Chester A., *74*
Brilhart, Aviation Radioman 3d Class J. C., 328
Briner, Lt. (jg) Richard R. (VB-1B), 69
Brinson, Storekeeper 1st Class C. R., 181
Bristol, Lt. Comdr. Horace, USNR, *329*
Bristol, Rear Adm. Arthur LeRoy "Roy," 8, 9, *9, 12,* 15, 19, 20, 21, *21,* 23, 34, 35, *38,* 43, 45, 46, 47, 48, 49, 56, 57, 146, 156
Brock, Ens. Sanford W., USNR (VF-12), 376
Brockway, Lt. John H., *154*
Brook, Paul (International News Service), 87
Brooklyn (CL-40), 228, 230, 233, 261, 270, 280, 287, 290, 291
Brooks, Ens. Ernest D., A-V(N) (VF-9), *206,* 226, 231, 238, 272, 281, 284
Brooks (DD-232), 79
Broome (DD-210), *137*
Brown, Aviation Radioman 3d Class J. C. (VS-42), 184
Brown, Lt. (jg) Warren A., A-V(N) (VF-4), *353,* 356, 357
Brown, Pvt. Frank S., USMC, 10

Browning, Lt. Comdr. Miles R., (VF-3B), 43, 60
Bruhns, Chief Yeoman F., 23
Buchanan, Pvt. R. M., USMC, 23, 24
Buchanan (DD-131), 29
Buckmaster, Capt. Elliott, 151
Budde, Lt. George H., 374
Buie, Lt. (jg) Paul D. (VF-3B), *59*
Bull, Lt. (jg) Richard S., Jr. (VS-41), 130, 146
The Bull Horn (ship's paper), 74, 132
Buracker, Capt. William H., 392
Bureau of Aeronautics (BuAer), 3, 15, 16, 25, 49, 96, 111, 140, 186, 354, 380, 382
Bureau of Construction and Repair, 3, 5, 139
Bureau of Engineering, 139
Bureau of Ships (BuShips), 142, 147, 148, 155, 156, 160, 165, 177, 181, 349, 350, 354, 358, 359, 360, 390
Burge, Constable L., 178
Burgess, Lt. (jg) John G. (VB-5B), 11, 12, *16*
Burnham, Lt. Fletcher H., *394*
Burns, Aviation Radioman 2d Class A. A., 360
Busic, Photographer's Mate 1st Class T. W., *21*
Butler, Aviation Radioman 3d Class James R., USNR (VB-42), 308
Butler, Second Lt. William H., USA, 262
Butler, Vice Adm. Henry V., 28, *28,* 31, 32, 35, 36, 56

C
Cadiz, 287
Cady, Ens. James M., USNR (VBF-80), 389
Caldwell (DD-605), 370
California (BB-44), 41, 118
Callen, Lt. (jg) Richard W. (VF-4), *353*
Campbell, Aviation Radioman 2d Class W. R. H., USNR (VB-4), 356
Campbell, Boatswain's Mate 2d Class John A., 381, *381*
Campbell, Ens. Archer B., USNR (VF-12), 374
Campbell, Lt. (jg) Clifford M. (VS-42), 94
Campbell, Lt. Norwood A. "Soupy", 154
Camp Craven, 58
Canal Zone, 28, 117
Cannon, Chief Yeoman J. H., 87
Capehart, Comdr. Wadleigh, 82
Cape Henry, 132
Cape Verde Islands, 202, 364
CAP flights, 207, 209, 226, 230, 231, 234, 235, 251, 256, 258, 262, 264, 265, 266, 268, 269, 270, 271, 275, 280, 281, 282, 283, 284, 286, 287, 289, 297, 328, 329, 342, 343, 344, 345, 347
Capps (DD-550), 354
Capshaw, Radioman 2d Class Ammon E., 170, 180
Caradoc, HMS (British light cruiser), 131
Carbovi (Spanish fishing vessel), 287
Card (CVE-11), 362, 363
CarDiv 11, 384
CarDiv 12, 379, 384
Caribbean Sea, 125, 130
Carll, Comdr. Francis W., *154*
Carls, Aviation Chief Machinists's Mate W. A. (VF-3B), 65
Carmody, Aviation Cadet Edmund O., USNR (VF-3B), 74, 75
Carpenter, Lt. Comdr. Gilbert C. (VS-41), 187
Carr, Ens. Kenneth J., USNR, 386
Carrier Aircraft Service Unit (CASU), 362
Carrier Air Groups:
  CAG-4, *329*
  CAG-18, 388
  CVG-1, 382, 383
  CVG-3, 366, 368, 370

Carrier Air Groups (*continued*)
  CVG-4, xiii, 25, 308, 309, 316, 317, 323, 326, 340, 345, 349, *353*, 356, 357, 370
  CVG-5, 380
  CVG-6, 372, 373
  CVG-11, 368
  CVG-12, 374, 375, 378
  CVG-14, 386
  CVG-17, 372
  CVG-18, 388, 390, 391
  CVG-44, 366
  CVG-80, 357
  CVG-81, 370
  CVG-84, 366, 374, *376, 377*
  CVG-98, 378, 386, 388
  CVG-100, 366, 370
  CVG(N)-42, 370
  CVG(N)-90, 368, 370
Carrington, Ens. Royal C., A-V(N) (VS-42), 179, 180
Carroll, Lt. (jg) Charles R., 42
Carter, Lt. George H. "Spanky" (VF-41), *210,* 212, 213, 215, 216, *216,* 228, 243, 247, 249, 254, *255, 261,* 267, 274, 275, 280, 283, 313, 330, 335, 336, 340, 344
Carver, Lt. Comdr. Lamar P. "Pete" (VS-41), 187, 209, 219, 220, 226, 228, 230, 232, *233*
Casablanca, 200, 207, 209, 210, 214, 219, 220, *220,* 221, 222, 224, 226, *227,* 228, 230, 232, 234, 236, 237, 239, 240, 241, 243, 244, 245, 246, 248, 251, 254, 255, 258, 259, 263, 269, 270, 271, 272, 273, 275, 276, 277, *279,* 280, 281, 282, 283, 286, 291, *363, 364*
Casco Bay, 301
Casey, Aviation Cadet Vincent, USNR (VF-4), 98
Casey, Radioman 2d Class H. L., 50, 69
Cassidy, Lt. Arthur J., A-V(N) (VF-41), *211,* 214, 227, 234, 235, 251, 256, 269, 283, 302, *302*
Catapults, 4, 364
Cazes, 213, 216, 218, 231, 235, 258, 275
Central Aircraft Manufacturing Compay (CAMCO), 149
CG-83492, 391
CGR-1996, 293
Chandler (DD-209), 87
Channing, Musician 2d Class C. H., 46
Chapman, Ens. Donald E., A-V(N) (VS-41), 226, 244, 260, 262, 278, 280, 284, 291
Chapman, Lt. Albert E. (VB-3), 118
Charger (AVG-30), 190, 196, *198,* 387
Charles, Ens. Nelson R., A-V(N), 292
Charleton, Radioman 3d Class J. R., 29
Charlotte Amalie, Virgin Islands, 146
Chase, Lt. Gordon P., A-V(N) (VB-4), 202, 203, *205,* 213, 224, 245, 328, 330, 373
Chaumont (AP-5), *137*
Chavez, Jorge (Peruvian aviator), 99, 104
Chenango (ACV-30), 283, 285
Chesapeake Bay, 192, 194, 292, *364*
Chester (CA-27), 33
Chicago (CA-29), 33
"Chicago Pianos," (1.1"/.75 Antiaircraft guns), 160
Chicopee (AO-34), 294
Childers, Lt. Kenan C. "Casey" (VF-9), *206,* 209, 226, 231, 238, 251, 252, 268, 269, 271, 277, 278, 283, 284
Childs (AVD-1), 375, 378, 384, 385, 386, 390
China, 3, 149
Christensen, Aviation Chief Ordnanceman A. L., 39
Christie, Lt. Comdr. Ralph W., 45
Christman, Ens. Albert B., A-V(N) (VB-4), 140, 141

Chugach Islands, 45
Churchill, British Prime Minister Winston, 183, 184, 188, 243, *321, 322,* 325
Cincinnati (CL-6), 173
Clark, Lt. (jg) Baylies V. (VB-1B), *50*
Clark, Lt. Thurston B., 89, *90,* 91
Clark, Rear Adm. Joseph J. "Jocko," 151, 202, 392, 393, 395
Clark (DD-361), 116
Claytor, Lt. Richard, A-V(S) (VF-4), *319, 353*
Clemons, Raymond G., 390
Cleveland (CL-55), 197, 201, 270, 291
Clifford, Capt. Nathaniel S., USMC (VMSB-131), 156
Clifton, Lt. Joseph C. "Joe" (VF-4), 138
Coar, Aviation Cadet Richard C. (VF-4), 115
Cobb, Lt. (jg) James O. (VB-3), 97
Cochrane, Rear Adm. Edward L., 358
Codman, Charles (*Saturday Evening Post*), 163
Coffin, Lt. Phillip R. (VF-3B), 69, 70
Coffman, R. A. (Federal Laboratories), 44
Coghlan (DD-606), 368
Cold Weather Test Detachment, 44, *46,* 47, 48, *49*
Cole, Seaman 2d Class C. F., 23
Collingsworth, (U.S. freighter), 19
Collins, Aviation Machinist's Mate 3d Class R. B. (VB-4), 98, 99
Collins, Ens. Harvey R., Jr., USNR, 386
Colon, Aviation Radioman 2d Class L. E. "Cy" (VS-41), 209, 226, 237, 257, 265, 272, 281, 288, 290, 318, 324, 328, 333
Colon 27, 117
Colorado (BB-45), 41
ComCarDiv 11, 366
ComCarDiv 12, 380
Commandant Delage, (French second class sloop), 271
Commander *Ranger* Air Group (CRAG), 110, 121, 123, 132, *136,* 150, 158, 159, 197, 232, 234, 244, 245, *246,* 282, 285, 286, 288, *288,* 289, 330, 336, 339
Commencement Bay (CVE-105), 380
Commick, Boatswain's Mate 1st Class R. M., *152*
Composite Squadrons:
  VC-5, 386
  VC-7, 380
  VC-33, 383
  VC-41, 383
  VC-63, 380, 383
  VC-68, 388
  VC-82, 370
  VC-83, 370
Conatser, Ens. Charlie N., A-V(N), 153, 154, 155
Congdon, Radioman 3d Class C. R., 109
Conner, Ens. Andrew B., A-V(N) (VF-9, VF-41), *210,* 212, 229, *229,* 238
Consolidated PB4Y Privateer, 366
Consolidated PBY Catalina, 82
Consolidated N2Y-1, 85
Contessa (U.S. freighter), *236*
Convoys:
  HX-156, 166
  PQ, 188, 189
  SC-48, 165
  WS-12X, 170
Conyngham (DD-371), *109,* 110
Cook, Adm. Arthur B., 111, 115, 126, 142, 147, 149, 150, 151, 156, 158, 161, 164, *164,* 165, 170, 171, 172, 173, 182
Cooke, Rear Adm. Charles M., Jr. "Savvy," 189, 190
Cook Inlet, 45
Corre, *Lt.* Pierre, 270

Corry (DD-463), 190, 191, 196, 270, 297, 319, 320, 322, 324, 325, 347, 349, 350, 351, 354
Corson, Chief Radioman M. D. (VF-4), 134
Costet, Capitaine de *Frégate* François, 224
Costley, Lt. Darwin S., USNR, 379
Craft, Seaman 2d Class Clayton, USNR, *367*
Craig, Lt. Earle F. "Buster" (VF-4, VF-41), *211*, 214, 223, 224, 230, 237, 256, 257, 262, 269, 270, 275, 281, 301, 324, 329, 343, 344, 347, *353*
Craven, Rear Adm. Thomas T., 58
Crawford, Lt. (jg) Nathan P. (VB-5), 380
Crews, Aviation Cadet Howard W., USNR (VS-42), 116
Crist, Lt. Comdr. Marion F. (VT-3), 97
Crochet, Signalman 3d Class Ernest L., 160, 199, 282, 354
Crommelin, Capt. John G. (VB-3), 118, 161, 396
Cronin, Lt. (jg) Robert C., A-V(N) (VF-4, VF-41), *210*, 230, 262, 275, 330, 340, 347
Crowder, Radioman 2d Class M. T., 106
Crowninshield (DD-134), 29, 65
Cuba, *26*, 28, 117, 119, *120*, 125, 132, 142, 143, *143*, 145, 190
Culebra, 119, 144, 145
Cullum, Cpl. Robert D. USMC, 8
Curry, Cpl. Gulledge E. "Squads Right," USMC, 8
Curtis, Radioman 2d Class L. A. (VB-4), 141
Curtiss H.75/75A Hawk, 211, 214, *214*, 216, 217, 218, *218*, 221, 245, 252, 253, 254
Curtiss BFC-2 Goshawk:
    BuNo 9274, 97
    BuNo 9332, 97
    BuNo 9333, 97
    BuNo 9338, 97
Curtiss P-36 Hawk, 211, 217
Curtiss P-38 Lightning, 363
Curtiss P-40E Warhawk, 181, 183, 184, 185, 275, 283, 294, *295*, 363
Curtiss P-40F Warhawk, 190, 191, *191*
Curtiss P-40L Warhawk, 297
Curtiss SB2C-3 Helldiver:
    BuNo 18707, 378
    BuNo 19639, 378
    general, *376*
Curtiss SB2C-3C Helldiver, 366
Curtiss SB2C-4 Helldiver:
    BuNo 18805, 382
    BuNo 19836, 384
    BuNo 19838, 386
    BuNo 19862, 386
    BuNo 19914, 382
    BuNo 20268, 380
    BuNo 20415, 383
    BuNo 20468, 383
    BuNo 20476, 386
    BuNo 20504, 381
    BuNo 20678, 382
    general, 384, 394
Curtiss SB2C-4E Helldiver:
    BuNo 19827, 386
    BuNo 20097, 386
    BuNo 65110, 386
Curtiss SB2C Helldiver, 345, 366, 379
Curtiss SBC-3 Helldiver:
    BuNo 0508, 140
    BuNo 0571, 115
    general, 111, 123, 141, 150, 151
Curtiss SBC-4 Helldiver:
    BuNo 1313, 156
    BuNo 1816, 156, 157

Curtiss SOC-1 Seagull, 121, 150, *162*, 209, 236, 290
Curtiss XBF2C-1:
    BuNo 9512, 27
    BuNo 9588, 27
    BuNo 9595, 26
    general, 13, 23, *25*, 32, 39, 44, 46
Cushing (DD-376), 87, 88, 89, 90
CV-4, The (Ship's paper)

D

Dahm, Lt. Odd (Norwegian), 328
Dale, Lt. (jg) Roland H., 80
Dalton, Aviation Machinist's Mate 1st Class B. M. (VT-4), 330
Dalton, Ens. George F., A-V(N) (VS-41), 226, 237, 238, 257, 284, 288
Damaskos, Lt. George (A1), USNR, 382
Danilin, Sergei (Russian navigator), 94
D.A.R. Trophy, 62, 96
Dargue, Maj. Gen. Herbert A., *159*
Darien, 54
Davis, Comdr. Ray "Jeff," 397, *397*
Davis, Lt. Comdr. Arthur C., 9, *14*
Davis, Lt. (jg) Sumner R., A-V(N) (VB-4), 328, 334, 335
Davisson, Lt. Comdr. Frederick A., 79
Dawidowski, Private Anthony, USMC, 178
Day, Rear Adm. George C., 24
DeChard, A. W. (Scintilla Magneto Company), 44
DeHaven (DD-727), 364, *365*, 366
de la Fuente, Nicholas, 19, 21
Delannoy, *Adjudant-Chef,* 211
Delareuelle, Ens. Robert R., A-V(N) (VB-3), 127
Deloache, Aviation Machinist's Mate 1st Class E. W. (VB-3), 127
de Montgolfier, *Adjudant,* 213
Denebrink, Capt. Francis C., 270, 280, 282, 287
Denoff, Lt. Reuben H. "Rube," A-V(N) (VF-9, VF-12), 198, *206*, 214, 230, 235, 256, 260, 268, 271, 281, 374
Deputy, Lt. (jg) Marshal P., Jr., A-V(N) (VF-4), 356
De Vall, Capt. Brenton A., USA, 262, *265*
DeVane, Lt. John M., Jr. "Count" (VS-41), 141, 209, 220, 221, 226, 232, 233, 244, 245, 256, 258, 259, 262, 263, 264, 268, 269, 272, 274, 286, 287, 288, 289
Devine, Aviation Radioman 3d Class L. J. (VB-4, VS-41), 209, 220
Dewey, Commodore George, 28
Dewey (DD-349), 28
Dewoitine, D.520, 211, *213*, 215, 220, 221, 228, 230, 263
Diamond Head, 32, 35, *36*, 76, 111
Dietrich, Aviation Machinist's Mate 2d Class B. J. (VS-41), 181
Dill, Lt. (jg) William E., A-V(N) (VB-4, VF-4), 328, 356
Dimmick, Lt. John B. (VF-3B), 62, 68
"Diving Panther" insignia, *110*
Dodson, Lt. (jg) Lucian F. (VS-1B), 53
Doerflinger, Lt. Carl R., 213
Dollfuss, Engelbert (Austrian Chancellor), 16
Dolphin (SS-169), 30
Dönitz, Vice Adm. Karl, 248
Dorion, Lt. Robinson H. (MC), *307*
Dostal, Ens. Howard F., A-V(N) (VF-4), 132, 138, 172
Dougherty, Tom (VF-41), 214, 241, 244, 246, 255, 266, 283
Douglas DB-7, xiii, 211, 215, 216, 217, 245, 252, 258, 261
Douglas SBD:
    Dauntless SBD, xiii, 197, *198*, 209, *218*, 221, 234, 237, 244, 251, 255, 258, 262, 263, 268, 269, 272, 273, *273*, 278, 279, 281, 282, 283, 284, 286, 287, 290, 301, 304, *304*, 308, 320, 329, 342, 343, 346, 362
    Dauntless SBD-3:
        BuNo 06619, 202, 203
        BuNo 06620, *242*

Dauntless SBD-3 (*continued*)
  BuNo 06628, 269
  BuNo 06634, 316, *316*
  BuNo 06641, *241*
  BuNo 06666, 301
  general, 226, 232, *264, 310*
Dauntless SBD-4:
  BuNo 06808, 310, 317
  BuNo 06812, 309
  BuNo 06826, 301
  BuNo 06827, 303
  BuNo 06866, 319
  BuNo 06897, 303
  BuNo 06920, 308
  BuNo 10516, 303
  BuNo 10778, 318
  BuNo 10785, 321
  general, 311
Dauntless SBD-5:
  BuNo 11011, 333, *333*
  BuNo 28605, 351
  BuNo 28609, 322
  BuNo 28636, 335
  BuNo 28660, 356
  BuNo 28709, 324, 325
  BuNo 28765, 349, 351
  BuNo 28811, 356
  BuNo 28949, 356
  BuNo 29041, 356
  BuNo 29090, 356
  BuNo 36154, 357
  BuNo 36907, 360
  BuNo 54127, 357
  general, 324, 328, 334, *334,* 345, 357
Douglas TBD-1, 111, 123, 150, 178, *180,* 183, *186*
Dowell, Capt. Jonathan S., Jr. "Dad," 87, 90, 93
Downing, Seaman 1st Class Clinton R., 119
Drayton (DD-366), 87, 89
Dresser, O. C. (NRL engineer), 165, 168
Duffin, Ens. Raymond P., USNR (VB-98), 383
Duffy, Ens. Charles J., A-V(N) (VS-41), 226, 228, 237, 238, 239, 240, *242*
Dugas, *Capitaine,* 253
Duke, Radioman 2d Class C. F. (VF-41), 239
Duke of York, HMS (British battleship), 327
Dunklee, Lt. (jg) Donald L., USNR, 384
Dunn, Aviation Machinist's Mate 2d Class J. S., 349
Dunn, Ens. Harry L., A-V(N) (VB-4), 324, 325
Dunn, Lt. Joseph B. (VS-1B), 83
Dunn, Machinist J. M., *306*
Durgin, Rear Adm. Calvin T. "Cal," 187, 199, 200, 201, *201,* 208, 270, 280, 282, 293, 294, 296, 299, 309, 315, 346, 392
Dussault, Capt. George A. "Goat," 395, *395,* 397
Dyer, Aviation Cadet Calvin Y., USNR (VS-1B), 71, 106

E

Eagle, HMS (British aircraft carrier), 188
Eardley, Aviation Radioman 1st Class Joseph M. (VB-4, VS-41), 209, 221, 226, 232, 237, 244, 250, 260, *263,* 268, 272, 277, 281, 285, 288, 328
Earhart, Amelia, xiv, 86, *88, 91, 92,* 93, *93,* 392
Eason, Lt. Richard B., USNR (VBF-1), 382
Eaton, Lt. (jg) Maxwell A., A-V(N) (VS-41), 209, 232, 233, 244, 245, 255, 258, 278, 279, 287, 288, 303, 304, 305, *305*
Eberle (DD-430), 149, 150, 151, 153
Edens, Aviation Radioman 3d Class Lloyd E. (VB-4, VS-41), 209, 232, 237, 239, 256, 265, 272, *274,* 288, 328

Edge, Lt. Clarence F., USCG, 44
Edison (DD-439), 271
Edward Rutledge (AP-52), 291
Edwards, Lt. (jg) Howard F. "Eddie" (VF-4), 300, *313, 353,* 354, 357
Edwards, Rear Adm. Richard S., 190
Edwards (DD-619), 370
El Hank, 243, 244, 245, *247,* 255, 259, 263, 269, 270, 271, 277, 279, 280, 283
Elkins, Aviation Machinist's Mate 2d Class F. J., 68
Elliott, Lt. (jg) James M. (VB-4), 104, 106
Elliott, Seaman 2d Class Eugene, 156
Ellis, Aviation Radioman 2d Class G. C. (VB-4, VF-4), 328, 351, 356
Ellis, R. E. (Standard Oil Company of New Jersey), 44
Ellis, Rear Adm. Hayne, 131, 141
Ellyson (DD-454), 183, 186, 190, 229, *229,* 238, 252, 270, 287, 289, 290, 295, 306, 357, *359,* 360
Elmore, Ens. Charles R., A-V(N), 127, 128
Embree, Lt. (jg) Ralph A. "Mac" (VS-41), 140, 209, 220, 221, 226, 228, 232, 233, 237, 238, 239, 240, 244, 245, 249, 250, 256, 260, 261, 262, *263, 264,* 268, 269, 270, 272, 273, 274, 277, 278, 279, 280, 281, 282, 283, 285, 287, 288, 289, 291
Emmons, Lt. Gen. Delos C., 159
Emmons (DD-457), 183, 190, 306
Emmy Friedrich (German tanker), 131
Enfield, Maj. William H., USMC, 392
Enterprise (CV-6), 85, 117, *119,* 121, 122, 125, 141, 181, 190
Eoff, Ens. James H., A-V(N) (VB-4), 128, *128,* 129
Erickson, Aviation Cadet Robert I., USNR (VB-4), 98
Erickson, Chief Electrician's Mate D. A., *306*
Erickson, Lt. John L., 310, 311
Escort Carrier Groups:
  CVEG-24, 379
  CVEG-40, 381
  CVEG-41, 390
  CVEG-49, 383
  CVEG-98, 384
Escort Fighting Squadrons:
  VGF-27, 235, 238, 240, 258, 264, 266, 269, 270, 271, 272, *273,* 276, 283
  VGF-28, 240, 264, 265, 269, 272, 275, 281, 283, 284
  VGF-30, 231
Escort Scouting Squadrons:
  VGS-27, 282
  VGS-28, 292
  VGS-29, 330
  VGS-30, 258, 264, 265, 272, 275, 281, 282, 284
Essex (CV-9), xiv, 142, 358, 359
Estafette (French surveying vessel), 235, 272
Etheridge, Aviation Radioman 2d Class Robert C., 213, 257
Eugene A. Greene (DD-711), 392
Evans, Lt. (jg) Joseph L. "Joe" (VS-72), 132
Evans, Lt. (jg) Myron T. "Empty" (VF-3B, VS-72), 41, 58, *59*
Evans, Radioman 2d Class C. L., 53, 106

F

Fabre, *Lt.,* 213
Fagervika, xiii
Fahrney, Lt. Comdr. Delmar S., 111, 114, 115
Fairfax (DD-93), 131
Fairlamb, Lt. Comdr. George R., 35
Fanning (DD-385), 370
Fanshaw Bay (CVE-70), 380, *389*
Farman aircraft, 214, 219
Farrell, Capt. Edwin J., USMC, *74*

Feasley, Lt. (jg) Harrison, A-V(N) (VF-9), *206*, 214, 230, 235, 244, 251, 260, 271, 281, 284
Feathergill, Lt. (jg) John P., A-V(N) (VB-42), 308
Fedala, 224, 228, 231, 233, 234, 235, 244, 249, *250*, 251, 252, 253, 254, 256, 258, 259, 262, *266*, 269, 270, 271, 272, 275, 276, 282, 283, 285, 291
Fenton, Aviation Radioman 3d Class R. L. (VS-41), 226, 237, 244, 257, 281, 288
Fenton, Lt. (jg) Charles R. (VF-3B), *59*
Ferguson, Chief Water Tender Harry A., 397
Ferguson, Homer L. (Newport News shipyard president), 3, *4*, 9
Feugnet, Pierre, 224, 226
Fields, Cpl. Lewis J., USMC, 8, 19, 23
Fighting Squadrons:
  VF-1, 126, 383
  VF-1B, 63, 82
  VF-2, 386
  VF-2B, 84
  VF-3, 82, 111, 122, 366, 367
  VF-3B, 38, 41, 42, 43, 50, *50*, 51, 52, 53, 55, *56*, 58, 59, *59*, 60, *60*, 61, 62, 64, 65, 66, 68, 69, 70, 71, 74, 75, 80, 81, 158, 164, 165, 177, 178
  VF-4, 29, 98, 103, *103*, *110*, 111, 115, 117, 119, 121, 122, 123, 125, 128, 131, 132, 134, 135, 137, 138, 140, 142, 143, 144, *144*, 145, 146, *150*, 151, 172, *211*, 214, 223, 224, 227, 228, 234, 243, 252, 269, 270, 296, 300, 302, 311, *313*, *314*, 318, *319*, 323, 327, 328, 329, 330, *331*, 332, 339, 343, 344, 347, *348*, 350, 351, 352, *353*, 354, 356, 357, 366
  VF-5, 151, *154*, *163*, 381, 382
  VF-5B, 38, 41, *50*, 51, *59*, 64, 65, 66, 68, 69, 71, 80, 81, 104, *110*
  VF-6B, 51, 80, 81
  VF-7, 131, 132, 133, 134, 135, 165, 360
  VF-9, 193, 194, *195*, 196, *196*, 197, *197*, 198, 199, *205*, *206*, 208, 209, *210*, *211*, 212, 214, 219, 221, 222, 224, 226, 227, 228, 229, *229*, 230, 231, 235, 236, 237, 238, 241, 242, 243, 244, 245, 251, 252, 253, 254, *255*, 256, 257, *257*, 259, 260, 261, *261*, 262, 263, 264, 265, 268, 269, 270, 271, 272, 273, *273*, 274, 275, 277, 278, 280, 281, 282, 283, 284, 286, 291, 311, 328, *335*, 374, 392
  VF-12, 198, *206*, 209, 214, 219, 226, 229, 230, 231, 235, 237, 244, 251, 253, 256, 257, *257*, 260, 264, 268, 271, 272, 273, 277, 281, 282, 284, 286, 373, 374, 376, 377, 378
  VF-18, 388, 390
  VF-27, 209
  VF-32, 384
  VF-41, 42, *59*, 135, 137, 139, 141, 142, 145, 146, *146*, 147, 148, 150, 151, 152, 157, 158, 159, 161, 165, *168*, *169*, 177, 178, 183, 187, *194*, 196, 197, 198, 199, 201, *205*, *206*, 208, *210*, 211, *211*, 212, 213, 214, 215, 216, *216*, 217, 218, *218*, 219, 222, 223, 224, 225, 226, 227, 228, 229, *229*, 230, 231, 234, 235, 236, 237, 238, *238*, 239, 240, 241, 242, 243, 244, 245, 246, 247, 249, 251, 252, 254, 255, *255*, 256, 257, 258, 259, 260, *261*, 262, 264, 265, 266, 267, 268, 269, 270, 271, 274, 275, 276, 279, *279*, 280, 281, 282, 283, 287, 289, 290, 291, 298, 299, 301, 302, *302*, 308, 309, 311, 313, *313*, 320, 321, 323, 324, 325, 328, 329, 330, 332, 333, 335, 336, *337*, 339, 340, *340*, *341*, 342, *342*, 343, 344, *345*, 347, *348*, *353*, 374, 392
  VF-42, 148, 158, 177
  VF-49, 214, 234, 384
  VF-72, 41, 58, *59*, 147, 150, 158, 178, 179, 181
  VF-78, 360
  VF-84, 374, *375*
  VF-100, 63, 370
Fighting Squadrons (Night):
  VF(N)-77, 357
  VF(N)-78, 357, 360

VF(N)-79, 357, 360, 362
VF(N)-102, 366
Firth of Forth, 349, 350, *350*
Fischer, *Hauptmann* Christian, 344
Fischer, *Uffizier* Alfons, 343
Fitch (DD-462), 191, 196, 290, 297, 306, 326, 347, 349, 351, 354
Fitzpatrick, Lt. James F. X., Jr. "Fitz" (VGF-27), 258, 266, 270, 283
Flanigan, Aviation Radioman 3d Class Earl F., 322
Flatley, Lt. (jg) James H. "Jimmy" (VF-3B), 59, *59*, 60, 62
Fleet Landing Exercise (FLEX) No. 2, 143
Fleet Landing Exercise (FLEX) No. 7, 145
Fleet Problems, xiii, 37, 82
Fleet Problem XVI, 29, 30, 32, *33*, 35
Fleet Problem XVII, 52, 53, 55, *56*, 57
Fleet Problem XVIII, 75, *75*, 79, 84
Fleet Problem XIX, *89*, 106, *108*, 110, *114*
Fleet Problem XX, 119, 125
Flowers, Pharmacist's Mate 1st Class K. N., 23
Flying Fleet, The (movie), 68
Flubeau, *Lieutenant*, 253
Foley, Lt. (jg) Francis D. (VS-42), 89, 93, *108*
Forbes, Lt. (jg) Lorenz Q. "Lorry" (VB-3B), 26, 44, *50*, *51*
Ford Island, *369*
Forrest, 1st Lt. Nathan Bedford, USA, *101*
Forrest (DD-461), 190, 191, 196, 304, 305, 319, 320, 322, 324, 325, 350, 351, 354
Fortune, Lt. (jg) William C. (VS-42), 99, 107
Foster, Lt. Comdr. Edwin D., (SC), 6, 392
Fougueux (French destroyer), 222, 224, 230
Fourniol, *Capitaine*, 261
Fowler, Private 1st Class Wallace V., USMC, 10
Fox (DD-234), 79, 132
Franger, Ens. Marvin J., A-V(N) (VF-9), *206*, 208, 226, 228, 231, 251, 260, 261, 272, 275, 281, 286
Franklin (CV-13), 397
Fraser, Adm. Sir Bruce, RN, 324, 327, 344, 345
Frazer, Ens. F. D., USNR, 386
Frederick, Capt. Theodore R. "Ted," *26*, 45, *50*, 368
Fredette, Ens. William A. J., USNR (VC-68), 388
Freshour, Lt. (jg) William M. "Mac" (VB-5B), 26, *50*
Friesberg, Lt. John L., 388
Frondeur (French destroyer), 222, 224, 230, 232
Fuchs, 1st Lt. Joseph P., USMC, 106
Fuller, Ens. Robert S., A-V(N) (CVG-4), 309
Fulnecky, Lt. (jg) John R. "Jack," 360
Furious, HMS (British aircraft carrier), 147, 322
Furney, Lt. Maynard M. "Bud," A-V(N) (VF-41), 135, 142, *210*, 212, 215, 230, 237, 241, 251, 256, 264, 275, 276, 281

G
Gaden, Lt. Comdr. Allan G., 271
Gagg, Rudolph (Wright Aeronautical Corporation), 44
Gaillard, Lt. (jg) William E. (VS-42), 122
Gamboa, 54
Gannet (AVP-8), 130, 132
Gansevoort (DD-608), 368
Gardemal, Lt. (jg) Louis G., *319*
Gardner, Lt. Comdr. Edward R., Jr. (VB-3), 118
Gardner, Rear Adm. Matthias B., 366, 368
Garner, Aviation Radioman 2d Class Shelton E. (VT-4), 301, 330, 339
Garrett, Ens. Jack, USNR, 372
Garrigan, Ens. Frank A. (VF-4), *353*
Garrison, Lt. (jg) Charles F. (VB-2), 96
Gates, Ens. Billy V., A-V(N), 134

Gavin, Capt. Arthur, 362, 363, 367, 368, *372,* 376, 380
Gawlik, Radioman 3d Class E. (VS-42), 158
Gazze, Lt. Sylvius (VF-3B), 51, 52, 55, *56, 59*
Gearing (DD-710), 392
Gendreau (DE-639), 366
George, Radioman 3d Class Joseph T., 128, 129
Gerhardt, Aviation Cadet Emerson D., USNR (VS-1B), 71
Gerhardt, Ens. Charles W., A-V(N) (VF-9), *206,* 209, 231, 251, 253, *255*
Germany, 125, 141, 148
Gervais de Lafond, *Contre-Amiral* Raymond, 222, *223,* 224, *225,* 226
Geyer, *Feldwebel* Heinz, 344
Ghormley, Rear Adm. Robert L., 131
Giavannoli, 1st Lt. R. E., USA, 44
Gibraltar, 286
Gibson, U.S. Ambassador Hugh S., 21, 23
Gibson, Aviation Cadet George D., USNR (VF-4), 98
Gibson, Lt. (jg) Charles E. (VS-42), 158
Giddings, Seaman A., RN, 178
Gilbert, Ens. George R. (VF-4), *353*
Gilbert Islands, 394
Gill, Capt. Charles C., 21
Gill, Lt. Cecil B., 42, 45
Gillon, Lt. Comdr. John F. "Jack" (VS-2B), 80, 81
Gilmer (DD-233), 131, *137*
Glass, Ens. David M., A-V(N), 172, 173
Glover, Lt. Comdr. Cato D., CO (VF-3B), *59,* 60
Gmyr, Radioman 3d Class W. A., 107
Gneisenau (German battle cruiser), 146, 148
Gold Coast, 184, 190
Goleta Field, Santa Barbara, 375
"Good Neighbor" policy, xiii, 16
Gordon, Lt. (jg) Prince H., A-V(N) (VB-4), 300, 328
Gordon, Seaman 2d Class Douglas, 151, *152*
Gouin, Lt. Marcel E. A., 21
Gowen, Aviation Cadet A. S., USNR (VS-1B), 71
Grace, Radioman 1st Class H. F. (VS-42), 38, 121
Graham, Ens. Thomas J., A-V(N) (VF-4), 343, *353*
Gran Chaco War, 21
Grant, Comdr. Vernon F. (VS-1B), 58
Grant, Ens. Robert F. (VF-4), *353*
Gras *Adjudant-chef,* 249
Grassy Bay, 178
Gray, Aviation Radioman 1st Class Reuben, USNR (VT-4), 330, 338, 342, 362
Great Lakes TG-2:
    BuNo 8713, 98
    BuNo 8715, 97
    BuNo 8725, 97
    BuNo A-8702, 41
Great Lakes XBG-1:
    BuNo 9220, 25
    BuNo 9501, 132
    BuNo 9502, 104, 105
    BuNo 9504, 45, 85
    BuNo 9505, 44, *51*
    BuNo 9506, 25, 133
    BuNo 9507, 98
    BuNo 9508, 31, *32,* 91
    BuNo 9510, 97
    BuNo 9511, 98
    BuNo 9514, 144
    BuNo 9534, 40, *41*
    BuNo 9536, 40
    BuNo 9538, 97
    BuNo 9543, 133
    BuNo 9548, 39
    general, 29, 35, 39, 44, 87, 91, *103,* 106, *108, 110,* 111, 117, 132, 134, 141
Greber, Lt. Comdr. Charles F. "Dutch" (VS-3), 24, 115
Green, Maj. Thomas C., USMC (VMO-1), 144
Greene, Lt. (jg) George M. "Joe" (VF-3B), 65
Greenland, 349
Greenlee, Lt. (jg) Archibald W. "Bill" (VS-1B), 75
Greenman, Comdr. William G., 6, 45
Greer (DD-145), *137,* 160, 360, 362, 364
Grell, Lt. Theodore A. "Tag" (VF-41), 152, 196, 212, 230, 235, 301
Grewingk Glacier, 46, *47*
Gridley, Capt. George V., 28
Grimes, Ens. Gerald, 321, 322, 349, 351
Gromov, Mikhail (Russian pilot), 94
Gross, Seaman 1st Class Edward J., 381, *381*
Groves, 2d Lt. Edward C., USMCR (VMF-512), 383
Grumman F2F-1:
    BuNo 9643, 69
    BuNo 9645, 62, 75
    BuNo 9648, 62
    BuNo 9649, 53
    BuNo 9650, 42, 58
    BuNo 9651, 42, 51
    BuNo 9652, 41
    BuNo 9654, 41
    BuNo 9655, 62
    BuNo 9658, 61
    BuNo 9659, 66
    BuNo 9663, 66
    BuNo 9664, 42
    BuNo 9665, 59
    BuNo 9667, 64
    BuNo 9673, 133
    general, 43, 44, 46, 50, 51, *59,* 60, *60,* 70, 80, 81, 84, 132, 134
Grumman F3F-1:
    BuNo 0216, 84, 115
    BuNo 0217, 68, 117, 131
    BuNo 0219, 135, 141
    BuNo 0220, 65, 98, 138
    BuNo 0222, 104
    BuNo 0223, 71
    BuNo 0225, 80
    BuNo 0227, 135
    BuNo 0228, 65
    BuNo 0229, 134
    BuNo 0235, *110*
    BuNo 0236, 98
    BuNo 0238, 140
    BuNo 0242, 135
    BuNo 0251, 99
    BuNo 0252, 71
    BuNo 0253, 132
    BuNo 0257, 134
    BuNo 0259, 138
    BuNo 0261, 134
    BuNo 0262, 138
    BuNo 0263, 134
    BuNo 0452, 142
    general, 52, 60, 76, 81, 111, 117, 121, 122, 132, 134, 137, 138

Grumman F3F-2, 111, *136*
Grumman F3F-3, 151, *154*
Grumman F4F Wildcat:
    BuNo 1565, 145
    BuNo 1854, 145
    BuNo 4090, 198, 199
    BuNo 11955, 347
    general, xiii, *171, 172, 205,* 218, 222, 224, 226, 228, 230, 235, 240, 242, 244, 252, 255, 258, 262, 264, 265, 269, 272, 275, 277, 279, 281, 283, 284, 289, 296, *304,* 316, 327, 329, 335, *340,* 342, *342, 343,* 346, *348,* 379
Grumman F4F-3 Wildcat:
    BuNo 1853, 157, 177
    BuNo 1859, 145
    BuNo 1862, 153
    BuNo 1863, 144
    BuNo 1870, 158
    BuNo 1879, 157
    BuNo 1886, 148
    BuNo 2518, 178
    BuNo 2521, 147
    BuNo 2524, 149
    BuNo 2526, 146
    BuNo 2530, 147
    BuNo 2533, 148
    BuNo 2536, 149
    BuNo 2538, 165
    BuNo 3862, 178
    BuNo 3863, 179
    BuNo 5034, 196
    general, 147, 150, *150, 162, 163, 167, 168, 169,* 177
Grumman F4F-4 Wildcat:
    BuNo 02136, 196
    BuNo 03396, 193, *193,* 194
    BuNo 03398, 199
    BuNo 03399, 194
    BuNo 03433, 354
    BuNo 03464, 311
    BuNo 4079, 187
    BuNo 4088, 183
    BuNo 4090, 183
    BuNo 4092, 187
    BuNo 11701, 298
    BuNo 11702, 197
    BuNo 11703, *216*
    BuNo 11704, 197, *197*
    BuNo 11705, 299
    BuNo 11740, 302
    BuNo 11743, 198
    BuNo 11747, 197
    BuNo 11863, 356
    BuNo 11927, 324
    BuNo 11950, 311
    BuNo 11951, 318
    BuNo 11953, 323
    BuNo 11956, 313, 354
    BuNo 11957, 325, 330, *331*
    BuNo 11995, 301
    BuNo 11997, 301
    BuNo 12001, 350
    BuNo 12002, 309
    BuNo 12040, 297, *299*
    BuNo 12042, 321
    BuNo 12153, 324
    BuNo 12158, 308

    BuNo 12186, 301
    BuNo 12196, 301
    BuNo 12209, 323
    BuNo 120000, 300
    general, *186,* 188, 208, 211, *213,* 214, *215,* 226, 237, *238,* 253, *255,* 256, *261,* 266, *266,* 268, 269, 270, 272, 275, 282, 287, 322, 328, 333, *341,* 345, *345,* 347
Grumman F4F-4P Wildcat (BuNo 5160), 351
Grumman F4F-B Wildcat (BuNo 11996), 356
Grumman F6F Hellcat:
    BuNo 41465, 370
    BuNo 65955, 379
    general, 345, *361,* 366, 379, 383, 389, *393*
Grumman F6F-3 Hellcat:
    BuNo 40248, 368
    BuNo 40458, 377
    BuNo 40563, 373
    BuNo 40977, 374
    BuNo 41118, 373
    BuNo 41182, 376
    BuNo 41271, 374
    BuNo 41820, *371,* 372
    BuNo 42131, 370
    BuNo 42324, 368
    BuNo 42433, 366
    BuNo 42513, 370
    BuNo 42777, 376
    BuNo 42818, 376
    BuNo 42945, 374, 375
    BuNo 42969, 377, 378
    BuNo 42989, 377
    BuNo 43004, 376
    BuNo 66234, 384
    BuNo 70061, 372
    BuNo 70601, 374
    general, 394
Grumman F6F-3N Hellcat (BuNo 40896), 357
Grumman F6F-5 Hellcat:
    BuNo 58592, 367
    BuNo 70628, 386
Grumman F6F-5N Hellcat (BuNo 40831), *358*
Grumman F6F-5P Hellcat, 366
Grumman F6F-6 Hellcat (BuNo 58484), 367
Grumman F8F-1 Bearcat (BuNo 94829), 390
Grumman FF-1 (BuNo 9376), 38
Grumman FM-2 Wildcat:
    BuNo 16367, 357
    BuNo 16397, 357
    BuNo 16763, 370
    BuNo 74363, 380
    general, 362, 370, 380, *381,* 387
Grumman J2F-1 Duck:
    BuNo 0169, 127
    BuNo 0172, *76,* 78
    BuNo 0176, *76,* 78
    BuNo 0187, 143
    general, 85, 150
Grumman J2F-3 Duck, *162*
Grumman J2F-4 Duck:
    (BuNo 1652), 142
Grumman J2F-5 Duck, 181, 356
Grumman JF-1 Duck:
    BuNo 9440, 37
    BuNo 9454, 53
    general, 21, 44, 45, 46

Grumman SF-1, 18, 23
Grumman TBF Avenger, 238, 239, 245, 284, 285, 286, *288,* 301, 308, 313, 330, 338, 339, 341, 345, 349, 362, 366
Grumman TBF-1 Avenger:
  BuNo 00524, 193
  BuNo 00582, 292
  BuNo 00618, 297
  BuNo 00676, 293
  BuNo 01770, 292
  BuNo 05922, *300*
  BuNo 06073, 296, *296*
  BuNo 06075, 295
  BuNo 06217, 296
  BuNo 06253, 297, *298,* 300, 301
  BuNo 06302, *319,* 336
  BuNo 06303, 305, 311
  BuNo 06378, 309
  general, 183, 220, 232, *246,* 269, 271, 272, *273,* 282, 286, 310, *325, 327,* 329
Grumman TBF-1C Avenger (BuNo 47921), 357
Grumman TBM Avenger:
  BuNo 8514, *395*
  BuNo 53091, *394*
  general, xiii, *304,* 379, 385
Grumman TBM-1C Avenger:
  BuNo 25179, 366
  BuNo 45462, 367
  general, 390
Grumman TBM-3 Avenger, 380, 394
Grumman TBM-3E Avenger:
  BuNo 56122, 388
  BuNo 86177, 388
Grumman TBM-3W Avenger:
  BuNo 22857, 388
  general, *385*
Gryt, Morten, 335
Guadalcanal (CVE-60), 391, 392
Guam, 88
Guantanamo Bay, 28, 117, 119, *120,* 125, 145
Gulf of Mexico, *394*
Gulf of Tehuantepec, 56
Gunnel (SS-253), *219, 220,* 221
Gurney, Aviation Cadet Alfred L., USNR (VS-41), 113
Guymon, Capt. Vernon M., USMC, 40, *41*
Gyatt (DD-712), 392
Gygax, Rear Adm. Felix X., 160

H

Haas, Naval Aviation Pilot J. W. (VT-3), 97
Hadden, Lt. (jg) Mayo A., Jr., A-V(N) (VF-9), 209, 219, 229, 235, 260, 261, 268, 271, 282
Hain, Lt. (jg) Vernon R. "Rex" (VB-4), 85, 91, *91*
Haines, 2d Lt. John P., USMC, 156
Haiti, 119, 125
Hale (DD-133), 65
Hale (DD-642), 322
Hale, Lt. (jg) Henry H. "Bill" (VF-3B), 50, 51, *59,* 62
Halibut Cove, 46
Hall, Cpl. Leslie J., USMC, 22
Hall, Lt. (jg) Finley E. "Pete," 68, 69
Halsey, Adm. William F., Jr. "Bill," 156, 392
Hambleton (DD-455), 183, 186, 198, 287, 357
Hamburg-Südamerikanische Dampfschiffahrts Gesellschaft, 330
Hamby, Aviation Machinist's Mate 2d Class E. C., 42
Hamilton, Lt. William H., 38, 147

Hammitt, Comdr. Frank M., *372*
Hammond, Lt. Keene G. "Kagey" (VF-41), *211,* 214, 222, 223, 227, 234, 235, 237, 241, 251, 256, 260, 262, 269, 281, 301, 325, 330, 340, *348, 353*
Hampton, Aviation Ordnaneman 3d Class G. H. (VF-4), *348*
Hamrick, Lt. (jg) Laurence L. "Ham," A-V(N) (VT-4), 300, 311, *319,* 330, 339
Haney, Aviation Ordnanceman 2d Class Harry E. (VT-3), 367
Hanley, Aviation Machinist's Mate 3d Class G. P. (VB-3B), 85
Hannegan, Lt. Edward A., 58, 100
Hanson, Lt. (jg) Murray, 99
Haraden (DD-585), 366
Hardison, Comdr. Osborne B. (VB-3), 118
Hardman, Lt. (jg) George F., A-V(N) (VGS-28), 292
Harlow, Ens. William R., A-V(N) (VS-72), 134
Harpoon, Operation, 188
Harrill, Rear Adm. William K. "Keen," 156, *157,* 160, *164,* 166, 168, 170, 171, 180, 183, 185, 186, 187, 374
Harris, Ens. Thomas, A-V(N) (VF-4, VS-41), 138, 144, *144*
Harris, Frank (Yard workman), 24
Harris, Lt. George E., A-V(N) (VF-41), 215, 237, 251, 256, 264, *341*
Harris, Lt. George M., Jr., A-V(N) (VF-41), 212, 230, 235, 237, 256, 264, 275, 281, 308, 328, 333, 342, *342, 353*
Harris, Lt. (jg) K. G., USNR (VF-2), 386
Harris, Lt. William S. (VB-3), 125
Harrison, Aviation Machinist Mate 2d Class J. F., 309
Harrison, Lt. Harry W., Jr., A-V(N) (VGF-28), 264, 275, 281
Harriss, Lt. J. Welsh, *319*
Harten, Aviation Radioman 2d Class Ben S., USNR (VT-3), 367, 368
Harter, Gunnery Sgt. Ora C., USMC, 8
Hase, Seaman 2d Class W. Q. (VF-4), *348*
Hastings, Lt. (jg) Burden R. (VB-4), 98
Hasty, Aviation Machinist's Mate 1st Class E., 41
Hausaman, George (Eclipse Aviation Corporation), 44
Haw, Asst. Eng. E. P., 54
Hawaiian Islands, 30, 32, 35, *36, 75,* 76, *79,* 82, 83, 88, 110, *113,* 173, 181, 366, 370
Hawkins, Ens. Hartwell R., A-V(N) (VF-4), 311, *314,* 323, 351, 352
Haynes, Aviation Radioman 1st Class William O., Jr. (VS-41), 209, 226, 232, 244, 256, 262, 268, 272, 287
Hayward, Lt. (jg) John T. "Chick," 23
Head, Mrs. Charles, 62
Hedrick, Ens. Roger R., A-V(N) (VF-4), 138
Heinkel HE-115B (WNr 1866), 343, 344, *344, 345*
Helen, (U.S. tug), 10
Heme, *Sergent* Lucien, 211
Hendricks, Lt. (jg) Charles G., Jr., A-V(N) (VB-4), 328
Hennekes, Seaman 1st Class J. W. (VB-3), 118
Henry, Capt. Clifford O., 8
Henry, Ens. Donald A., A-V(N), 357
Hensley, Ens. Lawrence A., A-V(N) (VF-4), 329, 343, 350, *353*
Hepburn, Adm. Arthur J., 86
Herbert (DD-160), 27
Hermite, French Ambassador Louis, 22
Herndon, Radioman 1st Class Glen A., 109, 116
Herriot, Radioman 3d Class Charles J., 101
Hershey, Ens. Merle M., A-V(N) (VF-9), 209, 219, 230, 235, 256, 260, 268, 270, 277, 278, 282
Hessel, Lt. (jg) Edward W. "Red" (VF-72), 178
Hestilow, Lt. Jack M., USNR (VB-5), 380
Hewitt, Fireman 1st Class Ernest G. "Spider," 12, 22, 23
Hewitt, Rear Adm. H. Kent, 201, 280, 282, 285, 286
Hibbs, Aviation Cadet Walter A., USNR (VT-2), 89
Hieber, Ens. Leonard L., USNR (VB-1), 382

Higley, Lt. (jg) Robert H., A-V(N) (VS-41), 209, 226, 237, 257, 259, 265, 272, 274, 281, 288, 290, 291
Hill, Charles, Jr., 54
Hill, Ens. David L. "Tex," A-V(N) (VS-41), 149
Hinds, Samuel S. (actor), 72
Hirsch, Ens. J. A., A-V(N), 153
Hitchcock, Photographer 2d Class M., 78
Hitler, Adolf, 125, 129, 159, 267
Hittel, Ens. Frederick A., USNR (VF-12), 377, 378
Hobbs, Lt. Comdr. Ira E., *185*
Hobson (DD-464), 190, 191, 196, 197, 198, 270, 297, 298, *299,* 300, 316, 319, 320, 322, 324, 325, 347, 354
Hogge, Radioman 1st Class S. F. (VS-42), 116, 122
Holden, Aviation Machinist's Mates 3d Class John H., 297
Holland (AS-3), 41, 80, 81
Holloway, Comdr. James L., 131
Holmes, Capt. Ralston S., 65
Home Fleet, 188, 322, 323, 345, 349
Homer Spit, 45
Honolulu, 32, 35, *36,* 82, 83, *113*
Hoover, Lt. (jg) Charles D. (VF-4), 138
Hoover, Mrs. Herbert C., 3, *4*
Hoover, President Herbert C., 3, 16, 21
Hoover, Seaman 1st Class M. L. (VS-1B), 53
Hopping, Lt. Halstead L. (VS-1B), 13, 15, 53
Hopson, Lt. (jg) Charles R. "Hoppy," A-V(N) (VF-4), *313,* 343, 344, *353*
Horne, Vice Adm. Frederick J., 56, 62, 67, 69, 74, 77, 84, 86, *107,* 359, 360
Hornet (CV-8), 181, 190, *371*
Horton, Gunner's Mate 3d Class W. S., 178
Hoskins, Comdr. John M. "Johnnie" (VS-42), 89, 109, 110, 147, *154, 163,* 201, 202, 203, *204,* 207, 267, 293, *296,* 392
Hospital apprentices ("Hossapps"), 19
Hoss, *Leutnant* Johannes, 343
Housatonic (AO-35), 190, 191
House, Lt. (jg) Herschel A. "Colonel" (VF-3B), *59,* 68
Houston, Lt. Hubert T. "Hubie," A-V(N) (VF-41), 197, 214, 223, 230, 237, 256, 262, 269, 270, 281, 309, *353*
Houston (CA-30), 39
Howard F. Clark (DE-539), 370
Howell, Ens. Harry E. "Pete," 147
Howerton, Lt. Charles C. "Chick", 127
Howland Island, 86, 89
Howorth (DD-592), 366, 368
Hoyt, Ens. Robert B. Hoyt, A-V(G), USNR, 58
Hubbard, Ens. Thomas M., A-V(N) (VS-41), 226, 237, 238, 257, 259, 281, 288, 290, 291
Huffman, First Lt. Wilfred J., USMC, 40
Hugget, Radioman 1st Class W. T. (VS-42), 165
Hughes, Capt. Thomas B., USMC, *154*
Hughes, Lt. Frederick T. "Joe" (VB-3B), *50*
Hugh L. Scott (AP-43), 291
Hulbert (DD-342), 383, 386, 388, 390
Hull (DD-350), 99, 106
Hullfish, Comdr. Wilson S., (SC), 118
Humphrey, Aviation Radioman 3d Class R. W. (VF-4), 357
Hundt, Commodore Lester T., 391
Hunter's Point, *73,* 74, 116
Hurst, Ens. Lane A., USNR, 101, 102, *102,* 127
Hurst Aviation Cadet Lane A., 110
Hustvedt, Rear Adm. Olaf M., 327, 345, 346, *350*
Hutcheson, Lt. Homer H. "Hutch" (VT-4), *313, 319,* 330, 338
Hutchinson, Lt. George L., 87
Hutsell, Seaman 1st Class D. L., 177
Huvet, *Capitaine* Robert, 214, 215

I

Iarrobino, Lt. (jg) John, 316
Ibis (steamship), 340
Iceland, 349, 354
Idaho (BB-42), 6, *15*
Identification, friend or foe (IFF), 333, 385
Ideus, Ens. Victor C., USNR (VB-98), 386
Illustrious (British aircraft carrier) HMS, 147, 162, 322
Independence (CVL-22), 392
Ingersoll, Adm. Royal E., 186
Intrepid (CV-11), 388
"Iron compass," 70
Irons, Lt. (jg) Alden H. "Rusty" (VF-3B), *50*
Iroquois, HMCS, (Canadian destroyer), 350
Isherwood (DD-520), 316, 320, 322
Italy, 125
I Was Chaplain On The Franklin, 397

J

Jackson, Aviation Ordnanceman 2d Class Charles P., Jr. (VT-4), 301, 330, 339
Jackson, Aviation Radioman 3d Class Roland O. (VGS-28), 292
Jackson, Wing Comdr. Eric R. S., FAA, 161
Jacobs, Aviation Radioman 3d Class B. L., 295, *296*
Jacobson, Radioman 3d Class Dale I., 172, 173
Jaeger, Aviation Cadet Thomas A., USNR, 108, 109, *109,* 116
Jaeger, Aviation Radioman 2d Class Robert H., 292
Jahncke, Assistant Secretary of the Navy Ernest L., 3
Jahncke, Mrs., Ernest L., 3
Jamaica, 143
James, Capt. Jules, 149
James, Lt. (jg) George S. "Buck," Jr. (VF-3B), 42, *59*
Japan, 125
Jason (AV-2), 8
Jean Bart (French battleship), 209, 220, 271, 272, 273, *273,* 274, 275, *276,* 277, *277, 278, 279,* 280, 282, 283, 363
Jennings, Rear Adm. Ralph E., 379, 384
Jett, Lt. (jg) Charles M., 38
Jettie Delure, 233, 251, 273, 277, 279, 283
Jettie Transversale, 273, 277, 279, 283
Jobe, Aviation Radioman 2d Class Kenneth W. (VB-4, VS-41), 209, 226, 237, 254, 269, 278, 281, 328
Johnson, Capt. Douglass P., 380, 382, 387, *389,* 390
Johnson, Ens. Ivan C., Jr., A-V(N), 347
Johnson, First Sgt. Josiah D., USMC, 8
Johnson, Lt. Cecil V. "Johnny" (VB-4, VS-41), 171, 172, 209, 226, 232, 237, 238, 256, 259, 265, 272, *275, 277,* 282, 283, *284,* 318, 319, 328, 333, 344, 394
Johnson, Lt. Comdr. Warren W., 147, *154*
Johnson, Lt. Howard L. (VGF-28), 272
Johnson, Lt. Jesse G., 118
Johnson, Lt. (jg) Harlan T. "Swede" (VB-3B), 31, 32, *32, 50*
Johnson, Lt. (jg) Thomas C., A-V(N) (VF-72), 181
Johnson, Lt. Seymour A. (VF-3B), *59,* 64
Johnson, Lt. William D., Jr., 33, 34
Johnson, Rear Adm. Alfred W., 125, *126,* 130, 131, 332
Johnston, Lt. Robert B. (VF-4), *353*
Jones, Aviation Cadet William H. Jones, USNR (VF-5B), 65, 66
Jones, Ens. Edwin R. (CVG(N)-90), 368
Jones, Ens. Robert C., A-V(N) (VF-4), 144
Jones, John Paul, Captain *xiv,* 6
Jones, Lt. (jg) Dee, A-V(N) (VF-4, VF-41), 212, 230, 237, 251, 256, 264, 269, 275, 282, 308, *313*
Jones, Radioman 3d Class W. H., 116
Joseph Hewes (AP-50), 181

Joseph T. Dickman (AP-26), 166, *169*
Juneau (CL-52), 190
Jung, Lt. (jg) Karl E. "Jug" (VF-3B), *50, 59,* 62, 69, 70, 71
Junkers JU-88D-1 (WNr 1682), 343, *343, 345*
Jupiter (AC-13), 3
Juracka, Storekeeper 3d Class J. F., 21
Justo, Argentine President Agustin P., 23

K

Kachemak Bay, 45, 46, *46*
Kaguir (steamer), 334
Kals, *Kapitänleutnant* Ernst, 291
Kanawha (AO-1), 32, *34*
Karlsen, Odd, 335
Karpiak, Aviation Metalsmith 2d Class Joseph (VT-4), 193
Karsemeyer, Aviation Chief Radioman Henry, USNR (VT-4), 330, 336
Kasaan Bay (CVE-69), 362
Kasilof, 45
Kaster, Radioman 3d Class Arthur L., 158, 162
Kauffman, Ens. David L., A-V(N) (VS-41), 184
Kearns, Ens. Elmer L. (VBF-98), 384
Kearny (DD-432), 149, 150
Keigher, Lt. (jg) Joseph P., Jr., A-V(N) (VS-41), 158, 209, *220,* 221, 232, 233, 244, 250, 260, 278, 280, 281, 282, 287
Keller, Chief Commissary Steward F. C. "Stew," 21
Keller, Ens. Clarence A., Jr., 45
Keller, Lt. (jg) Harold R., Jr., A-V(N) (VF-9, VS-41), 194, 196, *196,* 209, 226, 237, 256, 265, 272, 274, 284, 291, 311, 328, *335*
Kelley, Ens. Robert S. (VF-4), *353*
Kelly, Aviation Cadet Arthur N., USNR (VF-5B), 66
Kelly, Aviation Machinist's Mate 1st Class F. E. (VS-42), 94
Kelly, Lt. (jg) Edmund J., A-V(N) (VF-41), 187, 212, 216, 235, 237, 241, 251, 256, 264, 269, 283
Kelsch, Aviation Cadet Walter L., Jr. "Moose," USNR (VB-3), 118, 121, 122, 134
Kenai Range, 45, 47
Kenney, Lt. Francis V., 318, 319
Kennison (AG-83), 376, 378
Kerkplein (steamer), 340
Kidd (DD-661), 316
Killerece, Pvt. R. G., USMC, 112
Kimmel, Adm. Husband E., 148, 149
Kimpler, Lt. (jg) Joseph H., 69
Kinder, Ens. Billy N., A-V(N) (VF-4), 356, 357
Kindley Field, 164, 165, 179, 197
King, Adm. Ernest J., 9, 10, 15, 26, 79, 80, 82, 111, *114,* 144, 147, 148, 158, 181, 183, 189, 354, 370
King, Aviation Machinist's Mate 3d Class Donald L. (VT-4), 297, 330
King, Ens. Charles M., A-V(N) (VF-41), 137, 157
King, Lt. John W., 56
Kirby, Ens. Malcolm C., A-V(N) (VF-7), 133
Kirn, Lt. (jg) Louis J. (VT-3), 98
Kirsebom, Lt. H. (Royal Norwegian Air Force), 330
Kitsap Lake, 58
Kleiner, Aviation Radioman 2d Class Gerhard H. O. (VS-41), 209, 226, 232, 237, 256, 265, 272, *275*
Klies, Fireman 3d Class, 23, 24
Klinsmann, Lt. Comdr. George O. "Otto" (VB-4, VB-42), 319, 320, *326,* 328, 329, 330, 332, 333, 362
Knight, Lt. (jg) Mervin T., A-V(N), 294, 296, 297
Knox, Secretary of the Navy William F. "Frank", 148, 326, *326*
Kobelmann, A. H. (Walter Kidde Company), 44
Kohr, Lt. (jg) George L. (VF-3B), *59*
Komat, Ens. Stephen, USNR, 374

Koozer, Lt. (jg) Wendell S., A-V(N), 295, 296, *296*
Korecki, Aviation Radioman 3d Class John G. (VS-41), 209, 226, 237, 250, 262, 269, 278, 281, 284
Kozek, Aviation Radioman 3d Class C. (VB-41), 317
Kraft, Seaman 2d Class Clayton O., USNR, 367
Kreuter, Sgt. M. L., USMC, 156
Krieger, *Obergefreiter* Friedrich (radio operator), 343
Kriegsmarine, 327
Krol, Ens. Herman T., A-V(N) (VS-41), 157
Kugler, Ens. John C., USNR, 384
Kunze, Aviation Radioman 2d Class J. J., 316, *316*
Kuper, Aviation Ordnanceman 1st Class O. A., 78

L

Laake, Lt. (jg) Walter E., A-V(N) (VF-41), *210,* 212, 216, 237, 256, 264, 269, 281, 283, 311
Labyak, Ens. R. W., A-V(N), 297
La Chaux, *Lieutenant* François, 213
Lacy, Aviation Radioman 1st Class C. J. (VT-4), 330
Lagorce, M. Jean, 254
La Gracieuse (French second class sloop), 271
Lahaina Roads, 32, *34,* 77, 88
Laird, Lt. (jg) Dean S. "Diz," A-V(N) (VF-4), 318, 343, 344, *353*
Lake Champlain (CV-39), 358, 359, 360
Lakin, Ens. Benjamin M., A-V(N) (VF-7, VF-41), 135, 165
L'Alcyon (French destroyer), 222, 224
Lamson (DD-367), 87, 89, 90, 93, 110
Landau, Ens. Vincent L., USNR, 382
Landry, Aviation Machinist's Mate 2d Class R. W. T., 297
Lang (DD-399), 177, 178, 181
Langley (CV-1), 3, 6, 7, 23, 35, 43, 52, 56, 58, 85, *96,* 139, 156, 363
Laning, Vice Adm. Harris, 35
Lankowicz, Aviation Radioman 2d Class J. J. (VB-4, VS-41), 209, *220,* 226, 232, 244, 250, 257, 259, 260, 278, 281, 287, 328
Lanman, Lt. (jg) (VS-41), 109
La Plata (German steamer), 330, *331,* 332, 333, 339, *340*
Lapsley, Lt. (jg) Howard, A-V(S) (VS-41), 184
La Psyché, 220
Lapwing (AVP-1), 132
Larsen, Harry (Grumman Corporation), 52
Larson, Maj. W. T., USA, 44
Launder, Lt. (jg) Lloyd H., Jr. (VF-4), *353*
Laundrigan, Aviation Machinist's Mate 3d Class Edward L., 349
Lauritzen, Lt. Comdr. William C., 397
Lavie, *Sergent* René, 211, 213, 249
Lawrence (DD-250), 380
Lea (DD-118), 44, 45, 47, 49
Leahy, Adm. William D., 65
Leary (DD-158), 27, 28
LeBlanc, *Lieutenant,* 253
LeCalvet, *Lieutenant,* 253
LeCompte, Radioman 1st Class J. W., 115
Lee, Lt. Charles L., 109
Leeward Island, 120
LeGrande, *Sergent* Andre, *214*
Lemon, Lt. James N., USNR (VB-12), 378
Lend-Lease Act, 146
Leonard, Ens. George S., A-V(N) (VB-7), 132
Leonard Wood (AP-25), 166
Lepp, Ens. Louis K., A-V(N) (VF-4, VF-41), 320, 321, 328, 342, *353*
Leslie, Aviation Cadet James M. (VS-41), 109
Leslie, Lt. (jg) Maxwell F. (VF-5B), 51
Le Stum, *Lt.,* 213, 214
Levaçon, *Capitaine,* 247

Lexington (CV-2), xiv, 3, 4, 7, *15*, 18, 32, 35, 38, 39, 41, 43, 52, 58, 62, 63, 65, 73, 76, 80, 82, 84, 85, 87, 88, *88*, 89, *89*, 90, *90*, 91, *91*, 92, *92*, 93, 95, 96, 110, 111, *113*, 117, *119*, *124*, 125, 126, 148, 181, 188, 354, 392, 394
Light, Aviation Radioman 3d Class Oscar I. (VS-41), 209, 232, 237, 244, 251, 260, 272, *276*, 285, 291
Lightfoot, Aviation Chief Machinist's Mate 3d Class G. W. (VT-4), 295, 330
Lighthouse, Samuel, 178
Limon Bay, 117, *118*, *119*
Lincoln, Aviation Machinist's Mate 3d Class T. W., Jr. (VS-42), 177
Link, Lt. (jg) Everett M., Jr., 138
Liore et Olivier (LeO) 451, 214, 219, 227, 252, 258
Little, Adm. Sir Charles J. C., RN, 189
Livermore (DD-429), 149, 150
Lloyd, Aviation Chief Machinist's Mate Elmer B., 31
Lobos (British freighter), 184
Lobster (U.S. fishing vessel), 322
Lockheed Model 10-E Electra, 86, 89
Lockheed P-38 Lightnings, *363*
Long Beach, 70, 71
Long Island (ACV-1), 171
Longley, Lt. (jg) William H., A-V(N) (VB-4, VS-41), 181, 209, 226, 237, 250, 262, 263, 264, 269, 278, 280, 281, 284, 328
Loomis, Cadet Robert C., USNR (VF-3B), 66, 70, 71
Lorentzen, Aviation Radioman 2d Class A. W. (VB-4, VS-41), 209, 226, 237, 256, 265, 272, 284, 291, 328
Los Alamitos, 386
Lott, M. A. (Naval Aircraft Factory), 44
Lovejoy, Chief Machinist's Mate E. W., *306*
Lovelace, Lt. Donald A. (VS-41), 87, *88*
Lovell, Aviation Machinist's Mate 1st Class F. V., 143
Lovett, Lt. (jg) Benjamin B. C., 87
Lowe-class torpedo boat, 332
Lowndes, Ens. Andrew J., A-V(N) (VF-72), 178
Luce (DD-522), 322
Ludlow (DD-438), 224
Luftwaffe, 188
Luker, Lt. (jg) George R. "Luke" (VS-41), 109, *110*
Lusby, Chief Yeoman John, 21
Lützow, 322, 326
Lynnhaven Roads, 141
Lyster, Rear Adm. Arthur L. St. George, RN, 161, 163, 164, *164*

M
Maalea Bay, 78
Macomb (DD-458), 186, 187, 198, 357, *359*, 360
Macomber, Ens. Brainard T., A-V(N), *150*
Madden, Lt. Walter F. "Wally," A-V(N) (VF-41), 141, 145, 146, *146*, 148, *210*, 254, 258, 259, 269, 270, 271, 282, 283
Mahoney, Radioman 1st Class C. J., 110
Mahony, Lt. Jack A., Jr. (VGF-28), 240
Maine (U.S. battleship), 28
Maine, Rockland, *11*
Maison, Lt., 231, 236
Makassar Strait (CVE-91), 374
Malaga (German steamer), *335*, 336
Malinasky, Ens. Frank, A-V(N), 141
Malta, 188, 189
Mandarich, Lt. Stevan (VF-72), 179
Mangieri, Ens. Joseph, USNR (VF-12), 376
Manhattan. See *Wakefield* (AP-21)
Manuel C. Friere (Spanish fishing vessel), 287
Marcos, Master Sgt. Enrique, USMC, 226, *227*
Mare Island Navy Yard, 139

Marineartillerieabteilung 510, 335
Marine Bombing Squadron VMB-2, 97, 98, 111
Marine Detachment, 8, *12*, 19, 21, 22, 23
Marine Fighting Squadrons:
 VMF-1, *136*
 VMF-2, 63, 97, 99, 111
 VMF-111, 156, 157, 158
 VMF-112, 374
 VMF-123, 374, 375
 VMF-221, 374, 375
 VMF-351, 383
 VMF-451, 374, 375
 VMF-511, 374
 VMF-512, 374, 383
Marine Observation Squadrons:
 VMO-1, 143, 144, 145, 156, 158
 VMO-151, 158
 VMO-351, 374
 VO-8M, 59, 60, 63
Marine Scouting/Bombing Squadrons:
 VMSB-131, 156, 158
 VMSB-132, 158
Marine Scouting Squadrons:
 VMS-1, 141, 142, 143, 158, 162
 VMS-2, 97, 111
Marine Utility Squadrons:
 VJ-7M, 39
 VMJ-1, 143
 VMJ-2, 111
Marks, Lt. (jg) Robert R., A-V(N) (VS-42), 142, 192
Martin, Ens. Albert E., A-V(N) (VF-9), 226, 231, 251, 253, 264, 272, 273, 281
Martin, Ens. Charles L., II (VF-4), *353*
Martin, Lt. (jg) Marshall T. (VF-3B), 65
Martin 167 Maryland, 211, 252, *253*, 258
Martin BM-1:
 BuNo 8879, 98
 BuNo 8880, 58
 BuNo 8885, 83
 BuNo 9174, 66
 BuNo 9185, 65, 69
 general, *17*, *37*, *52*, 82
Martin BM-2:
 BuNo 9170, 89
 BuNo 9184, 56
 general, *37*, 42, 69, 82, 87
Martin PM-1, (BuNo 8295), 35
Martin T4M, *17*
Martinant de Preneuf, *Capitaine de Corvette* Charles, 224
Martinez, Chilean Ambassador Marcial, 22
Martinique, 181
Martins, (Brazilian Minister of Marine) Jorge, 395
Martlets. See Grumman F4F-4 Wildcat
Marx, Lt. (jg) Nathan, USNR, 386
Maryland (BB-46), 41
Mascots, 19
Mason, Ens. Singleton W., Jr., (D)L, USNR, 396
Massachusetts (BB-59), 209, 213, 220, 221, 230, 236, 239, 241, 257, 271
Massachussetts Institute of Technology–Radiation Laboratory (MIT–RL), 385
Matchless, HMS (British destroyer), 354
Maui, 32, *79*
May, Ens. William C., A-V(N) (VS-42), 177
May, Lt. Eugene F., 96
Mayer, Seaman 1st Class M. J., 143

Mayhew, Lt. (jg) Boyd N., A-V(N) (VF-4, VF-41), 196, 224, 230, 237, 241, 251, 256, 262, 269, 281, 287, 329, 332, 343, 344, *345*
Mayrant (DD-402), 166, 253
McAdams, Ens. William T. (VF-12), 376
McAdoo, Ens. C. W. (VF-17), 373
McAlister, Radioman 1st Class W. L. (VS-1B), 53, 55
McCain, Capt. John S. "Mac," 83, 100, *100*, 101, 104, *104*, *107*, 108, 112, 113, 120, 123, 126
McCalla Field, 131, 142, 143, 144
McCall (DD-400), 122
McCarley, Aviation Radioman 2d Class Donald W. "Mac," USNR (VB-4), 328, 334, 335
McCarthy, Capt. T. Donald, USA, 291
McCawley (AP-10), *161*
McClure, Lt. (jg) William H. "Mac" (VF-3B), 69, 70, 164, 165
McCormick (DD-223), 81
McCoy Reynolds (DE-440), 364, 368
McCracken, Lt. (jg) Reginald R. (VS-1B), 65
McCuskey, Ens. Elbert S. "Doc," A-V(N), 147
McCutchan, Comdr. George T., 368
McDaniel, Ens. Charles O., USNR (VF-12), 376
McDaniel, Radioman 2d Class John R. (VS-42), 99, 122
McDonald, Chief Commissaryman Lloyd W., 6
McDonald, Lt. David L., 173
McDougal, Brig. Gen. Douglas C., USMC, 39, 40
McDougal (DD-358), 153
McFadden, Ens. Harlan C., A-V(N) (VT-4), 297, *300*, 301
McFarland (DD-237), 372, 373, 374, 379, 380, 381, 382, 383, 384, 385, 386, 390
McGann, Ens. Robert M., A-V(N) (VF-9), 209, 219, 226, 235, 271, 282
McGeorge, Aviation Machinist's Mate 3d Class C. E. (VB-4), 98
McGown, Seaman 1st Class M. P., 23
McGuire, Lt. Comdr. Charles J. (VF-3B), 70
McKee, Lt. Carlos R., A-V(N), 367, *367*
McKinney, Ens. M., A-V(N) (VC-82), 370
McMenamin, Aviation Radioman 3d Class Edward J., USNR (VB-4), 357
McNally, Seaman 2d Class W. J. (VB-1B), 83
McNulty, Ens. Frank B., Jr., A-V(N) (VT-100), 366
McReynolds, Lt. (jg) John G., Jr., A-V(N) (VB-4, VS-41), 209, 232, 233, 244, 251, 260, 272, 274, *276*, 285, 328
McRoberts, Lt. Comdr. James J. (VF-3B, VF-41), 42, *59*, 158, 177, 178
McSary, Aviation Ordnanceman 3d Class Andy, Jr., 294
McVay, Lt. (jg) Woodie L., Jr., A-V(N) (VS-41), 209, 226, 237, 254, 255, 258, 269, 278, 280, 281
McWhorter, Adm. Ernest D., 182, 184, *185*, 190, 196, 197, 199, *202*, 208, 221, 258, 262, 272, 273, 280, 282, 284, 285, 286, 291, 292
McWhorter, Ens. Hamilton W., III, A-V(N) (VF-9, VF-41), *206*, *211*, 214, 231, 238, 245, 268, 271, 374, 392
Meade (DD-602), 370
Meadow, Lt. Comdr. Harold L. "Reverend" (VF-5B), *59*, 69
Mears, Lt. Col. Frank H., Jr., USAAF, 190
Meili, Aviation Cadet Walter L., USNR (VB-4), 98
Melton, Ens. Irwin E. (VB-98), 386
Melville, Storekeeper 2d Class Henry, 54
Melvin R. Nawman (DE-416), 370
Memphis (CL-13), 142
Menard, Lt. Lou (VF-9, VF-12), *206*, 209, 226, 231, 244, 251, 253, 257, *257*, 271, 284, 374
Mercier, *Capitaine de Vasseau*, 239
Meredith, Aviation Radioman 3d Class Herbert C., USNR (VB-4), 301, 328
Merrill, Adm. Aaron S., 395
Merrimack (AO-37), 184, 186, 191, 201

Merritt, Major Lewie G. "Griff," USMC, 39, 40
Messerschmitt Bf-109, 341
Messerschmitt Bf-110, 341
MFP-231 (German transport ferry), 338, 339
Michette, Electrician's Mate 2d Class A. A., *294*
Micka, Lt. Edward (VF-9), *206*, 209, 219, 230, 235, 236, 237, 260, *261*, 263
Midway Island, 32, 35
Mikronis, Ens. Christos E., A-V(N) (VF-41), 198, 199, 212, 215, 217, 218, 228, 231, 236, 237, 246, 257, 258, 291
Milan, (French destroyer leader), 222, 223, 224, *225*, 228, 230, 232, 233, 251
Millard, Lt. Junius, USNR, 147, 148
Miller, Aviation Machinist's Mate 1st Class Reginald H. (VT-4), 232, 234, 244, 282, 285, 286, 330, 336
Miller, Lt. (jg) Clayton L., 84
Miller, Lt. (jg) Norman M. "Bus," 44, 45
Miller, Lt. (jg) William, Jr. (VS-1B), 50
Milligan, Lt. (jg) Lloyd J., USNR (VT-5), 380
Mindoro (U.S. gunboat), 29
Miner, Aviation Chief Radioman Reginald A. (VB-3, VS-41), 125, 209, 226, 232, *233*
Minor Joint Army and Navy Exercises, 75, 76
Mississippi (BB-41), 18, 57
Mitchell Field, Long Island, 190
Mize, Chief Electrician's Mate Terry W., 20, *21*, 100, *100*
Mk. 8 bombsight, 217
Mk. 8 torpedoes, 132
Mk. 10 range-keeper, 96
Mk. 11 bombsight, 380
Mk. 17 depth bombs, 294
Mk. 19 depth charges, 297
Mk. 33 directors, 7, *63*, 182, *182*, *364*
Mk. 47 depth charge, 357
Moebus, Lt. Lucien A. "Fish," 29
Moffett, Lt. (jg) William A., Jr., 32
Moffett, Rear Adm. William A., 3
Moffett (DD-362), 142
Mohawk (YT-17), 10
Mokos, Photographer's Mate 2d Class M. D. (VS-41), 282, 283, *284*
Mole du Commerce, 279, 283, 363
Monahan, Aviation Radioman 2d Class R. J. (VS-41), *205*, 237, 250, 257, 260, 278, 284, 291
Monogram Field, 183
Montezuma (YT-145), 178
Montgomery, Lt. George C. (VF-3B), 41, *50*, *59*, 61
Montgomery, Rear Adm. Alfred E. "Monty," 67, *67*, *74*, 78, *100*, *104*, 139, 142, 148, 151, *154*, 156, *164*, 388, 394
Moore, Ens. Joseph, A-V(N) (VF(N)-79), 357
Moore, Lt. Comdr. Charles L., Jr. (CO, VF-4), 328, 329, 330, *331*, 353
Moore, Lt. (jg) Robert B. (VS-42), 115, 116
Moore, Lt. Waller C., Jr. "Moe" (VGF-27), 269, 271, 272, 276
Moore, Seaman, 2d Class G. F., 23, 24
Morgan, Ens. Russell I., USNR (VB-12), 375
Moroccan Submarine Flotilla, 219
Morocco, 200, 202, 203, 207, 208, 248, 252, 267, 275, 285
Morse, Lt. (jg) John H., Jr. (VF-5B), *50*
Mortensen, Radioman 2d Class Clyde S., 155
Moses, Ens. Francis, A-V(N) (VF-4), 356
Moss, Aviation Cadet William W. (VB-4), 98, 99
Mounce, Charles (UPI), 88
Mount Hood (AE-11), 364
Mount Vernon (AP-22), 166, 172

Moutenot, Lt. (jg) Charles L. "Moot," A-V(N) (VF-9), 214, 244, 256, 264, 268, 272, 273, 281, 286
Munn, Capt. John C., USMC, 156, 157
Murphy, Ens. Edward J., A-V(N) (VS-42), 128, 170, 173
Murphy, Lt. Comdr. William J., 132
Murphy, Technical Sgt. V. E., USMC (VMO-1), 144
Murray, Seaman 2d Class A. C., 38
Murray, Vice Adm. George D., 379
Musketeer, HMS (British destroyer), 354
Mussolini, Benito, 125

N

Narragansett Bay, 183, 186, 187, 190, 299, 356, 360, 362
Narwhal (SS-167), 30
Nash, Ens. James C., USNR (VF-12), 374
Nashville (CL-43), 161
Nation, Lt. Comdr. Milton A. (VS-1B), 33, 34, *50*, 220, 238
National Air Races, Los Angeles, 59, 60
Natoma Bay (CVE-62), *389*
Naval Aircraft Factory (NAF), 44, *88*, 160, 388
Naval Air Station (NAS):
  Alameda, 370
  Anacostia, 23, 128, 183
  Argentia, 303, 306, 308, 309, *310*, 317
  Coco Solo, 54, 83, 84, 126
  Hampton Roads, 12, 13, *18*, 23, 24, 28, 125, 129, *133*, 143, 149, 150, 158, 173, 177, 194, 292, 297, 364
  Jacksonville, 363
  Livermore, 373
  New Orleans, 390, 391
  Norfolk, *9*, 26, 127, 128, 134, 138, 142, 143, 187, 189, 196, 392
  North Island, 28, 35, 39, 48, 58, *59*, *60*, 62, 64, 66, 70, 72, 73, 85, *96*, 106, 374, 379, 384
  Palmyra Island, 299
  Pensacola, 29, 84, *128*, *144*, 186, 187, 363, 391, 396
  Quonset Point, 183, 186, 190, 297, 301, 303, 357, 358, *359*, 360, 362
  Ream Field, 374
  San Diego, 30, 35, 37, 38, 39, 44, 47, 48, 56, 58, 62, 69, 70, 82, 83, 84, 86, 88, 92, 93, 98, 106, 111, 113, 115, 116, 117, 140, 364, 366, 370, 373, 374, 378, 379, 383, 384, 388, 389, 390
  Seattle, 44, 374
  Squantum, 301
Naval Operating Base (NOB):
  Norfolk, 8, *13*, *16*, 23, 125, 131, 132, *137*, 141, 143, 147, 160, 162, *162*, 170, 181, 293, 294, 296, 297, 364, 397
  Trinidad, 186, 356
Naval Proving Grounds, Dahlgren, Virginia, 380
Naval Reserve Air Base, Long Beach, 30
Navy Material and Redistribution and Disposal Administration, 397
Navy Motion Picture Board, 72
NC-1, 57
Neal, Aviation Chief Machinist's Mate Thomas M. (NAP), 53, 54
Neblett, Lt. Thomas (VF-3B), *59*, 62
Nellie, (U.S. tug), 392, 393
Nelson, Aviation Radioman 3d Class C. W., 324
Nelson, HMS (British battleship), 188
Nemeth, Pvt. Andrew J., USMC, 170
Neptune Party, 92, 100
"Neptunus Rex", 20, 21, *21*, 56, 100, *100*
Neutrality Act of 1939, 146
Neutrality Patrol, 130, 141, 150, 153, 158, 160
Nevada (BB-36), 380

Newcastle Victory (AK-233), 395
New Guinea, 86
New Orleans (CA-32), 80
Newport News Shipbuilding and Dry Dock Company, 5
New York (BB-34), 18, *137*
Nicholl, Lt. Comdr. George W. R., RN, *326*
Nicholson, Ens. Robert G. (VF-4), *353*
Nicolini, Ens. Earl J., A-V(N) (VF-4), 356
Night Aircraft Carrier Training Unit (NACTU), 366, 367, 368, 370
Nimitz, Adm. Chester W., 379
Ninilchuk, 45
Nitro (AE-2), *137*
Nolan, Ens. Christopher A., Jr. A-V(N) (VS-42), 149
Nolan, Ens. John T., USNR, 42
Nonpariel, (U.S. tug), 10
Noonan, Fred J., 86
Norfolk, HMS (British heavy cruiser), 349
Norfolk Navy Yard, 8, *15*, 16, 23, 24, 126, 128, 139, 148, 155, 156, 157, 160, *161*, 166, 171, 177, 181, 192, *192*, 292, 296, 354, 356, 358, 360, 364
Norfolk Training Station, 24
Norman, Lt. (jg) Leo R., A-V(N), 328, 360
North American SNJ-5C Texan:
  BuNo 51761, 396
  BuNo 51950, 392
  general, 392, *396*
  landings, 391
Northampton (CA-26), 24
North Carolina (BB-55), 183
Northrop BT-1, 123, 151
  BuNo 0610, 154
  BuNo 0614, 153
Norway, xiii, 351
Norwegian Sea, 349
Nova Scotia, 166, 168, 321
Noyes, Capt. Leigh, 92, 93
Nugent, Frank S. (film critic), 73

O

Obdurate, HMS (British destroyer), 354
O'Brien, Lt. Comdr. Timothy J., 95, 96
O'Brien (DD-415), 143
Observation Spotter Squadrons:
  VOC-2, 380
Observation Squadrons:
  VO-1, 394
  VO-3B, 38
O'Callahan, Lt. Joseph Timothy, Chaplain, 187, 245, 267, *307*, 315, 397
O'Connor, Aviation Radioman 3d Class R. E. (VS-41), 209, 226, 232, 244, 250, 262, 269, 272, 281, 284, 290
O'Donnell, Aviation Chief Machinist's Mate (NAP) E. A., 41
Oerlikon machine guns, 182
Offenhauser, Seaman 2d Class W. W. (VF-41), 157
Offutt, Lt. (jg) Anderson (VT-2B), 58
Ogle, Lt. (jg) John N. (VS-42), 97
Okerson, Comdr. Glenn W., *389*
Okinawa, *371*
Oldmixon, Mr. G. T. (civilian pilot), 392
Oliver Mitchell (DE-417), 370
Olney, Lt. Alfred C., Jr., 24
Olympia (U.S. cruiser), 28
Omaha (CL-4), *137*
O'Mary, Lt. (jg) George W., A-V(N), 295

O'Neill, Lt. Hugh D., Jr. "Danny," A-V(N) (VF-9), 197, *197, 206,* 214, 222, 224, 230, 235, 260, 264, 268, 271, 281
O'Neill (DE-188), 363
Onslaught, HMS (British destroyer), 349
Onstott, Lt. Jacob W. "Jake" (VF-9), *206, 211,* 214, 222, 224, 227, 230, 235, 256, 264, 265, 268, 271, 272, 273, 281, 283
Operations
  Crossroads, 392
  FQ, 349
  Leader, xiv, 327, *355*
  Torch, xiv, 197, 198, *206,* 291, 293, 302, 303, 374
    Flight A-1(A) (VF-9), 209, 221
    Flight A-1 (VF-9), 208, 221
    Flight A-2 (VS-41), 209, 221
    Flight A-3 (VF-41), 212
    Flight A-4 (VF-49), 214, 234
    Flight A-9(A), 238
    Flight A-10 (VS-41), 232
    Flight A-11 (CRAG), 232
    Flight A-12 (VF-41), 234, 235
    Flight A-14 (VF-9), 235
    Flight A-15 (VF-9), 235, 236
    Flight A-16 (VS-41), 237
    Flight A-17 (VF-41), 237
    Flight A-18 (VF-41/VF-9), 237, 241, 242
    Flight A-19 (VF-9), 243, 244, 245
    Flight A-20 (VF-9), 244
    Flight A-21A (CRAG), 244
    Flight A-21 (VS-41), 240, 244
    Flight A-22 (VS-41), 244
    Flight B-1 (VS-41), 249, 250, 251, 256
    Flight B-2 (VF-9), 251, 252, 257
    Flight B-3 (VF-41), 251, 252, 256
    Flight B-4 (VF-41), 251, 256
    Flight B-5 (VF-41), 254
    Flight B-6 (VF-41), 254
    Flight B-7 (VF-9), 256, 259
    Flight B-8 (VF-41), 256
    Flight B-9 (VS-41), 256, 259
    Flight B-10 (VF-41), 256, 260
    Flight B-11 (VF-41), 256, 258, 260
    Flight B-12 (VS-41), 256, 257, 259
    Flight B-13 (VF-9), 260
    Flight B-14 (VS-41), 260, 261
    Flight B-15 (VF-41), 262
    Flight B-16 (VS-41), 262, 266
    Flight B-17 (VF-41), 262
    Flight B-19 (VF-41), 264
    Flight B-20 (VF-9), 264, 265
    Flight B-21 (VS-41), 264, 265, 266
    Flight C-1 (VF-9), 268
    Flight C-2 (VF-9), 268
    Flight C-3 (VS-41), 268
    Flight C-4 (VS-41), 268, 269
    Flight C-5 (VF-41), 269, 270
    Flight C-6 (VF-41), 269
    Flight C-7 (VF-41), 269, 270, 271
    Flight C-8 (VGF-27), 269
    Flight C-9 (VF-9), 270, 271
    Flight C-10 (VF-9), 271, 272
    Flight C-11, 272, 275
    Flight C-12, 275
    Flight C-13 (VS-41), 273, 275
    Flight C-15 (VF-41), 275
    Flight C-17 (VF-9), 277, 280
    Flight C-18 (VS-41), 277, 278, 280
    Flight D-1 (VS-41), 281
    Flight D-4 (VF-41), 281
    Flight D-5 (VF-9), 281
    Flight D-6 (VF-9), 282
    Flight D-7 (VF-41), *279,* 282, 283
    Flight D-8 (CRAG), 282
    Flight D-9 (VF-41), 282, 283
    Flight D-10 (VF-9), 284
    Flight D-11 (VS-41), 284
    Flight D-12 (VS-41), 284, 285
    Flight D-13 (VS-41), 285
    Flight D-14 (CRAG), 285
    Flight E-2A (CRAG), 286
    Flight E-2 (VS-41), 287, 289
    Flight E-3 (VF-41), 287, 291
    Flight E-4 (VS-41), 288, 291
    Flight E-6 (VS-41), 290, 291
    Flight E (VF-9), 286
    Flight "Q," 262
  Zitronella, 349
Oréade, (French submarine), 220
Oregon, (Battleship No. 3), 55
Oribi, HMS (British destroyer), 349
Orion, HMS (British light cruiser), 131
Orizaba (AP-23, AP-24), 166, *169*
Orkney Islands, 323, 324, 350
Orwell, HMS (British destroyer), 349
Ostrom, Lt. Charles H., 133
Otter (DE-210), 363
Overfield, Lt. Comdr. David B. "Bash" (CRAG, VS-42), 110, 158, 159, 232, 234, 244, 245, *246,* 282, 285, 286, 288, *288*
Owl (AM-2), 13

P

Page, Anita (actress), 68
Paglia, Cpl. B. A., USMC, 156
Palmer, Aviation Machinist's Mate 1st Class Keith F. (VS-42), 97
Palmer, Lt. (jg) John H. "Johnnie," A-V(N) (VT-4), *319,* 330, 336, 338
Palmore, Ens. W. K., *395*
Panama Canal, *27,* 54, 117, 368, 390, *391*
Paraguay, 21, 23
Paraiso (Canal Zone dredge), 54
Pargen, Aviation Chief Ordnanceman, 38
Parker, Lt. Comdr. Elton C. "Billy" (VF-4), 142, 145, 146, 151
Parkerson, Ens. Emmet, Jr., A-V(N) (VB-42), 317
Parrish, Aviation Radioman 1st Class Wilbert C. (VB-4), 328
Paskoski, Lt. John, 390
Patricia (U.S. cabin cruiser), 393
Patrol Force. *See* Atlantic Fleet
Patrol Squadron (VP) 6F, 35
Patterson, Aviation Radioman 3d Class Aubra T. "Pat" (VS-41), 226, 237, 239, 240, *243,* 265
Patterson (DD-392), 121, 122, 123
Patton, Maj. Gen. George S., Jr., USA, 249, *250,* 252
Pawlic, Seaman 2d Class H. M., 25
Pearl Harbor, 76, 88, 110, 173, 366, 370
Peck, Lt. Edwin R., 24
Pedro Miguel, *118*
Pennewill, Lt. William E., 127
Pennsylvania (BB-38), 30, 118, 119
Pentland Firth, 350
Perkins, Lt. (jg) Charles E. (VF-3B), *59*
Perkins, Willie (yard workman), 25
Perkins (DD-377), 87, 88

Perry, Aviation Radioman 3d Class G. H. (VS-41), 209, 232, 244, 256, 262, 272, 284
Perry, Lt. Robert M., *367*
Petach, Ens. John E., A-V(N) (VS-42), 149
Peterson, Ens. Carl W., A-V(N) (VF-4), 134
Peterson, Lt. Reuben F., A-V(N), *358*
Petitjean, 269
Petty, George, 178
Pevahouse, Firecontrolman 3d Class R., 96
Pfotenhauer, Lt. (jg) Fred D., 123
Phelps, Aviation Machinist's Mate 3d Class R. J., 127
Philadelphia (CL-41), 120
Philippine Insurrection, 29
Philips, Lt. Richard W. (VB-4), 328
Phillips, Dick, 333
Phillips, Ens. Francis B., USNR, 374
Pierce, Aviation Machinist's Mate 2d Class C. E. (VB-4), 91, 156
Pierce, Maj. Francis E., Jr., USMC, *389*
Pierce's Ferry, 58
Piper L-4 Cubs, 262, *265*
Piselli, Seaman 1st Class L. F., 395
Placentia Bay, 161, 303, *303*, 306, *306*, 309, 320
Plog, Ens. Leonard H., USNR (VB-98), 378
Polen, Radioman 2d Class B. A. (VS-42), 128
Ponce, Puerto Rico, 145
Ponsell, Baker 1st Class H., *373*
Ponton, Lt. Bruce E., USNR, 382
Pool, Ens. Tilman E., USNR, *371, 372*, 372
Popeye (*Ranger* mascot), 19
Porpoise (SS-172), 113
Portland (CA-33), 33
Port of Los Angeles, 37
Port Lyautey, 231, 235, 236, *236*, 251, 260, 261, 262, 265, 270, 275, 282, 283, 285
Port Royal Bay, Bermuda, 292
Port of Spain, *172*, 173, 191
Portugal, 286
Potez 29, 214
Pottage, Radioman 1st Class A. E., 133, 134
Potter, Henry C. "Hank" (film director), 73
Pottinger, 1st Lt. William K., USMC (VMB-2), 97
Pound, Aviation Cadet C. Addison, 103
Powers, Aviation Chief Machinist's Mate D. F., 78
Powers, Fireman 1st Class J. F., 178
Pownall, Mrs. Mary, 3
Pownall, Rear Adm. Charles A. "Baldy," 3, 6, 9, *12*, 20, 32, 56, 79, 389, 391, 394
Pratt, William V., Mrs., 3
Preston (DD-379), 122
Price, Aviation Machinist Mate 1st Class R. M. (VF-41), *218*
Primauguet (French light cruiser), 222, 230, 233, 237, 238, *240*, 244, 245, 251
Princeton (CVL-23), 392
Princeton (CV-37), 392
Project 157, 183
Project 337, 190, 192
Project Cadillac, *385*, 386, 388
Project NA-112, 385
Project NA-178, 385
Pryor, Lt. William L., Jr., 87
Puel, Seaman 2d Class A. F. (VB-4), 113
Puerto Rico, 144
Puget Sound Navy Yard, 57, 58, 62, *63*, 64
Puryear, Aviation Radioman 3d Class J. A. (VS-41), 284, 288
Pyne, Aviation Radioman 2d Class William E., 295

Q
Quarnberg, Lt. Paul A., A-V(N) (VF-100), 370
Quebec, 322
Queen Mary, (British steamship), *321,* 322
Quiberion, 74
Quincy (CA-39), 131, 150, 168, 172
Quonset Point, 192, 193, 293, 299, 354, 356

R
Rabat-Salé, 219, 231, 235, 238, 260, 262, 265, 270, 272, 275, 276, 334
Raborn, Lt. (jg) William F. "Red," Jr. (VF-5B), *50*
Raby, Lt. Comdr. John "Captain Jack" (VF-9), 193, *206*, 208, 214, 219, 226, 228, 231, 238, 244, 245, 251, 252, 254, 257, 260, 261, 262, 264, 265, 268, 272, 273, *273*, 274, 280
Radar:
  CXAM-1, 157, 160, 161, *161,* 165, *182,* 364
  FD, 182, *182*
  SC, 364
  SM-1, 364, 367
Radford, Lt. (jg) Jack F., A-V(N) (VF-4), 356
Rafferty, Lt. Comdr., William H. (ChC), 83
Ragsdale, Lt. Comdr. Van H., 45
Ramapo (AO-12), 88, 89
Ramirez de Arellano, Ens. Marion F., 96
Randolph, Aviation Cadet George B., USNR (VF-5B), 71, *110*
Ranger, The (ship's paper), 19, 20
Rangerion, 74
Ranger Maverick, 74
Reagan, Aviation Chief Machinist's Mate A. S. (VF-4), 356
Rector, Ens. Edward F., A-V(N) (VS-41), 149
Redfield, Lt. Comdr. Heman J., 39, 46
"The Red Rippers" (VF-4), *103, 110,* 111, 117, 119, 121, 123, 125, 131, 137, 143, *150, 211,* 214, 224, 243, 252, 296, 302, 326, 328, 329, 330, 347
Reed, Aviation Radioman 2d Class Henry H. (VB-4, VS-42), 179, 180, 301, 328
Reeves, Adm. Joseph M., 30, 35, 37, 39, 55, 126
Regia Aeronautica, 188
Reifel, Lt. Comdr. William M., 47
Reindeer (YT-115), 10
Reliance, (U.S. tug), *161*
Relief (AH-1), 54
Renfro, Lt. (jg) Edward C., 35
Renown, HMS, 183, 325
Reuben James, 131, 132, 165, 166
Reyne, Capitaine Elie, 214
Reynolds, Seaman 1st Class Marion M., *355*
Rhind (DD-404), 166, 172, 173, 177, 178
Rhoades, Comdr. George C., 21
Rhode Island, 149
Richards, Ens. Harry A., Jr. (SC), USNR, 181
Richards, Lt. (jg) Harold P. "Pay" (SC), 54, 55
Richardson, Aviation Cadet James J. (VF-5B), 71
Richardson, Aviation Chief Metalsmith 3d Class M. W. (VT-4), 330
Richard W. Suesens (DE-342), 368
Rigel (AD-13), 86
Rigg, Ens. James F., A-V(N) (VF-7), 134
Riggs, Lt. (jg) J. Clark, Jr. (VF-1B), 63
Riley, Lt. (jg) Herbert D. (VF-3B), *50, 59*
Roa, Mess Attendant 2d Class F., 87
Robbins, Lt. Comdr. Edward J., ChC, *152, 154*
Robert, Mrs. Henry M. (President General of the DAR), 141
Robert I. Paine (DE-578), 363, 364
Robertson, Comdr. James I., RN, 161

Robin (AM-3), *13*
Roches Noires, 271
Rodee, Lt. Walter F., 58
Rodman (DD-456), 297
Rodney, HMS (British battleship), 188
Rogers, Aviation Chief Radioman Elmer M. (VB-4), 320, 328
Rommel, Field Marshal Erwin, 200, 203
Roosevelt, President Franklin Delano, xiii, 39, 125, 130, 131, 148, 149, 160, 181, 183, 184, 322, 325
Roper (DD-147), 44, 45, 47, 49
Ross, Capt. R. H., USMCR (VMF-351), 383
Ross, Lt. (jg) Ralph W., A-V(N) (VB-4, VS-41), 209, 220, 221, 232, 233, 244, 257, 259, 278, 280, 284, 291, 328
Roswall, Lt. Comdr. Paul E. (VB-4), 89, *89,* 103
Rothe, Seaman 2d Class Merle B., *355*
Rouillard, Ens. C. S., USNR (VF-2), 386
Rouse, Ens. William E., A-V(N), (VS-41), 142, 162
Rowe, Capt. Gordon, 299, 305, 309, *312,* 324, *326,* 344, 345, 346, 347, 349, 350, *350,* 351, *352, 355,* 356, 360, 362
Rowles, Polly (actress), *72*
Royal Naval Air Station (RNAS) Hatston, 323, 324
Royal Naval Dockyard, Rosyth, Scotland, 349
Royer, Electrician's Mate 3d Class R. A., *294*
Rubin, *Lt.*, 213, 249
Ruchoux, *Lt.* Georges, 214, 215
Ruddy, Comdr. Joseph, Jr., 329, *329,* 330, 335, 339, 340, 344, 345, 362, *372*
Ruhsenberger, Lt. Comdr. John R., *185*
Rusbosin, Lt. (jg) Vincent, A-V(N) (VB-4), 356, 357
Rushing, Aviation Radioman 1st Class Joseph T. (VT-4), 162, 330
Ruth (U.S. freighter), 190
Ruth, Ens. Robert F. "Bob," A-V(N) (VT-4), 19, *319,* 330, 338, 362
Ryan XFR-1 Fireball, xiv, 386, 387, *387*
Rynd, Lt. (jg) Robert W. (VF-72), 181

S
S-30 (SS-135), 33
S-31 (SS-136), 33
S-32 (SS-137), 139
Saar (German submarine depot ship), *336*
Saguenay, HMCS (Canadian destroyer), 131
Saipan (CVL-48), 396
Salas, Spanish Ambassador Vicente, 22
Salinas (AO-19), 165
Sampas, 2d Lt. Michael, USMC (VMB-2), 97, 98
Sampson (DD-394), 149, 150
San Clemente Island, 41, 383
Sanderson, Capt. Lawson H. M., USMC (VB-1B, VMF-2), 63, 99
Sandnessjøen xiii, 330
Sands, Lt. (jg) John H. "Jack," A-V(N) (VF-9), 214, 231, 238, 271, 281, 284
San Francisco Bay, 30, 83, *86,* 381, 382, 383
San Francisco (CA-38), 80, 131
Sangamon (ACV-26, AO-28), 170, 198, 207, 231, 266
San Jacinto, 94, *95*
San Nicholas Island, 383, 386
Santee, Aviation Cadet Roger C., USNR (VS-42), 109
Santee (ACV-29, AO-29), *162,* 198, 207, 330
Saratoga (CV-3), 3, 4, 7, 18, 23, 30, 31, 32, 35, 39, 41, 51, 52, 54, 58, 63, 69, 72, 74, 75, 76, 80, 81, 82, 83, 84, 85, 87, 95, 96, 97, 98, 110, 111, *113,* 126, 181, 187, 190, 370, 394
Saska, Ens. Michael R., A-V(N) (VF-9), 194, 195
Saufley Field, 391, 396
Saunders, 1st Lt. William D., Jr., USMC, 44

Savannah (CL-42), 178, 181
Scapa Flow, 183, 188, 323, 324, 326, *326,* 327, *327,* 347, 349, 350, 351, 352, 354
Schader, Aviation Cadet Keith F. (VS-42), 97, 98
Schaeffer, Lt. Comdr. Valentine, 73
Scharnhorst (German battle cruiser), 146, 148, 322, 349
Schiff Trophy, 363
Schitter, Aviation Machinist's Mate 2d Class Ambrose I., USNR, 370
Schlatz, Radioman 3d Class W. (VS-1B), 75
Schleswig (German tanker), 332, *332,* 333
Schneider, Ens. Earl E., 45
Schoeffel, Lt. Comdr. Malcolm F. "Rojo," 32, 33
Schooler, Aviation Machinist's Mate 1st Class C. L., 128
Schrader, Lt. (jg) Frederick R. "Fritz" (VF-4), 117, 134
Schreffler, Radioman 2d Class R. (VS-41), 125
Schulz, Ens. Lester R., 23
Schulz, *Oberfeldwebel* Friedhelm, 344
Schumacher, Lt. Jules F. (VB-4), 106, 113, 115
Scourge, HMS (British destroyer), 344
Scouting Squadrons:
   VS-1B, 13, 15, *18,* 23, 32, 33, 34, 38, 39, 41, 44, 50, *50,* 53, 58, *61,* 65, 69, 71, 73, 75, 76, 80, 81, 82, 83, 91, 92, 106, 220, 238
   VS-2, 87, *93*
   VS-2B, 80, 81, 85
   VS-3, *93,* 111, 115
   VS-4B, 80
   VS-5, 123, 151, 158
   VS-8, 397
   VS-41, 69, 86, 87, *88,* 91, *93,* 94, 95, 100, *103,* 106, 108, 109, *110,* 111, 112, *112,* 113, 115, 117, *118,* 119, 120, 121, 122, 123, 125, 130, 131, 132, 138, 140, 141, 142, 143, 144, *144,* 146, 149, 150, 151, 152, 157, 158, 161, 162, *168, 169,* 171, 172, 178, 181, 183, 184, 187, 192, 194, 196, *196, 198,* 201, *205, 207,* 209, *218,* 219, 220, *220,* 221, 226, 228, 230, 232, 233, *233,* 234, 237, 238, 239, 240, *242, 243,* 244, 245, 249, 250, 251, 254, 255, 256, 257, 258, 259, 260, 261, 262, *263,* 264, *264,* 265, 266, 268, 269, 270, 272, 273, *273,* 274, *274,* 275, *275, 276,* 277, *277,* 278, 279, 280, 281, 282, 283, 284, *284,* 285, 286, 287, 288, 289, 290, 291, 301, 303, 304, 305, *305,* 311, 318, 319, 324, 328, 332, 333, *333, 334, 335,* 344, 362, 394
   VS-42, 85, 87, 89, 93, *93,* 94, 97, 98, 99, *103,* 106, 107, 109, *109,* 110, 115, 116, 117, *118,* 119, 120, *120,* 121, 122, 128, 131, 141, 142, 143, 147, 149, 150, 151, 152, *154,* 158, 159, 161, 162, *163,* 165, *166, 169,* 170, 173, 177, 178, 179, 180, 184, 190, 192, 201, 202, 203, *204,* 207, 232, 234, 244, 245, *246,* 267, 282, 285, 286, 288, *288,* 293, 296, 301, 328, 392
   VS-71, 131, 134, 135, 150
   VS-72, 131, 132, 134, 135, 143, 145, 150
Scrymgeour, Lt. Harper D. (VS-42), 121
Sears, Ens. Ferrell D. (VF-4), *353*
Seiler, Lt. Edward N. (VF-4, VF-41), 212, 235, 251, 256, 262, 275, 281, 323, 330, 336, 339, 343, 344, *353*
Seldovia, 46
Seligman, Comdr. Morton T. (CRAG), 121, 123
Sellar, Lt. H. D., A-V(N) (VF-81), 370
Semana Bay, 121
Servitor (British tanker), 170, 184
Seward, 45
Shackelford, Aviation Radioman 3d Class William T. "Bill" (VB-4, VS-41), *196,* 209, 226, 232, 244, 245, 255, 278, 281, 287, 303, 304, 305, *305,* 328
Shangri-La (CV-38), 358, 359, 360
Shannon, 2d Lt. J. K., 375
Shark (SS-174), 126

INDEX ■ 447

Sharp, Rear Adm. Alexander, 190
Shaw, Aviation Radioman 1st Class Robert N., USNR (VB-4), 191, 328
Shaw, Seaman 2d Class D. T., 156
Shea, Lt. (jg) John D. "Mike" (VF-6B), 51
Sheets, Apprentice Seaman W. J., 178
Shell, First Lt. John R., USA, 262
Shelton, Lt. (jg) Howard E. (VF-3B), *59*
Sherman, Comdr. Frederick C., 80
Sherrard, Lt. Frank C., D-V(G), 343, 347, 368
Sherrill, Lt. Wallace A. (VT-4), 178, 193
Shields, Lt. Charles A. "Windy" (VF-4, VF-41), *194*, 212, 219, 244, 246, 255, 266, 267, 283, 301, *353*
Shields, Lt. Ward T. "W.T." (VB-5B), 28, *50*
Shinty, Chief Water Tender A. G., *306*
Ship's paper. *See The Ranger, The Bull Horn, The CV-4*
Shōkaku, (Japanese aircraft carrier), 189
Shreffler, Radioman 2d Class R. (VF-4), 134
Shumway, Lt. (jg) DeWitt W. "Dave" (VS-1B), 76, 83, 91, 92
Sikorsky JRS-1, 128
Silber, Lt. Sam L., A-V(N), 230, 272
Simmons, Lt. George C. (VB-4, VB-41), 303, 317, 318, 324, 328, 332, 333
Simons, Rear Adm. Manley H., 155
Simpson, Cpl. Thomas H. "Pop," USMC, 8
Simpson, Wallis Warfield, 66
Simpson (DD-221), *33, 137*
Sims, Aviation Machinist's Mate 2d Class Thomas R., 305
Sinton, Capt. William H., 395
Skramstad (Norwegian steamship), 340
Sloan, Seaman 1st Class John W., 12
Small Carrier Air Group:
    CVLG-12, 374
    CVLG-30, 374
    CVLG-32, 384
    CVLG-33, 373
    CVLG-44, 368
    CVLG-49, 383
Smeeton, Lt. Comdr. Richard M., RN, 161
Smith, Aviation Cadet Maynard D., USNR (VB-1B), 66
Smith, Aviation Radioman 3d Class A. R. (VS-41), 209, 226, 232, 256, 264, 269, 273, 278, 281
Smith, Lt. Armistead B., Jr. "Chick," (VF-9, VF-12), *206,* 209, 219, 229, 235, 256, 260, 268, 271, 277, 278, 282, 286, 374
Smith, Ens. Hugh E., USNR (VF-12), 374
Smith, Lt. Allen, Jr. (VS-1B), 73
Smith, Lt. Donald H., USNR, 388
Smith, Lt. (jg) Allen W., A-V(N) (VS-42), 180
Smith, Lt. (jg) Lloyd A. (VS-42), 141
Smith, Radioman 3d Class L. R. (VS-41), 69, 171
Smith, Rear Adm. Arthur St. Clair, 9
Smith, Seaman 1st Class J. R., 127
Smith (DD-378), 98
Snider, Radioman 1st Class J. M., 33
Snow, Lorenzo (Pratt and Whitney Aircraft), 44
Solar (DE-221), 363
Solberger, Lt. Samuel (VF-3), 366, 367
Somers (DD-381), 120, 121, 122
Somerville, Adm. Sir James, RN, 183
Soucek, Lt. Apollo "Soakem", *50*
Soucek, Lt. (jg) Victor H. (VB-5B), 10, 11, *25*
Southard (DD-207), 87
South Boston Navy Yard, 322, 354
South Dakota (BB-59), 322
Southern Drill Grounds, 139, 141, 149, 156
Souza, Ens. Wilbur S. "Souz," *319*

Soviet RD 25-1 monoplane, 94, *95*
Soviet Union, 146
Sparks, Ens. Brian O. (VF-6B), USNR, 51
Spear, Aviation Cadet Frederick H., USNR (VS-41), 94
Speckman, Ens. Robert J., USNR, 382
Spell, Lt. (jg) Billie C., *393, 395*
Spencer, Comdr. Earl W., Jr. "Win," 56, 66, *66*
Spitsbergen, 349
Sprague, Comdr. Thomas L., 147, *152, 154*
St. Margaret (Steamship), 297
Stack (DD-406), 161
Stafford (DE-411), 366
Stallion (YT-120), 10
Stamm, Ens. A. G., USNR (VT-98), 388
Stancell, Chief Radioman L., 110
Standley, Adm. William H., 18, 26
Stang, Radioman 2d Class Harold (VS-42), 128
Stanley, Aviation Cadet Robert M., USNR (VB-1B), 83
Stark, Adm. Harold R., 130, 148, 149, 326
Starke, Ordnanceman 2d Class Ashton C., 294, 297
Staten Island, *363*
Stearman-Hammond JH-1, 114
Steel, Lt. (jg) James K., USNR (VF-12), 377
Steinhardt, U.S. Ambassador Laurence A., 102, *104*
Steinhardt, Mrs. Laurence A., 104
Stephens, Lt. (jg) Page P., *319*
Stepp, Aviation Machinist's Mate 3d Class D. L. (VF-4), 121, 122
Sterett (DD-407), 160, 161
Stern (DE-187), 363
Stevens, Ens. Harold H., A-V(N) (VT-3), 367, 368
Stevens, Lt. (jg) Lemuel M., Jr. (VS-41), 109, *112*
Stokes, Aviation Machinist's Mate 2d Class R. V., 133
Stoney, Ens. Rex W., A-V(N), 366
Stormes (DD-780), 384
Stouffer, Lt. (jg) Edwin, Jr., USNR (VF-18), 390
Stout, 2d Lt. J. E., USMCR, 380
Stradley, 2d Lt. J. G., USMCR, 392
Strait of San Juan de Fuca, 44
Stratton, Lt. Henry T., A-V(N) (VB-4), 328, 333
Straub, Radioman 3d Class Walter D., 153
Strickler, Lt. (jg) Robert L. "Strick" (VF-5B), 65, 104
Strother, Comdr. Edmund W., 16
Stuart, Comdr. William A., 240, 328, 342
Stuart, Hospitalman 3d Class C. T., 137
Sullivan, Lt. Claude F. "Sully" (VF-3B), *59,* 62
Sullivan, Radioman 1st Class Hobart B., 39
Sutton, Aviation Chief Machinist's Mate R. F., 56
Suwanee (ACV-27), 198, 202, 207, 209, 220, 226, 228, 231, 234, 235, 238, 240, 258, 266, 270, 271, 272, *273,* 275, 282, 283, 284, 285, 291
Swanson, Seaman 2d Class L. R., 116
Swanson, Secretary of the Navy Claude A., 23
Swanson (DD-443), 228
Sweeney, Lt. John R. "Jawn" (VF-41), 157, 158, *210,* 237, *238,* 241, 245, 262, 275, 280
Switzer, Lt. Comdr. Wendell G. "Windy" (VF-4), 103, 117

T
Tabberer (DE-418), 370
Table d'Aoukacha, 242
Tarbell (DD-142), 360, 362, 364
Tasker H. Bliss (AP-42), 291
Task Forces:
    TF-22, 183, 360
    TF-28, 360
    TF-34, *204,* 285

Task Forces (*continued*)
    TF-36, 184
    TF-121, 327
    TG 12.8, 364, 366
    TG 19.4, 366
    TG-27.1, 363
Tatom, Lt. (jg) Eugene (VF-3B), *50*, 51
Taylor, Aviation Cadet James O. (VS-1B), 69
Taylor, Aviation Machinist's Mate 2d Class James N., 31
Taylor, Comdr. Duane L., 147
Taylor, Comdr. Herbert, Jr., 89, *154*
Taylor, Lt. Comdr. David W., Jr. "Woot" (CO, VT-4), *319*, *326*, 330, 336, *337*, 349
Taylor, Lt. Comdr. William E. G., *163*
Taylor, Lt. (jg) William "W" (VF-4, VF-41), 212, 235, 237, 251, 256, 264, 275, 281, 287, 289, 290, 330, *337*, 340, *340*, *353*
Teal (AM-23), 54
Teel, Lt. (jg) Richard A. (VB-7), 132, 133
Terra, Gabriel, (Uruguayan President), 23
Tesseraud, *Adjudant-chef*, 253
Texas (BB-35), 8, 18
Thatcher, Ens. Avery, Jr., USNR (VF-32), 384
Theis, Aviation Radioman 1st Class Julius C., 321
Thomas, Ens. Gerald W. "Jerry," A-V(N) (VT-4), 309, 310, *319*, 320, 330, 339, 340, 341, 342, 351, 354, 360, 362
Thomas, W. (Pratt and Whitney Aircraft), 44
Thompson, Chief Radioman V. V., 33
Thompson, Ens. J. K. (VT-98), 388
Thompson, Lt. (jg) Warren R. (VS-1B), 53
Thompson, Pvt. F. E., USMC, 156
Thornton, Lt. (jg) Joseph T. "Joe" (VB-3B), *50*
Thrasher, HMS (British submarine), 354
Thrush (AVP-3), 130
Thurwatcher, Lt. Allen H., A-V(N), 303
Ticonderoga (CV-14), 362
Tighe, Radioman 1st Class T. U., 73
Tillman (DD-641), 235, 271
Tirpitz (German battleship), 322, 326, 327, 349, 351
Tobey, Lt. Carleton E., USNR (VF-12), 377
Toliver, Lt. Ens. James E. "Oliver" A-V(N) (VF-9), *206*, 209, 219, 235, 244, 260, 271, 272, 273, 284, 374
Tonnant (French submarine), 270
Topeka (German Steamship), 336, *337*, 338, *338*
Torpedo Squadrons:
    VT-2, 82, 85, 87, 89, *93*, 111
    VT-2B, 41, 58, 394
    VT-4, 19, 162, 178, *180*, *186*, 193, 232, 234, 244, 282, 285, 286, 295, 297, *298*, 300, *300*, 301, 305, 309, 310, 311, 313, *313*, *319*, 320, *320*, *325*, *326*, *327*, 329, *329*, 330, 335, 336, *337*, 338, 339, 340, 341, 342, 344, 345, 346, 349, 351, 354, 360, 362, *372*
    VT-5, 123, 158, 380
    VT-6, 380
    VT-12, 374
    VT-18, 390
    VT-44, 360
    VT-98, 374, 383, 388
    VT-301, 360
Towers, Capt. John H., 60
Townsend, J. W. (Solas Engineering Company), 44
Townsend, Lt. (jg) William E. "Slim" (VF-5B), 65
Tracey, Ens. Frederick W., A-V(N) (VS-42), 184
Tracy, Lt. John S. "Jack," 154
Tremblay, Aviation Machinist's Mate 3d Class R. A., 297
Tremolft, *Lieutenant*, 211

Trever (DD-339), 65
Trexler, Lt. (jg) Robert E. "Burt," A-V(N) (VT-4), *319*, 330, 338, 342
Tricaud, *Commandant* Georges, 210, 211, *212*, 215
Triche, Aviation Radioman 2d Class C. P., 300, 305
Trippe (DD-403), 142, 143, 172
Trott, Arthur, 178
Truman, President Harry, 389
Trumpeter, Ens. George N., A-V(N), 193, *193*
Truxtun (DD-229), 106, *137*
Tucker, Lt. Clyde A., Jr., A-V(N) (VB-4, VS-41), 183, 209, 232, 233, 237, 239, 256, 265, 272, 274, *274*, 282, 283, 328, 333, *333*, *334*, 344
Tumilovich, Aviation Machinist's Mate 2d Class E. L., 370
Tunisia, 200
Turner, Lt. Frank (VS-72), 134
Tuscaloosa (CA-37), 16, 131, *137*, 143, 149, 153, 209, 230, 233, 294, *304*, 316, 320, 322, 327, 349, 354, 357, *359*
Twiddy, Lt. (jg) Clarence A., Jr., A-V(N) (VS-41), 209, 220, 232, 244, 250, 262, 263, 272, 274, 281, 290

U

U-boats:
    general, 362
    U-86, 248
    U-91, 248
    U-103, 248
    U-106, 165
    U-108, 248
    U-130, 248, 291
    U-153, 190
    U-155, 248
    U-173, 248, 287
    U-185, 248
    U-404, 306, 364
    U-411, 248
    U-510, 248
    U-511, 248
    U-515, 248
    U-519, 248
    U-552, 165
    U-572, 248
    U-652, 160
    U-658, 165
    U-752, 248
Ulen, Comdr. Francis G., *154*
Upshur (DD-144), *137*, 360, 362
Uruguay, Montevideo, xiii, 16, 23
Utah (BB-31), also (AG-16), 21, 41, 66
Utility Squadrons:
    VJ-1F, 30
Utility Unit insignia, xiv
Utter, Lt. (jg) Harmon T. (VF-5B), 68

V

V-1 Division, 23
V-2 Division, *14*, 23
Vaagan (Norwegian steamer), 338, *339*
Van Deurs, Lt. George, 44, *50*
Van Keuren, Rear Adm. A. H., 160
Vann, Comdr. John W., (MC), *101*
Van Nagell, Comdr. John R., 147, *154*, 350
Vargas, Brazilian President Getulio Dornelles, 21, 22, *22*
Veeder, Lt. (jg) Volkert B., *307*
Venus, HMS (British destroyer), 354

Vera Cruz, 57
Vernadakis, Radioman 3d Class C. E., 178
Verrier, *Adjudant-Chef* Marcel, 211, 249
Vichy France, xiv, 181, 200, *213,* 220, *225,* 228, 231, *234,* 235, *240, 241, 247,* 252, 253, 254, 261, 270, 275, *277,* 280, 283, 291, 344
Victorious, HMS (British aircraft carrier), 188
Vietnam, xiv
Villaceque, *Sous-Lieutenant* Pierre, 211, *214,* 231
Vincennes (CA-44), 131, 150, 151, 168, 172
Virgin Islands, St. Thomas, 146, 147
Vita, Lt. (jg) Harold E., A-V(N) (VF-9), *206,* 209, 226, 231, 244, 251, 253, 264, 268, 272, 284, 374
Von Achen, Radioman 3d Class S. P., 84
von Bülow/*Kapitänleutnant* Otto, 306, *352*
Vosseller, Lt. James O. "Jimmy" (VF-4), 29, 145
Vought F4U Corsair, 366, *375*
Vought F4U-1C Corsair (BuNo 82289), 383
Vought F4U-1D Corsair:
   BuNo 57178, 383
   BuNo 57281, 383
   BuNo 57293, 383
   BuNo 57649, 384
   BuNo 57791, 374
   BuNo 82238, 384
   BuNo 82254, 386
   BuNo 82258, 384
   BuNo 82296, 382
   BuNo 82360, 382
   BuNo 82363, 382
   BuNo 82365, 382, 383
   general, 374, 375, *375,* 380, 384
Vought FG-1 Corsair, 366, 394
Vought FG-1D Corsair:
   BuNo 92109, 389
   general, 396
Vought O3U-3 Corsair:
   BuNo 8574, 38
   BuNo 9168, *76*
   BuNo 9318, 9, 10, *14,* 21, *26*
   BuNo 9734, 63
   general, 44, 46, 78, 85, 87, 111
Vought O3U-6 Corsair, 111
Vought OS2U Kingfisher, 213
Vought OS2U-3 Kingfisher, 209, 213
Vought SB2U Vindicator, *120,* 123, 125, *152, 168, 172, 186, 191,* 192, 193, 194
Vought SB2U-1 Vindicator:
   BuNo 0726, 179
   BuNo 0731, 127
   BuNo 0736, 183
   BuNo 0737, 123
   BuNo 0739, 125, 192
   BuNo 0743, 119, 177
   BuNo 0744, 121
   BuNo 0745, 134, 140
   BuNo 0746, 134, 141, 165, 184
   BuNo 0747, 162
   BuNo 0749, 157
   BuNo 0756, 170
   BuNo 0757, 171, 181
   BuNo 0758, 187
   BuNo 0759, 158
   BuNo 0760, *136*
   BuNo 0763, 162
   BuNo 0767, 142
   BuNo 0768, 194, *196*
   BuNo 0771, 142
   BuNo 0773, *136*
   BuNo 0774, 158
   BuNo 0776, 119, 128
   BuNo 9812, 137
   general, 111, 116, 117, *118,* 121, 122, 127, 128, 132, 134, 137, 141, 150, *169,* 172, 173
Vought SB2U-2 Vindicator:
   BuNo 1328, *166*
   BuNo 1346, 157
   BuNo 1348, 158
   BuNo 1358, 132
   BuNo 1360, 134
   BuNo 1365, 184
   BuNo 1373, 134
   BuNo 1382, 191
   general, 132, 134, 150, *169,* 184, 190
Vought SB2U-3 Vindicator:
   BuNo 0759, 179
   BuNo 2082, 156
Vought SBU-1:
   BuNo 9309, 125
   BuNo 9750, 115
   BuNo 9751, 141
   BuNo 9754, 128
   BuNo 9756, 116
   BuNo 9759, 100, 109, *110,* 112
   BuNo 9763, 99, 122
   BuNo 9764, 97, 109
   BuNo 9765, 99
   BuNo 9766, 109
   BuNo 9770, 94
   BuNo 9771, 53, 127
   BuNo 9775, 134
   BuNo 9776, 52, 55, 62
   BuNo 9777, 101, 102, *102*
   BuNo 9779, 81
   BuNo 9780, 116
   BuNo 9781, 109
   BuNo 9783, 107
   BuNo 9787, 138
   BuNo 9790, 109
   BuNo 9793, 122
   BuNo 9795, 109
   BuNo 9798, 99
   BuNo 9799, 83, 109
   BuNo 9800, 83
   BuNo 9801, 68
   BuNo 9802, *61*
   BuNo 9803, 53
   BuNo 9804, 69, 106
   BuNo 9805, 75, 108, *109*
   BuNo 9806, 121
   BuNo 9807, 69, 128
   BuNo 9808, 84
   BuNo 9810, 65
   BuNo 9811, 53, 71, 130
   BuNo 9817, 133
   BuNo 9820, *135*
   BuNo 9832, 76
   general, 44, 46, 47, 48, 65, 80, 81, 82, 87, *88, 103, 112,* 116, 117, *118,* 120, *120,* 121, 122, 132, 137
Vought-Sikorsky XPBS-1 *Flying Dreadnought,* 116

Vought SU-4:
  BuNo 9418, 39
  BuNo 9419, 13, 15, *18,* 94
  BuNo 9420, 39
  BuNo 9428, 34
  general, 33, 39, 50, 87, 94, 100

W

Wade, Photographer's Mate 2d Class William (VS-41), 282, 283
Wadi Sebou, *236*
Wagner, Lt. (jg) John E., A-V(N), 191
Wagner, Rear Adm. Frank D., 395
Wainwright (DD-419), 181
Wakefield, Pvt. Davies E., USMC, 10
Wakefield (AP-21), 166
Walker, Ens. George D., *319*
Walker, J. F., Mr., 153
Walker, K. W., Maj., USA, 44
Walker, Lt. Bert F., 380
Wallace, Aviation Chief Machinist's Mate H. E., 9, *14*
Walsh, Aviation Radioman 2d Class R. G. (VT-4), 330
Walsh, Quartermaster 3d Class Robert E., USNR, 355
Walsh, Sen. David I., 107
Warbler (U.S. salvage vessel), 132
War Brahmin, (British tanker), 178
Ward, Capt. Benjamin P., 391
Ward, Chief Radioman J. J. (VF-3B), 55
Ward, Ens. Felix E., Jr., A-V(N) (VT-4), *319,* 330, 338
Warrington, 395
Warta, Ens. Arthur L., A-V(N) (VS-41), 226, 237, 240, 250, 265, 269, 284, 291
Washington. See Mount Vernon (AP-22)
Washington, Port Angeles, 44
Washington (BB-56), 148, 183
Washington Treaty, 3, 6
Wasp (CV-7), 126, 132, 133, 134, 135, 138, 142, 145, 146, 147, 149, 150, 151, 158, 171, 178, 181, 188, 190, 354
Waterson, Aviation Radioman 2d Class Morris S. (VB-4, VS-41), 209, *218,* 221, 232, 256, 265, 278, 287, 328
Watts, 2d Lt. F. T., USMCR (VMF-512), 383
Way, Lt. (jg) Darrell E. (VB-4), 181, 328, 351
Weatherman, Aviation Machinist's Mate 1st Class N. G., 142
Webber, Chief Storekeeper, 67
Webster, Capt. Hugh P., 391, 392
Weddell, U.S. Ambassador Alexander S., 16, 23
Weeks, Lt. (jg) Cyrus F., A-V(N) (VB-4, VS-41), 209, 232, 233, 244, 245, 256, 262, 263, 272, 274, 284, 301, 328, 332, 344, 362
Weiler, Lt. Herold J., Jr. "Ham" (VF-41), 212, 215, 216, 230, 235, 251, 256, 259, 264, 265, 269, 270, 275, 276, 280, 282, 287, 289, 290, 291
Weitzenfeld, Lt. Daniel K. (VB-4), 316, *316,* 328, 332, 333
Welch, Seaman 2d Class B. F. (VS-41), 183
Well, Fireman 3d Class W. N., 178
Weller, Lt. Comdr. Oscar A. "Tex," *136*
Wellings, Lt. Joseph H., 65
Welsh, Lt. David J. (LSO), 69, 117
Welton, Ens. Chauncey G. (VF-4), *353*
Welty, Earl M. (AP), 88
West, Capt. Ernest R., USMC (VMF-111), 157
Western World (U.S. freighter), 22
Westhofen, Lt. (jg) Charles L. (VF-3B), *50*
Westmoreland, Aviation Machinist's Mate 3d Class James D., Jr. (VF-4), 354

West Point (AP-23), 166
West Virginia (BB-48), 18, 41, 394
Wheeler Field, 76
White, 1st Lt. John A. "Jack," *74*
White, Comdr. Allen H., *154*
White, Lt. (jg) Clarence M., Jr. (VF-4), 131, 134, 140
White, Lt. (jg) Clifford M., A-V(N) (VF-4), 228, *314,* 329, 332, 353
White, Lt. (jg) Horace R. "Hal," A-V(N) (VS-41), 209, 226, 234, *243,* 256, 264, 269, 273, 275, 278, 279, 280, 281
White, Maj., 164, 165
White, Supervisor P. A., 54
Whitehurst Auxiliary Field, Norfolk, 140, 141
Whitney, Aviation Machinist's Mate 3d Class William J., 370
Whitney, Lt. John P. (VF-3B), 53
Whitten, Seaman 1st Class Arthur G., 297
Wichita (CA-45), 149, 209, 230, 233, 239
Wilborn, Navy Diver 2d Class Jessie J., *195*
Wilhoite, Ens. Thomas M. "Willie," A-V(N) (VF-9), *206,* 209, 219, 229
Wilkerson, Ens. James M. "Silky," A-V(N) (VF-9), 197, *206,* 209, 226, 244, 260, 271, 277, 278, 284
Wilkes (DD-441), 203, 209, 213, 224, 228, 245, 373
Wilkinson, Seaman 2d Class John F., 364
Will, Lt. John M., 113
William B. Preston (AVD-7), 374, 375
Williams, Chief Photographer W. L., *26*
Williams, Ens. D. T., A-V(N) (VF-44), 366
Williams, Mess Attendant C. L., 178
Williams, Seaman 2d Class N. C., 25
Williamson, Comdr. Thomas B., 159, *159,* 164, 165, *185*
Williwaw, 45
Willson, Vice Adm. Russell, 190
Wilson, Lt. (jg) Albert H. "Jock" (VS-1B), *50*
Wilson, President Woodrow, 16
Wilson, Radioman 2d Class E. (VS-41), 109
Wilson, Radioman 2d Class H. (VS-1B), 65
Wilson (DD-408), 181
Wiltsie, Lt. Comdr. Irving D. (VB-3), 97
Winfield, Ens. Murray, USNR, 373
Wingard, Lt. (jg) Walter C. "Wing," 34
Wings Over Honolulu (movie), 72, 73
Winkle, Seaman 2d Class G. W., 23, 24
Winters, Lt. Theodore H., Jr. "Pedro" (VF-9), *206,* 209, 214, 219, 229, 230, 244, 256, 259, 260, 261, 270, 271, 272, 277, 280, 282, 283
Wolfe (British freighter), 173
Wood, Capt. Ralph F., 126, 131, 132, *140*
Wood, Lt. Ernest W., Jr. "Woodie" (VF-41), 139, 183, 187, *194,* 212, 215, 230, 237, 251, 256, 259, 264, 269, 283, 287, 289, 298, 299
Woods, Lt. Ralph W. D., 116, 122
Woolsey (DD-437), 287, 289, 290
Word, Technical Sgt. William E., USMC, 63
Wordell, Lt. Malcolm T. "Mac" (VF-41), 199, 201, 208, *211,* 214, 222, 223, 224, 225, 228, 230, 246, 247, 249, 267, 279, 280, 283, 301
Worden (DD-352), 99
Wright, Ens. David W., USNR, 397
Wright, Ens. Graydon D., A-V(N) (VT-4), 311, 313
Wright, Ens. Spencer D., A-V(N) (VB-7), 133
Wright, Lt. Comdr. Thomas K. (VF-27), 209
Wright, Lt. Jesse G., 19

Wright, Lt. (jg) James M. "Jim" (VS-41), 112, 113, 115
Wright (AV-1), 37, 82, 126, 156, 187, 380
Wright R-2600-8 Cyclone, 357
Wyoming (AG-17), *137, 162,* 394

Y

Yamashev, Andrei (Russian copilot), 94
Yarmouth, (U.S. Army transport), 165
Yarnall (DD-143), *137*
Yarnell, Adm. Harry E., 111
YC-270, 161
YE equipment, 157, 160, 161, 165, 168, 283
Yoho, Lt. John R. (VS-42), 165
Yonts, Aviation Machinist's Mate 3d Class E. M. (VT-2), 89
Yorktown-class ship, 142

Yorktown (CV-5), 85, 117, *119,* 125, 151, 153, *154,* 158, 161, 166, 168, 171, 181, 187
Youmans, Aviation Machinist's Mate 1st Class H. D. (VT-4), 330
Young, Chinese Minister Samuel Sung, 22
Young, Ensign George E., USNR (VB-5), 380, 381
Young, Lt. (jg) Joseph B. H., 97
Young, Lt. Rufus C., *25*
Youngblood, Boatswain's Mate 1st Class J. F., 177
YSD-8, 54

Z

Zalom, Aviation Radio Technician 1st Class Joseph L., USNR (VT-4), 330, 336
Zane (DD-337), 65
ZB gear, 283

ABOUT THE AUTHOR

Robert J. Cressman, the head of the Ships History Branch of the Naval Historical Center in Washington, D.C., is an award-winning author recognized internationally as a leading expert on the history of the U.S. Navy. His first book, *That Gallant Ship: USS* Yorktown *(CV-5)*, has been included on the recommended reading list of the master chief petty officer of the Navy. He lives in Silver Spring, Md.